Adventure Guide

Alaska Highway

4th Edition

Ed & Lynn Readicker-Henderson

HUNTER

HUNTER PUBLISHING, INC,
130 Campus Drive, Edison, NJ 08818
☎ 732-225-1900; ☎ 800-255-0343; Fax 732-417-1744
www.hunterpublishing.com

Ulysses Travel Publications
4176 Saint-Denis, Montréal, Québec
Canada H2W 2M5
☎ 514-843-9882, ext. 2232; fax 514-843-9448

Windsor Books
The Boundary, Wheatley Road, Garsington
Oxford, OX44 9EJ England
☎ 01865-361122; Fax 01865-361133

ISBN 1-58843-571-7
Printed in the United States
© 2006 Hunter Publishing, Inc.

This and other Hunter travel guides are also
available as e-books in a variety of digital formats
through our online partners, including
Amazon.com and Netlibrary.com.

This guide focuses on recreational activities. As all such activities contain elements of risk, the publisher, author, affiliated individuals and companies disclaim responsibility for any injury, harm, or illness that may occur to anyone through, or by use of, the information in this book. Every effort was made to insure the accuracy of information in this book, but the publisher and author do not assume, and hereby disclaim, liability for any loss or damage caused by errors, omissions, misleading information or potential travel problems caused by this guide, even if such errors or omissions result from negligence, accident or any other cause.

Cover photo: Mt. McKinley Highway Pass & the park road
© Ron Niebrugge/Alamy
Cartoons by Joe Kohl
Index by Nancy Wolff

Base maps provided by Lynne Readicker-Henderson
Maps by Kim André & Toni Wheeler © 2006 Hunter Publishing, Inc.

1 2 3 4

www.hunterpublishing.com

Hunter's full range of guides to all corners of the globe is featured on our exciting website. You'll find guidebooks to suit every type of traveler, no matter what their budget, lifestyle, or idea of fun.

Adventure Guides – There are now over 40 titles in this series, covering destinations from Costa Rica and the Yucatán to Tampa Bay & Florida's West Coast and Belize. Complete with information on what to do, as well as where to stay and eat, *Adventure Guides* are tailor-made for the active traveler, with all the practical travel information you need, as well as details of the best places for hiking, biking, canoeing, horseback riding, trekking, skiing, watersports, and all other kinds of fun. Cultural adventures might include cooking classes with a local chef, attending a wine-tasting event, learning a traditional regional dance or signing up for a language course.

Alive Guides – This ever-popular line of books takes a unique look at the best each destination offers: fine dining, jazz clubs, first-class hotels and resorts. In-margin icons direct the reader at a glance. Top-sellers include *The US Virgin Islands, The Cayman Islands* and *Aruba, Bonaire & Curaçao.*

One-of-a-kind travel books available from Hunter include *Best Dives of the Caribbean; London A-Z; Cruising Alaska* and many more.

Full descriptions are given for each book at www.hunterpublishing. com, along with reviewers' comments and a cover image. You can also view pages and the table of contents. Books may be purchased on-line via our secure transaction facility.

Contents

■ Maps

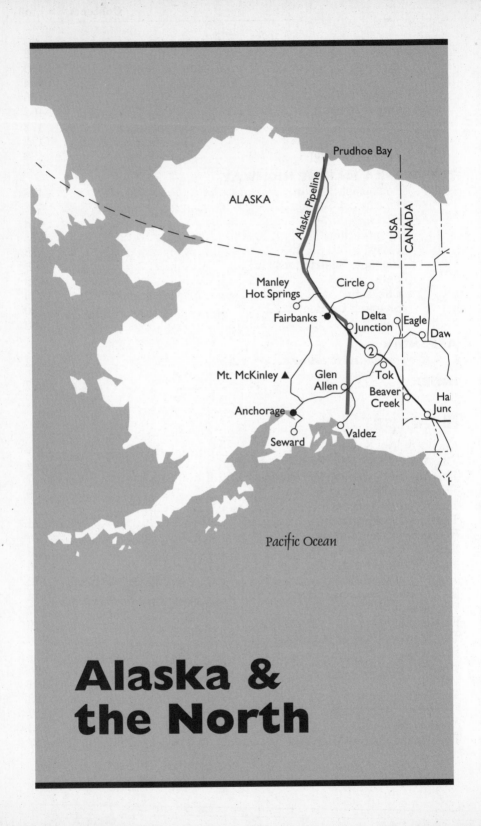

Alaska &
the North

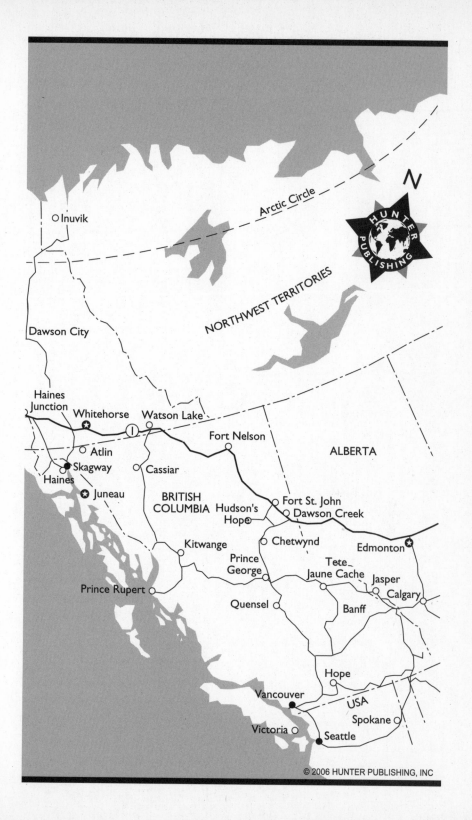
© 2006 HUNTER PUBLISHING, INC

Introduction

The Alaska Highway travels through some of the most pristine country-side in the Americas. Once a rugged dirt road few could travel – a road known to make military trucks disappear into deep mud – its 1,500-plus-mile route now is completely paved, frequently smooth, and open to anyone who wants to follow in the footsteps of the ever-hopeful gold rush prospectors, who wants to head as far north as the roads can go, toward spaces more wide open than most people can imagine.

The highway skirts lakes and rivers with water in shades of blue that defy description and with fishing where the reality surpasses the greatest lies told in the continental United States. It rounds the edge of the largest protected wilderness area in the world – the Kluane/Wrangell-St. Elias park system – a place so remote many of its mountains remain unnamed, a park bigger than most of the New England states combined.

When you're on the highway, there is wildlife everywhere you look. Black bears, moose standing seven feet tall, Dall and stone sheep, mountain goats, and even grizzly bears are often within easy sight of the road – sometimes they're standing on the road. And then there are the smaller animals: beavers, foxes, martens, porcupines, the ubiquitous Arctic ground squirrel. Along the coast you'll see sea otters, once the source of Russia's greatest wealth, smash clams on their bellies. You'll see humpback whales breach, raising their bodies 30 feet into the air before crashing back into the sea. For birders, 424 species have been spotted in Alaska alone; British Columbia and the Yukon are both on major migratory flyways. You might spot bald eagles, Arctic terns, red-throated loons, trumpeter swans, wigeons, canvasbacks, and redhead and ring-necked ducks. Over 100 species of birds nest in the Tetlin Wildlife Refuge alone, right on the path of the highway.

The modern Alaska Highway is a trip without hardship. Towns are mostly tiny – some that look like big cities on the map are really little more than crossroads – but frequent enough to keep you supplied with all the necessities. Campsites are among the best in the world. There are no language problems along the highway, only two currencies, hassle-free borders, and people who are unfailingly friendly.

Traveling the highway is an adventure of peace, beauty, and nature. It's the greatest drive in the world. North to Alaska.

■ How This Book is Organized

 This book is divided into three sections. Chapters 1-3 serve as an introduction to the North, including its history, geography, climate, and wildlife. This section also offers information on how to prepare yourself and your vehicle for the journey. The second part (Chapters 4 through 6) covers the approaches to the Alaska Highway, the highway itself, and the scenic alternate route north – the Cassiar Highway. In short, it gets you into the far North. Roads are described south to north, unless otherwise noted. Locations for the Alaska Highway are given by the old mile markers. Over the years, as the highway as been changed, these mile markers have ceased to be entirely accurate, although they are close to the actual distances. The old markers do, however, still exist, and they are the way businesses locate themselves.

The last section (Chapters 7-16) details the roads that lead off the Alaska Highway. These are presented in the order in which they appear if you're traveling the highway south to north. These roads are also described according to the direction in which they leave the Alcan (the Alaska Highway) – if the road heads south, we describe it north to south. If it leads north, we go south to north, describing it from the point it leaves the Alcan.

■ Who We Are, What We Do, & What You're in For

 We've been writing these books for 15 years; over that time, we've been lucky enough to get to see and do just about everything in the state. This book brings you the places and things that we think you're going to love.

However, let's admit to a couple of biases right up front: you go to the North to see the wild, to be outside, to see the best that nature has to offer. You don't go up there to eat or sleep at the exact same places you can find at home. Chain stores, in all their many permutations, make for mediocre experiences. We believe that you get the best trip when you deal with the people who live, work, and make a place their home. If you're planning to spend your trip eating two meals a day at McDonald's, this book isn't for you.

We also believe the best travelers, the happiest travelers, are the ones who know what they're looking at. That's why we spend so much time on history and culture. It ain't just like it is back home.

And we hope it never is.

Chapter 1

The Land & Its Inhabitants

British Columbia

■ Geography

British Columbia is defined by the chains of mountains that line the land: to the north are the **Cassiar** and **Omineca Mountains**; to the southeast, the **Columbia Mountains**; to the west, the **Coast Mountains**; and to the east are the **Rockies**. These mountains divide the province into sections of plateaus and valleys, rich for agriculture and animal husbandry, while blocking off huge tracts that are left to wilderness.

The Coast Mountains separate the rainforests of the coast with the drier Interior; farther north, the **Fairweather Range** includes the highest point in British Columbia, Mt. Fairweather – you can see it from 50 miles off, and it still looks huge.

At the far side of the province are the Rockies, dropping down to parallel the Alaska Highway, and then moving over towards the next province, Alberta, and one of the great park systems of the world: Jasper, Banff, Kootenay, and Yoho, which together form a UNESCO World Heritage Site.

The rivers of the province are no less impressive than the mountains. The largest of them, the **Fraser**, is 850 miles long and is fed by the Nechako, Quesnel, Chilcotin, and Thompson rivers. The **Kootenay** flows down to the **Columbia River** in Washington state, and westward to the Pacific, weaving a tortuous path between mountain ranges. More than a quarter of a billion birds stop along the **Stikine** – the fastest free-flowing river left on the continent – during the height of the migration season.

If all that wasn't enough, British Columbia has a long chain of islands, including **Vancouver Island**, the biggest on the west coast – almost the size of England, in fact. There are the delightful little **Gulf Islands** – Salt Spring issues its own currency – and farther north, the islands of BC mesh with those of Alaska, forming the Inside Passage. **Princess Royale** Island has kermodie bears, a rare subspecies of black bear – kermodies are white. Off the beaten track are the **Queen Charlottes** – home to some of the richest First Nations culture in Canada.

Alaska Highway
British Columbia

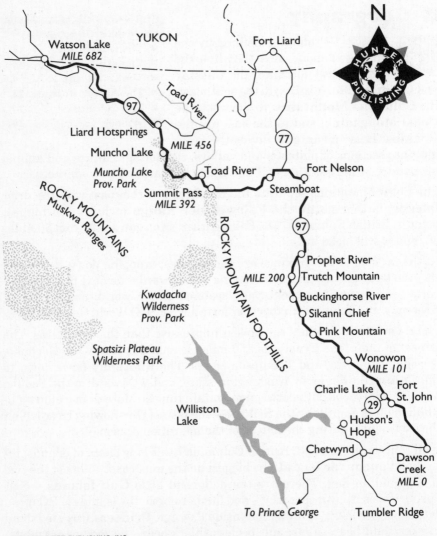

Watson Lake
MILE 682

YUKON

Fort Liard

N

Toad River

97

Liard Hotsprings

MILE 456

Muncho Lake

77

Muncho Lake
Prov. Park

Toad River

Fort Nelson

ROCKY MOUNTAINS
Muskwa Ranges

Summit Pass
MILE 392

Steamboat

97

ROCKY MOUNTAIN FOOTHILLS

Prophet River

MILE 200

Trutch Mountain

Kwadacha
Wilderness
Prov. Park

Buckinghorse River

Sikanni Chief

Pink Mountain

Spatsizi Plateau
Wilderness Park

Wonowon
MILE 101

Charlie Lake

Fort
St. John

29

Williston
Lake

Hudson's
Hope

Chetwynd

Dawson
Creek
MILE 0

To Prince George

Tumbler Ridge

Along the coast, there is the single greatest glory of the north, the Western red cedar (Thuja plicata). Its cones are oval, unlike the round yellow cedar cones. The Western red cedar was the department store for First Nations people. These trees can live over a thousand years. They rot from the inside, so a perfectly healthy tree may have a hollow that's 10 or 15 feet across and 30 feet high. They also provide a base for other forest growth: the biggest might have more than 50 plant species growing on them. You can't understand coastal life until you've taken a good look at these giants.

When William H. Seward bought Alaska from the Russians, his grand plan was actually to use it as leverage to allow the United States to annex British Columbia. The man knew a good thing when he saw it.

■ History

The land that is now British Columbia was first brought to European attention by **Juan Perez** in 1774; **Captain Cook** was the first European to land in the area, near Vancouver Island, in 1778, and he was quickly followed by **George Vancouver**. But the early explorers weren't really interested in British Columbia itself. They were actually just out there after a Northwest Passage.

So what finally got people interested in the territory? Fur hats. Plain and simple. Europe needed beavers to make felt for hats, and Canada had a lot of beavers. Prices were ridiculously high, and so traders and voyageurs headed into the Interior, looking for fur sources.

From the official standpoint, it was **Alexander Mackenzie** who opened the territory, when his 1793 expedition reached the Pacific Coast by land – a decade before Lewis and Clark ever turned their sights west. Mackenzie was not only the first to cross the continent, he was one of the greatest explorers the North has ever seen; after dipping his toes in the Pacific Ocean, he headed north, following what is now the Mackenzie River system to the Great Slave Lake and eventually to the coast of the Arctic Ocean. He wasn't really looking for what he found; he kept hearing stories about a big river to the west (the Yukon, no doubt), but while not finding it, he created the foundations for Canada's western provinces, mapping endless stretches of land that even today few venture into.

Where explorers first trod, tradesmen soon followed. After Mackenzie opened the West, Simon Fraser and George Thompson – names common to Canada's landscape today – followed in his footsteps, taking the trade out of the disorganized hands of the independent trader, and opening a series of fur-trading posts for the Northwest Company, which was later absorbed by the Hudson's Bay Company. The HBC, expanding as quickly as it could, sent men out to solidify its hold on trade and to fend off territorial encroachment by a variety of upstart fur traders.

The first whites to settle permanently in British Columbia were a ragged group of hunters and trappers, who either lived with the Natives (the term currently in use through much of Canada is First Nation peoples) or took advantage of them, seeking their fortune in furs.

From this beginning grew the modern province of British Columbia.

Actually, in the beginning, it looked like there were going to be three provinces, or at least three territories. The islands, including Vancouver Island, were not incorporated into the larger area until the middle of the 1800s. The Stikine River was also an independent administrative district, left to its own devices until the influx of gold miners made some kind of central control necessary.

Date modern BC to the territory joining the Dominion of Canada in 1871, and to the first railroad in the province, which joined BC to points east in 1875.

BC today is the best of Canada. More landscape, more scenery, plenty of open spaces. BC has found its niche in a diverse economy and vast natural beauty.

The Yukon

Famed as the home of the **Klondike gold rush**, the Yukon is one of the least populated areas of Canada. Only about 30,000 people live in the territory, or roughly one person for every 7 square miles of land. But if you take away Whitehorse, home to nearly two-thirds of the population, you're left with a territory that is home to only one person for every 26 square miles of land – plenty of room to spread out.

■ Geography

The Yukon is almost completely mountainous: the Rockies and the **St. Elias mountains** nearly fill the territory, and the Yukon holds the highest point in Canada: **Mt. Logan** is 19,850 feet high. Although considerably lower than Everest and a tad lower than McKinley, Mt. Logan is the largest mountain massif in the world. It rises from just above sea level on a base nearly 100 miles in diameter. Compare this to Everest, which rises to 27,000 feet, but starts from a plateau nearly 20,000 feet high and you'll understand how much bigger the mountains are in the Yukon.

Over half of the territory is drained by the **Yukon River**, which rises near Whitehorse, beginning a bare 15 miles from the ocean, and then threads its path north through the territory and into Alaska, ultimately reaching the ocean near Nome on the Bering Sea coast.

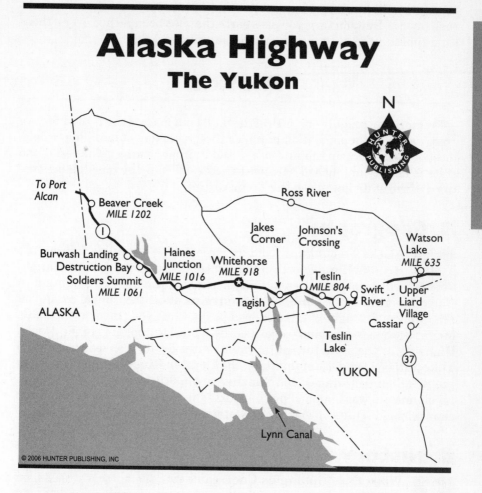

Alaska Highway
The Yukon

N

To Port Alcan
Beaver Creek
MILE 1202
Burwash Landing
Destruction Bay
Soldiers Summit
MILE 1061
ALASKA
Haines Junction
MILE 1016
Whitehorse
MILE 918
Jakes Corner
Johnson's Crossing
Ross River
Tagish
Teslin
MILE 804
Swift River
Teslin Lake
Watson Lake
MILE 635
Upper Liard Village
Cassiar
YUKON
Lynn Canal

■ History

The Yukon was first explored by **Robert Campbell** in the 1840s, under command of the Hudson's Bay Company. But it was another 50 years before the world took notice of the Yukon. On August 17, 1896, **George Carmack** struck gold on Bonanza Creek, and the Klondike gold rush began. Over the next few years a stampede of hopeful miners headed northwest, looking for the short road to riches – their boots wore paths in the hard rock mountains that are still visible today. During the height of the gold rush, their paddleboats, makeshift rafts, canoes, and dories created boatjams on the Yukon River.

Many died, and most of those who survived came back down the river a year or two later, not even carrying their hopes back. But the few who did strike it rich fueled the Yukon legend.

Mining is still a primary business of the Yukon. Driving toward the gold rush town of Dawson City, you pass earth that has been turned over a thousand times in the never-ending search for nuggets of gold.

Alaska

Comprising roughly one-fifth of the total land mass of the United States, Alaska has a population of under three-quarters of a million people, most of them living in the Anchorage and Fairbanks areas. The rest of the state is largely untouched wilderness accessible only by bush plane; one-third of the state lies above the Arctic Circle.

■ Geography

Alaska's mountains loom as large as the state itself. From the **Brooks Range** north of the **Arctic** Circle, to the **Alaska Range**, which includes Denali (Mt. McKinley), the highest mountain in North America, to the **Chugach Mountains** along the central coast, you are rarely out of sight of snow-capped peaks when you travel in the state. Mountains made overland travel an ordeal until the opening of the Alaska Highway, so the state turned to water routes for its transportation. The **Yukon River** fed most of the state; the **Copper River** brought ores from the rich Kennecott mines; and **Southeast Alaska**, home of the state capital of Juneau, was supplied by ships that threaded their way through the channels and straits of the coastal waterways.

■ History

When **Captain James Cook** came into the northern coasts, on his third voyage, only a few months away from being killed and eaten in Hawaii, he didn't find what he was looking for. He'd come north hoping to find the Northwest Passage, a shortcut from Europe to China. What he found instead was a land that he wasn't quite sure what to think of. His journal entry for October 10, 1778 reads that the Russians "call it by the... name... Alaschka.... From what we could gather from Mr. Ismyloff and the others, the Russians have made several attempts to get a footing upon that part of the Continent which lies adjacent to the islands [the Aleutians], but have always been repulsed by the Natives, whom they describe as a very treacherous people."

Of course, the Natives, the Aleuts and Athabascans, weren't thrilled to see yet another batch of white guys with big boats trying to take over their land. The Russians had already killed practically everything with fur along a thousand-mile swath of coast. They were looking for new killing grounds; Cook was just looking for a way home.

Alaska Highway
Alaska

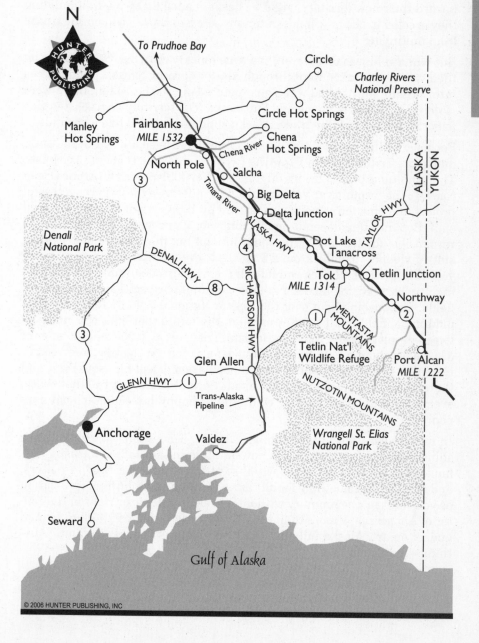

To Prudhoe Bay

Circle

Charley Rivers National Preserve

Circle Hot Springs

Manley Hot Springs

Fairbanks *MILE 1532*

Chena *Chena River* Hot Springs

North Pole

Salcha

Tanana River

Big Delta

Delta Junction

Denali National Park

DENALI HWY

ALASKA HWY

Dot Lake
Tanacross

Tetlin Junction

Tok *MILE 1314*

Northway

RICHARDSON HWY

MENTASTA MOUNTAINS

Tetlin Nat'l Wildlife Refuge

Glen Allen

GLENN HWY

Trans-Alaska Pipeline

Port Alcan *MILE 1222*

NUTZOTIN MOUNTAINS

Anchorage

Valdez

Wrangell St. Elias National Park

TAYLOR HWY

ALASKA
YUKON

Seward

Gulf of Alaska

© 2006 HUNTER PUBLISHING, INC

Alaska's history has been one of boom and bust. When the land was bought from Russia in 1867, for a bit over $7 million, or the famed two cents an acre, it was immediately dubbed "Seward's Folly" or "Seward's Icebox," after the man who engineered the sale. One reporter said of the sale, "We have been sold a sucked orange." And, in fact, Seward himself wasn't that interested in Alaska per se; he just thought owning it would make it easier for the U.S. to annex British Columbia and the Yukon. The U.S. attitude toward their new territory might be best summed up by the first building they erected in the new lands: a ten pin alley, in Sitka, to keep the troops from mutinying.

But when gold was discovered, the tune quickly changed. Stampeders on their way to the Yukon went through Alaska, turning Skagway and Haines into thriving towns. And when gold petered out in the Yukon, there were major gold strikes in Nome and Fairbanks. The territory also boasted rich fisheries and a brisk fur trade. Alaska suddenly seemed like a good idea.

For most of the past several decades, there has been a boom in the state due to the **Trans-Alaska Pipeline** (which, some fear, is about to go bust). This ambitious project brings oil from the North Slope, on the Arctic Ocean coast, to the terminus at Valdez, some 800 miles away. A largely successful project, the pipeline's image was tainted by 1989's tragic Exxon Valdez oil spill. But the state depends on oil money for its survival; oil revenues are responsible for the lack of personal income tax in Alaska and provide a state dividend – usually around $1,000 – to every citizen of the state, every year. The price of oil rises and falls, but cars continue to run in ever-growing numbers. Rising demand means continuing expeditions for more oilfields. The ongoing fight over the Alaska National Wildlife Refuge and its piddling oilfield is a prime example of the forces that split the state between developers and conservationists. There are 570,000 square miles of Alaska, or about a mile for every resident (ignore Anchorage, and you get two miles per person); put the same population density in New York, and there would be 16 people on Manhattan. So you'd think with all that space, everybody could do what they want and be happy, but so far, it's not happening.

In recent years, with pulp mills and logging concessions closing and oil's shine somewhat tarnished, the newest boom in the state is tourism. Perhaps no other state in the country is so attuned to the needs of its visitors, and Alaska has something for all tastes. You can be as far from civilization as you want in a community without wheeled vehicles, or right in the center of Anchorage, a more than luxurious city that spends 1% of its annual budget on art. Alaska fully lives up to its motto: "The last frontier." Anything can happen here.

The Gold Rushes

 Even a brief look at the history of the North shows that if it weren't for gold, there still might not be anybody north of Seattle. The Russians stuck pretty much to the coastline while Alaska was theirs – move 100 miles inland and it's almost impossible to find a Russian place name – perhaps because they had their own great North, and crossing Siberia had dimmed their ardor for Arctic land crossings. And while there were certainly explorers in the North, the basic and inglorious truth is that the land was opened up by prospectors with nothing on their minds but gold.

Gold made people crazy; it made them perform superhuman feats of strength and endurance. Long after anyone sane had turned around and headed south, would-be miners were standing knee-deep in snow, frozen and half-starved, thinking one more trip to the stream might be the lucky one. And if not this stream, then the next. Maps became hot commodities – trading for several thousand dollars each at a time when that much money could provide you a reasonable living for several years. Exploration became a byproduct of the search for gold.

The Klondike rush is the most famous and brings up the most romantic images – miners heading north over the Chilkoot Pass in winter, dragging their gear behind them; trails littered with dead horses; a mad rush to build boats to float the Yukon to the goldfields.

Rent Charlie Chaplin's movie *The Goldrush* for a taste of how this struggle was turned into legend.

But there were actually hundreds of gold rushes, from tiny creeks along the Fraser Canyon to the beaches at Nome. When the Klondike strike was made, setting off the largest stampede, a nearby strike at Circle had pretty much been played out and miners there were moving deeper into the territory. By the time the 30,000 hopefuls arrived from the US, miners from other rushes nearby already had most of the Klondike staked out.

The Alaska Highway passes the sites of hundreds of small gold rushes, from the Cariboo rush in BC, to the Resurrection Creek rush near Anchorage, to the Tanana River strikes near Fairbanks. It's safe to assume that nearly every creek in the North has been panned, mined, prodded, and poked by people looking for gold; and any time one person got lucky, everyone else within shouting distance came running. Throughout the North there are places named for their distance from the last big strike: Sixtymile, Fortymile.

These miners were not, for the most part, having a good time. They were freezing their butts off a long way from home, and, more often than not, coming up empty. Even their equipment, which should have made their lives easier, made things worse. Some early advice to would-be miners said that their most important bit of clothing would be "a good pair of well-nailed boots. They may be high or low, but should be over 18 inches." The same writer goes on to suggest a "nine-pound eiderdown sleeping bag" for summer. What these guys would have done for a chance to shop at REI.

THE THINGS THEY CARRIED

You always hear that "ton of gear" thing, but exactly what did that mean? Just what were these poor schmoes dragging along with them?

Here's what one popular guidebook of the day suggested:

- ❏ 150 lbs of bacon
- ❏ 400 lbs of flour
- ❏ 25 lbs of rolled oats
- ❏ 125 lbs of beans
- ❏ 10 lbs of tea
- ❏ 10 lbs of coffee
- ❏ 25 lbs of sugar
- ❏ 25 lbs of dried potatoes
- ❏ 2 lbs of dried onions
- ❏ 15 lbs of salt
- ❏ 1 lb of pepper
- ❏ 75 lbs of dried fruit
- ❏ 8 lbs of baking powder
- ❏ 2 lbs of soda
- ❏ 1/2 lb of vinegar
- ❏ 12 oz compressed soap
- ❏ 9 cakes of soap
- ❏ 1 can of mustard
- ❏ 1 tin of matches
- ❏ stove for 4 men
- ❏ gold pan
- ❏ set of granite buckets
- ❏ large bucket
- ❏ knife, fork, spoon, cup, plate
- ❏ frying pan
- ❏ coffee & teapot
- ❏ small assortment of medicine

- ❏ 1 shovel
- ❏ 1 whipsaw
- ❏ pack straps
- ❏ 2 axes, 1 extra handle
- ❏ 6 8-inch files
- ❏ drawing knife, brace & bits, jack plane, hammer
- ❏ 200 feet of 3/8-inch rope
- ❏ 8 lbs of pitch
- ❏ 5 lbs of oakum
- ❏ 10 x 12 tent
- ❏ 2 oil blankets
- ❏ scythe stone
- ❏ 2 picks
- ❏ canvas
- ❏ 5 yards of mosquito netting
- ❏ 3 suits of heavy underwear
- ❏ 1 heavy mackinaw coat
- ❏ 2 pr. heavy mackinaw trousers
- ❏ 1 heavy rubber-lined coat
- ❏ 1 dozen heavy wool socks
- ❏ 1/2 dozen heavy wool mittens
- ❏ 2 heavy outershirts
- ❏ 2 pairs of heavy, snagproof rubber boots
- ❏ 2 pairs of shoes
- ❏ 4 pairs of blankets
- ❏ 4 towels
- ❏ 2 pairs of overalls
- ❏ 1 suit of oil clothing
- ❏ several changes of summer clothing

 For a great history of the search for gold in the North, read Pierre Berton's *The Klondike Fever*.

GOLD CLAIMS

The tradition of mining claims continues, and much of the North has been staked out by miners who will be quite displeased if they catch you looking for gold on their claim. They'll probably let it pass if you're just standing in a stream for a few minutes, swishing your gold pan around – most miners today are well past that method, working with high-tech and expensive equipment – but you do need to be cautious and courteous. A flyer published by the Alaska Department of Natural Resources flyer says, "The gold you pan probably won't concern them as much as the possible vandalism of equipment, liability, or interruption of their operations." Then again, it might. Technically, you must have permission to be on someone's claim. The days when claim-jumpers were routinely shot are still not so far in the past. Claims should be marked off by highly visible stakes, so watch for them.

The flyer says, "Most streams originating in the mountains have color [gold flakes] in them and, by working the stream gravels, usually a few will be found." In other words, there's gold practically everywhere, at least in trace amounts.

There's still a lot of land out there that's not claimed, and many commercial operators will let you pan gold in their claims for a small fee.

AUTHOR TIP: *If you're in a stream, the best place to look for gold is where a bit of turbulence changes slow water to fast. Put a bit of gravel from the stream into your pan, add some water, and swish gently, allowing water and rocks to swish over the sides of the pan. Gold is heavier than gravel and, as you eliminate rocks and dirt from the pan, the gold stays behind.*

You've got to try panning for gold at least once – this is what brought people up North to begin with.

If you think a search for gold brought some of your people up this way, an electronic database called "Ancestors," put together by librarians at the University of Alaska and a professional genealogist, can help you search for your roots. You can check it out in Fairbanks at the **Rasmusson Library** (☎ 907-474-7261). The project incorporates magazine and newspaper articles, obituaries, mining reports, business directories, and more. If one of your relatives was in the North during a rush, you should be able to find traces here. **The Alaska Department of Natural R**esources (3601 C St., Ste. 1200, Anchorage, AK 99503, USA; ☎ 907-269-8721) publishes "Sources of Alaskan and Yukon Gold Rushes and Gold Rush Communities," which can offer some leads, as can the Yukon Archives, Box 2703, Whitehorse, Yukon Territory Y1A 2C6, Canada; ☎ 403-667-5321.

Climate

 Expect the unexpected. The weather bureaus of both Canada and the US have been compiling information on the climate of the North, and they can supply you with averages and expectations. As a general guideline, summers are mild and beautiful, with temperatures in the 50-80F range – usually in the lower end of that range – throughout most of the region. However, it might rain at any time, and snowstorms are not unknown at higher elevations in June and July. The mountains cool down quickly, and the larger mountains and big northern lakes create their own highly unpredictable weather patterns. You can find an area suffering from full flood conditions, facing a forecast with nothing but rain, while on the other side of the nearest mountain range people are fearing drought.

Overall, expect long summer days – Fairbanks has more than 20 hours of daylight in midsummer, and yes, it is very, very easy to get sunburned up there, particularly on your face and head. The weather is warm and sunny, punctuated regularly by rain and cold – how regularly is mostly a matter of luck. Nights tend to be quite cool.

For summer travelers, not much special clothing is needed. It is best to bring a light jacket and a sweater or two. If the temperature drops, it's better to have on several layers of light clothes, rather than one layer of heavy clothing, since layers trap warm air and keep you toasty. You'll need them, and there's no telling when.

In the winter, things are quite a bit harsher. The 60° daytime temperatures drop to well below zero. Forty below is a common winter temperature in Fairbanks, and 70 below is not unknown in many places along the Alaska Highway. Do not venture out into a Northern winter without appropriate clothing and preparation. The days are short – in many places, nonexistent – and the nights are incredibly cold. If you're planning to spend time in the North in the winter, bring the warmest clothes you can find, and pack a sunlamp – the dark is going to get to you long before the cold does.

The Landscape

 Let's start from the landscape of the south, moving north, with the highway, to the tundra above the Arctic circle.

What you hit first along the coasts of Alaska and Canada, stretching in as far as the Rocky Mountain divide, is a mid-latitudes rainforest.

∎ Identifying Trees

Sitka spruce (*Picea sitchensis*). Alaska's state tree, the Sitka spruce grows 150-225 feet high, up to eight feet in diameter, and lives 500-700 years. Its leaves are dark green needles, about an inch long, and they cover all the branches. At the top of the tree, light orange-brown cones develop, dropping to the forest floor and providing a favorite food for squirrels. Sitka spruce wood is commonly used for making guitars. The Russians used it for the beams and decks of ships that they built in their Sitka boatworks, and for housebuilding. In World War II, it was used for airplanes – the British made two of their fighters from Sitka spruce, and of course that's what went into Howard Hughes's *Spruce Goose*. Walking in the forest, you'll find huge spruce stumps. Notice the niches cut in them a couple of feet above the ground. Loggers, working a two-man saw, couldn't cut at the tree's base because their saws weren't long enough. Instead, they'd cut these niches, insert a platform on which to stand, then lop the tree from higher up, where the saw could go through.

Western hemlock (*Tsuga heterophylla*). Western hemlock are shorter than Sitka spruce – they grow to a maximum of about 150 feet – and they're thin, with a large tree only about four feet in diameter. Maximum lifespan is about 500 years. The leaves are wider and lighter green than spruce leaves, and the cones are a darker brown. Bark is a gray-brown. Western hemlock loves to come back in clear-cut areas.

Mountain hemlock (*Tsuga mertensiana*). It's not that easy to tell a mountain hemlock from a Western, but they are considerably smaller, growing to a maximum of 100 feet high and 30 inches in diameter. Their range is considerably more limited than the Western hemlock (Western can grow pretty much anywhere under the tree line, but mountain hemlock is restricted to the 3,000-3,500-foot elevation isotherm). The needles are more pointed than on Western hemlock, and the cones are bigger.

Yellow cedar (*Chamaecyparis nootkatensis*). The Forest Service is still trying to figure out why all the yellow cedar trees in Southeast are dying. The problem is, they've been dying off for a very long time, the last hundred years or more. It's a fairly delicate tree, temperature-wise, but scientists are not sure if the problem is a drop in temperature, too much snow during spring growing season, or a rise in temperature. Yellow cedars (which, like Western red cedars, are actually a kind of cypress), grow to about 80 feet, and perhaps two feet in diameter. They can live up to a thousand years, but they never get that big. The leaves are dark green and look almost like chains of beads; the cones are green and black, about a half-inch in diameter. Happiest at altitudes of 500-1,200 feet.

Western red cedar (*Thuja plicata*). Taller than the yellow cedar, the Western red cedar covers a wider range, from sea level to about 3,000 feet in elevation. The leaves are much like those of the yellow cedar, but more yellow-green in color. The cones are oval, as opposed to the round yellow cedar cones.

The Land & Its People

■ Alpine Meadows & Muskeg

 Muskeg is a mass of low, dead plants decomposing in a wet area. The dying plants make a rich soil that supports new plants ranging from the marsh violet and marigold, to sedge, juniper, and swamp gentian. Few of the muskeg plants grow more than a foot tall.

The most important plant in muskeg is sphagnum moss, which holds as much as 30 times its own weight in water, and so preserves the marshy habitat necessary for muskeg.

Muskeg covers more than 10% of the Tongass, and shows up as a large, mossy patch in the middle of a forested area. Flightseeing over Misty Fjords opens huge vistas of muskeg for view. From the ground level, walking on muskeg is kind of like walking on a trampoline. The trick is missing the spots where the plant life is not thick enough to support your weight: it's actually possible to drown in muskeg patches. Think of muskeg as a mat laid over a hole just like an elephant trap in an old Tarzan movie. But here the hole is filled with water.

Some contend that muskeg is the natural climax of the mid-latitudes rainforest, the place where the forest is heading, forming when the trees have died of old age and no new growth has come in. The acidic level of the muskeg keeps new growth out. This theory is debatable, as most of the forest is on slopes, while muskeg grows only on the flat.

Alpine meadows (technically, sub-alpine meadows) exist between the frozen peaks of mountains and the tree line. The soil here is thin and acidic, and only low plants survive (on a sub-alpine meadow, there will be bushes or shrubs; true high alpine will be without them). The meadows are thick with lupine, lichen, heather, low grass and sedge; a walk across such a meadow will show a complex of inter-nested plants and roots that looks as complicated as an architectural diagram. Like muskeg, the meadow plants are very fragile and can show scars for many years after damage. Stay on the paths and walk with care.

Lupine on the Kenai Peninsula.

ECO-AWARENESS: *There's no doubt that forests in the North are disappearing. Most of the disposable chopsticks used in Japan come from British Columbia. Most of Japan's comic book paper comes from Alaska.*

■ The Forest Service

A big part of the forestry problem is that, with no valid interpretation to work on, the National Forest Service makes the rules themselves. Their motto seems to be, "When in doubt, build a road and sell the timber for a loss." As Bill Bryson points out, there are over 378,000 miles of roads in national forests – that's eight times the length of the interstate highway system. In Bryson's book *A Walk in the Woods*, he writes that you show the Forest Service "a stand of trees anywhere, and they will regard it thoughtfully for a long while, and say at last, 'You know, we could put a road here.'" As you're bound to see on your travels in the North, your road-building tax dollars serve only to open up your national forests to being stripped by private logging concerns.

It is absolutely necessary to separate the Forest Service and the people who work for it. On your trip, you will probably meet lots of Forest Service people (Greenies, they're often called, not because of their jobs, but because of the color of the Forest Service vehicles, a sort of nauseating green). They are, with astonishingly few exceptions, good, helpful people who care very much about the wild. We've never yet met one who said he always wanted to grow up and become an official environmental terrorist for the government. The employees of the Forest Service are not the problem, but their bosses are, the people back East who have never seen an inch of unpaved territory in their lives. The ultimate boss of the Forest Service is Congress; that means we're the boss, because the people in Congress work for us. Take a look at the forest and take the time to remind them of that fact.

■ Reforestation

Although you'll pass by mile after mile of untouched, old-growth forest, any trip through the North is going to be an education in clear-cutting. You cannot miss the bald patches of mountains, scarred by landslides of rock no longer held in by tree roots.

Reforestation efforts are largely left to nature. It's easy to spot old clear-cuts: they are a brighter green than the surrounding forest, since the balance of plants is reversed. In the coastal old-growth areas, Sitka spruce is the dominant species, with Western hemlock second. However, in a clear-cut area, the hemlock quickly asserts dominance, leaving little room for the spruce to take root and grow. No surprise, then, that Western hemlock comprised 51% of logging activity – the companies are all for it coming back to dominate the land. Also in clear-cut areas, the usual lower-level plants –

the berry bushes, devil's club, skunk cabbage and so on – are pretty much absent from the grow-back. So, while from a distance the new growth looks at least similar, from up close it seems practically sterile.

Logging on government land is appallingly ugly, but strictly controlled. Cuts can cover only so many acres, and there have to be buffer zones between cuts and fragile areas such as streambeds. These restrictions do not hold for native-controlled land. The native corporations are free to strip entire mountains bare, to log right up to the water's edge, even in salmon spawning streams. And so they do. Logging in native areas makes the rest of the North's logged areas look like lovingly tended gardens.

The Canadians, as you'll quickly discover, belie their relaxed reputation when it comes to clear cutting. These people strip mountains down wholesale and, unlike the US, where there's at least usually a buffer left to hide the destruction from the road, the same is rarely the case in Canada. There are patches of BC that could make an environmentalist cry.

On the good side, Canadians are also much more careful about planting new trees. In a couple of hundred years, that'll really help, because no matter what you hear, it can take as long as 300-400 years for the natural balance of the land to reassert itself after a clear-cut, if it ever does. There are those – usually forestry officials – who say it takes only 40-100 years, but they're kidding themselves and lying to you.

Overall in the coastal forests, site of most of the logging, hemlock comprises 60% of the forest; Sitka spruce 30%. They share the forest with more than 900 other plant species. This includes 200 species of vascular plant, 100 or so of moss and liverwort, around 350 lichen species, and nearly 30 species of fern. In the mature forest, there are roughly 150 species of bird and mammal, plus thousands of insect species calling the place home.

■ Economics

Now for the other side of the story. Logging has long been second only to fishing as the most important industry in Alaska; for many years, especially before the oil strikes, it kept the entire state's economy afloat. The same holds true in BC. However, that's changing. The dive in Japan's economy (Japan imports more than $1.33 billion a year worth of Alaskan materials, three times more than Alaska's number two trading partner, South Korea) has dried up the timber market and the fishing market. (Now the Japanese will start bringing up all those logs they sank in a deep freeze in Tokyo Bay when the prices were good and the Forest Service was giving away huge swaths of forest for less than it cost to cut a road in.) Just between 1996 and 1997, Alaska's fishing exports declined more than 16%, and lumber exports were down more than 5%. That was before the serious slump hit Asia. Paper exports, once the staple of pulp mills around the state, declined 60.4% in just that year.

There are other problems with the extraction industries. With growing environmental awareness, methods are changing – which usually means becoming more expensive – and with price drops (largely due to serious deforestation efforts in the Third World), logging has become less viable. Southeast Alaska's logging economy has almost collapsed. This is great for the forest, but lousy for the economy of the towns and the state. There is nowhere for the people to turn; fishing has been decreasing throughout Alaska and Canada, and that really leaves only tourism. How many t-shirt shops can one small town support?

Any rational human being, no matter how green at heart, knows logging must happen. People need jobs, people need wood. We simply argue that it should be done not on the basis of politics, but on the basis of best available science and maximum sustainable yield.

■ Conservation Groups

 Before you write to your congressman, get the facts from both sides. **Alaska Rainforest Campaign**, 320 4th St. NE, Washington, D.C. 20002, ☎ 202-544-0475, on the Web at www.akrain.org, works on both the Tongass and the Chugach national forests. They're the central organization for forest conservation in Alaska, but the National Forest Foundation also concerns itself with the Southeast region, among others. Reach them at P.O. Box 1256, Norfolk, VA 23501. The Greater Ketchikan Chamber of Commerce, 744 Water Street Upstairs, P.O. Box 5957, Ketchikan, AK 99901, has information from the logger's point of view.

For Canada, the **Forest Action Network**, Box 625, Bella Coola, BC, V0T 1C0, ☎ 250-799-5800, maintains connections with a large network of conservation groups throughout BC, specializing in the coastal rainforest.

We feel that both conservationists and loggers are correct; the trick is getting them to meet in the middle on the basis of best available science and best long-term results. The question is whether they'll ever get a chance to do so, given the political wrangling in Washington and Ottawa. But the one thing any sane person should realize right away is that clear-cutting just ain't the answer.

■ Volcanoes

 The entire coast of Alaska is ringed by volcanoes, and active volcanoes dot the Southcentral Alaska landscape. **Augustine** erupted in 1986, and in 1993, an eruption of **Redoubt** shut down transportation in Southcentral's skies for days as the ash cloud billowed. While we were preparing the final touches on this book now in your hands, a volcano in Alaska blew five times in one day. But these events are the exception, not the rule for Southcentral. It is on the Alaska Peninsula and the Aleutians that the volcanoes begin to dominate. **Katmai**, the "Valley of

10,000 Smokes," saw the largest volcanic eruption ever recorded when, in 1912, a virtually unknown volcano, **Novarupta**, exploded. Prior to that, the landscape had been lush and full of wildlife. The eruption dumped 700 feet of ash in some places, and Katmai remains one of the most active volcanic regions in the world.

The best volcanoes views can be had along the road to Homer: on the west side of the Kenai, volcanoes dominate the view on a clear day.

■ Earthquakes

 Volcanoes kind of go together with earthquakes; where you've got one, you've likely got the other. And Alaska has earthquakes to spare.

Most famously, On Good Friday, 1964, a tremor measuring 8.4 (some say 9. 2) on the Richter Scale hit Anchorage. Tidal waves practically wiped out every city along the Southcentral coast.

A side effect of an earthquake created of one of the largest waves ever seen on the face of the planet. In 1958, a quake caused a rockslide in Lituya Bay, near Yakutat. The slide was so big that, for all intents and purposes, a mountain fell into the water from 3,000 feet. This kicked up a wave that on the opposite side of the bay, stripped the mountain bare to an altitude of 1,720 feet. The bay acted as a funnel, pushing the wave higher and higher. A branch of the wave moved toward the narrow open mouth of the bay at more than 100 miles per hour. Four square miles of forest were destroyed by this single wave, and two fishermen were killed.

■ Glaciers

 After a while the forest and ocean become overwhelming, and it's not certain you'll spot a grizzly bear or a whale. But one of the other great sights of Alaska and the North is always on display, and you will see at least one, if not dozens. These are the glaciers.

There are, literally, hundreds of glaciers in Alaska, the Yukon, and British Columbia, ranging from tiny cirque glaciers to the huge Matanuska Ice-fields, which cover an area bigger than Rhode Island.

How They Are Formed

Glaciers are, quite simply, old snow. Lots of old snow. They begin to form when newer snow falls on top of older snow, compressing it; more new snow comes in, and layer after layer forms. As the layers form, the crystals of snow undergo a slight change; where they touch, they squeeze out the air between them, and they near the melting point, allowing for an adjustment of the space between crystals. Individual snow crystals are packed in very, very tightly, keeping each other cool and forming thicker and thicker layers of ice.

The grand party time for glaciers was in the last ice age, which went from roughly two million years ago up to only 14,000 years ago. The glaciers you'll see were formed during this time, as the snows fell and the woolly mammoths cavorted.

Glaciers are not static entities; they can be considered frozen rivers and, like all rivers, they move. A glacier high on a mountain will obey the dictates of gravity and start to move downward. A few hot seasons will melt a glacier back. Most (but not all) of the glaciers in the North are retreating somewhat; this is partly due to global warming, and partly simply the way things are. We are, after all, just in a warm spot between ice ages, and the freeze will return sooner or later, if we humans don't irre-

Glacial ice.

vocably screw up world climate just so we can hang out at the mall. Glacier movement – forward or back – depends on a wide variety of factors, including weather, slope, and thickness of the ice. Sometimes one part of a glacier will move faster than another, causing a bulge of thick ice called a **kinematic wave.**

Glacial movement is not easy on the landscape around the glacier. While the ice itself isn't quite hard enough to do much damage, the stones and boulders that the ice picks up are abrasive on the ground. This is beautifully illustrated in the land around Exit Glacier in Seward: as the glacier has retreated, it has left behind land that is stripped almost to the bedrock. But after the land has had a little time to recover, the brush starts to spring up, and from that, the trees.

Because of the amount of rock and debris that a glacier carries with it, it leaves a clear record of its passing. When a glacier begins its retreat, it leaves a line of stones known as a **terminal moraine** to mark the peak of its advance. These are simply stones that were dropped or pushed by the leading edge of the glacier, and moraines can be huge and quite dramatic. There are also lateral moraines, where the glacier's sides once were.

Shapes & Colors of Glaciers

There are a considerable number of categories of glaciers – mountain glaciers and tidewater glaciers are among the major types.

- **Mountain glaciers** are found up on the peaks. A good example is Bear Glacier, near Stewart/Hyder, or the Juneau Icefields. That's also what you'll see if you drive up through Jasper and Banff.

- **Tidewater glaciers** come right down to the sea: for example, Tracy Arm, the glaciers in Glacier Bay, and the 20 glaciers that empty into Prince William Sound. These are the glaciers that let you see the drama of calving, when huge chunks of glacial face break off and fall into the water. Watching a berg the size of your house come crashing into the sea is not a sight you'll soon forget. Problem is, there really aren't any of these visible from the road, so you're going to have to get out on a boat to really see them. Yeah, life's rough when you have to go for a boat ride in the most beautiful landscape on the planet.

The final point to make about glaciers is their stunning blue color, which is due to the immense pressure that the ice is under and how incredibly compact the ice crystals are. A walk on a glacier will reveal shades of blue that you never before knew existed.

DON'T MISS: *The best places to get close to a glacier along the highway are Worthington Glacier, on the road to Valdez, and Exit Glacier, outside Seward. Portage Glacier, south of Anchorage, was once pretty accessible, but now it has retreated behind a bend in the mountain, and you can't see anything unless you take an overpriced boat ride. For more dramatic glaciers, head into Glacier Bay, or check out Harriman and College Glaciers in Prince William Sound – you can get to them by kayaking out of Whittier.*

The Bad News

Okay, Alaska's got a ton of glaciers. However, they're starting to disappear at an alarming rate. Call it global warming, call it a hot spell in world history if you like to rationalize. But when we started writing these books, 15 years ago, Exit Glacier was a more than a half-mile longer than it is now – today, the glacier is melting at a rate of three feet a day. Portage Glacier was visible from the road. The huge Matanuska Glacier filled valleys. Worthington Glacier was right outside the car.

It's not like that anymore.

The glaciers are going. Fast. It's that simple.

JOKULHLAUP

There's a little oddity, perhaps best grouped in as a side effect of glaciers, the jokulhlaup. It's not something you want to see, but it's an interesting in a scientific way.

The jokulhlaup occurs sometimes when a glacier blocks off a chunk of valley, leading to a large lake, choked off by ice. Because, ultimately, water is stronger than ice, the water can actually tunnel under the glacier; when it hits the end of the ice, it floods out into the glacier's usual silt stream. This can mean tons of water flooding out suddenly from under the ice. For all intents and purposes, it's a dam break, and the effects are like any other dam break: everybody downstream needs to head for higher ground.

After the lake is drained, the ice freezes up again, the lake starts to refill, and the whole process starts all over again. There's a jokulhlaup on the Snow River, emptying into Kenai Lake, which floods out about every three years. Statewide, there are more than 750 of them.

The Aurora Borealis

 Besides wildlife and the glaciers, people go to the north country hoping to see the aurora borealis – the northern lights. As most people travel in the summer, of course, it's too light to see the display unless you find yourself wide awake at 2 am or so.

The aurora is produced by a high-vacuum electrical discharge, created by interactions between sun and earth. What you see – the glowing curtain of lights – is charged electrons and protons formed by the sun hitting gas molecules in the upper atmosphere. The aurora can be compared to a TV picture. Electrons strike the screen (or the air), getting excited and making a glow. The most common color for the aurora is a yellow-green, caused by oxygen atoms roughly 60 miles above the earth.

The lights get more intense the farther north you go. People in Montana occasionally see a display. In Fairbanks, they're practically as common as the moon, with 240 displays a year. There are those who say they can hear the aurora sounds like a crackling but so far scientists haven't been able to prove or record it.

Head outside on cool, clear nights, and look north. You never know.

The Cultures

■ Southcentral

The dominant group in the western Gulf of Alaska and the Aleutians is the **Aleut Indians**. The Aleuts came over the Bering Land Bridge, liked what they saw right there at its base and stayed, making a living from the rich seas and harsh lands of western Alaska. For linguistic purposes, Aleuts are split into western, central, and eastern branches, but the language differences are dialectical and, unlike the Koniags (the other coastal Eskimo group), an Aleut from Attu can understand another from Chignik.

When the Russians first arrived in the area, they applied the term "Aleut" indiscriminately to every native they found. Because of this usage, which survives to modern times, the coastal Koniag Eskimos were also lumped into the "Aleut" category, despite the fact of their being from quite a different group, speaking an entirely different language. Physical differences are less marked. Athabaskan Indians also inhabited large parts of Southcentral, though they were not dominant along the coast.

Before the arrival of the Russians, Aleut culture thrived. They hunted from baidarka (animal skin kayaks) for whale, seal, sea lion, and otter, using tools made from bone and stone. Their clothing was made from animal intestines, which made it waterproof.

Aleut dwellings were communal and, usually, subterranean, covered with the excellent insulation of growing grass. Some of these underground houses are said to have been as large as 250 feet long. The houses had hatches in the ceiling to allow light in and smoke out; the ceiling was often held in place by rafters of whalebone, instead of scarce timber. Windows were made of translucent panes of otter intestine. In the hierarchy of society, the back of the house was always reserved for the most respected member of the dwelling. The Russians weren't very impressed with all this: "What is more revolting than all else is the filth around their huts, for the islanders do not go far away to do anything – and this gives one a very bad impression of their tidiness."

But while the Russians were out shivering in wool and living in houses entirely unadapted to local conditions, the Aleuts and Koniags were pretty comfy. In addition to the clothes made of intestines, the Aleuts had developed highly decorated and very practical garments. **Parkas** were made of sea otter skin or bird skin with the feathers worn on the inside, and so the down coat was invented. It took about 40 tufted puffins to make one parka, but cormorants were preferred for style and comfort. Aleut men wore **wooden hats**, shaped somewhat like a limpet shell, heavily decorated to show status and place in the community. The hats were especially important during visits to other villages. They also shielded the eyes to prevent the social gaffe of looking directly into someone's eyes (even the Russians noted how incredibly polite the Aleuts were, and how well their society ran). The Aleuts also wore complicated tattoos and labrets, small decorated ivory pieces stuck into the lips and cheeks.

In the eastern and central Aleutians, burial was usually by mummification. The deceased was buried with everything needed for the next life, from a baidarka and tools, to mats and eating utensils.

According to G.I. Davydov, who traveled the coast in 1802-1807 (an excellent translation of his voyage account is available from the Limestone Press), the coastal natives were fond of games, fairly indifferent to suffering, and extremely curious, always on the lookout for something new and diverting.

How badly the Aleuts fared when the Russians arrived is recounted elsewhere in this book. Davydov mentions that as of his trip, nobody had bothered to be interested enough in the locals to even make a collection of simple artifacts.

Here, suffice it to say that on August 21, 1732, when the Russian ship SV *Gavrill* headed for the "large country" they'd heard about (in an expedition that, incidentally, established that there was water dividing Alaska and Asia, fueling hopes for a Northwest Passage), the Aleut world came to a crashing end.

There are very, very few full-blooded Aleuts left today. The population was nearly destroyed by the Russian and U.S. exploitation of their hunting grounds, and it has been a long, slow road back. The Aleuts are back, however. The native corporations are helping the increasingly organized villages take care of business and fend off the outside world. With so much land in some of the richest fishing ports in the world, many of the villages are thriving – the Aleut village of Sand Point has one of the highest per capita incomes in the U.S.

▪ Southeast

 Although smaller tribes of Indians abounded in the Alexander Archipelago – Tsimshian, Nootka, Samish, Bella Coola – Southeast Alaska was dominated by two groups of Indians, the Tlingit and the Haida. The Tlingit controlled trade routes well into what is now the Yukon, while the Haida largely stayed to the southern coastal regions – about the only place on the highway that you're in what was once Haida territory is around Prince Rupert.

TLINGIT

It's pronounced KLINK-it by Americans. The actual native pronunciation of the word is closer to Khling-GET, but the sounds involved are unfamiliar to English speakers and the odds of saying it correctly are about zero.

As a general rule, the Haida occupied the southern reaches, from the Queen Charlotte Islands to the Ketchikan area, while the Tlingit lived on the islands farther north, as well as the inland areas of Alaska, Yukon, and British Columbia.

Culturally, the Tlingit and the Haida are remarkably similar. Blessed with living in a naturally rich area, they dined well on deer, bear, seal, otter, duck, and five varieties of salmon. Bushes hung low with fat berries ripe for picking. Survival was never a problem – there was no word in the Tlingit language for starvation, but there was the traditional saying: "when the tide's out, the table's set," reflecting the rich variety of sea life in the local diet.

Making use of time that most cultures had to spend searching for food, the cultures of the Tlingit and Haida developed in some amazingly complex ways.

Southeastern society was extremely hierarchical. Villages were headed by a chief (in the case of the Haida, up to four chiefs oversaw a single village). Everyone in the community had a particular rank in life, almost a caste. There was free mixing among the ranks in daily life, but there was little intermarriage between the low and high strata of society. Chieftainship was hereditary, usually passed from the current chief to a nephew. But being chief had few material benefits. Chiefs had no power to order the villagers to work on their behalf and, indeed, paid more for services because of their high rank.

Until European contact (and, some historians maintain, until well after), both the Tlingit and the Haida kept slaves, although only the higher ranks were allowed slave ownership. Slaves were usually obtained from captives of the many battles that raged among the villages; however, if you were born to a slave family, you would remain a slave.

The battles tended to be fought over trade routes. Trade in Southeast was rich long before the coming of the Europeans (who continued fighting over exactly the same trade routes). Again, the Tlingit controlled the northern routes, the Haida the southern.

Home life revolved around communal dwellings. Haida structures averaged 100 feet by 75 feet. Inside, there was little "furniture." Possessions were kept in bentwood boxes, decorated with totemic designs. Cooking was done in containers made of spruce-fiber; most food was boiled. Clothes were also often made of plant fibers, including cedar tree bark and spruce root. Special occasion wardrobes were made of otter, seal, and marten fur.

Within the hierarchical structure, a village was further organized around a dual structure of clan and totem. **Clan** was extended family. **Totem** was a little more complicated, and assured a genetically mixed village. One could not marry within one's own totem. Totems were distinguished by an animal sign: bear, eagle, raven, and whale are the most commonly seen in totemic design. Children became part of the same totem as their mother.

Totemic design defines the highly geometric, starkly black and red art that the natives used to decorate their homes, canoes, and blankets. It's a kind of cubism, flattening out drawings of animals, with an iconography of every gesture and posture. The art of the coastal Indians is as sophisticated as the most detailed architectural drawing, while simultaneously looking as modern and spontaneous as a Picasso.

■ Totem Poles

 Contrary to popular opinion, totem poles were never objects of worship. They were a heraldic emblem as well as a method of storytelling, a means of keeping a community memory. Although the poles used common elements and figures, any attempt to "read" a totem is possible only if you know the family and the story the pole commemorates. Usually this is possible only if there were written records of the pole raising, or if a member of the family that commissioned the pole still exists.

Poles were usually erected after a family had achieved some measure of economic success. Part of the fun of raising a pole was to show off to the neighbors. The largest poles were reserved for chiefs of extended family groups and those of higher social ranks.

Totem pole carvers were among the highest-status residents of coastal Alaska. They were tested on their knowledge of religion and mythology, as well as their carving experience, before being retained to carve a pole. They were welcomed in every village, enjoyed unrestricted freedom to travel, and were often wealthier and more famous than tribal chiefs. The downside of being a carver was that, if you made a mistake, you could be put to death.

Carvers were apprenticed when young, and they were expected to have the spiritual abilities of a shaman. Although the poles were not religious in nature, their importance to the community required a great deal of sensitivity and stamina: larger memorial poles could take over a year to carve.

Poles were invariably carved of cedar wood; larger poles were often hollowed first to make them more manageable. Tools, before European contact, were made of stone or bone. In the farther northern reaches of the pole-carving cultures, hammered copper was used.

Poles were not brightly colored. Because of the nature of cedar wood, which must be able to "breathe," painting the pole was the first step to destroying it. Native carvers used simple pigments made of plant materials, charcoal, and some oxides. Few colors other than black, red, and blue were used, and poles were seldom entirely painted. Instead, the colors were used as accents, and many poles were not painted at all.

Poles fall into seven basic types.

- ■ **Memorial poles** were erected to honor a deceased chief. These were heraldic in nature and were considered the finest of all poles. Very few examples remain in a well-preserved state.

- **Grave figures** are the most numerous of poles. Smaller than memorial poles, they showed the totemic figure of the deceased, identifying the grave site as that of a certain branch of a clan.

- **House posts** and pillars were probably the first type of pole developed, springing from the design of the long houses used along the Pacific Coast. The houses in this area were heavily decorated inside and out, and the posts and pillars were part of the adornments. Most of these disappeared with the houses, but they were once probably more numerous than the grave poles. The only limit to the use of house posts was the wealth of the owner and the space available.

- Similar to the house post was the house front, or **portal pole**. This was purely a measure of status, fronting a house to show who lived there by incorporating the family's crest or totemic figures.

- **Welcoming poles** were erected by the waterfront. These were usually unpainted, and in old pictures of villages in Southeast you'll see these standing in pairs. They were often constructed just for the occasion of a potlatch, or a large tribal gathering.

- **Mortuary poles** are related to the grave figures, but are considerably rarer. Only the Haida made general use of these poles, which were erected at a memorial potlatch.

There were the special poles that didn't fit into the above categories. These could tell stories of a successful hunt, but more often they were erected by chiefs out for revenge. The poles were designed to ridicule a specific person or group; considering the cost and difficulties of creating a pole, it's easy to imagine just how mad you'd have to be to put up a ridicule pole.

Poles were a vital part of coastal culture. A single village might have a hundred poles, and the raising of one was always a cause for celebration. A singer was hired to relate the history of the family and to narrate their accomplishments. The singer also hired and trained dancers to perform at the pole raising. Despite stories to the contrary, slaves were not sacrificed to the pole, nor buried beneath the base. Only a single skeleton has ever been found under a pole.

Despite the joy at their raising, poles were not necessarily meant to last; when their function was done, poles were allowed to fall into disrepair. The settlement of Alaska by Europeans forced many native villages to move, and the poles were left behind to rot. When hiking in remote areas, one sometimes encounters a moss-covered tree with a face – it's an old pole, turning into forest mulch.

POTLATCH

Pole raising often coincided with a potlatch. This term is a corruption of the Nootka word patshatl, meaning gift. Potlatches are famous in story as an opportunity for a family to give away all its possessions, showing its wealth, but they were a lot more complicated than that. A potlatch was given only with extreme protocol. Guests arrived on the shore in order, according to their status and rank. They were greeted by their hosts with great display. Then the feasting, which could last for several days, began. The pole raising was the height of the celebration. After the pole's story was told, the singing and the dancing finished, the gift-giving began. Gifts were carefully selected. An improper gift could be given as a purposeful insult and could lead to war. The generous spirit of the potlatch was not well understood by Europeans and the qualities of the poles were not generally appreciated. In 1884, Canadian law forbade potlatch ceremonies. This was merely another nail in the coffin for local villages.

Archeologists and anthropologists have done a remarkable job finding and preserving poles, but taken out of context they lose some of their beauty and become nothing more than museum pieces. Many such pieces suffer from the fact that early European efforts to preserve poles involved painting them, and so hastened the destruction.

After decades of neglect, totem carving is making a comeback. There are trained carvers working in several communities in BC and along the Alaskan coast, and the tradition is being revitalized with the incorporation of modern elements into standard designs.

TLINGIT RAVEN LEGENDS

According to the Tlingits, the raven is credited with stealing sunlight. At the time the world was created, it was all dark. The raven set out to obtain light, which was held jealously by a rich man. The raven seduced the rich man's daughter, and the resulting child was doted upon by the grandfather. The child began asking for larger and larger things. The stars were put into the sky at his request. Finally, the child made a grab for the sunlight, changed into a raven form, and delivered the sun to his father. In the earliest times, according to the legends, the raven was white. He earned his blackness when another scheme backfired. Escaping from a hut as he tried to steal water, he got stuck in the smoke hole. The smoke hole spirits held him there until his color had changed, and only then did they release him. There is also a raven story that is analogous to that of the biblical flood. The raven became curious about what was under the sea, so he had the Woman Under the Earth raise the waters so he could get a good look. The waters were raised slowly, so that the people could escape in their canoes.

Although the raven was the hero of most of their stories, the Tlingits were highly practical people as well. Their legends include this story about the first mosquito:

The sister to the chief was told she would never have children. Soon thereafter, however, she found herself pregnant. The fetus grew at an unnatural speed and was born after mere weeks. When he arrived, the child was covered with hair and had sharp teeth. His evil nature was proven when he was found killing animals for pleasure, not out of necessity. But, because he was the chief's nephew, nothing could be done. Finally, the chief himself got worried and fought the demon-child. The chief cut the demon with his knife, but no blood came out. Determined to rid his village of the evil, the chief began to wrestle with the demon. All night they wrestled. At the end of the battle, the chief managed to throw the demon into the fire, but the demon wasn't dead yet. From the fire came a voice declaring that the demon would drink the chief's blood for a thousand years. Ashes rose from the fire, and each ash became a mosquito.

At night, by your campfire, you may wonder how many of the thousand years are left!

Wildlife

Keep your camera ready, because this is where the North really shines.

Driving the highway, you've got an excellent chance of seeing moose, black bear, grizzly bear, Dall sheep, stone sheep, mountain goats, wolves, fox, beaver, deer, elk, and caribou, not to mention a host of smaller mammals, without ever leaving your car. The streams and lakes are teeming with king salmon, sockeye, Dolly Varden, grayling, char, and trout. In the sky, there are more than 400 species of birds: sandhill cranes, endless varieties of ducks and geese, the ubiquitous raven, and the near-legendary yellow-bellied sapsucker. Any time you stop for a picnic, a magpie is likely to land on the table and steal food. Bald eagles are so common in some cities that the locals don't even notice them.

Throughout this book, we have noted areas where you stand a good chance of seeing wildlife, be it caribou, bison, eagles, or bears. An in-margin icon indicates these spots. But it's best to be ready anywhere; animals go where they want to go. That's part of the fun of being a wild animal. Whittier has had bears inside its high school; Anchorage has moose warnings on major streets.

■ Catching A Glimpse

 What you will see of this amazing variety of fauna is largely a matter of luck, partly a matter of timing, and partly a matter of looking in the right places and being able to see the moose hiding in the brush. But keep in mind that no matter where an animal is supposed to be, it's always going to be where it wants to be.

Traditional wisdom says that the bigger animals come out in the early morning and late evening. In the far North in the summertime, 5 to 8 am and 7 to 10 pm are prime animal-spotting hours. On the highway, these times are good because there are fewer cars to scare the animals off.

Traditional wisdom also says to keep a close eye out by water, where animals go to feed. The banks of ponds, streams, and lakes are great spots to see bears.

> **WARNING:** The best way to see animals is from the comfort of your car. The signs saying "Moose Area" or "Caribou Area" are not jokes. The entire outskirts of Anchorage suffer from the road hazard of wandering moose. In a confrontation with a moose, both the moose and your car will lose, so drive with caution. All along the Kenai, you'll see signs of how many moose/car confrontations there were in the past winter; a number under 200 for any given town is a pretty good year.

The car is also your safest viewing place. The number one rule for safe animal viewing is this: Never get out of your car to follow an animal.

There are three simple reasons for this: first, as long as you're in your car, the animal isn't going to think you are food. Get out on foot, and guess what, you're back in the food chain, and you're a whole lot lower down on it than you're used to being. Even if they don't want you for food, you might set off their defensive mode. Every year people are attacked by moose. Invariably, the moose wins. Bambi does not live in the North.

Second, and a bit less extreme, is that even opening

Mountain goats near Skagway.

your car door might cause the animal to flee. Should you follow, you are endangering the animal's survival by taking it from its food source and possibly from its young, and by making it burn valuable calories. This is a crime, subject to arrest and fines. If you see someone hassling wildlife, take down the plate numbers and report them at the next ranger station.

Finally, you are depriving others of a chance to see the animal.

Never forget that these animals are wild and interested only in their own survival.

When you spot an animal, pull your car slowly to the side of the road. A Canadian Park Ranger told us that the biggest danger on the Alaska Highway is from people who do not follow this advice, thus causing accidents. Yeah, sure, park your car dead center in the road to gawk. The animals might get a kick out of watching a serious collision. It's more exciting for everybody to see a bear than to come around a corner and find someone stopped in the center of the road trying to watch a bear. So get your car off the road, and then shut off the engine. Make no sudden moves or sounds. Remember that you are invading the animal's home, and that its rights are foremost. The quieter you are, the more likely it is that the animal will look you over for a moment and then go back about its business, leaving you plenty of time for photos.

Never feed an animal (except the mosquitoes; there isn't much you can do about that), and keep all food at your campsite in scent-proof containers to discourage the curious. At all times, treat animals with respect; they, in turn, will treat you to a look at the beauty and the power of nature.

To keep track of Alaska's wildlife and the threats it faces, join the **Alaska Wildlife Alliance**, PO Box 202022, Anchorage, AK 99520. They've been fighting the good fight for more than 15 years.

The Alaska Department of Fish and Game produces an excellent brochure, "Southeast Alaska: Guidelines for Wildlife Viewing." Its most valuable chapter explains how to tell when you're too close to an animal and need to back off. Again, remember that bothering animals is against state law, punishable by up to six months in jail and a $1,000 fine. Help the Fish and Game people protect the wildlife by reporting violators, especially boats that chase down whales. Get the number of the vessel, take a picture, and make them pay for disrupting wildlife.

The three most common animals along the Alaska Highway are the moose, the bear, and the mosquito. Perhaps the most sought-after is the wolf.

■ Moose

 Moose are the largest members of the deer family, and the Alaska moose is the largest of all the moose subspecies: they stand from five to seven feet high at the shoulder, and the antlers, which grow only on the male, can measure six feet from tip to tip. Covered in thick, coarse brown fur, most people think moose are ungainly looking animals, but they can move with surprising grace and amazing speed, and we think they have a great amount of a kind of Zen dignity.

Moose are grazing animals, eating twigs, bark, grasses, moss, and water lilies. Willow is one of their favorite foods. Sometimes you can see where moose have been through because there will be a "hedge line" – all the plants cropped off at an even height.

Although moose live in small groups in the winter, during the summer months they tend to live alone, and the males are rarely sighted down from the mountains.

Moose breed in the fall. The males go through a fairly elaborate jousting routine, putting their antlers to good use while they try to establish dominance. Gestation period is about 240 days, with the calves born in May and June. Twin calves are not uncommon, and sometimes there are triplets.

More people are injured by moose than by any other wild mammal in the Americas. The only other large mammal in the world that can cause as much damage (besides people themselves) are the hippos of Africa. Moose are very territorial and protective, especially of their young. They are larger than you think, and their hooves are very sharp. Never think of a moose as a big, harmless galoot. Sit and watch them all you want, but do it from a safe distance. Only an idiot with a death wish tries to sneak up on a moose.

If the moose comes at you, run. This is the exact opposite of the advice for bear encounters. Moose just want you out of their territory. If they see you running away, they'll likely go back about their business.

We had a moose charge us once when we were on a motorcycle in Alaska. We came around a corner, and she was eating willows by the side of the road. She didn't know what a motorcycle was, but she was protecting her calf, and she was sure we were a threat; on our part, we were desperately trying to get the bike turned around and get out of there before she killed us. Seeing a moose, hackles raised, coming at you is not something you want to experience. Do not wait to discover what the moose breath feels like. Run. Run like you have never run before.

■ Bears

There's nothing quite like seeing a grizzly or a black bear walking in the woods or along the shore of a lake or stream hunting for fish. Or better yet, leaping into the water and coming up soaking wet, shaking itself.

Brown Bears

Brown bears, or grizzlies, are rarer and considerably larger than their cousins, the blacks. Your odds of seeing a grizzly along the highway anywhere but inside Denali Park are minimal. There are quite a few on the islands. Kodiak Island is famous for its huge bears, some more than 10 feet tall, and Admiralty Island in Southeast Alaska, near Juneau, has more bears than people. Grizzlies average seven to nine feet long, with males ranging from 400 to 1,100 pounds. Females run about 20% smaller. Brown bears can range from dark brown to blonde in color; the easiest way to distinguish them is by their hump on the back, just behind the head. Brown bears have a life expectancy of about 20 years in the wild.

These bears are bigger and faster and more dexterous than you can imagine. There is no thrill quite like watching a grizzly eat a fish, its claws moving as delicately as a pair of chopsticks. You can find t-shirts in some of the roadside shops in Alaska that show a grizzly paw the size of a dinner plate; the caption says "Actual Size," and it's not a joke. The biggest grizzly track we've found was 17 inches long, heel to pug. And that was in a place where there weren't really big bears.

Black Bears

Black bears are more common. You're almost sure to see at least one black bear (if not a lot more) along the highway. They range from three to five feet in length and weigh from 150 to 400 pounds. A good-sized black bear is easily mistaken for a brown bear because black bears are not necessarily black; their color can range from black to very light brown. In fact, two kinds of black bears are actually white: the **kermodie**, found around Princess Royal Island in British Columbia and around the junction of the Cassiar and the Yellowhead highways near Kitwanga, as well as the the gray-blue **glacier** bear, found near Yakutat.

Populations

Bear populations vary widely, depending on what the environment has to offer. Around Anan Bear Observatory, there are more than a hundred bears, living off the rich salmon stream; by contrast, at the North Slope, there may be only one bear (polar, this far north) per 300 miles. The average in the productive southern areas of the state in all the coastal regions served by the ferry, except the Aleutians, is maybe one bear per 15-23 square miles. Obviously, territories overlap, and a lot of bears may be sharing the same food reserves.

The life cycle of browns and blacks is similar. Cubs (one or two, very occasionally three) are born during the mother's hibernation. Black bear cubs weigh only a few ounces at birth, and their birth may not even wake the mother. They attach themselves to a teat, and mother keeps on sleeping.

INNOCENT OBSERVATION

In his 1555 book, *A Description of the Northern Peoples*, Olaus Magnus wrote that the "she-bear, a creature full of wiles, gives birth to shapeless cubs, which she licks with her tongue into a form like her own." Imagine a world full of such marvels.

Rising from hibernation, the bears spend the first week or two not quite awake. Their metabolism, shut down during the winter, is still pretty slow. They come out of their dens, dig up a few skunk cabbage tubers (which act as a laxative, helping to get things running again after the long sleep), and then go back to sleep for a while longer.

The bulk of the summer is spent eating, exploring, and teaching the young bears what they need to know. Bears are very playful and, while not particularly social, cubs can have a great time with each other.

Come fall and the first touch of colder weather, the bears seem to enter a kind of frantic mood, as they try to pack on enough fat to last them through the winter. They move down to salmon streams and start to gorge themselves on the return. A bear can eat part of 50 fish a day – stomach, brains, some skin, the roe, the parts with the most fat – leaving the rest behind for birds to scavenge.

Come winter, the bears hole up in their dens. One of the last things they do before hibernating is eat some clay if it's available – sometimes you'll see scratch marks in clay banks, where a bear has tried to find some better tasting clay. This is thought to help plug up the digestive tract for the winter.

Bears are omnivorous – they will eat anything. They are also highly intelligent and extremely curious. And, when threatened, surprised, or angered, they are extremely dangerous.

Bear Safety

While virtually every story you've ever heard about bear attacks is likely to be untrue, you do not want to mess with bears in the wild. They are not like Yogi waiting to steal a picnic basket. They're animals with jaws strong enough to take off your leg, and if you provoke one, it will react.

However, the bears really have no interest in you at all. In fact, they're usually appalled that you're even there, and most of the time they'll do anything they can to get away from you. This makes it fairly easy to stay safe. All you have to do is make sure the bear sees you first. To avoid untoward encounters with bears, there are a few simple precautions you should take.

- The easiest thing to do is **avoid contact**. When hiking, make some noise to alert bears of your presence. Talk loudly, bang a stick against trees, or drop a few pebbles into an empty soft drink can and tie it around your waist so it clanks. Some people use small bells, which most Alaskans tend to call "bear dinner bells." We just call out "Hey, bear," at fairly regular intervals.

- **Never smell interesting**. Bears have a keen sense of smell, and poor eyesight. They are both curious and hungry. Bears are omnivores, like humans, and they'll eat pretty much anything – berries, fish, squirrels, whatever looks good. They are also known to eat camping gear if the right mood hits them. Cooking inside a tent is an invitation to disaster, as are strong perfumes or soaps. Keep all smells away from your campsite, and keep your food in a bearproof container or up in a tree, hanging from a rope (see the Camping section for more details). If you're keeping food in the car, the trunk is safer than the interior – at least that way they won't tear up your upholstery if they want your pretzels. Bears have only about six months to get fat enough to make it through hibernation, and so they get touchy about their food supply. When you consider a squirrel is only about 2,000 calories, you know it takes a lot of eating to fill a bear.

- **Stay away from cubs**. Period. If you see a bear cub, head back the way you came, away from the cub, as quickly as possible, without showing signs of distress. Just go back the way you came, because where there's a cub, there's a protective mother nearby. There are more stupid people/bear altercations because of people wanting to pet the cute bear cub than all other causes combined. People see a cub out playing, and don't bother to remember that Mom has claws big enough to whack your head off with a single blow.

- **Bears always have the rights to berry bushes and fishing streams.** A single bear can eat 2,000 or more berries in a single day (and you have to wonder who counted seeds in bear scat, and for how long, to come up with that number), so a loaded bush is always tempting for a bear. Stay out of thick patches of bush, make noise. The bears don't want to see you – they just want to eat and get on with their business. Try not to walk into the wind; bears don't see well, but they do have excellent senses of smell and, face it, you don't smell as if you belong there. If the wind is behind you, your scent is carrying news of your approach, and that gives the bears time to leave.

- **Never let a dog loose** in the forest. It's generally better to leave your dog at home. Dogs and bears don't get along. Even the calmest dog tends to freak out and think it's tougher than the bear as soon as it gets the first whiff of bruin. We've known people with weiner dogs that thought they could attack bears. Bears make dogs really, really stupid.

If you see a bear, don't run. Food runs, so the bear's impulse is to chase. You will lose any race you have with a bear. On a dirt road, we once startled a bear. We were driving nearly 30 miles per hour; the bear passed us, and ran straight up a hill and out of sight faster than we could put on the brakes. This was not unusual; black bears have been clocked at well over 30 mph, and browns at 41 mph – that's 100 meters in under six seconds. You don't stand a chance if you run and the bear decides to chase you.

If you see the bear from a distance, detour around it. If you see a bear cub or an animal carcass, leave the area as quickly as you can without showing distress. Just go back the way you came, because where there's a cub, there's a protective mother. The carcass has likely already been claimed by a defensive bear.

Close Encounters

In closer quarters, the advice of bear experts is to stand your ground and speak to the bear in a firm tone of voice. If the bear stands, it is not necessarily a threat sign: since bears have lousy eyesight, they stand to get a better look at things. Keep talking to the bear, let it know you're there and not interesting. Do not turn your back to the bear. Do not, under any circumstances, run. Again, that's what food would do. If the bear stands, try to look big – fan out your jacket, wave your arms, or if there's a group, everybody stand together. You can yell. If the bear doesn't leave, you can try to back away slowly – still facing the bear – but if the bear starts to follow, hold your ground. If you can, and if you have to, back up to a tree and start to climb. Climb high, though, because grizzlies can reach quite a ways. Climbing won't work against black bears: they can climb better than you.

- **Don't make eye contact**. That's a threat.

- If you're facing a bear and the bear woofs and runs, even in your direction, that's okay. **Hold your ground.** But if it holds its own ground and woofs, or pops its teeth together, it's time for you to back up. Keep facing the bear, don't run, don't panic, but give the bear some room.

- If the bear turns sideways, that's not a good sign. It's a **threat posture**. Just like you wave your arms to show the bear you're big, the bear is showing you its flanks to prove how big it is. Take this as a sign to start backing up, slowly.

- If the bear follows you, **drop your hat or jacket**, something that smells like you but doesn't smell like food. Most bears will investigate what you drop, and be satisfied.

- Absolutely **do no imitate the bear's sounds or postures**. This is the number two stupid thing people do, next to trying to pet cubs. If the bear is in a threat pose, you want to submit, not mirror it back.

- If the bear is being obviously aggressive, you can try being aggressive back. Sometimes it's enough to deter – like backing down the bully. If you're being stalked by a bear, grab something and prepare to defend yourself. Chances are at least reasonably good that if you fight back, even for a second, a potential attack can be warded off.

- **Play dead** only as an absolutely last resort. Curl into a fetal position, keep your pack on for extra protection, and cross your arms behind your neck. Reports vary on which attacks are worse. Grizzlies tend to maul and get it over with. Black bears hang out and nibble, and are more likely to think you're food, or at least a really fun toy that they can swat around for a while. If you're attacked, hold still for as long as possible. Something that doesn't move loses its entertainment value, and the bear will probably get bored and leave pretty quickly. There's a new school of thought that believes instead of curling up, you're better off playing dead by laying flat on your stomach, hands laced behind your head. Nobody really wants to test this theory.

- **Guns** are pretty much useless against bears. Unless you're either very lucky or a crack shot with an ice cool head, calm enough to make Clint Eastwood look like he needs Ritalin, you'll just piss the bear off. **Pepper sprays** can work from about 20 feet, but it's best not to get that close in the first place. These sprays are the choice of locals. However, there are two warnings about it. First, it doesn't really work on wet bears. The potent molecules don't bond with water – this is why you should head to the sink after you mace yourself with the stuff, which is what usually happens to people who carry sprays. But it's not a good idea to go merrily tromping off into the bush figuring the pepper spray will protect you. The stuff is a last resort, at best. There have been a number of recent cases of people figuring that pepper spray, since it deters bears when sprayed in their faces, would also act as a kind of bear repellent. These people have sprayed pepper spray all over their backpacks and tents. The problem is, old pepper spray smells like dinner. Bears come running for it. If you're going to carry the spray, remember it works only when fresh – and not always then – and when the bear is standing right there looking at you.

Here's a sourdough story of what to do in the last resort, when you're being attacked by a bear: jam your fist down its throat and block it's air hole. Maybe before the bear finishes chewing off your arm, it will suffocate. Maybe.

All of these precautions work in theory, but still depend upon the bear's mood. If the bear doesn't feel like being placated, it won't be. The bear doesn't know and doesn't care about the rules.

 Most forest service offices have a free brochure, *Bear Facts: The Essentials for Traveling in Bear Country*, that offers more details.

A FED BEAR IS A DEAD BEAR

Finally, do not ever, for any reason, feed a bear. Bears are very, very smart. If they get food from a person once, they're likely to think it can happen again, and that's how you end up with bears in garbage cans and rummaging around houses. When that happens, sooner or later, Fish and Game will have to kill the bear.

Why don't they just relocate them, you ask? Because bears are smart, and they know where home is. Relocated bears will do just about anything to get back home. They've been known to swim hundreds of miles, just to get back to that trash can. Even if they don't head right back, they're likely to start looking at human settlements as sources of food.

Bear Watching

Like any other time when people meet nature, there's going to be controversy. That's the case at many of the places in the North where people go to watch bears. As more visitors head to the top of the globe, there are more people anxious to see bears; but rather than go out and try to meet the bears on their own terms, the popularity of places like Katmai, Pack Creek, and Chinitna Bay increase: places where there are lot of bears who are mostly too busy gorging themselves on the salmon run to pay attention to the Gore-Tex clad hordes snapping their pictures.

But at what point do the bears start to notice?

At Chinitna, where day trippers fly in from Homer and the Kenai Peninsula, there are airboats blasting up and down the rivers where the bears are trying to fish. The boats destroy the riverbeds, and that destroys the salmon habitat, and that means the bears either starve or find a new place to go find lunch.

Downside number two: as bears get more and more accustomed to there being people in particular places, the bears become less afraid/wary of those people. If you meet a bear in the wild, odds are the bear is as unhappy to see you as you are to see it; but if they're acclimated to people, you suddenly have a dramatic increase in the potential for confrontation. The bears treat you as part of the scenery – over which they have always had mastery – and the people treat the bears like they were part of a tame theme park.

What can you do about it? The exact same thing we suggest whenever you encounter wildlife: try to be invisible. You don't belong there. The animal does. Watch all you want, but never make an animal change its habits.

The best bear pictures were taken by Michio Hoshino; they're in his book *Grizzly*. The one true, cautionary bear tale we will tell is that Hoshino, who spent his life around bears and knew the rules as well as he knew his cameras, was killed by a grizzly, somewhere in Siberia. Hoshino was sleeping; the bear took offense at the color of his tent, or something. It's impossible to know. The point is that, in the end, the bears will do exactly what they want.

We're not going to comment on Timothy Treadwell. We were on the beach where he was killed a week or so before it happened. Alaskans tend to have one idea about Treadwell, the rest of the world another, and in a rare display of tact, we're staying out of it.

Bear attacks are extremely rare. Take proper care, and don't worry too much. We hiked in bear country for four years before we even saw one.

THE FUN SIDE OF PEPPER SPRAY

The odds are, that if you carry pepper spray with you long enough, you're going to either blast yourself in the face with it, or blast the face of someone you're with. Because, really, what are the odds you're going to aim the thing the right direction when the bear is standing there and you're shaking in your boots?

If it happens, you have two immediate problems: first, anything strong enough to stop a bear is not going to be that much fun on you.

If it's in your eyes, head for the nearest stream and wash your eyes with clear water for at least 10 or 15 minutes. If you've got contacts in, go ahead and toss them; you'll never want them in your eyes again.

On your skin, there are two schools of thought: one says that washing just spreads that capsaicin, the stuff that stings; the other says try to get the damn stuff off you by rinsing until you can rinse no more. If you've got some cooking oil or vegetable oil with you, rub that on; it will dissolve the capsaicin, and then you can wash the oil off so you don't smell like lunch.

Which brings up problem two, mentioned above: loose pepper spray to a bear is like the smell of bacon to a truck driver. Because you've got this stuff all over yourself, you now smell like a good snack. Leave. Go find a hotel. Take a long shower. Toss your clothes in the garbage.

Pepper spray is good stuff; it's what people who spend their time in the woods all carry. Just be sure you're aiming it the right way.

■ Wolves

 You're not likely to see one, but keep your eyes peeled. A wolf sighting is more exciting than just about any other thing you'll see in the North.

The first wolf we ever saw chased us. We were on a motorcycle, and the wolf was crossing the highway. It heard us, its ears twitched, and it was off. The only sad part was that we were going too fast to enjoy watching the wolf.

The first thing you have to be sure of when you spot a wolf is that it isn't a coyote. There are a lot more coyotes in the North than wolves. Coyotes are smaller in both body and head. Wolves have short, rounded ears, while coyote ears tend to be longer and pointed. If you're tracking, you'll see a wolf has front paws larger than its rear paws; it's the other way around on a coyote.

There are estimated to be between 5,000 and 8,000 wolves in Alaska. This works out to roughly one every 100 square miles. Yet, because of the massive negative publicity wolves have gotten ever since Little Red Riding Hood went home and lied her fool head off, there is a legal hunting of 1,500 wolves per year in the state – and probably that many more are killed illegally. The population is barely holding its own, and it's likely to slip fast if there's a bad year for the food supply.

NATIVE BELIEFS

It wasn't always like this. The wolf was considered a powerful animal by Northern Native Americans. The Kwakiutl believed that if a bow or gun was used to kill a wolf, the weapon became unlucky and had to be given away. Wolves were guiding spirits and companions. They were – and are – simply beautiful animals to watch as well.

The **gray wolf**, *Canis lupus*, averages between 40 and 80 inches long, nose to tail. They can be three feet high at the shoulder, and weigh up to 130 pounds. We have a plaster cast of a wolf track, taken off the Stikine River, that's over six inches long. They can get big. They are a mixture of browns, tans, and grays; usually the muzzle is a lighter color than the rest of the body.

Wolves are quintessential pack animals, feeding on caribou, deer, sheep, goat, moose, or whatever else they can hunt. In hard times, they go after squirrels, marmots, and other small game.

Wolves stick to their own territory. They are so territorial, in fact, that it is believed prey animals are often able to find the "no man's land" between two wolf packs and so travel through an area safely. For the wolves, being so territorial makes them easier to hunt. The most famous pack was the

Headquarters pack in Denali Park, but the last of those wolves was killed in 1995.

The gray wolf once ranged over nearly all the land north of what's now the Canadian border. They are reduced to pockets now.

There are a lot of **wolf-hybrid farms** along the highway, where you can stop in and see these wolves. It's fun, but nothing like the real thing. The wolf-hybrids also tend to be a little off in their personality. The domesticated part of them wants to be a lap dog; the wolf part wants to rip your throat out. It makes for a squirrely animal, and that's why you'll just about never see wolf hybrids pulling as sled dogs; physically, they'd be perfect, but personality-wise, they're kind of lacking.

 For a great movie with some of the best wolf photography ever, try *Never Cry Wolf*, based on the book by Farley Mowat (you can meet the man who trained the wolves for that movie, and see a couple of their descendants, in Haines; see page 297). Support Friends of the Wolf, at PO Box 21032, Glebe Postal Outlet, Ottawa, Ontario K1S 5N1, Canada.

■ Other Mammals

The coastal regions are host to a variety of smaller mammals: voles, beaver, weasels, mink, squirrels, mice, marten, porcupines, and so on. Most of these live quite deep in the forest and you're unlikely to spot them, although you might get a mouse or a vole wandering into your campsite.

■ Whales

Spend some time on the coast, and you're going to see whales. They might be just the little beluga whales, the stately humpback, or the incredible, giant fin whales, but spend time on the water, and sooner or later you're going to come across something. Your best bets are around Haines, Skagway, and the Kenai Penninsula; there's also some really good whale watching out of Prince Rupert. If you're serious about whale watching, take the ferry (see our other book, *Adventure Guide to the Inside Passage and Coastal Alaska*) and get the camera ready. Whales are as common as dogs to Alaskans (a ferry was once stopped for several hours because the entire channel was full of whales and the ship couldn't get through), but nobody ever gets tired of seeing a breaching humpback.

There are roughly 500 humpbacks that summer in Alaskan waters between the months of April and November. There are some whales that hang out year-round, but it rarely seems to be the same whales each year. Scientists are still working on which ones stay and why.

Humpbacks

Humpbacks are most commonly seen in Southeast. Humpback whales grow to 50 feet, but most are closer to 40. They are distinguished by the way they swim and their shape at the waterline: their back forms a right angle as they dive. Whales do not generally show their tails above water unless they are sounding or diving deep – when you see the tail, that's usually the last you'll see of the whale.

 DID YOU KNOW: *Humpback tails are as distinctive as human fingerprints, and scientists use the patterns on their huge, broad tails as means of identification.*

One of the main points of study with humpbacks is their **song**. Scientists all over the Alaskan coast are dropping hydrophones in the water to record whale song, which has definite rhythms and repetitions. Whales have been known to stop a song when leaving Alaska for the warmer waters of the south, and then pick it up on exactly the same note when they return the following year.

BREACHING

The premier animal sighting in Alaska is a breaching whale. Humpbacks come all the way out of the water – it's amazingly slow, the whale just keeps moving up and up and up before falling back down on its side. Whales like to flop back and forth, beating the water with their flukes. Some of the reasons for this behavior are unknown, but often it's seen when the animals are feeding. Breach behavior is also thought to be simply for the fun of it, and sometimes as a sign of agitation. There are less scrupulous whale-watching tour operators who will take out a dozen small boats, surround a group of whales from a legal distance, and thrill their clients with the whales coming up out of the water – which the whales are doing because they're seriously pissed off and feeling threatened by the boats. The best breach behavior we ever saw was in the Aleutians where three humpbacks seemed to be playing leapfrog. One would jump, then the next, then the next, and they kept at it as long as we kept them in view before the boat went around a corner, maybe 45 minutes.

Humpbacks feed only in Alaska – they fast during the winter months in Hawaii. In the rich waters of Alaska, the whales create a "bubble net" by swimming around a school of krill and trapping them in their exhalation. The animals then lunge up through the krill, mouths open, scooping up tons of krill and sea water. The water gets squeezed out through the baleen, long spiny plates that take the place of teeth in many species of whale.

When watching the sea, look for the spout, the whale's breath, which is visible from quite a distance. It looks like a small palm tree of water and, from a distance, is much easier to spot than the body of the whale.

Minke Whales

Minke whales, also common along the coast, have an almost invisible spout, and they don't stay on the surface for very long when they breathe, making them very difficult to spot; they're also likely to stay up only for a couple of breaths at most. Minkes are often mistaken for large porpoises, very small humpbacks or, occasionally, orca. The smallest of the rorqual whales, minke whales run up to 31 feet for females, 27 feet for males, weighing up to perhaps 10 tons. They are characterized by a triangular snout. Their body color is black above and white below, and many have a band of white in the middle of their flippers. Their dorsal fin is considerably back of the center, giving them an oddly sleek, racy look. Minke are not particularly endangered: there are estimated to be more than 500,000 of them. They mostly travel alone.

Fin Whales

The other species of whale you might spot is the fin whale, but you'll have to be pretty far west, off the range of the Alaska Highway to see one. Fin whales are giants of the sea, with some approaching 80 feet in length. They are dark grey to brownish-black on the sides and white on the underside. Their head shading remains dark further back on the left side than the right. Like humpbacks and minke whales, fin whales have baleen and feed on krill, straining the tiny animals from the water. Fin whales are rarely seen breaching; usually you can see the spout, then a small black fin, and then an incredibly long back.

Beluga

Just south of Anchorage, there's a place called Beluga Point. Believe it: it's a great place to watch for beluga whales passing by. On the trip to update this book, we watched a pod of 30 or so swim slowly past while we sat on the beach and caught up on our notes.

Belugas are among the smallest of the true whales. An adult male is only about 13 feet long, and weighs about 3,000 pounds. When they're born, belugas are about five feet long and weigh only 100 pounds or so.

They start off a dark grey, but by the time they're five years old, they've faded to the familiar white color. A beluga can live up to 35 years.

Belugas like to live in groups; while recent newspaper reports in the Kenai suggest that the populations are way down, you'll still see belugas in bigger bunches than any other kind of whale. There have been sightings of more than 1,000 whales in a single pod in the Arctic. There are about 70,000 belugas in the world, so they're not on the endangered list. Native hunting in Alaska takes two or three hundred a year.

Belugas swim quite slowly, looking for fish, crabs, clams, and squid to chow down on. They've got sensational sonar, among the best of the whales, and that, combined with their size, means they're frequently in much shallower water than most whales. That makes it easier to watch them.

Whaling

Killing whales isn't as difficult as it once was. If you're a Norwegian with no recriminations, or a Japanese hiding behind the facade of scientific research (but that doesn't explain the whale meat stores all over Japan, does it?), you chase them down in a large ship, aim a harpoon cannon at them, and when the harpoon hits the whale, the tip explodes, hopefully killing it before you have to waste another couple of hundred bucks on a second harpoon.

But it wasn't always like this, and there's no real way to look at the history of the North without looking at the history of whaling. From the 1600s into the 1900s, whales provided lamp oil, corset stays, perfume bases, and a hundred other must have items.

The best account of traditional whaling is, of course, *Moby Dick*. Melville had done his time on a whaling ship, and he knew what he was talking about. When a sailing ship spotted a whale or a group of whales, they lowered whaleboats – about 20 feet long – and chased after the whale. They drew close enough to lance it and harpoon it. This meant getting right on top of the whale. Then the crew held on for the ride, trying to stick more lances in the whale and injure it enough to slow it down. It was incredibly dangerous, bloody work, and a whaling ship that didn't lose a few of the crew to accidents was a miracle ship.

Let's let Melville tell it:

> *A short rushing sound leaped out of the boat; it was the darted iron of Queequeg. Then all in one wild commotion came an invisible push from astern, while forward the boat seemed striking on a ledge; the sail collapsed and exploded; a gush of scalding vapor shot up nearby; something rolled and tumbled like an earthquake beneath us. The whole crew were half suffocated as they were tossed helter-skelter into the white curdling cream of the squall. Squall, whale, and harpoon had all blended together, and the whale, merely grazed by the iron, escaped.*

European and American hunters set out in ships a hundred feet or more long, getting near the whales in the small boats only at the last moment. Eskimo and Inuit hunters paddled out after whales in their kayaks. The killing technique was essentially the same: lance it, wear it out. But the Native hunters were doing this in boats not much bigger than your couch at home.

By the way, if you're wondering, whale meat tastes kind of like greasy, rubbery tuna fish.

Orca

Orca, or killer whales, are one of the most exciting animals to spot in Alaska. They are not actually whales; rather, they're the largest member of the porpoise family.

Orca can be more than 30 feet long, and the dorsal fin on a male can be as much as six feet high. At birth, orca weigh roughly 400 pounds. A full-grown orca can weigh up to nine tons, and can swim 34 miles per hour.

Orca travel in pods, with anywhere from three to 25 animals moving together. There are no accurate estimates for how many orca travel in Alaskan waters, as the animals move very quickly and scientists are never sure if they've counted the same one twice.

In the past few years, the orca population has been at the forefront of a problem all over Alaska: changing weather is changing feeding patterns due to changing weather conditions. The seal population of the Aleutians has crashed; the orca are switching to eating sea otters, but otters aren't nearly as nutritious as seals, so not only is the otter population taking a hit from being turned into snack food, the orca population is decreasing because of the simple fact of starvation.

The most distinctive feature of the orca is the black and white coloration. Dall's porpoise, which are similarly marked, are often mistaken for orca. However, the Dall's porpoise grows only to six or eight feet. There are a couple of other differences in the coloring: an orca has a white patch behind each eye, which is not usually present on a Dall's, and their flukes are white on the underside, whereas a Dall's is usually white at the edges.

■ Porpoises

Dall's Porpoise

Dall's Porpoise, which grow to a maximum size of 300-450 pounds and five to seven feet long – by killer whale size – travel in fairly large groups, usually numbering 10-20 animals. They forage at all levels of the ocean, and are known to dive to depths of more than 1,600 feet. These are highly playful animals; if you see porpoise playing with the ship, they'll be Dall's. Extremely fast swimmers, able to top 35 miles per hour, Dall's porpoises will happily chase boats and play in the wake unless the boat drops below 12 miles an hour or so; then the porpoise seem to lose interest and drop away, looking for something more fun to do.

Harbor Porpoise

Harbor porpoise are also a fairly common sight from the ferry, but you don't see them for long. They are darker, more sedate in their movements, and more shy in their approaches than Dall's porpoise. They are much smaller than a Dall's, growing to only 125-145 pounds, and perhaps four to six feet in length. They travel in small groups, no more than five animals, and they come up only briefly to breathe, making sightings fairly short-lived.

■ Seals

 Harbor seals, like harbor porpoise, are shy and difficult to spot. They come up quietly, take a quick look around with only their head and nose protruding above the water – and the black color can make them almost invisible – then they disappear. Estimates of how many harbor seals there are in Alaska run in the 200-300,000 range.

They're covered with short hair, and are usually colored either with a dark background and light rings, or light sides and a belly with dark splotches. They generally stay within about 150 miles of where they were born. They do not migrate, but they will wander about to find food – walleye, cod, herring, salmon, squid, and octopus, among other sealife. You'll sometimes see them surprisingly far upstream on bigger rivers, as they follow the salmon. We've seen them a hundred miles up the Stikine River.

DID YOU KNOW: *A harbor seal can dive to 600 feet, and stay down for over 30 minutes. When it dives, its heart rate slows to 15-20 beats per minute, about a quarter of its heart rate when it's at the surface.*

■ Sea Lions & Sea Otters

While harbor seals disappear when you spot them, sea lions and otters, on the other hand, are showmen. Sea lions jump, splash and play constantly, as do the otters. Steller sea lions can grow to 1,200 pounds or more, and there's nothing quite like watching them at a haul out. They are also known to be much less shy than seals – a diver told us of a few sea lions coming up behind them on a dive and repeatedly swimming in fast circles around the divers while occasionally giving someone a playful nudge. Both seals and sea lions like to pull themselves out of the water and bask in the sun atop rocks. Another good place to watch for them is on channel markers and buoys.

SEA LION OR SEAL?

How do you know if what you're looking at is a seal or a sea lion? It's really pretty easy.

- Seals have short, clawed front legs; sea lions have long, broad front flippers.
- Seals don't have visible ears; you can see the ears on a sea lion.
- When they're out of water, seals lie down; sea lions sit up.

A CLOSE CALL WITH EXTINCTION

The Russians killed whatever seals and sea lions they came across – why not, they were out hunting anyway – but what they were really after were sea otters.

Sea otters were once hunted almost to extinction as fur traders made fortunes on their rich, luxurious pelts – the first sealing expedition, in 1741, brought back 900 pelts; in 1800, Alexander Baranov estimated that in the previous 10 years, more than 100,000 pelts had been taken. It was noticed quite early on that this couldn't continue – already by 1818, it was reported that "along the whole expanse of coast from Cape Ommaney to Kenai Bay, only two places remain where we can still hunt, namely, Lituya Bay and Yakutat; but even there, they are no longer native, but hide someplace farther along the coast to the southeast where they are more protected." The Russians were letting the locals do all the killing, and contemporary reports show that they were really, really good at it, even without threats of violence from the Russians. "The Aleuts are the only people born with a passion for hunting sea otters. When they spot a sea otter, they surround it, and the person closest... gets to shoot him with a dart and has the right to claim the kill."

For more on Russian sea otter hunting, see K.T. Khelbnikov, *Notes on Russian America*, beautifully translated by Serge LeComte and Richard Pierce. It's one of the best accounts you can find of what the Russians were doing in Alaska.

Why were the Russians killing off the otters? So they could sell the pelts to China and trade for tea. The English had their opium trade for the exact same reason.

Now sea otters, quite well protected by law, are back, and there's a healthy population that can be spotted almost anywhere along the Alaskan coast.

Sea otters grow to six feet and live, somewhat communally, in kelp beds. Rather odd is that while they live in groups, they don't really interact with each other; there may be some play fights and mating behavior, but other than that, they pretty much pretend the other otters aren't there. Their diet consists largely of fish, marine bivalves and sea urchins, and they're famous for using rocks to bash open tough shells. There's a flap of skin under their forelegs in which they can stash food or rocks.

FURRY FACTS

The fur of a sea otter is a miraculous thing: otters have up to 125,000 hairs per square inch, more than double just about any other mammal. This high-density fur makes otters the prime target for coats, hats, boots, and anything else for which a dead animal might be useful. The thickness of the hair is an evolutionary development in lieu of layers of subcutaneous fat. Most marine mammals have thick fat layers to keep them warm in the cold waters. Hair is all the otters have, and this is part of why they were so susceptible during the oil spill in Prince William Sound: the fur, matted with oil, lost its insulating capabilities and the oiled otters literally froze to death.

Even when it's working well, the thick fur has some drawbacks. A sea otter has a metabolic rate two times higher than average for an animal its size. The body is working overtime to maintain its core temperature. You'll see that sea otters generally keep their feet lifted out of the water – this helps keep the wet surface area to a minimum, and keeps the otter warmer. Should the otter get overheated, there is a solution: like polar bears, sea otters have extra blood veins in their feet. They can send blood through these veins, close to the surface of the skin, and cool off. It's estimated that 80% of the excess heat can be shed this way.

Although sea otters are very unpopular with local fishermen (who claim they ruin the fishing grounds and depopulate the fish), they're actually a very important species for the maintenance of a healthy environment along the coast. Sea otters eat urchins, abalone, and other animals that eat kelp. Without the otter predation, the kelp beds, which shelter numerous schools of young fish, would quickly be gone.

■ Fish

 Considering that Alaska has something like 10 million lakes and the longest coastline in the U.S., it comes as no surprise that there are a fair few fish around. The species tally is about 300, really an astounding variety.

That said, most people who come to Alaska are interested in only salmon and halibut.

Salmon

There are five types of salmon in Alaska: pink (humpie), chum (dog), coho (silver), sockeye (red), and the prize of them all, the king, or chinook.

Now that we've said that, we're going to list a sixth type, the steelhead. Steelhead, long classified as a type of trout, were just officially moved into the salmon category a few years ago. For reasons that require explaining more about fish biology than you're probably interested in, there are a lot of fish experts who aren't happy with this move. Yes, steelhead move from freshwater to salt water and back. But that's about it on the similarities list, and the same attribute isn't enough to push the Dolly Varden (an ocean-going trout, which is what everybody thought steelhead were) into salmon land. All over the country, there are Ph.D. candidates getting dissertation material out of the debate. There aren't enough steelhead to make them important commercially – according to Fish and Game, of the 331 known steelhead streams in Southeast, only 12 support more than a thousand fish.

All salmon share the trait of returning to the waters in which they were born to spawn and die. During the summer months, this means rivers clogged with dying fish, and a lot of very happy bears.

The **chinook**, Alaska's state fish, is what all the fuss is about: they grow up to 100 pounds, and 30-pound fish are common. They also fight. (A few years ago, a man had a chinook on the line for over 24 hours. He lost it when his guide used the wrong sized net and snapped the line.)

The chinook is considered abundant all along the Alaskan coast. The run is usually from May through July. The chinook is rather astounding in its run, traveling more than 2,000 miles in only two months – but there are some that, over their lifespan, travel more than 10,000 miles. Once returning to the site of its birth, the female lays up to 14,000 eggs. The fish in the run may be anywhere from three to seven years old; there is not a clear cycle for chinook.

A full-grown fish has black spotting on its back and dorsal fin, and a line of black along the gum line.

> **AUTHOR TIP:** *Trolling is your best bet for catching chinook, using herring as bait. There are strict regulations on catching chinook, particularly in Southcentral; check with Fish and Game before heading out.*

While the chinook is the trophy fish, a lot of people prefer the coho for eating. Coho, which grow from eight to 12 pounds, don't have the tail spots that kings do. Fins are usually tinted with orange, and the male has a hooked snout.

Coho spend a fair amount of their lives in freshwater; after hatching, the fish may hang out in estuaries through the summer and then move back into freshwater for the fall. They may spend as much as five years in freshwater before their salt water period, which averages about 18 months.

> **FISHING TIP:** *Like fishing for chinook, your best bet is trolling with herring for bait. The run lasts from July into September, and coho fight enough to make chinook seem like logs.*

Sockeye, or red salmon, are probably the biggest part of the fishery, and they have been for thousands of years. They spend one to four years in the ocean, and then do the run home. Their average weight is four-eight pounds at maturity, but they can get bigger; some around 15 pounds have been caught.

There are a few places where you can find a landlocked species of sockeye, called **kokanee**. These stay pretty small, and you're not that likely to run into them. It's the ocean-going type that everybody's after, and they find them in abundance. In Bristol Bay alone, there are 10-20 million sockeyes caught every year. Most of them are caught with gill nets, which are a small step up from the drift nets you read about.

Alaska offers tranquil fishing in spectacular surroundings.

If you're fishing for them, troll like you would for any other salmon. There have been a number of closures on the Kenai for sockeye of late; the long-term effects of the Valdez oil spill are just now making themselves clear.

The other two species of salmon are caught more on a commercial than a sport basis. The pink, or humpback, grow to about four pounds. They're steel blue on top and silver on the side. They get their nickname, humpie or humpback, from the hump and hooked jaws that develop when they enter freshwater. Pink salmon mature in only two years. These are the primo fish for commercial fishermen; more than 45 million fish a year are taken, roughly half the total salmon catch.

Chum salmon, which are green-blue on top with small black dots, mature after roughly four years. They spend most of that time at sea, primarily in the Bering Sea or the Gulf of Alaska. A full-grown chum will weigh seven-15 pounds. There is a huge commercial fishery for chum in Alaska, primarily through gillnetting or seining; about 11 million fish a year are taken.

We've already mentioned the steelhead controversy – once a trout, now a salmon. There is another kind of very salmon-like trout, the Dolly Varden.

Dolly Varden are a mottled olive-brown, with dark marks. Mature males are bright red on their lower body, while the fins are red-black with white edges. They also develop a strongly hooked lower jaw.

The Dolly Varden run is from mid-August into November. They actually move in and out of freshwater for most of their lives, not migrating into the sea until they are three or four years old. They're still quite small at this time, only about five inches long. Spawning generally happens when the fish is five or six years old, and unlike other salmon, roughly 50% of Dolly Varden live to spawn a second time (steelhead also do this, which is one of the reasons for the controversy about whether they're salmon or anadromous trout). The fish can live as long as 16 years.

Dolly Varden never reach the size of coho or chinook – a full-grown fish is only about four pounds – but they are around all year.

THE LIFE CYCLE OF SALMON

The life cycle of all the types of salmon is more or less similar – it's a matter of how long they do what that really changes.

At hatching, what you've got is called an alevin; this is a tiny little bit of a fish, with the yolk sack – that they're still living off of – remaining attached. They live in the gravel where they were born, six to 12 inches down in the streambed.

The next stage is the fry stage, where they start to look like real fish. They're about an inch or two long at this point, and they start to get vertical bar marks – like they'll get later when they're packaged and barcoded in the supermarket – to help them hide in the streambed. This stage lasts a couple of months.

Next, they turn into fingerlings, or parr. They've gotten bigger now – a couple of inches or so – and they may stay in this stage for anywhere from a couple of months (pink and chum) up to a couple of years for sockeye and chinook. The bar lines have gotten darker, and they're really just building up strength for their final freshwater stage.

That's the smolt. They're better than six inches long now, and they've lost the bar marks as they become silver for better camouflage in the open ocean. At this stage, they undergo a massive physical change, getting ready for the change from fresh water to salt water: their gills essentially reverse, and their hemoglobin changes to cope with the loss of oxygen that comes with salt water.

As soon as the fish hits salt water, it changes from a smolt into an adult salmon. It's time to go out in the open water.

At their end of their lives, the salmon come back. Walt Disney taught you in school in all those nature films that they always come back to the stream where they were born. That's mostly true – salmon navigate by a sense of smell that can detect "one drop of vermouth in a 500,000-gallon martini." They know where they're going. However, there are always a few that don't want to go along with the crowd – about 8% decide that home ain't good enough, so they head out for other streams. This is good, as it can help populate new areas; it's bad, because, as we'll explain below, it gives alien fish a chance to move in where they don't belong.

AN UPHILL STRUGGLE

There is a bit of salmon behavior you're bound to see if you're traveling during the run months: salmon, gathered near a stream mouth, jumping. You'll hear various explanations for this behavior, ranging from "they're trying to catch bugs to eat" to "they're trying to shed scale parasites." The jumpers are female fish, loosening their eggs before heading upstream.

Salmon populations, like those of so many other things, are declining rapidly. Some of this is due to over-fishing, some to climate changes. Each year, there are more fishing closures along the Kenai, and the commercial catch in Southeast declines as each year, the returns are getting a little smaller. Over the past hundred years, 232 genetically distinct strains of salmon (that's strains, not species) have become extinct. Due to decreasing runs, the value of the salmon catch dropped almost by half between 1994 and 2000. Having an oil tanker worth of poison spilled into the ecosystem didn't do anybody any favors, either.

That said, there is some hope. The return of pinks was so large in 2001 that most canneries stopped taking them; there were too many to process. Fish return run in cycles; there's hope that this huge return is a marker of the end of the bad years.

The Negative Impact of Hatcheries & Fish Farms

So, what to do about this overall decline in fish population? Screw with nature, of course.

The first idea was hatcheries – you can see them in work in a lot of towns along the coast. The idea here is that, if nature lets about one out of a thousand eggs actually grow into salmon and return to spawn, why not scoop some eggs up and increase the odds?

Hatcheries raise the fish in controlled environments. This makes sure that the salmon don't have any chance to develop the wild smarts they'll need to survive. It's a lovely way to dilute a gene pool, particularly when the hatchery-raised salmon breed with wild. Think how smart chickens are after centuries of domestication, how well they'd do in the wild. Same thing with hatchery fish.

Once a hatchery is up and running, it gets its own return of salmon. The fish are imprinted with marks, so they can be tracked. Once they make it up to the home hatchery, they're pulled out of the water, gutted, and the roe and smelt are mixed by hand. Oh, and all that valuable protein, the fish that once was, is discarded. It's the rule.

The life stages are then led in tanks, rather than the stream. Rather than having anything to do with Darwinism – which works for most species – survival becomes a matter of luck.

A big part of the luck is surviving the diseases and filth that hatcheries tend to breed.

So the next bright idea is fish farms, which are illegal in Alaska, but common in Canada. The first problem here is that most fish farms stocked with Atlantic salmon – nothing like bringing in alien species. Farms are built in streams, with holding pens for different stages. The concentration of fish in one batch of step ponds means there's a whole lot of fish waste churning out into the ocean – as much as from a town of 10,000 people. The fish are also packed in so tightly that they can hardly swim. The fish themselves are more susceptible to disease and pollution in this cradle-to-the-table captive cycle. Of course, that means they get antibiotics pumped into their food.

Canadian fish farms are allowed to shoot any marine mammals that might come by and see these pens as a free lunch – about 900 seals and sea lions are shot a year.

There's also the little detail that farm-raised fish are eating fish-meal pellets – ground up bits of other fish. The Worldwatch Institute looked into this and discovered that for every gram of farm-raised salmon that hits your dinner table, five grams of other fish were turned into salmon food. This really helps the part of the worldwide fishing industry that's out to strip the oceans bare. Estimates are that in British Columbia alone, this means an annual waste of 90,000 tons of edible protein.

Because the fish are eating unnatural food, they don't come out looking nice and healthy and pink like you want them to. But dyes fix that.

One more thing while we're on the subject – the increase of fish farms has devastated the traditional culture of the coasts. Towns that used to support 40 or 50 fishermen now support two or three.

Shall we talk about Frankenfish? Genetic engineering is turning out salmon that mature in a fraction of the time it takes nature. Like most genetic engineering products, there's no idea what the long-range effects of this might be. And if you think the fish are confined to pens, forget it: Fish escape. Aliens enter the gene pool and the wild streams – Atlantic salmon have been found in quite a few Alaskan rivers. In 1997, a single fish farm in Washington State "lost" over 350,000 Atlantic salmon in one whack. Try and think of any way this is a good thing.

In 1980, 1% of the salmon market was comprised of farmed salmon; today that number is 56%.

Other Uses for Salmon Besides Your Dinner

Salmon aren't just out making salmon dinners. They're a vital part of the entire ecosystem, almost the base level, the cornerstone of the Pacific

Northwest's economy, ecology, and culture. You can't understand anything about the Alaskan coast without taking salmon into account.

Besides yourself, there are 137 other animal species that depend on salmon at some stage of their life for animal protein – everything from bald eagles to bears, seals, sea lions, and everything in between.

The forest also depends on salmon. The rotting fish that die in streams after the spawn provide 17% of the nutrients found on the rainforest floor along a stream. About 60% of the nutrients that freshly hatched salmon depend on comes from their spawned-out parents.

Disappear the fish, you disappear the forest; and that disappears it all.

Halibut

Halibut are a kind of flatfish, like enormous flounders. Like many fish, they're darker on the upper side than on the lower – the idea is that a predator fish getting under the halibut will look up and think the light color is just a patch of sky. Or so the theory goes.

FISHERMENS' TALES

This is one of those great Alaska stories, the kind of thing that could never happen anywhere else. A man was out fishing, and he caught a halibut. Not a little one, mind you. Estimates later put the fish at around 460 pounds. The man got the fish on deck, using a crane, but the fish wasn't quite dead, and it began to thrash around. The man slipped; the halibut's tail hit him in the head. Death was probably fairly fast for him, rather slower for the fish.

Halibut live on the bottom of the ocean, sometimes at great depth – up to 1,800 feet. Once hooked, a large halibut may get dragged to the surface and still find the strength to go back down six or seven times, diving several hundred feet. Most halibut fishermen carry guns to try and keep this game to a minimum. Gaffs just make the fish madder.

Halibut migrate in a clockwise manner, heading south and east through the Gulf of Alaska. Older fish are more likely to stay put. A halibut reaches maturity around the age of eight, and a female might lay as many as three million eggs a year. A halibut might live more than 25 years.

Halibut are extremely strong swimmers, as anyone who has hooked one can tell you. This allows them to eat pretty much anything they want to. The halibut's digestive tract is extremely small for an animal its size, so to maintain its metabolism, it eats all the time.

AUTHOR TIP: *In Alaska, the vast majority of halibut fishing goes on around Homer, at the bottom of the Kenai Penninsula. If you're after flatfish, head there.*

BARN DOOR HALIBUT

Four hundred-pound halibut are rare, but one or two are caught every year, and probably thousands of hundred-pound halibut are caught each season. Fish this big – a hundred-pounder will be about six feet tall and three or four feet across, and maybe six inches thick – are called "barn door" halibut. They're the ultimate trophy, but the truth is, the little ones, 20 pounds and under, make for better eating.

Cooking Your Catch

Once you've made your catch, it's time for dinner. We offer here two of our favorite recipes, courtesy of Wrangell's Alaskan Vistas outfitters (see the Stikine River section).

■ FOR SALMON

Mix up a marinade of ½ cup of soy sauce, ½ cup of brown sugar, and ½ teaspoon of liquid smoke seasoning. Marinate fillets for at least six hours, turning them a couple of times. Grill on a low fire. Slide the fish back and forth in the pan, and use olive oil to prevent sticking. Turn over only once. Cook until the fish is no longer transparent – about five minutes per side, maximum.

■ FOR HALIBUT

Mix ½ cup of real butter, ½ cup of soy sauce, ¼ cup of lemon juice, and 2 tablespoons of Worcestershire sauce. Coat an aluminum tray with olive oil or nonstick cooking spray. Place halibut on the tray and cover with the sauce mix. Cook until the meat is no longer transparent (shouldn't take more than 10 minutes, tops). Use very low heat – halibut is very easy to overcook.

CATCH & RELEASE

If you're not hungry, follow these basic steps to release the fish:

- Land the fish quickly and carefully.
- Don't lift the fish entirely out of the water.
- Use only a soft or knotless mesh net, and keep your hands wet while handling the fish.
- Use barbless hooks, and keep the fish underwater while you're pulling it. If you can't get the hook out, cut the line off the hook – sooner or later, the hook will rust out.

- Stick the fish into the current, or swish it back and forth in the water to revive it. Make sure the gills are working, and let the fish swim out of your hands.

A lot of catch-and-release fish still end up dying due to improper release techniques. Some basic care keeps them out there and alive.

■ Birds

Eagles

 Most people go to Alaska hoping to see a bald eagle, but the truth is, it's harder not to see them. They're everywhere. These birds, which can easily weigh more than 20 pounds, were so common in Alaska that, from 1917 until 1952, there was a bounty on them. Hunters were paid as much as $2 per pair for talons. The bounty was put in place on the assumption that eagles ate too many fish. It was discontinued in 1952, when the birds joined the list of federally protected species.

There are more than 10,000 adult bald eagles in Southeast Alaska, and a few thousand more young eagles. Thousands more live inland.

Adults are distinguished by the trademark white head; adolescent eagles are a dull brown and are harder to spot. Most nests are close to the water.

> **DID YOU KNOW:** *Eagles build the largest bird nests in the world, weighing up to 1,000 pounds. A pair of eagles will return to the same tree year after year, making the nest a little bigger each time. It is abandoned only when the tree threatens to give way.*

Eagles themselves are easy to spot, once you get the hang of it: look at the tops of trees and keep looking for a white patch. Eagles are amazingly patient and can sit, almost unmoving, for hours on end. They do not generally hunt by circling around, looking for prey, the way you're probably used to seeing hawks. In Southeast and Southcentral, they're more likely to sit until something catches their eye – and they have great eyes, with vision roughly 20 times better than 20-20, and the ability to filter glare off water so they can see the fish moving beneath the surface.

Eagles dive for fish. An eagle's talons lock when they are under pressure and cannot be released until the pressure is alleviated. They can put as much as 6,000 pounds of pressure into each talon. All this means if the eagle grabs a fish that weighs more than it can lift, the eagle goes face first into the water. It doesn't happen often, but it's a memorable sight. After the face plant, if the eagle is unable to swim to shore with the prey, it is entirely possible that the weight of the would-be victim can actually exhaust and drag the eagle down, drowning it. Eagles are good swimmers, though, using their wings like arms to swim. Young eagles get a lot of swimming practice, because they have to learn to keep their wings up when they hit the water; wings down, they don't have the necessary strength or lift to get back up in the air, and they have to swim to dry land to take off. When you see an adult eagle hit, the wings are up and extended fully, ready for the powerful thrusts needed to get airborne again.

Eagle-Spotting

Good eagle-watching spots include city dumps, outside the fish processing plants, and around boat harbors. Haines is famous for the number of eagles that nest there – as many as 3,000 a year. Homer and Cordova also have large eagle populations.

If you're looking for bald eagles, here are some tips.

- First, look for white spots in the tops of trees. Eagles like to find the highest point they can, then sit there endlessly, doing a remarkable impression of life after taxidermy. Young eagles don't have the white heads that help you to pick them out against the dark backdrop, but they'll head for high points, too.

- If you come across an eagle on the ground, stay back. As with all wild animals, if you make the bird move, you're endangering it and making it burn calories it has better uses for.

- If you want good bird shots, you'll need a telephoto lens, fast film, and some luck.

- Find out when fishing boats are dumping leftover bait (usually in the late evening) and head down to the docks. There's nothing quite like watching a full-grown, 20-pound eagle hit the water at full speed.

Other Birds

There are more than 400 other bird species in Alaska, British Columbia, and the Yukon, the majority of which are coastal animals, or like to hang out around rivers. Many people go out to the Aleutians just to watch birds: mile-long rafts of **shearwaters, mureletts, puffins** flying everywhere like whirligigs. The trip is especially famed as a chance to see the **whiskered auklet**, but you don't need to get that far into the boonies.

In Southcentral, near Valdez, the Copper River Valley near Cordova provides an important migratory flyway for **trumpeter swans** and several species of ducks. The Copper River Delta is the only known breeding area for dusky **Canadian geese**.

The fun birds to watch along the coast are the alcids: the **auks, murres,** and particularly the **puffins**. Alcids are birds that can "fly" underwater. The Audubon Society describes them as "chunky, penguin-like seabirds, chiefly dark above and white below, with short wings and large webbed feet located far back on the body." This doesn't quite do them justice. Puffins, the ones you're most likely to spot (take a trip out in Resurrection Bay, near Seward), are kind of a symbol of the far north. Their colorful beaks and the way they fly – flailing their wings like whirligigs – makes them seem a kind of clown of the sea. And there are some oddities about them: for instance, their jaws are not hinged, but rather open and close something like a crescent wrench. This means they can stuff a lot of fish in their mouths at one time – one puffin biologist we know counted 42 fish in one bird's beak at a single time – but when they're done eating, they're so heavy they can't take off. If, say, the wake of a boat disturbs them, they try to get airborne, but just end up smacking face-first into the first wave they hit.

This does not mean that they're not amazing birds. A tufted puffin (the other common species in Alaska is the horned puffin) can dive a lot deeper than you can; and while it's down there, air squeezing out of the space between its feathers, it's as graceful as a seal. You can watch puffins underwater at the Sealife Center in Seward.

The Alaskan coast is noted for its huge tidal fluctuations. When the tide is out, shorebirds appear in full force, feeding off the exposed marine life. Sand pipers, plovers, several types of gulls and ducks, ravens, and more swoop down at low tide to feed on blue bay mussels, steamer clams, wrinkled whelk, file dogwinkle, sea urchins and even the occasional starfish left high and dry by the receding waters.

> Even if you're not a birder, it's useful to have a field guide for the trip. The definitive book is Herbert Brandt's *Alaska Bird Trails*, if you can find a copy, but that's going to run you at least $200. For something cheaper, see *Other Reading,* page 483.

▪ Bugs

Guess what? Once you're in the North, you're quite a few steps farther down the food chain than you're used to being.

Mosquitoes

A much bigger threat to your health and sanity than bears or moose are mosquitoes. They are bigger, meaner, and more abundant than you ever imagined. Shops in the North sell three-inch-long bear traps labeled mosquito traps, and they're not joking. There are 27 species of mosquito in Alaska, all of them waiting to bite into your soft hide. During the summer months, the biomass of mosquitoes in the North outweighs that of the caribou – there are actually swarms of mosquitoes in the far north of the state bigger than Rhode Island. The Alaskan mosquito's bite is enough to raise welts on a moose. There are many stories of animals going insane from mosquito bites; and there are reputable reports of caribou so drained of blood after a trip through bad mosquito country that they died. They're big, they're mean, and they're everywhere. And, as if the mosquitoes weren't enough, there are black flies, no-see-ums, snipe flies, and moose flies.

Anywhere you go in the North, something will want to eat you. So what chance do you have against them?

Simple measures are the best protection.

- Mosquito **repellent** is quite effective, especially those that include the chemical DEET. The more DEET the better, but if putting serious toxins on your skin doesn't thrill you, there are people – you can usually recognize them because they're busy scratching – who swear by Skin So Soft lotion.

- Wear **long-sleeved clothing**, and tuck the cuffs of your pants into your socks.

- Try to camp where there is a **breeze** – a wind of five mph will keep the mosquitoes down. In your RV, camper, or tent, make sure the screens are made of the smallest netting money can buy.

- In hotels, check the **window screens** before opening the window. Mosquito coils are popular, but they're not going to work outside of an enclosed area, and who knows what that smoke is doing to you?

No-See-Ums

Where the mosquitoes leave off, the no-see-ums start in. The same precautions work against these huge clouds of biting bugs. If you're camping, check all screens: they can get through the tiniest opening.

 If you're interested in knowing your enemy, get a copy of *The Mosquito Book*, by Scott Anderson and Tony Dierckins. The subtitle says it all: "More than you'll ever need to know about... the most annoying little bloodsuckers on the planet."

You will get bit. **Hydrocortisone cream** can help stop the itching, and there is a variety of specialized products designed to do the same. Pick up a tube or two, and then prepare to accept the mosquitoes. They're as much a part of life in the North as the midnight sun itself.

Finally, rest assured in the knowledge that there are no poisonous snakes or spiders indigenous to Alaska.

Chapter 2

Practicalities

When to Go, For How Long

Keeping climate information in mind, most people travel between the months of June and September. The Alaska Highway is most crowded in July and August, but people who go in the shoulder seasons of May to June or September to early October find the land just as hospitable and quite a bit emptier. Most seasonal businesses shut down somewhere between the beginning and end of September, and remain closed until mid-May or

the beginning of June, which makes it more difficult to find needed services; but there's always something open. With patience and careful planning, you can make a successful and enjoyable trip at any time of year. If you're looking to avoid crowds, there's no better time than the middle of winter. Pack your long johns and cross-country skis. You'll have a great time.

Without seriously hurrying, you can drive from Seattle to Fairbanks in six days – 10 if you want to stop and really enjoy yourself. Anchorage, Denali Park, and south-central Alaska take another week or so; and then there is the return trip. Most people head north on three-week vacations; a month or two is better. You can save a few days by taking the ferry through the gorgeous Inside Passage one direction, but it's nearly impossible to squeeze all the splendor of the North into two weeks. No matter how much time you have, you'll wish you had longer.

Costs

Now for the bad news; there's nothing cheap in the North. Even if you're planning on tenting, it's doubtful you can travel for under $75 a day. That's figuring $15 for the campsite, $20 for a tank of gas, and $30 for food, plus ten bucks mad money. It obviously doesn't take into account actually doing anything.

RVers should add $15-20 per night to that figure for hookups, and figure your gas according to the abilities of your rig. If you manage a full day of driving for under $125, call it lucky.

If you're heading to hotels, figure about $90 and up per night.

There are ways to cut this figure down, thus freeing up cash in the budget for expeditions. You'll discover that you want to spend entire days just sitting and looking at scenery. This is quite cheap. Pack sandwiches for lunch, eat donuts or fruit, depending on your health ideas, for breakfast, and save the eating out money for dinner. People with tents can reasonably camp virtually anywhere that's not private land. This means you can just head off into the bush and pitch a tent for free – just remember the bear precautions.

We figure you've been saving for this trip for a while and have enough put aside to let you drop some bucks from time to time. We list some very expensive expeditions – and they're worth it. But you can also have a killer time for $25 touring kennels in Fairbanks. And a day hiking is free.

As a guideline, figure a day of fishing will cost you $200, a day of kayaking around $100, a full-day trip on a tourist boat $100-150.

One place not to skimp is on your gear. We've seen a lot of trips ruined because people weren't properly outfitted. This doesn't mean go spend a fortune on the same gear climbers use on Everest. But you'll be a lot happier in waterproof boots than in tennis shoes, and there's a simple reason why everyone you meet in the North has a closet full of Gore-Tex: it works, and it's comfortable, and it works.

In other words, travel in the North is not cheap; if you're scrimping every penny, you'll find yourself not having much of a trip. On the other hand, it's still costs less than a trip to Europe, and the scenery is much, much better.

Here are some final numbers, courtesy of the state of Alaska: their figures indicate that the average package tourist spends $60 per day, in addition to the original cost of the tour. The average independent traveler spends about $160 per day.

And here's a real fun fact: the most recent set of numbers we found say the average out-of-state fisherman spends $930 to catch a king salmon, and $230 to catch a halibut.

Tourist Information

i In nearly every city, town, village, and hamlet along the highway, you'll find a tourist information booth. These vary from tiny, empty offices to huge buildings stocked with free literature. The staff of these centers are uniformly friendly and usually offer a gold mine of information. They also can steer you in the right direction in case of emergencies. Don't fail to make use of these treasure troves – and don't neglect to sign their guest books; the government looks at those when deciding on continued funding.

Tourist bureaus can be helpful even before you leave home. Write and tell them where you are going and what you want to see. They'll soon fill your mailbox with flyers. Write to:

Tourism Department of British Columbia, 1130 W Pender St., Suite 600, Vancouver, BC V6E 4A4, Canada. ☎ 800-663-6000, www.hellobc.com.

Tourism Yukon, PO Box 2703, Whitehorse, YT, Y1A 2C6, Canada. ☎ 867-667-5340. The Yukon is on the Web at www.touryukon.com.

Alaska Division of Tourism, PO Box 1180, Juneau, AK 99811-0801, USA. ☎ 907-465-2010, www.travelalaska.com.

For information on the Northwest Territories:

Economic Development and Tourism, PO Box 1320, Yellowknife, NWT X1A 2L9, Canada. ☎ 800-661-0788.

For **Alberta**: PO Box 2500, Edmonton, AB, Canada T5J 2Z4, ☎ 800-ALBERTA (800-252-3782), www.travelalberta.com.

For driving throughout the region, **Tourism North** is a great resource: www.northtoalaska.com.

Shopping

You'll find no shortage of places to spend your money along the highway. The majority of shops carry identical items, but there are a few unique places.

In Whitehorse, Anchorage, and a few smaller cities, **co-ops** run by Natives sell authentic Indian and Eskimo (in Canada, First Nations and Inuit) art. For **ivory** and **whalebone** articles, the co-ops are generally cheaper and the quality considerably higher than the tourist shops; and you can be sure that your money is getting back to the artist. Items made from certain animals cannot be sold unless they have been "significantly altered" by a Native artisan; this is why virtually all items made from whale are carved or have paintings on them. There are ways of getting around this, of course. The interpretations of what significantly altered means is highly debatable. Some think polishing a piece of baleen is enough – and then you can get yourself a piece without the tacky carvings on it. Some paint walrus skulls with watercolor paints and then tell you, nudge nudge, wink wink, never get it wet. Others turn the material into masterpieces of carving and painting. If you look around enough, you'll find something you love.

Often at the co-ops, you meet the artisan him- or herself. Sometimes, you meet the hunter.

Besides whalebone and ivory, watch for the exquisite **soapstone** and **jade** carvings done by Natives. In the southern areas of the region, you'll find the highly geometric art of the Tlingit and Haida Indians, usually carved and painted on wood, although artists are adapting traditional methods to modern means, producing stunning lithographs and prints. Several Native tribes specialize in **beadwork**. And don't forget the attractive, functional **clothing**: mukluks and anoraks are widely available. For the kids, pick up an Eskimo yo-yo, usually made of seal skin. The yo-yo is two balls of skin connected by a string. You make it work by getting the balls spinning in opposite directions.

Furs are another common purchase; you'll find fox, mink, sheep, and bear. Prices range from $50 or so for a beaver pelt to upwards of $20,000 for a polar bear skin. The fur trade isn't what it used to be, of course; between 1926 and 1937, $24 million worth of furs were shipped out of Alaska alone. That brings up the next point: a lot of these furs are coming off animals that are now considered endangered.

> **IT'S THE LAW:** *Goods made from endangered species cannot be imported into the US or Canada. Goods made from non-endangered species are still subject to special regulations. See the* Customs *section, below, for details.*

■ Ethical Issues

Although many of the products for sale in Alaska and Canada are made from endangered species, strict controls are enforced in both countries. The bone, ivory, and baleen (a kind of strainer that replaces teeth in some kinds of whales; pieces of it can be 10 feet long) come from animals that were hunted under subsistence regulations and used for food by Native villagers. This might be sometimes abused – reports of headless walrus carcasses are not uncommon. There's also the question of what defines subsistence. In theory, it's an animal killed for your own use, but the law also allows kills to be used for trade. And here's where the gray area comes in.

As with most Native cultures, Alaskans believed waste was a bad thing; it was an insult to the land and the animals. Interpret this however you want, but it's a commonsense idea: when one bad salmon run can mean your whole village starves, it's in your best interest to keep the salmon coming back.

Now, of course, you can just run out to the grocery store.

This means that there are some – and they are a minority – who are killing the animals under subsistence regulations, but letting the bulk go to waste, or doing something with it that the law did not quite have in mind. For instance, in the July/August 2000 issue of *Sierra*, Nancy Lord writes,

> *Beginning in the early 1990s, it became apparent that increasing numbers of Eskimo hunters were harvesting increasing numbers of Cook Inlet belugas for their own use, and, as broadly provided for under [law], for "trade and barter." This provision, meant to accommodate exchange in a village situation, created a large loophole that encompasses the legal (sometimes expressed as "not illegal") sale of beluga muktuk. Some Native hunters were in fact engaged in commercial whaling – selling the muktuk of Cook Inlet belugas to others.*

What all this means is, you need to be aware of what you're buying when you buy a product made from animal hide or bone or ivory.

However, when all's said and done, the abusers are not as many as those using the law and their traditional rights correctly. For the most part, when you buy these products, you are supporting a traditional way of life, one that predates European civilization by thousands of years.

Photography

 While you're up here, you might as well get pictures. Every person you talk to along the way will have different advice for taking good photographs. Below are just a few general guidelines.

- No matter how tricky they seem, with tiny zoom lenses, flashes, and so on, the popular little pocket cameras really won't give you great pictures. Little cameras give you little pictures. More importantly, they give you poorly resolved little pictures, and there is virtually no hope of pulling out detail later if you want to enlarge something. The same holds true for digital cameras without serious megapixels. Pocket cameras are fine for snapshots around the campsite, but to capture the glory of the North – especially the wildlife – you need a single lens reflex camera, the kind that offers through-the-lens viewing and has interchangeable lenses. Essentially, whether you're dealing with a fancy SLR film camera, or the newest digital, big zooms and wide angles are both good.

- Remember when framing your shot to include something that will give depth: a nearby tree, your friend, a stream. Just aiming at distant mountains gives a flat, uninteresting picture.

■ Catching Wildlife on Film

 The best time to photograph animals is in the dawn and dusk hours. In summer, these hours, for all practical purposes, extend from about 5 to 8 am and 7 to 10 pm. In the winter, it may be noon for sunrise and 3 pm for sunset. Remember, though, that animals don't always do what they're supposed to. We have yet to see an animal when and where all the advice tells us they'll be, so keep a sharp look-out at all times of day, especially around water sources.

When you spot an animal as you're driving, do not stop your car in the road. Get your vehicle completely off to one side, or skip the picture. No photograph is worth causing an accident. Also, do not jump out of your car to chase after animals. Respect them. If you go running off into the woods trying to get a better shot, all you'll find is that the animal can run faster than you can. Chasing after an animal is a needless hassle for both of you, and it can be dangerous. An animal could be startled away from its young, who would be left vulnerable. And as for you, it's all too easy to fall and get hurt if your attention is not on your feet.

> **WARNING:** Do not, under any circumstances, get out of your car to photograph bears or moose, unless you want to become part of ranger folklore about the many stupid ways people find to kill themselves.

Try to take animal shots from far enough away that you don't spook the creature. This is why you carry the telephoto or zoom lens. Move slowly, don't speak or make any sudden noises (like slamming the car door), and the animal will probably just look at you for a moment and go back to its business, leaving you a great opportunity for pictures. The calmer you are, the more relaxed the animal will be, and the less likely it is to go bounding off into the woods before you've gotten your camera out.

> **AUTHOR TIP:** *A small, soft pillow propped on your windowsill makes a good, stable emergency tripod. Some folks recommend a beanbag, but a pillow has lots of other uses in a crowded car.*

Finally, remember to bring all your accessories with you, including spare batteries and a camera cleaning kit.

■ Video Photography

There are only two general guidelines to keep in mind here: Smaller is better, and a huge power zoom makes everything better.

In some of the smaller towns, electricity is supplied by a generator, so the current may be erratic. When charging your battery, watch carefully for unusual heat output or an unusually long charging time. Should this occur, unplug the camera and wait for the next town. You probably won't damage your battery, but it's better not to take any chances.

You make a tradeoff with video. It's a lot more like being there when you get home, but you're never going to get the single stunning image that sums up the whole trip for you. You'll never get the detail that a still camera can offer. On the other hand, a still camera won't take you back to the way streams sound when they're flowing north.

And one final warning about video cameras: we spend a lot of time hanging out with tourists. It's alarming how many of them never look up from the viewfinder. It's as if every minute of the trip simply has to get onto the tape. So remember to get your face out of the camera from time to time. One of the saddest things we ever saw was a couple who filmed a grizzly bear in Glacier Bay for under a minute and then spent the next 10 minutes winding and rewinding their video to make sure they got it okay. Meanwhile, the bear was diving, fishing, and acting like a bear the whole time. The couple with the video camera missed it all.

Accommodations

Along the road you'll find many types of places to stay. Hotels and motels are usually the most plentiful and generally the most expensive. There are the familiar chains, as well as a variety of family-run establishments. The chains tend to be larger; they are usually more expensive and more likely to fill up with groups. You stand a much better chance of finding last-minute lodging at a locally owned place. Prices start at $50 for a single and $70 for a double, and can go as high as you're willing to pay.

HOTEL PRICING
Prices are in US dollars.
under $50 . . . . $
$50-$100 . . . . $$
$100-$150 . . . . . . $$$
above $150 . . . . . $$$$

> **AUTHOR TIP:** *Many places also have weekly rates; if you're planning to stay for more than a couple of days in one place, it's worth asking about.*

As a general rule, prices increase as you move away from populous areas and as you head farther north. Prices also increase once the summer season proper gets going – around June 1. From then through the end of August, you don't often have the chance to be picky about where you're staying; even Anchorage can be entirely sold out on a July weekend. If you know your schedule and aren't simply winging it as you go, getting reservations a couple of days ahead can save you a lot of worrying.

∎ Bed & Breakfasts

Bed and breakfasts are scattered along the road, but tend to be near the larger towns. There's a large turnover in the B&B business; the best place to check for current listings is the bulletin board in the nearest visitors center. In Anchorage, the visitors center will even make reservations for you. Prices throughout the region start around $80-100 for a double. It's not any cheaper than a hotel, and this always comes as a surprise to travelers from Europe, where B&Bs don't have themes and are actually cheap alternatives to hotels.

■ Roadhouses

Roadhouses are found along many of the more remote areas of the highway. They are usually a good value and are convenient if you're traveling in a group. You can rent cabins that sleep two to four people, often in scenic areas, and they make good bases from which to explore the wilderness. However, most of the roadhouses come with a bar. That's why it's there, right? Make sure your room isn't over it.

■ Camping

The best way to enjoy the great outdoors is to camp, and campgrounds are plentiful along most of the road. They vary in services, but most private sites offer RV hookups and a few tent sites. Many also have showers, washing, and shopping facilities. Figure on $20-25 a night for full hookups.

Besides the numerous private campgrounds, British Columbia, the Yukon, and Alaska all maintain excellent government campgrounds. Although they do not have hookups for RVs, they boast locations in scenic spots, clean facilities, and often free firewood (you'll need a small ax, since the wood is usually rough-cut). If you're in a tent, these are the places to head for – you probably already know that places that cater to RVs tend to have all the ambience of a parking lot. The state and provincial campgrounds are almost never crowded – usually, they're not even half full – and the prices can't be beat; typically, they run $10 to $12 per night. At most larger campgrounds, a ranger comes around in the early evening to collect; smaller places operate on the honor system. There used to be a seasonal pass you could buy that would let you stay in all of the Alaska state campgrounds, but that's now available only to residents.

The National Recreation Reservation Service, ☎ 877-444-6777, on the web at reserveusa.com, can hook you up with campgrounds all over the state, up to 240 days in advance – useful if you're thinking of going somewhere popular. They can also book you into Alaska's other great resource, the Forest Service cabin, up to 180 days in advance.

■ Forest Service Cabins

One of the best ways to see the Alaskan bush is to rent one of the Forest Service cabins that are dotted throughout the state.

Very, very few of these cabins are accessible by land; access to nearly all of them requires chartering a boat or plane. When chartering, be sure the pick up time and place are well understood. Go prepared for weather delays – bring a couple of extra days worth of supplies in case you get fogged in and the pilot can't reach you.

Reservations

Reservations for cabins can be made 190 days in advance. If you know when you'll be in an area, it's a good idea to call in right on the 190-day deadline and ask what's available and which forms you'll need to make your reservation. The best cabins are booked up without a break.

The local ranger stations keep notebooks with the vital statistics of each cabin. These include attractions in the area, fish most often caught, and visitor comments, which can be useful for determining a cabin's condition. The visitor comments also tell of any recent bear activity.

Your reservation will be confirmed no sooner than 179 days in advance. All applications must be accompanied with payment – most cabins run $25 a night. You can get a cabin for seven days between April 1 and October 31, or for 10 days the rest of the year. Checkout time is noon. It is usually possible at any time of the year to get an immediate booking for the less-popular cabins. Even those are lovely and offer a real taste of life in the Alaskan bush.

To book a cabin, you'll need a credit card; payment is due when the reservation is made. You can make a tentative reservation on the phone (not on the Web), but they have to get your payment within 10 days (cashier's checks or money orders only) or the reservation is canceled. Cabins are reserved on a first-come, first-served basis, and, again, the most popular cabins book up almost immediately. Phone ☎ 877-444-677 (toll-free) from 4 am to 8 pm Alaska time between April 1 and Labor Day; the line is open 6 am to 3 pm the rest of the year. You can visit their website at www.reserveusa.com. For more information, phone the Forest Service Information Center at ☎ 907-586-8751.

The only drawback is that by getting your reservation this way, you'll miss the chance to pick up local info on which cabins are the best.

Cabin Types

There are four types of cabin used by the Forest Service: A-frame, Hunter, Pan-abode, and Alpine. The A-frames have a second floor, which opens up a bit more sleeping space. The others have similar interiors, but only a single floor. All of the cabins can hold at least four people, and usually six.

Many of the cabins have oil-burning stoves, but stove oil is not provided. Check the type of stove in the cabin; if you need oil, five or 10 gallons is plenty for a week's stay. Wood is provided for those cabins with wood stoves, but you'll have to split it yourself.

The cabins do not have any bedding, electricity, or cooking utensils. There is no running water, and stream water should be boiled for a full five minutes before using. There's no such thing as a safe stream.

> **RESPONSIBLE TRAVEL:** *Cabins are run on an honor system: take care of them, and pack all your garbage out.*

Access by Charter

To get to the Forest Service cabins, or simply to get out and enjoy the beauty of Alaska away from the towns, you'll need to charter.

Charter operators are listed in each town section in this book, but they represent only a fraction of what's out there. You can charter a tiny boat, a huge yacht, or a plane that holds anywhere from two to six people, or more. Need a helicopter? It can be chartered.

Flight companies all work on a similar basis. They have a flat per-hour charge, which varies with the size of the plane. With a six-passenger plane fully loaded, chartering can be surprisingly cheap – less than $100 per person. For a plane that holds three passengers and a limited amount of gear, the going rate is around $400 per hour of flight time. The planes can fly you into forgotten lakes where the fish are just waiting to bite, or a customized sightseeing package can be arranged.

> **AUTHOR TIP:** *If you're being dropped off, always allow for delays due to inclement weather on the pick up.*

■ Youth Hostels

Youth hostels are found mostly in areas not accessible by main roads, as well as in the larger cities. Sleeping arrangements typically are dormitory-style, and there are curfews in some hostels. Alaska has set up a central office for their hostels: Alaska Council, AYH, PO Box 91461, Anchorage, AK 99509-1461.

Reservations

Summer is the busiest season, so if you're traveling then, it's highly advisable to make reservations in advance, especially in the more remote areas and in the bigger cities. If you haven't booked, start looking early in the afternoon. Often, every hotel in town is full by 4 pm. The same holds true for campgrounds close to towns – if all else fails, though, just drive out 30 or 40 miles, and you should find a campground with plenty of space.

Many places are open seasonally, so between September 1 and April 30 you should check on accommodation availability in advance. The dead of winter is not the time to find out you're going to have to rough it.

Transportation

 There is a wide variety of transportation on the highway, and the one you choose will dictate what you see and the shape your trip takes. We've done the road in a variety of cars and on a motorcycle (there's nothing quite like the adrenaline rush you get when you're charged by a moose bigger than your mode of transportation). While RVs outnumber everything else on the road, you'll see everything from Jeeps to old VW buses; and every year people do the highway by bicycle.

It's more than 2,500 miles (4,000 kilometers) from Seattle to Fairbanks, and there are endless side trip possibilities. Whatever vehicle you choose, you'll be spending a lot of time in it. Keep in mind that on the highway the traveling is the end, not the means to an end. So whatever transport you choose, make sure it's a choice you'll be comfortable with, something that will enhance your journey, not distract from it. Also remember that all side trips are not equally accessible to all vehicles; a 40-foot RV won't go where a Jeep will. We've met a lot of people whose trips were ruined by the wrong means of transport. And anybody who's traveled in the North can tell you about all the people they saw who might have driven a 40-foot rig just fine on the interstate down south, but once they got to the narrow, twisting roads of the North were huge accidents waiting to happen. Whatever you're in, make sure you're comfortable with it.

■ Precautions

The main road is essentially paved; at any given time, however, there may be extensive construction, and some sections are still gravel-paved. Although the gravel is oiled and compacted, it still makes for rougher traveling than asphalt. It's a good road, but it can be demanding on vehicles. For this reason, make absolutely sure your vehicle is in top shape. There are plenty of garages and service stations along the way, but they may not have the parts you need, or the services may be 100 miles down the road from where you have trouble. Before you leave home, take your vehicle to a trustworthy mechanic and have everything checked and repaired as needed. Don't leave with a worn-out belt or hose, hoping it will hold another 10,000 miles. While a broken hose won't end a vacation, it will certainly slow you down.

No matter what you are riding or driving, you should carry a full-sized **spare tire, a jack, a lug wrench**, and a **puncture repair kit**, and know how to use them. The half-sized spares now included with most passenger cars are not suitable for the Alaska Highway. No matter how much extra trunk room it takes, bring a full-sized spare. If you're planning extensive side trips on dirt roads, bring two. Although blowouts are more common than punctures, a few cans of compressed air and puncture sealant can be useful, too. Get the more expensive kind with nozzles that thread onto the valve of your tire.

You should also take along a spare **fan belt** and **radiator hose**. Since you've done all your repairs in advance, you probably won't need them; but if you do, you'll need them badly. Not all garages will have all supplies, and having the appropriate belt or hose with you means you won't have to wait while one is ordered. There's really no such thing as overnight package delivery in most of these parts – delivery more likely will take three or four days.

Also take along an **emergency kit**: jumper cables, flares, a flashlight, duct tape, a crescent wrench, a small socket wrench set (before buying your socket set, check to see if your car is on the metric or inch system), pliers, and a large knife. Most auto repair shops carry prepackaged repair kits. Take one of these as a base, and build it from there. If you don't know exactly what you need, find someone who does, and ask.

While you may not end up needing all this stuff – we never once have – you're likely to meet up with someone who does. There is a strong sense of fraternity in traveling the Alaska Highway, and you'll frequently find people crawling under each others' cars to check for leaks at campgrounds. Carrying spares is good for you and for everyone around you.

Many people put **screens** over the front of their cars to protect them from flying gravel. Also, cheap plastic **headlight covers** can save you from buying new, expensive glass ones at the end of your trip. There are places where the gravel flies thick. The AAA tells you that, because of the gravel, you will break your windshield. That's not necessarily true, but there's a pretty good chance, so make sure your insurance covers the possibility. On our trips, we have ranged from zero to six cracks in the windshield (our record is five cracks in one day), and we never leave home without double-checking our insurance coverage. Also, **towing insurance** could save you a fortune should something go wrong – you really don't want to be footing the bill for a 200-mile tow just because you didn't spring for $20 of towing insurance. Give your insurance agent a call to see what is covered and to make sure your policy is good in both countries. Get a proof of insurance card for traveling in Canada. It is mandatory to be insured in Canada, and they will ask about this at the border.

For those traveling in RVs or campers, before leaving home check all the **window screens**; make sure they are of the smallest mesh you can buy. Also outfit your vehicle with mudflaps, to help control the problem mentioned below.

One side effect of the road construction is that, after awhile, the **tail lights** of most cars are completely obscured. Always check when you stop for gas, to avoid having mud instead of brake lights.

At each stop for gas, check all the other **fluids** in your car as well; it's easy to be complacent if you just checked the oil yesterday – but that might have been nearly 1,000 miles ago. Make it a habit at each stop.

Gas is readily available all along the highway; the only long stretch of the Alaska Highway – the Alcan – with no services in the summer is between Whitehorse and Haines Junction, about 100 miles. Gas prices are much higher than in the continental US, and Canadian gas prices are considerably higher than those in Alaska. For those with political leanings one way or the other regarding the oil spill in Prince William Sound, Exxon is Esso in Canada.

In the Yukon and in many parts of Alaska and BC, the law says you must drive with your headlights on at all times. This is an excellent idea to follow everywhere. It's often difficult to see cars against the dark backdrop of trees, and headlights are a great help. Seatbelts, of course, are a must everywhere.

Finally, take along a simple **repair manual** for your vehicle and a couple of blankets. These small precautions can prevent a lot of discomfort waiting by the roadside. Don't worry in advance. Just take all the proper precautions and use care.

■ Racking Your Gear

 While you can rent canoes, kayaks, and bikes in a lot of towns, you're really going to want them outside of town. This means bringing your own along, which usually requires a rack.

Just about any car, van, truck, or camper can be outfitted with a roof or rear-end carrier. Manufacturers are increasingly customizing their hardware to accommodate specific makes and models so, no matter what you drive, you'll find something that fits. Prices range from about $50 for a basic bike rack to $500 for a customized rooftop carrier.

There are a few things to consider when you're hauling your gear on the roof or tail of your vehicle:

- Many of the nuts and bolts on car racks are unique to the manufacturer and may be hard to replace on the highway. Bring extra parts along with you. Washboard roads will loosen even the tightest bolts over time. Be sure to check all connections periodically to make sure everything is still tight.

- Road conditions in the North can be rough. You'll need to protect your gear from mud, gravel, low-flying birds (we've had several smack into us), and other hazards. While canoes and kayaks can be washed – hey, they're meant to get wet – with a bike you must carry along extra lubricant. Good bike supply shops have mesh shields you can stretch across the front of the bike to reduce flying gravel dings.

- After you've tied your gear to the roof and locked it (good boating stores sell kayak and canoe locks; bikes are a lot easier to chain down), be sure all straps are tight and any slack in the tiedowns is tied off properly. Loose straps will sound like an army of bees heading toward you when you hit highway speed. They're also a hazard, especially long ends. Remember, Isadora Duncan died when her scarf got tangled in a car wheel. Tie down straps can do the same trick.

Even if you aren't taking along a canoe or bike, you might want to look into a rooftop carrier, especially if you've got a small car. Getting the laundry out from under your feet and into a box on the roof can make the whole trip a lot easier.

ROAD WISDOM

Here is one final warning for travel in all kinds of vehicles: Keep in mind at all times that you're not really going anywhere, you're just going. Too many people lose out on great moments of their vacation by trying to hurry along to the next spot, the next goal. We are so accustomed to getting in our cars and going somewhere, that we don't know how to just go. And we tend to look for goals, for those dots on the map – but once you get to them, they're probably smaller than the mall back home. As Anthony Trollope wrote in another place, "One seems to ride forever and come to nothing, and to relinquish at last the very idea of an object." That's what you want to do. Relax. Be willing to stop for anything that intrigues you. Don't worry about the 12 slow RVs you just now finally got around. Don't set goals. Take a lesson from the Zen masters: Be here, now. Or from Lao Tzu: "A good traveler has no fixed plan and is not intent on arriving." If the Alaska Highway offers any lesson at all, it's that there's an amazing amount of highway.

Getting Off the Road

■ Boating

 For most travelers, a trip to the North isn't complete until they get on the water. There are 10 million lakes in Alaska alone, not to mention the rivers and, of course, the ocean. There can be lines of cars on the highway, but the lakes will be completely empty. Throughout this book we offer suggestions for where to get into the water.

One of the first things early explorers to the North noticed was that the locals had better boats. While the Europeans sailed bulky ships that could barely turn, the locals, according to George Stellar (after whom so many Northern animal species are named, including the Steller sea lion, the incredibly common Steller jay and the now-extinct Steller sea cow – and yes, it usually is spelled differently; it all depends on who's doing the transliteration out of Russian), were in boats "about two fathoms long, two feet high, and two feet wide on the deck, pointed toward the nose but truncated and smooth in the rear.... On the outside [the] frame is covered with skins, perhaps of seals, and colored a dark brown." Stellar had spotted a kayak, and it didn't take the Europeans long to figure out that these tiny boats could do just about anything. Meanwhile, in the Interior, explorers and trappers were heading up the rivers in bark and skin canoes, some 30 feet long.

Precautions

The water up North is still great – still perfect for paddling. But whether you canoe one of the wild rivers, kayak the fjords to watch glaciers calve, head out fishing or cruising, or just want to sit in a boat and watch the sky overhead, there are things you have to keep in mind. Many of the Northern lakes remain wild and remote, so excursions onto the water require a high degree of planning and self-sufficiency.

- Always file a float plan and itinerary with an agency, authority, relative, or friend. Should you end up late, stranded, or in need of rescue, a search can be underway a lot more quickly if someone knows where and when to start. Details of the float plan should include the type, color, and length of your boat, the number of people, and even the color of clothes everybody's wearing when they head out (remember, it's a lot easier to spot a red jacket than a green one).

- Get an accurate weather forecast before you set off and watch for any signs that conditions are deteriorating. Keep your eyes on the horizon and peaks for clouds coming in. Carry an emergency supply of food, clothing, and essentials separate from your other gear, in a waterproof container. This can save your life if you have to weather a storm.

- Have PFDs (personal floatation devices – life jackets) and wear them at all times.

- Be aware of the dangers, conditions, symptoms, and treatment of hypothermia – see the Health section, below. Northern waters are always cold, and getting wet can kill you.

- Watch out for bears, marine mammals, and other wildlife. Salmon-spawning streams and berry bushes are prime bear spots. Marine mammals should be viewed only from a distance. It's illegal and dangerous to chase after an animal – an angry seal can easily capsize a boat. And remember, to most marine mammals, a guy in a kayak looks just like a killer whale. Respect the animals.

- If you're going out into the ocean, be aware of tidal races and fluctuations. Have – and use – charts and tables to ensure safe boating. The tides can move very fast in some spots, and the tidal variations are often extreme. Remember this when you're pitching your camp – stay well above the high water mark, high enough so that wakes and unusual waves won't bother you.

■ Boil and purify all drinking water, no matter where you land, and practice eco-sensitive rules of waste and sewage disposal. No-trace camping is the only way to go.

■ Take some kind of signaling device with you for an emergency, such as a VHF radio, an EPIRM (emergency position indicating radio beacon), flares, and mirrors. More than one person on a trip should know how to use these.

■ Have a contingency plan in case anyone in your party gets separated. Pick a spot to meet, and choose regular times to check in by walkie talkie; don't count on your cell phone signal working everywhere.

■ Finally, you need to plan a rational approach to threatening situations. Remaining calm is the first thing to do. Then you can make a clear assessment of the emergency and take proper corrective measures. Find shelter, food, water, and keep a level head. That will just about ensure survival and rescue.

The odds of an emergency are remote – more likely, you will enjoy peace and safety on the water. But the more prepared you are for an emergency, the more relaxed your days on the water will be.

If you haven't brought up your own boat, they're easy to rent, for about $40 a day for a single kayak. You will have to prove that you know what you're doing with one; it's annoying for the outfitters to have to go hunt down yahoos who got in over their heads. So if you can't do a water re-entry, forget renting, and just stick with guided trips.

All time spent on the water is good time.

WHITEWATER CLASSIFICATION

Class I: Almost flat water, maybe a few riffles. No obstructions or real waves.

Class II: Easy rapids, waves up to three feet high. Not a real problem for anybody who understands their boat.

Class III: Rapids with irregular waves; may need some serious maneuvering.

Class IV: Long, difficult rapids, possible need for very precise maneuvering. You may need to scout the route from shore before you do the rapid, and only experts have any business in a canoe in Class IV. Kayakers must know how to Eskimo roll. Anybody going through a Class IV had better know how to swim.

Class V: Think Class IV, but a whole lot worse. You have no business being out here unless you've done a lot of rivers already in your life.

Class VI: Forget it. A cold and wet way to commit suicide.

■ Charters/Outfitters

Once you get out of the car, you're probably going to end up hiring a charter operator or two to take you farther into the bush. Throughout the North, hundreds of operators are anxious and ready to take you fishing, hiking, biking, canoeing, kayaking, parasailing, bungee jumping.... You name it, you can pay somebody to help you do it.

When chartering or booking with an outfitter, be up front about what you want to do and what you hope to accomplish – but be reasonable. Even the most experienced boat captain can't guarantee you'll catch a fish. But different species need different tricks and lures, and a good captain is up on where and when your chances are best. A good captain also is going to tell you this himself, without promising record catches. The same holds true for rafting trips. So maybe the last group went Class IV without anybody pitching out of the boat. But how often does someone go overboard (if they tell you never, they're lying).

Before booking the trip, find out exactly how long a half-day or whole-day charter is. Find out how long different operators have been working the area, and ask about their licenses or affiliations. Ask what they do for you. You'll find rafting trips where you sit while other people paddle. This is great for many people, but others like to take a more active part. There are fishing charters where the guides hardly let you touch a line until it's time to reel in. Others sit back and let you do everything yourself.

Find out what gear they supply, and what you need to bring yourself. If it's an all-day trip, do they supply lunch, or do you need to pack your own PB&J? (We're developing a theory that you can gauge the quality and quantity of fishing charter operators in any city by the number of Subway sandwich shops.)

If one charter company is more expensive – or cheaper – than any of the others, find out why. At a basic level of service, boat charters should include all fishing gear, some kind of refreshments, and at least some help on processing the fish.

Some charters run cheaper trips not because they skimp on the service, but because they run in different areas. This might mean a float trip that takes a less crowded fork in the river, a kayak operator who paddles a different stretch of coastline, or an operator who is simply trying something completely different. For example, in Homer, the lower-cost charters stay out of the deep, rougher water where the really big fish are; but they can take you into hidden, quiet bays, and they often offer more excitement, since they use lighter tackle.

For fishing and water sightseeing, find out what kind of boat you'll be on. Charters range from Boston Whalers with Alaska cabins – basic, serviceable, and far from comfortable, but great for serious fishing – to luxury cabin cruisers.

If you're booking a kayak trip, you should find out how far from town you're going, what kind of things you're likely to see, and how long you'll be in the boat. Kayaks move slowly; five miles is about as far as most novices can paddle without beginning to hurt in the legs or hands. Also, because kayaks are slow, where you start paddling is usually a pretty good reflection of what you'll see. Most good outfitters will have pictures of trips for you to look at. We have never yet come across a kayak outfitter who wasn't very good with the beginning paddle/safety demonstration. Have no fear: even if it's your first time, you'll know what to do when you get in the boat.

The only way to ensure you get what you want out of a charter or booked trip is to let the operator know what you're after. Operators don't want to take you out if they don't have what you want – it just means you waste your money and they end up with an unhappy client, making everybody miserable. Make your expectations known, match the trip to your needs, and you'll have a great time.

■ Wilderness Hiking

 The roads in the North open only a tiny fraction of the land. There is so much of British Columbia, Alaska, and the Yukon to explore beyond the highway that you could easily spend a hundred lifetimes hiking in the backcountry and still have plenty to see.

The backcountry is wonderful if you're prepared, a terror if you're not. Throughout this book, we emphasize the importance of preparation before you set off on any hike into the bush. Here are a few of the details you'll need to take care of before you lace on your (broken-in) boots.

First, get maps. Topo maps are available in most cities; if you don't know how to read one, get a good explanation before you head out. All the modern global positioning systems (which are fine if it's not too cloudy) and tricky radios won't be as useful as topo maps and an old Boy Scout compass.

For any lengthy hike, tell somebody where you're going and when you expect to be back. Nobody will go out to search for you if no one knows you're lost.

Practice no-trace camping. Nothing rains on the parade of your wilderness experience faster than ending a 10-mile hike and finding old cans where you wanted to pitch the tent. According to the Forest Service, here's what you've got to do:

- Plan ahead. This makes sure you're not in over your head. Nothing messes up the wilderness like a good search party looking for someone where they shouldn't have been to begin with. Planning ahead also means knowing what to do when you're face to face with a moose, bear, or a case of hypothermia.

- Stick to harder surfaces wherever you can. The forests and tundra are a lot more fragile than you might think; in tundra, it can take more than a decade for a footprint to disappear. So stay on the trails if there are any, and if you can, camp where somebody else has camped before you.

- If you pack it in, pack it back out. You can make this easier on yourself by getting rid of excess packaging material before you head out. It's amazing how much garbage is simply packaging.

- Human waste gets buried, at least six inches deep, at least 200 feet from water. Same deal if you're going to wash your dishes after dinner: keep your soap away from water sources.

- Don't mess with the wild. This means no chopping down trees, no messing with what you find when you're out there. Leave it as you find it.

- Finally, skip the campfire. Pack in a stove, and use that for cooking. If you've really got to make a fire, use only dead and down wood, and try to build it where someone else has already had their fire. Remember, a fire is not out until you can run your hands through the ashes and feel no heat.

Make sure to pitch your tent above the tide line if you're on the coast. Tides can raise the water dramatically, and it's not at all uncommon for novice campers to wake up right before the tent floats off. Even a mile or two up a river, the tide can change the water level by several feet. Find good high ground to pitch your tent.

Current thinking is that big tarps under your tent just funnel rainwater to where you're sleeping. A footprint tarp under the tent takes care of this and still protects the bottom of your gear.

Boil all water before drinking it.

Read the section on Wildlife and know what to do if you run into a bear or moose.

Know your limitations. It's not at all uncommon for novice hikers to get in over their heads in the bush. Know the conditions of the hike before you set off. Local ranger stations are great for this.

Always stick to the trail whenever possible. The land in the North is extremely fragile, and has a very short growing season. Just a few footprints can take years to disappear.

It's a good idea to pack a copy of *The Outward Bound Wilderness First-Aid Handbook*. It will get you through most emergencies, from having to splint a break to treating beaver fever.

River Crossings

If you're hiking in the backcountry, sooner or later you're going to have to cross a river. To avoid swimming – not at all what you want to do in water that's running maybe 45 degrees – here are the basic rules:

- Cross early in the day, and never cross after a storm. Watch for storms in the same watershed – water levels can change dramatically and rapidly.

- You're probably going to look for a narrow place to cross, but narrow usually means deep and fast. Rivers tend to be slower and more shallow in wide spots. You're wet an extra few yards, but it's worth it. Head for the wide places.

- Keep your boots on. They've got better traction than your feet.

- Keep your pack loose, so you can get it off if you swim. Make sure anything you can't allow to get wet – like your sleeping back and a set of dry clothes – are in dry bags. If you can't roll your pants up high enough, take them off. Hypothermia can strike just from wind hitting wet clothes.

- If you've got a rope, and want to be safe, loop it around a tree. You can only cross a river that's half as wide as your rope is long – that loop lets you get it back once you're safely on the other side.

Finally, if you do swim and the current grabs you, assume river swim position: like you're sitting in an easy chair, feet in front of you, body upright. If you can't see your toes, your legs are too low. Taking it like this means your feet – not your head – are the first to encounter river obstacles.

■ Fishing & Hunting Rules

 A few weeks of fishing in the North will spoil you for the rest of your life; you'll never want to return to the streams and lakes at home. The size and diversity of fish are unmatched anywhere else in the world. From the mighty king salmon to the delicious grayling, there is hardly a nonglacial stream out there where you won't catch something.

For hunters, the challenge is just as large in spirit, and a whole lot larger in size. Bear, moose, even musk ox are hunted, although the fees for a nonresident hunting permit may be staggering – well over $1,000 for a musk ox. Hunting trips must be planned well in advance to qualify for tag drawings.

For those unfamiliar with the area, your trip might be a lot more enjoyable with a hired guide. There is no shortage of them, anywhere along the highway and beyond.

Fishing licenses are available in many local shops along the way; hunting licenses must be obtained in advance. For detailed information, write to the appropriate address below.

In British Columbia, there are separate licenses for saltwater and freshwater fishing, and even for a few separate species of fish.

For information on saltwater fishing, write: **Department of Fisheries and Oceans**, 555 W. Hastings St., Vancouver, BC V6B 5G2, Canada.

For freshwater rules, and information on hunting, write: **Ministry of Environment, Fish and Wildlife Branch**, 780 Blanshard St., Parliament Buildings, Victoria, BC V8V 1X4, Canada.

For the Yukon, contact: **Yukon Government, Fish and Wildlife Branch**, PO Box 2703, Whitehorse, YT Y1A 2C6, Canada.

The address in Alaska is: Alaska Department of Fish and Game, PO Box 25526, Juneau, AK 99802, USA.

To simply obtain a license by mail, write: **Alaska Department of Fish and Game Licensing**, 1111 W. 8th St., Room 108, Juneau, AK 99801, USA.

Health

 There are no major health hazards involved in traveling along the Alaska Highway; nor are there any inoculations required by either country. Still, there are a few things to keep in mind.

■ If you are currently taking any medication, be sure to carry an adequate supply for the length of your trip. If you have allergies, take along some antihistamines. A lot of flowers bloom along the road.

■ It's a good idea to pack a first aid kit. You can buy a perfectly good one at any camping store. It should include several sizes of bandages, disinfectant, a small pair of scissors, mole skin, pain reliever, antiseptic cream, and tape. When choosing your kit, keep in mind the number of people who will be using it.

■ Should you go far from the highway, beef up your kit accordingly. Add more bandages, a lot more mole skins, and a broad spectrum antibiotic.

■ For those who are hiking and camping, a means of water purification is a must. No matter how clear the streams may look, you really don't know where the water has been, and you should not assume it's safe to drink. Purifying drinking water is a simple precaution against a lot of possible discomfort. You can use filters, which are expensive but don't alter the water's taste, or you can buy iodine or chemical tablets, which are cheap and taste terrible. With either product, follow the manufacturer's directions carefully. The third and easiest way to purify water is to boil it. Bring the water to a full boil for five minutes. If you're in the mountains, increase the boiling time by one minute per 1,000 feet over 5,000 feet of altitude. An alternative are the new sterilizing pens, which use soundwaves to kill the nasty stuff, and don't alter the taste at all.

■ If you insist on trusting nature and not purifying your water, pack more of the broad spectrum antibiotic and remember that most diarrhea goes away in three or four days. If it does not, or if there is blood or fever, see a doctor.

■ Take along sunblock. There can be more than 20 hours of daylight per day on the highway; the farther north you go, the greater your risk of sunburn. Choose a sunblock with an SPF number of 15 or higher. It's perhaps not surprisingly difficult to buy sunblock in most northern drugstores.

■ Perhaps most important, take along a massive supply of mosquito repellent. Those with the chemical DEET work best; they're more expensive (which means you can get a bottle for two bucks instead of one), but they're worth every penny. If you don't want to put such a toxic chemical on your body, there are those who swear by Skin So Soft, a lotion available in most drug stores, and now jazzed up with a special repellent ingredient. If you're using DEET, remember to wash it off with warm water and soap, and be sure to clean your hands before touching food.

DEET ALERT

DEET is nasty stuff, but mosquito experts (yes, there are such people, squinting through microscopes to identify the dozens of species that inhabit Alaska alone) swear it's the only thing that truly works. There are a couple of other warnings about DEET. Children should not use a concentration higher than 10%. You should never use DEET on broken skin, nor should you apply it under your clothes (although a drop on the top of your hat brim will keep mosquitoes away without you having to put poison on your face). Don't mix DEET with any kind of skin lotion – the lotion drags the DEET down into your system through your skin, where you really don't want it. If you use DEET on your clothes, wash them as soon as you take them off. Remember that DEET is highly toxic, and treat it that way.

- Whatever you do about mosquitoes and other things that bite, take along some hydrocortisone cream to soothe the itch when mosquitoes and other biting insects have no respect for modern chemistry.

There's a useful brochure, **Help Along the Way: Emergency Medical Services for Alaska's Travelers**, that you can find at Info Centres along the road, or write to the Southern Region EMS Council, 6130 Tuttle Place, Anchorage, AK 99507-2041. It's well worth having a copy in the car.

■ Hypothermia

Hypothermia is the number one killer of outdoorsmen, but it can be avoided easily. Hypothermia occurs when the body is unable to maintain its core functioning temperature; to save the vital organs in the middle of the body, it begins to shut down the extremities. Wet and wind in combination are the main causes. Victims of hypothermia may display uncontrollable shivering, loss of coordination, and sudden sleepiness. Often, they are unwilling to believe anything is wrong with them. Should a member of your party show signs, get him or her out of the elements immediately and into dry clothes. Hot drinks can help in a minor case of hypothermia, but in more extreme cases, they can be a choking hazard. Put the victim into a sleeping bag. If the symptoms are severe, strip both the victim and yourself, and get into the sleeping bag together. Try not to let the victim fall asleep, and do not give him or her any alcohol. It's also recommended that you not rub them vigorously in hopes of restoring circulation. In a severe case, get the victim to a hospital as quickly as possible. With hypothermia, quick action saves lives. From personal experience, we can tell you that the person suffering from hypothermia has no idea what's happening. From the inside, it's actually rather peaceful. So watch out for each other.

One Highway, Two Countries

■ Legalities & Customs

There are a few things to keep in mind when crossing the border between the US and Canada:

- Technically, US citizens entering Canada and Canadian citizens entering the US need not have passports or visas. However, as of this writing, there is potential of this undergoing considerable change. Check with the respective governments for the latest regulations. In the paranoid new world, who knows what rules are going to kick in.

- Although recently Canadian Customs have gotten more careful with searches (particularly looking for illegal animal products and guns), as a general rule Customs at both borders are quick and easy. If you look less than clean-cut and prosperous, Canadian Customs usually asks if you have adequate funds for your planned stay in the country. People have been turned away at the border for having less than $150.

- Fruits and vegetables may be inspected or confiscated. This is especially true when you enter Canada from Washington; remember this when you're driving past the fruit stands that line the highway in the miles before the border.

- Dogs and cats over three months old must be vaccinated for rabies; you must have a certificate from a licensed veterinarian that the shot has been given within the past three years.

- You cannot take pistols or any firearm with a barrel length of less than 18.5 inches into Canada. "Long guns" – rifles – are allowed, at least hunting rifles and shotguns. Semi-automatic weapons are forbidden. Canadian Customs will ask if you are carrying any weapons, and the penalty for bringing in an illegal firearm is stiff.

- Do not even think about bringing illegal drugs into either country. Carry copies of your prescriptions – this speeds matters up if they want to check the pill bottles, and it makes it easier if you lose your bottle and need a refill somewhere along the way.

- Both countries prohibit import of products made from endangered species. This becomes confusing, because there are products made from whale, walrus ivory, bear, seal, and wolf in gift shops all along the highway in both countries. However, if you buy one of these items in Canada, you will not be allowed to transport it into the US; if you buy it in Alaska, you will not be allowed to transport it through Canada on the way home without a special permit. You can avoid this hassle altogether by boycotting endangered species products. If you must purchase something and have doubt, call the local Customs office for details before making your purchase and trying to ship it. You can buy fossilized ivory and whalebone, legally transporting it through either country. If you have any questions, contact the local Fish and Wildlife Office or its equivalent. (As for the ethical questions of buying products made from endangered species, see the section on Shopping, above.)

- When you return to your home country, Customs officials will assess duty on items purchased abroad. For US citizens who have been out of the country for less than 48 hours, the duty-free allowance is $25; after more than 48 hours, it's $800. Canadian citizens are allowed $20 after 24 hours, $100 after 48 hours, and $300 after seven days.

▪ People who are not residents or citizens of the US or Canada should check with local embassies or consulates for current entry requirements. A multiple-entry visa is needed for both countries to complete a round-trip of the highway.

For the latest information on Customs, write to: **Department of the Treasury**, US Customs Service, Washington, DC 20041, or your local Customs office.

In Canada, write: **Customs Offic**e, 1001 W. Pender St. Vancouver, BC V6E 2M8, Canada.

▪ Currency

$ Although each has nickels, dimes, quarters, and dollars, the US and Canada have separate currencies. To save time and trouble, convert as much as you think you'll need, either at home or at the first town over the border.

Any bank should be able to handle the transaction, but commission rates are not fixed, so it's a good idea to shop around. One bank may charge a simple fee of $1 for the entire exchange; others may charge as much as $5 per traveler's check. For the current exchange rate, check the newspaper, and always ask the bank about its commission rates.

On the other hand, your ATM card will work fine in both countries, and you get the bank rate on exchanges, which is a lot cheaper.

International boundary, marked by a clearcut section and a post.

Many businesses in Canada – particularly gas stations – will accept US dollars in payment, at slightly less than the going exchange rate. The same does not hold true for Canadian dollars in the US. It's better to change your money. You lose a lot tossing US dollars around at Canadian businesses, and it's not worth the apparent convenience. Besides, it's just rude.

Mastercard, Visa, and American Express are pretty much universally accepted along the highway, as are all major traveler's checks (in the proper currency). Always carry some cash, though, for the exceptions or for the trip into the bush.

If you head away from the highway, don't expect to find an open bank or a lot of shops. You'll need to be very much self-sufficient. Remember that most of the people who live in the bush are there at least partially to get away from the pressures of a market economy.

■ Electricity

 Both Canada and the US run on 110-120 voltage, and the plug shape is the same, so no adapters are needed. Be aware, however, that many of the smaller towns use generators to supply their power, so there may be minor fluctuations. When charging a rechargeable battery item, such as a video camera or a personal computer, watch for unusual heat or unusual charging time. Should this occur, unplug your machine and try charging it again in a larger town.

■ Telephones

 The best telephone systems in the world cover Canada and the US. The only thing you need to worry about is area codes. With the exception of Stewart/Hyder, all of Alaska is 907; all of the Yukon and the Northwest Territories take area code 867; in BC, everything – including Stewart/Hyder, but with the exception of Vancouver – is 250; Alberta is 403. Vancouver is 604.

■ Metric Conversion

 Officially, Canada uses the metric system; however, a lot of Canadians haven't realized this yet, and if you ask most of them a weight or a distance, they'll answer in pounds and miles. In this book, we use the US system, because it is more readily accessible to both countries.

Recommended Outfitters

If you stick to the highways in the North, you're seeing maybe 1% of the accessible territory. We don't have the space in a book to go into all the options of heading farther afield – guidebooks can hardly scratch the surface – but here are some choice outfitters who can get you into the lovely deep boonies.

Alaska Discovery, part of the Mountain-Travel/Sobek family, runs trips all over Alaska, from kayaking Glacier Bay to rafting the Hulahula, a considerable ways north of the Arctic Circle. First-rate company. ☎ 800-586-1911, www.akdiscovery.com.

Alaska Mountain Guides, ☎ 800-766-3396, www.alaskamountain guides.com, runs big mountain climbing trips – if you feel like taking on Denali, these are the guys to call – and offer skills schools, rock and ice climbing trips, and more.

Alaska Vistas is one of our favorite outfits anywhere. Trips on the Stikine River, and into the best of Southeast Alaska. ☎ 866-874-3006, www. alaskavistas.com.

Alaska Wildland Adventures, ☎ 800-334-8730, www.alaskawildland. com, runs fantastic trips in Southcentral Alaska, from the Chugach down the Kenai, and north into the Arctic.

Nome Discovery Tours is all you need to know about the great gold rush town of Nome – where it's not unusual to see musk oxen near the high school – and the surrounding area. Richard is one of Alaska's great, most entertaining guides. ☎ 907-443-2814, or email him at discover@gci.net

Serious river freaks should try **NOVA**, ☎ 800-746-5753, www.novalaska. com, for the Talkeetna, the Copper, and more.

The Beauty of the Wild

Finally, remember this: Much of the North is wilderness, meant to stay that way. There are huge areas where no roads are allowed. Once you set off into these places, you're on your own. In Juneau, you can buy postcards with a quote from the *Idaho Law Review*. Nothing we've seen better sums up the beauty of wilderness areas.

A venturesome minority will always be eager to get off on their own... let them take risks, for God's sake, let them get lost, sunburnt, stranded, drowned, eaten by bears, buried alive under avalanches – that is the right and privilege of any free American.

Chapter 3

The History
of the Highway

A Highway Is Born

On February 2, 1942, the US War Department called Brigadier General Clarence L. Sturdevant to a meeting. Sturdevant was the Assistant Chief of Engineers, and the War Department, shaken by developments in

the Orient, decreed a new project: the construction of a highway to Alaska. If this project were proposed today, you could figure on 10 years of study, at least a 100% budget overrun, and engineers trembling at the thought of cutting a road through nearly 2,000 miles of bush and mud. But in the 1940s, the country was preparing for war. Only two days after the meeting with Sturdevant, a comprehensive plan was presented by the Chief of Engineers. The Alaska Highway was about to become a reality, and the North was about to explode in a frenzy of activity.

The Alaska Highway was designed to provide a military supply route to the threatened fringes of America; it was also to provide a supply line to a series of air bases – the Northwest Staging Route – which stretched in a chain from Edmonton, Canada, to Fairbanks, Alaska. The Northwest Staging Route had been established the year before, and the tiny airports – not much more than Quonset huts and dirt landing strips – were already overloaded with the influx of war materials as planes were ferried along the route from the US to the beleaguered forces of the Soviet Union, which had nearly collapsed under the Nazi advance.

By February 16, orders had been given and military engineers were heading North. Dawson Creek, in British Columbia, was chosen for the southern end of the highway; the city was served by a small dirt road, and it was the northern terminus of the Northern Alberta Railways, so it was a relatively easy place to bring supplies.

In order to get the road built as quickly as possible, a three-pronged attack was planned. Construction crews were to begin not only from Dawson Creek, but also from Fort Nelson, BC, Whitehorse, YT (where supplies could be brought via the White Pass & Yukon Route Railway), and Big Delta, Alaska (today, Delta Junction), where the existing road from Fairbanks turned south.

The original plan was to build a simple, fast, and serviceable pioneer road, to open access to Interior Alaska as quickly as possible. Standards were established. The clearing had to be at least 32 feet wide, the grades no more than 10%, the curves no less than a 50-foot radius, with a minimum of 12 feet of surfacing. The specs called for exactly enough road to get a military truck up, nothing more. The official orders said, "Further refinements will be undertaken only if additional time is available." However, once construction started and they found out exactly what was involved, refinements came about with amazing speed, almost on the heels of the pioneer road.

■ A Tough Road to Build

On March 9, 1942, nine days before the Canadian government officially agreed to allow the US to build a road through Canadian territory, troops began arriving in Dawson Creek. They were met by deceptively warm weather – about 50°. But within days, they discovered the real character of the North. The temperature plummeted to 30° below zero, and snow and ice covered the ground and the tents where the soldiers lived. Less than a week after the first troops arrived, there were more than 1,100 soldiers in Dawson Creek. This was but a fraction of the more than 10,000 soldiers who would soon be involved in the construction, and they were all to learn the same lesson: Living conditions were not going to be easy. Early March isn't exactly the best time to start a construction project in the North. Even today, all construction is done during the summer season, and only a few maintenance crews venture out in the dead of winter.

The highway was to cut through completely uninhabited country for most of its length; the few towns that did exist were tiny and unprepared for huge influxes of soldiers. Dawson Creek had a population of less than 500; Whitehorse had 1,000. The soldiers were forced to live on what they could carry.

Road construction moved along so quickly there was no chance to build permanent settlements or even refined living quarters. The soldiers lived in tents, although a few later changed to small shacks mounted on skids that could be dragged forward as the construction progressed. They were not supplied with cots, but fashioned their own beds from boughs and government-issue sleeping bags.

The food they ate was equally basic: dehydrated potatoes, powdered milk, canned chili, and corned beef. As sections of the road opened up and transportation problems eased, the menu changed slightly. Fresh meat and vegetables were brought in at the first opportunity. But, in general, the meals were monotonous, enlivened only when a soldier happened to kill some fresh game.

If the only problems had been food and shelter, the soldiers could have easily taken it; after all, life in the Army has never been luxurious. But working in the North brought a new array of problems. The soldiers were attacked by clouds of mosquitoes and biting flies. The mud was so deep in places that entire tractors sank. And then there was the weather: freezing cold, day after day, with temperatures reaching 40 and 50 below, and no place at all to get warm. (The miserable weather made the section of road around Muncho Lake one of the most popular for the workers; Liard Hot Springs was nearby.) When it wasn't freezing cold, other elements tormented the exhausted workers. On June 7, 1942, 4.47 inches of rain fell on Fort St. John. The workers were living in tents; the road became an impossible morass that could not be approached for two weeks. In December of 1942, just after the pioneer road had opened but long before the work was finished, the temperature in Whitehorse did not rise higher than 20 below for two weeks, bottoming out at 67 below – cold enough to freeze exposed skin and to explode tires when the air inside them froze.

Historic photo of tree-clearing during the Highway's construction.
Photo courtesy of Anchorage Museum of History & Art

These problems, coupled with the difficulty in getting mail through and the lack of news from the Lower 48, led to serious morale problems among the workers. One entertainment they devised was to elect a "Sweetheart of the Al-Can." The sweetheart they chose was Rita Hayworth. The soldiers pooled their money and sent Lt. Jim Blackwelder to Hollywood, where he met Ms. Hayworth and took her picture. The story made the front page of The Los Angeles Times on June 11, 1943.

Despite all the difficulties, the road got built at a lightning pace. Workers cut trees down by the thousands; bulldozers followed closely behind, leveling a roadway. Construction moved forward at such speed that surveyors did their work from atop the bulldozers – barely able to keep ahead of the machinery. By the first of August, 858 miles of road had been laid out, 611 miles had been completed, and there were an additional 183 miles under construction.

But this incredible pace wasn't fast enough. The road had to be finished before hard winter set in. To support the Army, the Public Road Administration (PRA) joined in during the late summer. Its workers followed behind the troops who were creating the pioneer route, and began to improve and maintain the road, getting it ready for all-season operation. At the peak of operations there were 17,000 civilians working on the road, using 7,000 trucks, bulldozers, and cars.

The work, for troops and civilians alike, was arduous. Workers faced terrain conditions that had never been encountered before. Muskeg was one of their first threats. A swampy area covered by low plants, muskeg looks solid, and sometimes is, but other places give way to the deep waters beneath. The muskeg areas were feared to be impassable, but the engineers developed skills at spotting them, and were able to loop the road around many of the boggy areas. There were times when it couldn't be gotten around, however. On one three-mile stretch, the muskeg, three to four feet thick, had to be cleared by a dragline. Then the road bed had to be backfilled with dry clay transported from a considerable distance away.

Permafrost was a more serious threat. Delicate, frozen ground, the permafrost melted and sank the first attempts at roadbuilding, when the workers stripped the topsoil and tried to grade the ground beneath. The longer the permafrost was exposed and the underlying ground was allowed to melt, the worse the conditions became. Finally, the engineers developed the technique of leaving the topsoil and increasing its insulating qualities by laying a bed of logs and brush; on top of that went the road surfacing. More than one vehicle was swallowed by the gaping, melting earth before engineers struck upon this idea.

The North is a land of water. More than 200 bridges were built, plus countless culverts and drainage areas. The roadbuilding crews worked miles ahead of the bridge builders, so equipment had to be forded across streams and rivers. There are accounts of tractors being taken through water so deep that only their air intake and exhaust pipes were visible above the water surface.

Bridges and culverts were built with whatever material came to hand, often the very logs that had been cleared from the water's edge. Just 10 days before the opening of the highway, the bridge over the Smith River was carried away by water and ice. Three days after that, 200 feet of the bridge on the Peace River was swept away.

Historic photo of trucks stuck in mud.
Photo courtesy of Anchorage Museum of History & Art

When the PRA came along to erect permanent bridges, they faced the diffi-culty of attempting to work with steel in weather of 40 or more below zero. A touch on bare skin was torture, and even the thick gloves worn by the workers didn't provide full protection.

Under the demands of the thousands of men and machines working on the highway, local transportation systems, such as they were, became over-loaded. When the Army took over the White Pass and Yukon Route Rail-way, the railway's engines and rolling stock were decrepit and out of date. Yet they were the only means of getting equipment from the harbor in Skagway, up the 2,900-foot White Pass, and on to Whitehorse. Meanwhile, near Dawson Creek, more than 1,000 freight cars jammed the yards; there was no equipment to unload them and take the cargo farther north.

And still the work went on at a furious pace, taking its toll in both ma-chines and men. Near the Kluane River stands a monument to Lt. Roland Small, one of the soldiers who died during the construction.

What did the workers earn for their efforts? A laborer working for a con-tractor under the PRA made as little as 96 cents an hour. Tractor drivers made $1.60 for an hour of freezing cold. Crane operators earned $2 an hour. Room and board cost the workers about $2 per day. The workweek was 70 to 77 hours long (of course there wasn't much to do but work), and

History of the Highway

almost no overtime was paid. An ad for workers in the New York Times included this enticement, "Temperatures will range from 90° above zero to 70° below zero. Men will have to fight swamps, rivers, ice, and cold. Mosquitoes, flies, and gnats will not only be annoying but will cause bodily harm."

■ A Road in Use

By September 1, 1942, the entire road had been laid out; 837 miles were completed. On September 4, as part of the final push, the War Department created the Northwest Service Command, bringing all the disparate construction and transportation units under one command. And on September 28, the route from Dawson Creek to Whitehorse was given its baptism by fire. The first truck to take the road traveled the 1,030 miles in only 71 hours – at an average speed of 15 miles per hour. More trucks quickly followed; by the beginning of October, there were regular cargo runs from Dawson Creek to Whitehorse.

The cold weather was coming. The lakes and rivers began to freeze, and there was widespread flooding. Against all odds, on November 20, 1942, the road was officially opened where the 18th Engineers and the 97th Engineers linked up the northern and southern sections at Soldier's Summit, on the shores of Kluane Lake. The road was completed, but not finished.

The day before the road opened, the first convoy left Whitehorse for Fairbanks. It arrived only three days later. The first convoy to travel the entire route, Dawson Creek to Fairbanks, did so in 210 hours.

The pioneer road was in business, but it was rough, crooked (partly because the surveyors had worked from the tops of bulldozers, and partly to protect convoys from enemy aircraft), and so tiring that convoy drivers were changed every 45 to 90 miles.

But the goal was to have more than a seasonal tote road. The furious construction continued, to provide an all-weather road by the end of 1943. Thaws in the spring of 1943 had shown weaknesses in the road. Transportation was interrupted, and men were stranded as the road turned into a long ribbon of mud. Brigadier General Ludson D. Warsham, who was in charge of the Northwest Division, ordered an all-out effort to get the road into shape. His challenge was met. Over the next few months, the road was straightened, ballasted, surfaced, and widened. Permanent bridges were erected and, by October 15, 1943, the Alaska Highway was open for year-round use by military traffic.

The road opened to civilian traffic in 1949, but only a few intrepid and self-reliant motorists tried it. The trip was still months long, freezing cold, and terribly muddy. It wasn't until the automobile boom of the late 1950s and early 1960s that traffic began to increase; services along the road multiplied as the number of cars grew.

Improvements have continued over the years: paving, smoothing, construction of new bridges. A road that could once be traveled at only 15 miles per hour is now easily and comfortably traveled at 65 (unless you're behind RVs, which all too often seem to top out at 40). Towns along the highway have grown and thrived, and the road has opened endless possibilities for recreation and commerce, as it has opened the northwest section of the continent.

Western Approach

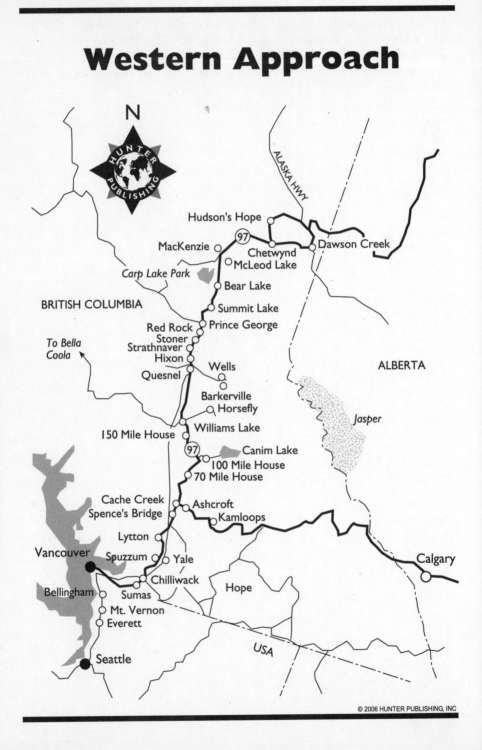

N

BRITISH COLUMBIA

To Bella Coola

ALBERTA

Jasper

Hudson's Hope
MacKenzie
97
Chetwynd
McLeod Lake
Dawson Creek
Carp Lake Park
Bear Lake
Summit Lake
Red Rock
Stoner
Strathnaver
Hixon
Prince George
Wells
Quesnel
Barkerville
Horsefly
Williams Lake
150 Mile House
97
Canim Lake
100 Mile House
70 Mile House
Cache Creek
Spence's Bridge
Ashcroft
Kamloops
Lytton
Vancouver
Spuzzum
Yale
Chilliwack
Bellingham
Sumas
Hope
Mt. Vernon
Everett
Calgary
USA
Seattle

Chapter 4

Approaches to the Highway

The purpose of this book is to get you on the Alaska Highway and to points north. However, the simple fact is that the Alaska Highway starts in the middle of nowhere, and it's quite a trip simply to reach it. So, before you can start your Alaska Highway vacation, you've got some miles to drive. You could – and many people do – happily spend an entire vacation in the area we're going to cover in just a few pages here (and if you want to do that yourself, you need one of our other books, *Adventure Guide to British Columbia*). But for this book, we want to get you onto the highway as quickly as possible.

There are two main ways to get to the Alaska Highway. The Western Approach takes you from Seattle north, along the path of the gold rush, following the evolution of transportation routes – from pony trails, to the railroad, to the highway itself – through some of the least hospitable road-building country in the world.

The Eastern Approach takes you through some of the most spectacular scenery the Rockies have to offer, as you drive through Jasper, Banff, and Kootenay parks. There's not much history here, but the views will take your breath away – and give your brake foot a serious workout.

The Western Approach – North from Seattle

■ Seattle

 Seattle might be one of the most livable big cities in the country (as long as you don't have to drive anywhere – the freeways are

Highway Approaches

more like parking lots than you can believe). It's here that most people start their trips north. After all, this is where the miners started when they headed north looking for gold. Seattle is worth a visit in itself, but for the highway traveler there are a few points of special interest in town.

Head for the **Pioneer Square** area, downtown. At 117 S. Main St. is the **Klondike Gold Rush National Historical Park**, which features an interesting display of artifacts and archives on the gold rush. It's a good stop to get you in the mood for what lies ahead. Just around the corner at Main and 1st is **Eliot Bay Books**, a Seattle institution, and one of the best bookstores anywhere in the United States. Load up for the trip ahead.

Nearby, learn about the life of a city – there aren't many cities in the North – by taking the **Underground Tour** through the old sewers of the first town to have a Skid Row. Buy tickets at the corner of James St. and 1st Ave.

Head a block down to the waterfront for another assortment of interesting shops. The best of these is **Ye Olde Curiosity Shop & Museum**, at Pier 54. Inside, among the souvenirs, is an assortment of oddities, including a two-headed cow and a mummy.

You can get a nice view of Seattle and the surrounding area on a clear day by taking a **Washington State Ferry** from Pier 52. The 40-minute ride to Bremerton costs only a few dollars and it offers some lovely views of Puget Sound.

North from Seattle

Heading north from Seattle on I-5, you pass through an industrial zone and then a large agricultural zone, which extends all the way to the Canadian border. Interstate 5 is just as charming as you'd expect an interstate to be, but don't despair – it's about to get much better.

In 1989, the Alaska Marine Highway system moved its southern terminus from Seattle to **Bellingham**, 85 miles north. Bellingham is a beautiful city, full of Victorian homes and streets that change their names every couple of blocks, so even people who've lived there for years get lost. To reach the ferry terminal, take Exit 250 and follow the signs. The ferries are heavily booked in the summer. If you don't have reservations, there's a chance you can get in on standby, but only a chance. (For more information on the ferry, see Chapter 16; for even more detail, as well as a complete write-up on the glories of Bellingham, see our book *Adventure Guide to the Inside Passage and Coastal Alaska*.)

Continuing through Bellingham, the easiest way to the Canadian border is Route 546, which goes through old farm towns, with lots of cows and dilapidated barns. The turnoff for Route 546 is Exit 256A. Alternatively, you can follow Route 539 and Route 9. They both take you to the border at Sumas.

Crossing into Canada

Buy gas before you get to Sumas. The difference in price can be a penny a mile as you get closer to the border – and you'll be a lot happier if you have a full tank before you get into Canada.

Just on the US side of the border, there are hotels (expensive), gas stations (very expensive), and fruit stands galore. The fruit is cheap and looks good, and there is every chance you'll have to dump it at the border. Apples are a special no-no; the entire Northwest has been suffering from an infestation of apple maggots for years, and Canada has been desperately trying to keep it out. If they're running fruit patrol, cooperate with the border police; they're not likely to check, but they do have reasons for what they do.

From the border, take Canada's **Highway One East**. No one we asked was able to explain why a road that goes almost due north is called East. Along Highway 1, stop at Fort Langley, site of the first European settlement in the Fraser Valley. This is also the best place to jump from the north to the south side of the river, or vice-versa, via the **Albion Ferry**, ☎ 604-467-7298. It's free, it runs every 15 minutes, and it's worth getting on just to say you crossed the mighty Fraser.

Visitor Info in Fort Langley is at 23245 Glover Rd., ☎ 604-513-8787.

But the main reason to stop in town is to see **Fort Langley National Historic Park**, one of the refurbished HBC posts. The first post was built here in 1827; that didn't work out too well, so in 1838, they built a new fort, farther upstream. That didn't go so well, either: it burned to the ground only two years later. They tried one more time, a bit farther upstream, and that location is where the park is now.

At its peak, this was one of the busiest posts in Canada, and it served as a central depot for other HBC posts, sending out nearly forty thousand pounds of Fraser River salmon to more distant forts each year.

This spot was important enough that when BC officially became a crown colony, in 1858, the announcement was made here, in the Big House; Fort Langley was actually the first capital of the new province, but that lasted only a year. By 1866, there was no need for the post at all; it was shut down, and left to rot, until 1923, when preservationists got hold of it.

Today, you can wander around the reconstructed post (only the storehouse remains from the original fort), and ask questions of the very knowledgeable staff, who hang out in period costumes (this is a great summer job for university history majors).The park is open daily from March through early November. Admission is $5, and it's money well spent to see how the HBC became the second-largest empire the world has ever known – only Kubilai Khan ruled over more territory. ☎ 604-513-4777.

Just a bit farther up the road, in the town of Langley, is the **Canadian Museum of Flight**, at the Langley Airport, Hangar 3. ☎ 604-532-0035. For aeronautical fans, the big draw here is a Handley Page Hampden bomber, one of only two in the world. This one was dredged up from the Straits of Georgia in 1986, restored, and put on display here.

Keeping on Highway 1, the first town of size you hit is **Abbotsford**. The city is one of Canada's largest berry-producing areas, growing strawberries, raspberries, and blueberries. It's also the first Canadian city you'll hit if you're coming north from Seattle. There is no shortage of banks in the city center ready to change your US dollars for much more interesting-looking Canadian dollars. Not much other reason to stop, though.

The road winds northeast, getting closer and closer to the mountains. Snow-covered much of the year, these are the Coast Mountains, which extend for nearly 1,000 miles inland.

There's a helpful tourist information stop outside **Chilliwack**, and for people who've just driven up from Washington State, this should be one of your first stops in Canada, if only to take a look around the first of the wonderful BC Tourist Info Centres. Stop here – 44150 Luckakuck Way (how can you go wrong with a street name like that?), ☎ 604-858-8121 – and load up on brochures of the nearby parks and activities. The city itself has the **Minter Gardens**, 52892 Bunker Rd, ☎ 800-661-3919, a world-class botanical array. In summer, when the flowers are in bloom, it's a great place to laze away a few hours while you rest from driving. You'll see the entrance from the highway, off exit 135.

Also in Chilliwack is the **Canadian Military Engineers Museum**, the first of many transportation/engineering museums along the BC highways. This one focuses on how the CME has helped develop this part of Canada. The museum is on the Canadian Forces Base, 45820 Spadina Ave, ☎ 604-795-5210. There's also a city museum and archives, both on Yale Road. Take the same exit as for the CME museum, but turn west.

There are plenty of places to sleep and eat around Chilliwack, but if you've got the energy for another 45 minutes or so of driving, continue toward the mountains, to Hope. Along the way there is the very popular **Cultus Lake Provincial Park** (fishing, boating, almost 300 campsites; ☎ 800-689-9025). The word Cultus comes from the First Nation's Sto:lo language: it means "bad, worthless." It's one of the most popular parks in this part of the province, even though there's supposed to be a Slellucum – a giant spirit bear – that lives around here.

On summer weekends, this park is an escape valve for Vancouver, and can be very full.

The road also passes **Bridal Falls Provincial Park** – which has the sixth-highest waterfall in Canada, at 403 feet – and **Harrison Hot Springs**, where you can soak away the pains of driving (especially useful if you're heading south at this point). The hot springs are at the southern edge of Harrison Lake, and they've been in constant use for as long as anybody can remember – the Salish used them, and when gold miners came into the area, they found out this was the place to be to soak out the sore muscles they got from failing to strike it rich.

If you want to get out for a soak yourself, you have two choices. You can stay at **Harrison Hot Springs Resort**, 100 Esplanade, ☎ 604-796- 2244, and shell out $150-350 or so for a double in the very, very nice lodge with access to pools, a spa, restaurants. Or you can go to the public pool, downtown, on Harrison Hot Springs Rd. $7.50 gets you in, and you can camp at the **Bigfoot Campgrounds**, 670 Hot Springs Rd, ☎ 604-796- 9767, which has fully serviced sites.

Near the springs is the **Agassiz-Harrison Museum**, housed in an original 1893 railway station. It now sits on the property of Agriculture Canada's Agassiz Research Station. Check for the current schedule of summer tours – usually offered in early afternoon.

EAST OR WEST

Every road has a direction it should be driven. We're describing this one, Highway 1, the direction you're most likely to go: west to east. And it's beautiful that way, as the mountains draw ever closer, before the road heads right between peaks. But if you find yourself coming back out this way, east to west, you'll discover that it's even more dramatic, with coming out of the mountains being like coming out from under a very beautiful thunderstorm, into broad daylight.

The road follows the path of the **Fraser River**. The mountains generate a lot of clouds, and it can get cold here very fast. The Fraser River is one of BC's most important rivers – the canyon it has cut is one of the province's most dramatic spots. There are several provincial parks along the river, with great camping in each and every one. Alongside the water used to be the Cariboo Wagon Road, which from 1862 to 1870 took more than 10,000 miners north to the Cariboo goldfields. One miner imported 23 camels to haul packs on the trail and, until his camels died, he probably got a lot closer to rich than most of the would-be miners. The Fraser is great for whitewater rafting, especially around Lytton, which is at the north end of the canyon, at the junction of the Fraser and Thompson rivers.

■ Hope

Hope was just a quiet little spot in the middle of nowhere until it burst into the world's view in 1982, when it was chosen as the site for filming *Rambo: First Blood*. Many of the shops have autographed pictures of Stallone and, for the movie buff, there is a self-guided Rambo Tour, which points out all the infamous backdrops for the movie.

Of course, once everybody forgot the movie, the town went back to being a quiet little spot in the middle of nowhere. However, it's a very, very pretty little spot, with quite a venerable history.

The first settlement was built in 1848, when the HBC put up a trading fort. Only 10 years later, the place became a boomtown, when gold was struck in the nearby Cariboo region. Hope was a jumping-off point, serving steamboats on the Fraser River; shops and sawmills soon followed.

Unlike most boomtowns, Hope outlasted the gold rush, thanks to a silver rush – just as everybody was about to pack up and go home, there was the fortuitous discovery of silver on Silver Peak in 1873. The early 1900s brought the railway, which ensured continued slow growth. The town was officially incorporated in 1928.

Hope is a scenic little town with plenty of attractions to justify getting off the highway for a little while.

A good place to start your tour is at the **Tourist Info Centre**, 919 Water Ave, ☎ 604-869-2021, and museum ($). In front of the building is a funny-looking contraption, a restored gold mill. Inside you'll find interesting farm and mining tools, as well as many objects from everyday life, such as a gentleman's mustache teacup with a special ceramic plate covering part of the cup so that a mustache couldn't get wet. There is no admission fee; the staff in both the museum and Info Centre are informative and helpful.

ON LOCALE

One thing the staff will want to point out is that Rambo isn't the only movie ever to have been made here. A couple of dog movies – *White Fang II*, and *Far From Home* were both filmed here, and much of the excellent mountaineering movie *K2* was filmed in the Fraser Canyon. Jack Nicholson and Sean Penn hung out in town to film *The Pledge*, and Sidney Poitier was here for *Shoot to Kill*.

Hope claims to be the "Chainsaw Carving Capital." This is partly an indication that people go a little stir-crazy here in winter, but also recognition of a genuine Canadian art form. It started off in 1991, when a tree in Memorial Park had to go, because of root rot. A local artist argued for making this into something worthwhile, so he hacked away with his saw until there was a carving of a bald eagle with a salmon in its talons. Now there are a couple dozen giant carvings scattered around town. If you really are interested, there's a pamphlet on the tour at the Infocentre, but it's more fun to just stumble on these and be surprised. There are several bears, a mountain goat, and more.

On the corner of Park and Fraser is a church that claims to be the oldest in mainland Canada still on its original foundations. It was consecrated 1861, and services have been held ever since.

Just outside the town are the **Othello/Quintette Tunnels**, a set of railroad tunnels built in 1910 as part of a project to link this area with the BC coast. The cost of building in this area was tremendous, averaging $136,000 per mile, and one mile held the record for being the most expensive in the world, at $300,000. Of course, modern roads often cost that much per foot now. You can visit the tunnels at any time, except during the winter months; there are no hours or fees. A walk in the beautiful Coquilla Canyon is peaceful and relaxing, and there are picnic tables along the way. The tunnels are fairly dark, so a flashlight is a good idea. Continue through the tunnels and you'll pass over a gorge cut by the roaring Fraser River. Getting the trains through here gave the engineers nightmares for years.

Hope is a good place from which to launch side trips into the wilderness. There is excellent fishing and river-running in the area, as well as hiking, winter sports, and gold panning. Hang-gliders from around the world come here to jump off the mountains. Ask at the Tourist Info Centre for additional information.

You won't have any trouble finding a place to stay in Hope: there are plenty of choices, most under $85.

Best Continental Motel, 860 Fraser Ave, ☎ 604-869-9726, www.bcmhope.com, is right off Highway 1. It has good views, and all the rooms have fridges. $$. **Inn Towne Motel**, 510 Trans Canada Hwy, ☎ 604-869-7276, has jacuzzi suites if the road has been getting to you. $$.

HOTEL PRICING
Prices are in US dollars.
under $50 . . . . $
$50-$100 . . . . $$
$100-$150 . . . . . . $$$
above $150 . . . . . $$$$

Maple Leaf Motor Inn, 377 Old Hope-Princeton Way, ☎ 604-869-7107, www.mapleleafmotorinn@telus.net, has newly renovated doubles. $$. Another good choice is the small but nice **Colonial 900 Motel**, 900 Old Hope Princeton Way, ☎ 604-869-5223, www.colonial900motel.com, $$.

For campers, **Othello Tunnels Campground & RV Park**, 67851 Othello Rd, ☎ 877-869-0543, is just 10 minutes away from the tunnels. It has tent sites, full hookups and showers. **Coquihalla Campground** verlooks the Coquihalla River. It has treed sites, showers and a laundromat. ☎ 888-869-7118.

If you're not in your own car, Hope is a stop for **VIA Rail** (☎ 800-561-8630) and **Greyhound** (☎ 800-661-8747).

 HIGHWAY TIP: The road continues along the Fraser River, through Hell's Canyon. It's scenic and amazing, and it's very dangerous driving, so use caution.

North from Hope

Route 1 follows the Fraser River, from Hope north. This is a beautiful road, lots of twists and turns and dramatic canyon views. There are also a few really cool places to stop along the way and, if you're a river rafter, this is the place to be.

It's about 62 miles/100 km from Hope to Lytton, the first town of size you'll hit, but don't plan on hurrying through this stretch. There are plenty of

Highway Approaches

things to see, places to stop, and it's well worth the time simply to plan on an hour or so watching the river flow.

The Fraser has always been BC's most important river. It cuts through the heart of the province, emptying just south of Vancouver. Really, it's the river that made the province, as it was used by early explorers, by First Nations traders, and by military expeditions. The HBC never could have dealt with BC without the Fraser opening the landscape for them.

Alexander Mackenzie and his men used the river to explore BC in 1793. Mackenzie and his men started their work in 1789, looking for a freshwater route to Cook Inlet – where Anchorage, Alaska, is today. That didn't quite happen. First, they went north along the Peace River, ended up in the Great Slave Lake, and found what's now the Mackenzie River, in the Yukon and Northwest Territories. It empties out in the Arctic Ocean, a long, long way from Cook Inlet.

In 1793, he gave it another shot, heading down the Fraser. The Fraser is kind of a tricky river: it's huge, wide, and flat in some places, but in others, it gets a little nasty. The town of Yale marks the southern boundary of the nastiest section. It was here that the river was blocked by Lady Franklin's Rock, a huge black boulder in the middle of the river, which kept steamers from going any farther north.

LADY FRANKLIN

Lady Franklin is a story in and of herself. Her husband was the great lost cause of the mid-1800s, a man who was once governor of Tasmania, and then got in way over his head as an Arctic explorer. In 1845, Franklin, at the command of two ships, went north looking for the Northwest Passage. By 1847, it was clear that he was deeply lost, and for the next 20 years – yes, 20 years – search parties went out looking for him from every conceivable angle. In doing so, they mapped out half the geography of the northeast Arctic, and the career of one of the greatest polar explorers ever, John Ross, was nearly destroyed when he gathered evidence from the Inuit that, in their last days, the remnants of the Franklin Expedition had resorted to cannibalism.

Lady Franklin herself never gave up. She was sure her husband – by this time in his 60s – was still out there, alive and well. She came to the Fraser thinking that Franklin and his men may have made it as far as the mouth of the Mackenzie, and then worked their way down. Didn't happen, but there's the rock here that bears her name, a monument to a lady who absolutely would not quit.

If the story intrigues you, one of the best books on the search for the northwest passage is Canadian author Pierre Berton's *Arctic Grail*, a classic.

Waterwheel on the outskirts of Hope.

■ Yale

Yale is a pretty, small town today, but it was once a boomtown: because river traffic had to stop here, it was a transshipment point, the origin of the Cariboo Wagon Road, which led north and serviced the 1858 Cariboo gold rush. At one point, more than 30,000 people lived in Yale. Now there are fewer than 200. But it's worthwhile to pull off and take a look at the **Yale Museum**, 31179 Douglas St, ☎ 604-863-2324, which has good displays of the gold rush history. In summer, the museum offers walking tours of the town.

Yale also has the oldest church in British Columbia that's still on its original foundation, **St. John the Divine Church**, on Highway 1. It dates back to about 1859, and it's worth a quick stop to see.

The Fraser and the nearby Thompson rivers are the place to raft in British Columbia, and Yale is the home to one of the best outfitters, **Fraser River Raft Expeditions**, ☎ 800-363-RAFT, www.fraserraft.com. You'll see their headquarters off the highway (there's also a really nice little B&B on the grounds, a restored 1864 house, with Fraser views and nice, simple rooms, $$; it's a very quiet and peaceful stay). The company runs single- and multiple-day trips on both float rafts and power rafts – the power rafts are more stable, you're a lot less likely to go in the water, and you get to see more scenery because you can move more quickly through the river's slow spots. On the other hand, your wilderness experience will include the sound of a motor. Their trip on the Thompson, which runs just over $100, takes you from Spence's Bridge down to Lytton, and includes Class IV rapids – the full-day version of this trip takes in 25 separate sets. If you're looking for an experience more like the earliest travelers had, take their power raft trip on the Fraser, which includes shooting Hell's Gate (see below), for the same price. For longer trips, there are three days on the Ashcroft, ending at Yale, for $450, or six days, from Soda Creek to Lillooet – amazing scenery all the way, rapids that will leave you screaming – for $1,450. This is a good operation – you'll be glad you went out with them.

North from Yale

Leaving Yale, the road hugs the river and mountains; there are seven tunnels along the way, as well as the tiny town of **Spuzzum** (population about 30), and **Alexandra Bridge Provincial Park**, 13 miles/22 km past Yale. The first bridge across the Fraser was built near here in 1863, as part of the Cariboo Wagon Road. That was replaced in the 1920s; the bridge that you drive across now is the third. From the park, there are lovely views, and if you're looking for a picnic spot by the river, this is the place to be.

Another five miles/eight km up the road, you come to the **Hell's Gate Airtram**.

THE CONQUERING OF HELL'S GATE

Hell's Gate stopped more than its share of explorers over the years. Mackenzie's crew got through the first batch of rapids leading up to the gate, but then quit when they saw what was up ahead.

How did the Fraser River get its name? Because Simon Fraser wasn't going to let something like a suicidal stretch of river stop him. He got past the stretch that stopped Mackenzie and kept going, noting along the way that there were paths carved along the cliff faces, and that the First Nations men had developed techniques to stand in the river and spear fish, even in currents that should have knocked them down. And, as George Bowering writes in his marvelous *Bowering's BC*, Fraser noticed "many graves covered with small stones all over the place."

They did not shoot Hell's Gate in their canoes. They weren't quite that dumb or determined. Leaving all their gear behind (except their guns, of course), they set out on the same paths the locals used, paths upon which, according to Fraser, "no human being should venture." Fraser bought new boats near what's now Yale, and finished his first descent of the river. It took modern rafting technology to make shooting Hell's Gate possible, and it's actually kind of sad that anybody with a hundred bucks or so can rip right through a passageway that stopped people for centuries.

Today, Hell's Gate is a tourist attraction. You can ride the airtram across the canyon for $10.50, and you get great views (the canyon is actually even worse now than when Fraser was here, after a 1914 rockslide). Once you're across, the **Salmon House Restaurant** is a good place for lunch. The tram is open in summer from 9-6. ☎ 604-867-9277.

The small town of **Boston Bar**, north of the gate, is the put-in spot for rafting trips through the canyon. This was one of the more important mining spots during the Cariboo rush, but not many people have stuck around since.

REO Rafting runs the **Nahatlatch River Resor**t, right outside Boston Bar, ☎ 800-736-7238, www.reorafting.com. With them, you can run the Thompson for around $100, or do Class V on the Nahatlatch for around $150. They've also got multiple-day packages. Stay at the resort in a tent cabin ($$), teepee ($), or log cabin with a private bath ($$$$). Rates are cheaper in the middle of the week.

■ Lytton

There's not much else but scenery between Boston Bar and the town of Lytton, the biggest town between Hope and Cache Creek, with nearly 400 residents. It's a pretty town, right at the junction of the Fraser and Thompson rivers, and there are actually quite a few things to see around town.

Start at the **Info Centre**, 400 Fraser St, ☎ 250-455-2523. Open daily in summer, weekdays October through May. The main thing you'll need here is a map to the Stein Valley Nlaka'pamux Heritage Park (see below) and a map to the nearby Pit House. It's also well worthwhile to stop in the museum next door, where there are good displays of Cariboo history and some great historical photos of the region.

The **Pit House** is up the road to Lillooet; you'll pass a few horse ranches, then see what's really nothing more than a turn off and a gate. Hike down the road (or drive, if the gate happens to be open), and you'll eventually come to a traditional pit house, of the sort the First Nations people in this region used for thousands of years. More than half the house – a circular structure – was underground, with a log roof covering it. It was warm in winter, cool in summer, and easy to defend – the perfect dwelling. Check at the Info Centre, as there are rules and regulations regarding access to the area.

To get to **Stein Valley Nlaka'pamux Heritage Park**, cross the Fraser via the reaction ferry (open daily, runs on demand from 6:30 am to 10:30 pm). From there, drive three miles/4.5 km to the parking lot at the edge of the park. The main attractions here are some good hikes and views of the Stein River. If you like what you see, you can string together a multi-day hike, from the parking lot all the way back to Tundra Lake, 62 miles/100 km away. There are campsites along the way, and a couple of suspension bridges and cable car crossings – not for the person afraid of heights. This takes you through Lytton First Nation Reserve land, so show respect, and camp only in the designated sites.

Headed the other way, northeast from town, you hit **Skihist Provincial Park** right outside of town. There's a campground and a day-use area. A hiking trail that leaves from campground takes roughly 2-3 hours for the whole thing, and you get some really nice views, as well as an education on the health of the forest – this is the unlogged area that's closest to Vancouver, so there's a mix of new and old forest. Like so much other forest in BC, this is under attack by pine beetles, spruce beetles, Douglas-fir beetles, and an assortment of worms. None of this does happy things to the trees, but nobody's figured out a cure yet.

If you haven't booked your rafting trip from one of the outfitters mentioned earlier, try the **Kumsheen Rafting Resort**, ☎ 800-663-6667, www.kumsheen.com, in Lytton. Day trips on the Thompson start around $125, or check into multi-day trips on the Thompson and Fraser. They've got quite a few combo packages available, with multi-sport trips and stays at the lodge. Another option is **Hyak**, which charges about the same and has been running the rivers here for more than 20 years. ☎ 800-663-RAFT, www.hyak.com.

If you're looking for something a little more sedate to do around Lytton, try gold panning. There's a three-mile/five-km section of the Fraser that's set off for public hand-panning. No, you probably won't get rich, but it was gold that brought people here in the first place, and you owe it to yourself to take a shot. For kids, stop by **Caboose Park**, which looks more like a model train than the real thing.

One of the beauties of Lytton is that it's where the Fraser meets the Thompson. It's worth some time simply to sit and watch these two mighty rivers blend – and we've seen bears right at the confluence, as well, so you never know what might walk in to your photos.

Lytton is a tiny town, but it's a good place to spend the night, especially if you're planning a raft trip. The town's **Acacia Leaf Café** is actually quite good, and the **Totem Motel & Lodge**, 320 Fraser St, ☎ 250-455-2321, is a cottage-style place, nicely kept up, and off the highway. $$. A good place to call it a day.

North from Lytton

It's an easy and scenic 50 miles/85 km from Lytton to Cache Creek. You'll go through the small town of Spence's Bridge – not too far from here was where the drove the final spike on Canada's Northern Pacific Line.

Ashcroft, another 25 miles/40 km north and off a small side road, is worth a look. In 1862, a couple of lawyers from England came here to start a ranch. They held races, and when they couldn't find any foxes for traditional fox hunts, started out after coyotes. Their house, Ashcroft Manor, is now a museum, with a teahouse and the inevitable gift shop. It's a nice testament to what people can do when they have vision. Nearby is the Ashcroft Museum proper, which has First Nations displays, as well as a good explanation of the importance of the Chinese to the region. This seems particularly appropriate now, since a newspaper headline in late 2003 stated that nearly half the people living in lower BC were actually born outside of Canada – any walk around Vancouver leaves you wondering just how many people stayed in Hong Kong for the turnover. Maybe a half dozen, at most.

From Ashcroft, take the road north out of town, and that will lead you out of the forest and the canyon to the town of Cache Creek.

■ Cache Creek

Cache Creek, despite the dry-looking land around – almost like the bad-lands – is actually on a floodplain; most of the town nearly washed away during the floods of 1990. Overall, it's an unusual land-scape, plopped right in the middle of mountains and lakes. This is land that hasn't quite recovered from the last time a volcano erupted here,

HOTEL PRICING
Prices are in US dollars.
under $50.........$
$50-$100 .... $$
$100-$150 ..... $$$
above $150.... $$$$

and the cactus and sagebrush make it look like Clint Eastwood would be perfectly comfortable riding his horse around.

That said, there's not a whole lot here, and since the faster Coquihalla opened, traffic through the town has dropped considerably.

Because it was once a major crossroads, there's a good assortment of places to stay; many people make it their first stop on the way to the Alaska Highway, as Cache Creek is a comfortable day's drive north of Seattle. Try the Sandman (☎ 250-457-6284, 800-SANDMAN, www.sandman.com), $$; the Best Value Inn Desert Motel (☎ 250-457-6226), a bit cheaper; or the Sage Hills Motel (☎ 250-457-6451, 888-649-9494), also at the low end of the $$ scale. There's camping at the Brookside Campsite (☎ 250-457-6633), a mile east of tow. Full hookups run around $20.

Another good option, if you're camping and don't mind a few more minutes in the car, is to head to Hat Creek Ranch, seven miles/11 km north of town. The ranch was first opened as a roadhouse around the 1860s by a man named Donald McLean, a deeply unpopular man, who was later killed. Three of his sons took after dear old dad, and ended up hanged in 1881 for murder.

You do have to give the family credit for recognizing a beautiful place to live, though. Hat Creek Ranch today is a BC Heritage Trust Site, and the buildings you can tour (free, although they ask for donations) include the roadhouse, barns, and a blacksmiths shop. You can also book trail rides here. They have a very small campground. ☎ 250-457-9722. Pitch your tent in the Old West for a night.

Highway Approaches

North from Cache Creek

Continuing northbound, you're headed towards a long series of what were once stops on the Cariboo Wagon Road. The road parallels the Bonaparte River, and now that most people take other roads, there's a nice, remote feeling to this stretch. The tiny town of **Clinton** was the junction of a pair of roads to the gold fields, and today it's well-known in BC as being the kind of town where people who just don't quite fit in elsewhere end up. There's a good **museum** at 1419 on the Cariboo Highway (☎ 250-459-2442), which will help you get a handle on the most important gold rush in BC.

Just north of Clinton is the turnoff for **Big Bar Lake Provincial Park**, ☎ 250-398-4414. Come back here for the camping, or a chance to hike glacial eskers. There's also a pretty good chance of seeing marmots in the area – think guinea pigs on steroids.

Chasm Provincial Park is on the main highway, 14 miles/22 km north of Clinton. It's worth the stop here to see Painted Chasm, a slice in the volcanic landscape that has some pretty dramatic color to it. The volcanoes went off as long as 25 million years ago; the chasm was carved out by glacial meltwaters at the end of the last ice age, about 10-12,000 years ago.

The towns on this stretch of road have numbers as frequently as they have names. **70 Mile House** was 70 miles from the start of the wagon road in Lillooet. There's a roadhouse here you can tour, but not much else. Still, this is ranching country, and that means they do things big here. **Gang Ranch** is west of the highway on Meadow Lake Road. It's about a 30-mile/50-km trip back to the ranch, which was once the largest cattle ranch on the continent; even today, considerably smaller, it covers more than a million acres. In addition to running cattle, they also run a small B&B, ☎ 250-459-7923, which offers a good chance to spend the night and see what real cowboys (with more land than some Eastern states) have to do to get through the day.

100 Mile House, the biggest stop between Cache Creek and Williams Lake, has about 7,000 residents. It's a center for all the ranches that surround the town, as well as for logging concerns. **Visitor info** is on the highway at the Chamber of Commerce building, ☎ 250-395-5353. It's easy to spot, since there's a pair of giant skis outside, in yet another one of those BC shots at having the world's biggest something: gold pan, skis, fishing pole, whatever. You really have to wonder who in the city councils thinks these things up, but they make for interesting stops and a good peek into the psyche of lesser-traveled regions in Canada.

Right behind the center is a small wetlands. The helpful info staff can tell you the birds you're likely to see – there's a display board as well – and direct you to a larger wetlands, about five miles away. It's a good place for birders to have a picnic and perhaps add a waterfowl or two to the lifelist.

AUTHOR TIP: *There are great fishing lakes all around 100 Mile House. Try your luck at **Mahood Lake, Hathaway Lake, Horse Lake, Ruth Lake,** or **Canim Lake**. These are all excellent moose sites, as well.*

The 100 Mile District Historical Society has been hard at work at the **108 Heritage Site**, where they've gathered buildings from around the district and put them up here, in one spot. If you missed Hat Creek, here's another chance to see what ranch life was like at the turn of the century. There's a ranch house, telegraph house, and a log barn that they say is one of the biggest in Canada. The site is open late May into September. ☎ 250-791-5288.

Lac la Hache bills itself as "the longest town in the Cariboo" – maybe they couldn't think of a giant something to put outside the town, so they hit on this instead. Or maybe they were just too busy looking at the beautiful lake to care. Fish the lake for trout, camp at **Lac la Hache Provincial Park**, eight miles/13 km north of town (☎ 250-389-4414). Just past the campground is **Cariboo Provincial Nature Park**, a walk-in only park that has some easy walks to show you beaver ponds and birding areas.

Look over the lake with the **Shoreline Resort**, ☎ 250-396-7441, which has parasailing and jet ski rentals. Ten minutes in the air attached to a sail will run you about $40.

■ Williams Lake

Williams Lake started off as a big stopping point for miners headed to the goldfields. However, when a local refused to loan money to the builders of the Cariboo Road, they bypassed the town and it pretty much died. Today it's home to one of Canada's largest rodeos (July 1 – book well in advance or plan on staying far outside of town). For birders, there's excellent watching in the marshes around town.

AUTHOR TIP: *If you're planning to go to Barkerville or the Bowron Lakes, Williams Lake is actually a much nicer, more scenic place to stay than Quesnel, where most people end up.*

The **Info Centre** is at the south end of town, on the highway. ☎ 250-392-5025. They'll tell you the place to go in town is the **Museum of the Cariboo Chilcotin**, which includes the BC Cowboy Hall of Fame. It's at 113 4th Ave, ☎ 250-392-7404, open Monday-Saturday in summer, 10-4, for only a couple of bucks. Inside, you will find out more about ranching and cowboys than you ever thought you'd need to know. It's a lot of fun.

If that's a little sedate for you, stop by **Red Shred's** on 1st Ave. This is information central for rock climbers, mountain bikers, and other adrenaline junkies. It has all the gear you need, and ideas on where to use it. **Esler Lake** has good climbing routes already established if you're traveling with your own gear.

If you have a rodeo boat and know what to do with it, try the **Quesnel River**, between Likely and Quesnel Forks. Pick up a map at Red Shred's, prepare for class IV.

Fishermen just need a copy of *Cariboo-Chilcotin Fishing Guide*, from the information center. No matter what lake species you're after, this will point you to the right place.

Of course, the big deal in town is the **annual rodeo**, and if you can get reservations – or don't mind driving in from a ways out – it's worth coming. There are more than $100,000 worth of prizes, and rodeos daily, as well as tractor pulls, raft races, and barn dances. Pretty much anything you can think of that might go with a rodeo is happening here. All you have to do is grab your hat, pick up a corn dog from one of the food vendors, and dive in to the action. Phone (well in advance) ☎ 800-717-6336 for tickets; it's online at www.williamslakestampede.com.

Williams Lake has all the usual road food choices, but for something different, try **Laughing Loon Neighborhood Pub**, 1730 S. Broadway. It has a nice atmosphere and a very large menu. Note that when they say one of the dishes is hot, believe them. It took five Cokes to get through the very delicious stir-fry we tried – and that was the medium heat.

HOTEL PRICING
Prices are in US dollars.
under $50.........$
$50-$100 ....$$
$100-$150 ......$$$
above $150.....$$$$

First choice for a place to stay is the **Drummond Lodge Motel**, overlooking the lake (☎ 250-392-5334, 800-557-4555, www.drummondlodge.com. Good rooms, nice people, and fantastic lake views. Get a room with a balcony, $$-$$$, and you're set for the night. There's also an RV park here.

Other good choices include the **Sandman**, 664 Oliver St, ☎ 250-392-6557, 800-SANDMAN, www.sandman.com, $$$, and the **Overlander Hotel**, 1118 Lakeview Crescent, ☎ 250-392-3321, 800-663-6898, www.overlanderhotel.com, $$.

Campers can go to the **Williams Lake Stampede Campground**, 850 S. Mackenzie St, ☎ 250-398-6718, which has full services for around 20 bucks. If you're in a tent, go north of town to the **Wildwood Campsite**, eight miles/13 km outside of town, ☎ 250-989-4711, which has shaded tent sites.

North from Williams Lake

Heading north, between Williams Lake and Quesnel (pronounced Kwenel), you pick up the Fraser River again. At the tiny **Soda Creek Xats'ull First Nations site**, 20 miles/33 km north of Williams Lake, there's a traditional pit house village where in summer, there are salmon bakes and cultural programs. Check at Xats'ull Information, ☎ 250-297-6323, to see what's going on. The Xats'ull have been here for a couple of thousand years, making use of the rich resources of the Fraser. Soda Creek was once a lot busier than it is now, as it's the southernmost point of navigability on the upper Fraser. From here, you can head north 400 miles or more on the river without hitting anything horrible, like Hell's Gate. The gold rushers came this far, then switched to the paddlewheelers that once roamed the river.

There is a reaction ferry at **Marguerite Ferry**, 39 miles/62 km north of Williams Lake. It'll hold one car, and there's not much reason for you to use it, but it's kind of nice that these things are still around. In winter, when the river freezes, there's a hand tram.

■ Quesnel

 Quesnel bills itself as – get ready for it – "home of the world's largest gold pan." It's the last major city between southern BC and the Cariboo – the area you've been traveling through – and the nearly empty but incredibly scenic northern reaches of the territory, which begin at Prince George.

The fact that the best the town can come up with is a huge gold pan should tell you that the interest lies outside the town itself. But it is a nice little town with all the services you'll need, and it's a perfectly reasonable place to stop for a day. Except for the third week of July, when it hosts Billy Barker Days (see Barkerville, below), there's not a whole lot going on in the town itself.

Quesnel **Info Centre** is a little tricky to find, but it's at 705 Carson Ave, ☎ 250-992-8716. Follow the signs off the main road, and be prepared for at least one U-turn. They can fill you in on everything in the scenic town, including a one-hour walking tour of the downtown area that's a nice way to get out of the car and stretch your legs. They also have a checklist of local birds, everything from the green-backed heron to the Calliope hummingbird. They even get white pelicans through here, just one of the 259 species on the checklist.

One reason Quesnel gets a lot of BC tourists is that they've got a casino. The **Billy Barker Casino Hotel**, 308 McLean St, ☎ 250-992-5533, 888-992-4255, www.billybarkercasino.com, is

Chainsaw grizzly bear outside Quesnel.

actually quite nice, with rooms in the $$ range, and if you're in a gambling mood, it's one of your only choices in the entire province.

Or you can try striking it rich the old-fashioned way, by **panning for gold** at the city-owned area at the confluence of the Quesnel and Fraser rivers. Outside of this spot, most of the land is somebody's gold claim, and it's best to steer clear.

Heritage Corner is at Carson and Front streets. There are the remains of an old riverboat here, as well as the **Heritage House Restaurant**, 102 Carson Ave, your best bet for food in town. It's in an old HBC trading post. If road food is getting to you, **Karin's Deli & Health Foods**, 436 Reid, downtown, has salads, sandwiches, and organic choices. Another good choice for fresh food is the Saturday **farmer's market**, held from May to October, at 97 and Kinchant, downtown. It's a must stop if you're going through on the weekend.

Once a year, the entire town turns out for **Billy Barker Days**, which include one of the biggest rodeos in BC. It can be hard to find a place to stay during this frantic time. Downtown is closed off for an open-air crafts fair and the parade, and everybody wears period costume. For details and a schedule, ☎ 250-992-1234.

BILLY BARKER

Billy Barker was an old Cornish gold miner who struck it rich in 1862, triggering the Cariboo rush. Billy pulled out $1,000 in gold during the first two days he worked his claim. Remember, for comparison, that the Klondike rush was started on about $40 worth of gold and a lot of speculation.

The rest of the year, you won't have any trouble finding a place to stay. Quesnel's main drag is one hotel after another. As we mention above, Williams Lake is a bit more scenic, but if you need to stop in Quesnel, you'll still have quite a nice evening.

There are the usual chains in town: **Sandman**, ☎ 250-747-3511, 800-SANDMAN, www.sandman.com, $$$, is at 940 Chew Ave; **Travelodge**, ☎ 250-992-7071, 800-665-6995, $$, is downtown at 524 Front St. The **Fraser Bridge Inn & RV Park**, ☎ 250-992-5860, www.fraserbridgeinn.com, 100 Ewing Ave, is a good budget choice, $$.

■ Barkerville & the Bowron Lakes

 Outside Quesnel is Barkerville, a fun old mining camp/tourist trap sort of place. It's a pleasant half-hour drive outside of town, with a good chance of seeing moose on the way. Barkerville is a restored gold mining town – over 100 structures – with people around to interpret the various exhibits. The town of Barkerville originally sprang up right after Billy hit it rich. For a while it was the largest city west of Chicago and north of San Francisco, with more than 10,000 people running around, but it was pretty much a ghost town by 1900. Today, it's a very, very popular spot, especially for people from BC. Take the kids out for a stagecoach ride, or just pretend there's a chance you're going to strike gold in the river – they'll let you take a shot at panning in the Cottonwood River. Some people will find what's left of it hokey, but most folks really enjoy the town. Adult admission is $8, and the park is open daily, 8-8 (however, if you're heading out in winter, call first). ☎ 250-994-3332

There are three campgrounds at Barkerville, plus a couple of hotels. **Kelly House**, ☎ 250-994-3328, www.kellyhouse.ca, offers rooms in a heritage house, $$$. **The St. George**, ☎ 250-994-0008, 888-246-7690, www. stgeorgehotel.bc.ca, is nice, and a few dollars more.

Near Barkerville is the **Bowron Lake Provincial Park**. Head east on Highway 26; then turn off on the gravel road right by Barkerville. If you've got a canoe, this is the spot you've looked for all your life. The chain of lakes, rivers, and streams adds up to about 70 miles of the best paddling you'll ever find. You can pick up a map of the circuit in Quesnel. To be sure that everyone gets a primo experience on the lakes, reservations and registration are required – no more than 50 people are allowed on the circuit in a day. For reservations, ☎ 250-992-3111. The circuit is open from May to October, and you have zero hope of just rolling in and getting on the lake. You'll have to plan this one ahead.

At the main parking lot, there's a visitor center where all travelers must register, and, before they go out on the lake, watch a video. If you're going to do the full circuit, there's a $50 fee; just the west side runs $25.

There's a campsite by the center, but once you're out there, you'll find cooking areas and cleared spaces for three to seven tents. There are a couple of cabins along the way, but they're for emergency use only.

You can fish for your dinner along the route, but you will need a license. Remember that this is bear country, and take all appropriate cautions. All the camping areas have bear-proof food caches.

The beginning of the route is almost enough to make most people turn back: a 1.5-mile/2.4-km portage from the center to Kibbee Lake. After just a very short paddle there, you get to portage again, this time 1.2 miles/two km to Isaac Lake. Once you're that far, though, you're made. Isaac Lake is 24 miles/38 km long, and although it is prone to high winds, if you stick reasonably close to the shoreline, you should be okay.

At the south end of the lake is an entrance to the Isaac River. The current is pretty fast here, so be careful. You're on the river for only 1,300 feet/400 meters before you'll see the portage sign – don't miss it, because if you go any farther, you'll be in whitewater. It's a short portage to McLearly Lake, Indian Lake, and Kibbee Lake. Part of this takes the Cariboo River, where there are a lot of sweepers and a strong current. On Lanezi Lake, stick to the north shore.

AUTHOR TIP: *Get off the Cariboo at Unna Lake, unless you think you can successfully navigate your canoe over a 80-foot/24-meter waterfall.*

Take Unna Lake to Babcock Creek, and be sure to use the portage through the rapids. From there, it's pretty straightforward, as the lakes link up. The entire route is 72 miles/116 km, with about seven miles/11 km of portages.

Obviously, the quick description here is not enough to see you through. Get good maps, and ask for current advice from the registration center. And be sure to plan early.

If you want to see some of the scenery without paddling, keep driving past the registration center to Kruger Lake Forest Service Road; turn west and keep going until the road dead-ends at Littlefield Creek. From here, you can pick up the **Goat River Trail**, part of Canada's National Hiking Trail. The other end of the trail is at Crescent Spur, eight or nine days away, off the Yellowhead Highway.

Although the hike does run along a few forest service roads, it's mostly deep wilderness hiking, and you've got to be ready to be alone out here. Take all bear precautions, and be sure to let the forest service know where you're going and when you expect to get out.

You can pick up a basic brochure on the hike, but it has nothing more than a paragraph or two on the 34-mile/54-kilometer middle section of the trail. Get good topo maps in Quesnel, or check with the Fraser Headwaters Alliance, ☎ 250-968-4490, www,fraserheadwaters.org, for the latest on the trail.

North from Quesnel

Back on 97, north of Quesnel, you're faced with pasture land, farms, tree-covered hills in the distance, and lots and lots of wildflowers in season. There's gas, food, and lodging available at regular intervals, and some nice provincial parks for camping, including Cottonwood River and Ten Mile Lake, before you roll north to Prince George, where southern BC meets its great North.

HIGHWAY TIP: Prince George offers a choice of directions. You can continue north to the Alaska Highway, or take the shortcut and head west along the Yellowhead, connecting with the Cassiar Highway.

■ Prince George

Prince George itself is the largest city in northern Canada; if you're heading north on the Alaska Highway, it's the last chance before Whitehorse to stock up on necessities at something that resembles a reasonable price and to get your fill of junk food.

Prince George is a transport city: the railway runs through here, the river traffic runs through here. That makes it important, but not exactly the most exciting spot for visitors. Still, it's a decent spot to stop and recharge for a night. There are some good, cheap restaurants, and a couple of attractions that are well worth your time. The train museum is astounding

Museums & Attractions

Start at the **Visitor Info Centre**, on the corner of Victoria St. and Patricia Blvd, open year-round. This is a must-stop, as they have stuff on the entire northern region, as well as many points south. Whichever way you're thinking of going from George, they've got you covered. ☎ 250-562-3700, www.tourismpg.bc.ca.

The main attraction in town is the **Prince George Railway and Forestry Museum**, 850 River Rd, ☎ 250-563-7351. It's open from May-October, admission $3.50. This has a great collection of railway machinery; there's also a good display of early fire trucks and heavy equipment. It's all laid out in a huge field, so you can just walk around and see what interests you. Many of the cars are open, so you can get in – don't skip the caboose, to see how early trainmen lived. The highlight of the collection is the 1903 Russell snowplow, which is made out of wood and is truly a thing of beauty.

The **Fraser-Fort George Regional Museum**, at the end of 20th Ave, has lots of displays on the area's history – both natural, with lots of stuffed animals, and cultural, with displays of Carrier arts. There's a theater, lots of stuff for kids, and an Internet café – those can be a bit scarce on the next section of the road, so you may want to stop just for that. Admission $8, ☎ 250-562-1612.

Across the street is **Fort George Railway Station**, which has a half-mile mini steam train that runs on summer weekends. This whole area is the original site of Fort George, an HBC fort established by Simon Fraser. Fraser, as we point out elsewhere, was just a fun guy. More than anyone else, his drive and precision and control-freak nature opened BC to exploration. He was of a generation of explorers that simply doesn't exist anymore, able to cross frozen streams, eat nothing but rotted biscuit, and still have time to break treaties with the locals. Okay, that sounds snide, but Fraser was, really, a marvel.

A FRASER EXPEDITION

In May 1808, Fraser left Fort St. James with four canoes, nineteen voyageurs, a pair of First Nations guides, and some flunkies. They got to Prince George (then Fort George), did a bit of trading, and, despite all sanity, headed south along what's now the Fraser River. Fifteen years earlier, Alexander Mackenzie had been turned back by the rapids at Hell's Gate. Fraser went through, passing, as he wrote, "where no human being should venture." He and his crew – after a few days of hanging on cliff sides, wishing they were mountain goats, lining their canoes through impossible rapids, and trying to cling to the cliff-sides with rickety ladders – were the first people to shoot the length of the Fraser River. When he got to the end, he turned around and went back. People were different in those days.

If you're in town on a Friday night from August-October, take a look at the Prince George Astronomical Society's **telescope**. The public can attend open houses. Admission is by donation, but do call first – ☎ 250-564-4787 – to make sure they're on that week.

From May to September, stop at Prince George's Saturday **Farmer's Market**, in Courthouse Plaza, first thing in the morning. This is the center of BC's farming districts, and the only other place in the province where you can get produce like this is in the Okanagan (BC's wine-growing district; for more on that, see our *Adventure Guide to BC*).

Prince George has long depended on the huge stretches of surrounding forest for its robust economy. The single largest Canadian forestry company is based in Prince George, and in summer, you can take a tour that shows you the whole process, from seedlings to pulp. It's a four-hour excursion, and it's free. Check at the Visitor Centre at the intersection of Highways 16 and 97. ☎ 250-563-5493. There's also a demonstration forest, east of town on Highway 16.

For serious hikers, **The Alexander Mackenzie Trail** is accessible from Prince George. It stretches from here to Quesnel, then along the Dean Channel (near Bella Coola on the Pacific Coast). It takes about three weeks to hike the entire trail, which began as an Indian trading route, with furs and obsidian as the main goods. Alexander Mackenzie, the first white guy to cross the Americas from coast to coast, reached the Pacific in 1793 (well before Lewis and Clark) and used this route for the last part of his trip. Mackenzie was one of the great ones, a mad explorer who was not happy unless he was in the middle of nowhere (although he did retire fat and rich in England). The Mackenzie River, which runs from Great Slave Lake in the Northwest Territories to the Beaufort Sea, was one of Mackenzie's better-known canoe trips (see Chapter 9 for more on the Mackenzie).

> **WARNING:** You'll need topos, and be sure to get the latest information from locals. Know what you're doing before you even think about getting on the Alexander MacKenzie Trail.

Food

PG is not exactly a luxury dining kind of place. All the usual fast food suspects are here.

Our first choice is **Moose McGillicuddy's**, 1778 Highway 97, ☎ 250-563-8667, a local landmark in Hawaii; here, the food is every bit as good. It serves the best hamburgers we've had in this part of the country, and the service is great. In and out for under $20.

Foodteller, 508 George St, ☎ 250-563-2946, makes for a nice night out. It offers steaks, pasta, seafood, and more, for around $20.

Ric's Grill, 547 George St, ☎ 250-614-9096, is part of a mini-chain, with a couple of other locations in BC and Alberta. Steaks and seafood, reasonable prices.

Accommodations

PG is used to people coming through for a night, so there are many quite reasonable hotels in town. At the low end, under $75, try the **97 Motor Inn**, 2713 Spruce St, ☎ 250-562-6010, for comfortable budget accommodation, or the **Carmel Motor Inn**, 1502 Hwy 97, ☎ 250-564-6339, 800-665-4484.

HOTEL PRICING
Prices are in US dollars.
under $50 . . . . $
$50-$100 . . . . $$
$100-$150 . . . . . . $$$
above $150 . . . . . $$$$

To move up a little on the luxury and price scale, there's a **Sandman** in town, 1650 Central St, ☎ 250-563-8131, 800-SANDMAN, www.sandman.com, $$$, and a **Coast Inn**, ☎ 250-563-0121, 800-663-1144, www.coasthotels.com, with a pool, sauna, gym, and three restaurants. $$$-$$$$.

Prince George has a good B&B association that offers a free booking service. Reach them at ☎ 888-266-5555, www.bbcanada.com (click on BC, then Prince George). They book some very nice properties, so just tell them what you like in a B&B, and they'll set you up.

Campers can head out to the **Prince George Municipal Campground** at 4188 4th Ave. Sites are priced from $12. Other choices include the **Blue Spruce RV Park**, on Kimball Rd, just west of Highway 16, ☎ , with pull through sites and full hookups, around $20.

North from Prince George

Once you're through Prince George, it's an easy drive to Dawson Creek, the start of the Alaska Highway. You'll be going through farmland, some very tiny villages, and not much more. From here on out, until you get to Whitehorse, or Fairbanks, or Anchorage, your vacation is going to be mostly in the great big, beautiful empty North.

North of Prince George, you are in prime gold rush area. The scenery is pleasant, but not spectacular, and the services are frequent, as the road continues north through **Chetwynd**. Chetwynd is a place to stay if you can't make it to the beginning of the highway at Dawson Creek; otherwise, buy gas, and keep on moving.

There is a way to head north along Hudson's Hope Loop from Chetwynd, bypassing Dawson Creek and intersecting with the highway at Fort St. John. The loop is more scenic and you can stop in the museum at Hudson's Hope for a look at dinosaur bones dug up locally; but if you take the loop, you can't say you've driven the entire length of the Alaska Highway.

The last miles to Dawson Creek are through lush farmland; watch carefully so you don't mistake moose for cows.

The Eastern Approach

Far more scenic than the Western Approach, the Eastern Approach takes you straight through the heart of the Rocky Mountains – and some of the most unspoiled and scenic country in the West. There are a variety of ways to get this far. You can go through Montana, stopping in Glacier Park and Alberta's Waterton Park, or you can head up through Idaho, past wheat fields and, in season, berry vendors lining the roads. If you're heading through Idaho, the easiest thing to do is drive through the stunning mountainscape of Yoho and Kootenay parks, then hook up with Highway 93N – the Icefields Parkway – through Jasper and Banff. From a more easterly direction, once you're in Canada, head north through Calgary, continuing to Edmonton on Highway 21 and then northeast to Dawson Creek, or east along the Yellowhead Highway straight through Jasper – which offers an easy detour to Banff.

 **EARTH-FRIENDLY:** *This region of Yoho, Kootenay, Banff, and Jasper national parks, along with a number of provincial parks in the area, has been declared a World Heritage Site by the United Nations. It's one of the world's largest protected wilderness areas.*

The advantage to the Eastern Approach is, simply, the scenery. There are few places in the world with better alpine scenery this accessible, and you'll hurt your neck craning to see the tops of the snow-covered peaks. The disadvantage is the continual presence of the many bus tours – plus the hordes of other tourists – going through the same area. Either make your reservations well in advance if you're planning to stay in an inn or motel (and spend a lot more money per night than you would if you went up the Seattle route) or plan on camping – and you'll need to reserve your campsite or stop very early in the day.

Eastern Approach

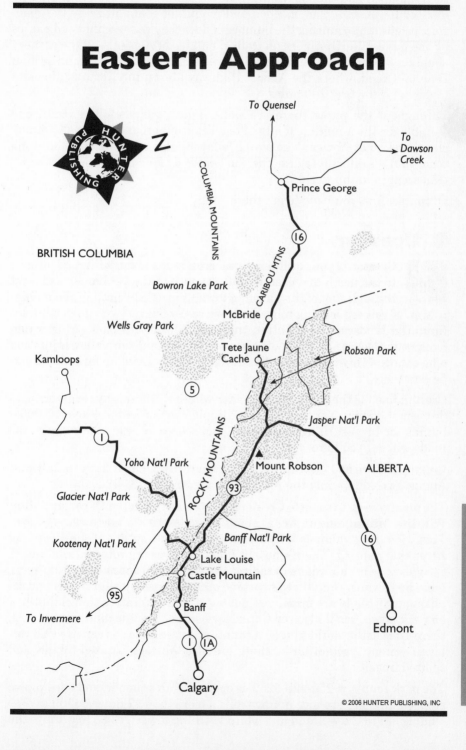

To Quensel

To Dawson Creek

Prince George

COLUMBIA MOUNTAINS

BRITISH COLUMBIA

CARIBOU MTNS

16

Bowron Lake Park

McBride

Wells Gray Park

Kamloops

Tete Jaune Cache

Robson Park

5

Jasper Nat'l Park

ROCKY MOUNTAINS

1

Yoho Nat'l Park

Mount Robson

ALBERTA

Glacier Nat'l Park

93

Kootenay Nat'l Park

Banff Nat'l Park

95

Lake Louise

Castle Mountain

16

To Invermere

Banff

1 1A

Edmont

Calgary

Highway Approaches

There aren't really all that many specific attractions along this route. It's the road itself and the mountains that surround it that are the draw. The Rockies tower and loom, caribou and mountain goats graze by the roadside, people stop counting the number of deer they've seen, the road passes by the largest North American icefield outside of Alaska, and the scenery simply never ends. If you come this way, once you hit the flat land around Dawson Creek, where the Alaska Highway starts, the Alcan is almost a letdown for the first 200 miles.

Throughout the parks there are well-marked, easy-to-follow trails, one suitable for the ambition of any hiker. The campgrounds are well tended, clean, and quiet. You can't go wrong following this route – there's only one road – but it's difficult to describe. Just be ready for some of the most beautiful scenery in the world.

Of course, first you have to get there.

■ Creston

 Creston is your quintessential crossroads town, with road options to the north and east as well as south to the US border and west through a lot of tiny farming towns, eventually getting you to Vancouver. If you are looking to go west, we really suggest you go north a bit first. The landscape gets better, the road a little less frustrating. From Creston to Osoyoos, at the southern end of the Okanagan Valley, is just one long string of tiny towns with traffic lights, punctuated by farm fields and forest.

Creston itself is the agricultural center where all these tiny towns come to do their shopping. Not a whole lot of people live in Creston – about 5,000 – but it's the biggest thing in the area, and sooner or later, all southern BC roads will get you here.

Creston **Info** is at 1711 Canyon St, on Highway 3. Open daily in July and August, weekends only the rest of the year. ☎ 250-428-4342.

The main reason to come to Creston and stay awhile is the **Creston Valley Wildlife Management Area**, about six miles/10 km northwest of town. This wide, long valley is a floodplain, taking the waters of the Kootenay River every spring. There's nearly 7,000 hectares of protected wetland in the valley, so it's a birder's paradise. More than 250 species come through, including swans – and there's nothing quite like seeing wild swans and realizing they really are birds, not just big stupid decorative things that live on park lakes. You'll also see Canada geese, snow geese, and more. In all, there's one of the world's highest counts of nesting species right in this valley. If you get tired of birds, there are also Western painted turtles and spotted frogs.

The park center, ☎ 250-428-3259, is open daily in summer, and once you've stopped in, there are nice hiking trails – more than 22 miles/35 km in all – leading out to the wetland and a birdwatching tower. It's $3 to get into the center, and they have guided trips out onto the water that are well worth your time. Stop in and make a few ticks on your life list.

Creston is a crossroads, so there are plenty of fast food choices, and no shortage of hotels. Try the **Creston Valley Bakery**, 113, 10th Ave at breakfast – or pick up a sandwich for a picnic later. **Munro's**, 1403 Canyon St, has steak and seafood, and is one of the more popular places in town.

All the hotels are easy on the budget, $$ all the way. **Bavarian Orchard Motel** is, as you might guess, set in an orchard. It has suites and some decks, 3205 Highway 3, ☎ 250-428-9935, 800-663-9544. **City Centre Motel**, 220 15th Ave, ☎ 250-428-2257, 877-506-2211, is only a block off the highway. Despite the name, it's a quiet location, and you can walk to most of

HOTEL PRICING
Prices are in US dollars.
under $50 . . . . $
$50-$100 . . . . $$
$100-$150 . . . . . . $$$
above $150 . . . . $$$$

the town attractions. **Sunset Motel**, on Highway 3, ☎ 250-428-2229, 800-663-7082, is another good choice in the same price range.

Go east from Creston, you cross the Purcell Mountains into a wide valley region between here and the Rockies. There are a few things worth stopping at along the way, as you head east and north into Banff.

■ Cranbrook

The biggest town in southeast BC, Cranbrook doesn't have a whole lot to make you stop. Driving through, it's large, ugly, and industrial. Two things make it worth the trouble, though – the Canadian Museum of Rail Travel and Fort Steele Heritage Town.

Tourism Info is at the junction of Highways 3 and 95, open year round, ☎ 250-426-5914.

The **Canadian Museum of Rail Travel**, 1 van Horne St North, ☎ 250-489-3918, is, plain and simple, the best train museum in BC. Any train fan is going to simply love it here. There are beautifully restored cars – including luxury sleepers, a dining car, a solarium, and more. Tours take you through each car, including a caboose, where you see that maybe it wasn't really the best place on the train to be. These are all in like-new condition; nowhere will you get a better idea of what travel was like during the classic age of rail. There's also a very nice movie shown, and a model train set up. Get there around lunchtime and you can have tea in the restored Argyle dining car. It's open 10-6 daily in summer, with regular tours.

> **AUTHOR TIP:** *The short tour is enough for most people, the $10 long tour a better choice for serious train nuts.*

Fort Steele Heritage Town, 15 minutes out of town on Highways 93/95, is open year-round, although not as much happens in the winter. It's set up to look like a town in the 1890s, when this was a booming mining community. Killed when the railroad passed it by, the town's now restored with a theater, a bakery, a general store, horse-drawn wagon rides, and more. This is a good place to take the kids for a day. ☎ 250-417-6000. Admission to the park is $6 (free in winter), with extra charged for theater shows.

If you end up spending a night in Cranbrook, you're going to be mostly stuck with road food. There just aren't many fine dining options. You'll find lots of places to stay, though, befitting the largest town in the region. Go to Cranbrook Street and take a look around. You're not going to have any trouble finding a place.

The Heritage Inn, 803 Cranbrook St, ☎ 250-489-4301, 888-888-4374, www.heritageinn.net, has nice rooms and some suites, $$$. Cheaper are the **Kootenay Country Comfort Inn**, 1111 Cranbrook St, ☎ 250-426-2296, 800-862-2823, and **Lazy Bear Lodge**, 621 Cranbrook St, ☎ 250-426-6086, 888-808-6086, both of which run at the low end of $$. Clean, good choices.

In the same price range is the **Nomad Motel**, 910 Cranbrook St, ☎ 250-426-6266, 800-863-6999, which has a heated pool. Every room has a fridge and a microwave.

 HIGHWAY TIP: If, for some reason, you want to skip the Rocky Mountains and the incredible scenery therein, there is a quick way through to Alberta, taking Highways 3/93 out of Cranbrook, east to Fernie and into Alberta at Crowsnest Pass. If you're in a hurry to get to Calgary, this would be the route to take.

There's not much reason to stop in **Fernie** in the summer, but in winter, the **Fernie Alpine Resort** comes alive, and it has some of the best – and least discovered – skiing in BC. The Vertical rise is over 850 meters, and the weather patterns bring plenty of snow – as much as 30 feet a year, with great bowl skiing. If you come in summer, put your bike on the lift and blast down the slopes. ☎ 250-423-3555. If you're coming in winter, be sure to ask your hotel about lift/lodging packages. It's how they make their business.

The Best Western, 1622 7th Ave, ☎ 250-423-5500, www.bestwestern fernie.com, is quite convenient, and some rooms have fireplaces and jacuzzis. Doubles from $$-$$$. If you want to stay right next to the slopes, try **Lizard Creek**, 5346 Highline Dr, ☎ 250-423-2057, www.lizardcreek.com, which offers some kitchenettes and fireplaces, $$$. Also nearby is the **Stanford Inn Fernie**, 100 Riverside Way,

HOTEL PRICING
Prices are in US dollars.
under $50 . . . . $
$50-$100 . . . . $$
$100-$150 . . . . . . $$$
above $150 . . . . . $$$$

☎ 250-426-5000, 877-423-5600, www.stanfordinn.net/fernie. It has hot tubs, a sauna, and even a waterslide that's open year-round. Doubles start under $100 and run nearly $900 at the high end.

North from Cranbrook

Highways 93 and 95 lead you to the parks. From Cranbrook, you're looking at a few hours yet to get into Banff. It's a nice drive, though, with mountains to either side and good river scenery. Stop for the night to camp at **Whiteswan Lake Park**, a popular provincial park near Canal Flats. There's a nice big lake and good walks along the shoreline. ☎ 250-422-4200.

From Whiteswan, you can take the logging road back to **Top of the World Provincial Park**, which has hiking and good backcountry camping in the shadows of Mt. Morro, which is more than 10,000 feet//3,000 meters tall.

Stay on the main highway – which parallels the Columbia Wetlands Wildlife Management Area, so it's a good place to have your spotting scope at the ready – up to the Dutch Creek Hoodoos, 12 miles/20 km past Canal Flats, at the north end of the lake.

HOODOOS

Hoodoos are pillars left by erosion: what usually happens is that a capstone prevents the pillar itself from eroding, while everything around it is worn away. It's a classic and fascinating geological trick.

Just beyond the hoodoos you'll get good views of the Columbia River. This river was somewhat problematic in the early days, as both Canada and the United States wanted it. Canada put forts as far south as Oregon (that's why there's a Vancouver in Washington State), and the US nearly started a world war over what it saw as its divine right to own most of British Columbia. The river still is a point of tension, as fishing rights and water rights – the new battle for the new century – are ongoing issues.

Fairmont Hot Springs Resort is near where the river hits the lake. It offers golf, a ski area restricted to hotel guests, and the less exclusive hot springs pools, which you can get into for $7. The lovely lodge rooms run $$$$; ☎ 250-345-6311. If you're the lodge sort, you'll have a good time here. Otherwise, you might be a little happier up the road at Radium.

The small towns of Windermere and Invermere are along the river banks. Finally, you come to Radium Hot Springs, the gateway to Banff.

■ Radium Hot Springs

 It's the most important town in this chunk of road, and it's really nothing more than a crossroads lined with hotels. Still, it's a good place to stock up on picnic supplies before you head into the parks – everything is cheaper here than it is in Banff – and if you're coming out of the parks, soak your hiking-weary muscles in the springs.

Visitor Info is right on the highway, 7585 Main St, ☎ 800-347-9704, 250-347-9331. It's next to a grocery store, so it's a convenient one-stop spot.

The hot springs themselves have been a destination since the 1890s, when the first pools were built. Today, there are several pools, the hottest of which has water just under 100° F. There is indeed radioactive material in the water, which people figure is bound to cure something. Don't worry: you won't come out glowing. A day pass is $10, and between soaks, there are some hikes right by the pools. ☎ 250-347-9485.

The town of Radium Hot Springs isn't really much more than a line of hotels. If you want an early start in the park, you'll save a lot of money starting here, instead of in Banff.

Apple Tree Inn, 4999 Highway 93, ☎ 250-347-0011,800-350-1511, has some suites and kitchenettes. You can walk to the hot springs from here. $$-$$$. **Big Horn Motel** gets you off the main road, 4881 St. Marys, ☎ 250-347-9522, 800-552-4881, www.bighornmotel.ca. $$. **Park Inn**, 4873 Stanley St, ☎ 250-347-9582, 800-858-1155, www.parkinn.bc.ca, has some rooms with full kitchens, some with jacuzzis. There's also an indoor pool. $$-$$$. **Chalet Europe**, 5063 Madsen Rd, ☎ 888-428-9998, www.chaleteurope.com, is a bit swanker, with some suites, some rooms with balconies and fireplaces. $$$. **Radium Hot Springs Lodge**, 5425 Highway 93, ☎ 250-347-9341, 888-222-9341, www.radiumhotspringslodge.com, has saunas, whirlpools, suites, and more. Good ski packages. $$$-$$$$.

You can go on into Kootenay to camp – we cover that on page 128 – but here there aren't many choices. **Canyon RV Resort**, on Sinclair Creek Loop Rd, ☎ 250-347-9564, has nice sites along the creek.

On to the Parks

This whole region has been declared a World Heritage Site by the United Nations. It's one of the largest protected wilderness areas in the world, and there's a good reason for it: mirror-still lakes, roadsides with mountain goats, towering peaks that are part of the most dramatic mountain landscape we've ever seen anywhere in the world.

The disadvantage to all this beauty is the continual presence of the many bus tours – plus the hordes of tourists. Either make your reservations well in advance if you're planning to stay in an inn or motel, or plan on camping – and you'll need to reserve your campsite or stop very early in the day.

But like heavily traveled areas anywhere in the world, it's surprisingly easy to get away from the crowds. Most people never leave the roads. Get onto a trail, look at the back country, go out later in the evening, and any time of year, you're likely to have this glorious place all to yourself.

> **AUTHOR NOTE:** *One note, right up front – this area is worth a guidebook all to itself. All we can do here is give you a good listing of the highlights and make some suggestions of where you might look for more. Once you're in the park system, the possibilities are truly endless.*

RULES

To get into the park system, you've got to pay. There are fee gates, where you pay $5 per day; the pass gets you all the way from here to the other end of the park system, beyond Jasper. Keep your ticket on the windshield; these things are regularly checked.

The parks are open year-round, but some of the roads get snowed under during winter. Obviously, Japser and Banff both depend heavily upon winter traffic for their livelihood. You can check current conditions, rules, etc., at www.parkscanada.ga.ca.

■ Kootenay National Park

Kootenay is the only national park in Canada with both glaciers and cactus. For the most part, the park is rugged limestone cliffs and red rock country dotted with hot springs. While the scenery is much the same as in the other parks – Kootenay is drier and sometimes hotter – Kootenay is considerably less crowded than Jasper or Banff, which gives you a better chance to see the stunning assortment of wildlife: elk, bear, moose, mountain goats, several varieties of wild sheep, and more. It also means that you'll have the place more as you want: all to yourself.

There are fewer services and hiking trails in Kootenay. Really, most people never do more than drive through on their way to Banff. It's good that way, because it means there's lots out there for anybody who wants to get off the road.

Kootenay also has maybe the most dramatic entryway of any of the parks. From Radium Hot Springs, you enter a cleft into the mountains, just like out of a fairytale. Get through the narrow defile, and it's like you're in a completely different world.

The region has always been part of a major north-south route, first used by the Kootenai First Nations people. Nowadays it's an active migration route for animals – when you're driving through the park, watch for mountain sheep in the southern cliffs and mountain goats in the Mt. Wordle area. The mountain goat is the symbol of Kootenay, and it is amazing to watch, especially when one decides to run straight up what looks like a perfectly smooth cliff.

For a quick hike, there's the very short **Marble Canyon Trail** – it takes about 20 minutes, round-trip – which crosses over narrow gorges more than 100 feet deep in places, filled with blue-gray glacial runoff. The trail ends at a lovely, roaring waterfall.

Another nice stroll leads to the **Paint Pots**, three ponds of different colors, created by different oxides in the water. There's a red, orange, and yellow pool; of course, something this good was extremely important to the First Nations people, who used these pigments for their art. It's a .6-mile/one-km walk from the hiking area back to the pots.

Kootenay National Park

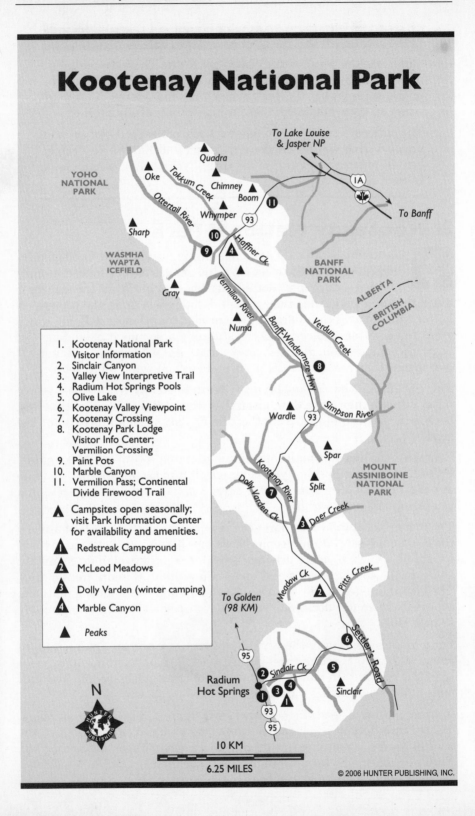

YOHO
NATIONAL
PARK

To Lake Louise
& Jasper NP

1A

To Banff

Quadra

Oke

Tokkum Creek

Chimney

Boom

11

Whymper

93

Ottertail River

Sharp

10

9

4

Haffner Ck.

WASMHA
WAPTA
ICEFIELD

Gray

Vermilion River

Numa

Banff-Windermere Hwy

BANFF
NATIONAL
PARK

Verdun Creek

ALBERTA

BRITISH
COLUMBIA

8

Simpson River

Wardle

93

Spar

Kootenay River

Dolly Varden Ck.

7

Split

MOUNT
ASSINIBOINE
NATIONAL
PARK

3

Daer Creek

1. Kootenay National Park
    Visitor Information
2. Sinclair Canyon
3. Valley View Interpretive Trail
4. Radium Hot Springs Pools
5. Olive Lake
6. Kootenay Valley Viewpoint
7. Kootenay Crossing
8. Kootenay Park Lodge
    Visitor Info Center;
    Vermilion Crossing
9. Paint Pots
10. Marble Canyon
11. Vermilion Pass; Continental
    Divide Firewood Trail

▲ Campsites open seasonally;
   visit Park Information Center
   for availability and amenities.

1 Redstreak Campground

2 McLeod Meadows

3 Dolly Varden (winter camping)

4 Marble Canyon

▲ Peaks

Meadow Ck.

Pitts Creek

2

To Golden
(98 KM)

Settler's Road

6

95

2 Sinclair Ck.

5

Radium
Hot Springs

1 3 4

Sinclair

93

95

N

HUNTER PUBLISHING

10 KM

6.25 MILES

© 2006 HUNTER PUBLISHING, INC.

If you're just getting warmed up after that, there's a nine-mile/15-km trail from the pots back to **Helmet Creek**, which ends at a waterfall. Along the way you get glacier views. It's a tough hike, so figure five hours each way, but there is a campground at the end of it.

Another good hike out of the paint pots is to **Tumbling Creek**, 6.5 miles/10.5 km, with an altitude gain of about 2,500 feet/750 meters. You get good creek views, and if you don't feel like doing the full vertical hike, there's a turnaround place at Rockwall Pass.

The **Stanley Glacier hike** is about six miles/nine km, round-trip, with not too much elevation gain (about 1,100 feet/350 meters). The trailhead is just west of the Continental Divide, and that's the point of the hike: to get views of where the waters part, and of Stanley Glacier, where the water got frozen and now is melting back.

There are some longer, multi-day hikes in the park. To do the full Rockwall hike, which covers upwards of 31 miles/50 km, will take you four or five days – more, depending on how much the mountains slow you down. *The Canadian Rockies Trail Guide*, by Brad Patton and Bart Robinson, is the book you need to get farther into the boonies. Also, before you head for the backcountry, be sure to check in at a ranger station to get the latest conditions.

Camp in Marble Canyon or McLeod Meadows if you have a tent (beautiful sites, no services) or Redstreak, near the West Gate, if you need hookups. They don't take reservations at any of these parks, so show up early to claim your spot.

HIGHWAY TIP: Highway 93, the main road through Kootenay, crosses the Vermillion Pass, and then joins the Icefield Parkway about halfway between the towns of Banff and Lake Louise in Banff Park, so when you leave Kootenay, there's plenty more scenery to come. We're going to go south, then head back north.

■ Banff

Banff was Canada's first national park, and today, if you asked most people to name a park in Canada, Banff is what they'd come up with. It's the quintessential resort town, world-famous for skiing, hiking, and the huge numbers of Japanese tourists who descend upon it each year. They do, however, stick to the roads. Because of the sheer volume of traffic, regulations on using designated areas for camping, picnics, and such are much more tightly enforced than in some other parks. However, if you head out into the backcountry (remember, permit and registration are required), you're going to be all alone.

Get out of town – pick any direction – and in about 10 feet, you'll hit one of the best wildernesses in the world.

Stop at the Tourist Info Centre in Banff, Lake Louise, or Jasper to pick up a copy of the *Backcountry Visitor's Guide* or *Drives and Walks*.

The City

The town of Banff can be a little overwhelming. Why is it inevitable that as soon as a place becomes known for being beautiful, developers come along and screw it all up? It's not as frightening as, say, Whistler, from a strictly aesthetic point of view – certainly not anywhere near as sterile – but it's like the architects were intimidated by the stunning natural scenery, and so decided all their buildings should be as mediocre and uninteresting as they possibly could be. Add in serious parking problems, tons of people walking the streets every day of the year, and it's a fairly normal reaction, upon getting to Banff, to figure out how quickly you can get back out of it.

But take a deep breath and look around. There's some good stuff in town, and it's worth the stop, before you head back into the wild.

Start at **Banff Visitors Centre**, 224 Banff Ave, ☎ 403-762-0270; there's a Parks Canada office in the same building, ☎ 403-762-1550. If you come into town in high season without a hotel reservation, and you're hoping to spend the night, come here first. They'll help you out as best they can – there's a board listing hotels that still have rooms, and they'll call around. They also have all the usual useful stuff on the town and what you can do nearby. Get your backcountry permit from the Parks Canada side of the room.

From wherever you parked to get into the Info Center, leave your car and take a walk on Banff Ave, the main shopping street in town. There's a lot of generic stuff, with some better than average stuff mixed in, but it's the main drag, and even if you're not interested in buying from The Gap, it's worth hanging out for awhile to people watch.

For the best selection of books on the parks, stop in at **Banff Book & Art Den**, 94 Banff Ave, ☎ 403-762-3919.

The best activity in Banff is the mountain hiking, but if you're looking for water, you have a few good options. **Wild Water Adventures**, ☎ 888-647-6444, and **Kootenay River Runners**, ☎ 800-599-4399, both take trips out of Banff to the Kicking Horse, one of the best whitewater rivers around. A day of Class 1-IV water, including transport from Banff, runs about $100-150.

To get an overview of the town, hit the **Banff Gondola**, a tramway that takes you about 2,200 feet up to an observation deck at 7,486 feet (2,281 meters). Once you're on the top, you get absolutely killer views of the Rockies, a good chance of seeing big horn sheep and maybe some marmots (think of a weasel on steroids) and of course, there's a restaurant and gift shop up at the top. Rides are $20.

Nearby is the **Upper Hot Springs**, part of the heavy geothermal activity in the Rockies. If you didn't take a dip at Radium, try it here. It's $7.50 for a day pass, and they're open year-round.

Food & Lodging

Most of the town's restaurants are right in downtown Banff, along Banff Avenue. Try **Guido's**, 116 Banff Ave, for Italian dishes from $12. Nearby is the **Maple Leaf Grill**, 137 Banff Ave, which is maybe the best place for a cheap lunch – fish and chips or burgers for under $10. A half-block off Banff Ave is **Bruno's**, 304 Caribou St, another local favorite that's laid back and cheap. **Melissa's**, 218 Lynx St, is one of the oldest eateries in town. It's open for all meals, and on a nice summer day there are few better places to hang out than the patio. For dessert, hit **Rogers' Chocolates**, 133 Banff Ave.

Banff is a busy, busy place, and hotels can be an issue. If you're showing up in town without a reservation, check at the Info Centre, and try calling **Banff Central Reservations**, ☎ 877-542-2633. Still, it's not a bad idea to come into town with a backup plan.

Prices are high, and they can do it because they're full most of the time. You really don't have a lot of choice except to shell out. There is a hostel in town, **Banff Alpine Centre**, ☎ 403-762-4122, about two miles/three km from downtown, but even here, just a dorm bed is going to run close to $30 a night. A decent hotel room is going to run around $200 or up. Sorry, that's just the way it is. There are just a few choices under $200.

The Arrow Motel, ☎ 403-762-2207, on the grounds of the Ptarmigan Inn, 337 Banff Ave, is a reasonable budget choice. $$$$ gets you a double that will serve nicely as a place to crash. If you want a little more amenity, the Ptarmigan, at the same address and phone number, $$$$ – standard Banff rates – has some nice rooms with balconies and fireplaces.

HOTEL PRICING
Prices are in US dollars.
under $50 . . . . $
$50-$100 . . . . $$
$100-$150 . . . . . . $$$
above $150 . . . . . $$$$

Banff Voyager Inn, 555 Banff Ave, ☎ 403-762-3301, is another good budget choice, $$$. There's a pool and a sauna, making this a good choice at the lower end of the price range. The **Spruce Grove Inn** shares the sauna and pool with the Voyager. Spruce Grove, 545 Banff Ave, ☎ 403-762-3301, $$$$. It's a new property, still pretty shiny clean.

Just a bit more expensive is the **Red Carpet Inn**, 425 Banff Ave, ☎ 403-762-4184, $$$$. Some rooms have jacuzzis, and some have balconies so you can watch the world go by.

If you're willing to go over $200 a night, your options get a little wider. **Banff Traveller's Inn**, 401 Banff Ave, ☎ 403-762-4401, has a steam room, nice balconies, and a good ambience. In the same price range is the **Dynasty Inn**, 501 Banff Ave, ☎ 403-762-8844, where some rooms have fireplaces and balconies.

Highway Approaches

Brewster's Mountain Lodge, 208 Caribou St, ☎ 888-762-2900, keeps you downtown but gets you off Banff Ave. It's a kicky old-fashioned sort of place, with log furniture.

Move up some, to the $300 neighborhood, and you can try the **Mount Royal Hotel**, 138 Banff Ave, ☎ 403-762-3331, which has some rooms with fireplaces and fridges, as well as jacuzzis. It's a really nice place to spend the night, if you can take the price point.

Finally, to really blow the budget, there's the **Fairmont**. You've seen pictures of it all your life: the quintessential mountain castle-style hotel. $500 a night should see you through.

Lots of good **camping** in Banff. Problem is, you can't make reservations, so show up early in high season to claim your spot. Once you've registered, you're safe, so you can head right back out without worrying about claim jumpers. Most sites run around $25.

Closest to town is **Tunnel Mountain Village**, a trio of campgrounds; only Tunnel Mountain Village 1, open in summer, allows tents.

North of town are the pair of **Two Jack** campgrounds – main and lakeside. These are rather nicer than the Tunnel Mountain sites, and a whole lot better if you've got a tent or don't want to spend the evening looking into the windows of the vehicle parked next to you.

Huge **Lake Louise Campground** is right outside the village. There are interpretive programs, full hookups, and decent showers. One caveat is that it's right next to the railroad tracks, which can get a little distracting.

The Park

Once you're settled in the town, it's time to head out. Try Johnston Canyon (off the Bow Valley Parkway; it runs parallel to the Icefields Parkway for about 50 miles), an eight-mile trip through alpine scenery with clear, startlingly blue lakes, waterfalls, and meadows full of wildflowers.

Of course, **Lake Louise** is the main draw in Banff. Nobody comes to the park without coming here. Because the very tiny lake acts as a perfect mirror, Lake Louise is one of the most photographed spots in all of the park system, and the lodge on its shores is justifiably famous. It's also bigger than the lake itself, which is really more pond-sized than lake-sized. Unless you've got a wide-angle lens, it's very difficult to get good photographs.

For mountain views, go to **Moraine Lake**, about 10 miles from Lake Louise. A great 14-mile hiking trail, **Valley of the Ten Peaks Trail,** runs between the two lakes. Take a day and see the countryside the way people did for the thousands of years before tour buses were invented.

Another good view is at **Lake Minnewanka**, the biggest lake in the park, formed by a dam built back in the early years of the last century. It's northeast of town, and once you're there, **Lake Minnewanka Boat Tours**, ☎ 403-762-3473, has 90-minute cruises that get you nice mountain views.

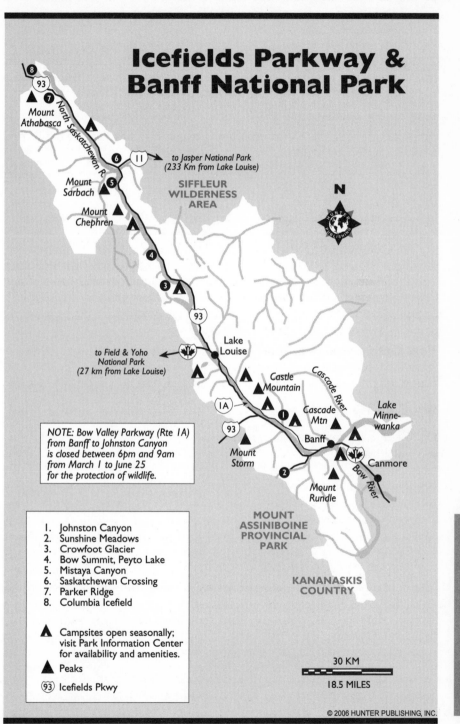

Icefields Parkway & Banff National Park

to Jasper National Park
(233 Km from Lake Louise)

Mount
Athabasca

Mount
Sarbach

Mount
Chephren

**SIFFLEUR
WILDERNESS
AREA**

to Field & Yoho
National Park
(27 km from Lake Louise)

Lake
Louise

Castle
Mountain

Cascade River

Cascade
Mtn

Lake
Minne-
wanka

Banff

Mount
Storm

Canmore

Bow River

Mount
Rundle

NOTE: Bow Valley Parkway (Rte 1A)
from Banff to Johnston Canyon
is closed between 6pm and 9am
from March 1 to June 25
for the protection of wildlife.

**MOUNT
ASSINIBOINE
PROVINCIAL
PARK**

**KANANASKIS
COUNTRY**

1. Johnston Canyon
2. Sunshine Meadows
3. Crowfoot Glacier
4. Bow Summit, Peyto Lake
5. Mistaya Canyon
6. Saskatchewan Crossing
7. Parker Ridge
8. Columbia Icefield

▲ Campsites open seasonally;
visit Park Information Center
for availability and amenities.

▲ Peaks

⑨③ Icefields Pkwy

North Saskatchewan R.

N

30 KM

18.5 MILES

© 2006 HUNTER PUBLISHING, INC.

Highway Approaches

Driving through the park, you can get off the main highway and onto **Bow Valley Parkway**, which runs parallel. This is the back way between Banff and Lake Louise, a narrow, twisty road, but there are lots of places to get off the pavement and take a look around. It's also, of course, a lot prettier than the main highway, since you're running back in closer to the trees. The best things along the parkway are the wetlands areas: **Backswamp** and **Muleshoe**, both of which are birder paradises.

Some nice hikes are right off the parkway. **Cory Pass** (four miles/six km one-way) has great views of Mt. Louis. The trailhead is at the Fireside Picnic Area. This trail tops out with a very long, steep ascent, so all your gasping is worth it. If that's too much climbing, try **Edith Pass**, a forest walk leading out of the same picnic area. It doesn't have the great views, but is a good leg-stretch walk at just under three miles/five km.

In **Johnston Canyon** (take the Johnston Canyon road where Bow Valley meets the Trans-Canada), you can walk the edge of the canyon – not the biggest around, but pretty – or head out to the **Ink Pots**, a batch of cold mineral springs. It's 1.7 miles//2.7 km from the trailhead at the Johnston Canyon Lodge, back to the Upper Canyon falls, which drop about 100 feet. From there, it's another two miles/three km back to the Ink Pots.

From Lake Louise, where the Bow Valley meets the Trans-Canada meets the Johnston Canyon Road, you have a couple of choices of which way to go. We're thinking what's behind door number 1 – the Trans-Canada down to Yoho – is a nice option.

■ Yoho

 A nice side trip – or an alternate to the more standard route – is into Yoho. If you're coming into the parks system from Golden, this is where you'll start off; it's easy access to central British Columbia.

Yoho is, like Kootenay, kind of underutilized. People drive through it, but they don't think about stopping. This means if you can't find a campsite in Jasper or Banff, this isn't a bad place to try. Yoho has the same stunning scenery as the other parks, but it rains more, and cloudy days are more frequent on the western side of the Rockies.

From Lake Louise, it's a dramatic downhill run to the small town of Field. Along the way, you'll pass **Spiral Tunnel Viewpoint**, which lets you see just how determined they were when they built the first transcontinental railway in Canada. They tried laying a regular line, but failed because the grade was so steep – all they got was a bunch of dead trains. The solution, then, was to build two spiral tunnels through the mountains. The tunnels are 1.2 miles/two km long, and brought an end to the train crashes, although they did kind of perturb people who didn't like running circles in the dark.

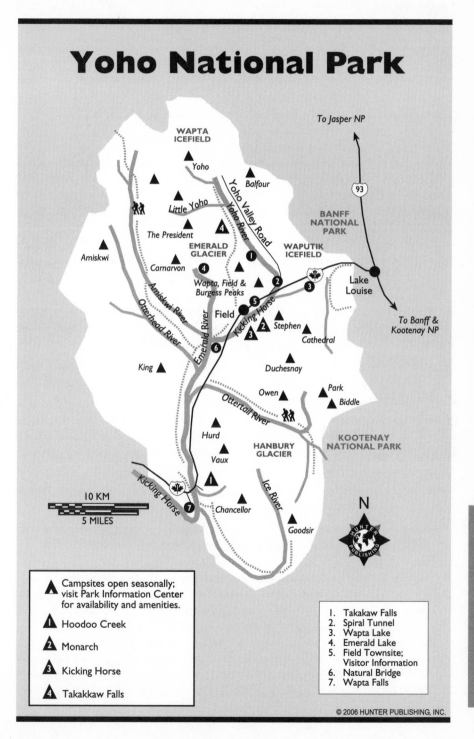

Yoho National Park

WAPTA ICEFIELD

To Jasper NP

Yoho

Balfour

Little Yoho

The President

EMERALD GLACIER

Amiskwi

Carnarvon

Wapta, Field & Burgess Peaks

Field

King

BANFF NATIONAL PARK

WAPUTIK ICEFIELD

Lake Louise

To Banff & Kootenay NP

Yoho Valley Road

Yoho River

Kicking Horse

Stephen

Cathedral

Duchesnay

Owen

Park

Biddle

Amiskwi River

Otterhead River

Emerald River

Ottertail River

Hurd

Vaux

HANBURY GLACIER

KOOTENAY NATIONAL PARK

Kicking Horse

Chancellor

Ice River

Goodsir

10 KM
5 MILES

N
HUNTER PUBLISHING

Campsites open seasonally; visit Park Information Center for availability and amenities.

1 Hoodoo Creek

2 Monarch

3 Kicking Horse

4 Takakkaw Falls

1. Takakaw Falls
2. Spiral Tunnel
3. Wapta Lake
4. Emerald Lake
5. Field Townsite; Visitor Information
6. Natural Bridge
7. Wapta Falls

© 2006 HUNTER PUBLISHING, INC.

Highway Approaches

HIGHWAY TIP: Just for fun, remember that the main highway you're driving on follows the original rail route, the one that caused so many train crashes.

Just a little farther downhill is a viewpoint where you can see where the Yoho and Kicking Horse rivers meet. The Kicking Horse is some of the finest whitewater in BC.

There's a turnoff from the main highway to Yoho Valley Road. Follow this back nine miles/14 km to **Takakkaw Falls**, more than 800 feet/250 meters high, rumbling out of a glacial river. This is well worth the side trip. There's an easy walk that gets you better views than you'll have from the parking lot. From the parking lot, the **Twin Falls** hike runs five miles/eight km past more waterfalls than you're going to want to count. At the end, there's the Twin Falls Chalet, where you can pick up a snack or drink before heading back.

The main highway flattens out at the small town of **Field**, where there's the Visitor Information Centre (open 8 am to 8 pm). You need to stop here to see what the **fossils** from the Burgess Shale (see below) really look like. Quite frankly, most people walk away wondering what kind of drugs the paleontologists were on, to get those creatures out of those fossils, but this is going to be your best view of some of the most important fossils ever found.

Hikers in Yoho should try the trails to **Twin Falls** or **Emerald Lake**. Both are fairly flat, with lovely water views. For the more ambitious, the overnighter to **Lake O'Hara** offers alpine scenery at its best.

Yoho is more remote and less traveled than the other parks. It's climate is also different, all of which means that hiking here is different than hiking elsewhere. And you owe it to yourself to get out of the car once or twice.

The most popular hike is probably the **Emerald Lake Loop**, just over three miles/five km along the lakeshore. This is an easy walk with lots of scenery, a perfect after-dinner stroll.

THE BURGESS SHALE

The best reason to visit Yoho is to see firsthand why we're driving cars and not sludging around in the mud at the bottom of the ocean somewhere. Inside the park boundaries is the Burgess Shale, one of the most interesting fossil finds in the world. The shale was formed about 530 million years ago. Only 10 feet thick and 100 yards or so long, more different types of life have been found here than in any other spot on the planet. Life, essentially, has narrowed its choices since the shale was formed, keeping only a few species of animals. In the Burgess there is evidence of the processes of life going on a wild experimental binge, producing incredible shapes of animals – beasts that looked like walking tinker toys, with five eyes, what paleontologist Stephen Jay Gould called animals "whose mouth was a circular nutcracker."

Although it wouldn't be hard to find paleontologists who would argue with his theories, Gould's book, **Wonderful Life**, is a great history of the find and the implications of the incredible variety of animals in it.

Perfectly fossilized in the shale formations are 20 to 30 kinds of arthropods (spiders and lobsters are modern arthropods) that don't fit into any modern group. In other words, entirely new kinds of life developed and disappeared.

The fossils here were discovered by Charles Walcott in 1909. Walcott was the head of the Smithsonian Institution, and today you can tour the quarry that has been named after him for $45. It's an all-day trip on a 12.5-mile hike and will take you to the best part of the formation. If that's a bit more than you have in mind, there's a shorter hike, to the Mt. Stephens Fossil Beds, where mostly trilobites have been found, for $25 per person. It's a 3.7-mile round-trip hike. While both hikes are considered moderately difficult, the shorter one actually has the steeper grades.

Tours run from July to September or October, depending on weather conditions. Reservations are required. Phone the Yoho Burgess Shale Research Foundation at ☎ 800-343-3006 for details. (However, they're notorious for not bothering to answer their phone, so be ready to be persistent.) Bring your own lunch and prepare to be amazed. Why sit through a video of computer-generated dinosaurs when the real miracle of prehistoric life is right here?

If you can't get in on the tour, stop by the Yoho Visitor Centre, which has some of the fossils on display. Looking at them, you're going to be struck most strongly by wondering what kind of freaks scientists are. Compare the fossils to the drawings of the animal the way they think it looked before it got flattened out. There are things the specialist's eye catches that you and I will never see.

The gift shop has good trilobite postcards and copies of *The Fossils of the Burgess Shale*, by Derek Briggs, Douglas Erwin, and Frederick Collier. This is a serious book – it runs upwards of $40 for the paperback – but well worth it for the dino-inclined. Check out the hyoliths, which look like octopus who got bred with crossbows; or the chelicerata, distant relations to scorpions and spiders, and nothing at all that you'd ever want to see crawling at you. In all, about 170 species have been found at the Burgess Shale.

Food & Lodging

The choices are minimal in Yoho. It's a good place to plan a picnic. Try the **Truffle Pigs' Café**, downtown, for a huge menu and crowds of locals not in the mood to cook. A good place.

Hotels are a little cheaper than in Banff or Jasper, but not a whole lot. **Emerald Lake Lodge**, ☎ 250-343-6321, has nice rooms in chalets, with fireplaces, a hot tub, and a sauna. $$$-$$$$. **The Kicking Horse Lodge**, ☎ 250-343-6303, is outside of town in a beautiful, quiet location. Some of the rooms have kitchenettes, and there is a restaurant on the grounds. $$$-$$$$.

Cathedral Mountain Lodge & Chalets is out toward Takakkaw Falls. Stay in a log cabin, walk along the Kicking Horse before dinner. Around $200 and up.

On the road to Takakkaw Falls is **Kicking Horse Campground**, the park's biggest. If you're in a tent, though, keep going back to **Takakkaw Falls Campground**, a walk-in only facility. **Hoodoo Creek**, southwest of Field, is also a good choice, with trees and flush toilets.

North from Lake Louise

The **Icefields Parkway** leaves Lake Louise, heading for Jasper. Traffic can be slow, especially in the long, narrow valley along the continental divide, but you'll want to be driving slowly anyway to take in the view. Watch for wildlife along the entire route: goats and sheep in the south, more elk and deer toward Jasper.

It's 143 miles/230 km from Lake Louise to Jasper, but it's best to figure on a full day to do the trip. There's plenty to get out to see, always a good chance of wildlife along the road – elk, mountain goats, maybe bear – and there are plenty of places to get out and walk around.

> **HIGHWAY TIP:** A lot of people can be on this road in summer. Drive carefully. Because it's such a good road – wide, with generous shoulders – there can be a lot of bike traffic.

Any time you're coming around a blind corner, slow down. There's no telling what's on the other side of it, be it an animal, a bunch of people stopped for an animal, or somebody on a bike.

The road is open year-round, although it can sometimes be closed for a little while in winter due to avalanches.

All that said, it's one of the prettiest stretches of road you'll ever be on. Get the camera ready.

Distances we list here are from Lake Louise.

The **Crowfoot Glacier viewpoint** is 20 miles/33 km north of Lake Louise. Crowfoot is shrinking fast, so you'd better see it now. The name comes from what look like three toes coming down off the main glacial face; one toe is gone, the other two won't be hanging around much longer.

Another 2.5 miles/four km up the road is **Bow Lake**, source of the Bow River, and it's all fed by the Bow Icefield and glacier. The water can be mirror still – if you didn't get the mountain reflections you wanted at Lake Louise, try here.

The road heads uphill from here to **Bow Summit**, just over 6,500 feet/2,000 meters high. Then it's all downhill to Jasper – which is why most people on bikes are going north, not south.

Peyto Lake, 25 miles / 40 km from Lake Louise, is just behind the Bow Summit parking lot. It's an easy walk back, and you really shouldn't miss this. Get all the pictures you can, because it's going to take proof when you get back home and tell your friends about the colors of the water. Depending on how the sun is hitting it, you can get anything from emerald green to a dark blue; the color changes seasonally, as well, depending on glacial melt. You don't want to miss this.

Pretty much everybody stops at the **Columbia Icefield Visitor Information Centre**, almost the halfway point between Jasper (65 miles/105 km north) and Lake Louise (82 miles/132 km south) – it's huge, with a cafeteria, dining room, and an impressive interactive glaciation display. That's reason enough to come in, but while you're here, if you've never walked on a glacier before, now's your chance. The center is just across the highway from **Athabasca Glacier** (part of the immense Columbia Icefields, the largest in the Rockies), and there are regular trips that take you out onto the glacier itself. Buy a ticket from the booth upstairs in the center; they'll tell you when the next bus is leaving. It goes across the road and along a glacial moraine. You then load into snowcats, huge treaded buses that take you down the moraine and onto the ice of the glacier. These things move very slowly – they top out around four mph – but you're probably not in a hurry, as you can get terrific ice and mountain views. The end of the ride comes at a large, cleared area. Okay, face it, it's a parking lot carved into the glacier. If you've been on glaciers before, this is going to come as a bit of a disappointment, as you can't get any farther into the ice. If you've never been on a glacier, this is a good introduction. It's also easily accessible for people with mobility issues. Tickets are $33.95. ☎ 800-565-7547, www.columbiaicefield.com.

The Columbia icefield is melting fast, but in places, the ice sheet is still more than 1,000 feet thick. Meltwater from the icefield feeds the North Saskatchewan, Columbia, Fraser, Athabasca, and Mackenzie rivers.

Highway Approaches

HYDROGRAPHIC APEX

Mt. Snow Dome in the park is the "hydrographic apex" of North America. What this means is that a drop of water balanced at the absolute top of the mountain stands an equal chance of ending up in the Atlantic, Pacific, or Arctic ocean. It's a three-way continental divide.

Drive away from the center, and the mountain views are, to use a cliché, breathtaking. Any direction you look on a nice day, you'll see steep slopes, thick forest, ice-capped mountain peaks. The tallest mountains top out at over 10,000 feet; the tallest in the park is Mt. Forbes, 12,000 feet/3,630 meters, which you can see on the way to Sunwapta Pass.

The pass is the border between Jasper and Banff, but the scenery doesn't change any. Stop at **Sunwapta Falls**, 34 miles/55 km south of Jasper, if you haven't had your fill of waterfalls yet.

The last miles into Jasper are tree-lined, pretty, perhaps a little less dramatic than farther south. Jasper makes you work just a little harder to be dazzled, but there's no shortage of the spectacular in the park; actually, we like it best of the whole system.

■ Jasper

The Town

Jasper bills itself as the "Gem of the Canadian Rockies," and that's no joke. With probably the prettiest scenery of the four parks (although it's hard to compare superlatives), Jasper has the usual mountains, gorges, lakes, and streams, but somehow they're put together even better here. Whereas the other parks are a little more sedate, Jasper is where people come for serious, hard-core outdoor action. If you're packing a canoe or planning some rock climbing, you're going to want to spend your time here.

If you thought Banff was a little hurried and harried in town, the town of Jasper is a whole lot more laid back. It doesn't have the shopping or the fine dining that Banff does, but it has families sunning themselves on the lawn in front of the Visitor Centre, and a slower, more laid-back feel to it. It's a mountain town that hasn't been ruined yet by its proximity to the mountains.

There's no way to miss the **Info Centre**: it's right downtown, in a beautiful old stone building. ☎ 780-582-6176. There's also a Parks Canada office in the same building, if you're wanting to get backcountry access.

Everything you need in town is within walking distance of the Info Centre. The main stretch of road has plenty of restaurants and souvenir shops. Nothing outstanding, but you won't have any trouble here if you've got money burning a hole in your pocket.

Food & Accommodation

Mountain Foods Café, 606 Connaught, is the place to hit for breakfast and fresh baked goods. For later, pick up a sandwich or wrap. **Jasper's Pizza Place**, 402 Connaught, is a local favorite, with small, wood-fired pizzas that will set you back about $12.

One street back from Connaught is **Patricia St**, where Spooner's is upstairs at 610 Patricia. Balcony seats let you watch the people moving by, and inside, there's good light sandwiches and salads. A nice place for lunch.

For dinner, try **Villa Caruso**, 640 Connaught, for steak and seafood, from $15. At the fancier end of things is **Andy's Bistro**, 606 Patricia, with local ingredient specialties.

As far as hotels go, Jasper is cheaper than Banff, and you stand a better chance of rolling up and finding a room on short notice, but it's still best to plan ahead.

Rocky Mountain Reservations, ☎ 780-852-9455, 877-902-9455, can book you into hotels anywhere in the parks. They are worth a call if you haven't planned ahead. You can also try **Banff Accommodations**, ☎ 877-226-3348, which will book Jasper hotels. **Becker's Chalets**, ☎ 780-852-3779, is just south of town in a pretty location. Some of the rooms have balconies and fridges, but none has a phone. Good, clean and comfortable, $$$-$$$$. **The Astoria Hotel**, 404 Connaught, ☎ 780-852-3351, is downtown. It's comfortable, with clean rooms, all with a fridge. $$$$. **The Athabasca Hotel**, 510 Patricia St, takes you one street back from the main drag. Some good touches include high-speed Internet access. $$$.

HOTEL PRICING
Prices are in US dollars.
under $50 . . . . $
$50-$100 . . . . $$
$100-$150 . . . . . . $$$
above $150 . . . . . $$$$

Jasper Inn Alpine Resort moves you up the comfort and price scale. A lot of the rooms have real wood fireplaces. There's a heated pool on the grounds, plus a sauna and steam room, but you're in the over $200 range here. **The Maligne Lodge**, 925 Connaught, ☎ 780-852-3143, has room with balconies, some with fireplaces. $$$$. **The Tonquin Inn**, 100 Juniper St, ☎ 800-661-1315, is another good choice at around $200. It's at the end of town, but still walking distance. Some rooms have fireplaces.

At the top of the economic scale is the **Fairmont Jasper Park Lodge**, with everything you expect from a Fairmont. It's on Highway 16, just outside town, ☎ 800-441-1414, with doubles from $550.

Whistlers Campground is the biggest in the parks, just a couple of kilometers south of town. It's huge, but its layout leaves you with some feeling of privacy and being in the woods. It has everything from tent sites to RV sites with full hookups.

Another 1.2 miles/two km south of town is the **Wapiti Campground**, which is still huge. If you're coming in winter, this is your only option.

Highway Approaches

You can't make reservations at these campgrounds; you have to show up and hope. Check out time is 11 am, so plan accordingly to claim your spot during high season.

The Park

Take Highway 93A for views of **Mount Edith Cavell** reflecting in a glacial melt lake. Off Highway 16 East, there are hot springs, waterfalls, and frequent traffic jams caused by elk herds. One of the more popular drives is back to **Maligne Lake**. Head back on Maligne Lake Road, just outside of town. There's a nice stop at **Maligne Canyon**, where you can take a short, easy hike along the gorge. When you hit the end of the road – which has gorgeous mountain and river views, some of the best anywhere in the parks system – you can launch your canoe on Maligne Lake, the second-largest glacier-fed lake in the world, more than 14 miles long. Boat rentals are available from Maligne Lake Boathouse.

A tramway goes up **Whistler Mountain** (just south of the town of Jasper), past Whistlers Campground. It climbs 973 vertical meters/3,200 feet, taking you 2,300 meters (nearly to 8,000 feet) atop the mountain, with hiking trails leading to the summit. Allow an hour and a half to get to the peak and back. This is a really dramatic ride, and if you've got a clear day, you're going to run out of film very quickly after you hit the top. Watch for marmots galumphing along the trails. It's a nice place to see what the high alpine landscape is really like. The round-trip is $20, and cars depart every 12 minutes. Go early, as it can get really crowded as the day wears on.

Good hiking trails include the **Pyramid Lake Trail**, about 12 miles and fairly strenuous, or the ambitious 18-mile **Saturday Night Lake Circle**, which runs past a string of lakes. You can access the trail from town. Once you take any of the trails out of town heading up the mountains to the west, you are on a huge network of interlacing trails that could keep an experienced hiker busy for weeks. A good quick hike is the **Lake Annette Loop**, only a mile and a half or so. The trailhead is on Maligne Road.

From Whistlers Campground, walk up the road toward the tramway, then hit the **Whistlers Trail**, which leads off south. This is a steep, switch-back trail, but once you're at the top, you've got killer mountain views and a chance to see some of the high alpine landscape. It's eight km/five miles each way – figure as much as five hours up, three hours down.

 There's a free brochure, *Summer Trails in Jasper*, that lists some good hikes. If that's not enough for you, we again suggest the marvelous *Canadian Rockies Trail Guide*, by Patton and Robinson.

Of course, with all the snowmelt, there's great whitewater rafting in the park on several rivers. **Maligne Rafting Adventures** (☎ 866-625-4463, 780-852-3370, www.mra.ab.ca) runs trips on the Maligne, the Athabasca, and the Kakwa – from quick trips for $44 to three-day runs for $450 and up.

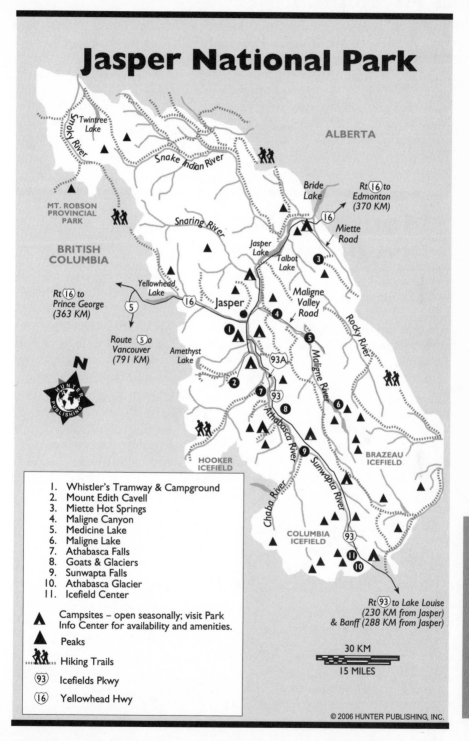

Jasper National Park

ALBERTA

Twintree Lake

Smoky River

Snake Indian River

MT. ROBSON PROVINCIAL PARK

BRITISH COLUMBIA

Snaring River

Bride Lake

Rt (16) to Edmonton (370 KM)

Miette Road

Jasper Lake

Talbot Lake

Rt (16) to Prince George (363 KM)

Yellowhead Lake

Jasper

Maligne Valley Road

Route (5) to Vancouver (791 KM)

Amethyst Lake

Rocky River

93A

HOOKER ICEFIELD

Maligne River

Athabasca River

BRAZEAU ICEFIELD

Sunwapta River

Chaba River

COLUMBIA ICEFIELD

Rt (93) to Lake Louise (230 KM from Jasper) & Banff (288 KM from Jasper)

N

HUNTER PUBLISHING

1. Whistler's Tramway & Campground
2. Mount Edith Cavell
3. Miette Hot Springs
4. Maligne Canyon
5. Medicine Lake
6. Maligne Lake
7. Athabasca Falls
8. Goats & Glaciers
9. Sunwapta Falls
10. Athabasca Glacier
11. Icefield Center

▲ Campsites – open seasonally; visit Park Info Center for availability and amenities.

▲ Peaks

👣 Hiking Trails

(93) Icefields Pkwy

(16) Yellowhead Hwy

30 KM

15 MILES

Highway Approaches

© 2006 HUNTER PUBLISHING, INC.

■ Mt. Robson

 If you're heading from Jasper to Prince George, you'll pass through **Mt. Robson Provincial Park**, a relatively small park just west of Jasper. People come here to see the mountains and to camp in sites that are usually much less crowded than those in the nearby parks. Best views are of Mt. Robson (you can't miss it – it's the mountain view that makes you stop your car), the highest peak in the Canadian Rockies, at over 12,000 feet. Rearguard Falls (about 13 miles west of the park headquarters) and Overlander Falls (a mile east) make for nice stops. Hikers can take a quick 90-minute walk out of Overlander.

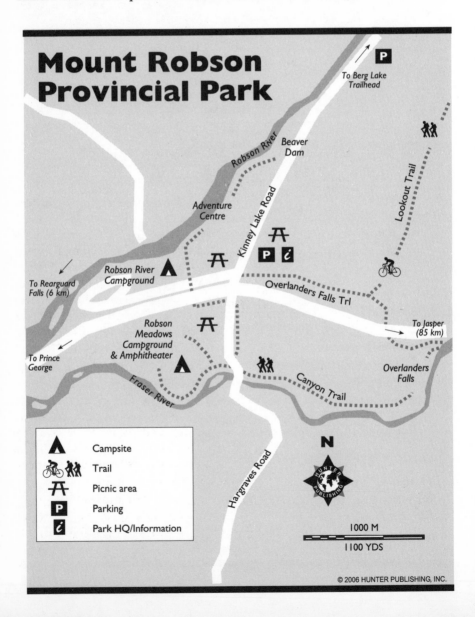

Mount Robson Provincial Park

To Berg Lake Trailhead

Robson River

Beaver Dam

Lookout Trail

Adventure Centre

Kinney Lake Road

Robson River Campground

To Rearguard Falls (6 km)

Overlanders Falls Trl

Robson Meadows Campground & Amphitheater

To Prince George

To Jasper (85 km)

Overlanders Falls

Fraser River

Canyon Trail

Hargraves Road

N

▲	Campsite
🚴🏃	Trail
⅂	Picnic area
P	Parking
i	Park HQ/Information

1000 M

1100 YDS

© 2006 HUNTER PUBLISHING, INC.

If the campsites by the road are full, shoulder your pack and try the **Rockingham Creek** crossing site: it's 3.7 miles from the trailhead (at the Yellowhead Lake boat launch). Head up another 6.8 miles and you're in beautiful alpine lakes.

For a week in the backcountry, take the **Berg Lake Trail**, 13.6 miles long, which links up with **Moose River Trail**, for a total of just over 50 miles. Along the way you pass more than a dozen glaciers. The trailhead is 1.5 miles past the Visitors Centre, where you must register before leaving.

The Canadian Rockies are one of the premier destinations in the world for outdoors people. We only have time to scratch the surface here. But let's close the chapter with this: we go through these parks all the time. Every time, we find something new to do, something we never expected.

For thorough coverage of the Rockies, pick up *Canadian Rockies Adventure Guide*.

Out of the Parks

■ The Yellowhead Highway from Jasper to Prince George

If you're coming out of the parks, through fantastic vistas in Banff and Jasper, the Yellowhead is going to be more than a little of a let-down. As it goes, the road from the parks to Prince George is good but fairly uninteresting, mostly following the course of the Fraser River. Farms and ranches dot the landscape, and the forests are a mixture of evergreen and deciduous trees. Be aware: there really isn't anywhere to stop and camp along this road. There are a couple of motels near the northern park entrances, but once you've left the park behind, you're pretty much stuck on the road until you get to Prince George. And after an hour or two of it, you're going to feel quite stuck.

You hit Highway 16 just a couple miles out of the park. To your left, as you're heading west, is **Mt. Terry Fox Provincial Park,** named after one of Canada's great heroes. Fox was born in Winnipeg and grew up in Port Coquitlam, near Vancouver. He was diagnosed with osteogenic sarcoma, bone cancer, at 18 and had his right leg amputated six inches above the knee in 1977. But instead of lying down and quitting, while he was still in the hospital, Terry decided to run across Canada to raise money for cancer research. This became what he called the **Marathon of Hope**.

As soon as he could, he started training. Eighteen months and 5,000 km (3,107 miles) later, he began his run across Canada in St. John's, Newfoundland on April 12, 1980. Not many people cared at first, but it didn't take all that long for this man – who really did run, with a kind of hop in his step – to start getting attention. Lots of it.

But Terry didn't make it all the way across the country. On September 1, after 143 days and 5,373 km (3,339 miles), Terry had to stop running, just outside of Thunder Bay, Ontario because cancer had appeared in his lungs. He died on June 28, 1981 at age 22.

But the work went on. To date, the annual Terry Fox Run, held in cities all over Canada and overseas, has raised more than $300 million for cancer research. His run, his refusal to quit, is still making a lot of lives better.

It's quite fitting that one of the most beautiful mountains in Canada is named after the guy. He towered above most of us.

The junction with Highway 5 is at Tete Jaune Cache (5 takes you south toward the Okanagan). **Tete Jaune Cache** has 150 residents and stretches out along the banks of the Fraser River. You can get gas, maybe something to eat, but don't count on it. If you can, stretch it out to McBride, 60 km farther east. The town has about 2,500 residents. Visitor Info is in the caboose at Robson Square Shopping Centre, ☎ 250-569-3366.

The trailhead for the **Goat River Trail** is off Loos Road, 15 km/nine miles west of McBride. This is eight- or nine-day hike that takes you to Route 97 and the Bowron Lakes Canoe circuit (see page 114). Know what you're doing, and let people know you're headed into the middle of nowhere. The **Fraser Headwaters Alliance**, ☎ 250-968-4490, fraserheadwaters.org can give you the latest on trail conditions.

For the next 200 km, until you get to Prince George, you're paralleling the Fraser. There are a few attractions along the way, including **Kakwa Recreation Area**, up a branch road just outside Kidd. You'll need a 4WD car to get the 87 km to Kakwa, but once you're there, you'll have the place to yourself. Fantastic wildlife country, with moose, black and brown bear, and more. **Purden Ski Village** is 60 km/37 miles east of Prince George. It's a T-bar hill and a double chair – nothing compared to what you get around Banff or in Whistler, but you could kill a winter day here. **Bowron River Rest Area**, five km/three miles farther up the road, is day-use only. What's interesting here is the state of the forest. There was a ferocious spruce beetle infestation here, so it was opened for logging to try and get the beetles under control before they spread. Now it's the largest silviculture plantation in the world, covering upwards of 130,000 acres.

The **Willow River Forest Interpretation Trail**, 34 km/21 miles out of PG, is a two-km/1.2-mile trail through a variety of ecosystems. It's a good place to see animals, get off the road and stretch your legs. Watch for moose 30 km/19miles out of Prince George. There's a raised platform off the north side of the highway over a good moose marsh. **Tabor Mountain Ski Resort** – another small one – is 20 km/12 miles outside of town. Popular with locals, it's got a triple chair, but a vertical drop of only about 800 feet.

Prince George comes up in a tangle of railway lines and industrial buildings. It's not the prettiest spot in the province, but it is the most important town in the northern reaches, and it's the last big town travelers for the Alaska Highway hit until they get to Fairbanks or Anchorage.

Chapter 5

The Alaska Highway

Dawson Creek

■ History

Dawson Creek is Mile Zero on the Alaska Highway, the place where construction started. Now it's the place where every Alaska Highway traveler stops to buy their first souvenirs of the road.

Dawson Creek and the surrounding area were first explored by a governmental boundary commission in 1879. Named for George Mercer Dawson, the area was first settled about 1912. Dawson was the kind of explorer who just doesn't exist anymore. He started off as a geologist, and in 1873-74 he set off to explore the 49th parallel from the Lake of the Woods to the Pacific, despite having bone tuberculosis. Instead of staying home and feeling sorry for himself, Dawson set out to see and study everything. If all that weren't enough, he's also credited with being "the father of Canadian Anthropology."

The town site of Dawson Creek was originally two miles west of its current location, but it was moved in 1930 to become the railhead for the Northern Alberta Railway. The railway became the life's blood of Dawson Creek. As the northernmost and westernmost railhead in Canada – called "the end of steel" – it was the only possible choice as the base for construction of the Alaska Highway. In 1941, the area's population was under 500; in 1942, it was 20,000, as soldiers and engineers moved in to begin the highway. Things have slacked off since then, and today about 11,000 people call the beginning of the Alaska Highway home.

■ Things to Do

We asked a local resident what there was to do in Dawson Creek; he replied, "Leave." It's not quite that bad, but there's no reason to plan a long stop here, either.

The main attraction in town is the cairn that says you are entering the Alaska Highway, the **Mile Zero Cairn**. To reach it, turn left when you en-

Dawson Creek, Mile 0.

ter the town from the south. The Mile Zero marker you see today is not the original; that one, which was in a slightly different location, was hit by a car. The new post is 10 feet tall and located at 102nd Ave. and 10th. It does not sit at the geographical start of the highway, but the city fathers decided it was better for business to plunk it smack dab in the center of downtown. Let's face it, there aren't a whole lot of other reasons to go downtown.

One Halloween, the sign was stolen and replaced by a wooden privy.

The other attraction in Dawson Creek is the **Info Centre** itself, at 900 Alaska Ave. (☎ 250-782-9595, www.tourismdawson creek.com). It's all housed in a converted railway station. It has the standard array of brochures – a good place to stock up to see what lies ahead. But more interesting in the same building is the lovely **Dawson Creek Station Museum**, housing railroad artifacts, recreating the look of a working station in the time before the highway, with a ticket office, baggage room, and stationmaster's quarters. The museum also has an excellent display of pioneer items and a geological and wildlife display – including serious mammoth bits, bigger than you're likely to see elsewhere. There's also a good photo history of the building of the highway, with a video shown at regular intervals. Both sides are well worth a look. Open May to September, 8 am to 7 pm; entrance fee, $1.

Outside the Info Centre, take a look at the train engine built in 1933. Next door is an old wooden grain elevator, now the **Grain Elevator Museum**, one of the last survivors of the many that once lined the tracks. Housed inside is an art gallery that features the works of locals, as well as traveling collections. It's open June to August, 10 am to 5 pm.

Dawson Creek is either your first or last chance – depending on which direction you're heading – to get an "I survived the Alaska Highway" T-shirt. A surprising amount of the town's economy depends upon the sale of "official" highway merchandise.

Two and a half miles south, on Highway 2, is the **Walter Wright Pioneer Village** (☎ 250-219-4714), open May to August; suggested donation, $5. At the village you'll find old pioneer buildings and an array of farm machinery. Tours ($10) are available from the end of May through Labor Day, 10 am to 6 pm. If you're wondering what it was like to live here a hundred years ago, this will give you some idea.

■ Out & About

Dawson Creek is part of the Peace River drainage, so there are some great hiking and boating opportunities around. **Bear Mountain Hike** is 7.5 fairly easy miles (it's used by cross-country skiers in winter). Access is 3.7 miles south of town by the bypass road turn-off – the same turnoff trucks carrying hazardous cargo are supposed to use. If you've got a day to kill, take the Hart Highway to the Heritage Highway past Tumbler Ridge; turn left (away from Chetwynd) and take the Quintette Coal Mine Exit. If all this sounds complicated, the payoff is worth it. From Quintette there are turnoffs into the **Kinuseo Falls Provincial Park.** Take the Murray River left fork (there are signs), jump on the trail, and hike 21.5 miles back to Kinuseo Falls. It's too far for heavy hiker traffic, and the reward is a waterfall that's higher, at 225 feet, than Niagara.

There are a bunch of hikes around **Tumbler Ridge**. It's best to ask around town for suggestions and detailed directions. The Info Centre does have a handout on the hikes, but it won't tell you much. Easiest to reach – although not to take on – is **Bald Spot**. The trailhead is right on the highway, just past Tumbler Ridge. It's two km/1.2 miles straight up, but you get views that leave you gasping, if you have any breath left. Much easier is the five-km/three-mile hike to the **Flatbed Pools**, with the trailhead a kilometer southeast of Tumbler Ridge. There are a bunch of canyon and waterfall hikes in the area, including a 10-km/six-mile hike to **Bergeron Falls**, which, at 330 feet, is the biggest fall in the area. Look for the trailhead at the gravel pit, 16 km/10 miles northeast of Tumbler Ridge.

■ Food

The stop of choice for lobster, pasta, hamburgers, gourmet coffee, and a small dose of history, is the **Alaska Café**, in business since 1936, at 10209 10th St. Prices range from $7 up. They've also got steak and seafood. It's really the only restaurant you need in town, but if they're full, try the **Mile Zero Café**, 1091 Alaska Ave.

■ Accommodations

The **Lodge Motor Inn and Café**, at 1317 Alaska Ave., has clean and comfortable rooms. $$. ☎ 250-782-4837 or 800-935-3003, www.lodgemotorinn.com.

The **Dew Drop Inn**, downtown, ☎ 250-782-7998, www.alaskahotel.com, is great for those on a serious budget: rooms start at $35.

The town also has a **Ramanda**, ☎ 800-2-RAMADA, at Mile 1, and a **Super 8**, ☎ 888-482-8884, 1440 Alaska Ave. $$-$$$.

Camping

Mile 0 Campground (☎ 250-782-2590) is at Mile 1 on the highway. The 85 sites are nice and grassy. **Northern Lights RV Park** (☎ 250-782-9433) is another half-mile down the road.

Dawson Creek to Fort St. John

The highway starts off as a good two-lane road, with wide shoulders on both sides. The surface is smooth, and the driving is easy. There's also, though, not a whole lot of interest right along here – a lot of factories and strip mall kinds of places – so you can move towards the better stuff farther north pretty quickly.

Two miles out of Dawson Creek, there's a repeater station for the Cantel telephone/telegraph lines. When this line was first put in, it stretched from Alberta to Fairbanks and was one of the world's longest open-wire circuits.

■ Kiskatinaw Provincial Park

At Mile 17, there's a turnoff for Kiskatinaw Provincial Park. The park contains a section of the original Alaska Highway, which was abandoned for a straighter, easier path. You can follow this road for 4.5 miles, joining today's Highway again after crossing the Kiskatinaw River, over an old wooden bridge that offers dramatic views of the river. The bridge was the first of its kind built in Canada; it's the only wooden bridge still on the highway – old or new sections – today. It's a **three-span trestle bridge**, and it curves nine degrees over its length. You've really got to wonder just what the engineers were thinking. Just before crossing the river, there is a nice campground, the Kiskatinaw Provincial Park, with 28 graveled sites, some overlooking the river. Water is available – boil it before you drink – and there are outhouses that adhere to the spotless BC standards. The road is rather tight inside the campground, so larger RVs should use caution. You can fish for grayling on the river, but prepare to be eaten alive by mosquitoes.

The Kiskatinaw River is popular with canoeists, but only experienced paddlers should try it during high water levels. The river hasn't been graded, but figure it at least at a Class III. Not a bad place for some practice with your rodeo kayak.

■ Peace Island Regional Park

 The road enters Peace River Valley, with sweeping views to the northeast. More camping is available at Mile 34, in Peace Island Regional Park, on an island in the middle of the river connected to the shore by a causeway. There are 20 sites, open from May to September. There is no room for RVs, and you'll have to supply your own firewood. Every year in August, they hold the **World Gold Panning Championship** here.

> **WARNING:** There are two dams on the river, and the water levels can change dramatically, so use caution.

■ Taylor

 The town of Taylor is at Mile 35. Before the highway, Taylor was a ferry town for travelers crossing the Peace River. During WWII, the Alcan Ferry was used here to help transport the Army while the bridge was under construction; it was the main transport link connecting the north and south. The original Peace River suspension bridge, the longest on the highway, collapsed in 1957. From this piece of road, you can see a long suspension bridge used to carry a gas pipeline.

Taylor **Visitor Information** is on the north side of the highway in a small log cabin (☎ 250-789-9015). Taylor is the official town sponsor for the World Individual Gold Panning Championships in August, held back down the road at Peace River. Novices are welcome, but if you're planning to come for the event, remember the town overflows and you'll probably have to commute from a distant campground. Because of the river and its rich soil deposits, there are excellent market gardens around town; in the summer months Taylor is a great place to stock up on vegetables. It's only other claim to fame is the "world's largest golf ball," an old fuel tank that's been painted. Hey, winters can be long up here.

Taylor is a good pullout point if you want to put a canoe into the Peace River. You can put in at Hudson's Hope, at the old ferry landing, and then take out at Taylor, the Halfway Bridge, or Clayhurst. It's a one- to four-day trip, not getting much beyond Class II. You can set up your tent on river islands.

■ The Peace River Area

The Peace River is one of the first shots you get at wild Northern territory. The Peace runs on a slight arc, one that is followed by roads roughly from beyond Taylor to Hudson's Hope. Farther west, the river runs into Dinosaur Lake, which eventually flows into the huge Williston Lake. If you've got a canoe or kayak, you can happily spend weeks out here without seeing anybody; and when you get tired of paddling, you can hunt for fossils on shore. There is an endless chain of rivers and parks to explore. Get topo maps in Fort St. John at **BC Maps** (10600 100th St.), stock up on freeze-dried chow, and head out. It's mostly Class II paddling, with some nastier stretches.

 An outstanding brochure, ***Peace River Alaska Highway Canoeing***, is available in local tourist spots. Highlights include the Heather-Dina Lakes circuit, outside of Mackenzie. There's a loop of six lakes with only small portages required. See the Mackenzie section (below) for full details.

There's also great hiking along the rivers. We've listed hikes from the towns closest to the trailhead.

Fort St. John

■ History

 One of the oldest non-Native settlements in mainland BC, Fort St. John has been bounced from pillar to post along the Peace River, as the fortunes of the Hudson's Bay Company rose and fell. It was a headquarters for the fur trade from its establishment in 1794 into the early 1800s, and then became a full-fledged city with the influx of workers for the highway, when it was one of the two biggest camps and the field headquarters for the eastern sector of construction. Before the highway, the only way north from here was on dog and pack trails. The area, which was described by early surveyors as "one big morass," became completely impassable with spring thaw.

Today, Fort St. John calls itself the "Energy Capital of British Columbia," due to the large oil and natural gas fields in the area.

■ Things to Do

As in Dawson Creek, it's better if you don't ask the locals what to do. One answer we got was, "work and go to bars." For the visitor who isn't working or drinking, most of the attractions are in one place: at the **Info Centre**, which is easy to spot since it's behind a 140-foot oil derrick at 9323 100th St. (☎ 250-785-3030, www.fortstjohchamber. com). Hours are 8 am to 8 pm. The building houses a nice museum (admission, $4) with an excellent display of artifacts from the Hudson's Bay Company and an interesting case of objects the army issued to highway workers. They've also got all the usual items of area history and prehistory, but it's better arranged than most local museums, with reconstructed rooms of early homesteaders and the first store in Fort St. John. There's also a nice little museum shop.

For good views of the Peace River Valley, drive south on 100th St. to the end of the road, at **Lookout Park**. There are good mountain biking trails in the park.

Canadian Forest Products offers a tour of how they reforest after clearing timber. It's free, but you need to call for a reservation (☎ 250-785-8906). If you're tired of looking at deforestation, you can see what comes next here. There's also the **Fish Creek Community Forest** just north of town, beside the Northern Lights College. Self-guided tours offer a look at the local flora and fauna.

■ Food

Jade's Garden, at 10108 101st Ave., offers Chinese specialties and a quiet atmosphere. Takeout is available. Dinners from $4 to $15. **Wilson's Pizza**, 10503 100th Ave., has Italian dishes in the same price range.

■ Accommodations

The town is unusual because it's actually just as full in winter – when the oil and gas surveyors appear – as it is in summer. Most hotels in the area are at the cheap end of things, $50 to $75 per room. There's rarely a shortage of places to stay, even in summer.

Northwoods Inn (☎ 250-787-1616), 10627 Alaska Rd., has a coffee shop and lounge, $$. It also has a cabaret and pub. The **Four Seasons Motor Inn** (☎ 250-785-6706), downtown, is simple and cheap. $$.

For something a little more luxurious and corporate, there's a **Best Western** in town, ☎ 888-388-9408, and a **Ramada**, ☎ 250-785-9255, both $$-$$$.

The **Alexander Mackenzie Inn** is close to the same price, with rooms from $$. ☎ 250-785-8364.

Camping

The most convenient – though far from scenic – place to camp is **Fort St. John Centennial RV Park**, right behind the Info Centre. It's open May to September, and some sites have hookups. There's lots of grass, but no trees, and if you're looking to camp, it's nicer to drive the six miles north to Charlie Lake (see below).

Fort St. John to Fort Nelson

Camping is available at Mile 49.5, **Beatton Provincial Park**, on the east end of Charlie Lake. It's one of the oldest provincial parks, and the lake has good fishing for walleye and pike. In winter, there's excellent cross-country skiing and ice fishing. The park has a boat launch, a playground, and swimming. There are 37 sites, open May to October.

Still on Charlie Lake, there's **Charlie Lake Provincial Park**, with 58 sites. It's very quiet, in a beautifully treed area, right on the edge of the lake. There's water, a kitchen shelter and a nice picnic area, plus a .7-mile hiking trail. There are also lots of mosquitoes, and some of the spaces are very tight; if you're in an RV, be prepared to back up. The park campground is a popular end point for mountain bikers, so watch out as you walk.

For canoers, Charlie Lake has excellent, flatwater paddling. There are quite a few spots around the lake where you can get out of the boat and explore. Although there's some heavy algae in late summer, you'll find good fishing for walleye, northern pike, and perch.

Charlie Lake is the site of some of the oldest settlements in BC. It was on the migration trail, and the animals got narrowed into the valley. According to archaeologists, this was the place to be even before the ice age.

Along the highway, the area is pastureland punctuated by forests. It was all combed for gold, but the miners came up empty and headed farther north. As the highway does the same thing, the road conditions improve slightly.

Just past Mile 72 is what was once the Beatton River Flight Strip, one of the four gravel airstrips built during Highway construction to provide emergency services for the military.

■ Wonowon

 Wonowon is really at Mile 102. Not much more than a Husky gas station and a café/hotel today, during WWII, Wonowon was a control station, a military checkpoint set up to make sure no Japanese were trying to head north along the road.

You'll find a different kind of danger along Mile 110. There are a lot of natural gasworks in the area, and signs are posted: "Dangerous Gas Area – no parking or camping." Check in Wonowon for the latest details.

More gas – the safe kind for your car – is available at Mile 143, at **Pink Mountain Campsite & RV Park** (☎ 250-774-5133). RV sites and tent sites are available, and there are basic cabins.

There's good fishing in the **Halfway River** in August and September. Rig your lures for lake trout and Dolly Varden. For paddlers, take the turnoff at Mile 147 to the bridge (about 10 miles). The upper portion of the river is a Class III; the lower, a Class II, suitable for intermediate paddlers.

 From here to the end of the Trutch Mountain stretch – about the next 40 miles – you're in serious moose territory.

Mile 148 is what was called Suicide Hill when the highway went in, as it was the most treacherous hill on the road. Travelers found this greeting posted at the beginning of the hill: "Prepare to meet thy maker."

Mile 168.5 has a turnoff road (which is rutted) to the **Sikanni River Falls**. Ten and a half miles in (where the road starts to widen) is a trailhead that takes you down a short hike to steep cliffs and some lovely waterfalls. Plenty of hiking trails thread around the falls and canyon, and you have a chance to see goats or bears. It's worth a quick side trip.

There's camping at **Buckinghorse Provincial Park** at Mile 173. The park offers quiet sites along the river.

At Mile 176 is the beginning of the **Trutch Mountain** bypass, where a part of the original highway is visible to the east. The original road climbed to a pass of over 4,100 feet, the second highest pass along the route first laid down. As soon as the engineers had time (well, about 40 years later), they found a more level route, which is what you travel on today.

Prophet River Provincial Park, Mile 217, offers a nice hike from the campground to the river; but it's in a bear area, so be sure to make some noise as you walk. Gas, food, and lodging are available at the tiny settlement of Prophet River, at Mile 233.

Camp at Mile 265 in the **Andy Bailey Provincial Par**k, seven miles off the highway. With 35 campsites, a boat launch, swimming, and fishing for pike, the park is deep in a lovely spruce forest, but the road is narrow, and there is only one place wide enough to turn an RV around.

The highway crosses the Muskwa River (the name means "bear" in Slave Indian) at Mile 281. This is the lowest point on the highway, at 1,000 feet.

Fort Nelson

■ History

Named for the famous British Admiral Lord Nelson, Fort Nelson was established in 1805, as a fur trading post. The word "fort" in the town name – or in Fort St. John and many other small towns – is appropriate. The fur trading posts were truly forts, designed to hold off the enemy in a siege. Depending on the area, Indian attacks on the trading posts were common. A more serious danger, though, were attacks from a rival trading company. In the historical annals of the Hudson's Bay Company are countless stories of attacks by rival companies, such as the North-West Company, and by independent traders (called peddlers), who took advantage of HBC's policy of letting the furs come to them. While the HBC cowered behind walls, the independent traders were opening up Western Canada.

With a population today of around 4,000, Fort Nelson is the biggest city between Fort St. John and Whitehorse. Once fur trading halted, the city depended for years upon the world's largest chopstick manufacturing company for its economic survival. The chopsticks were made from the huge poplar forests that surround the city; they were sent to the Orient, where each set was used once and thrown away. Take a good, long look at the trees while you drive around. These are the survivors of years of government-subsidized deforestation. Once the subsidy was gone, the factory packed up, causing a nightmare for the town's economy, until they found somebody else to buy the trees.

The **Info Centre** is on the highway, at the north edge of town, in the rec center. It's small, but helpful. The staff can often arrange tours of local businesses; check with them if you see a place that interests you. They're open 8 am to 8 pm in summer. ☎ 250-774-6400, www.northernrockies.org.

■ Things to Do

 Fort Nelson Heritage Museum is next to the Info Centre, and it's open from 10 am to 9 pm daily. Admission is $5 for adults, $3 for kids and seniors. Inside, they show the Trail of '42 video, an excellent work compiled from government films on the construction of the highway. It's the best look at just how difficult it was to put the road through: vehicles swallowed by mud, workers freezing, mosquitoes as thick as clouds. The soldiers – more than 2,000 of them were here at the peak of construction – felt incredibly isolated, and it shows on their faces.

Another interesting display in the museum is an exhibit explaining the steps to build a birch bark canoe – a necessary skill for a Native or a trapper (if it whets your appetite, get a copy of John McPhee's book, *Survival of the Birch Bark Canoe*). Out behind the museum is a reconstruction of a trapper's cabin and some old shop fronts. In the front and side yards there are vintage cars and construction vehicles restored by the museum's curator, Marl Brown. Each one is in running condition.

■ Seasonal Activities

 During the summer months, Fort Nelson presents a **Welcome Visitor** program at Town Square, just east of the Info Centre. These free programs include slides and discussions of the Northern lifestyle, including the interesting quirk of grass burning – you burn the grass so it will grow back greener. Unfortunately, this activity also tends to take a few barns and garages with it, keeping the local fire department jumping. The programs are run from May 15 to August 15, at 6:45 pm, Monday through Thursday. ☎ 250-774-6400.

■ Food

 Dan's Neighborhood Pub, at Mile 300 on the highway, is the most popular place with the locals. It's got a lively pub and the best food and drinks in town. Steaks, seafood, even vegetarian fare, from $6 to $20.

Inside the **Provincial Motel** there's a restaurant with good stir-fry and other Chinese and Western dishes. Prices range from $6 to $25. The **Northern Deli**, downtown, is the place for cheap food; also the place to pack up on cheeses for the road ahead.

■ Accommodations

 The Bluebell Inn, ☎ 774-6961, has nice rooms, some with kitchenettes. $$. 4203 50th Ave. S. Another choice is the somewhat fancier **Woodlands Inn**, ☎ 250-774-6669, 888-966-3466, www.woodlandsinn.bc.ca, which has basic rooms from $$, working up towards suites at twice the price.

There is a **Ramada**, ☎ 866-774-2844, and a **Super 8**, ☎ 888-888-5591.

Camping

Near the museum is the **Westend Campground**, with 110 camping spaces in a nicely wooded lot. Showers, laundromat, and ice are available. It's the only campground with full services in the area, but the spaces are small and it feels crowded. ☎ 250-774-2340.

Fort Nelson to Muncho Lake

The road worsens noticeably in this section of the highway, but the scenery is beautiful enough to take your mind off any troubles. The old Alcan is visible in some spots to the north. The old road, even more curved than the new one, is being eaten up by vegetation.

 HIGHWAY TIP: Allow some extra time for driving this section; although the narrow turns and gravel patches will slow you down, the photo opportunities will slow you down even more.

Leaving Fort Nelson, you pass through large groves of poplars. Early in the summer, the road is also lined with wildflowers. Off in the distance, to the south, the Rockies are visible, snowcapped year-round.

At Mile 320, the road begins a long, steep climb to the top of **Steamboat Mountain** (3,500 feet). This piece of road seems to be under construction almost every summer. Grades through the area reach 10%, and the higher you get, the better the views get. This is especially true around Miles 348 to 350, just before you start heading down the mountain at Mile 352.

Take the pullout at Mile 350 for a lovely view down through the Muskwa River Valley and over to the Rockies.

The down side of the mountain is in worse shape than the up side. The road gets worse, the turns get sharper. There are glimpses of the river valley through the thick forest, and at Mile 361 you can see Indian Head Mountain dead ahead, its profile formed by erosion caused by receding glaciers. Another erosion feature, Teetering Rock, is on the horizon to the north, at Mile 363.

If it's late in the afternoon or looking like it might storm, consider pulling off to camp for the night around the Tetsa River.

> **WEATHER ALERT:** Farther ahead, at Stone Mountain and Muncho Lake, the weather can turn mean very quickly. Especially for tenters, if there are dark clouds in the sky, stop down here.

Tetsa River Provincial Park is at Mile 365. It's quite a nice spot, with some sites having good river views. It's also pretty quiet and rarely crowded. Pitch the tent, park the camper, and go for a walk along the river banks. This is kind of an undiscovered treasure along the highway. There's good fishing for grayling and Dolly Varden.

You enter **Stone Mountain Provincial Park** at Mile 371.5. The next section of road is one of the most hazardous on the entire Highway. For the next 100 miles, the road travels through the habitat of the stone sheep. The sheep themselves are only an occasional hazard. They come down near the road to look for salt. The true danger is people stopping their vehicles on blind curves to take pictures.

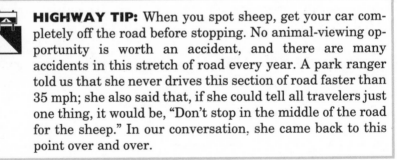

HIGHWAY TIP: When you spot sheep, get your car completely off the road before stopping. No animal-viewing opportunity is worth an accident, and there are many accidents in this stretch of road every year. A park ranger told us that she never drives this section of road faster than 35 mph; she also said that, if she could tell all travelers just one thing, it would be, "Don't stop in the middle of the road for the sheep." In our conversation, she came back to this point over and over.

The government is trying to solve the problem by putting in artificial salt licks, with overlook points, but so far their efforts to move both the sheep and the road hazards have not been successful.

STONE SHEEP

Stone sheep are considered to be a geographical variation on the better known Dall sheep, their northern cousins. Stone sheep are brown, with white patches around the muzzle and rump; Dall sheep are a creamy white color, except for a few dark hairs occasionally found along the spine and tail. A full-grown stone sheep male averages just over three feet at the shoulder and weighs 200 pounds; a Dall male is about the same height, but as much as 40 pounds lighter. Both varieties live on grasses and sedge, and are preyed upon by lynx, wolverine, wolves, and grizzly bears. The sheep prefer to live in high, rocky areas, where they have a good view of anything coming up at them.

The sheep in this area are very used to cars; they will not bolt when you stop. Sometimes, they even begin to come closer, and this is a good time to drive away. They are not usually being aggressive, just curious. But curiosity draws them into the middle of the road. There are frequent pullouts in the area. For everyone's safety, get to one before stopping your vehicle.

From here, the road narrows, but it is in good condition as it follows the rocky-bottomed Tetsa River. The banks of the river are lined with forest.

The road climbs to Summit Lake, and at Mile 392 is the **Summit Lake Lodge**, offering gas, food, and lodging. The lodge is known for its enormous, delicious cinnamon rolls. Also good burgers. ☎ 250-232-7531.

The view from here is of the barren Stone Mountain Range, with a few peeks of the peaks of the Rockies behind. Summit Lake lies at an altitude of 2,680 feet; the mountains around it climb to over 7,000 feet. The most dramatic of these is Mt. St. George, at 7,419 feet. On a very still day, it is reflected in the blue-green waters of the lake with dramatic effect. The lake's color is caused by copper-oxide leaching into the water from the limestone bedrock. It's worth spending a day here just to watch the water's color change as the light hits it from different angles.

Summit Lake Campground, right on the edge of the lake, offers 28 sites in a clean, graveled area. The campground itself isn't exciting – in fact, considering the location, it's pretty bleak, just a gravel pad jammed in between the road and the mountains – but the scenery around it can't be beat. Watch for sudden weather changes. If the wind kicks up, you could easily find your tent in the lake. There's a boat launch in the campground – no boats with motors allowed. Fish for lake trout, grayling, whitefish, and rainbow.

There are quite a few **hiking trails** in the area, two of them beginning right at the campground: a 2.5-mile round-trip hike to **Summit Peak,** where there are good alpine views (plan for up to five hours to make it there and back), and a 3.5-mile hike to **Flower Springs**, which offers alpine lakes, flowers, and waterfalls. For the more ambitious, there's hiking along the **MacDonald Creek Valley**. A one- to three-day hike takes you through prime moose, caribou, and sheep country.

Another option is to hike through the pristine **Wokkpash Valley, Forlorn Gorge**, and the **Stepped Lakes**. Access to the trail is at Mile 400, on

Churchill Mine Rd. It's 12 miles back, and only four-wheel-drive vehicles will make it past the river. Check at the Fort St. John park office – ☎ 250-787-3407 – before you go. It's a 15.5-mile trail with an elevation change of nearly 4,000 feet. Figure on at least two days.

There's an even longer option, 43.5 miles, which takes you from MacDonald Creek along the valley, then back to the Creek and the highway. Don't go without a topo map. The astounding hoodoos are what makes these hikes popular.

HOODOOS

Hoodoos are created by rain wash. During a storm, each droplet of rain impacts at about 20 mph. The hoodoos are eroded out of glacial debris, soft stone left behind by the receding glaciers. As the rain hits this, the softest stone erodes, revealing boulders beneath. The boulder then provides a cap for the pillar, protecting the softer rock underneath. The ground around the boulder continues to erode, leaving a pillar. When looking at a group of hoodoos, you can see some with the cap, and some that have not yet found the cap and so are less defined. Generally, hoodoos are found in semi-arid regions, at the edges of steep slopes. Hoodoos are easily seen at Mile 394, where there's a very short viewing hike.

Wokkpash Protected Area, which is just south of Stone Mountain Provincial Park, covers 93,000 acres of pure wilderness: no road, no nothing. If you hike into it, know what you're doing, and be sure to take all proper bear precautions.

Just 112 miles from the lowest point of the highway is its highest point: Mile 392, altitude 4,250 feet at the summit. Engineers had to blast through rock to make this pass.

Camp at **One Fifteen Creek Provincial Park**, where there's fishing for Dolly Varden and a close-up look at beaver dams and lodges.

Mile 422 has the **Toad River Lodge** (☎ 250-232-5401), with gas, café, and motel, $$, and okay campsites. They've also got a collection of more than 6,000 hats hanging from the ceiling. It's a good place to stop for lunch, and the store has a small assortment of CDs, their biggest sellers. "You know how often we get told drivers are sick and tired of listening to the same dozen records?"

Muncho Lake

Muncho Lake Provincial Park, which covers nearly 90,000 hectares, begins at Mile 427; at 428, there is a view of Folded Mountain, an interesting combination of erosion and plate tectonics.

HIGHWAY TIP: For the next 37 miles, a "watch for wildlife" warning is in effect on the road. The warning is primarily for stone sheep, but there are also a lot of moose in the area, as well as caribou, elk, black bear, mountain goat, mule deer, and the very occasional grizzly bear. The road narrows, and in many places there is no shoulder; do not stop on the road. Also, watch for landslides. The mountains are steep and treeless, and can come down without warning.

The river running alongside the road is the Toad, headed north. In June, this is an excellent area for wildflower viewing, especially wild roses, sweet pea, and yellow daisies. You'll also see yellow lady's slipper and bog orchids, one of the northern species of orchid.

Muncho Lake itself comes into view at Mile 454. The lake is 7.5 miles long and has virtually no shore; it just drops off, as deep as 200 meters in places. Highway crews were practically standing in the water trying to cut the road through. Like Summit Lake, Muncho Lake's brilliant color is caused by copper-oxide leaching in from the bedrock. But at Muncho Lake, the color is deeper, more arresting. Staring into it is one of the highlights of a trip on the highway. Best photo ops are at the viewpoint at the north end of the lake. Along the way, you'll pass several alluvial fans, evidence of the great forces of water and ice that formed the lake.

"Muncho" means "big lake" in the Tagish language. It's the longest lake in the Northern Rockies – technically in the Terminal Range of the Rockies, which end near here (or begin, depending upon your point of view), 1,850 miles from their other end in New Mexico. The next range of mountains north, the Mackenzies, are geologically quite different, and also have much longer lakes – Teslin Lake is about 80 miles long.

■ Things to Do

The best activities at Muncho Lake are on the water. **Canoe** and **boat** rentals are available at the hotels, as are boat excursions. The lake offers good fishing, too. You can catch trout, grayling, Dolly Varden, and whitefish. In July, try your luck at the annual **Muncho Lake Fishing Derby**. The lake has Class I paddling, suitable for a novice, but be careful of sudden strong winds.

There's also abundant **hiking** in the area; ask at the hotels or restaurants for a trip to fit your ambition. Remember the bears, and be sure to make some noise. A couple of trails right off the highway lead back and pretty much straight up.

There are a couple of good, easy, short hikes. **Strawberry Flats** starts at the campground of the same name, goes three km/1.8 miles (one way) along the old Alaska Highway, for views of the lake. **Sheep Flats** is a four-km/2.4-mile round trip that follows an alluvial fan to a salt lick popular with stone sheep. If you didn't see any standing in the middle of the road, this may be your chance. The same goes for the **Trout River Mineral Lick Trail,** which is a 1.5-km/one-mile circuit right off the road that takes you to another favorite lick spot.

■ Accommodations

There are three motels, and each of them offers campsites. There are also places for campers only. All of these fill early. Make reservations at least a day ahead.

HOTEL PRICING
Prices are in US dollars.
under $50. . . . . $
$50-$100 . . . . $$
$100-$150 . . . . . . $$$
above $150 . . . . . $$$$

The nicest of them is the **Northern Rockies Lodge**, at Mile 462. They've got beautiful cabins on the water's edge, $$ There are also rooms in the lodge – the largest log building in BC – with rooms from $$-$$$. There are also 30 camping sites, with electricity, water, and sewer available. There's a small store, a fantastic restaurant, a gas station, and a laundromat. The lodge rents canoes and boats ($20 to $40 for five hours). They also run long tours into the mountains, do fly-in fishing excursions, and offer flight-seeing trips. ☎ 250-776-3482 or 800-663-5269, www.northern-rockies-lodge.com. One caveat: this place gets heavy European traffic, and it's really geared towards German tourists. This means it's a great place to buy a schnitzel lunch, but they may also be full up from package tours.

J & H Wilderness Resort, 1.5 miles farther down the road, at Mile 463. The motel is small (doubles go for $60); the campground has more than 70 good sites by the lake, hookups available. There's a laundromat, showers, and a licensed dining room. Boat rental is available. ☎ 250-776-3453.

Finally, there is **Muncho Lake Lodge** at Mile 463. It's open May to October. $$, camping sites have hookups and showers are available. The nice thing here is for tenters is the huge chunk of lakefront property; you can pitch pretty much anywhere you want. Some great views. They've also got a restaurant, laundromat, and gas station. ☎ 250-776-3456.

There are two camping-only sites at Muncho Lake: **Provincial Park Campground** at Strawberry Flats (Mile 457) and **MacDonald Campground** (Mile 462.5). The two provide only 30 sites in one of the most beautiful spots in Canada. Both campgrounds have boat launches. MacDonald fills up faster, but you can't get any closer to the lake.

Muncho Lake to Watson Lake

After briefly following the lake, the highway begins to climb and the landscape gets a little greener as the road heads off along the Trout River. Behind the front range of mountains you'll get glimpses of higher, rocky and snow-covered peaks.

At Mile 473 is a turnoff for a mineral lick. From the turnoff parking lot, there is a short, uneven trail leading to an overlook. If you haven't seen any sheep or other beasts so far, try here, especially in the early morning. It's a little less than a mile loop. But around here, animals are much more often in the road than they are at the lick. Still, this is a nice place to get out and stretch your legs while looking at the limestone, dolomite, and shale formations.

> **NOTE:** *The area code is 250 until you cross the Yukon border at Mile 590, Contact Creek, when it changes to 867.*

At Mile 490, the road begins to follow the **Liard River.** This river can be taken in a canoe, from Muncho Lake all the way to Liard Hot Springs. The highway hugs the river for the simple reason that it made laying out the lines a lot easier for the highway engineers. The Liard River itself drains into the Mackenzie River, which ultimately drains into the Arctic Ocean. The Liard River Bridge is the last suspension bridge on the highway. It's a local favorite spot to fish for grayling, and if you look a hundred yards or so upstream of the bridge, you'll see some ruins of old squatter cabins.

■ Liard Hot Springs

Located at Mile 496, Liard Hot Springs Provincial Park is a great place to soak out some of your sore driving muscles. There are two pools for a bath. The first, Alpha (up to 127° F), is about a quarter-mile from the parking lot. The second pool, Beta (a cooler 104° F – good hot bath temperature), is about the same distance from Alpha. Both pools are accessed by wooden walkways. The Beta pool is more for swimming than soaking. Both pools offer changing rooms and bathing platforms. Park rules require that all bathers wear something, but they don't say what. If you didn't pack a bathing suit, just jump in with your clothes on.

During the peak summer months, a ranger is on constant duty near the path to the pools who will answer your questions about the area, or just fill you in on details about the wildlife. Moose, bear, and deer also like the pools, although they'll stay away when people are around. Nature walks are given daily, and they're worth taking. The flora around the hot springs is like nowhere else on the highway; it's almost tropical. Look for ferns and orchids, as well as a few carnivorous plants, including sundew and butterwort. The hot springs have caused a microclimate, the warm air allowing plants and animals to thrive that would otherwise freeze this far north. More than 250 species of plant are found around the springs, at least 14 of them much farther north than their normal range. There have been sightings of 28 mammal species and more than 100 species of bird here. A short path leads back from the pools to the hanging gardens, where a cascading spring has made a beautiful tiered area.

The hot springs have been a popular stopping point since the first French trappers came through looking for fur. The word "liard" is French for poplar, a nod to the trees that surround the area. In the days of the gold rush, miners would pause here to gather strength. During construction of the highway, being posted to this area was a prime assignment, since it was the only warm area during the winter. Workers bathed daily here, and once a week the springs were cleared for women to use.

There is a campground near the entrance to the springs with 53 sites, and they fill up early.

Just past the springs is **Liard Hotsprings Lodge** (☎ 250-776-7349, www. liardhotsprings.ca), rooms $$, campsites nearby, open year-round. This is a nice log-cabin lodge, very clean and comfortable.

Leaving Liard, the road is narrow and there is a lot of broken pavement. This area is frequently under construction, but the wild roses offer a distraction from the gravel, which is mostly hard-packed; there is quite a lot of washboarding in some places. The road climbs and drops, with some very steep hills.

At Mile 514, there's a turnoff for a hike down to **Smith Falls**. You can get a look at the two-tiered falls from the road.

Mile 543 is the Coal River Bridge, where the Coal meets the Liard. There was a forest fire here not long ago, and it's interesting to see how the woods are regenerating.

There's a turnoff for "do it yourself camping" here – a few fire rings and a clearing – and you can hike around the rapids of the Liard. The river, which is really moving at this point, has thrown trees as far as 75 feet from the normal flow level. You can climb around on the rocks here, which is dangerous but a lot of fun.

Contact Creek Bridge, at Mile 588, is one of the points where the highway construction crews met up, connecting two sections of the road. They met here on September 25, 1942, and there's a turnout with an informational plaque on the spot.

Food, gas, and lodging are available at Mile 590; gas is two or three cents a gallon cheaper here than it is farther up the road at Watson Lake.

By this point, you've already crossed into the Yukon several times; there's no official notice of that fact, other than a lone sign telling you that it's the law to drive with your headlights on.

 HIGHWAY TIP: Driving with your headlights on is a good idea on most of the roads in the North; a dark car is almost invisible against a background of forest.

Altogether, the road crosses back and forth over the Yukon/BC border seven times. The road is poor overall, with a lot of dirt, gravel, washboarding, and construction to Watson Lake.

There's a **Yukon Government Campground** at Mile 615 with 55 sites, some by the lake, where you can fish for grayling, trout, and pike, and there's a boat launch and good swimming in the lake.

There's a turnoff for Lower Post at Mile 626. It's an old Hudson's Bay Company trading post, but no services are available today. By the turnoff is the **Lucky Lake** picnic area, which has water slides into the lake. Leading from the area is a two-mile trail, an easy walk heading up Liard Canyon. Across the river is a cabin dedicated to Robert Campbell, said to be the first white man to enter the Yukon.

Watson Lake

Before the advent of the white traders and trappers, this was the home of the Kaska Indians. The lake was originally known as Fish Lake, and it's still a great place for fishing.

■ History

The first settlement was Sylvester's Landing, part of a series of trading posts. By the 1870s, with the discovery of gold, the area was booming, and the city got its new name from Frank Watson, a hopeful miner from Yorkshire, England. He was on his way to the goldfields, but stopped here, became a trader, and married a Native.

In the 1930s, mail planes began to land on Watson Lake, which grew as a fueling stop, but the real boom came when the Alaska Highway construction began and Watson Lake became a supply center. The airfield was upgraded to handle fighter traffic headed for Russia along the Northwest Staging Route.

Today, Watson Lake, at Mile 621 on the Alaska Highway, thrives on logging and tourism; its population of around 2,000 makes it the third largest city in the Yukon.

■ Things to Do

The big attraction in town is the **Alaska Highway Interpretive Centre**. Just look for the signs and the RVs at the junction of the Alcan and the Robert Campbell Highway. The center is open from 8 am to 8 pm, mid-May to mid-September (☎ 867-536-7469). Inside you'll find tourist information, a photo mural showing construction of the highway, and a real Army tent, set up the way it was for the workers. A three-projector slide show on the history of the highway is shown at regular intervals. The show is unique to this center, and well worth watching. The center also broadcasts a visitor radio show on 96.1 FM.

The Alaska Highway

Outside the center is the famous **Signpost Forest**, which now boasts more signs than any sane person wants to keep track of, and is growing at a rate of a couple of thousand a year. It was started in 1942 by a homesick GI named Carl Lindley, from Danville, Illinois, who put up a sign pointing to his hometown. Other workers followed suit. Maintaining the tradition, anyone with a hammer and nail can put up a sign today. A part of the forest was taken down and displayed at Expo 86, in Vancouver, at the Yukon Pavilion. Gotta admit, we find the whole thing a little creepy on an existential level, especially the way the number of signs has boomed over the 15 years we've been writing these books.

The other big attraction in town is the **Northern Lights Centre**, a sort of planetarium devoted to the aurora borealis. It boasts a 110-seat theater, interactive exhibits, and several different shows running about every hour during the day. If you're traveling in the summer, you're not likely to see the aurora – it's never dark enough – so this is a good substitute, although it ain't nothing like the real thing. $10. ☎ 867-536-7827, www.northernlightscentre.ca.

If you want to get out of town, you can pan for gold. Be sure to stay away from regions between white stakes with silver heads; those mark off claims, and people get very touchy about them. There are a number of hiking trails around, but your time is probably better spent elsewhere. You could charter a helicopter from here to **Coal River Springs Territorial Park**, a weird landscape of limestone and calcium carbonate formations.

▪ Food

Other than the hotel restaurants, there are only a few places to eat in Watson Lake. The **Pizza Palace**, at the corner of the Signpost Forest, has good chicken and pizza dishes, from $5 to $20. In the same building is a gas station and a laundromat.

For something a little fancier, the **Nugget Restaurant** has Western and Chinese food, and serves breakfast all day ($2 to $10), lunch ($7 to $12), and dinner ($8 to $20).

▪ Accommodations

Watson Lake is seriously pricey. It's better to stay north or south of it, but you may not have that option.

Watson Lake Hotel (☎ 867-536-7781), next to the Visitors Centre, is the most popular place in town. $$$. There's a good dining room, with breakfasts and lunches starting at $5, dinners at $11. Book your room early. **Gateway Motor Inn** (☎ 867-536-7744), also right on the highway, is comparable, but a couple of dollars more expensive; some of the rooms have kitchenettes. The **Belvedere Motor Hotel** (☎ 867-536-7712) is open year-round, and in the same price range. Some Jacuzzi rooms. The three hotels have joined together with a single webswite, www.watsonlakehotels.com.

Big Horn Hotel (☎ 867-536-2020) keeps you in the same price range, perhaps a bit less. While Watson Lake Hotel gets more business, the rooms are nicer here. There's a Jacuzzi suite, and even the regular rooms are huge.

Much more basic is the **Cedar Lodge Motel** (☎ 867-536-7406, www.cedarlodge.yk.net), $$. Some rooms have kitchenettes. The motel also rents bikes. The cheapest rooms are at the **Air Force Lodge**, just west of town. Very clean, very simple rooms – and we mean simple, bed, table, that's it – with a shared bath. ☎ 867-536-2890. $$. Good atmosphere, nice people.

HOTEL PRICING
Prices are in US dollars.
under $50 . . . . $
$50-$100 . . . . $$
$100-$150 . . . . . . $$$
above $150 . . . . . $$$$

As soon as you're out of Watson Lake, prices begin to drop. **Upper Liard Village**, at Mile 643, and Junction 37 Services at Mile 648, where the Alaska Highway meets the Cassiar Highway, have some cheaper options, and even when Watson Lake is jammed, you can usually find a room here.

Camping

For camping, the best spot is the **Gateway to Yukon RV Park**, at Mile 635. There's a Husky Gas Station, a large store, and a restaurant. This is much nicer than most of the private RV parks. ☎ 867-536-7448

Campground Services, ☎ 867-536-7448, has 140 spaces on the southeast side of town. **Green Valley RV Park** (☎ 867-536-2276), Mile 641, has grassy tent sites, full hookups.

Watson Lake to Teslin

In Watson Lake is the turnoff for the Campbell Highway, a shortcut to Dawson City. (See the section in *Chapter 9*, page 304, for details.)

At Mile 648 is the junction with the Stewart-Cassiar Highway, which leads due south to join up with the Yellowhead Highway. (For details on that run, see *Chapter 6*, page 235.)

Northern Beaver Post, at Mile 650, is one of the better souvenir stands along the highway, with wood and jade carvings, candles, crafts, and more T-shirts than you can count. Nearby is the **Alaska Highway's Best Coffee Shop**, open in summer. This is much better food than you can find back in town.

The road through this section is rough, with a lot of unpaved sections and washboarding. The surface is extremely slippery when wet. If you need to get off the road, there's the day-use-only **Big Creek Recreation Site** at Mile 674, with nice picnic tables and a kitchen shelter. By Mile 693, the

Cassiar Mountains begin to dominate the horizon, and there are some steep grades on the road.

 HIGHWAY TIP: It's important to stop and clean off your headlights and tail lights after going through muddy sections of road; after a few miles, they may be invisible under the dirt.

There is a major geographical point at Mile 722: the **Great River Divide**, the point where the two watersheds meet. Rivers on one side flow to the Arctic Ocean (the Mackenzie River system) or into the Pacific (the Yukon River system). Two miles farther is the Continental Divide, dictating the east and west motion of the rivers. At Mile 733 is the **Continental Divide Lodge**, with a café and B&B deal. There are also RV sites (no hookups). ☎ 867-851-6451.

Nearby, the road dips back into BC and gets rougher for a few miles. Services are available at Miles 775 and 797.

At Nisultin Bay, Mile 803, is the longest bridge on the highway.

Teslin

Teslin, at Mile 804, is an old Tlingit (pronounced KLIN-kit; the Natives themselves pronounce it more along the lines of Kling-GET, but the odds of you hitting the sounds right are pretty small) fishing village. The name comes from the Tlingit language and means "long and narrow waters." Teslin Lake is about 80 miles long, and only two miles wide.

The Tlingits live primarily in Southeast Alaska, but by the time the Russians arrived in the late 1700s, the Tlingits were well-established as traders far into the Interior of Canada and Alaska, taking trade goods up the Stikine River into the Interior; most of the routes the gold rushers used were also originally Tlingit trade routes.

Today the Tlingit are famous for their art, which is highly geometric and features semi-abstract representations of animals and natural items. They are probably best known for their totem poles, which can be seen in Southeast Alaska. Sitka, which was for a while the Russian capital of Alaska, was also a Tlingit trading center.

The most important animal to the Tlingits is the raven; today it is the official bird of the Yukon. The bird ranges throughout the areas inhabited by the Tlingits, and its cunning and guile are the stuff of numerous legends and folktales (see page 29 in the *Introduction*).

The town of Teslin is home to about 450 people, one of the largest Native settlements in the Yukon. It was moved to its present location from the north end of the lake in 1903. Before that time, it served as a stopping point for miners on their way to the goldfields.

Today, the main attractions in Teslin are hunting and fishing. The lake is home to trout (up to 40 pounds – yeah, really), grayling, whitefish, and pike. During the late summer salmon run, there are chinook and chum. Game ranges from waterfowl to moose. There is no shortage of guides around town who will be happy to take you on a hunt.

■ Things to Do

The **George Johnson Museum** (☎ 867-390-2550) is on the south side of the highway. It holds the collection of George Johnson, who photographed the people of the area between 1910 and 1940, along with many early Tlingit artifacts (notice their development of cubism, long before Picasso) and displays from the gold rush era. The museum is open 9 am to 9 pm, late May into early September. Well worthwhile.

The **Tlingit Heritage Centre**, just north of town, ☎ 867-390-2526 is the newest attraction in Teslin, and in this part of the North, it's the best chance you'll have to get an idea of what First Nations life was like before contact. Well worth the stop, and if you've come up from the coast of Southeast Alaska, it's interesting to see how the inland Tlingit did things differently than their coastal kin.

Nisutlin Trading Post (☎ 867-390-2521), founded by R. McCleery in 1928, was one of the first stores in Teslin and is still a good general store. Fishing licenses are sold here. From the George Johnson Museum, follow Nisutlin Drive to the first southbound street. Take this to its end and turn right. The store is on the south side of the street. Closed on Sunday.

For birders, **Nisutlin Bay** is a major migratory stop. All around Teslin and Nisutlin, watch for bears, moose, wolves, and eagles.

Nisutlin Bay Marina, 2.5 miles north of town, runs charter fishing on the lake, and they also rent canoes and can give you the scoop on the best directions to paddle. You can get to the Dawson Peaks trailhead in about six hours of paddling if you're looking to mountain climb. To put in on the Nisultin, the best approach is to drive up the South Canol Road about two hours, then paddle back down to the bay. Before heading out on the lake, stop at the Nisutlin Trading Post for fishing licenses, camping gear, and tackle.

Gas is more expensive in Teslin than in Watson Lake.

■ Food

Mukluk Annie's Salmon Bake is the place to go in Teslin. It's open from 11 am to 9 pm daily. The café is open for breakfast, and they have RV services. They also have great packages of take-out smoked salmon. They're on the highway, Mile 812, nine miles north of town.

The motels in Teslin also have restaurants.

■ Accommodations

 There are several places to stay. The nicest is **Dawson Peaks Resort**, which has cabins, $$-$$$, and tent sites. The resort boasts a restaurant that serves Mexican specialties – widely considered some of the best food on the highway – and offers guided trips out on the river. Good people and a very nice place. ☎ 867-390-2310, www. dawsonpeaks.ca.

The **Yukon Motel** has seven nicely kept rooms; $$, and there are some well-grassed tent sites. The motel also has a nice restaurant with good food at very reasonable prices. Outside is a gas station, manned by a mechanic. Open year-round. ☎ 867-390-2575, www.yukonmotel.com.

Camping

Besides the sites mentioned above, at Mile 813 you'll find the **Teslin Lake Campground**. It's got 27 gravel sites right on the lake, with great views.

Teslin to Whitehorse

The road in this section is mostly good, and there are abundant services along the way, spaced out every 10 to 15 miles. Long, slow grades follow the crossing of the Teslin River Bridge, at Mile 837. Just before that, at Mile 836, is a marker commemorating the Canadian Oil Project, designed to keep the Northwest Staging Route fueled and running. The project involved more than 600 miles of pipeline.

There's a territorial campsite at Mile 848, on **Squanga Lake**. Here you'll find quiet sites set back in groves of trees, a boat launch nearby, and good fishing.

You pass the junction of the Alcan and the Atlin Road at Mile 865.2. Follow the Atlin Road for a lovely side-trip to Atlin Provincial Park (see *Chapter 7*, page 267).

The **Marsh Lake Campground** is at Mile 888. Marsh Lake is more than 20 miles long. As in every other lake in the area, you can fish here for grayling and pike.

At Mile 895, the highway crosses the Yukon River, the greatest river in the North and once the lifeline for all the miners and trappers who called the area home.

The Yukon, which rises a mere 15 miles from the Pacific Ocean (or 60, depending on whom you believe as to the river's source), takes a meandering course through Canada, into Alaska, and finally empties into the Bering Sea, 2,300 miles later, making it the third longest river in North America, after the Missouri-Mississippi system and the Mackenzie River. At this crossing, navigation for larger boats is difficult, if not impossible. This determined the placement of the city of Whitehorse. It was as far down the river as the big paddleboats could safely go.

At Mile 906 is **Wolf Creek Territorial Campground**. This has beautiful tent sites, but is more crowded than some of the other places around.

If you want to go to Skagway or Carcross (see *Chapter 7*), take the turn at Mile 905. Mile 912 is the turn for **Miles Canyon**, a popular picnic area for the locals of Whitehorse. And Mile 914 is the turnoff for Whitehorse itself, capital of the Yukon.

Whitehorse

■ History

The first people in the area, the Southern Tutchone Indians, called the region "Kanlin," or "water flowing through a narrow passage." From its beginnings, the area that is now Whitehorse has been defined by the mighty Yukon River, which flows through it.

The name Whitehorse also comes from the river. The rapids in nearby Miles Canyon were described as like the wild manes of white horses. The Indians had a better name for it though: *"klik-has."* That translates, roughly, to "very bad."

Still, by 1887, the name Whitehorse was in common use. In 1895, the Northwest Mounted Police sent 19 men into what was then part of the Northwest Territory, basing them near this spot.

Still, it was another year before the world was to hear of Whitehorse, and then not because of the town itself, but because of what was north of the town. In 1896, much closer to Dawson City than here, George Carmack, Skookum Jim, and Tagish Charlie found gold. And not just a little bit of gold. During a time when getting 10 cents to the pan was considered riches, these men suddenly struck an area that yielded as much as $4 per pan. And they hadn't even struck the rich part of Rabbit Creek – soon to be renamed Bonanza Creek – a tiny tributary of the Klondike River.

A NOTE ON NAMES

Thanks to a wide variety of people with no lives who want everybody else's to be just the same, there has been much debate and rewriting of history in the Yukon over the past few years, most of it having to do with Skookum Jim and Tagish Charlie. The word "skookum" is a First Nations term meaning "husky." Skookum Jim earned his nickname by carrying more than 150 pounds of bacon up the nightmare Chilkoot Pass in a single load. Harmless enough, right? Maybe not. Skookum is dropping out of favor.

Even worse is what has happened to poor Tagish Charlie. "Tagish" is both a place and a group of people who lived at that place. Nothing more. But the revisionists are now going back, like a scene out of 1984, and changing Tagish Charlie to "Yukon Charlie." There is no good reason for this at all. Period. Do not play along. Whenever you hear some tourism goomer say "Yukon Charlie," say, "Do you mean Tagish Charlie?" Let's mess with their heads until they have brains again.

Remember that classic definition of Puritans: Somebody who is sure that someone, somewhere, is having fun.

The goldfields were a long way off, but Whitehorse was the closest thing to them in the way of what could pass for a town. The boom times began.

To understand why the gold rush was such a boom, such a bonanza, so much the basis for stories and legends, you have to look back at the times. The world was in a deep economic depression; with the gold standard in force, the world's nations were running out of gold with which to back their money – and without that, countries might as well have been playing with Monopoly money. The times were stifling and sad, the future bleak. Word of gold in the Klondike blew all the clouds away.

 The best book on the rush is Pierre Berton's **Klondike Fever**. Nobody else has ever come close to a chronicle of the rush days so entertaining.

The goldfields were 400 miles northwest of Whitehorse, but the city prospered on river traffic and on hopeful miners passing through. Miners would hike up past the border, build boats at Lake Bennett or Laberge, then try to float the Yukon River up to the goldfields. Seeing that not many of the miners had a clue about building boats, and taking into account the immense haste with which the boats were built – nobody was thinking of anything but getting to the goldfields first – it's not really surprising that in the first few days of the rush that first spring, more than 150 boats were swamped and 10 would-be miners drowned. Once word spread, there was actually a boat jam while people tied up and looked at the rapids, searching for a safe way through.

Those not willing to shoot the rapids emptied their boats and pulled them through the rapids by a line leading to shore, the miners walking, the boats getting tossed in the water. Jack London worked here one summer, pulling boats through the rapids.

However, lack of skill in boat-building opened up opportunities for those who knew what they were doing, and it wasn't long before huge paddleboats began making the voyage downstream from Whitehorse to Dawson City, headquarters of the gold rush. The first paddleboat to shoot the rapids was the *Bellingham*, which made it through the canyon in 1898.

The one small problem was that the boats couldn't make it back upstream past the rapids. The operators eventually began running two fleets of boats, one above and one below Miles Canyon.

Only the wealthiest miners could afford to travel on these floating luxury palaces. Most of the prospectors headed up-river on log rafts, badly made dories, and anything else that might stay afloat long enough to get to the goldfields.

Whitehorse was the last touch of civilization, the midway point between the horrors of Chilkoot Pass and the promise of riches in the Klondike. About 30,000 people passed through the town in the two years of the rush, triggering a construction boom of hotels, bars, brothels, and banks.

In 1898, a tramline was built on the east side of the river, from the entrance of Miles Canyon to the end of the rapids. The tramline was four miles of rails atop wooden poles, and the company that ran the tram, the Canyon and White Horse Rapids Tramway Company, charged 3 cents a pound for gear and $25 for boats to get them past the river's rough stretch. At the peak of the operation, the tram hauled up to 90 tons of freight a day.

The heyday didn't last long, however. By 1899, the rush was beginning to slow, the town beginning to shrink. An operator who built another tramway on the west side of the river quickly went bust. The river runners – professionals who took boats through the rapids for miners, for anywhere from $10 to $100 – began to disappear, although they got a second wind when the Mounties decreed that all boats heading through the rapids had to have a professional pilot. Mounties superintendent Sam Steele also declared that women and children were not allowed on the rapids and had to walk the portage.

The river became nearly irrelevant in 1899 with the completion of the White Pass and Yukon Route Railway, with its terminals in Skagway and Whitehorse, marking the first easy access to the Interior of the Yukon. No longer was it necessary to carry everything on the backs of porters and mules. Before the railway opened, the passes were littered with the bones of pack animals and the river was lined with dead boats; with the advent of the railway, it was possible to take a ship from Seattle to Skagway and the train to Whitehorse, then board another ship above the rapids, a ship that could follow the Yukon clear to the Bering Sea. A whole world was opened, and Whitehorse was one of the hubs.

Even after the Klondike rush petered out or was completely staked out, men kept heading north hoping for gold. If nothing else, this kept the Mounties jumping; by 1903, there were more than 350 Mounted Police in the area, centered at Whitehorse.

Of course, being a transportation hub for an area where virtually no one lived was not a great distinction. The entire population of Alaska and the Yukon during the years after the gold rush wouldn't have filled a decent-sized city. Whitehorse lost residents year by year, the nexus of the settlement moving from downstream to where the trains met the boats. But as long as the river boats continued plying the waters north to the mines, the town hung on. In January of 1942, about 800 people called Whitehorse home.

Three months later, in April of 1942, the population of Whitehorse was 40,800. The war had brought the town's hub status to the forefront once more, as Whitehorse became one of the most important construction centers for the Northwest Staging Route and the Alaska Highway. Since there was access via the railway to the sea – the same railway that had allowed miners to transport their gear to the Interior now allowed the Army to transport construction materials – Whitehorse was made the western sector headquarters for the highway. During the nine months of Highway construction, Whitehorse was a boomtown once again. And, just as before, the boom turned to bust. But with a difference this time: There was a road. And where roads go, commerce follows.

Twenty years after the highway's construction, Whitehorse was a sleepy town of 6,000. Today, it's a bustling city, with around 30,000 people in the area. Over two-thirds of the population of the Yukon call it home (the second biggest city in the Yukon, Dawson City, has a population of not much more than 2,000), and it is the territorial capital of the Yukon.

Traveling is a little easier now, and there's probably still gold in the creeks. Whitehorse is a great place to stop and stretch your legs for a couple of days.

QUICK TOUR: Walk along the riverbanks to see the water that brought everybody here to begin with; then hit downtown and a last chance to stock up before Fairbanks.

DON'T MISS: Tour the S.S. *Klondike II*, for those gold rush/ Huck Finn dreams.

■ Things to Do

 Start your tour at the **Visitor Reception Centre** on 2nd Ave. and Hanson St., downtown, next to the Yukon Territorial Government Building. Open from mid-May to mid-September, 8 am to 8 pm, the center offers all the usual tourist information on Whitehorse, including high-tech interactive audio/visual shows on the Alcan, the Dempster Highway, Dawson City, and the gold rush. You'll also find an interesting booklet for sale that guides you on a walking tour of Whitehorse's historic sites. Check here for gold rush activities. Contact the center at ☎ 867-667-2915, or visit them on the web at www.touryukon.com.

More information is available on **96.1 FM Yukon**, which offers radio broadcasts of gold rush history, Indian heritage, and announcements of local activities.

The most interesting attraction in town is the **S.S. *Klondike II***, a stern-wheeler built for the river trade and today dry-docked for tours.

Steam-powered boats were first used on the Yukon in 1866. Because of the many narrows on the river, the side-wheelers that plied the Mississippi River were adapted to stern-wheelers. The typical stern-wheeler was 170 feet long, 35 feet wide, and could carry from 200 to 250 tons of cargo, while drawing only four feet of water. Many of the ships also pushed barges, complicating navigation, but doubling their load capacity. Between 1866 and 1936, about 250 of these ships were used on the Yukon and its tributaries. Every winter, the ships were dragged out of the river and onto solid ground to prevent the coming ice from crushing their sides. The first true sign of spring was the ships back in the water.

The greatest of all the ships was the S.S. *Klondike II*, built from the scrap of the *Klondike I*, which had run aground in 1936. The *Klondike I*, built by British Yukon Navigation Company (a subsidiary of the White Pass and Yukon Route Railway) in 1929, boasted a revolutionary design that allowed an increase of 50% in cargo capacity. Capable of carrying 300 tons, the *Klondike I* was the queen of the river; when she died, the *Klondike II* carried on the tradition.

The S.S. *Klondike II* was built in 1937 and ran the river until 1952. Although it was mostly a cargo ship, it also carried up to 75 passengers – in what passed for great comfort at the time and in this part of the world, although because of the narrowness of the river, the passengers and crew were nearly eaten alive by mosquitoes.

The trip down to Dawson City (remember, the river flows north; downstream is up on a map) took about 36 hours. The northbound ship's cargo consisted largely of supplies for the miners in the North: food, whiskey, a few luxury goods. Before its trip back up the river, the ship stopped at Stewart Landing to load silver, the main cargo bound for Whitehorse. The trip upriver took four to five days and required three times as many stops for wood as a downstream run. Wood was available every 50 miles; headed downstream, the ship burned one to one and a half cords of wood per hour. Wood had to be loaded into the firebox every 30 seconds; the man doing this back-breaking work made $85 a month.

The S.S. *Klondike II* is 210 feet long, 41.9 feet wide, and has a gross tonnage of 1,362.5 tons. It could carry 300 tons of cargo and was manned by a crew of 23. It could operate in surprisingly shallow water. Fully loaded, it drafted only about 40 inches.

The opening of an all-weather road between Whitehorse and the mines at Mayo spelled the end for the big ships. Trucks could take the road any time, while the river was open only four to five months a year, despite some innovative efforts on the part of the ship companies. As Lake Laberge especially was late in thawing, workers spread lamp black on the ice to melt it and open leads for the ship. In the 1920s, a dam was built on Marsh Lake; water was released in waves, in hopes that it would break up the ice.

The S.S. *Klondike II* had a brief, unsuccessful career as a cruise ship, and then was dry-docked, alongside two other retired stern-wheelers. Those two were burned when some boys were camping inside one and their campfire got out of control. The *Klondike II* was saved, and was moved down the town's main street to its current location; every citizen in the town turned out to watch.

Today, the vessel has been lovingly restored and is open for tours from mid-May to mid-September. Before taking the tour ($5), stop in and see the 20-minute historical film in the tent near the ship's bow. The 25-minute tour takes you from the cargo hold, where the engines are, up to the second deck and the fancy dining room, and from there to the wheel house, where Yukon law kept the windows open, no matter what the weather. There's a nice lawn nearby for a picnic and an information center with still more historical background. Plan at least two hours for this. It's fascinating.

The **MacBride Museum**, at 1st and Wood St., is open from May 12 to September 30, 10 am to 6 pm, ☎ 867-667-2709, www.macbridemuseum.com. Admission is $6. The admission is good for the entire day, so you can go in and out. Built for Canada's centennial, the museum is housed in a log building with a sod roof, the traditional materials of the North. The upstairs has a variety of the area's animals, stuffed and mounted, and patches of their fur that you can touch. In the hallway is an air pump used by divers working on bridge foundations on the highway. Most of the original bridges were made of logs, but the only one of these that survives is at Canyon Creek, in the Yukon. Downstairs in the museum is an assortment of dioramas showing the entire history of the region, including some really good displays of just how the gold rush worked, and what the miners had to do to get the gold out. The Indian artifacts are of the highest quality, and the overview is unusually sympathetic. Be sure to pause at the moose skull on your way out. The museum offers daily slide shows and has excellent historical photos of Whitehorse. The gift shop has a couple of items not available elsewhere and is worth a look.

The yard of the museum has original cars and buggies, a steam engine, and the cabin of Sam McGee, who was later immortalized by Robert Service.

The **Yukon Transportation Museum**, at the Whitehorse airport, is open in the summer months from 10 am to 6 pm. ☎ 867-668-4792. Admission is $6, or get a combo pass with the Beringia Museum for $9. This museum shows the history of transportation in the Yukon – the building of the highway, the White Pass and Yukon Route Railway, and 1920s aviation. You'll also find a nice display of snowshoes and stage coaches. One of the highlights of transportation in the Yukon is the first use of the integrated container concept. Trailers would be shipped up by barge, moved to the train, then moved on to trucks. This method is used everywhere in the world now – any time you see a freight train loaded with truck trailers, remember that this is where the idea got its start – and it all gets explained in the museum on a video tour of the White Pass and Yukon Route Railway. Also in the museum you can check out the bush pilot exhibit and a full-sized rep-

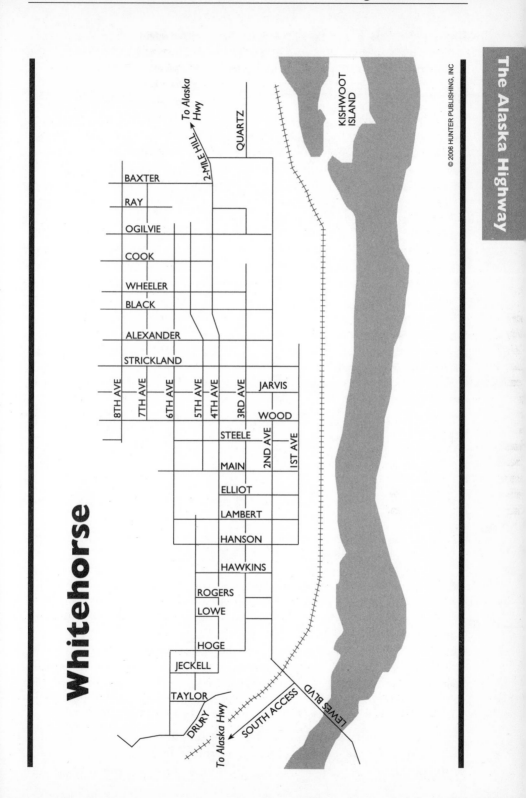

© 2006 HUNTER PUBLISHING, INC

lica of the *Queen of the Yukon* monoplane, a sister ship to the *Spirit of St. Louis*. This is a good place to stop for a while, and one of the best of the many transportation museums along the highway.

Next door is the **Yukon Beringia Interpretive Centre**, ☎ 867-667-8855, www.beringia.com, $6, or do the $9 combo pass with the transportation museum. The first lesson of the Beringia Centre is that what you probably thought about the ice age was most likely dead wrong. Not so much Whitehorse, but farther north of here – Dawson and up – was actually ice-free, part of a huge transcontinental steppe. This means, instead of being a frozen wasteland, the place was actually chock full of beasts. The Centre has great exhibits of prehistoric life: the scimitar cat (a saber-toothed tiger with attitude), the short-faced bear (bigger than modern grizzlies), and, of course, the woolly mammoth, a member of the elephant family. The display's centerpiece is a life-sized cast of the largest woolly mammoth ever found. There are also multimedia exhibits and a reconstruction of the Bluefish Caves archaeological site, which dates from the time of the first human incursion into the area. Afterward, you can go outside and try throwing an atl-atl, the height of caveman hunting technology.

The Yukon has always been great for archaeological and paleontological exploration, mostly because miners, looking for gold, have dug up practically every inch of dirt in the territory. They didn't always strike it rich, but they often struck bones, and the Beringia Centre is a great place to see some of them.

The Yukon Gardens, S. Access Rd. and Alcan Junction, are open 9 am to 9 pm from April to September. Possibly the northernmost botanical gardens in the world, the 22-acre site displays both wild and commercial flowers – more than 100,000 varieties, including the 17 species of wild orchid found in the Yukon – huge vegetables (some for sale, great if you're tired of road food), fruit trees, and a medicinal garden. Admission is $10. You can catch a bus from the city center out to the gardens.

The **Old Log Church Museum**, Elliot and 3rd Ave., is open daily 9 am to 6 pm, from late May through Labor Day; 12:30 to 4 on Sundays. The church was built in 1900, and claims to be "the only wooden cathedral in the world." While that's debatable, it is certainly the oldest building in town. Today, there is a nice museum emphasizing the history of the Anglican Church in the North. There are bibles in Native languages, a variety of Native and non-Native artifacts, and an audio/visual show on the history of the Anglican Church. While there are certainly ongoing questions about how much the Natives lost when the missionaries – of any persuasion – came in to teach them how to read, pray to different gods, and give up ways of life that had kept them happy for thousands of years, a stop here is certainly worthwhile for one side of the picture. Admission is $2.50 for adults.

The **Yukon Archives and Arts Centre** is at 2140 2nd Ave., next to the library. Open Tuesdays and Wednesdays from 1 to 9, Thursdays through Saturdays 10 am to 6 pm (☎ 867-667-5321), the building has a photo collection of more than 57,000 prints, covering every aspect of Yukon history. The library section of the archives contains 11,000 volumes and many unique manuscripts, plus more than 8,000 maps. If you've got any special interests in the North, this is the place to do your research. Admission is by donation, and the displays in the arts center can be surprising, including original Edward Weston prints.

For guided walks around the city, try the tours that start downstairs in the Heritage Building. They last about 45 minutes and are run by the **Yukon Historical and Museums Association** (☎ 867-667-4704), located at 3126 3rd Ave. Cost is $2. Tours are run regularly every day of the week from May through late August. If you can't get in on a tour, the association also offers a walking tour booklet, so you can do it yourself. All proceeds from the tours go toward preservation efforts. Another option are the guided nature walks given by the Yukon Conservation Society. These walks cover a variety of areas and last from two to six hours. ☎ 867-668-5678.

Miles Canyon, just outside the city, was a dangerous point for gold seekers during the Klondike gold rush. Headed for the fields in homemade boats, would-be miners hit these rapids and some never made it any farther. Today it's a popular picnic area, with good views of the river and a footbridge from one side to the other. (See below for more details on the canyon and the rapids.)

At the end of Nisatlin Dr. is the **Whitehorse Dam** and **Fish Ladder**. It's usually open from mid-July to late-August, 8 am to 10 pm. This place offers a chance to see the chinook salmon on their annual migration. The fish ladder allows them to get over the dam and continue along one of the longest fish migrations in the world. Some of the salmon travel over 1,600 miles to spawn and die. Check out the underwater windows that let you peek into the ladder itself. The hatchery at the dam can handle up to 400,000 fry a year. Each year they take about 75 female and 60 male chinook from the river and collect sperm and eggs. Survival rate to the fry stage in a hatchery is about 80%; in nature, it's about 10%. So, with the heavy depletion of salmon stock in rivers throughout the North, they're doing good work here.

Takini Hot Springs is a concrete pool with natural spring water. It's a popular place to soak away a morning and a nice place to camp. To get there, take the highway 9.5 miles north to the Klondike Loop Highway. Follow that for three miles, turn left, and a six-mile road takes you to the hot springs. Open from 8 am to 10 pm; admission is $5 for adults, $3.50 for seniors and students. They've also got horseback riding trips available, and you can camp here.

Farther out the road is the **Yukon Wildlife Preserve**, featuring elk, bison, caribou, moose, mountain goat, musk ox, and more. ☎ 867-668-3992.

▪ Out & About

You can cruise the river on the **M.V. *Schwatka***, taking a two-hour Miles Canyon cruise, narrated by guides on points of historical interest. Tours leave twice daily from June through August, and the cost is $25 from the dockside or a bit more from most of the hotels. Children under 11 are half-price. ☎ 867-668-4716, www.yukon-wings.com. A nice combo deal with a 20-minute float plane ride for $79.

Other operators running soft trips on the river include **Atsua Ku Riverboat Adventures** (☎ 867-668-6854), which takes you five miles down the Yukon to a First Nations camp. The tour takes three hours, and there's an overnight option. Prices start at $50.

The historic **White Pass and Yukon Route Railway** still makes its run, although not all the way from Skagway to Whitehorse. It's a tourist railroad now, the original steam engine taking you as far as the old train sheds, where it's traded for a diesel that follows the tracks through spectacular scenery loaded with history. Construction of the line was begun in 1898. It was finished two years later, at a cost of $10 million. The line ran continuously until 1982, when service stopped. In 1988, it was resurrected as a tourist line. Although most people book the train from Whitehorse, the train doesn't actually go through that far. It runs from Skagway to Lake Bennett. From there, you catch a bus back to Whitehorse. See the Skagway chapter (chapter 7) for details. The train runs from May 21 to September 21, and reservations are recommended. Any travel agent in town can book for the railroad, but prices can vary. ☎ 800-343-7373, 800-478-7373, or 907-983-2217.

Several local companies offer out-of-the-ordinary tours: whitewater rafting, sightseeing and flightseeing on the Yukon, fishing, horseback riding, and so on. These offerings can change rapidly, so check at the Visitors Centre, where all the companies put up their brochures.

Hiking

For hiking, try **Miles Canyon** or a longer (up to 10 days) hike through the **Donjeck Valley**. In winter, you'll find world-class cross-country skiing at **Mt. McIntyre Recreation Centre**. An extensive network of trails crisscrosses the area.

River Trips

Whitehorse has always been centered around the water, and it's still a great place to get out and get wet. If the river trips listed above are too sedate for your taste, **Kanoe People** (☎ 867-668-4899, www.kanoepeople. com) rents canoes and kayaks. They've also got any odds and ends you might need, right down to a helmet if you're experienced enough to try the rapids.

Kanoe People can also arrange one-way trips to Carmacks or Dawson City. If you want to do the Dawson City run, they figure a 16-day rental for the 460-mile trip. Guided tours range from little day trips to 10-day wilderness masterpieces.

You can get to the Tatshenshini, the Alsek (see *Chapter 8* for details), or the Firth from Whitehorse. These are wild rivers; you should either know what you're doing or have an experienced guide with you.

For something smoother, take your canoe to **Takhini River Campground**, where you can put-in on calm water. Also, **Kusawa Lake** is a popular site; you can float back to town, portaging one small rapid.

Mountain Biking

Once you've had your fill of water, Kanoe People (above) rents mountain bikes for $25 a day. The best biking is out in the **Ibex Valley** or on the **Canol Road**, which was built to link oil wells in Norman Wells, Northwest Territory, to Whitehorse. It's now a Heritage Trail. There are a few patches where you'll have to carry the bike across streams, but it's wild and uncrowded and a beautiful ride.

Horseback Riding

Finally, **White Horse Riding Stable** rents horses. ☎ 867-633-3086.

▪ Seasonal Activities

In February, try the **Frostbite Music Festival**, which features musicians from all over North America. It's a three-day lead-in to the **Yukon Sourdough Rendezvous**, a nine-day festival that culminates in the Yukon Quest sled dog race, a 1,000-mile course from Fairbanks to Whitehorse (for more on the Quest and mushing, see the *Fairbanks* section). During the festival, you'll see leg wrestling, climbing the Chilkoot, and snowshoe races.

In March, **ski touring races** of 40, 20, and 10 kilometers are held. There's a **square dance jamboree** in May, and the **Yukon International Storytelling Festival** in June, on the summer solstice. This is one of the town's biggest events – solstice parties are often held in the North – and it's good to plan ahead if you can. Stories from Native groups around the North are told; one year they had offerings in 23 different languages. Call ☎ 867-633-7550 for a schedule of events.

▪ Nightlife

The **Frantic Follies Vaudeville Review** at the Westmark runs once or twice a day from May through September. This 1890s saloon show features can-can dances, skits, turn-of-the-century gold rush songs, and the poetry of Robert Service. Sounds hokey, and it is, but it's also a lot of fun. The show lasts about 90 minutes. Get tickets at Atlas Tours in the Westmark Hotel, ☎ 867-668-3161.

The **Frostbite Music Society** hosts a summer concert series and a winter music festival. ☎ 867-668-4921.

■ Food

Whitehorse is your only chance for junk food between Prince George and Fairbanks, with McDonalds, Dairy Queen, Subway, Pizza Hut, and a Kentucky Fried Chicken.

Now that you've decided to avoid all of those, the place to go is **Klondike Rib & Salmon Barbecue**, ☎ 867-667-7554, 2116 2nd Ave, next to the Westmark. Operating in the oldest building left in town, with tables on porches in the front and back. Once you wait through the line, you're in for the best food in the Yukon, from simple fish and chips to dishes with exotic ingredients like caribou and musk ox. Prices start around $10.

Tung Lock Seafood Restaurant, 404 Wood St., is open for lunch and dinner, offering seafood from $15, vegetarian specialties from $8, plus an assortment of other dishes. Takeout service is available.

Also highly recommended by the locals is the **No Pop Sandwich Shop**, 312 Steele. They mean it with the name.

The **Westmark Village Garden**, inside the Westmark Hotel, has an excellent breakfast buffet. Cold dishes are $7, hot are $10.

For a good night out, try **The Cellar**, downstairs (big surprise), at 101 Main. Nice wine list, good entrées, the place to go for a good surf and turf dinner.

3 Beans Natural Foods is a health food store with an organic juice bar. At 308 Wood St., this is a good stop after a day in a kayak.

■ Accommodations

Whitehorse can be the most difficult town along the highway for getting a hotel room. Show up early or book in advance.

The **High Country Inn** (☎ 867-667-4471, 800-554-4471, www.highcountryinn.yk.ca), 4051 4th Ave., was recently renovated. $$$$. Multi-night packages can save you some bucks. **The Edgewater Hotel** (☎ 867-667-2572, 877-484-3334, www.edgewaterhotel.yk.ca), 101 Main St., is the most pleasant of the luxury hotels, but you're paying for it. It also has a very good, reasonable restaurant, lounge, and gift shop.

The **Yukon Inn** (☎ 867-667-2527 or 800-661-1454, www.yukoninn.com) at 4220 4th Ave. has nice rooms, $$$, and a restaurant, lounge, and café.

The **River View Hotel**, 102 Wood St., ☎ 866-949-7800, www.riverviewhotel.ca, takes pets, has a nice restaurant, and makes for a good choice. $$$. Out on the highway, the **Airport Chalet**, ☎ 866-668-2166, is walking distance from the Beringia Centre. Good choice away from downtown. $$$.

The **Westmark** can be full of package tours, but the location is great, and you can walk almost anywhere from the hotel. ☎ 800-544-0970, www. westmarkhotels.com. $$$$.

If you'd like to try a bed and breakfast, easiest to hit the Visitor Centre, as these things come and go quickly.

Camping

Close to downtown is the **Robert Service Campground**, on South Access Rd., with 50 tent sites. There are washrooms, showers ($1 for five minutes), free firewood, and drinking water. This is a tent-only campground, and you'll have to walk in to your site. There are some good hiking trails start at the campground and go along the river. If you've got a tent, come here and don't bother looking anywhere else, unless you absolutely have to.

Pioneer RV Park has serviced sites. It's a huge place, with a total of 134 sites. The park also sells gas and offers a nightly show with a Klondike theme. Open May through September.

Hi-Country RV Park is at Mile 913 on the highway, near the Yukon Gardens. Laundry, ice, and showers are available, and they've got a small wildlife display. Open April through September.

Mackenzie's RV Park, open year-round, is at Mile 922.5 on the highway. This is a good location, although there's a bit too much gravel.

Whitehorse to Haines Junction

There is no gas available between Whitehorse and Haines Junction, so gas up in town, unless you know how to get gasoline out of muskeg.

Miles Canyon is right outside Whitehorse; the turnoff is at Mile 911.5. It's in Miles Canyon that the city of Whitehorse got its name, from the Whitehorse Rapids. Going through the canyon, the Yukon suddenly narrows. Squeezing all the river's water through a slot roughly 15% the width of the rest of the river creates a .6-mile-long rapids that nearly gave the first white explorer – US Army Lieutenant Frederick Schwatka, in 1883 – reason to turn around and go home.

The walls of the canyon rise to 100 feet around the boulder-strewn, whirlpool-full rapids. A report from a later explorer noted that these rapids were "never run... in boats, except by accident." They are a little tamer now. Thanks to the technological wonders and ecological disasters of modern dam construction, the river isn't in quite the same narrow course it was

100 years ago. And since modern rubber boats and rodeo kayaks can go where no 1890s dory sailor could dream of, it's kind of fun out on the river.

If you don't want to get wet, there's Miles Canyon Road, which runs between the White Pass and Yukon Route Railway tracks and the river, offering great views of the Yukon. The dam is just south of town. It was built in the late 1950s, backing the river up for 17 miles. Just below it is the world's longest wooden fish ladder, a 1,180-foot slideway that lets salmon get up beyond the dam.

Just past Mile 916 is **Cairns**, which was a station run by the Royal Canadian Engineers for maintaining the highway between 1946 and 1964. It was here, in April of 1946, that the US Army turned over the Canadian section of the highway to the Canadian Army; they, in turn, handed it over to the Federal Department of Works.

On the east side of the road at Mile 916.9 is the north access road to Whitehorse; on the west side is the turnoff to the Mt. McIntyre Recreation Centre. Unless you're looking for a side-trip, forgot something back in town, or are trying to get out from behind a particularly large herd of RVs, there's not much reason to take either turn.

 HIGHWAY TIP: For those who want to take the Klondike Highway to Takhini Hot Springs, Carmacks, and Dawson City, the turnoff is at Mile 922.5. This road heads north to the gold and silver fields, following the Yukon River and the paths tracked by endless miners. (See *Chapter 7* for travel along this historic route.)

A remnant of the original Alaska Highway can be reached from Mile 929, on a three-mile loop road. The original section is two lanes and mostly in good shape, although there are some sections of broken pavement. During the construction of the highway, the surveyors ran just ahead of the logging crews – sometimes, in fact, they were trying to lay out the road's route from atop moving bulldozers – so they rarely had time to choose the best line for the road. Instead they simply chose the first line that looked reasonable. Over the years, a lot of the curves they laid down have been straightened out, leaving small sections of the original Highway abandoned and cut off like a river's ox-bows.

Takhini River Campground is nine miles off the road at Mile 958.5. It's only got eight RV/tent sites, so if it's full, continue down the same road another five miles to **Kusawa Lake Campground**, which has 48 RV/tent sites. Both have water and cooking shelters available. You can also fish or boat at Kusawa.

Along this section of the road, watch closely for Arctic ground squirrels. They live in small tunnels near the side of the road and take great delight in running in front of cars. Looking rather like fat prairie dogs, they are a favorite food of many Northern predators, and there are seemingly billions of the bite-sized critters, so everybody can chow down. If you really wonder, we can tell you from experience: boiled Arctic ground squirrel tastes a lot like – no, not chicken: dark turkey meat.

In Denali Park, the Arctic ground squirrel is the main source of meat protein for the Toklat grizzlies, despite the fact that one squirrel provides only around 2,000 calories. If a grizzly bear can catch a six-pack or so of squirrels, it's had a pretty good day.

Providing coverage for the squirrels are the abundant wildflowers in this area. In summer, watch for wild rose, lupine, and sweet pea.

■ Champagne

Champagne is at Mile 974, and it's a good place to look at a couple of old miners' shacks. In the summer, the flowers outside are impressive. The village was once a stopping point on the old Dalton Trail, which leads up to the Dawson goldfields. It was complete with a roadhouse and trading post that acted as a supply center for two of the area gold rushes (the Bullion and Burwash Creek rushes, in 1924).

FRIENDLY TRAVEL: *Please notice the sign on the Indian cemetery that it is not a tourist attraction; the village is now home to the local Champagne-Aishihik Indians.*

People first arrived in this area around 10,000 years ago, trudging across the Bering Strait when there was a land bridge there, in the same migration that ultimately took the Hopi to Arizona and the Maya to South America. The people who stayed in what's now the Yukon and Alaska found the living relatively easy, if a little chilly at times. Game was plentiful and, if you could take the winters, spring and summer offered berries, caribou, and endless tons of fish. The earliest settlers spoke languages from the Tlingit and Athabascan language groups, and they were hunter-gatherers, moving from camp to camp according to what was in season, stashing food and supplies along the trails for future use. The usual traveling group was the family or extended family.

Between Miles 976 and 994, as the road runs along the Dezadeash River, watch for bison, the great lumbering animals that were hunted to near extinction a century ago. Several transplanted herds thrive in Canada and Alaska. No longer endangered, bison are farmed for a variety of commercial purposes throughout the West, including for steaks. Looking south along this section of road, you can also see the Dezadeash Range, but these mountains are quickly overshadowed by what lies ahead.

One of the most spectacular sights of the highway comes into view at the turnout at Mile 986. Due north are the foothills of the **St. Elias Mountains**. These form the natural border to Kluane Park, part of the largest wilderness area in the Americas. On a clear day you can see Mt. Kennedy, at 13,969 feet, and Mt. Hubbard, at 15,104 feet.

We're covering, in just a couple of pages, enough scenery to keep you enthralled for days. The mountain views never stop. Everywhere you look, it seems like there's another river, and the wildlife viewing is limitless. Don't let the quick description fool you: this is a really, really beautiful stretch of highway.

More camping and fishing (grayling, lake trout) is available at **Aishihik Lake**, Mile 995.6, 26 miles off the highway. This is prime wildlife area, especially for moose, bear, and caribou, but because of the altitude and the influence of weather patterns bouncing off the nearby mountains, the lake may have ice in it as late as June.

The massive **Kluane Icefields** come into view by Mile 997. At Mile 1,008, there's a pullout with an information plaque about the Kluane Range. The view here is astounding, with the highway stretching straight into distant ranges, the icefields, and the St. Elias Mountains to the west.

Kluane Range.

Camp in the shadow of the mountains at **Pine Lake**, Mile 1,013 (33 sites, water, restrooms, firewood available), or drive the last three miles into Haines Junction.

At Mile 1,016 is the highway's junction with the Haines Highway. To continue on to Beaver Creek, Tok, Anchorage and Fairbanks, turn right. If you're heading down to Haines and the ocean, keep going straight, but buy gas here, as there isn't any more until Kathleen Lake (there's also camping there). (See *Chapter 8* for details on one of the most scenically stunning roads in the world, the Haines Highway.)

Haines Junction

Headquarters of **Kluane National Park**, Haines Junction was originally built as a Highway construction camp for workers who were linking the inland Highway with the coast at Haines and the Lynn Canal, to make a sea-link with the Lower 48. Today, Haines Junction still depends on the highway for most of its livelihood, but the creation of the park gave it a draw for tourists and some diversity of employment for the locals. Situated on the eastern boundary of Kluane Park, at the junction of the Alaska Highway and the Haines Highway, on a clear day Haines Junction is a town you never want to leave – except to get into the park.

■ Things to Do

 Okay, there isn't much to do in Haines Junction except stare at the scenery. But there are a few things that can get you started on your trip to Kluane. Head for the **Kluane National Park Visitor Reception Centre** (open 8 am to 8 pm daily in the summer; ☎ 867-634-2345), just east of the highway. The center offers interpretive displays of area history and an excellent 30-minute slide show (admission is $3 for adults). Since there are no roads leading into the park, this slide show is the only chance most people have of seeing past the border range of mountains. A couple of times a day, they show, flat out, the best film ever made on what to do in a bear encounter. A must-see for anybody headed into the backcountry. The rangers at the park are helpful and extremely knowledgeable about the area; if they can't answer your questions, they have a reference source that can. The rangers also offer interpretive programs and hikes. Check at the center for the current schedule of events. These range from a simple guided walk that takes about two hours and costs $5 to longer hikes, up to six hours, for $10. Well worthwhile if you're not heading out on your own.

If you're going into the park, you will need a wilderness permit. For one night, this runs $5; you can also buy an annual permit for $50. Bear-resistant food containers are required in many areas because of the number of bears around (the center is a good place to find out who's seeing bears where). You can rent them at the center, but there's a $150 deposit required. The center can sell you a fishing license, or even rent you a personal park interpreter for the day (two week advance notice is required; cost is $300). If you're going into the park, this is also the place to get your topo maps.

■ Food

 Besides the hotel restaurants, there aren't a lot of choices in Haines Junction for dinners out. **The Village Bakery**, across the street from the Visitors Centre, has excellent baked goods (try the strudel) and serves sandwiches, soup, quiche, and drinks.

There's a good **general store** in town, which has an excellent selection of groceries and baked goods, plus fishing tackle and camping supplies. There's also a post office window inside. It's open daily.

■ Accommodations

 The nicest place is **Cozy Corner** (☎ 867-634-2511), on the main road, at Mile 1,016. Open year-round, $$.

HOTEL PRICING
Prices are in US dollars.
under $50 . . . . $
$50-$100 . . . . $$
$100-$150 . . . . . . $$$
above $150 . . . . . $$$$

From March to the end of September, there is also a café here. The **Kluane Park Inn** (☎ 867-634-2261), also on the main road, is another good choice. It's got 20 rooms and is open year-round; $$. It's right by the other hotels.

Alcan Motor Inn, at the junction, ☎ 888-265-1018, takes pets, has a sports lounge, and is the newest, shiniest motel in town. $$-$$$.

Just outside of town at Mile 1,022 is the lovely **Bear Creek Lodge**. Open from May to September, they have seven rooms, with doubles around $$. They've also got serviced campsites. In addition, the lodge offers a restaurant, laundromat, showers, gas station, and convenience store. ☎ 867-634-2301.

Camping

Kluane RV Kampground is open May through September. There are showers, a laundry, a store, and an unbeatable view of the mountains. The campground also rents canoes and does fishing charters. ☎ 867-634-2709.

Kluane National Park

Kluane National Park is one of the newer parks in Canada; it was formed in 1972. The name Kluane – originally the name of the territory's largest lake – means "place of many fish," and today the park's 13,209 square miles (22,015 square kilometers) is a UNESCO World Heritage Site, along with its neighboring park, Alaska's Wrangell-St. Elias. In 1993, the addition of the newly formed **Tatshenshini-Alsek Wilderness Park** (see *Chapter 8* for details), which abuts Wrangell-St. Elias and Kluane, made this region the largest protected area in the world. Entire countries could get lost inside the borders of these three parks.

■ History

The first people in the region were the Southern Tutchone Indians, who hunted, fished, and trapped in the rich lands. Archaeologists have found evidence of bison hunting as far back as 8,000 years ago; 1,000 years ago, Natives were using local copper for ax heads, arrow heads, and knives.

In 1892, Jack Dalton improved the old Indian trading site south of the modern-day park and built the Dalton Trail – the first overland toll route to the Yukon goldfields.

Gold was discovered in Kluane in 1903, at Sheep Creek and Bullion Creek. Remains of the old mines are still visible. To cash in on the miners, Frenchmen Louis and Jean Jacquot built a trading post at Burwash Landing, supplying the miners with necessities and lightening their burden of gold.

The end of the gold rush brought quiet times to Kluane, until the highway was pushed through. A wildlife reserve was created in 1942, in part as a reaction to the number of people running through the area, and that formed the nexus of today's park.

■ Geography

The park is dominated by the **St. Elias Mountains**, which are made up of two ranges: the **Kluane**, which is what you see from the highway, and the **Icefield Ranges** farther west, which include Mt. Logan – at 19,520 feet, the tallest mountain in Canada and the second highest in North America. Because of its huge base and rise from near sea-level, Mt. Logan is the largest massif in the world. The icefields themselves are also the world's largest outside of the polar regions; they cover nearly half of the park's area. Moist Pacific air reaches the mountains and dumps huge amounts of snowfall annually. The two ranges of mountains are set apart by the Duke Depression, which creates a dramatic contrast of highs and lows.

There are so many peaks in these ranges, so much unexplored territory, that some mountains remain unnamed and unclimbed. The park has 20 mountains that are over 16,000 feet; and, if you know what you're doing, there are countless climbing possibilities. Of course, if you don't know what you're doing, trying to head up one of these mountains without proper preparation is just a complicated and fairly expensive way to die.

There are a number of glaciers in the park, the longest of which, the Lowell, is over 40 miles; the glacier used to extend over the current site of Haines Junction. When an ice-dam broke at Lake Alsek as the glacier retreated, the flow of water was thought to match that of the Amazon River.

■ Flora & Fauna

But Kluane is not all mountains and ice. Along the glacial fringe is a belt of green meadows and forest, chock-full of animals, including about 4,000 Dall sheep, primarily in the Sheep Mountain area. There are mountain goats in the south and the largest subspecies of moose in Kluane. A herd of caribou is occasionally found in the Duke River area. The grizzly bear population stays largely in the alpine meadows and valleys. At the Visitors Centre is a map of recent bear sightings, but these are mostly the smaller black bear. The Kluane region has the Yukon's greatest concentration of grizzly bears.

Besides the large animals, the park supports populations of wolf, wolverine, muskrat, mink, marmot, red fox, lynx, beaver, and snowshoe hare, just to mention a few. Some 118 species of bird nest in the park, and 160 species have been sighted, including Arctic terns, falcons, and golden and bald eagles.

The tree line in the park varies from around 3,400 to 4,000 feet. There are more than 200 varieties of alpine flower in the park, from Arctic poppies to mountain heather.

■ Climate

Weather in the park is generally dry and cold; the south is just a little warmer and wetter. The summers are short, and the winters are long and bitter; frost is possible at any time of year, and ice begins forming on the lakes in October. The average January temperature is about -5° F; in June, it's 50° F, although it can range from -50° F to nearly 90° F.

■ Out & About

Fishing

Kluane took its name from the fish in the lake. There are plenty of fish to be had, from lake and rainbow trout (catch and release only) to Arctic grayling, northern pike, and a landlocked form of sockeye salmon. Get your license at the Visitors Centre in Haines Junction. There are a number of regulations to keep in mind. Check at the Visitors Centre for current catch limits, which vary with season and conditions.

- Fishing is prohibited from two hours after sunset to one hour before sunrise.
- You can't leave a line unattended or use more than one line at a time.
- You can't use fish or fish parts – live or dead – as bait.

If you've got a canoe or kayak, head for **Kathleen Lake** or **Marsh Lake** for the best paddling.

> **WEATHER ALERT:** Keep a close eye on conditions, because the mountains cause unpredictable weather. Strong winds can come up without any warning, easily whipping up whitecaps on the water. The term for the extent of water exposed to the wind is "fetch" – and it's huge in this area. You do not want to take a swim here. The water is very cold and you'd be minutes away from hypothermia.

Hiking

You must register at the park headquarters before setting out on your own into the park. While no one is sent away, weather conditions can change with frightening speed, and the rangers need to keep track of where everyone is. You can register at Haines Junction, Sheep Mountain, or with any ranger.

Kluane is one of the prime wilderness experiences in the world; it is only truly accessible by foot or on horseback. Facilities are extremely limited, so go into it fully prepared. Know how to treat animals, take care against hypothermia, and do not carry anything in that you are not willing to carry out. Practice all aspects of minimum-impact land use, and all proper bear precautions.

There are quite a few hiking trails in the park, ranging from strenuous week-long treks to day hikes that follow old mining roads. A small topo map is available at the Visitors Centre, and the rangers can fill you in on the flora and fauna you might see, as well as give detailed route descriptions. There's also a pamphlet, *Hiking in Kluane,* that you should pick up. All overnight hikers must register at either the Haines Junction or Sheep Mountain Visitors Centres. You can register by phone – don't forget to call when you get back – at ☎ 867-634-2345.

Kluane Park is one of the few places in Western Canada where they take the metric system seriously; in this section, we give measurements in both systems.

Among the most popular hikes is the **Sheep Creek Hike**, a 3.8-mile (6.4-km) one-way hike which begins at Mile 1,029 (Km 1,707), outside the Sheep Mountain Interpretive Centre and across from Soldier's Summit, on the Alaska Highway. The trail follows an old mining road, and there's good animal viewing along the way. This hike is a side-trip off the longer Slims River West Trail – follow the signs from the Visitors Centre.

Aurist Trail, a nine-mile (15-km) round-trip hike, offers lovely mountain views and a walk through the sub-alpine areas. It starts at Mile 149 (Km 248.3) on the Haines Road, not far from the Visitors Centre. A similar hike is the one to **St. Elias Lake**; 3.8 miles (6.4 km) one way. Mountain goats are often spotted on the south side of the trail. The trailhead is at Mile 117 (Km 196) on the Haines Road, and the hiking is easy.

For the ambitious, there is the **Cottonwood Trail,** a 50-mile (85-km) round-trip. From Dezadeash Lodge to Kathleen Lake, it takes about five days to hike, and the trail crosses two mountain passes, where there is often snow. It's the best hike for animal viewing. Moose, goats, sheep, eagles, ptarmigan, and bear (with the very occasional grizzly) are common. The trail also passes some interesting mining relics.

Finally, the most popular trail in the park is probably the **Dezadeash River Trail,** which starts directly outside the Visitors Centre. It's a 2.4-mile (four-km) loop, and there's a good chance of seeing moose and beaver along the way. It's one of the most popular hikes with birders.

Kluane Park to the Alaska Border

This section of the highway through the park is an occasionally narrow, two-lane road with graveled shoulders. Mostly it's in good condition, although there is some patching, and you may encounter construction.

Twelve miles out of town, at Mile 1,028.6, the highway reaches **Bear Creek Summit**. At 3,294 feet, this is the highest point on the highway between Whitehorse and Fairbanks. From here it descends slowly, headed toward Boutillier Summit (3,280 feet), the second highest point on the highway. Between these two summits, watch for the stunning view of the Kluane Mountains to the west. Besides the mountains, there are low forested valleys and marshlands perfect for moose. As the road runs along the mountains, there are vast arrays of wildflowers in season, including sweet pea, lupine, and fireweed.

Boutillier Summit, at Mile 1,050.4, brings the first look at Kluane Lake, the largest lake in the Yukon, encompassing over 153 square miles. The color of the lake changes remarkably as the sun shifts during the day. The mountains to the east of the lake are the Ruby Range; their red color comes from mineral deposits in the rock.

> **WEATHER ALERT:** If you go out on the lake, remember that storms cook up fast and the winds can get nasty. Know what you're doing.

There's a turnoff for the ghost town of **Silver City** at Mile 1,053.3. Silver City thrived from 1904 to 1924, as a trading post, a roadhouse, and the barracks for the Royal Canadian Mounted Police. It was a stopping point on the wagon road between the Kluane goldfields and Whitehorse. From here, travelers took boats onto the lake to look for a fresh bit of land to dig for gold. During the highway construction, the town served as a depot for carrying materials across the lake. The ruins of the town are visible from about three miles off the highway. It's well worthwhile to take a side-trip down. The buildings are reasonably intact, and you can see how the original town was laid out. Beautiful fuchsia fireweed grows up between the boards in the summer, and you'll see Arctic ground squirrels with no fear at all.

Mile 1,061 brings a point of interest on each side of the highway. To the north is the **Sheep Mountain Interpretive Area and Visitors Centre**, open 9 am to 5 pm, May through September. Sheep Mountain is the home of a large herd of Dall sheep. The center has a viewing telescope, or you can take the Sheep Mountain Hike (see *Hiking*, above). Your best chance to see them is from August through the winter and into early June.

Just past the center, on the opposite side of the road, is **Soldier's Summit**, the site of the official opening ceremonies of the highway. A plaque commemorates the ceremony, which took place on November 20, 1942, when troops from the 97th Engineers, who were working eastward, met troops from the 18th Engineers, headed west, and the two sections of the highway were joined on the shores of Kluane Lake. The ribbon was cut by E. L. Bartlett, Alaska's delegate to Congress, and Ian MacKenzie, an MP from Ottawa, while the grunt soldiers stood around in blizzard conditions and no doubt wished they could go home. The site was rededicated for the highway's 50th anniversary on November 20, 1992.

The road continues to skirt the lake; there are many pullouts that make good picnic spots or places to stop for photos.

Camp at **Congdon Creek**, with 81 sites at Mile 1,070.5. It's on the lake, and during the summer months the rangers give interpretive talks about the park and animals. If you need hookups, **Cottonwood RV Park**, Mile 1067, is the place to go.

Destruction Bay, at Mile 1,083, started as a construction camp for the highway. It served as one of the relay stations (they were spaced about every 100 miles) for truck drivers to take a nap and get their trucks fixed. It was named when a storm broke off the lake in 1942, destroying much of the camp.

The **Talbot Arm Motel** makes for a good stop for the night if you're running tired. $$$, and maybe not the greatest decor for the price, but it's just about the only game in town. They have 16 partially serviced RV sites as well. Open year-round, there's a gas station and a restaurant. ☎ 867-841-4461.

■ Burwash Landing

 Burwash Landing, at Mile 1,093, was established by the Jacquot brothers in 1904 as a trading post, at the height of the gold rush in the Kluane area. (Burwash, like Kluane, means "place of fish" in the local First Nations dialect.) Besides doing business with the miners, the brothers also traded with the Southern Tutchone Indians, the region's original inhabitants. It was an active settlement when the highway was being built. The historic marker notes, "After months of rough camp life, American soldiers were surprised and delighted when they reached this prosperous little settlement, which seemed like an oasis in the wilderness. Burwash also became the home of Father Eusebe Morissett, an Oblate missionary, who served as an auxiliary chaplain of the American Army." There's no note on what the locals thought about having a missionary move in.

Some artifacts from the Indians can be seen at the **Kluane Museum of Natural History**, right on the highway, open from May to September, 9 am to 9 pm. Admission is $3 for adults, $1.50 for kids. This is an excellent museum, not only for learning about the Indians but also for seeing the animals of the area. Virtually every small town has a few stuffed animals in their museum, but here there is greater variety, and more effort has been made to put the animals into the kind of setting they might actually inhabit. There are also casts of many kinds of paw prints and swatches of fur. This is far and away the best of the dead animal wildlife museums along the highway, and really a class act, despite the "world's largest gold pan" out front.

Burwash Landing also has an excellent hotel, the **Burwash Landing Resort.** It offers tours of the lake and glaciers, gold panning, a restaurant, showers, a gas station, and a fantastic view. $$. For campers, there are 16 serviced sites. Open year-round. The staff can also arrange fishing tours, lake excursions, or park tours from here. ☎ 867-841-4441.

Dalan Campground has 25 sites, a laundromat, showers, and so on. It caters more to the RV than the tent. It's a mile off the highway on Kluane Lake. ☎ 867-841-5501.

■ Kluane Wilderness Village

 The highway follows the Kluane River northward to Kluane Wilderness Village, at Mile 1,118. There's a motel and campground here, along with saloon, gas station, and restaurant. ☎ 867-841-4141.

The point of interest for stopping at the village is the **burl shop**, recognizable by the burl-flanked driveway. A burl is a peculiar deformation in wood, caused by fungus or insect damage. Rather than growing straight, the wood bulges out, forming a bump with a beautiful grain. The shop sells plain burl sticks, which can be used for anything from lamp posts to walking sticks, as well as some beautiful items made from burls. Don't miss looking at the bowls inside and checking out the burl furniture. It's also worthwhile to read the philosophy of life and crafts that the owner, Scully, has hand-lettered on signboards in the place.

The Alaska Highway

Burl Workshop, Mile 1118.

Looking around from the burl shop or the hotel, there are views of the St. Elias Mountains to the south and southwest, including, on a clear day, views of Mt. Logan. To the northwest you'll see the Dawson Range. The roadside looks like soft velvet when the flowers are in bloom – fuchsia, pale yellow, and white.

From Mile 1,130, you hit what was one of the toughest sections of the highway to build. From the Donjek River to the Alaska border, it was all swamp, with a layer of permafrost skating on the top. There were hundreds of creeks and lakes and huge areas of muskeg. The milepost marker reads, "These braided mountain streams would flood after a heavy rainfall or rapid glacial melt, altering the waters' course and often leaving bridges crossing dry ground."

 HIGHWAY TIP: The Yukon puts out an annually updated pamphlet on driving the Alcan, which advises travelers of the possibility of construction, as well as listing Royal Canadian Mounted Police – RCMP or the "Mounties" – stations and the local radio stations to tune in to for conditions. You're going to need that information, because from here the road deteriorates considerably. For the next 100 miles, it's narrow, winding, and very bumpy, with a lot of breaks in the pavement from frost. Don't expect to move too fast.

The forest is very dense through this area, as well; there are abundant small lakes and beaver ponds.

Pickhandle Lake, at Mile 1,158, presented the start of an unusual problem for the road engineers. It was here that they first encountered permafrost.

PERMAFROST

Permafrost is simply frozen ground that lies beneath a thin layer of topsoil. There are two bands of it: the continuous, in the far North, and the discontinuous, as you'll see at Pickhandle Lake. Areas of discontinuous permafrost are surrounded by areas that are not frozen. You can spot the areas by the trees, which are smaller and stunted. Permafrost reaches depths of a thousand feet in places (in this area, its average depth is only about a foot), and it is a nightmare for builders. Anything constructed over it tends to melt the ice, subsiding the ground and sinking the structure.

During the Alaska Highway construction, the road sank, as did the vehicles used to build it when the engineers used standard Lower 48 road-building techniques of stripping off the topsoil and grading what lay beneath. A massive roadbed was eventually constructed, which left the topsoil in place and added further insulation with a layer of fallen trees and brush, and the road went through. The trees in most permafrost areas are largely black spruce, which thrive under the harsh conditions. Watch for areas where the spruce lean to one side; the ground underneath them has partially melted and refrozen. In the forests around Beaver Creek, there are also willow, birch, and evergreens.

The road leaves its course along the edge of the St. Elias Mountains here, but there are still lovely views in every direction: the St. Elias to the southwest, Nutzotin to the northwest, the Wrangell Mountains on the far western horizon.

The last campground before entering Beaver Creek is at Mile 1,188.8. **Snag Junction**, a Yukon government campground, offers a kitchen shelter. The 15 sites are near the lake, with excellent boating and swimming.

■ Beaver Creek

 The last settlement in Canada before you reach the Alaskan border – and the westernmost in the country – Beaver Creek began its history around 1909, when the area was prospected for gold. On the supply route between the White River and Chisana goldfields, not much stopped here until 1955, when it became the Canadian Customs post. And, although Soldier's Summit gets all the publicity, Beaver Creek is also noticeable as the place where the highway was finally finished. When the crews linked up here on October 28, 1942, travel was possible from Dawson Creek, British Columbia, to Fairbanks, Alaska.

In the summer of 1975, there were rumors of a new gold rush. More than 800 claims were staked in the Moosehorn Mountain area, outside Beaver Creek, but not much has come of it. Today, Beaver Creek survives on the Customs Post, a highway construction and maintenance camp, and tourists. Prices reflect this; it's one of the most expensive towns along the highway. Unless your gas tank is empty, wait until the Alaska border, 55 miles down the road. The price of gas falls considerably when you cross the border.

There's really nothing to do in Beaver Creek. The **Visitors Centre** is opened from May to September, 8 am to 8 pm (☎ 867-862-7321), and there are a few interesting displays. Across from the Westmark there is a small, Native-run souvenir shop that's worth stopping in to see the bead work. Other than that, there are only the hotels.

The top-of-the-line hotel in town is the **Westmark**, which is large, comfortable, and often full of bus tours. ☎ 867-862-7501 or 800-544-0970.

The **1202 Creek Motor Inn** has rooms, an RV park, a service station and café. ☎ 867-800-764-7601 from Alaska; ☎ 867-800-661-0540 from the Yukon or BC. Or stay at **Buckshot Betty's**, ☎ 867-862-7111, with cabins and a café. $$.

CUSTOMS CONTROL: Canadian Customs, at Mile 1,203.5 just outside Beaver Creek, is open 24 hours a day, all year, and all traffic entering Canada must stop. Recently searches at this station have increased. Look back at the Customs section in Chapter 2, so you can avoid items that will cause problems. US Customs is located at Mile 1,221.8. It's open 24 hours a day, year-round; all traffic entering the US must stop.

The Canadian Customs station is not actually at the border, however. The actual border between Canada and the US is marked by a clear-cut strip of trees that extends in a perfectly straight line for 740 miles. The trees were originally cut between 1907 and 1913, as both countries tried to clear up the vagaries of the deed of sale to Alaska written by Russia. The strip is 20 feet wide, and there's a stone marker centered in it. It's an interesting piece of national vanity.

The 18 miles of road between Customs posts is rough, narrow, and winding, rather suitable for a no-man's land.

Alaska Border to Tok

>
> **HIGHWAY TIP:** Once you get past the Customs post, the road improves as you travel into Alaska. However, there are some good-sized frost heaves and some breaks in the pavement, enough to keep speeds down a few miles an hour around here. The road stays poor until Northway Junction.

At the border, reset your watch – moving into Alaska, set clocks back one hour. Alaska has its own time zone – Alaska Time – while the Yukon is on Pacific time. Almost immediately past the border, the price of gas on the Alaska side drops considerably, compared to Canadian prices. Ah, all that nasty tax they put on stuff for things like... well, universal health care.

■ Tetlin National Wildlife Refuge

The refuge begins at Mile 1,223. It covers three-quarters of a million acres that were set aside as an important waterfowl breeding and migration area. Among the most beautiful of these waterfowl are the sandhill cranes. Many mammals also make their home here, including moose, caribou, Dall sheep, black bears (whose color may be black, blue, brown, auburn, white, or off-white), grizzly bears, and wolves. Oddly for a refuge, hunting, trapping, and fishing are allowed. Ask at the office.

History

The refuge takes in the Tanana region, which was first explored and settled in the late 1800s. By the 1870s, trade contact had been made with the Athabascan Indians in the region, and a few gold miners were sifting streams. The first official survey was done in 1885, and it included the area from the Copper River to Tanana. This survey was followed by another, in 1899, by the US Geological and Geographical Survey. Traders had become common by the early 1900s, and several trading posts sprang up along the rivers. The trade routes were enlarged, and as the traders introduced the Indians to new food, tools, and so on, the lifestyle of the Indians began to change from a nomadic pattern to a village pattern. This didn't do anybody any favors, but it's a pattern you see all over the world. People who own houses are never happy seeing people who don't want to own houses, and forced settlement usually follows upon the establishment of a government.

The gold rush came late here. In 1913, the Chisana stampede began, flooding the valleys with hopeful placer miners. It went bust as quickly as it had boomed.

Access to Tetlin was difficult until 1942, when the Alcan brought the world to the North. The creation of the refuge and the situation of the site, next to

Wrangell-St. Elias/Kluane Park, has kept the area in a nearly pristine state, where the birds and other animals thrive. There are some remnants of hunting and fishing camps, as well as a few old mining trails, but primarily the land is untouched.

The forest contains a lot of black spruce, one of the few plants that thrives on permafrost; a tree with a trunk two inches in diameter may be over 100 years old though, the growing season is so short and the conditions so unfavorable. Black spruce do not release their seeds except during a forest fire. Large areas of the refuge burned in the summer of 1990, and the new growth forest is now starting to look like real trees. In addition to black spruce, there are aspen, poplar, balsam, and paper birch trees in the refuge.

Inside the Refuge

The highway skirts the northern edge of the refuge, and there are no roads leading inside. To get to the interior, you need a boat or strong legs.

As the road enters the refuge, the first features are wetlands. At Mile 1,224.5, there is an interpretive display explaining the waterfowl habitat below in the Scotty and Desper Creek bottoms. At Mile 1225.6 is a boat ramp into **Desper Creek,** for canoes or other small boats. Arctic loons are a common sight through here, as are a variety of ducks. You may also see eagles and osprey. The best bird-watching is done away from the road, during the months of May and June, and then again in August through October, but no one, at any time of year, goes away without seeing something.

Tetlin is one of two national refuges within Alaska (there are another 16 state refuges, which total more than 87 million acres); it is required by law to educate people, to interpret the environment for the benefit of those who visit. This is accomplished at the **Wildlife Refuge Visitors Center**, at Mile 1,229 (the refuge's main center is in Tok). Open from May to September, 7 am to 7 pm, the center offers an information booth, an observation deck with descriptive plaques and identified bird calls, a nice pressed wildflower display, and earphones you can put on to hear bird calls. There are also a few taxidermied animals. Over by the bathrooms is a board that gives current road conditions on the major roads in Alaska, as well as one offering information on fishing: who's biting what, where. The fishing around here is excellent. Northern pike average about two feet in nearby Deadman Lake.

At Mile 1,240, notice the vertical roadside culverts. They were built to try and prevent permafrost thaw. The deteriorating road condition shows that the efforts were not entirely successful. Remember, there are only two seasons in the North: winter and construction.

A kind of sand dune can be seen in many of the road cuts; these are built from glacial silt blown by the wind from old river beds.

To the north, the Mentasta Mountains come into view. These are part of the Alaska Range, which culminates in Denali, the highest point in North

America. To the southwest, you may get a glimpse of the Wrangell Mountains; to the south, the St. Elias.

Camp at the pretty **Deadman Lake Campground** (Mile 1,249.3), which offers 18 sites, or at the **Lakeview Campground** (Mile 1,256), which has eight. Deadman has a boat launch. Lakeview can take only small vehicles and it's fairly primitive – perfect for tenters looking to get away from RV herds. Lakeview also has a display to explain the waterfowl in the area. At either campground, watch for birds, and take a look at the wildflowers along the road, including sweet peas, poppies, Indian paintbrush, and Labrador tea.

The highway begins to parallel the Chisana (pronounced shoe-SAN-naw) River at Mile 1,263.5. A half-mile after meeting the river, there is a turnoff for **Northway Junction**, one of the stops on the old Northwest Staging Route. The town itself, an Athabascan village, is about seven miles off the highway, and gas, food, and lodging are available. Right on the highway at the turnoff is the **Naabia Niign Athabascan Indian Crafts Store and Campground**. The name "Naabia Niign" means "our village along the river." In addition to the excellent selection of authentic crafts (take a look at their mukluks, bark baskets, and the extraordinary beadwork – you can also buy beads to try your own hand at it), there is a restaurant, gas station, and grocery store.

Northway Junction is often the coldest place in Alaska. This far inland, the weather patterns are influenced by the shape of mountains and plains, and the wind can howl through here in the winter. At least one or two days a year around January, the village will see temperatures dropping past 50 below.

The road begins to improve again here, smoothing out under good surfacing. Notice the glass insulators on the telephone poles; collectors haven't raided Alaska yet (nobody wants to risk the bears, mosquitoes, etc.).

There are good views of where the Chisana and Nabesna rivers join to form the Tanana River, which is the largest tributary to the mighty Yukon, at Mile 1,269. A sign points out the pertinent features. There are several pullouts for photos of the river valley.

Mile 1,284 marks the northern boundary of the refuge, and pretty **Midway Lake** is to the south at Mile 1,289. The lake was the site of a contractor's camp during Highway construction in 1943. Its inhabitants were called "dirt pushers." From here you'll see the Mentasta Mountains to the southwest, the Wrangell Mountains to the south.

Tetlin Junction, at Mile 1,301.7, offers a turnoff to the Taylor Highway, and the Top of the World Highway, Dawson City, and Inuvik, via the northern route.

HIGHWAY TIP: Before taking this route, check with the Tok or Tetlin Visitors Center, or with the state Highway Commission. Road conditions change quickly, and fires close off sections of the roads nearly every summer.

Fuchsia fireweed carpets old burn areas. The worst sections of the Taylor Highway are the very beginning, and again approaching the Canadian border. From the Canadian border to Dawson City, the road is a joy to drive – unless you're coming after heavy rains and before the graders. See *Chapter 9* for details.

WARNING: In summer the fire danger in this area is high, and all campfires should be carefully controlled. The Tok area averages nearly 20 human-caused fires a year. Lightning strike fires, like the massive Tok River fire, add to the firefighters workload. Within the Tok forestry district, roughly 5,000 acres are burned by fires started by careless people every year. Make sure your campfires are entirely out, with nothing left smoldering. Stir the ashes and feel them with your bare hands. If there's still heat, you need to work on putting out the fire. After a forest fire, firefighters have to go through every inch of the burned land, checking for hot embers to ensure there's nothing that's going to rekindle the blaze.

CUSTOMS CONTROL: The US/Canadian border crossing on the road up toward Dawson is not open at night, so time your travel accordingly. The post is open 9 am to 9 pm, Pacific Time – note the hour difference with Alaska time.

The road was first carved out by miners heading up to Eagle. **The Eagle Trail**, built in the early 1900s, stretched as far south as Valdez. Later, during the Fortymile gold strike, the road was flooded with hopeful miners en route to the Klondike. Small pieces of the original trail are still visible.

From here on out on the Alaska Highway, you've got company to Fairbanks. The Alcan runs along the path of the Tanana River almost all the way to town. Sometimes the river is out of view behind the trees or away from the road, but when it's on view, you'll have great views of the river; watch for swallows swooping around bridges.

Tok River State Recreation Site, at Mile 1,309.3, is a lovely spot that was saved from the fires of 1990 by the river. There are 25 campsites, interpretive signs, and a nature walk. Sites are $10 per night.

Tok

Nearly destroyed by a massive forest fire in the summer of 1990, Tok is a major crossroads in central Alaska; it provides access to Dawson City, Fairbanks, Valdez, and Anchorage. Although there's little to it except hotels, it's a surprisingly enjoyable place to spend a day.

There are conflicting stories about the town's name. One holds that it was originally called Tokyo, and the name was shortened during the war because of anti-Japanese feelings. Another story attributes the name to the Tok River, the word "tok" meaning "peace crossing" in an Athabascan language. The region was an Athabascan peace gathering area long before the arrival of the whites. There's also a theory that the town's name came from a husky puppy that lived at the site when the Alcan was going through.

Area of forest in Tok scarred by fire.

■ History

Like so many other towns along the road, Tok began its life as a Highway construction camp; after the war ended, it became a camp for the Alaska Road Commission, with all the same duties under another name and boss. The town itself was formed in 1946, the same year the Alcan opened to civilian traffic, and it has thrived on that traffic ever since. About 1,000 people call Tok their home today.

The fire of 1990 nearly brought an end to the peace of the town. During the first days of July, a fire caused by lightning strikes miles from the town began to push northward, coming up to Tok past the airport, jumping every firebreak the firefighters created. The highway was closed and parts of the town evacuated, as fire raged on both sides and firefighters fought the blaze house to house. Finally, the weather gave them a much needed break, as winds shifted the blazes away and a sprinkling of rain fell, saving the town. Both sides of the highway had burned, from the Tok River to the edge of the parking lot of the easternmost hotel in town, one that had just opened for business before the fire. The exhausted fire crews then had to rush off to fight another fire on the Taylor Highway.

It will be many years before the forest comes back to its mature state; thousands of acres burned, extending from Tok through the wilderness into the Tetlin Refuge. But even a week after the fire, signs of resurgent life could be glimpsed through the haze of the smoldering trees: birds feasting on insects, small mammals tentatively looking for food away from the burn. In the fire, the black spruce opened up their seeds; so in another generation, the forest should be new and vibrant. Ten years after the fire, things are looking relatively well, but fires come all too close to the town every year. And as hot as the past few years have been, with as many fires – in the Yukon alone, more land burned in 2004 than in all the rest of Canada combined – as there have been lately, the fine people of Tok do keep a very close eye on their trees.

■ Things to Do

 Tok has one of the best visitors centers along the entire Highway. The big log building is located on the north side of the road, just east of the junction with the Glenn Highway. You can't miss it. During the 1990 fire, the parking lot was turned into a campground while stranded travelers waited for fire crews to clear the road. The center is open daily from 7 am to 9 pm, from May 1 through October 1; and from 8 am to 4:30 pm in the winter (☎ 907-883-5887).

Tok Visitors Center (or, as it is officially called, the Alaska Public Lands Information Center, as the two places have more or less melded into one) offers a huge variety of informative brochures for places of interest all over the state. There is also a computer that can deliver information on public lands throughout the state. There's a small museum on the history of Alaska and the highway, a few wildlife displays, and an excellent slide show on the building of the highway. The helpful staff gets the same questions about the road to Dawson a thousand times a day, so they're the best place to check for current information. They also dole out free coffee.

Those heading west should stop by **Tetlin National Wildlife Refuge Headquarters**, inside the US Fish and Wildlife office (☎ 907-883-5312) in town, next to the grocery store. It's open from 8 to 4:30 daily in the summer. For more on the refuge, see the Tetlin section, a few pages back.

Mukluk Land (☎ 907-883-2571), at Mile 1,317, is open from June 1 to August 31, from 1 to 9 pm. It's got movies on Alaska, bush miniature golf (if you're really trying to kill time), gold panning (with success guaranteed), the world's largest mukluk, the world's largest mosquito (a claim to be debated by anyone who has done much camping in the state), and "a tent in Tok" (which is a tent that a family lived in for 13 months, enduring temperatures as low as 69 below). Maybe it's kind of hokey, but there's not a whole lot else to do in town. If you like this kind of thing, or if you've got kids who've been sitting in the car too long, you'll love this place. If you don't like this kind of thing, the river's not far away and the hiking is excellent. Admission is $5 for adults, $2 for kids.

Tok bills itself as the "sled dog capital of Alaska," and it hosts one of the largest races in the state, the **10K Race of Champions**, on March 31. Those going through in summer can still get a look at sled dogs at the **Burnt Paw**, just west of the junction. Monday through Saturday during the summer months, at 7:30pm, they put on a free demonstration of sled dogs, explaining the gear used, the conditions, and the history, and telling you about the dogs before they hitch four of them up and let them run. The dogs love to run, and they are not in the least bothered by the weight in the sled (a 50-pound dog can pull a 1,000 pounds). It's a fascinating look at an Alaskan tradition, and if they draw your ticket number in the free lottery, you'll get a ride on the sled. If the howling makes you wish for a pup of your own, you may be able to buy one from the Burnt Paw from about $100. Only worthy owners who understand how much these dogs love to run need apply.

■ Out & About

There's not a whole lot going on in or around Tok. The city began as a crossroads, and it's still mostly a nice place to stop on your way somewhere else. The fun of the place is just to hang out and watch the world go by for a little while.

One of the more unusual outdoor opportunities is the paved **bike path** that follows the highway from Mile 1,313 to Mile 1,326, and again for about two miles on the Tok Cutoff. There are prettier rides in the state, but if you're bored and need to stretch, here it is. In winter, there's great cross-country skiing and snowmobiling.

For bird-watchers, Tok and the entire upper **Tanana Valley** are on one of the major flyways for the **Arctic migration route,** bringing in Canadian geese, swans, pintails, wigeons, and a hundred or so other species of bird.

Tok also hosts a more exotic, and perhaps more endangered species: it's hitchhiker central – thumbers line up here looking for rides. If you're going to try it, don't so much as bother to wave at cars with out of state plates; only Alaskans will even think about picking you up. Keep your bottle of DEET handy while you wait for a ride. Overall, Alaska is one of the last places in the US where hitchhikers can find rides; it's a fairly safe state, most people are already armed for bear, and you have to feel sorry for some hitcher standing out in the rain in the middle of nowhere. We're not suggesting you try hitching, or that you pick people up; your choice, either way.

Fishing is good in most of the nearby lakes, or try for turbot in the rivers.

Most of the hotels in town have some kind of gold panning action. For the finished product, after the gold gets cleaned, polished, and shaped, take a look at the **Jack Wade Gold Co.**, just down the cutoff. It's a good place to see how gold is mined and processed, with some historical displays. ☎ 907-883-5887.

■ Food

The best place to eat is the **Tok Gateway Salmon Bake** on the north side of the main road, Mile 1313. It's run by a husband-and-wife team. He grills outside, she takes your money and hands you a plate. You eat outside in a covered area with picnic tables. This is widely considered one of the best salmon bakes in the state.

If getting delicious halibut or salmon cooked over a wood fire doesn't thrill you, there are other options in town.

Fast Eddie's, at Mile 1,313.3, is the place to go for Italian food, offering good lasagna and pizza. There's a big salad bar, too – try the Polar Bear salad. Prices range from $4 to $19. For baked goods, try the **Valley Bakery**. It sells meat and cheese by the pound, fresh breads, and baked goods. Stock up here for the drive ahead. Try the straw bread – not only is it good, it keeps for about 10 days.

Finally, the **Sourdough Campground** has a good breakfast café, open from 7 to 11 in the morning. It serves up lots of food at very reasonable prices.

The cheapest food in town is at **Frontier Foods**, directly across from the Visitors Center. The grocery store has a deli and a bakery, and it's a must-stop if you're heading up the Taylor Highway, down the Tok Cutoff, or taking another route into Canada, where the prices jump dramatically.

■ Accommodations

Tok is a city of hotels. Driving through, it looks as though the rooms could never be booked up, but during peak season they fill early. Make your reservations in advance if you can. At least the prices are reasonable – $100 is a really expensive room in Tok, and you can probably get something under $75 without much trouble.

One of the best deals in town is the **Golden Bear Motel**, two miles down the Tok Cutoff. It offers 52 rooms, some with kitchenettes at no extra charge. $$. The motel also has a good campground, set back in the trees –

best tent spaces in town – and there's full hook-ups for RVs. There's also a laundromat and free showers with unlimited hot water. For tent campers, there's the nearly unheard-of luxury of heated bathrooms. The motel also offers gold panning and a gift shop. ☎ 907-866-883-2561.

HOTEL PRICING
Prices are in US dollars.
under $50 . . . . $
$50-$100 . . . . $$
$100-$150 . . . . . . $$$
above $150 . . . . . $$$$

The **Snowshoe Motel** (☎ 907-883-4181) is across from the Visitors Center. It's small, but pleasant and recently fixed up. In summer months the motel offers a free continental breakfast. $$. Comparable is **Young's Motel** (☎ 907-883-4411) at Mile 1,313, next to Fast Eddie's Restaurant. You'll find a laundromat, gas, a mini-store, and plenty of parking. $$

If you're planning to hang out at the **Burnt Paw** for the sled dog demos, you can also stay there. They've got four very nice cabins, $$. They are usually booked, so you'll need to plan ahead. ☎ 907-883-4121.

For luxury accommodation, try the **Westmark**, at the junction of the Tok Cutoff. It has 72 rooms, as well as a good restaurant, a gift shop, car wash, gas station, and the only bookstore in town. While Westmark's lodging is at the upper end of the price scale, the hotel chain's restaurants tend to be surprisingly reasonable and good. ☎ 907-800-544-0970 or 883-5174, $$$$.

There are a few B&Bs in town, if you're looking for a change of pace. Check at the Visitors Center for new B&B openings.

Old standards include **Cleft of the Rock** (☎ 907-883-4219), $$ and **Off the Road House** (☎ 907-883-5600). It's open year-round, $$ and an art gallery on the premises.

Camping

While the hotels sometimes fill up, there's almost always a place to park for the night. Besides the **Golden Bear Motel's** campground, there's the **Bull Shooter RV Park**, at Mile 1,313.3. Open May to September, it offers showers, a camping shop, and a nice location among the trees. There are 50 sites. ☎ 907-883-5625.

The **Sourdough Campground** is a half-mile south of the cutoff, on the Glenn Highway. Open May to September, it has 75 sites, with room for everything from tents to 70-foot RVs. Besides the usual services, it also offers slide shows and a small museum. This is a good place to stay, but it's more popular with the RV crowd than with tenters. ☎ 907-883-5543.

Tok RV Village, Mile 1,313.4, is open May to October. It has the biggest lot in town. It's not as scenic as others, but is clean and organized. There are 95 sites; tenters may want to look elsewhere. ☎ 907-883-5877. **Tundra Lodge and RV Park** is at Mile 1315, with 77 sites. ☎ 907-883-7875.

As mentioned above, there's camping at the **Salmon Bake**, Mile 1313, good for those who might overindulge in some of the best fish in Alaska. A

nice place with good people. Open mid-May through mid-September.
☎ 907-883-5555.

Tok to Delta Junction

Agood but narrow and sometimes winding road takes you from Tok to
Delta Junction. As on most roads in the North, there are areas of frost
heave and some patching on the road surface.

Along the road you'll see the Alaska Range to the west and the St. Elias
Mountains to the south. But for the most part, from here to Fairbanks,
you're not exactly in the most stunning scenery around. Flatland and forest sums it up.

Mile 1,332 offers you a chance to camp among the poppies – white, orange,
yellow, and pink – at the **Moon Lake State Recreation Site**. No services
are provided, but 15 good gravel campsites, and small boat access and good
swimming in the lake. Watch for moose in the area.

You cross the Robertson River at Mile 1,355; the river is frequently partially frozen as late as mid-June.

Excellent **fishing** abounds in the many lakes. Try **Jan Lake** at Mile 1,359;
the lake is about a half-mile off the road, and it's a good place to try your
luck for rainbow trout.

Dot Lake, at Mile 1,361.3, has a small lodge and a gas station. They're
open year-round, except on Sundays. The roadside culverts are simply
brimming with wild iris in season.

Between Mile 1,390 and Delta Junction, there's a good chance of seeing bison toward the southwest in the 3,000-acre **Bison Sanctuary.** Bison once
ranged wild from Alaska to Florida, but you all know the stories of what
happened there (and no, they're not buffalo – that's a different species, native to Asia and Africa). Over a six-year period, coinciding with the coming
of trains to the West, the animals were slaughtered, millions upon millions
of them left to rot in the sun.

The herd here, which numbers about 375 animals, is the result of a trans-
plant of 23 bison from Noiese, Montana, in 1928. The Delta Junction region
was chosen because wildfires had replaced the trees with grasses. The
herd grew as large as 500 animals during the 1950s; however, space and
forage availability, as well as strictly controlled hunting, has lowered the
number. About 10,000 hunters annually apply for the 50 to 75 permits allowed each year.

The bison have developed a slight migratory pattern. They summer and
calve along the Delta River, to the southwest of Delta Junction; in winter,
they spend their time in the Delta agricultural region, giving the local
farmers fits. The Department of Fish and Game is working on getting the

bison to winter away from the farms by planting forage in new areas, but so far their success has been limited.

In the summer, the best place to see the bison is on the turnout at Mile 242.5 on the Richardson Highway, about 20 miles south of Delta Junction. There's a large sign on the west side of the highway. Even from here, however, they are usually a long way off; binoculars or a telephoto lens are a must.

At Mile 1,409, a marker that says, "The Alaska Highway exposed Alaska to all the good and bad in civilization we always thought was so far away." Luckily, most of it remains far away.

There are good views of the Alaska Range to the south at Mile 1,410. As you approach Delta Junction, there is a place to stay outside of town.

Mile 1,415 is the turnoff to **Clearwater State Recreation Site and Campground**. It's about 8.5 miles off the highway. There are 16 sites next to the Delta-Clearwater River. It's a good place to check on the spring and fall migrations of sandhill cranes, geese, and other waterfowl, and there are the usual boating and fishing opportunities: grayling, whitefish, and, in the fall, silver salmon.

At Mile 1,415.4 is the **Alaska Homestead and Historical Museum**, with a log house, gardens, historical farming and logging equipment, sled dogs, and such. Run by the Dorshorst Family (you actually tour the family's house), admission is $4 for adults, $3 for kids. ☎ 907-885-4431.

Delta Junction

Congratulations! You have just finished driving the Alaska Highway! That is, if you choose to believe the Delta Junction Chamber of Commerce. The Fairbanks Chamber of Commerce will disagree mightily – although signs are they're coming around to the truth.

The controversy here at Mile 1,422 is as old as the highway itself. When construction began, the Richardson Highway, leading from Fairbanks to Valdez, already went through Delta Junction before turning south. This was the old Valdez-Fairbanks Trail, a route used by hopeful miners looking for gold – branching off towards Circle and the Klondike, or towards the Tanana strikes, or even farther out to Nome. It was turned into a real road in the early 1900s, and the highway engineers on the Alcan used the established road as the last leg of their own project. In that sense, Delta Junction is, indeed, the end of the Alaska Highway; at least, it is the end of what was built during that frenzied period in 1942. You're at the end here, and Fairbanks – although a recent newspaper article admitted Delta Junction was the end of the highway – can fuss about being the real end all it wants. It's your tourist dollars they're fighting over.

Still, no matter the truth behind Delta Junction's claim, the destination for the highway was always Fairbanks. If the Richardson Highway hadn't been there, the engineers would have simply gone on carving out more road for a couple of hundred miles. After what they'd already been through, it would have been a piece of cake.

■ History

 Throughout its history, Delta Junction has been a stopping point on the way to somewhere else. During the Fairbanks gold rush, the trail for the miners led from Valdez north, through Delta Junction. Roadhouses were established, and a town of trappers, miners, and those who were to serve the trappers and miners slowly developed. One of these roadhouses, Rika's Landing, still stands as the main attraction at the Big Delta State Historical Park.

Delta Junction was also called Buffalo Center during the early days, due to the large herd of bison. The town has grown from the influx of travelers on the Alaska Highway and the Richardson Highway, and because of the Alaska Pipeline, which is nearby. Today, about 1,200 people live inside the city, and another 4,000 live in the surrounding areas. Farming and tourism are the main industries, since the pipeline boom passed.

A bit of extra life is injected into the town by Allen Army Base (now called Fort Greely), built as a transfer point for the Lend-Lease program with the Soviet Union, which sent US aircraft overseas. Today, it is home of the Northern Warfare Training Center and the Cold Regions Test Center, which gives equipment the stress test under extreme conditions.

■ Things to Do

 There's not much to do in Delta Junction; it's still just a stop on the way to somewhere else, and few people stop here longer than it takes to stretch their legs. However, the **Visitor Information Center** (☎ 907-895-9941 or 907-895-5069) is well worth a stop. It's open in the summer from 9 am to 6 pm, and just outside the door is a large sign proclaiming the end of the highway. There are also some cross sections of pipeline, to give you an idea of what was involved in bringing oil down from the North Slope. You'll also find free coffee, a nice garden, a good selection of books on Alaska, and films running throughout the day, and you can buy a certificate – "End of the Alaska Highway" – proclaiming your success at surviving the Alcan.

■ Out & About

The **Sullivan Roadhouse Historical Museum** is right by the Visitor Center. It's the oldest roadhouse in Alaska's Interior, and it's been jazzed up to let you see what life used to be like up here. Lovely garden outside, and admission is free. Well worth stopping in.

The Alaska Highway

A nice side-trip from town is to climb or drive to **Donnelly Dome**, about 23 miles south of town on the Richardson Highway. The Dome is 2,400 feet above the surrounding area and offers excellent views of the Alaska Range and the Tanana Valley. In the Alaska Range, you'll see Mt. Shand (12,600 feet), Mt. Moffit (13,020 feet), and Hess Mountain (11,940 feet). The tallest mountain visible is Mount Hayes (13,832 feet). Hayes is 43 miles southwest of Delta Junction, and it was first climbed on August 1, 1941. While you're on the Dome, take a look at the wildflowers; it's the best wildflower viewing spot in the area.

Fishing is especially good on **Quartz Lake** and **Clearwater Lake**; you can try fly-fishing for grayling or fishing for trout and silver salmon, which are stocked in Quartz Lake. Clearwater is better for grayling. There are a lot of lakes and streams around Delta Junction, enough to keep anglers happy for weeks. Some other good choices include Shaw Creek, Birch Lake, and the Salcha River. Check current conditions at the Visitor Information Center – also check on current regulations, since there are catch-and-release-only periods. **Granite View Sports and Gifts**, just across from the Visitors Center, can sell you lures, local maps, and a fishing license.

▪ Food

Outside of the hotels, there aren't many restaurant choices in Delta Junction.

Try **Pizza Bella Restaurant**, across from the Visitor's Information Center. Open 10 am to midnight, seven days a week, it offers great pizza, steaks, and Italian food, with fun, sassy service, at prices ranging from $4 to $12. This is far and away the best food in town; the booths have been worn threadbare by all the tourists sliding in and out.

For something a little different, there's **Delta Meat & Sausage Company**, Mile 1413.5. Not a restaurant, but a food store. Where else can you get buffalo steaks for your lunch and reindeer sausage for your breakfast? They're open Monday-Friday, 8-5, Saturdays from 10-4.

▪ Accommodations

The **Alaska 7 Motel** (☎ 907-895-4848, www.alaska7motel.com), at Mile 270.3 on the Richardson Highway (about five miles out of town), is open year-round. $$. A few dollars more is **Kelly's Alaska Country Inn** (☎ 907-895-4667, www.kellysalaskacountryinn. com). Right at the intersection of the Alcan and the Richardson, it has nicely done rooms and is probably the best bet between here and Fairbanks.

Camping

Campers with tents should head for the **Delta State Recreation Site**, at Mile 267 on the Richardson Highway, a mile west of town. Open only in the summer, it offers good views of the Alaska Range.

> **HIGHWAY TIP:** From here on out mile numbers are the mileposts on the Richardson Highway. The road is wide and good, with the usual frost heaves.

Delta Junction to Fairbanks

■ Big Delta State Historical Park

Rika's Roadhouse, at Mile 275, is one of the many roadhouses that lined the trail from Valdez to the goldfields north of Fairbanks. Located at Bates Landing, at the confluence of the Delta and Tanana rivers (which was originally the location of an Athabascan fishing camp, and later a military communications center), the roadhouse was built to service a ferry run by the federal government that once took travelers across the Tanana River. They only charged people who were northbound. The land was bought in 1906 by John Hajdukovich, and he enlarged the existing roadhouse into a trading post for fur. He also ran a steamship up the Tanana River and guided hunting parties. John eventually ran into debt to Rika Wallen, a Swedish immigrant who worked at the roadhouse. He owed her so much in back wages that he was forced to sign the deed of the house over to her in 1923. She also owned a homestead that adjoined the property, and the roadhouse stayed in business until the late 1940s.

Now a historical state park – technically known as the Big Delta State Historical Park – Rika's Roadhouse has been completely restored and opened for visitors. Admission is free. There's a self-guided tour, which takes about 30 minutes, and you can see the roadhouse, barn, smithy, gardens, and a variety of farm animals. A small museum is located in a sod-roofed building in front of the roadhouse. Inside the beautifully restored roadhouse itself there is a good but pricey gift shop. After taking the tour, don't miss the restaurant. It serves some of the best pastries – especially bear claws (the baked kind!) – in the entire state. It's open 9 am to 5 pm and is best when there isn't a bus tour around. It's a beautiful spot to get out and look around. ☎ 907-895-4201, www.rikas.com.

Continuing past Rika's Roadhouse, the next place of interest is at Mile 275. 5, where there's a pullout to view the Alaska Pipeline as it is suspended above the **Big Delta Bridge**. There are interpretive signs to explain everything. You're also back in moose country now.

For those wanting to fish or camp at Lost Lake and Quartz Lake, the turn-off is at Mile 278.5. **Quartz Lake State Recreation Park** has often-crowded campsites (you're really in the distant suburbs of Fairbanks here – or at least within commuting distance), plus another 77 places to park your RV. **Lost Lake** is much less crowded, has a nice picnic area, better scenery, and good beaches; it's also got only 12 sites.

You have great views of the Alaska Range from Mile 288. Look south and you can see Mt. Hayes (13,832 feet) and Mt. Deborah (12,339 feet).

The highway begins to climb a bit past Birch Lake, and at Mile 321.5 you'll see the **Harding Lake State Recreation Area**, with 89 great camping sites. It's a popular summer place for Fairbanks residents. Just a bit farther down the road, at Mile 323, is the free **Salcha River State Recreation Site**. It's smaller, but hey, it's free, and just as good as Harding Lake. In salmon season, though, come dressed for combat and ready to stand and fight for your spot by the water.

If you didn't buy burls back near Haines Junction and have since regretted it, there's another chance at the **Knotty Shop**, at Mile 323.3; watch for the burl animals in front of the store. They've got good ice cream in the shop for only a buck a cone.

The final stretch of the road begins with a divided highway at Mile 341. The road is excellent but crowded, particularly during shift changes at Eilson Air Force Base.

Chena Lakes Recreation Area turnoff is at Mile 346.7. It's popular with Fairbanks residents and very busy. First built by the Army Corps of Engineers, it has 80 campsites, swimming, good fishing in the stocked lake, and some hiking trails. Fee for both camping and day use.

The largest Santa Claus in the world is at Mile 349, at **Santa Claus House** in North Pole, Alaska. Any kind of Christmas decoration you might ever want can be found here, and you can meet Santa Claus year-round. Stop in, and you can get letters from Santa sent to anybody, anywhere in the world. They've also got an RV park if you don't want to take the last few miles into Fairbanks.

The town of **North Pole** was started in the 1940s by residents hoping to attract a toy manufacturer to the area. They could just see the riches coming in and the cachet the toys would have, being manufactured at "the North Pole." Unfortunately, the idea didn't quite pan out, but the town's sticking to the name and the theme, even though more people make their living off the two refineries than they do from Christmas. The streets have whimsical names, such as Mistletoe Lane, and the post office is incredibly busy during the Christmas season, giving out the "North Pole" postmark (a right now usurped by many other local post offices in the area). North Pole gets about 100 letters to Santa Claus per day. You can drop your letter off in the sack at the Information Center, where it will get hauled to the post office.

You can bypass Fairbanks and head directly down to Denali and Anchorage at the exit to the Parks Highway, at Mile 360.5. If you want to go to downtown Fairbanks, turn left on Airport Way; continue straight for the Steese and Elliot Highways, which lead north to Manley Hot Springs and the Dalton Highway – and up past the Arctic Circle.

Fairbanks

O kay, we're cheating. In Delta Junction we told you Fairbanks wasn't part of the Alaska Highway, and here we are including it in the Alaska Highway section.

That's because no matter where the roads were or weren't, Fairbanks was the end. It was the goal. After months of slogging through mud, muskeg, brutal freezing temperatures, hundreds of truck breakdowns, and long nights in unheated tents, Fairbanks came upon the highway construction crews like a day in paradise. While the road itself did not have to be built this far – Fairbanks is on the Richardson Highway, not the Alaska Highway – the town was always considered the final goal of the Alaska Highway. Once you've made it here, you've finished the Alcan, driven a good chunk of the Richardson, and taken the route whose creation moved men and machinery at unimaginable speed through the wild. Remember, it took the first truck convoys weeks of steady driving to make it this far – at an average speed of about 15 miles an hour.

Fairbanks is the second-largest city in Alaska, with a borough population of upwards of 100,000 people. It is also the home of the University of Alaska, and it's one of the northernmost major cities in the world. Always in a rivalry with Anchorage, Fairbanks is a reversal of the maxim, "It's a nice place to visit, but I wouldn't want to live there." Fairbanks is a lovely place to live – there are great restaurants, fascinating seasonal events, lovely neighborhoods tucked away in the trees, and only the occasional winter day when the temperature gets worse than 50 below; for most visitors, however, Fairbanks is just a stopping point on the way to Denali. Give the place a little more time, though, and you'll find some really nice surprises.

■ History

Fairbanks history began in 1901, when Captain E. T. Barnette set up a small trading post on the banks of the Chena River. Barnette, though, had wanted to be somewhere else; this spot on the riverbanks was just a transfer point. Actually, he was headed for where the Tanana River and the Valdez-Eagle Trail intersected to set his trading post up there, much closer to the action. However, he wrecked his own boat, and then the boat he hired was stopped by shallow water. Barnette was sitting by the riverbank, his gear piled high around him, selling what he could and trying to figure a way east, when Felix Pedro discovered gold nearby. (Some people have all the luck.) Barnette quickly turned his temporary trading post into a permanent one.

The sudden influx of miners and those seeking to make a few bucks off the miners brought in enough population for the town to incorporate in 1903. By 1908, there were 18,500 people in the area.

The name "Fairbanks" came about in a bit of wheeler-dealery and power trading. Senator Charles Fairbanks got a town named after him, and Judge James Wickersham got a permanent seat for his court in return.

Fairbanks grew slowly and steadily, gaining the railroad and the university, until the next boom came with the oil pipeline. The town became the northern headquarters for construction of the project (although most of the main offices for the pipeline were in Anchorage). This was another reason for the rivalry between the two cities; rumor says that Fairbanks was just too greedy, and the oil barons decided to leave things in Anchorage as much as possible. Nonetheless, workers flooded the area. The tide has receded today, leaving behind a pleasant small town with many of the amenities of a big city. The town maintains the main campus of the University of Alaska (incoming freshmen get a flyer detailing camping near campus, with the warning, "It takes most people about three weeks to find an apartment"). The Ft. Wainwright Army Post and Eielson Air Force Base are also here.

■ Climate

 What sets Fairbanks apart from most other places you may have been is its rather unusual weather. Over the course of a year, the city can have temperature swings of 150° or more. There are winter days that hit 50 or 60 below, and summer days over 100° hit once every couple of years.

However, for the most part, in the summer, Fairbanks has glorious weather: long, sunny, warm days with an average temperature of 72° in July. The sun is still blazing at midnight – the city has "continual functional daylight" from May 17 to July 26. This doesn't mean the sun is up all that time – you're well below the Arctic Circle here – but twilight and dawn blend into each other, so it's never really pitch dark. The winters are the payback, however: dark and freezing – an average of 10.3° below in January – with daytime temperatures often hitting 40° below. Go to any store in town and you'll see signs that say "Please turn off your engine." This may puzzle you until you've tried to start a car with a cold motor in serious sub-zero weather. On the shortest day of the year, there are only three hours and 42 minutes of daylight.

THE NORTHERN LIGHTS

However, there is beauty in the winter, as well. There are few places as suited to viewing the northern lights as Fairbanks. The winter displays are awe-inspiring. The university issues a weekly aurora forecast, predicting when and where the best displays of northern lights can be seen. If you want a great view in the winter, head away from the lights of the city and up toward Chena Hot Springs or the town of Circle.

QUICK TOUR: Fairbanks is very spread out. Head up to the **college** to check out the attractions there, then down towards **Creamer's Field**. A quick spin through **downtown**, and then it's time to hit all the attractions at the edge of town.

DON'T MISS: The **U of A museum** is one of the best in the state.

BEST FREE THING TO DO: Check out the **musk ox** at the Large Animal Research Station (although you get a better look with the tour), or **birdwatch** at Creamer's Field.

■ Basics

Fairbanks is a sprawling city with attractions often very widespread. Start your visit in the downtown area. This is where you'll find the log cabin **Visitor Information Center**, at 550 1st Ave. (☎ 907-456-5774 or 800-327-5774, www.explorefairbanks.com). The center is open daily from 8 am to 8 pm in summer and 8 am to 5 pm in winter, weekdays. The staff is endlessly helpful and can load you down with promotional brochures, including ones on walking and driving tours of Fairbanks. The full tours are not really worth the time; choose what interests you and skip the rest. There are also smaller visitor booths at the airport and the Alaska Railroad depot.

There are **weekly concerts** in the plaza outside the Visitors Center. Offerings can range from a polka band to Dixieland; check for the current schedule.

Nearby, at 250 Cushman, is the **Alaska Public Lands Information Center**, in the basement of Courthouse Square, open 9 to 6 daily in the summer, and 10 to 6, Tuesday through Saturday in the winter. This is where you can get information and recreation ideas on any of Alaska's public lands. There is a small bookstore with books, prints, and slides, and there are daily films, short videos, interpretive exhibits, and stereoscopic viewers with slides of historic events. The best of these displays are the short pieces on the different regions of Alaska. In 20 minutes or so you get the highlights of the whole state to help you plan where to go next. The staff is friendly and extremely knowledgeable. Go here before you head out for any of the parks. (However, remember that the staff does not handle reservations for any park.) There are some state cabins in the Fairbanks area, but most of them are geared more toward winter use, so if you're here in the cold, the office will fill you in on avalanche safety and so forth.

Alaska Public Lands hands out a weekly schedule of the films they're showing – from half-hour documentaries on traditional Native life or local kayaking to hour-long films about sled dogs. It's worth picking up as soon as you get there so you can plan ahead. There's also a schedule of their excellent naturalist programs. If you're here in the winter, they have a great lecture series that covers things like hiking the Chilkoot. Best of all, it's all free.

If you're about to head out of Fairbanks and need more information on where you're going, call the **Alaska State Department of Transportation** (☎ 907-451-2210). They can give you up-to-date conditions on any of Alaska's roads.

■ Things to Do

The big attraction in town is **Alaskaland**, a free theme park. Okay, first of all, it's really called **Pioneer Park**, but everybody in town still calls it by its old name, Alaskaland. Either way, it's at Airport Way and Peger Rd., and open from Memorial Day to Labor Day, 11 am to 9 pm. You get in free, but then there are separate charges for the attractions. Originally built for the commemoration of the 100th anniversary of the Alaska Purchase, the most interesting feature of Alaskaland is the array of old cabins, moved here from their original sites all over the state. Carefully restored, the cabins now house gift shops and restaurants. In addition, there is a reconstructed gold camp and examples of Indian houses. There are three museums, including one on pioneer aviation and one on the gold rush; a railroad car used by President Harding; the sternwheeler, S.S. *Nenana*; and a steam shovel that was used to help dig the Panama Canal. A train is available to take you on a circular tour of the grounds, and there are daily shows of the Big Stampede, a pictorial history of the gold rush era. There is also a variety theater show at the Palace Theater. Check the signboard outside for show times.

S.S. *Nenana*, on the grounds of Alaskaland, is the second-largest wooden ship in the world today, at 237 feet long and 42 feet wide. The ship drew an amazingly shallow six inches during its operational years, making a 774-mile trip from Nenana to Marshall. Heading downstream, the ship could cover 17 miles an hour. If you missed the riverboats in Whitehorse, this is a good second chance to see how things moved in Alaska before the highways.

There's a salmon bake at Alaskaland that's a good value, and the halibut nuggets are great. Dinner only. See the *Accommodations* section (below) for details on staying overnight here.

The **Large Animal Research Station**, at Mile 2, Yankovich Rd. (☎ 907-474-7640), offers a chance to see musk oxen, reindeer, and caribou. You can go at any time and see the animals from viewing platforms, or you can take a tour. Tours run June through August on Tuesdays and Saturdays at 11 am and 1:30 and 3 pm, or in September on Saturdays at 11 am. Cost is $10 for adults, $4 for seniors, $2 for students, or the whole family for $10. Children under age seven are free.

MUSK OX

The musk ox was once hunted to near-extinction in Alaska; the entire population in the state today is the result of a successful breeding program, bringing animals in from Canada and Greenland. Musk oxen do not produce musk and they are not oxen. Although they somewhat resemble bison, they are more closely related to sheep and goats. Historically, they are a remnant of the last ice age, one of the oldest animals on the continent. Frenchman N. Jeremie first described the musk ox in 1720, when they were plentiful. However, their own defense mechanism – gathering into a tight circle to fend off predators and keep the young protected in the center – was their downfall. Hunters killed entire herds, merely for the sport of killing.

In 1933, musk oxen were re-introduced to Alaska. Thirty-four of them were captured in central Greenland, and then dogsledded to the coast. From there, they were put on a ship to Sweden, with connections to New York. In the Big Apple, they got stuck in quarantine for three weeks while Customs tried to figure out just what they were. Then they were put on a train to Seattle, a boat to Seward, and finally a train to Fairbanks. Incredibly enough, all 34 survived. Eventually, these musk oxen got moved off to Nunivak Island. For the story from there, pick up a copy of Peter Matthiessen's book *Oomingmak*.

There are about 3,000 musk oxen in Alaska today, and valued for both their beauty and their wool, they are well protected.

The qiviut wool grows underneath the longer guard hairs, which can reach two feet long on the neck. Despite their bulk – a male in the wild can reach 650 pounds, or 1,450 in captivity – the musk ox is surprisingly agile and can run very fast when threatened (let's not talk about the time the guide in Nome was screaming "Get out of there," just because the musk ox wanted to be sure we knew he knew that we were there). Before the advent of white hunters, their only enemy was the wolf; their lives were relatively peaceful, as they grazed on willow, sedge, rushes, and grasses.

Don't miss your chance to see these wonderful animals, either here or at the Musk Ox Farm in Palmer (see the section on Palmer in *Chapter 10*).

It's a fascinating tour – although it's not so much a tour as a good lecture while you watch musk ox eat branches, and then a second equally interesting lecture while you watch the reindeer do much the same. It provides a good opportunity to get a close-up look at some of Alaska's most interesting animals. The farm has about 70 musk oxen and 40 or so reindeer. In the mornings, the animals are closer to the fences as they graze. By afternoon, binoculars are a good idea. The gift shop sells T-shirts, posters, and musk ox wool. This stop is highly recommended. (It should be noted that the station exists for research, not for harvesting qiviut, the beautiful musk ox wool – not that they let the stuff go to waste.)

REINDEER

Okay, Santa Claus has them, so just what are reindeer? The simple answer is that they're lazy caribou, caribou that don't move around much.

The more complicated answer is that they are caribou that have, over hundreds of generations, been selectively bred to make them more amenable to domestication. When the Samis of Finland were looking around for a way to make a living out of the cold north, what they came up with were caribou. Rather than chasing the migrating herd around, over time, they were able to breed caribou for more useful traits: like a disinclination to migrate. Reindeer are also heavier and thicker-boned than caribou, with more meat.

Genetically, reindeer are just a subspecies of caribou; the University of Alaska has done testing, and breeding is possible in male caribou/female reindeer or female caribou/male reindeer directions.

The other don't miss attraction to Fairbanks is on the campus of the University of Alaska: the **U of A Museum** (☎ 907-474-7505 for the 24-hour information line; on the Web at www.uaf.edu/museum). Admission is $5 for adults, $4.50 for seniors, $3 for ages seven through 17. The museum is open daily 9 am to 7pm, June through August; from September to April, it's open weekdays 9 to 5 and weekends noon to 5.

This is probably the best museum in Alaska (only Sheldon Jackson in Sitka might also vie for that honor), and it's been getting better, with a massive expansion. Still, the museum's main attractions are are just about of the right number to allow you to remember what you are seeing without being worn out, and it's detailed enough to answer any questions you've

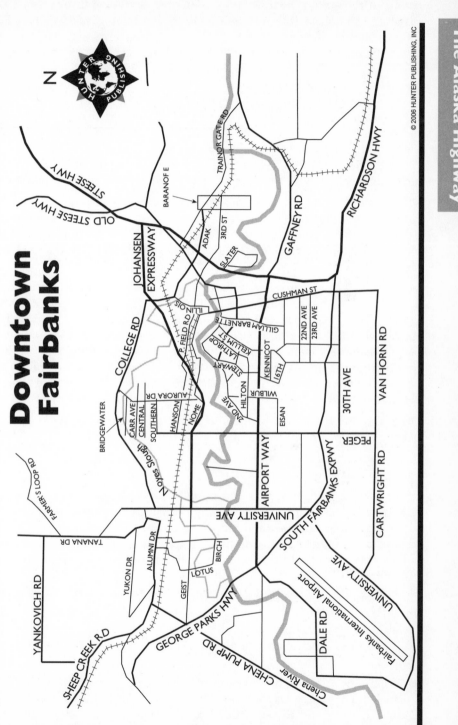

Downtown
Fairbanks

The Alaska Highway

got about the state. The museum's main area is divided into sections, corresponding with the different areas of the state. Their prize display is Blue Babe, a 36,000-year-old bison found partially intact, its skin and internal organs frozen in the permafrost. There's also an excellent variety of Indian and Eskimo artifacts, mammoth bones and tusks, a few assorted dinosaur pieces (including a rare skin impression), and a 12-foot stuffed grizzly bear with a rather bewildered expression. When you're looking at the caribou skeleton, notice the construction of the ankle bones; this is what causes caribou to click when they walk. It's said that when a large herd is migrating, the clicking can be heard for miles. The theory goes that a tendon slings the foot back into a stepping position, reducing the effort the caribou needs to exert to walk; they are the most efficient walkers on the planet.

Other primo displays include a 3,500-pound chunk of jade and a 5,495-pound copper nugget. Don't forget to look up at the skin kayaks hanging from the ceiling. The gift shop has some odd stuff you're not likely to find elsewhere. There are also daily slide shows and films on the aurora. Check for schedules.

The new part of the museum includes a permanent exhibition of the photos of Michio Hoshino, probably the best wildlife photographer ever (he was killed in 1997, when a bear dragged him out of his tent in Kamchatka, Russia). We've talked to a lot of people who traveled with Michio, and everybody absolutely loved him, although he apparently could get a little frustrating: set up his camera on, say, a tundra flower, then walk away, simply checking back on it from time to time until he got the light he wanted.

Other parts of the new area include paintings from the museum's permanent collection, a much larger display of Native art, and a café.

If that weren't all enough, the gift shop has some of the best Native items you're going to find in Fairbanks.

In summer, the museum puts up a tent to host the Northern Inua, displays of Eskimo games. When we went, none of the kids performing were Eskimo – they were all Athabaskan – but they put on a great show of traditional games, including ear pulls and high jumps. It's a lot of fun, and you won't believe the strength it takes to balance on one hand and then kick a hanging ball.

Out in front of the museum you can join a walking tour of the campus at 10 am, Monday through Friday. Also on campus, there are tours of the Geophysical Institute, Thursdays at 2 pm. If you're a summer traveler, this is where you can see the aurora borealis through some of their special machinery.

The U of A has its own botanical garden, the **Georgeson**. It's at the Agriculture and Forestry Experiment Station on West Tanana Drive, off the Parks Highway and Sheep Creek Extension. Admission is $2, and it's a good place for a picnic.

You can see Denali from the campus, but the weather conditions have to be perfect. Take a peek, but don't expect much.

Creamer's Field, at 1300 College Rd., is a turn-of-the-century dairy farm and an excellent place to go bird-watching, especially in early and late summer There's a two-mile nature trail that goes beyond the front fields into the woods – but you should see the sandhill cranes in the field as soon as you park. Creamer's Field is on the migratory path of over 100 species of birds, from the sandhill crane (mid-April through mid-September) to the plover. If you've never seen a four-foot-tall bird in the wild, here's your chance. We've sat here and watched what must have been close to a thousand of them, grumbling at each other and the geese who dared to try and share the field.

It's also a good place for moose and fox and a prime mosquito area, so dress accordingly. There are free guided nature walks offered several times a week. Stop in at the Visitors Center, Tuesday through Friday 10 am to 5 pm, or Saturdays 10 to 3. ☎ 907-452-5162.

There is an ongoing attempt to tag and chart the birds going through; volunteers check the mist nets hourly, then weigh and tag any birds that are caught. Capturing and tagging birds is a skill, and the people here are very, very good at it. Stop by to take a look.

HOW DO YOU WEIGH A BIRD?

Stick it upside down in a film canister (or a similar container, according to the size of the bird), and then put that on the scale. The bird, too puzzled to move, just waits to be turned over.

Fairbanks is the home of the **Yukon Quest dogsled race**, a race that almost makes the Iditarod look like a walk in the park. It's shorter than the Iditarod, but it's through rougher terrain. The Yukon Quest was started by people who thought the Iditarod had become too commercial. It travels along the gold rush trails between Whitehorse and Fairbanks for 1,000 miles. The race alternates starting points, and it takes roughly two weeks to complete, although the past couple of winners have done it in a couple of days less. You can visit the Yukon Quest headquarters and commercial shop at any time, downtown at the corner of 2nd Ave. and Cushman. It's open from 10 to 5. The Yukon Quest is run with fewer dogs and checkpoints than the Iditarod; professional mushers consider it by far the harder of the two races.

Fairbanks is sort of dog mushing central, and it's the best place to get an idea of what mushers and dogs go through in the races. There are several kennels that offer tours, but if you're going to go look at dogs, why not look at the best? **Trail Breaker Kennel** is run by the first person to ever win the Iditarod four times – Susan Butcher – and Yukon Quest champ David Monson. There are about a hundred dogs or so on the property, and each and every one of them is probably better taken care of than your dog back home. These are dogs that love to run – when they see the trainer coming with a harness, they start howling for sheer joy.

Tour the kennel, play with puppies, pet a ton of dogs, and watch the dogs play on the dog-go-round, a training tool that is really just a big hydraulic merry go round pulled by dogs. There's a demonstration of the equipment that mushers use, and at the end, a team gets hitched to a wheeled sled and taken out around the lakes. It's a must stop for all dog lovers.

Phone for reservations at ☎ 907-479-3825, and make sure to get directions while you're talking to them; the kennels are near the airport, but a little confusing to find.

SLED DOGS

The Eskimo and the Inuit were the first to discover how useful a dog could be when pulling a sled. Dogs are able to get through territory a man on his own could never cross, and they do it at up to fifteen miles an hour.

When the first Europeans came to the Arctic, they looked down their long, pointed noses at this. Most of them then proceeded to die while hooked up to man-hauled sledges across the ice. After a few hundred years of this, they caught on that maybe dogs were a good idea. From the late 19th century on, dogs were integral parts of expeditions to both poles.

The traditional idea of a sled dog is a husky – which is a generic term, just meaning a dog that pulls things. Think sled dog, you see a Siberian Husky, that thick silver coat and the blue eyes.

However, that's not what makes for the best dogs. The husky breeds are strong and great in the cold, but if you want a first-rate sled dog, you want to breed in a little hound for speed and personality. Susan Butcher's championship dogs are about 50% husky, 50% hound/German pointer.

Sled dogs have got great lives. At a professional kennel, they're weaned at four to six weeks. At three or four months old, they're tethered out with the other dogs, getting them socialized and used to being in a crowd. They start being harnessed to run at around six-nine months of age, depending on the dog. They'll get harnessed up with a couple of retired dogs, who will show the puppies what to do. Dogs this young can pull on fun races up to about three miles. There's no competition, because you want the dogs to enjoy themselves, not feel pressure. By the time they're nine months old or so, they're in fun races of up to 10 miles. A sled dog hits its prime between the ages of four and seven. Most are retired around age eight, although some keep pulling until they're as old as 12.

For mature dogs, a race up to 20 miles is considered a sprint. A first rate 20-dog team can average 20 miles per hour on a race that short – remember, one 50-pound dog can pull close to 1,000 pounds, and rider and sled weigh only a couple of hundred pounds. Most of the force and speed come from the first couple of dogs.

For a race of 30-300 miles, you'd use between six and 12 dogs on your team; a good team can easily average 10-14 miles per hour over that kind of distance. For the longer races, those of 300 miles or more (although Susan Butcher says she's just getting warmed up around 500 miles into a race) you'd use 10-20 dogs, pulling on a tether that stretches out 10-12 feet in front of the sled. Officially, the Iditarod uses 16-dog teams; the Yukon Quest, 14.

During a longer race, a dog eats a 10,000-calorie-a-day diet, mostly of fish and fat. Running that long is hard work; a dog can easily burn as much as 12,000 calories a day.

When the musher comes into a checkpoint, there's a very specific order of events: first, the musher signs in. Races have to make sure nobody is lost out there in the snow (although everybody not in first place has a pretty good path of footprints to follow). Then a vet checks over all the dogs, to make sure they're all healthy. Notice nobody is looking at the musher to make sure he or she is still in one piece. Next, the musher spreads straw out for the dogs and checks them over. Finally, the dogs get fed. Only then does the musher get to sit down and rest for a few minutes.

The standard is to run for six hours and then rest for six hours. However, there are some – such as Doug Swingley, who has been dominating the Iditarod for the past several years – who can keep their dogs running for up to ten hours with only three or four hours of rest. Other mushers wonder how he's breeding bionic dogs, but they're too far behind him – he holds the Iditarod speed record – to find out.

Nobody gets rich from mushing. Prize money might cover the dog food and vet bills for a year, but don't count on it. A competitive musher will have as many as a hundred dogs, and the dogs are pampered like you would not believe. Despite all publicity otherwise, mushing is more than humane – it's letting the dogs do what they love to do. There are few happier animals than a husky pulling a sled.

Sled dogs are not only used for races, though: in many remote villages, they're simple transportation. A lot of the North is without road, and in winter, there's no way to get anywhere if you don't have dogs. Unlike snowmachines, dogs don't break down and require new parts.

In the winter of 2000-2001, there was a crisis in the Alaska bush when the salmon runs fell well short of expectation. Dog owners count on the runs, stocking up on fish to feed their teams over the winter. With the fish shortage, many dog owners were facing the hard choices of which dogs they would have to kill, while still keeping enough dogs alive to handle the sleds so necessary in the bush during winter. Once word got out, there was a massive relief effort undertaken – 50,000 pounds of fish were sent up from Prince William Sound, and several dog food companies sent up tons more food. Other kind souls donated straw – which was also running short – so the dogs would have places to sleep. It didn't solve the problem, but it cut it down.

 For more on dogs and mushing, there is a magazine, *Mushing*, published six times a year. Contact them at ☎ 907-479-0454, or online at www.mushing.com.

 For books, try *Dog Driver*, by Miki and Julie Collins; our friends who mush consider it the classic of dogsledding books. And, of course, for a bit of rousing mushing fiction, there's always Jack London's *Call of the Wild.*

The **Dog Musher's Museum**, on Farmer's Loop Road, ☎ 907-456-6874, is open from June 1 to September 4, 10 am to 6 pm. It's the home base of the Alaska Dog Musher's Association, and they've got sled dog demonstrations, slides and videos, and a gift shop. Nearby is the racetrack, with sleds and equipment. There are good views of the city and the surrounding mountains from here. ☎ 907-456-MUSH.

You saw them in Whitehorse and at Alaskaland, but now you can ride one. The **Stern Wheeler Riverboat** *Discovery* (☎ 907-479-6673, www.riverboatdiscovery.com) is your chance to ride on an authentic paddleboat, the kind that used to ply the rivers, carrying supplies up to the miners and gold down to the Lower 48. To get to the dock, take Airport Rd. west to Dale Rd., and then turn on Discovery Drive. The ship cruises the Chena and Tanana rivers, and the 3.5-hour trip includes a sled dog demonstration and a visit to an Athabascan Indian village. The ship leaves at 8:45 am and 2 pm. This is heavily popular with group tours, but if you can ignore the crowds, it's a nice way to spend half a day. The trip will run you $45.

The other big hit with group tours are gold mines: First, outside of town, on Mile 9 of the Old Steese Highway, is **Gold Dredge Number 8**. Built in 1927, it was used for 32 years (Fairbanks was the second-richest gold area in Alaska). A gold dredge operates by scooping up dirt and separating the gold by sluicing and screening through progressively finer meshes. The dredge moves by creating a dam in a small creek, then floating in the pool that's created. Eventually it mows the dam down and starts the whole process over again. Gold Dredge Number 8 could displace more than 1,000 tons of earth at a time, chewing up the rivers whole, and it produced more

Above: Beginning of the Stewart-Cassiar Highway.

Below: Delta Junction Museum blacksmith shop.

Above: Baby caribou.
Opposite: Musk oxen, near Palmer.
Below: Old cannery building, Prince Rupert, BC.

Above: White Pass & Yukon Route railway cresting a peak near Skagway.
Opposite: Bakerville, BC, on a sunny day.
Below: Signpost forest, Watson Lake.

Above: Bear Glacier, Stewart-Cassiar Highway.
Opposite: Kluane Range.
Below: Weighing the catch, Homer.

Above: Million Dollar Falls, near Haines.

Below: Kennicott Mines. © Trainer/Hall

than 7.5 million ounces of gold during its years of operation. It's open from mid-May to mid-September. Admission is $23, including your own chance to pan for gold. There's a "miner's lunch" deal for another ten bucks.

Next door and across the road is a modern **gold mining operation**. You can see some of the equipment from the road. The piles of rocks strewn about are tailings – what's left over after they've sifted the rock for gold.

Another gold mine on view is the **El Dorado**, 1.3 miles up the Elliott Highway (about nine miles from downtown). It's a working gold mine where you can go inside a permafrost tunnel – and finally see what's making all those trees lean – and pan for gold yourself or take a short train ride with the tour. The train goes through the permafrost tunnel and past several mining technique exhibits, the highlight of which is the giant sluicebox demonstration.

If seeing the permafrost gets you in the mood for ice, **Fairbanks Ice Museum** has 40,000 pounds of ice on display. If you've never seen real ice sculpting – we're not talking swans in the middle of a dinner table here, but life-sized miner's cabins, a carousel, and more – it's worth the stop. Open 9 to 9; ☎ 907-451-8222. $6.

The closest place to town to view the pipeline is at about Mile 8.5 on the Steese Highway. There is a pullout with an information plaque. This is only worth the trip if it's on your way; otherwise, see the pipeline by Rika's Landing or in Valdez.

■ Out & About

A quick **gold-panning trip** can be made to the memorial statue of Felix Pedro, about 20 miles out of town on the Steese Highway.

Most people looking to take an excursion from Fairbanks want to head farther north, to the Arctic Circle. If you don't want to drive yourself (see the Dalton Highway section in *Chapter 12*) and want just a quick look at the land where the sun doesn't set, there are quite a few outfitters ready to fly you over the Circle.

Northern Alaska Tour Company (☎ 907-474-8600, 800-474-1086, www.northernalaska.com) runs quick flights to the Arctic Circle for $289. Their Anaktvuk flight, which includes a tour of the village, is $399. Other options include fly/drive to the circle, visit the Brooks Range, or multi-day arctic trips.

Princess (☎ 800-452-0500) and **Grayline** (☎ 800-544-2206 or 907-456-7741) also both run motorcoach tours to Prudhoe Bay. Prices, which include lodging, are steep, but they're worth it if you don't want to drive yourself and are determined to get all the way to the top of the world by land.

Alaska Airlines runs seriously touristy trips to Kotzebue or Nome from Fairbanks or Anchorage. ☎ 800-468-2248. Kotzebue is a Native village on the Bering Sea Coast; Nome was strictly a white city, built up around the discovery of gold on the beaches. Unfortunately, many Kotzebue Natives have gotten so tired of having tour groups descend on them that you can't really get a look at Native life; especially on the day tours, you're getting a kind of Arctic Disneyland.

River Trips

Alaska Log Raft Adventures has a different take on the river – you float it on a large log raft, with tents for comfort. You can take side trips in the canoes or riverboats they have along. It's really comfortable, really unusual, and a trip you won't forget. ☎ 800-628-0282, or check them out on the web at www.lograft.com.

Of course, the Yukon is a ways out of town; the Tanana runs right through it. For $99, **Alexander's River Adventure**s will take you on a 4-hour trip on the river, heading out to a fishing camp; for $125, you get a trip on the river and a tour of Nenana. ☎ 907-474-3924.

If you want to fish, kayak, or canoe on your own, leave town. The best water is on the Chena and Tanana rivers.

Hiking

Hikers are also better off heading out. However, for a quick walk right around town, one of the more popular spots is the **Birch Hill Trail System**, right off the Steese Highway. There are quite a number of trails, ranging from 1.5to 3.5 miles. In winter, it's the place to go for cross-country skiing. But again, the real action is farther out.

Fishing

Fairbanks is on or near quite a few rivers, so there's a lot of fishing around.

Interior AK Adventures, ☎ 907-388-4193, www.aktours.net, runs day fishing trips on the Chena River, from $105. Lots of longer offerings, too.

North Country River Charters, ☎ 907-479-7116, www.ncrc.alaska.com, and **Arctic Grayling Guide Service**, ☎ 907-479-0479, www. wildernessfishing.com, both take trips out to local rivers, including the Yukon.

Chena River & Hot Springs

This is the most popular side-trip around Fairbanks. If you don't want to brave the roads to the North (see the *Chapter 12*), an hour's drive to Chena Hot Springs can take you into some really nice territory with minimal effort.

Leave Fairbanks on the Steese Highway; at Mile 4.9, take the Chena Hot Springs Road. It's 56 miles to the end of the road and the springs, but along the way there's great hiking, fishing, and camping.

Chena River State Recreation Area starts at Mile 26. It doesn't reach all the way to the hot springs but, while it lasts, it's one of the best small parks in Alaska. The road follows the Chena River, which is excellent for paddlers. You can pretty much put in and take out anywhere. It's Class I water, but heavy rains can fill the rivers with hazardous debris. Watch for mosquitoes in slack water. Fish for grayling (catch-and-release only), pike, whitefish, and even the occasional king salmon. Check in Fairbanks for restrictions. If you need to rent your canoe, try **Beaver Sports**, in town, 3480 College Rd., ☎ 907-479-2494.

There are also outstanding hikes in the area. The most popular is the short (just under four miles) **Angel Rocks Trail**, which starts at Mile 48.9. If you turn east at the top of the Angel Rocks Trail, you link up with a ridgeline trail that takes you all the way to the hot springs resort, 8.5 miles away. Walking on the ridge gives wonderful views, and the hike isn't too difficult.

Other good hikes are the **Granite Tors Loop** (15 miles, trailhead at Mile 39), which takes you up above the tree line into alpine country, or the **Stiles Creek Trail** (15 miles, trailheads at Miles 31.6 and 36.5). Stiles Creek is accessible to ATVs, and hikers might want to think about a different route if they hear that buzzing.

For the ambitious hiker, the **Chena Dome Trail** is considered one of the best hikes in the state. It's 29 miles long, with the trailhead at Mile 50.5. The trail is very steep, taking you up and down, above and below the tree line, leading up to the peak of Chena Dome at 4,421 feet. There is a shelter cabin about 17 miles in on the trail (after you've peaked out), but it's really just a box to shelter you from the rain. Bring your own water, extra food, and a cook stove – open fires aren't allowed.

There are two **campgrounds** in the rec area: the **Rose Hip Campground**, at Mile 27, and **Tors Trail**, at Mile 39. Rose Hip is a little more scenic and a lot more popular; there's better river access from Tors, and it's the easiest place to stay the night if you're going to do the Granite Tors Trail. For RVs, stay at Rose Hip. Canoers should stop here, too, to check the information board.

It takes a bit over an hour to drive all the way to the hot springs and the **Chena Hot Springs Resort**. The resort itself is a great display of woodworking skills, and the huge fireplace in the lounge shouldn't be missed. There's camping (kind of wet; you'll probably be happier pitching your tent down the road), and RV sites from $10, cabins from $$, and rooms in the lodge from $$$. This lovely spot is close enough to Fairbanks that it gets pretty crowded on weekends and holidays. Locals will come out for a day in the pool or a nice dinner in the lodge restaurant. ☎ 907-451-8151 or 800-478-4681, www.chenahotsprings.com.

There are three old trapper cabins on the grounds. One has been converted to a massage room, the other two are being turned into a museum. The lodge is also a great place to come in winter to warm up in the springs or head out cross-country skiing. The area around the springs is beautiful, heavily forested with birch and spruce.

You don't have to stay at the lodge to use the pools. It's $10 for a day pass.

■ Seasonal Activities

 If you hit town at the right time, Fairbanks can be more fun than just about anywhere in Alaska. Sled dog racing can be seen in January and February, leading up to the **Limited North American Championship Sled Dog Race**, a three-day event in March. Also in March is the **Open North American Championship**, the oldest continuously run mushing event in the world. Races begin and end downtown.

In late February or early March, there's a **Festival of Native Arts**. All the different groups of Alaska Indians gather and demonstrate dances and arts and crafts.

Also in March is the **World Ice Art Championships**, held on the spring equinox to celebrate the end of winter. There are snow sculptures, dog races, ice carvings, parades, a triathalon, and a lot of people trying to remember what daylight looks like. Ice sculptors come from around the world to compete. A two-person team gets 7,200 pounds of ice to work with; larger teams get 36,000 pounds and three days. The ice gets sculpted into jousting knights, castles, miners, and more. They are especially impressive at night, when the sculptures are lit from behind.

June brings the **Yukon 800 Marathon** boat race, from Fairbanks to Galena and back. Pick a comfortable spot on the river and watch the boats go by.

For the summer solstice on June 21, check out the **Midnight Sun Baseball Game**. It's played at midnight, with no lights. You won't have any trouble seeing it, just problems getting a seat. As with most towns in Alaska, the solstice brings out some wildness. There are games all over town, races, band performances, and more.

The **World Eskimo-Indian Olympics** are held over a four-day period in July every year. Events include the ear pull – two people, a string tied to their ears, a lot of pulling, and a fair amount of pain – fish-cutting competitions, greased pole climbs, muktuk-eating contests (muktuk is whale blubber), and more sedate dance competitions. It's well worth timing your trip to Fairbanks to get in on a day or two of this. You may not ever get another chance to eat muktuk yourself. If you can't make it for the games, though, you can at least get a taste of what they're like at the Northern Inua show on the U of A campus (see above).

July is the busy month in town. **Golden Days** commemorate the discovery of gold near Fairbanks in 1902. The business people dress in period costume, and sometimes those not in costume or not wearing a commemora-

The Alaska Highway

tive lapel pin are arrested by the Golden Days Jail. Lots of contests and other activities.

Finally, there is the **Fairbanks Summer Arts Festival**. For three weeks, top performers from all over the world come and give concerts, workshops, dances and theater shows. Musical offerings range from classical to jazz, opera, and cabaret. There are Shakespearean plays, and you can take lessons from many of the visiting artists. For advance information on who's coming when, write PO Box 80845, Fairbanks, AK 99708. On the Web, it's www.fsaf.org.

Tanana Valley State Fair is in August. This is where you can see 60-pound cabbages from the Matanuska Valley. In November, try the Athabascan Old Time Fiddling Festival for three days of fiddling action.

For up-to-date information on any of these events, ☎ 907-456-INFO.

Finally, if you're here in the winter, go skiing at the **Aurora**, about a half hour north of town on Cleary Summit. Just be aware that they're only running from 10 am to dusk, which can hit awfully early in winter.

■ Nightlife

Of course, in the summer there are no nights, and the local scene reflects that. **The Marlin**, at 3412 College Road, is smoke free, and has good live music. **The Blue Loon**, 2990 Parks Highway, also has live music, dancing, and concerts. The **Howling Dog Saloon**, at Mile 11 on the Old Steese Highway. A little more sedate is the **Pump House,** at 13 Chena Pump Rd. They've got a cigar bar and good eats.

More cultural are the shows at **Alaskaland** or at the **Malamute Saloon** at the Ester Gold Camp, Mile 8 on the Parks Highway. The saloon features nightly shows with comedy, singing, and the poems of Robert Service (see *Chapter 13* for more details on Ester.)

■ Shopping

As a general rule, you'll find that prices and selection are better in Anchorage than in Fairbanks on most arts and crafts items. That doesn't mean there aren't good places to check out.

Our favorite is the gift shop at the **U of A Museum of the North**. Quality pieces, reasonable prices. See the museum section, above, for more.

Just across the street from Alaska Public Lands is the best of the millions of other gift shops in the Fairbanks area, the **Arctic Traveler's Gift Shop**. It's got a wide variety of Native crafts in every price range. There is serious, high-quality art here, from Athabascan, Yupik, Inupiat, Tlingit, and many other groups. The better works are signed by the artists and come with a card telling about the local craft traditions. The store also carries just about anything else you could want – ulus, birch bark baskets, baleen, ivory, and more. If you strike out there, practically next door is **Arctic Wonders**, 301 S. Cushman, which also has a great assortment. If you're still not finding what you're after, wander the neighborhood, you'll get it.

The Great Alaskan Bowl Company turns out lovely bowls from birchwood. They'll also put together a bowl gift basket with syrup, teas, herbs, and more. Located at 4630 Old Airport Road, the company is open year-round and well worth a visit.

Alaska Rare Coins, 551 Second Ave., has gold jewelry, raw gold, coins, and a great selection of Alaskana books. **Alaska Prospectors and Geologists Supply**, 504 College Road, is the place to go for your gold pans, mining books, pumps, dredges, and more. **Beaver Sports**, 3480 College Rd., has the most complete selection of outdoor gear in the city. They rent canoes.

■ Food

 Fairbanks has something to satisfy every hunger, if not every budget. If you're trying to save money, stick to the chain restaurants. If you're willing and able to spend, however, there are some memorable meals ahead.

Sam's Sourdough Café, 3702 Cameron, is the best place for breakfast – good, filling, and cheap, from about $5. Another excellent breakfast choice is **The Bakery**, at 69 College Ave. It serves six kinds of French toast, sourdough pancakes, and more, all day. Prices from $5.

Soapy Smith's Pioneer Restaurant, on 2nd Ave. near the Visitor's Center, is a good choice for a burger lunch. It also serves chicken, shrimp, and sandwiches. Prices from $7.

For more formal meals, try the **Alaska Salmon Bake**, at the corner of Airport Way and Peger Rd. (off to the side of the Alaskaland parking lot). This is the best of the many area salmon bakes, and it's also got ribs, steak, and seafood from $20. Most people think this is the best salmon in town – it's flown in fresh from Sitka.

Souvlaki, 310 1st Ave., has fast Greek fast food from $7; it's a local favorite.

The **Pump House Restaurant**, 13 Chena Pump Rd., in an old gold pump house, has a cigar bar, a regular restaurant, a bar, and prices starting at $15. You can actually skip the restaurant and just have bar food – the appetizers are dinner sized – and get out a little cheaper. You'll need reservations for weekend evenings. This is very popular with locals, especially the bar.

Pike's Landing, on Airport Road (☎ 907-479-6500) is the place for Sunday brunches and some of the best dinners in town. It's pricey, but worth it. Reservations suggested.

For pizza, just head straight to **College Town Pizzeria**, 3549 College Road. Best in town.

The **Wolf Run Coffee and Dinner House**, at the corner of Geist Rd. and University Ave., ☎ 907-458-0636, is in a nice converted old house. Good place to go for dinners in the moderate price range, or just show up for coffees and desserts.

If you're not stuffed yet, head to **Hot Licks** for dessert. It's on College Road, right by the university, and serves homemade ice cream.

Finally, if you want something good to take to your campsite, the **Tanana Valley Farmers' Market** is a must-stop. The market is held Saturdays from 11 am to 4 pm, mid-May through mid-June; from then to mid-September, it's 11 to 4 on Wednesdays. You'll find fresh blueberries, strawberries, and the biggest vegetables you'll ever see, plus a good variety of baked goods, jams and jellies, honey, and flowers to decorate your campsite.

Carrs Foodland, at Cushman and Gaffney, is a supermarket supreme, with a sushi bar, a Chinese kitchen, a deli, and all the normal supermarket stuff – plus reindeer sausage.

■ Accommodations

During the high season, Fairbanks can be a difficult place to find a bed. It's best to make reservations at least one night ahead, and don't expect any bargains. B&Bs come and go with great regularity. If you want to stay in one, you're best off calling the Info Center to find out who's in business. Or check out the website of the **Fairbanks Association of Bed and Breakfasts**, at www.ptialaska.net/~fabb.

HOTEL PRICING
Prices are in US dollars.
under $50 . . . . $
$50-$100 . . . . $$
$100-$150 . . . . . . $$$
above $150 . . . . . $$$$

That said, as soon as you know what days you're going to be in Fairbanks, run, don't walk, to the phone and make reservations at the **Forget Me Not Lodge/Aurora Express**, ☎ 907-474-0949. $$$-$$$$. Ask for the caboose – yeah, you read that right. They've got train cars converted into very swank, very comfortable rooms, with attention to detail that shows what a labor of love this place is. The cars are fully plumbed, and more comfortable and with better views – you can take in practically the entire Tanana Valley from the trains – than any hotel room you're likely to find. The magnificent caboose is quite suitable for a couple, whereas the 85-foot long car "The Arlene" has plenty of room for a family, with two bedrooms. Flat out, one of our favorite places in Alaska to stay. And, oh, on the off chance you're one of those rare people who don't like trains, they've got rooms inside the house, from $85. You can check them out on the web at www.aurora-express.com; however, don't count on responses to e-mail. Call for reservations.

For the hotel scene, you've got a lot of choices.

Downtown is the extremely nice **All Seasons Inn**, at 763 7th Ave., ☎ 907-451-6649. Regularly rated one of the best places to stay in Alaska, the rooms are large, with nice touches, and breakfasts bigger than any you've seen in your life. $$$-$$$$.

A nice spot is the **North Woods Lodge**, on Chena Hills Dr. It's comfortably rustic, with a Jacuzzi and hiking and biking trails nearby. Rooms start at only $65; cabins from only $45. They also have a hostel, with spots for $15, and tent sites from $12. A great bargain all around. ☎ 907-479-5300 or 800-478-5305.

The **Fairbanks Hotel** (☎ 907-456-6411), 517 Third Ave., is the oldest hotel in town, but it's been newly renovated. It offers smoking and nonsmoking rooms, brass beds, and the feel of an older time. Rooms start at $65 for a shared bath and $85 for private. There are also four apartments.

Groups should try the **Ambassador Inn**, at 415 5th Ave. Rooms start around $85, all with kitchens, some with two bedrooms. It's an old apartment building and not overwhelmingly attractive, but a good deal. ☎ 907-451-9555.

The chain hotels are all here, in all price ranges. The **Super 8** chain has a hotel at 1090 Airport Way that's up to their usual high standards. ☎ 907-451-8808 or 800-800-8000. There's also a **Westmark** at 813 Noble St. (☎ 800-544-0970), and a **Comfort Inn**, at 1908 Chena Landings Loop (☎ 907-479-8080 or 800-201-9199), overlooking the Chena River.

The **Bridgewater Hotel** (☎ 907-452-6661) at 723 First Ave. has a nice restaurant and lounge. Easy walking distance to downtown. $$$$. The **Sophie Station Hotel** (☎ 907-479-3650, 800-528-4916) at 1717 University Ave., near the airport, is convenient and quiet. The place is huge, with nice, quiet gardens. Rates go from $$ in winter to $$$$ in summer. The same people also run the quite upscale **Wedgewood Resort**, 212 Wedgewood Dr. (☎ 800-528-4916), which is the place to go if you need a suite. All three of these properties are online at www.fountainheadhotels.com.

If you're putting out a lot of money for a room, go to the **Regency Fairbanks** (☎ 907-452-3200, 800-348-1340, regencyfairbankshotel.com), 95 Tenth Ave. It has a good location and has every amenity you can think of. $$$$.

A few other choices at the high end of things are the **Captain Bartlett Inn**, 1411 Airport Way, ☎ 907-452-1888, 800-544-528, www.captainbartlettinn.com, with a nice Alaska-atmosphere bar, or **Pike's Waterfront Lodge**, at 1850 Hoselton, ☎ 907-456-4500, 877-774-2400, www.pikeslodge.com. One of our favorites.

If you want to do the hostel thing, call the **Fairbanks International Youth Hostel**, 456-4159.

If you don't mind driving, a nice place to stay is outside Fairbanks, at the **Chatanika Gold Camp**, at Mile 27.5 on the Steese Highway in Chatanika. A registered National Historic District, the buildings date from 1921, when this was a working gold mine. There's a restaurant, a saloon, and a lot of atmosphere. $$. ☎ 907-389-2414.

Camping

It's easy to camp in Fairbanks without going more than a couple of miles from downtown.

The most popular sites are at the **Chena River State Recreation Site**, 1155 University Ave. It's near the college, and has both tent sites and hook-ups.

Also near the college is the **Tanana Valley Campground**, at 1800 College Road. It offers 50 treed sites, showers, and a laundromat. It's clean, well run, and has friendly hosts. Try to check in early to get a space away from the road. If you're in a tent, this is a better choice than Chena River.

The **River's Edge RV Park** (☎ 907-474-0286), 4140 Boat St., is (obviously) right on the river. It's huge, with 180 RV sites and 10 tent sites. Full hookups and tent sites. They've also got 48 cottages ($$$$). This place is kind of a one-stop wonder. They'll book tours, there's an incredible restaurant on the grounds, and it's just a good place – although better for RVs than tents. The **Norlite Campground**, 1660 Peger Rd., is next to Alaskaland. It's got 250 sites, showers, and a laundromat.

The cheapest spot for RVs is the parking lot of **Alaskaland**. There are no services, but overnight camping in a self-contained vehicle is only a few bucks. Of course, you are camping in a parking lot in Alaska, and how are you going to justify that to your friends back home?

Chapter 6

The Yellowhead & Stewart-Cassiar Highways

Western BC opens up via the Yellowhead Highway west from Prince George. The Yellowhead is in excellent shape: smooth, wide, not heavily traveled. It stretches through alternating patches of forest and farmland, with a few glaciers in the mountains and hints of things to come along the way. If you take the Yellowhead all the way to its end, you get to Prince Rupert, a lovely town that feels more like Alaska than Canada – and in fact, Alaska is only a few miles up the coast.

The other reason to get on the Yellowhead is to take the alternative to the Alaska Highway, the Stewart-Cassiar Highway: it's shorter, rougher, and so much more scenic than the Alcan that it's impossible to even compare the roads. This is the one we pick to head north on.

Along the Yellowhead

You leave Prince George on the same kind of low, rolling scenery that you come in on. Cross the bridge over the Fraser River, the city's earliest lifeline, and you're out of there. This is farming country, and you can plan on getting through the first stretch of the road pretty quickly.

About 45 km/28 miles from Prince George, you'll see **Bednesti** Lake on the south side of the road; this was an important village site for the Dakelh First Nations people who lived here before the coming of the HBC. There's a plaque here that gives a little history, if you need to get out and stretch.

Just over 29 km/18 miles farther up the road, you hit the geographical center of British Columbia – it's on the other side of the trailer park, if this kind of stamp collecting is your thing.

Vanderhoof

 The first town you hit moving west from George is Vanderhoof, with a population of a bit under 5,000. It's a logging town, and a ranching center for the outlying areas.

There's not a whole lot to do in Vanderhoof, but it's a nice little town. Stop in at the **Visitor Info Centre**, just north of the highway on Burrard St., ☎ 250-567-2291.

AN ODD BEGINNING

The town name comes from Herbert Vanderhoof, a man who was a PR flack for the Canadian railways in the early part of the 1900s. He thought this spot would make a perfect writer's retreat, and so he started to plan one, along with a luxury hotel. Neither ever came off, but the loggers loved the spot, and the town, named after a failed dream, started to grow.

Heritage Village is on the western edge of town. There are reconstructed buildings from the 1920s here, and a small museum that has stuffed birds, and all the things you would have needed to survive here 80 years ago – lots of tools. Worth a quick look, and it's only $2. Open daily 10-5, ☎ 250-567-2991.

The other big attraction in the area is the **Vanderhoof Bird Sanctuary**, at the northern edge of town, along the banks of the Nechako. They get upwards of 50,000 migrating birds through here in spring and fall. Out of migration season, it's a nice spot for a picnic.

Take Stoney Creek Road 11 km/seven miles south of town to the village of **Sai-K'uz**, a Dakelh village. Head for the Potlach House, which has some arts and crafts for sale.

If you need to stay in Vanderhoof for the night, there's a campground at Sai-K'uz, at the **Riverside Park Campground**, 3100 Burrard Ave., ☎ 250-567-4710, or at **Dave's RV Park**, 1048 Derkson Rd., ☎ 250-567-3161. Hotels are nice and cheap here. You can get a good basic room at the **Grand Trunk Inn**, 2351 Church Ave., ☎ 250-567-3188, the **North Country Inn**, 2645 Burrard, ☎ 250-567-3047, or the **Siesta Inn**, on Highway 16, ☎ 250-567-2365, all in the $$-low $$$ range for a double.

■ West from Vanderhoof

When you're leaving Vanderhoof to head west, don't get right back on Highway 16 quite yet. There's a wonderful side trip to take first, up Highway 27 to Fort St. James. It's about 50 miles, but it's well worth the effort.

Fort St. James, which was a Hudson's Bay Company headquarters site. Today it's a "living history" park, where visitors can wander around restored sites and talk to people costumed as 1800s trading post folk. This is actually well worth the side trip. The fort is in a beautiful location, on the edge of a huge lake, and the people inside really know their stuff.

The HBC was the single most important force in settling western Canada, and it was all on the basis of a single, very simple idea: fur sells. The Fort St. James warehouse has a good display of the different furs the HBC dealt in, from the luxurious otter pelt to weasel skins and scent glands from minks. You'll see the presses where the skins were flattened for easy shipment, and get a good idea of the kind of insular world these people created for themselves. To quote Peter Newman's outstanding book *The Company of Adventurers*:

> *The Company's wilderness settlements were eventually modeled on contemporary defensive architecture.... They were situated inside a quadrangle of wooden bastions mounting various gauges of cannon, joined by palisades of upright logs, sometimes with iron points. The main buildings were meant to be unassailable redoubts with parapets pierced by embrasures for fixed eight-pounders.*

Fort St. James was actually taken over by First Nations forces at one point in its history. Really, despite their fortifications, the HBC posts were here because they were allowed to be here; the men inside were desperately outnumbered, and entirely dependent upon the goodwill of the Natives for everything they needed.

In 1828, James Douglas, the man who turned the HBC into what it was in the western reaches of Canada – Douglas was driven, organized, and utterly fearless; he was also married to a First Nations woman who could help him get around in the local languages – heard that a man named Tzil-na-o-lay, who had been accused of murder five years before, was living near Fort St. James. The fugitive was hanging out in the house of a man named Kwah, who had been a good friend to the HBC – he'd once saved Simon Fraser and his crew from dying of starvation, and he was the driving force behind much of the fur trade in the area.

Douglas, though, in an unusual mood for a trader, put Western justice above practicality, and went out after Tzil-na-o-lay, who ended up beaten to death.

Kwah didn't much care for this abuse of his hospitality, so he and a bunch of his men went out and captured Ft. St. James. Didn't take much doing. As the story comes down, Kwah had Douglas pinned to a table, a knife at his heart, when Douglas's wife came in to save the day. She went straight for the pile of trade goods, and started throwing presents at the warriors, telling them that if they left her husband, they could have it all.

Kwah was insulted by the attack on his house, but he was a practical man, too. Reparations struck him as being a good idea, so he and his men loaded up on goodies and headed out. He was banned from the fort for six months.

Douglas got it a bit worse. He'd been diminished in the eyes of the locals, and there began to be regular threats against him, small skirmishes, just enough to keep him on his toes. It wasn't long after the confrontation with Kwah that Douglas got transferred to Fort Vancouver – nowhere near what's now Vancouver, but much farther south, in the disputed region around the Columbia River – to be the accountant.

Take the side trip. There's nowhere else in BC where you can see how the western expansion of Canada came about. Where else are you going to find out that an HBC clerk made the princely wages of 50 pounds a year, more than double what an interpreter would make for explaining to the clerk exactly what the hell was going on?

Fort St. James is open May-September, 9-5. There's a small museum and reception center on the grounds, which is open year-round, but in winter, you're not going to get to see much else. Admission is $4, and entirely worth it.

If you've come out this far, you can go just a bit farther north to Germanson Landing North Road, which opens up the **Takla-Nation Lakes**. There's a multi-lake canoe route through here, as well as a wide variety of hiking trails.

■ North from Vanderhoof

Once you get back on the Yellowhead, you'll pass **Fort Fraser**, a tiny community on the site of one of the first trading posts in BC, and **Beaumont Provincial Park,** which has nice campsites (☎ 800-689-9025 for reservations). There are, though, better campgrounds farther ahead.

The scenery starts to get a little more wild as you enter the foothills of the coastal mountains. By **Burns Lake**, you're in the pretty stuff. There's not a lot to see in Burns Lake, but there is the **Heritage Center**, ☎ 250-692-3773, if you need to get off the road and stretch a bit. Burns Lake is a popular recreation area, with lots of fishing and boating; it's also the access point for **Tweedsmuir Provincial Park**, the biggest in BC, with nearly a million hectares.

Tweedsmuir has no road access or facilities from this side of things – the road to Bella Coola, farther south, cuts through the park and there are a couple of ways into it from there – but you can get at it by crossing Ootsa Lake (if you've got your own kayak, you could easily spend a couple of days on the lake), which forms the northern park border. Once you're inside, you're on your own. This is bear country.

Serious paddlers can link up a chain of lakes: from Ootsa through Whitesail, Eutsuk, Tetachuck, and Natalkuz, which will take you back to Ootsa. You'll need to do some portaging, and if you don't know how to boat in the wilderness, this is really just a cold, wet way to commit suicide.

Highway 16 starts to head north here, past the small towns of **Houston** (home of the "world's largest flyrod" – 60 feet long and 800 pounds) and

Telkwa (which made *Ripley's Believe It or Not* for having three bridges over two rivers, all anchored on the same rock – Ripley was maybe having a slow week). The bridges are long gone, but the town is a pretty little spot, and there's a heritage walk, with about 30 stops; pick up the free pamphlet at the museum, on Highway 16, ☎ 250-846-9656.

There's good camping at **Tyhee Lake Provincial Park**, just north of Telkwa. It's wheelchair accessible, and has good bird watching.

Smithers has about 6,000 people, almost every fast food restaurant known, and not much else. It's a good halfway point between Prince George and Rupert on the coast, but unless you're really tired, there's not much need to stop. It is another of those BC spots with the weird history. In the early days, it was a way-point for people headed to the Klondike, but because the government had decided the region was fertile and would make for good farming, they hatched a plan to move 8,000 Boer War veterans here. Problem was, they couldn't find 8,000 who wanted to come. Only a hundred applied, and about half of those sold off their allotment of 160 acres to speculators.

Smithers was also going to be passed by on the rail line: the plan was to send the train through Aldermere. Much like the Boers and their unwanted land, though, Aldermere didn't want the railroad; they were afraid it would turn their lovely little town into nothing but a huge collection of squatter shacks, and so they pushed to get the train through Smithers – which ended up, for a time, being called Squatterville.

If you're looking to get into the bush, take the road out to **Babine Mountains Recreation Area**. Along the way, you'll go through **Driftwood Canyon Provincial Park**, which has some nice fossil beds. Most of them are plant fossils, but there are also a few fish and insects. Don't go up on the canyon walls after fossils – these are fragile, and you'll end up bleeding. It's okay to check the slope below, though.

Out by Babine Lake, you've got a no-roads park that covers 34,000 hectares. Here you can try the eight-km/five-mile **McCabe Trail** for good views of alpine meadows.

The **Adventure Smithers Group**, ☎ 250-847-3499, 877-610-8075, www. adventuresmithers.com, is a co-op of outfitters who can get you into the extraordinary bush around town. This ranges from flightseeing and easy hikes, to trips deep into the Spatsizi. Check them out.

You can take a whitewater raft trip on the Buckley River with **Suskwa Adventure Outfitters**, ☎ 888-5-GO-RAFT, www.suskwa.com. It's a stretch of about 30 rapids, but nothing too hairy.

Back on 16, another 60 km/37 miles down the road, you hit the complex of **Hazelton**, **South Hazelton**, and **New Hazelton**. It's a lot of names for about a thousand people. The towns are overlooked by Mt. Rocher Deboule, or Rolling Stone Mountain – so named by miners who kept getting nailed by landslides. It was a bit more important to the First Nations Gitxsan, for whom it was kind of the center point of their civilization.

ONCE IS ENOUGH

Over in New Hazelton, there's a fun historic oddity: Russian anarchists robbed the railway's payroll. It worked once, so they thought they'd try it again. You know that scene in *Butch Cassidy and the Sundance Kid* where they're surrounded by the Bolivian Army? The Russian anarchists – boy, were these guys lost – ended up playing that out.

All three Hazeltons share the same **Info Centre**, at the junction of 16 and 62 north. ☎ 250-842-6571. The big guy out front is Jean Jacques Caux, a packer, a *voyageur*, legendary for the size of loads he carried on the trails. As the stories come down to us, the guy was also famous for only changing his clothes once a year – whereas, let's be realistic here, most other guys out working in the bush probably changed clothes two or three times a year.

The Hazeltons do open up two of the more interesting First Nations villages in the area. **'Ksan** is just outside of town. It's a reconstruction of a traditional Gitxsan village, very beautifully done. Set on a quiet meadow overlooking a rive, there are classically constructed tribal houses, complete with totem poles, and other carvings and paintings. It gives a very good feel for what these villages must have been like. Tours ($8) leave every hour, and it's worth it: you go in the different buildings, see the quite wonderful regalia room and carving room, while the guide tells you stories about the village and the culture. This is really very well done. If you don't want the tour, but just want to walk around the village, that's $2, but it's worth paying the extra to get inside. There's also a quite large gift shop and a good museum. The village also runs the **Kitanmax School of Northwest Coast Indian Art**, which offers a four-year program that passes on the traditional styles and techniques. There aren't many groups who've gotten this organized with passing on their heritage. Tours are May-October, and the village is open from 9-6. ☎ 250-842-5544. There's also a decent campground.

The other nearby village is **Kispiox**, also a Gitxsan village. It's 16 km/10 miles north of Hazelton. Come out here for the totem poles if you're still looking for more after 'Ksan.

From the Hazeltons, Highway 16 starts to dip south, running along the Skeena River and heading for the coast. The mountains that are dominating every view you have on a clear day are the Seven Sisters, some of the prettiest mountains in BC.

Along here, you enter kermodie bear territory. Kermodies are a white subspecies of black bear. They are very, very rare, and you stand a better chance of being struck by lightning than seeing one. The only other place in

BC where there's a population of these (also called spirit bears) is on Princess Royal Island.

LUCKY KERMODIE SIGHTING

Here's a fun kermodie story, told to us by a BC tourism official. It was his job to guide media people to what they wanted to see. When Michio Hoshino, the best bear photographer ever, wanted to see a kermodie, it took weeks. When Jack Hannah decided to bring in his camera crew, he had a couple of hours. They had to get in, get the bear, get out. Impossible. Wasn't going to happen. The BC guide tried to talk them out of this, but Jack insisted.

They landed on Princess Royal, and within two hours had all the bear footage they needed.

Lightning is more cooperative for some than others.

To get an idea of what a kermodie would look like if you were that lucky, stop by the **Terrace Visitor Centre,** right on Highway 16, ☎ 250-635-2573. You could also give **Silvertip Eco Tours** a call, ☎ 250-635-9326, www.grizzlytours.ca. They guide bear trips – as well as jet boats and kayak trips – and might be able to make your kermodie dream come true.

Terrace has always made its living off the river, the downhill slide to the ocean. It's a good town for fishing, and in August, there's a local festival, the **Sternwheeler Days**, to hark back to the time when giant paddlewheel ships worked the Skeena.

While you're in town, stop by the **Heritage Park**, 4113 Sparks St., ☎ 250-615-3000. Guided tours take you through buildings dating from the early days of Terrace, to give you that wild west feeling. Displays cover mining, trapping, and more. $3.50.

If you're really looking for something to do, there's a 80-km/50-mile one-way side trip to the Nisga'a Lava Beds, a lava flow about 18 km/11 miles long, left from an eruption around 1775, that might have killed as many as 2,000 people and rerouted the Nass River. According to the Nisga'a, the eruption was nature's retaliation: their children had begun to torment salmon. There are a couple of short trails into the lava, and in summer, you can get on a guided four-hour hike. ☎ 250-638-9589 for reservations.

Terrace has more hotels than any town between Prince George and Prince Rupert. **Northern Motor Inn**, 3086 Highway 16, ☎ 250-635-6375, www.innbc.com, is basic but comfortable, $$. There's also a couple of the standard Canadian chains: **Sandman**, 4828 Hwy 16, ☎ 250-635-9151, 800-SANDMAN, www.sandman.com, $$$, and Coast Resorts, 4620 Lakelse Ave, ☎ 250-638-2258, www.coasthotels.com, $$-$$$.

If you've got a tent, go back east on the road to **Kleanza Creek Provincial Park**. It's tiny, but there are sites right along the river. This is one of the most perfect campsites we've ever stayed in.

Your other nearby camping option is at **Lakelse Lake**, on the road down to Kitmat.

Side Trip to Kitmat

If you have time, you can make a pleasant side trip from Terrace down to Kitmat. It's 57 km/35 miles from Highway 16 to the end of the road in Kitmat.

Locals all go out to play on **Lakelse Lake**, which has more than 150 campsites, and can be very, very crowded in summer with families. For reservations, ☎ 800-689-9025. The lake has a winter population of trumpeter swans and is a very popular fishing lake. There's also a hot springs nearby, at Mount Layton – skip the natural pools, which are too hot, and try the pool at the **Mount Layton Hot Springs Resort**, ☎ 800-663-3862.

Kitmat is a port town and a smelter town; most of the population makes its living off one or the other. There's not really a whole lot to see in town, but the road in is quite pretty, and if you drive to the far end of town, there's the **Radley Memorial Campground**, which has BC's oldest Sitka spruce tree – better than 30 feet in circumference, 150 feet tall, and 500 years old.

If you want to see how the industrial side of British Columbia works, you can set up tours at Alcan Kitimat, Eurocan Pulp and Paper, or Methanex – ask at the Visitor Info Centre, which is on the east side of the road as you come into town, ☎ 250-632-6294.

Once you're back on Highway 16, the scenery starts to look more Alaskan than Canadian. You're entering the great rainforest of the coast, which covers most of the area from Seattle all the way up to Haines and Skagway, Alaska. The mountains are rolling, the trees thick, the clouds low. The road runs right along the banks of the Skeena – there are some pullouts for views, but keep any eye out for the heavy truck traffic when you're getting back on the highway.

The river opens to the ocean, the road bends north, and you enter Prince Rupert, a town that, since it's beginning, has been designed to be the end of the line.

Prince Rupert

■ History

Founded in 1900, Prince Rupert is now home to about 18,000 people. The original idea for the town was that it was to be the terminus of the Grand Trunk Pacific Railway. The Grand Trunk was one of those great plans that didn't turn out quite like anybody thought it would. In preparation, more than 12,000 miles of territory were surveyed for the best route, nearly 900 miles of right of way was blasted through solid rock, and costs rose to more than $10,000 per mile before the line was completed.

Plans for Prince Rupert were equally grandiose, and publicity started early. First, there was a contest to name the town. The rules were that the name had to have 10 letters or fewer, and represent the Northwest coast. Prince Rupert – yeah, it's got too many letters, they allowed the cheat – was second cousin to Charles II and son of Fredrick of Prussia. His Northwest connection came because he was the first governor of the HBC. For this marvelous bit of sucking up, three $250 prizes were awarded to contest entrants.

The original plan was for the town to have as many as 50,000 people. This would have made it one of the biggest cities west of the Rockies at the time, but everything changed when Charles Hays, the man who was spearheading all this building effort, went down on the *Titanic*. With him, the grandiose plans for the port – situated in the third-largest and deepest ice-free harbor in Canada – went down with him. When he died, there were about 200 people in the town.

That wasn't necessarily a bad thing. While Hays envisioned something to compete with Vancouver, what happened instead was slow, controlled growth, leaving behind a pleasant little city that still maintains a very busy port, especially for pulp and coal.

■ Basics

i In addition to access from the Yellowhead Highway, the **Alaska Marine Highway** ferry system uses Prince Rupert as its secondary southern terminus. Southbound ferries that terminate here – ships that go on to Bellingham usually do not stop in Rupert – leave you with a very enjoyable drive farther south, on the Yellowhead Highway and into southern B.C., or you can hop a B.C. Ferry and go a bit farther south, to the northern tip of Vancouver Island, before you start driving. Either option is more than scenic. The local AMH number is ☎ 250-627-1744.

In summer, there's a BC Ferries run every other day from Rupert to Port Hardy on the tip of Vancouver Island. The trip takes 15 hours and it is always run in daylight to provide maximum scenic enjoyment. Ferries also go from Rupert to Skidgate in the lovely Queen Charlotte Islands. Local phone number in Prince Rupert for BC Ferries is ☎ 250-624-9627; toll-free in BC, ☎ 800-663-7600.

For local charter flights, call **Harbor Air**, ☎ 250-627-1341, or **Island Air**, ☎ 250-624-2577.

Greyhound Bus connects Rupert to Prince George and Edmonton, with daily departures. ☎ 800-661-1145.

Rent a car at **Tilden Rental**, ☎ 250-624-5318.

Yellowhead & Stewart-Cassiar Highways

Skeena Taxi, ☎ 250-624-2185, serves the Prince Rupert area.

There's an excellent **Visitor Information Center** next to the small boat harbor in Cow Bay. It's open from 9 am in summer. ☎ 250-624-5637, ☎ 250-800-667-1994, or write Box 22063, Prince Rupert, BC, V8J 4P8.

Internet access can be had at **Java Dot Cup**, 516 3rd Ave. West, ☎ 250-627-4112.

> **QUICK TOUR:** Rupert has great displays in the **Museum of Northern British Columbia**. Stop in and see how the HBC used to live. Then head over to the **Kwinitsa Railway Museum** to see how trains changed Canada.

> **DON'T MISS:** The **archaeological tours** offered by the museum are a great value and a good way to get onto the water. The **North Pacific Historical Fishing Village**, just outside of town, shows you how lucky you are never to have been a fish canner. These people worked for their money.

■ Museums & Attractions

Rupert is a walking town. Just take a stroll from the archaeological museum down to the train museum, around the point towards the ferry terminal. Look one way, there's a beautiful town; look the other, nothing but ocean and islands and fishing boats coming and going.

Still, there isn't a whole lot to do in Rupert except soak in the exceptional scenery – the town is most useful as a way to get somewhere else, as it's a port for both the Alaska Marine Highway and the BC Ferry system – but you're not going to regret a couple of days wandering the pleasant streets, either. It's one of the prettiest, nicest small towns in British Columbia.

Start touring the town at the **museum**. Check for guided heritage walking tours of the downtown area. The museum has a good assortment of Native artifacts, including a reproduction of a petroglyph known as "Man who fell from the heaven." It's a full-sized outline of a human body. There are elaborate displays of Native basketry and other utensils, and it's pretty easy to lose track of time in here, the quality of artifacts is so good. There are also regular guided programs to the carving shed behind the museum, which offers a look at a totem pole in the making, and in which films are shown on the history of totem poles. Admission is $5.

In the summer, the **Museum of Northern British Columbia** runs archaeological tours, selling tickets in the Tourist Info Centre. The tour, which is really more historical than archaeological, takes you out on a boat to the old village of Metlakatla, stopping along the way at other points of interest. A knowledgeable guide fills you in on how to spot old Native villages (watch for green swaths of land or parallel rows of rocks leading into the water), and offers a history of settlement in the area. It's a good introduction to local Native culture, and the price can't be beat: $24 for a 3½-hour trip. For more information, contact the museum at PO Box 669, 100 1st Ave. East, Prince Rupert, BC V8J 3S1. ☎ 250-624-3207.

The **Firehall Museum** details Rupert's historical fire stations, with the highlight of the exhibition being a 1925 Reo Speedwagon fire engine. It's just up the street from the Tourist Info Centre. Admission is by donation. ☎ 250-627-4475.

*Walk west along the waterfront to reach the **Kwinnitsa Railway Station Museum**. Along with an interpretive exhibit – a detailed history of how the railway has influenced Prince Rupert – the museum also features videos and has a good gift shop. It looks small on the outside, but this is a must-see. After all, the railway was what started the town, and of all the railway museums in British Columbia, this one gives you the best idea of what life was like at the stations – most museums concentrate on the trains. Good photographs of railway workers and their tools, and a great place to get an idea of what working on the railroad really was like. Admission is by donation, suggested at $1. ☎ 250-627-8009. Another great thing about the museum is the location: right on the waterfront, with a little park nearby. It's the perfect spot for a picnic.*

The other standard attraction is a few miles out of town. Head out on the Yellowhead Highway and take Route 599 – there's only one way to go and you can't get lost. Follow 599 for six miles, and you'll reach the **North Pa-**

Abandoned cannery building.

Yellowhead & Stewart-Cassiar Highways

cific Cannery Historic Fishing Village. Like coal mining communities in the Eastern US, cannery communities in the West were towns unto themselves, with housing, stores, entertainment, and more. The North Pacific Cannery opened in 1899, and ran continuously until 1981. It's been reopened as a museum, showing the details of the canning process and how the canneries stayed alive. The museum offers excellent displays (ever wonder how they made cans before the machinery took over?) and good interpretive signs. Tours are run every hour, or you can walk the grounds yourself. Admission is $10 for adults, and well worth it.

Khutzeymateen/K'tzim-a-Deen Grizzly Bear Sanctuary

A lot of the operators listed below in the out and about section say they run trips into the Khutzeymateen wilderness, and that's sort of true. But they're really running on the very edges of it, in the Khutzeymateen Inlet, just outside the actual sanctuary. That doesn't mean you won't see bears – there are a lot of bears out there to see (roughly 50 make the area home, which is quite a high density for grizzlies), and your chances are extremely good of getting a close-up view. But be sure to clarify whether you're going into the very restricted reserve, or simply into the area.

The Khutzeymateen was Canada's first wilderness area set up to specifically protect grizzlies and their habitat. It covers a bit over 44,000 hectares of land, ranging from the coast to 6,000+-foot mountains. The official provincial park handout on the sanctuary says it all: the land is there for the bears, and "any human activity in the area is secondary.... While visitor use of this sanctuary is not encouraged, controlled viewing is permitted."

And they keep a tight control on the viewing. This isn't a place you can just turn up to and take a look around. All visitors must register at the ranger station at the head of the inlet. Once you're there, they're going to keep close track of you. Only one group per day – 10 people maximum – is allowed into the estuary, the prime bear-watching spot. They'd really rather you never even got out of your boat, and just watched from the water, at least 100 yards from any bear. If you've got your own boat, you can turn up and anchor in the inlet, but you can't get off the boat unless you're accompanied by a park official.

In other words, Canada is trying hard to make this a very inconvenient place to go. It's better for the bears that way, and we've got to encourage that. Bears have enough trouble. Let's give them some room, and applaud Canada's efforts to tightly control the area. Ten people a day is enough.

For more information, contact BC Parks Khutzeymateen office, ☎ 250-798-2277.

If running on the edges of the sanctuary isn't enough for you, contact **Ocean Light II Adventures**, ☎ 604-328-5339, an official guide into the sanctuary itself. Four-day trips run about $1,500, coming in on the company's swank boat. These people know what they're doing, and they're serious about bear conservation and the protection of bears inside the sanctuary. For true bear fans, this is the chance of a lifetime.

■ Out & About

 Prince Rupert is **salmon** country. Mid-May to mid-July, the place is a fisherman's dream come true. Even as late as September, you can pick up on the coho run.

There are a ton of local operators. Check with the Info Centre first, since they know the operators and can set you out with the people who will best match your needs. Remember, always before booking a charter, see what you're getting yourself in for, what's provided and what isn't, and what kind of boat you're going to be on. There are plenty of choices out there, and something that's just right for you.

Once you've caught the fish, **Dolly's Seafoo**d, #7 Cow Bay Road, ☎ 250-624-6090, can freeze or vacuum pack your catch.

If you're looking to kayak, contact **Eco-Treks**, ☎ 250-624-8311, right next door to the Info Centre. They've got quick paddles for novices, from $40. If you're looking for something more, there's a six-hour paddle at Lucy Island, where you've got a good chance of spotting seals and more – blue lagoons, white sand beaches. The $150 fee includes a Zodiac ride out there. For birders, there's the Kayaking Quest tour, for $60, which takes in a rhinoceros auklet sanctuary. You have to wonder just what kind of bad day Mother Nature was having when she came up with these birds, which are even more clumsy than most of the auk family. Eco-Treks also runs longer trips, including excursions to Khutzeymateen to see grizzlies, for $595, in June and July, or overnight paddles to go watch humpback whales, for the same price. And they rent kayaks, but you've got to know what you're doing before they'll send you out alone with one.

Harbour Air, ☎ 250-627-1341, runs flightseeing trips, including flyovers of the Khutzeymateen wilderness – Canada's only grizzly sanctuary. A look at it will run you about $250. **Inland Air**, ☎ 888-624-2577, also runs charters to Khutzeymateen, as well as quick flightseeing trips closer to town.

Palmerville Adventures, ☎ 888-580-2234, runs trips to Khutzeymateen, starting with a flight to the inlet, and then two hours of boating to watch for bears. Prices start around $250.

Seashore Charters, ☎ 250-624-5645, in the trailer across from the museum, has wildlife watching, fishing, and town tours. Fishing charters start at $200/person for all day, with a minimum of four people. Whalewatching trips run around $75, with a good chance of seeing humpbacks, and possibly minkes or grey whales. Trips out to see bears run about $200.

■ Food

 The place of choice is **Smiles**, at 113 George Hills Way, in Cow Bay. The menu includes seafood, wonderful carrot cake, and other desserts. In business since 1922, it's the best food in town, and the most popular – you may have to wait for a table. Prices start around $6. Nearby is the reservations-required **Cow Bay Café** (☎ 250-627-1212), at 205 Cow Bay Rd. The meals change according to what's fresh, but the food is always outstanding. Prices from $12.

For a nice night out, try **Boulet's Seafood** (☎ 250-624-9309), in the Pacific Inn. They serve crab, salmon, and more in a deluxe atmosphere (with deluxe prices). Reservations are required.

At the other end of the scale is the **Green Apple**, at 310 McBride. Stop in for a quick fill up of fish and chips. This is Prince Rupert's place of choice for a quick meal.

■ Accommodations

 Most of the town's hotels are along 1st, 2nd, and 3rd Avenues, between the ferry terminal and downtown.

HOTEL PRICING
Prices are in US dollars.
under $50 . . . . $
$50-$100 . . . . $$
$100-$150 . . . . . . $$$
above $150 . . . . . $$$$

Crest Motor Hotel, ☎ 250-624-6771, 800-663-8150, www.cresthotel.bc.ca, 222 1st. Ave. West, is the nicest place to stay in town. $$$. The **Moby Dick Inn**, ☎ 250-624-6961, 800-663-3760, www.mobydickinn.com, 935 2nd Ave. West., is conveniently located, features room/car packages, and has a pretty good restaurant on the premises. $$. **The Inn on the Harbour**, ☎ 250-624-9157; 800-663-8155, www.innontheharbour.com, at 720 1st Ave. has good views, $$.

The Aleeda Motel, ☎ 250-627-1367, at 900 3rd Ave West, is out near the ferry terminals. $$. In the same neighborhood is the **Totem Lodge**, 1335 Park Ave., ☎ 250-624-6761 or 800-550-9161, $$.

As with most towns, turnover in B&Bs is huge. It's easiest just to ask at the Info Centre, where there will be plenty of brochures on local spots.

Camping

There are two places to camp in Prince Rupert.

Park Avenue Campground is just a mile from the ferry terminal. Not much atmosphere here, but it's very convenient. Tents can get in anytime; RVs need reservations. The place is a big grassy patch by the roadside. ☎ 250-624-5861.

Just 14 miles outside of town on the Yellowhead Highway is **Prudhomme Lake Provincial Park Campground**, which features 18 nice spots, no facilities, but lots of trees and scenery.

■ Leaving Prince Rupert

 Despite all its charms, the main reason to come to Prince Rupert is to leave. The **Alaska Marine Highway** uses Prince Rupert as its secondary southern terminus. There are six north-bound runs and six south-bound into Prince Rupert each week. Ships that stop in Prince Rupert do not serve Bellingham. ☎ 250-627-1744 or 800-642-0066.

 For extensive details on the AMH and its routes, pick up a copy of our *Adventure Guide to the Inside Passage and Coastal Alaska*, also from Hunter Publishing.

To get farther south by sea, take the **BC Ferries**. There's a run every other day from Prince Rupert to Port Hardy, on the tip of Vancouver Island. Ferries also go from Prince Rupert to Skidgate in the lovely Queen Charlotte Islands. ☎ 250-624-9627; or toll-free in BC, 800-663-7600.

 For more on the Charlottes, see our other book, *Adventure Guide to British Columbia*.

The Stewart-Cassiar Highway
The Quick Way North

The Alaska Highway is not the only road route into the great North. There's also the Stewart-Cassiar (usually just called the Cassiar), which picks up from the Yellowhead Highway just south of Kitwanga and comes out 21 miles west of Watson Lake, in the Yukon. The Cassiar is faster, more consistently scenic (although there is nothing to match the grandeur of Stone Mountain or the Kluane Range), and considerably shorter. It's also in lousy shape, only occasionally punctuated by good stretches, and full of trucks going too fast for conditions. There are even a few places where the road doubles as an air-strip.

Start of the Stewart-Cassiar Highway.

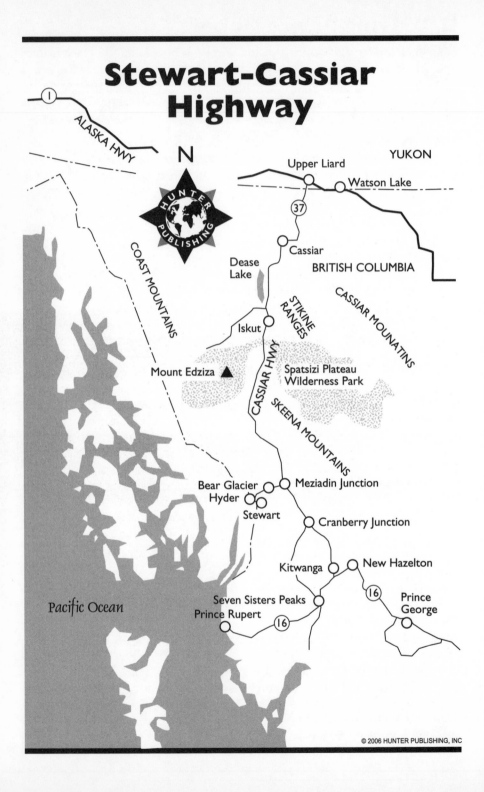

Stewart-Cassiar Highway

N

Pacific Ocean

© 2006 HUNTER PUBLISHING, INC

There's always that chance of spotting a kermodie along the way. Okay, so maybe your chances for winning the lottery are better. Still. It's enough for us to keep our eyes peeled.

Mile markers are almost nonexistent on the Cassiar; what's given here is mean distance, so keep an eye on your odometer. We're giving distances in miles rather than kilometers, because of the Cassiar's longstanding place as an alternate to the Alcan – there was actually quite a controversy over changing the Cassiar over to the metric system.

The junction for the Cassiar is in the middle of nowhere, but it's well signed, 365 miles west of Prince George. Be sure to gas up in Hazelton, which is spread out along the highway about 25 miles before the junction. Hazelton was a wintering spot for miners and prospectors working the Interior; pack trains traveled the Telegraph Trail and ended up here.

Around you at the junction are the Seven Sisters Mountains. In this area there is some possibility of seeing a kermodie bear, a rare subspecies of black bear. Kermodies are cream-colored – it's a form of albinism – and found only around here and on some coastal islands. The other mainland spot where you might see them is in Terrace, farther along the Yellowhead toward Prince Rupert.

■ Kitwanga

The first village you hit on the Cassiar is Kitwanga (turn east on the side road a quarter-mile after the junction). It has a National Historic Site commemorating the fight at Battle Hill; the first such site honoring of the activities of the Natives in Western Canada. It's not exciting – it's a 40-foot manmade hill – but it's worth a quick drive by. This was the site of a Gitxsan fortress, which included hidden chambers, trap doors, and booby traps. The leader of the forces was a man named Nekt, who went into battle dressed like a grizzly bear. Luckily for him, he was killed in battle a while before the Europeans first showed up.

There are also some nice **totem poles** in the village and **St. Paul's Anglican Church**, a prime example of Canadian wooden church architecture, which dates back to 1893. The bell tower is especially lovely. Kitwanga – or Gitwangak, as it was traditionally called – was on the trading route for candlefish oil (it was called the Skeena Grease Trail), which braided and branched as far as the Bering Sea.

Kitwanga is part of what's billed as the Northwest Kultural Tour – Kitwanga, Kitwancool (properly Gitanyow), New Hazelton, K'san, and Kispiox – a day trip of about 125 miles that takes in some of the First Nation villages in southern BC. K'san boasts a reconstruction of a Gitksan village; Kispiox has great totem poles. These are all simple villages, not really tourist attractions, except for K'san, which is quite developed. You're perfectly welcome, but be polite.

Gitanyow is a recent change in name to the village of Kitwancool, at Mile 5, where you take the short spur to the west. Your map may show either name, but outside the village, more people are still calling it Kitwancool – it'll take a while for everybody to get used to the change. Gitanyow is home to an impressive collection of totem poles, including what is believed to be the world's oldest that is still standing in its original location; the pole is titled "Hole-in-the-Ice." More than 140 years old, it tells how a man saved his village from starvation by his skills in ice-fishing. The art of totem carving is still very much alive in Kitwancool; half-carved poles lie on the ground among the poles that have been erected. Common figures on the poles include ravens, frogs, and killer whales. For more on totem poles, see the *Introduction*.

Check at Gitanyow's Information Centre, next to the carving shed, to see if there's anybody around who feels like talking to you about the poles.

Heading north, the road travels alongside Kitwanga Lake, with the Kispiox Mountains to the east. To the west are the massive Coast Mountains, which form a barrier between the shore and the Interior of BC.

The first camping facilities are at **Cranberry Junction**, at Mile 53 (about km 74). You'll find good fishing on the nearby Cranberry River, especially during salmon season. No services are available here; there's just the campground.

Nass Road heads west at Cranberry Junction, leading back down to Terrace. The road is paved and improved gravel, leading past logging operations and a few First Nation villages. For scenery, there are dried lava flows in places. At any campground in this area, watch for black bears. There's quite a population around.

Continuing north, the road follows the **Nass River**, which is one of BC's best salmon runs, and crosses the Meziadin River on a one-lane bridge nearly 200 feet long at Mile 87.9. In autumn, you can stop and watch the salmon run in Hana Creek, at Mile 94.4. A salmon run is an amazing thing – on a large one, the water will be completely full of fish, packed gill to gill. The fish are struggling upstream, a little closer to death each minute, as they can hardly breathe in the fresh water. It is illegal to fish in a running stream, and it is illegal to harass the fish in any way. They've got enough problems without you. And, as you might recall from the incident of Canadian fishermen blockading an Alaska Marine Highway ship during the summer of 1997, fish are taken very seriously around here.

The highway reaches the banks of Meziadin Lake at Mile 99. Here is the junction with the road to Stewart and Hyder, two interesting old towns. At the junction, at Mile 96.2, is the **Meziadin Lake Provincial Park**, with 46 campsites and great views of the Coast Mountains. Some of the sites have great water views, too. You're in bear area here, so keep your camp accordingly. Sites are $12, and there's a boat launch, with good canoeing and fishing on the lake. Gas and repairs may be available at Meziadin Junction

Services, which also operates a small RV camp and restaurant on the shores of the lake. ☎ 250-636-9240.

Stewart-Hyder

The side trip to Stewart and Hyder is an interesting one. It's a 40-mile access road, smooth and delightful, traveling between tight mountain ranges. You'll see several glaciers along the way; the Bear Glacier, at Mile 15, is the best. Come here in early morning light for top notch photos. There's a pullout where you can look across the river to the glacier. Look up at the old highway, several hundred feet up. The glacier used to reach all the way across the valley. A few miles farther is a huge accumulation of snow, which looks like a glacier, but is in reality the remnants of avalanches.

The scenery on the road in is nothing short of stunning. In addition to the glacier are mist-covered streams, steep mountains, and that feeling that you're entering a different world as you head downhill from the interior's plateau to the coast. If you've never seen the coast of Southeast Alaska, this is what it looks like: trees, water, mist, like a Chinese landscape painting run riot.

Stewart, despite being the northernmost ice-free port in Canada, has the most snow of anywhere in the North. Its record is 1,104 inches during one 12-month period.

These weather conditions have made Stewart the town of choice for filming Hollywood movies. *The Thing* (the John Carpenter version), *The Iceman*, and *Bear Island* were all filmed here. More recently, the Robin Williams-Al Pachino film *Insomnia* came to town. Most of the crew stayed out on the yachts the producers brought in, but locals will tell you quite elaborate stories of Robin Williams getting crazy in the woods.

The town of Stewart (population 1,200), which is in Canada, is primarily interesting for its juxtaposition to Hyder (population 100), which is in Alaska. Hyder residents tend to use Canadian money, attend Canadian schools, and use the Canadian time zone. Hyder, in a very real sense, tries as hard as it can to be invisible – as soon as you cross the border into the Alaska town (you will have to stop at Canadian customs on the way back in, so be aware if this presents visa issues for you), the road goes to hell, for example, in an effort to keep people away. However, because of Canada's tax structures, the grocery store in Hyder is much more popular than the one in Stewart. Hyder also has more bars per captia than pretty much anywhere else in the world.

The two towns create an odd but very interesting juxtaposition, so it's well worth the couple of hours it takes to come down here.

■ Museums & Attractions

 The Stewart **Info Centre** is in the Chamber of Commerce Building on 5th Ave.; it's open in summer, and they've got a good variety of brochures, etc. on the area.

The towns lie at the head of the **Portland Canal**, a 90-mile-long salt-water fjord. George Vancouver came up this canal on July 29, 1793, looking for the northwest passage. Obviously this dead end wasn't it, but he wrote about this place, "salmon in great plenty were leaping in all directions. Seals and sea otters were also seen in great numbers." Actually, had communications been better at the time, Vancouver might have skipped the canal entirely (his diary entry when he left said he was "mortified with having devoted so much time to so little purpose"). In August 1791, the *Columbia-Rediviva*, a US ship, was in the canal when "one canoe came alongside in which was six men extraordinarily well armed with spears daggers bows and arrows covered with mats in the bottom of their canoe." There was a bit of talk, a bit of trade, and a landing party was put ashore. It didn't come back, so the ship tacked in closer, and there "I saw my worthy friend Mr. Caswell laying dead in the bottom of the boat . . . stabbed upwards of twenty places." The ambush was apparently retaliation for the actions of yet an earlier ship (Vancouver was really behind here), the *Hancock*, which had opened fire on the locals.

The US Army Corps of Engineers came here in 1896, and with the big gold rush in the Klondike two years later, the area was swamped with would-be prospectors. A few got lucky here, and both towns boomed for a brief period. Just before World War I, there were 10,000 people in town. When the boom went bust, about a dozen remained.

This area was originally going to be the terminus of the transcontinental railway, but the terrain leading in was simply too rough to cut a train line. The terminus got moved south to Vancouver, and Stewart/Hyder languished until the 1960s, when mining concerns moved in. The biggest of them, a copper mine, shut down in 1984. Today both towns are quiet, but pleasant.

There's not a whole lot to do or see in the towns. People come here for the drive in, the glaciers, the bars, and the bears. That's about it, but it's really more than enough to justify the drive.

Hyder is worth a visit for a look at the **bars**. The walls are covered in money, a tradition from the days of the miners. A miner would tack a bit of cash to the wall, scribbling his name across it. It was insurance against coming back broke from prospecting. The big deal, of course, is to get "Hyderized" at the Glacier Inn – knock back a shot of 190-proof in one swallow, you get a genuine Hyderized card to show your friends and make them wonder just what's wrong with you. The cards are numbered, and among Alaska and BC residents, there's a certain amount of bragging right involved in having a lower-numbered card.

Wildlife

Once you're across the border in Hyder, head right to **Fish Creek**. The **Fish Creek Wildlife Observatory** is three miles outside Hyder; it's the easiest access of any of the bear observatories in Southeast. From July into September – as long as the fish run holds out – both black and brown bears show up to gorge on the salmon return here. There are very few rivers that the two types of bear share – Anan in Southeast Alaska is the only other accessible one – but you're not likely to see both kinds on any given day.

A viewing platform stretches out parallel to the creek. There are Forest Service personnel are on duty from 6 am to 10 pm. Bring lots of film (or a full memory card for your digital), and read the bear section in the *Introduction* for how to behave at the platform. And remember: bears don't like flash bulbs. Never surprise anything with a mouth bigger than your head.

That's the good side of the platform. In season, you will likely see a bear, and because it's a small creek, you'll probably see the bear closer than you've ever seen a bear before. The downside is, because the platform is so accessible, it can get jammed. On a recent visit here, we came up with one bear and easily 150 people pushing to get the best angle with their telephotos. The bears have got to be really, really puzzled by all this.

Once you're done with the bears, if you're in a decent car, keep heading out the road to **Salmon Glacier**. The best views are about 35 km/22 miles from the Hyder border, but if your appetite was whetted by Bear Glacier, it's worth the drive.

■ Seasonal Events

The towns get a little wild at the beginning of July for a combination **Canada Day/Independence Day** celebration, with parades, fireworks, pig races, and more.

■ Out & About

If you're looking for a place to hike or boat, head to **Clements Lake**, seven miles northeast of Stewart. Other options are the **Sluice Box Trail** (the trailhead is near the dump), which is a nice short overview trail; or the **Titan Trail**, with the trailhead off Salmon River Road. The hike is 4.7 miles up to the Titan Mine.

■ Food

The **Bitter Creek Café** has pizza and Mexican dishes. For the trip ahead, stop in at **Brother's Bakery** for rolls, fresh sandwiches, and a good selection of meats and cheeses.

■ Accommodations

There are some nice places to stay in town. All hotels, whether in Alaska or Canada, use the 250 area code, and prices are quoted here in Canadian dollars. Canadian hotels tack on a 15% bed tax to their rates.

The **King Edward Hotel** (☎ 250-636-2244) is the town's standard. It's downtown. Some rooms have kitchenettes, and the dining room serves passable dinners. $$.

The **Ripley Creek Inn** (☎ 250-636-2344) is a bit smaller and a bit more swank, with a sauna and a few other perks. It's off the main road, and there are some rooms with kitchens. $.

Camping

Campers can head to the **Rainy Creek Campground**. It' nothing exciting, but it'll do, with 98 sites. Across the border in Hyder is Camp-run-a-muck. Again, pretty basic, but you're a little closer to the bears.

The Cassiar, continued

The Cassiar used to be a nightmare of packed gravel and broken pavement. Not so much anymore. In fact, the road is pretty smooth for the most part, and the pavement is in good shape. There's not as much maintenance along here as there is on the Alcan, and there are more long-haul trucks taking advantage of the shortcut to Alaska, but as long as you're paying attention – there are still places with no center lines and a lot of curves – everything will be fine. This is a remote road; once you're on it, there are only a couple of places with services, so time your days out accordingly.

The payoff on the Cassiar is that it is so very much prettier than the Alaska Highway. The Alcan has stretches of more dramatic scenery, but just for mile after mile of stunning, there aren't many roads that can match the Cassiar. It's quite scenic through here: mountains all around, lovely forests.

It's prime bear area, so keep a close watch by streams for the bears who might be fishing. Those who want to try their luck at fishing should keep an especially close eye out before dropping their lines. There are also extensive patches of berry bushes, a bear favorite. And, with all the water around, there are numerous moose, beaver, and smaller mammals.

Your first chance for a break comes at Mile 153.6, **Bell II Lodge**. Gas, food, and lodging, available year-round. ☎ 888-655-5566.

> **WEATHER WARNING:** You're in serious avalanche territory from about Miles 160 to 175. Use extreme caution in winter and spring.

Mile 178 passes the **Dominican Telegraph Line**, which linked Dawson City and Vancouver. Built at the turn of the century, the line was also used as a trail to Atlin. You can still see a few telegraph cabins submerged in Echo Lake and a few stretches of the old trails that haven't been completely swallowed by forest.

Kinaskan Lake Provincial Park Campground is at Mile 225. It has 50 sites for $12; and you can fish the lake for rainbow trout. Good moose country.

Mile 248 has the **Red Goat Lodge**, on Eddontenejon Lake, which rents canoes. Park your RV or stay in the lodge, $$. ☎ 250-234-3261.

Mile 250 has the **Mountain Shadow Campground and RV Park**, a nice place tucked down in a valley away from the road. Clean facilities, and both wooded and gravel sites.

Gravel patch of the Cassiar Highway, headed south.

Yellowhead & Stewart-Cassiar Highways

■ Iskut

The tiny town of Iskut, Mile 250, has several hotels. **Tatogga Lake Resort**, Mile 240.7 (☎ 250-234-3526), has a restaurant, gas station, and a campground. **Trappers Souvenirs** has a gift shop and a few cabins at Mile 256. Plan to stop early in the day, if possible.

Iskut, spread out and nearly empty, is a Taltan Indian town. The site forms the boundary between the **Mt. Edziza** and **Spatsizi Provincial parks**. Spatsizi is a wilderness park with no road access. You can enter on trails or fly in. On the river, there's a great week-long paddle trip. If you've got a mountain bike, the old railroad beds are just there waiting. Mt. Edziza Provincial Park is also a wilderness area, with no vehicle access. Again, you have to get in by plane or trail; easiest access is from Telegraph Creek.

You cross the **Stikine River** at Mile 275. The Stikine is one of the last great rivers, yet to be tamed. Boating is excellent along its length (see below). West of the bridge is the Grand Canyon of the Stikine (with rock walls nearly a thousand feet high), the river runs Class V+, and you can camp along the shores elsewhere.

Watch for bears, and expect masses of mosquitoes in season.

■ Dease Lake

Dease Lake, at Mile 307, is the only town of any size along the Cassiar. The Natives called it "Tatl ah" (head of the lake), and its modern history goes back to 1838, when Robert Campbell was first opening the area for the Hudson's Bay Company. The lake was used as a boat building site during the Cassiar gold rush (1872-1880), and the boomtowns that sprang up during this period – Laketon and Porter's Landing – are now ghost towns that make for an interesting side trip. Gas, groceries, and lodging are available year-round. Try the **Northway Motor Inn** (☎ 250-771-5341), right on the highway, with doubles from $75, or the **Arctic Divide Inn**, ☎ 250-771-3119, about the same price.

There's an interesting side trip from Dease Lake, down the **Telegraph Creek Road**. The road was cut in 1874 by William Moore. Later this route was used to haul supplies to Alcan construction camps – from Dease Lake, the supplies got ferried on the Dease River.

HIGHWAY TIP: The road to Telegraph Creek is gorgeous, but should be attempted only by those in sturdy vehicles. An RV isn't going to make it. Check at Dease Lake for road conditions and a weather forecast before heading down.

■ Telegraph Creek

 The road is about 70 miles long, and takes you to the town of Telegraph Creek, population about 400. Traders came in and tried to kick out the Taltan Indians during the early 1800s. The Taltans had the interesting habit of hunting bear with dogs. They bred a special type of dog, now believed extinct, that was insane enough to leap at a bear. Well, actually, almost any dog is insane enough to leap at a bear – we've seen weiner dogs go amok – but the Taltans had dogs that could win in the fight, instead of just becoming bear appetizers.

As with every other wide spot in the North, gold was eventually found near Telegraph Creek (in 1861), and a boomtown followed. During the Klondike rush, Telegraph Creek boomed again when it was on the "all Canada" route to the goldfields, with miners heading up the Stikine to Teslin Lake, then on the Teslin and the Yukon rivers to Dawson City.

This was not a happy route. It took would-be miners from the coast to the Interior faster than any other means, and it didn't have any of the nasty mountains or glacier crossings that other routes did. The big problem was getting from Telegraph Creek up to Teslin Lake, where you could load gear onto a boat and head north. The *Klondike News*, on April 1, 1898, wrote, "The portage of 150 miles from Telegraph Creek to Teslin Lake is one that the traveler will never forget, even though made over a wagon road, and we would advise our friends to wait until the long-talked-of railroad is completed and go over this route by Pullman Car." Of course, if you had waited, you'd still be waiting.

And so, although hundreds of miners tried this route in the first years of the rush, not many made it. The miners traveled in winter, and the first thing that got them was the fairly constant 60-mph headwind that howls down off the glaciers all winter long.

Actually, not much that was ever supposed to happen at Telegraph Creek ever really did. The town was founded to support the telegraph line – it was easily accessible by river, a nightmare to reach by land. Rosemary Neering describes some of the hassle in her book *Continental Dash*:

> The trip was the most miserable of all Morison's experiences in the region. For ten days, he was constantly wet, wading in cold water under teeming rain or soggy snow. He arrived at his destination, the miners' settlement known as Buck's Bar, now renamed Telegraph Creek in honor of the planned telegraph line, to find just two or three shacks and a dozen miners washing gold. These were the last holdouts of the hundreds who had flocked here in 1862. Most had returned down the coast on the H.M.S. Devastation, sent to rescue them from hunger, cold, and despair.

So, more than once, Telegraph Creek was going to be the next big boomtown. Never happened.

Yellowhead & Stewart-Cassiar Highways

There's not much in Telegraph now. There's an airport, where it looks like the terminal is an abandoned truck camper (but no – there really is no terminal), and a few dozen houses, about half of which seem to be falling down. There's one store, and there is the small church, which is really quite lovely but impossible to get a decent picture of because of the way the phone lines frame it.

You go to Telegraph Creek for the river.

■ The Stikine River

If you want to be alone in the most beautiful countryside you can imagine, the Stikine River is for you. John Muir called it "a Yosemite 100 miles long," and we're convinced the only reason he didn't rave more was that he didn't have time to go upriver any farther.

The Stikine River – the name comes from the Tlingit for "Great River" – is about 400 miles long, starting deep in British Columbia. Fed by literally dozens of glaciers, the water in the river is a murky silver, laden with silt, and yet somehow enormous runs of salmon return to the river each year.

The watershed of the Stikine is one of the largest on the continent, and it is the largest (over 20,000 square miles) that is un-dammed.

At its widest, the river is a bit less than a mile across, but most places are considerably more narrow, perhaps averaging a hundred yards or so from bank to bank.

Outfitters

*The best way on the river, unless you're a crack camper and kayaker, is to let somebody else do the work. The fine people of **Alaska Vistas** are the only outfitters to run raft trips down the Stikine. For a paltry $2,400 – only a bit more than hiring a jetboat just to get you back to Telegraph – you get first and last night at a hotel in Wrangell and five days traveling and camping on the river. Each evening is capped off with the best food you have ever eaten in your life. You travel in an 18-foot self-bailing river raft, with plenty of time to get out and hike around, enjoy the scenery, and sit back and relax in camp. This is one of the best deals in the state, and the trip's river time will be five of the best days of your life. Contact them at ☎ 907-874-3006, or via their website, www.alaskavistas.com. We have been lucky enough to experience a lot over the decade we've been writing these books. This is, quite simply, the best thing we've done in the North, and there's no way to recommend it highly enough.*

Kayaking

You can't kayak the river above Telegraph Creek. Right past the town is the Grand Canyon of the Stikine, an area with Class IV and V whitewater. Below the town, there's nothing more than Class II, and the very fast current (about five knots) that makes running the river a gentle, easy blast – all 150 miles down to the river's mouth by the Wrangell airport.

Glaciers

Above the river is the Stikine Icefield, whose 2,900 square miles includes the LeConte Glacier. Most trips to the Stikine will stop by the glacier (actually closer to Petersburg than Wrangell).

LeConte Glacier is a favored pupping ground for harbor seals, who have their pups on the ice floes that calve off the glacier. There are also moose aplenty, bear, and even a few packs of wolves. In migration season, the Stikine sees as many as a quarter of a billion birds. Snow geese, teal ducks, sandpipers, eagles, and more flock to the rich shoreline.

TRAVELING SAFELY ON THE STIKINE

The main complication of traveling the river is that the channel is never the same twice. Huge amounts of silt are coming down the river, and the soft banks are cut away as the river digs new courses for itself. The lower reaches of the river, in particular, are heavily braided, with as many as 10 or 15 small channels reaching out. No chart can keep up with the river. In winter, storms howl through the Stikine valley, combining with deep freezes; you can pass acres of trees where the tops have been simply sheered off through a combination of freeze and breeze. This means that, at any time of year, there is a lot of debris in the water, snags and entire tree trunks waiting to reach out and grab your boat. There are log jams and sweepers (trees that extend into the water but are still attached to the bank) that need to be watched for. The lower reaches of the river are tidal, which can cause other problems. Plus, the water is really, really cold. Should you fall in, not only are you going to be dealing with the possibility of hypothermia, you've also got to worry about so much silt getting between the fibers of your clothes that it can drag you down before you have time to get hypothermia. The river requires attention and respect; it's not a simple float.

There is no really fast water on the river below Telegraph. There are some riffles, rated as Class II, but nothing at all to worry about. You're not going to find yourself ripping down uncontrollable whitewater on the lower part of the river (up in the canyon above Telegraph is another matter entirely).

Because of the remoteness of the river and the very few people traveling on it above Shakes, you have to assume you're on your own when you head out. Be prepared for emergencies. There is enough jetboat traffic running between Wrangell and Telegraph that you can't go for more than a day or two without seeing a boat go by – unless you're in one braid and they're in another.

However, even if a passing boat sees you, they're not going to stop unless you're signaling – they don't want to interrupt your wilderness experience. To the usual first aid kit and emergency equipment, add a good signaling device.

Camping

Camping on the Stikine is one of the great pleasures of life. There are plenty of wide beaches, sheltered by alder, pine, and spruce. Camp well above the water level – floods are generally seasonal, but anything is possible – and practice all bear safety precautions. We've been ashore on very few beaches without bear sign. You can get your water out of the river, but either boil it and wait for the sediment to settle, or filter it. If you're going to filter, keep in mind what all the sediment is doing to your equipment.

Preparation

Anybody can go on the river at any time, although there are a lot of times you wouldn't want to be out there. No permit is required. Prime season for running the Stikine is May-August. There are heavy spring floods before that, and in late summer the wind begins to howl up the river, making paddling downriver a bit of a nightmare. In winter, the entire thing freezes up.

If you are going to run the river on your own, the put in point is Telegraph Creek. As mentioned above, you can get there by driving in from the Cassiar Highway, or you can hire a jetboat in Wrangell to take you up. You can also fly, but regulations make it impossible for you to fly your boat into Telegraph, unless you can collapse it and fit it inside the plane. Canada no longer allows boats strapped to the outsides of airplanes.

Alone, the trip will cost you between $1-1,500 to get a jetboat ride from Wrangell to Telegraph. The ride takes about eight hours. Keep this in mind if you're leaving your car in Telegraph while you hit the river.

> **AUTHOR TIP:** *Telegraph is your last chance to stock up on anything and, as there is only one store, don't plan on finding much. Get what you need before you get to the river.*

It's about three to four days (six hours a day) in a canoe or a kayak to get downriver from Telegraph to the mouth of the Stikine. Obviously, the more you want to get out and explore, the longer it's going to take.

For however long you plan to stay on the river, remember that you are on your own. You need to be entirely self-sufficient.

NATIVE GLACIAL MYTHS

Native mythology has quite a story about the Great Glacier on the Stikine. It seems that, when they were first moving into the area, they found the river entirely blocked off by the glacier. There was, though, an opening in the glacial face through which water moved. They sent a couple of people up over the ice to see if the water came out anywhere, then sent a log through to see if it made the trip okay. Then they sent the most expendable member of the society, someone's grandmother. When she got through alive, everyone else decided it was okay for them to follow, and the journey continued.

Accommodations

There are two B&Bs on the river, one just below the **Great Glacier,** one on **Farm Island.** There's no real way to contact them in advance; if you're interested, just show up, and the odds are there will be room available. There are also six **Forest Service cabins** on the river, plus another six on the delta, which are not quite as nice in the scenic department but still great places to stay.

Most people plan on their pick up around the Great Glacier. There is a developed picnic site here, and it's an easy place to tell your ride home where you'll be. There's an easy half-hour hike back to the glacier's pond, with great views of the glacial face and floating icebergs. If you fly over the area, you can see that the glacier once reached much farther ahead; there are two concentric rings, moraines, that show how far up the glacier once moved.

Side Trips From The Stikine

A popular side trip on the river is to **Chief Shakes Hot Spring**s, which is on a slough by the Ketili River. It's about two miles off the main channel, and at high water levels, paddling up to the spring is quite doable; if the water is running fast, particularly at the mouth of the slough, you can pretty easily line your boat up past the rapids. Once you hit the springs, you'll find the water is a toasty 122°. There is another hot springs on the river, **Warm Springs**, across from the Great Glacier and just above the Choquette River, marked on many maps, but it has leeches.

 Before hitting the river on your own, pick up a copy of *Stikine River: A Guide to Paddling the Great River*, by Jennifer Voss.

Conservation

The mere fact that the Stikine River is huge, remote, and fairly pristine means that there are a lot of people who want to do something to it. The additional fact that many of its tributary rivers are rich in coal, gold, and other goodies, means that the Stikine is facing serious threats. It's the last great undammed river on the continent, but that may not be true much longer.

The Iskut, perhaps the Stikine's main tributary, has been the site of mining activities for years. When you're on the lower reaches of the river, you may see a large plane flying low overhead; it's taking ore out of the mines on the Iskut, two or three loads a day. Before the plane was used, a hydroplane was used, a behemoth that literally killed the river. The turbulence it kicked up in the Iskut entirely changed the river's habitat, rendering the area largely sterile. Additional silt flowing into the Stikine, where the boat also went, made the river shallower and wider, greatly increasing bank erosion.

The mines on the Iskut are one problem; the huge coal deposit on the Spatsizi is another. There is simply no way to extract it without damaging the Stikine's downriver flow.

Finally, there have been plans for years to dam the Stikine at the Grand Canyon (above Telegraph Creek). The river depends on regular flood cycles to maintain its equilibrium; without them, the river will die, the fish in the river will die, and the world will have lost another beautiful natural feature just so people can run their hairdryers.

FRIENDS OF THE STIKINE

The Friends of the Stikine have been around for a long time, trying to keep the river alive. They lobby actively for preservation of the river and its headwaters and, while a few of their positions may verge on over-conservation – in Wrangell and Telegraph Creek, there are fears that the FOS is trying to outlaw jetboats, which would cut off Telegraph and send Wrangell's economy into a tailspin – they are the only ones fighting for the river. Friends of the Stikine, 1405 Doran Rd., North Vancouver, BC, Canada, V7N 1K1. ☎ 604-985-4659.

◾ The Stikine River Corridor

If you look east or west of the bridge over the Stikine, as you cross the river on the Cassiar, you're looking at the Stikine River Corridor, a protected area that leads to Mt. Edziza Park, to the west, and to the east, the Spatsizi Plateau Wilderness Park. This is a huge area of protected wilderness; except for the road town to Telegraph Creek, the only way in is by boat or float plane.

Mount Edziza Provincial Park covers over 230,000 hectares of the Tahltan Highlands. It's a park of nature run wild: there's a volcanic landscape of perfect cones, lava flows, cinder fields, and more. Mt. Edziza itself, at 2,787 meters/9,144 feet, is, according to the Canadian Park Service, "a composite volcano consisting of thin basalt flows and a central dome of andesite, dacite and rhyolite with a glaciated crater nearly 2,500 metres/8,200 feet in diameter. The eruption that built the mountain and its central cone began four million years ago. Successive lava flows raised the dome above the encircling plateau and spread lava over an area 65 by 25 km/213 x 82 feet. The last basalt flow occurred only 10,000 years ago, at which time it solidified in place and plugged the central vent."

What all this boils down to is a landscape that looks like pictures of Mars – but with animals. On one fly-by of the mountain, we watched a wolf trot right out to the ridge line to watch us. There are caribou everywhere, and the biggest bears we've ever seen have all been along the Stikine River.

To the east side of the river, at the upper reaches of the Stikine, is **Spatsizi Plateau Wilderness Park**. There is no road access to this at all – it's 656,000 hectares of the middle of nowhere, so go in only if you know what you're doing. But, as Parks Canada says, it's "True wilderness atmosphere, outstanding scenery and varied terrain make this park an excellent place for quality hiking, photography, and nature study. Lands within the park have an excellent capability for supporting large populations of wildlife."

This is remote enough that there aren't a lot of operators who can take you into the parks. Book a plane from Telegraph Creek, or from Smithers, down on Highway 16. If you're looking at the river, east, into Spatsizi, is doable. Just don't even think of going west towards the canyon.

The Cassiar, continued

Back on the Cassiar, the road follows Dease Lake for a considerable distance; and once you've passed Dease Lake, there is a daisy chain of other lakes, all with excellent fishing.

This area has produced some of the richest gold finds in Canada, including a 72-ounce nugget pulled out of McDame Creek in 1877, near the gold rush town of Centreville (Mile 381). Most of the gold is long gone, but there are still extensive jade mines – check out **Jade City** at Mile 370 – and, until 1992, there was a huge asbestos mine in the city of Cassiar, 10 miles off the highway. You can't get back there anymore, but it was amazing to drive into the town and see the oddly glowing green hill that dominated the buildings around it. The hill was made up of tailings from the mine, grown over by mosses; but in the proper light, you could swear it was alive. It was a creepy place.

Boya Lake Provincial Park, at Mile 394, has nice campsites on the lake, good boating, and fishing on cloudy days. On clear days, the clarity of the water allows the fish to get a good look at you and know what's coming. The campground has 45 sites. It's a nice place to spend the night, with surprisingly few bugs.

The last 35 miles of the road are paved, but the condition of the pavement may not be the best. The road is narrow and twisting, and there are many one-lane bridges, as the road crosses the French River, the Blue River, Cormier Creek, and dozens of others. At Mile 444 you leave British Columbia and enter the Yukon. If you've been driving with your headlights off, turn them on now, according to Yukon law. No more services are available until you hit the junction with the Alaska Highway at Upper Liard, 23 miles west of Watson Lake.

Chapter 7

Roads to Skagway

The Atlin Road

From Jake's Corner, Mile 866 on the Alaska Highway, you have a choice of two roads. The first goes to Atlin Provincial Park, a hardly visited byway on the highway. The road was built by the Canadian Army Engineers in 1949. It's 58 miles long, with the first 40 miles gravel, the last 18 miles paved. You can camp at Mile 16.5 and at Mile 20.5.

■ Atlin

Atlin is the most northwestern town in British Columbia. In 1899, at the height of its boom days, Atlin was called the Little Switzerland of the North, and it was supposed to be a lovely town, very advanced for the day. It was on the phone and telegraph lines quite early, and after the gold petered out there was a tourist boom that lasted into the 1930s. It was actually the second richest goldfield found, surpassed only by the Cariboo, with more than $23 million of gold taken out. Upwards of 8,000 people lived here at one time, all looking for the glimmer of gold.

Today it's a tiny town overlooking the huge (85 miles long) **Atlin Lake**.

At the southwest tip of the lake, if you're in the mood for a long paddle, is the gigantic **Llewellyn Glacier**, which extends almost to the coast at Juneau. The glacier is in one corner of Atlin Provincial Park; in fact, about one-third of the park's total area is glacier.

If paddling doesn't do it for you, but you want to get out on the lake, rent a boat from **Norseman Adventures** (☎ 250-651-7535). The lake is big and makes its own weather, so it's not really a place for you if you're not comfortable with running boats.

The **Tourist Info Centre** is at the museum on 3rd St., in the old school building. It houses great historical photos of Atlin's salad days and on the history of the local Tlingits. There's a walking tour that takes in some good historical buildings, and you can look at the MV *Tarahina*, a 1916 luxury lakeboat built by the White Pass Company to handle the people and cargo the mining brought up.

For hikers, try the **Monarch Mountain Trail**; two hours gets you great panoramic views. Trailhead is off Warm Bay Road. If you're a birder, you can add a few of the 200 species of bird that call the area home.

Take the highway to its end at **Atlin Provincial Park**. The park is beautiful. In fact, it's remote enough – and more than beautiful enough – that it was used as the setting for filming much of the movie *Never Cry Wolf*, the best movie ever made about wolves. If you've seen the movie, you've probably already pointed the car down the road, just to get a look at this place.

The best thing you can do in the park probably is paddle Atlin Lake. There are some beautiful, remote campsites on **Sloko and Griffith islands**, and at **Lake Inlet**. There's enough lake here to wear out a set of paddles.

For hikers, the **Telegraph Trail** leads from the lake along the Pike River, uphill to Kuthoi Lake, and beyond. This is the route the telegraph originally followed, but it's mostly overgrown now. Still, if you've got time and you're ambitious, it's lovely.

The Tagish Road

The second road leading out of Jake's Corner is the Tagish Road, a shortcut to Carcross and the road to Skagway. It's gravel as far as Tagish, then paved from Tagish to Carcross. Camp at Mile 13, Six Mile River, just before the town of Tagish – the word means "fish trap" in the local language.

Two miles south of town is Tagish Post, originally **Ft. Sifton**, a Mounties checkpoint where they kept track of stampeders headed to the Klondike. The Canadian government used the checkpoint to collect duty and make sure the miners were properly prepared and not going to drop dead on Canadian soil.

The road ends at Mile 34, the junction with the South Klondike Highway. Turn left for Carcross and Skagway, right for Whitehorse.

The South Klondike Highway

Note: Miles are read from Skagway.

The junction of the South Klondike and the Alaska Highway is at Mile 905 on the Alcan. The South Klondike Highway essentially follows the same path the would-be miners used to get up to the Klondike goldfields. The road goes along the tracks of the White Pass and Yukon Route Railway, which was built on top of rocks worn smooth by the footsteps of the miners.

There's an old **White Pass and Yukon Route Railway** shed at Mile 86.7, and the remains of the old **Robinson Roadhouse**. At Mile 73, you'll see the stunning **Emerald Lake**. There is no way to describe the color of this piece of water – *emerald* doesn't do it justice.

In contrast to the beautiful water, at Mile 66.9 is the **Carcross Desert**, the smallest desert in the world, at about 644 acres. The area was originally covered by a glacial lake, but as the glaciers pulled back, this sandy "desert" bottom was left behind. Strong winds kept the plant life to a minimum.

As you're driving along here, you'll think you see an animal, way up on the hillside. You'll pull into the nearby parking lot for a better look. Then you'll consider driving off again. Don't. **Caribou Crossing**, Mile 67.9, bills itself as "Yukon's Premier Wildlife Museum," and that's really not a bad description. What you get inside, in addition to an ice cream parlor, pizza place, gift shop, and the usual tourist stuff, is a pretty amazing display of taxidermied animals. Big ones. Really, really big ones. And not just the usual suspects: they've also put together displays to show you some of the ice-age mammals that lived around here (for more of that, check the Beringia Centre, in Whitehorse). For your $6, it's a really interesting place to stretch your legs for a half-hour. And dry camping is free for RVs with museum admission.

The junction with the Tagish Road is at Mile 66.1, and the town of Carcross, population 400, is a tenth of a mile farther on.

■ Carcross

Carcross was a depot town for the White Pass and Yukon Route Railway; it later served as a supply center for the Conrad Mine, on Tagish Lake, and as a transfer point for cargo headed to Atlin. The town was originally called Caribou Crossing because of the regular caribou migration in the area.

The **Tourist Info Centre** is at the old White Pass and Yukon Route Railway depot. Open daily in summer from 8 am to 8 pm. For a small town, it's a better-than-average center.

There's a stern-wheeler dry-docked next to the interpretive center. This kind of boat was used to move people and freight on the area lakes – notably Lake Bennett, where miners switched from walking to floating. The people who started it all, Skookum Jim and Tagish Charlie, are buried in the **Carcross Cemetery**, half a mile south of town.

TAGISH CHARLIE

Let's take a little side trip here down the path of political correctness. You'll still hear about Skookum Jim when you're in the North, but Tagish Charlie has been PC'd – he's now usually called Yukon Charlie. Tagish is, of course, a group name, a perfectly acceptable one, pointing to one of Canada's many First Nations bands. Somebody somewhere, though, got their undies in a bunch over this one and decided to erase a hundred years of history with a whine. Their cries reached the ears of those in power, who decided joining in on stupidity was easier than risking losing the votes of ill-informed fanatics.

It's Tagish Charlie. Don't play along.

As you head out of Carcross, watch for sections of the old wagon road, visible from the highway.

Mile 59 has a pullout with overlooks of the **Windy Arm** of Tagish Lake, and at Mile 52 you can see the remains of the **Venus Mill**, an old gold and silver mine.

 CUSTOMS CONTROL: The Canadian border is open from 8 am to midnight from November 1 to March 31, and 24 hours a day the rest of the year. Remember, Canada is an hour later than Alaska. If you're traveling in winter, remember that these are Canadian times – an hour ahead of Alaska. See the Alaska Highway section at the end of the book for more details. Also, check locally before you head out. The world is changing pretty fast right now, security-wise, and it's annoying to have to turn around. Don't go to the border until you've made sure it's open.

The summit of White Pass, 3290 feet, is at Mile 14.4. Look across the canyon for the White Pass and Yukon Route Railway tracks. The road drops here, twisting and corkscrewing its way down to US Customs at Mile 6.8.

At Mile 2.3 is the junction of the Dyea Road (see below for details), and then you're in the historic town of Skagway.

Skagway

A "ton of gold" was carried off the docks into the small town of Seattle in July 1897. A full year had passed since the stuff of dreams had been discovered in the Klondike, on Rabbit Creek, a tributary of the Yukon River; but it was only when the ship hit Seattle, wallowing gold-heavy in the light swells of Puget Sound, that the rest of the world had its first news of the gold strike.

The very next ship heading north from Seattle was overflowing with hopeful prospectors. The rush was on, and it all channeled through Skagway, the northern port for the would-be rich.

▪ History

Skagway became one of the most famous cities in the world in 1897. There was hardly a newspaper printed in the continental US. that year that didn't have an article on the gold rush and the trip north. It was from Skagway that thousands headed up the murderous **Chilkoot Trail**, bound for the goldfields of the Yukon, 600 miles to the north. The Chilkoot actually started in nearby Dyea, which would have been the boomtown if ships could have gotten to it more easily, but a huge mud flat meant ships stayed well away – although at one point, the town founders of Dyea put up a dock a mile long to help ships get in, it took them so long to make it the back end was crumbling before the front end was done.

So you had two choices: you could go straight to Dyea, unload on the mud flats, and try desperately to get all your gear ashore before the tide came in and washed it away, or you could get out, safe and dry, in Skagway, but then have to schlep your gear a dozen miles or so to the Chilkoot trailhead.

Or – and not many were foolish enough to try this option – you could take the Dead Horse Trail, the White Pass. It was shorter, but it was infinitely harder, and it earned its name for a reason. Only 5,000 people tried the White Pass that first winter; they managed to kill off 3,000 pack horses along the way. Within two months, the trail had become almost impassable from overuse and the impossibility of getting around the carcasses.

CAPT. WILLIAM MOORE

Captain William Moore, anticipating the gold rush by almost a decade, had staked claim to 160 acres at the mouth of the Skagway River nine years before the first strike and begun construction of a wharf. When the first load of miners arrived in his would-be village of Mooresville, a group that included surveyor Frank Reid forced Moore and his claim aside, drew up a new town plan, and renamed the town Skaguay, after the Tlingit "Skagua," or windy place. Moore never did make his fortune, though after years of court battles he finally received a small part of the value of the land.

Skagway was the largest Alaskan town during the gold rush years, with a population between 10,000 and 20,000. It also had a reputation as lawless and dangerous. Many stampeders never reached the goldfields but instead lost everything to one of the myriad of conmen waiting at the docks. Many more lost everything in the mud, on the trail, or they simply came to their senses – not many in this last category – and headed back home. One estimate is that a grand total of 100,000 people started off for the goldfields. Half made it to Alaska. Roughly a fifth made it to Dawson. Maybe fewer than 50 actually got rich.

During the first year of the gold rush alone, about 20,000 to 30,000 gold-seekers headed up the Chilkoot Trail from Dyea. After starting from the port in Skagway, the trip took an average of three months. As the Canadian government required that each person carry a year's supply of food and necessities – the Canadians weren't that interested in finding a lot of dead hopefuls on their land – a lot of hiking back and forth between Dyea or Skagway and the top of the pass was required. Because of that ton of gear, you didn't just hike the trail once; you hiked it maybe 40 times before you were done. On average, it took three months to get the gear the 25 miles from Dyea to the top of the pass.

For an idea of just how much stuff they had to carry, check the *Introduction*, page 12.

Figuring that a miner's gear cost a total of roughly $500-2,000, you know there were plenty of people waiting and hoping to sell stuff. It was the only sure way to get rich off the gold rush (one estimate says that within two weeks of the first ship of gold docking in Seattle, local merchants sold $325,000 worth of mining gear). Along the way, boomtowns sprang up, some considerably bigger than modern Skagway.

There is actually still a company in business that started by making clothes for the stampeders. The **Filson Company**, in Seattle (☎ 800-624-0201, www.filson.com) continues to make oil cloth clothing and bags the same way they did more than a hundred years ago. We love the stuff – Filson rain hats are absolute Alaska essentials. Filson gear is utterly indestructible, and of the highest quality imaginable; you can plan on who inherits it, because it will outlive you.

As for the miners – many no doubt wearing Filson duds – once atop the pass, miners built rough boats on the lakes and floated the Yukon River up to the goldfields. Sounds simple, right? Maybe not. Most of these people had never built a boat before, and of course, there weren't hardware stores handy for buying boat kits. They had to go into the woods, cut down the timber, whipsaw it into planks – if you've never used a whipsaw, think of two people with a flexible, six- or eight-foot piece of metal between them, trying to draw it in a straight line through a knotty piece of wood. Yeah. Lots of partnerships broke up during the whipsaw phase of things.

The ice broke up that first winter, and 7,000 boats took to the water. The miracle was that only about 150 of them sank right off, and only 10 men were killed in the water.

All those pictures you see of the stampeders, all those miners trudging through knee-deep snow, all the stories of hardship, all come from the winters of '98 and '99. The Chilkoot Pass was about to become completely unnecessary.

In 1898, construction began on the **White Pass and Yukon Route Railway** (WP&YR), which still operates today. The line didn't get finished until June 8, 1900 – after the bulk of the rush was past. Getting the line through meant the trip to the goldfields was cut from six months to six days, but the traffic was already thinning. The Nome strike, when there was gold on the beaches of the Bering Sea, was already drawing hopeful crowds.

After the Gold Rush

The railroad was leased by the U.S. War Department in 1942 for the duration of World War II, and used to transport supplies and men for the construction of the Alaska Highway. Everything arrived by barge, was transported to the army's base camp in Whitehorse, and then moved out to the work sites along the highway. During the months of construction, the line moved 15 tons of freight every two weeks – more than it had moved in the 40 years previous. There were up to 17 trains a day running through the pass. It was on this railroad that the idea of container shipping was first tried. Truck trailers came off barges, were loaded onto the train, then transported north to the road. Now used worldwide, the idea started right here.

There are two excellent books on the gold rush and the White Pass, detailing the early history of Skagway and the trials of the miners: *The Klondike Fever*, by Pierre Berton, covers the gold rush; *The White Pass*, by Roy Minter, is a fascinating history of the WP&YR railway.

Skagway Today

Except when the cruise ships are in, Skagway is considerably calmer than it once was. As one long-time resident put it, "In the gold rush days, we had 20,000 people walking the streets with guns; now we just have seven or eight thousand tourists walking around with credit cards." This sleepy town of 850 year-round residents faces more tourist jams than guns now. From 9 am to 9 pm, there can be as many as 9,500 cruise ship passengers on the street – yes, there's really only one – of Skagway, all of them come to see a town that's being restored to its full 1898 glory. In 2004, Skagway got just over 800,000 cruise ship passengers to visit over the summer months. The main shopping/tourist area is one street, six blocks long. Prepare for combat tourism, but don't let the numbers put you off. Skagway is a beautiful city in one of the most dramatic settings in Southeast. During ship hours, head for the mountains; when the ships are out, come in and walk around the beautiful town.

There are those who complain that Skagway is becoming a kind of Disneyland of the far north – an unreal town living only for the tourist trade – but few visitors go away disappointed. We were here with our parents last summer, their first visit. Ed's father, overwhelmed by the crowd, was ready

Roads to Skagway

to flee. We went one block away from Broadway, and that was all it took. "Oh. This is a nice town," Dad said, as soon as he could move his elbows.

Final fact about Skagway: it's where we lived while finishing up writing this book. We kind of like the place.

■ Basics

i Skagway and Haines are the only places where you can switch from the Alaskan road highway to the Alaska Marine Highway for trips south. The ferry terminal is about half a mile from downtown. See the *Alaska Highway* chapter at the end of this book for details on linking up to the road system. Local phone for the AMH is ☎ 250-983-2941. Do be aware that the road from Skagway into Canada isn't anywhere near as beautiful as the road from Haines.

Cruise ships dock right at the edge of downtown. Head inland. You'll strike shops.

Rent a car from **Avis**, ☎ 250-983-2247 or 800-331-1212, or **Sourdough Car Rental**, ☎ 250-983-2523.

Sockeye Cycle rents mountain bikes, ☎ 250-983-2851; Sourdough Car Rental does as well. Check at their office on 6th, off Broadway. Rates start at $10/hour. Finally, **The Skagway Fish Co.**, ☎ 250-983-3474, also rents bikes.

Charter a helicopter from **Temsco**, ☎ 250-983-2900, which also has heli-flightseeing tours of the local glacier area. **L.A.B.**, ☎ 250-983-2471, and **Skagway Air**, ☎ 250-983-2218, also charter and run similar tours in fixed-wing planes, as well has having regularly scheduled runs to nearby towns.

Haines-Skagway Water Taxi, ☎ 888-766-3395, offers a good way to take a day trip to Haines, get some good views of the Lynn Canal and possibly some wildlife, and still be back in Skagway in time for dinner. The trip takes roughly an hour each way; the taxi makes two round-trips per day. Fare is $35 round-trip. $90 puts you on the fast boat to Juneau.

The **Fjord Express**, ☎ 800-320-0146, runs fast ferries to Juneau, for $129 round-trip.

To take a bus to the Interior, call **Alaska Direct Bus Line**, ☎ 800-770-6652. It'll run you about $230 from Skagway to Anchorage.

The **Information Center** is right downtown, in the old AB Building. You'll recognize it because of the herd of tourists out front taking pictures of its beautiful driftwood exterior. It has the usual assortment of stuff and a map of the Skagway walking tour – Skagway is one of the most beautiful towns in Alaska to walk around in. If you're doing the tour, though, take a good look at the map first and check for shortcuts to the places you're really interested in. Nothing is very far away. The Info Center is open daily 8-5 in the summer, 8-12 and 1-5 the rest of the year. ☎ 250-983-2855.

The **National Park Service Visitor Center** is in the old WP&YR offices, right in the center of downtown. They're open daily 8-7 in summer, 8-6 in May and September, and 8-6 Monday through Friday the rest of the year. ☎ 250-983-2921. See below for more details.

Get **Internet access** at **Glacial Smoothies/Seaport Cyber,** on 3rd, just off Broadway.

The zip code for Skagway is 99840.

QUICK TOUR: Skagway is four blocks wide and 22 long. Use your imagination.

DON'T MISS: Rail buffs, here's your chance to ride the **White Pass and Yukon Route**. If you're looking for something to do with your feet, head over to Dyea and hike the **Chilkoot Trail**. You'll appreciate the train all the more.

BEST FREE THING TO DO: People watch. There's nowhere in Alaska so perfect for it. Find a comfortable place to sit, and sooner or later every tourist in the state will walk by. And when you're done with that, take the five-minute hike out to **Yakutania Point** and watch the ocean to remember why you came to Alaska to begin with.

■ Museums & Attractions

 Skagway's attractions are all pretty close together, and you can walk to everything. It's a great town for walking, too, because ocean and mountain views come out and surprise you around the edges of Victorian houses everywhere you turn. Despite the madding crowd, Skagway is a fun place to hang out. Even if the ships sometimes make downtown look like an old fraternity gags – how many people can you stuff into a VW Bug? – don't let it get you down. There's no way around it, the town is still a blast, and on the off chance there's no ship in, most of the attractions will be closed anyway. (If there's no ship in, call and check to make sure what you want to do is still open: the train runs, the plane runs, all that kind of stuff is still going.)

Klondike Gold Rush National Historical Park, Broadway and 2nd, is open 8 am to 8 pm June through August, 8 to 6 in May and September. Once the depot for the WP&YR, it's now the forest service and park head-quarters and marks the beginning of a seven-block corridor that houses many restored buildings dating to gold rush days. The center has daily film shows, and it's the starting point for free guided walking tours of the town (check early to book ahead). The tours take about an hour and are well worth joining. The 30-minute film is usually shown on the hour, and is way above average for this kind of thing – it's really worth your time. There are daily ranger talks at 10 am and 3 pm, as well. They've also got some great displays of old mining items next door in the museum, including a pile of goods to represent the ton of stuff miners had to haul with them. Really, we've said it before, we'll say it again: these people were insane. ☎ 250-983-2921

 Be sure to pick up a copy of the *Skaguay Alaskan*. *The Skagway Trail Map* is invaluable if you plan to do any hiking.

The park maintains two other buildings in town: the Mascot Saloon, which is just up Broadway at 3rd, and the Moore House, just off Spring and 5th.

The **Mascot Saloon** is a replica of a gold rush-era saloon, complete with mannequins drinking. Whereas most of the original gold rush buildings were false front – put up an impressive building front, and maybe nobody would notice that behind it was a tent or just a bunch of planks nailed together – the Mascot was a full building, and it's the only original gable-roofed structure left from the era. Good displays on what probably took up a good portion of the stampeders' lives: drinking and trying to forget what they had gotten themselves into.

The **Moore House** is one of Skagway's older buildings. First erected in 1897, it's been beautifully restored to show how buildings changed as the town got more permanent, and to show what home life was like a hundred years ago – surprisingly luxurious. Right next door is the family's original cabin, put up when Captain Moore was mapping out the idea of Skagway – before somebody took it from him. Don't miss it.

There's a Park Service brochure, *Gold Rush Buildings in Skagway*, which lists 17 townsites. There's not a lot to see at many of them – maybe you can peek in the windows – but restoration is an ongoing process, and walking the town with the brochure in hand offers a nice way to put the town in its historical context.

White Pass & Yukon Railroad is next door to the old depot; the new depot becomes a hive of activity when the train pulls in to start the trip up the White Pass. All the publicity shots show a steam train on this run; sorry, it's not gonna happen. They use the steam train only for special occasions, and odds are high all you'll see moving is a diesel. Still, the carriages are either originals or beautifully made replicas, and the scenery is simply astounding. There's no feeling quite like looking out of the train at places where miners wore paths down into bedrock as they hauled their gear. It's a must-do for train buffs (and everybody loves a choo-choo train, right?). The four-hour trip up to the summit and back is a great way to spend the afternoon. Nobody comes off this ride without a smile on their face. Tickets are $89 for adults, $45 for kids age three through 12. For more information, ☎ 250-983-2217, 800-343-7373, www.wpyr.com. The train does have wheelchair access.

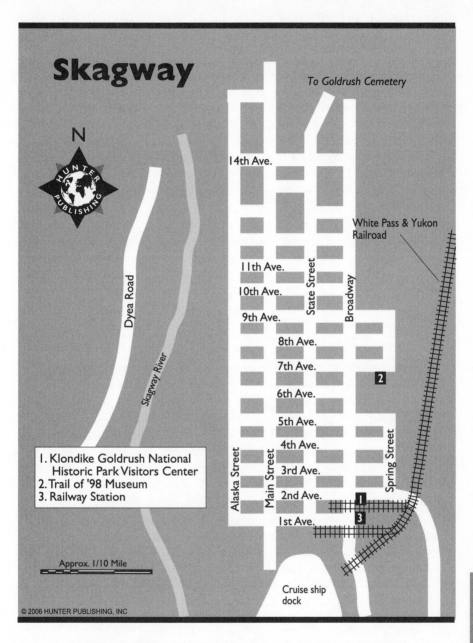

Skagway

To Goldrush Cemetery

N

14th Ave.

White Pass & Yukon Railroad

11th Ave.

10th Ave.

9th Ave.

8th Ave.

7th Ave.

6th Ave.

5th Ave.

4th Ave.

3rd Ave.

2nd Ave.

1st Ave.

State Street

Broadway

Dyea Road

Skagway River

Alaska Street

Main Street

Spring Street

2

1

3

1. Klondike Goldrush National
   Historic Park Visitors Center
2. Trail of '98 Museum
3. Railway Station

Approx. 1/10 Mile

Cruise ship
dock

© 2006 HUNTER PUBLISHING, INC

AUTHOR TIP: *The railway climbs more than 2,800 feet in only 20 miles, and because the line follows the curves of the mountain, there are some great chances to lean out the windows and catch pictures of the train even when you're on it. If you want to shoot some pictures of the train as it goes by, stand along Spring Street. Back in the old days, the tracks actually ran down the center of State Street; the train yards are still there, to the north of town.*

Roads to Skagway

Train fans should check out the **Train Shoppe**, inside the depot. It's got a large selection of train stuff, from whistles and books to videos and models.

Other White Pass excursions include the **Chilkoot Trail Hiker's Service** – the train picks you up at Lake Bennett – for $35, and a nice long ride up to Lake Bennett, for $135 ($160 on Saturdays when they use the steam engine for part of the run). For $95, you can take the train to Fraser, BC, then get on a bus that will take you into Whitehorse. You can even charter an entire car for yourself and your friends in the ballpark of $650 for a caboose or $2,500 for a luxury railcar from the days when people had more fun with their money than they seem to now.

Around town you'll see people selling White Pass bus tours, claiming that the road offers the same scenery as the train, for a fraction of the price. That both is and isn't true. Yes, you're still going up to the White Pass, and the road is a pretty one. But it's on the opposite side of the draw as the railroad, and the waterfall and river views aren't anywhere near as nice.

Coming out of either the Park Service building or the WP&YR station, you'll see the **Red Onion Saloon** right across the street, a lively place with music and crowds until late in the evening. Once a brothel, it's now a restaurant with good food and a very interesting atmosphere, if you can get past the crowds. There are also (somewhat dubious) rumors of a ghost.

GHOSTS OF ALASKA

With all the people who dropped dead in Skagway, there have to be at least a couple of ghosts. We've never heard reliable reports of the one in the Red Onion, but there's not much doubt about the one in the town's oldest hotel, **The Golden North**, built in 1898. Although the hotel was converted to gift shop storage a couple of years ago, there's a long history of guests regularly spotting the ghost, even seeing it wander through the dining room.

That's not the only ghost in town. Across the street in the **Eagles Hall**, we've got very reliable reports of another one. The building has lots of nooks and crannies, and it's a natural place for a haunt. Unfortunately, the haunted parts aren't open to the public.

The Trail of '98 Museum/Skagway City Museum is in the old City Hall. It displays artifacts pertaining strictly to Skagway and its history and the gold rush. Among the attractions is some early gambling equipment from the time when Skagway was at the very edge of the Wild West. There are some very nice displays of Native artifacts, and a section on building the Alaska Highway. It's one of the better local museums. Open daily in the summer; admission is $2. The **Old City Hall** is on 7th Street; turn east off Broadway. The building was the first granite building in Alaska, and it's worth a look even if you're not interested in the museum. It was recently renovated, and over the next few years it will be fascinating to watch the new stone blend in with the old. They did a great job with it.

The **Corrington Museum** is inside a gift shop, but that's not what's important. It has a nice collection of Aleutian baskets and ivory, with good model displays. It has some of the best scrimshaw you can find. This is the only place in town to show anything about the Russians in Alaska. The museum is free and open daily in summer. 5th & Broadway. Well worthwhile.

Gold Rush Cemetery is the final resting place for, among others, two people who made Skagway history: Soapy Smith, a gang leader who held the town under his thumb for years, and Frank Reid, the man who killed Soapy on July 8, 1898. Soapy had just enough time to shoot back, and Reid died 12 days later. The cemetery is two miles north of town, near the WP&YR lines. Sadly, they've put up replica stones next to the real ones – mostly too aged to read – and it ruins a lot of the effect. Still, it's a pretty walk back to the cemetery, and interesting to see how young most of these people were when they died. If it gets too oppressive for you, there's a short trail back to Reid Falls, quite a lovely waterfall.

SOAPY SMITH

You can't talk about Skagway without bringing up Soapy. Okay, Frank Reid killed him and got credit for saving the town. But what was he saving the town from?

Soapy – Jefferson Randolph Smith – came to Skagway in 1897, setting up business with his friend "Reverend" John Bowers. Their idea of business was largely fleecing the hopeful miners hitting town, and they were pretty creative about it. They set up a telegraph office – the wires ran straight into the ocean, but oddly, the return replies usually requested that the miners send money home – sold faulty supplies, took kickbacks, offered guiding services without guides, and generally had a very good time at everybody else's expense.

But while he was doing this, Soapy was also looking to be the town's legitimate power base. He gave to charities, helped build the town's first church, and started an "Adopt a dog" program. On July 4, 1898, he was the grand marshall of the town's Independence Day parade, hanging out with the governor of Alaska.

The fall came only four days later, when members of his gang robbed a man named J.D. Stewart of about $2,800 worth of gold dust. A vigilante committee was quickly formed – the "Committee of 101" – which gathered on the Juneau Co. Wharf. Soapy went down to break up the meeting, figuring he could talk his way out of anything.

Didn't work out like that.

One person buried in the cemetery who you might overlook is a man named **Martin Itjen**, a man to whom the city owes much. Itjen, more or less all by himself, decided that since gold was no longer keeping Skagway alive, perhaps the memory of gold could. In other words, Itjen invented tourism in Skagway. He arrived in the town in 1905, with the idea of becoming an undertaker. Not enough people died to keep him busy, though, so he started to run streetcar tours of the town, in a boxy, wooden-sided car. It cost 25 cents a ride and, as a big sign on the car told you, there was "Nothing Like It In the WORLD." Itjen even drove his car from Seattle down to Hollywood, where he hung out with Mae West.

Kondike Gold Dredge Tours, ☎ 250-983-3175, www.klondikegold dredge.com, lets you see just how far people would go in their search for gold. They've taken a huge dredge – one of those machines that ate rivers whole – and opened it up for tours. For $30, you get a movie (try to stay awake if you can), a tour of the dredge, and you get to try some gold panning yourself. Best for those who like big machinery, but the gold panning is always a hit. Remember, this ain't exactly right on a historical basis: there was never any gold in Skagway, except what got carried down from the north.

Eight miles on a bumpy gravel turnoff leads to the ghost town of **Dyea** (pronounced DYE-ee). Once almost as big a boomtown as Skagway, living off the miners headed north, the town collapsed when the WP&YR was completed. All that remains are a few skeletal, collapsed buildings and Slide Cemetery. However, the drive out is lovely, there's a good chance of seeing seals in the bay, and Dyea is the trailhead for the Chilkoot (below).

Dyea had been the end of a trading trail for centuries, part of the extensive trade network the Tlingit operated in Southeast, connecting them with the Interior. The first trading post was built in 1880, and seven years later, there were nearly 200 people in town. Right after the news of gold got out, though, the town boomed to nearly 8,000 people. As with any boomtown, though, this didn't last long. As a port, Dyea sucked. Literally – the mud flats exposed at low tide swallowed more than one miner's gear, and ships couldn't get anywhere near the town. If the trail hadn't been there, nobody would have come near the place, and after an avalanche in April 1898 killed more than 60 wannabe miners, even more of the traffic moved over to Skagway and the White Pass Trail. By 1900, only two years after the gold strike, the town was back down to 250 people. By 1903, there were all of three people rattling around what had once been one of the largest towns in Alaska.

The site is now a National Historical Park, with all the protection thereof. There's lots of stuff under the brush and grass, but leave it there. The Park Service has daily walks of the townsite at 2 pm in the summer. You'll pass a false-front building – only the front remains – and the collapsed warehouse that once stored most of the miners' gear. It's a pretty walk through the woods, with views of the channel beyond, and a wide marsh. Worth the trip. Meet at the parking lot in Dyea.

For more than half a century, the Fraternal Order of the Eagles has been putting on the **Days of '98 Show** in the Eagle's Hall at 6th and Broadway. It gives a good, entertaining history of Skagway – complete with the fight between Soapy Smith and Frank Reid, plus a few chorus girls. The evening show features "mock gambling." Daytime shows are at 10:30 am and 2 pm, for $14; the evening performance, $16, has gambling starting at 7:30, with the actual performance beginning at 8:30. It's a good way to spend the evening; these people work hard to entertain. ☎ 250-983-2545.

▪ Out & About

 With the cruise ship market requiring maximum scenery with minimum effort, there are plenty of town tours available. If you've got only a few hours, these are well worth looking into. They're all going to do pretty much the same thing: take you past some of the Victorian houses, the Gold Rush Cemetery, and up to the White Pass summit, stopping at a couple of the spectacular waterfalls along the way. The number of operators out there selling these tours keeps them all pretty decent, with good buses, for around $55.

Klondike Tours, ☎ 250-983-2075, www.klondiketours.com; **Frontier Excursions**, ☎ 250-983-2512, www.frontierexcursions.com; **M&M Brokerage**, ☎ 250-983-3900, www.skagwayadventures.com; and **Southeast Tours**, www.southeasttours.com, ☎ 250-983-3544, all have the same basic program.

If you are an experienced **kayaker** and have your own boat, you can easily paddle the 15 miles to Haines, getting a good look at both the Lynn Canal and the Taiya Inlet. Rent a kayak from the **Mountain Shop**, at 4th near Broadway.

The best paddle is probably over to **Haines**, or turn up the **Lutak Inlet** and paddle for the old town of **Chilkoot**. If that's too much, just try the easy paddle over to **Dyea**, which is nicely protected, very scenic, and you can always have somebody pick you up at the other end if you only want to go halfway.

Klondike Water Adventures, ☎ 250-983-3769, www.skagwaykayak. com, has introductory paddles on Lake Bernard.

Skagway Float Tours, ☎ 250-983-3688, www.skagwayfloat.com, has a really nice combination hike/float, for $80. You hike a bit under two miles on the Chilkoot Trail (not the steep part, but there is a pretty good uphill portion), and then load into rafts for a nice float back downstream on the Taiya River. The trip takes about four hours, and it's a lot of fun – plus you get to claim that you've hiked at least part of the Chilkoot Trail. If the hike is more than you're in for, just the float runs $70.

Skagway Float Tours also has a rafting trip on the Tutshi (pronounced Too-SHY) River that they don't widely advertise – locals kind of keep it to themselves. For $100, you drop 10-foot waterfalls, take enough class IV and V to make you wonder why you ever thought this was a good idea to begin with, and in general have the kind of good time that Mountain Dew commercials leave us wanting. It's about six hours from the time you leave town until you get back, and you're in a full dry suit for the water run. This is one of the better whitewater trips around; do it before it gets discovered.

Packer Expeditions has a great trip that gives you the best of Skagway – you helicopter up over the Juneau Icefields to Glacier Station; once there, you do a five-mile hike along the Skagway River, over to Laughton Glacier. Finally, you return to town on the WP&YR train. The trip runs $299. They've also got a cheaper full-day hike up the Denver Trail; you take the train five miles to the trailhead, then hike back to the head of the valley, past waterfalls and into the old growth forest. You're going to need to be in shape for these hikes, but you'll have the time of your life. ☎ 250-983-2544, or stop in at the Mountain Shop, on 4th Ave. just west of Broadway.

Alaska Sled Dog Adventures, ☎ 250-983-3990, www.alaskasleddog. com, has dog demos, where you get to ride around on a wheeled cart. Sled dogs are more a part of Alaskan history than the greed for gold. There's nothing quite like watching a half-dozen huskies blast off. The ride, demo, and getting to play with puppies runs about $85.

To get an overview of what it's all like, take a ride with **Temsco Helicopters**. The best deal is the "Pilot's Choice" ride, which includes two landings and, probably, good views of the Juneau Icefields and more. It's what locals put their relatives on when they come visit. There's a shorter, $199 ride that includes a single glacier landing, or for $359, you can fly up onto the glacier and go mushing with sled dogs. ☎ 250-983-2900, www. Temscoair. com.

Not many people come up the Lynn Canal to go fishing; as in Haines, there simply aren't a lot of charter operators working.

Dockside Charters, ☎ 877-983-3625, has been working in town for years. Half-days, $135; full days, $225. If they're booked, try **Choctaw Charters**, ☎ 250-983-3306, or **Chilkoot Charters**, ☎ 250-983-3400.

Hiking

The best hiking is obviously on the Chilkoot (see below), but there are a lot of other options that aren't quite so strenuous.

There's a quick viewpoint hike out to **Yakutania Point**. Take the footbridge past the airport and head left. Good place for a picnic.

The easiest hike is the **Lower Dewey Lake Trail**, only .7 miles. Go from 2nd Ave. and head east. There's no way to miss the signs. From Dewey Lake, you can hook up with the **Northern Bench Trail**, another mile that takes you back toward town. The trailhead is at the northwest corner of the lake. If you want to see Upper Dewey Lake, it's only another two miles, but you're going to work for it. It's one of the harder local hikes, and although it does start off quite steep, it does eventually level out, ending up in a muskeg meadow.

Another good hard route is the **Denver Glacier Hike**, a three-mile hike from the trailhead at Mile 5 on the WP&YR, or a two-mile hike from the parking lot at the Gold Rush Cemetery. You go through spruce and hemlock forests typical of Southeast Alaska's mid-latitudes rainforest, then climb up the mountain along the banks of the East Fork Skagway River, through an area covered with alder and devil's club.

A hike up **AB Mountain** will kill a full day. It's 10 miles round-trip, and it has an elevation gain of around 5,000 feet, so you'll be hurting by the top. Pick up the trailhead on the Dyea Road, and make sure you don't lose the trail once you get above the treeline.

The **Lost Lake Trail** leaves from Dyea, climbing 1,400 feet over a 2.9-mile route. You can camp up at Lost Lake, a nice spot most of the way up the mountain.

 Pick up a *Skagway Trail Map* at the Info Center or at the Forest Service Office.

The Chilkoot Trail

 Not to be attempted lightly, the Chilkoot is still open for hikers. It takes three to five days to hike this historic route, and it can be a bit crowded in the summer. About 3,000 people hike the trail each year. At the end of the trail, you'll be given a certificate by the Canadian Park Service documenting your accomplishment.

Before setting out, stop by the National Park Visitors Center (across from the old train depot, in what was once Martin Itjen's house) for mandatory registration, and for their useful handouts on the trail. They'll also know the latest trail conditions. If you're going to hike the trail, plan on spending some time talking to these people.

Parks Canada now requires $50 (Canadian dollars) for a permit to hike the trail; only 50 people a day are allowed. Call well in advance of your planned trip for reservations: ☎ 800-661-0486. You can book only parts of the trip – the US side requires a US $15 fee (but you have to make your reservations through the Canadians), the Canadian side, CDN $35.

Go fully prepared, taking all necessary camping gear, food – including a cookstove and a water filter – and personal items, keeping in mind that the weather can change dramatically and quickly. There are no shelters on the trail. Bring your own tent.

There are 10 designated camping areas along the way; **Canyon City, Sheep Camp, Deep Lake**, and **Lindeman** are especially nice. However, they also tend to be crowded; when you're making your reservations, check to see how many people have booked in which camps; it may be that by hiking just a couple extra miles, you'll get the place to yourself.

Roads to Skagway

WARNING: None of the water is safe for drinking, so be sure to boil it first. All camps are in bear country, so keep the camp clean.

 There's a good guidebook specific to the trail, *A Hiker's Guide to the Chilkoot Trail*. You can pick it up in town, or order it from the Alaska Natural History Association, ☎ 250-274-8440, www.alaskanha.org.

ARTIFACT ETIQUETTE

Along the way, there are many artifacts dropped by the tired miners: Do not touch these. Nearly a century of being exposed to the elements has left them extremely fragile, and they are part of a living museum protected only by state law and your courtesy. Take photographs, and leave the objects untouched for other hikers and the researchers, who are putting back together a picture of life on the trail.

The trail goes from sea level to a peak of 3,000 feet. At its base, you are in a rainforest; at the top of the pass, you've entered an alpine tundra zone, which means that for quite a stretch you're above the tree line and there's no protection from the elements at all.

Pick up the trail right before the Taiya River bridge at Dyea. The first dozen miles or so are a fairly gentle climb followed by a long flat. At the mouth of the Taiya River Canyon, not quite eight miles up the trail, you'll pass what was once the booming town of **Canyon City** – as many as 1,500 people lived here in 1898, providing a resting spot for people headed up the trail. At its peak, the town even had a doctor and a post office, all basking in the glow of electric lights, but by 1899, the place was deserted. **Sheep Camp**, 13 miles up the trail, was another boomtown, and in its very brief day, it was even bigger than Canyon City – there were five doctors here, as well as three saloons and two dance halls. Everything the eight thousand or so miners needed to get ready to go over the pass.

Because only three miles past sheep camp, things got nasty for the miners.

The first stop was **The Scales**, at Mile 16. This is where you had to prove to the good folks of Canada that you really had your ton of gear, and that you weren't going to drop dead from being unprepared in their country. If you'd hired packers to help you carry your gear, this is where things became considerably more expensive, as well, since the next half-mile of the trail was the trek up the pass.

And that's the section you've probably seen in photos. It was a 45-degree climb from The Scales to the pass. During the gold rush, steps were carved into the ice on the slope – and yes, you had to pay to use them – but it didn't help that much when you were hiking up the trail for the fifth time that day with 60 pounds of bacon on your back.

Of course, not many people were strong enough to do it five times a day. Many could manage only one trip, and it could easily take more than two dozen trips to get all your gear up to the summit. There were so many people climbing the Golden Stairs that if you stopped to rest, you lost your place in the human train, and might not get back in for hours. This climb is what everybody thinks of when they think of the gold rush. Insane people, standing in line in deep snow. Nothing better sums up their hope and desperation.

During the peak of the rush, three trams ran between The Scales and the Summit. These were powered by horse or by steam. The longest of them, built by the Chilkoot Railroad and Transport Company, featured 45 miles of line, stretching between Canyon City and Crater Lake. If you could afford it, they'd haul your gear from Dyea all the way up to Lindeman, at the head of Lindeman Lake, and where you could start building your boat, for just seven cents a pound – so $150 or so for the whole lot. Of course, if you had that much money, you probably didn't need to be here desperately scrambling for gold.

The tramways were a great idea, and highly profitable. They were also, clearly, a threat to the planned White Pass & Yukon Route Railway. The WP&YR bought out the tramways and tore them down. Monopolies are fun.

There's nothing too difficult about the last portion of the trip, unless the weather turns bad.

The Park Service actually considers it easier to go up this slope than down and they try to discourage people from hiking the trail in reverse for fear of injuries.

You hit the ruins of **Lindeman City** at Mile 26. During the stampede, you could use the lake – which was frozen over – as a quick route to Lake Bennett; in summer, ships made the trip. Every tree within miles of the lake was cut, whether to provide lumber for more boomtown buildings, or to go into the makeshift boats. That winter, the town had about 4,000 people; by the next year, no one would ever live here again.

The whole point of the Chilkoot Trail was to get to Lake Bennett. You get up here while the lake was still frozen, and start building your boat. The instant the ice breaks up – it was on May 29, 1898 – you get your boat in the water and run the connecting lakes that take you to the Yukon River, which you can then use to get all the way to Dawson City. That stampede winter, there were 20,000 people here, waiting for the ice to move, and when it did, 7,000 boats headed north.

The only thing left of the town is the St. Andrews Presbyterian Church, and the ghost of a lot of hope.

The final stop on the trail is the **Log Cabin**, which you reach via a cut-off trail heading back south. The Cabin, which was the old Northwest

Mounted Police customs post, is where your previously arranged transport will pick you up.

You can make reservations to ride the WP&YR back to Skagway from Lake Bennett (daily service in the summer) if you don't have a ride waiting for you at the end or don't have the time to hike the trail round-trip.

It's a memorable hike, and not a terribly difficult one if you're fit. The trail is well marked, well traveled, and hard to miss. For the first two or three miles, you may well end up sharing the trail with a cruise ship tour, but they tend to fall off quickly.

Just follow the rules, talk to the Park Service first, and prepare for every contingency.

If you'd rather do the trail with a guide, talk to **Packer Expeditions**, in the Mountain Shop, ☎ 250-983-2544.

■ Shopping

It's a small town, designed for handling masses of cruise ship passengers in a very short time. You're not going to have any trouble finding the stores.

The Mountain Shop, on 4th Ave. just west of Broadway, has a full line of outdoor gear, a lot of it at prices cheaper than you're going to find down South. ☎ 250-983-2544.

A Fine Line, on Broadway near 6th, has beautiful trade beads – one of the best selections in the state.

Corrington's Alaskan Ivory, at 5th and Broadway, ☎ 250-983-2580, is worth stopping in for the free museum; they've also got the standard tourist fare, but with some interesting twists.

Lynch Kennedy has two locations – one on Broadway near 4th, the other up the street between 6th and 7th. You'll see some interesting new takes on traditional designs at the larger store near 4th, some beautiful skin boats at the one near 7th, at the Skagway Inn. ☎ 250-983-3034.

Inside Passage Arts is on 7th, just off Broadway, ☎ 250-983-2585, has a nice selection of traditional Southeast Alaskan crafts, and some newer stuff, too. Good carvings, nice trade beads.

The Skaguay News Depot, ☎ 250-983-3354, on Broadway between 2nd and 3rd, can take care of your reading needs for books on the town's history.

■ Food

You can eat quite well in Skagway.

The Skagway Fish Company (☎ 250-983-3463) and the **Stowaway Café** (☎ 250-983-3474), both on the east side of the boat harbor, are the places to go for the best food in town. Try the halibut and brie at the Fish Company, or one of the Cajun specialties at the Stowaway. You're not going to be sorry. Entrées start around $15.

The **Red Onion Saloon**, mentioned above for its possible ghost, has sandwiches, nachos, and pizza, $12-22. Lots of atmosphere, but serious crowds on cruise ship days. ☎ 250-983-2222.

The **Corner Café**, 4th and State, has great lunches and big breakfasts. It's quite cheap – ten bucks or so fills you up. ☎ 250-983-2155.

The **Sweet Tooth**, Broadway and 3rd, is a converted saloon that now serves a great breakfast of eggs, sausage, and excellent hash browns. You'll get out for about $10. It gets crowded here around 7:30 in the morning.

Glacial Smoothies, on 3rd, just off Broadway, has wraps and pitas. Best choice for healthy food in town, with prices starting around $5. ☎ 250-983-3223.

Sabrosa's, on Broadway, across from the post office, offers something a little different, with Tex-Mex fare. Try the King Ranch Casserole.

If you just need a quick cup of espresso or hot chocolate, the little stand inside the **Train Shoppe** has the best prices.

For something different, **Olivia's**, at the Skagway Inn, does a combo town tour/cooking demo, with fresh produce from the Inn's garden. ☎ 888-752-4929.

■ Accommodations

HOTEL

There are no bargains in Skagway, and early reservations are a must.

Sgt. Preston's Lodge, ☎ 250-983-2521, sgt.prestons@usa.net, is a good bet. Centrally located on 6th, a block west of Broadway. They have a courtesy van, too. It's off Broadway, so it's pretty quiet. $$-$$$.

HOTEL PRICING
Prices are in US dollars.
under $50 . . . . $
$50-$100 . . . . $$
$100-$150 . . . . . . $$$
above $150 . . . . . $$$$

Smaller but quite nice is the **Skagway Inn B&B**, 7th & Broadway, ☎ 250-983-2289, www.skagwayinn.com, with doubles in an 1897 Victorian house. The Alice Room – with a glassed-in porch overlooking Broadway – might be the nicest in town. Their restaurant features herbs from their own garden. $$$.

Mile Zero B&B is one of those lovingly run places that just amaze you when you stay. All rooms have private entrances, and, rarity of rarities, soundproof walls. At 9th and Main, ☎ 250-983-3045, www.mile-zero.com. $$$.

At the White House, ☎ 250-983-9000, www.atthewhitehouse.com, is a nice B&B set in a building listed on the National Register of Historic Places. Private baths, cable TV, nice comfortable touches. $$$.

Roads to Skagway

Chilkoot Trail Outpost is 8½ miles out on the Dyea Road, so if you're looking for a quiet place, this is a nice choice. Cabins have microwaves and fridges, and you can use the Outpost's bikes. $$$-$$$$. ☎ 250-983-3799, www.chilkoottrailoutpost.com.

The bargain choice – if you can get in – is **Skagway Home Hostel**, at 3rd and Main, ☎ 250-983-2131, www.skagwayhostel.com. Rooms in the dorm start at $15. The other hostel choice is **Alaskan Sojourn Hostel**, ☎ 250-983-2030, www.alaskansojourn.com, with dorm rooms from $20. Both of these can fill with summer workers.

If everything else is full, try the **Westmark**, which has more rooms than the rest of the town combined. Be aware it's often filled with package tourists. ☎ 250-983-6000, www.westmarkhotels.com.

The Forest Service runs one of the nicest places to stay: a converted caboose, five miles up the train line. Like any Forest Service cabin, bring your own gear. Reservations on line at www.reserveusa.com.

Camping

Skagway has recently increased its camping facilities, so your chance of finding a spot is much greater than it used to be. Still, things can get really busy when a ferry arrives, full of people who don't want to start the drive into Canada for another day. So check in early. **Pullen Creek RV Park**, ☎ 250-983-2768, is down by the ferry terminal. Full hookups are available.

More scenic are the RV and tent sites at Broadway & 14th, in **Mountain View**, which is the best place for watching the steam engine of the WP&YR go by. Phone for reservations, ☎ 250-983-2768, but the place is often full of summer workers.

Garden City RV Park, ☎ 250-983-23RV, 15th & State, is another possibility.

If you want to get out of town, drive to **Dyea** and stay at the **National Park Service Campground** there. The road to Dyea is not recommended for RVs, and this makes the campground a haven for tenters. There are 22 sites, and you just need to show up and see if there are any spots available.

Chapter 8

The Haines Highway

Somewhere along the road to Haines, you run out of superlatives. By the time most people have gotten this far, they've seen some of the most beautiful territory around – the area by Muncho Lake, the stunning parks in southern BC – and they think it's not going to get any better. Then they drive to Haines.

The road leaves from the town of Haines Junction, starts to climb, passes Kathleen Lake, and ends up high between mountain ridges, with glacial melt ponds lining the wide, smooth road, snow-covered peaks everywhere, and rainbows chasing the traffic, jumping from pond to stream. You have to keep stopping the car so you can gawk. If all that wasn't enough, the road then drops down off the ridge and the Chilkat Pass – once crowded with miners headed north – and catches up to the Chilkat River, running alongside the banks for the last stretch into town. It's probably the most beautiful drive in the North. And almost no one does it, so the road is wide open.

Camp along the way at **Kathleen Lake**, Mile 134 (where you can pick up the trailhead of the 53-mile loop Cottonwood Trail; figure four days to finish it, with much of the hike along old mining roads). Or stop at **Dezadeash Lake**, Mile 119, **Dalton Post**, Mile 99, or the truly marvelous **Million Dollar Falls**, Mile 96. 2, which has a lovely board walkway down to the river and the steep falls beyond. You also stand a good chance of moose nosing around your campsite. Watch for mountain goats on the peaks.

Million Dollar Falls.

CUSTOMS CONTROL: Canadian Customs is closed between 11 pm and 7 am, but you can go through after-hours if you stand in front of the camera and follow the directions. However, *before* you head to the border, double check this information. Everything has been changing lately, and it's a long way back to town if you get stuck here, waiting for customs to open. You must have proof of insurance for your car at customs. Officers can also ask about your finances: You must have $50 for 48 hours in Canada, $200 for more. Plastic is okay. The Customs station is at Mile 42 on the Haines Highway. US Customs is at Mile 40.4.

The last stretch of road is along the banks of the Chilkat. The Chilkat – wide and tree-lined to one side of the road, while the other side is mountains heading straight up – is home to as many as 3,000 bald eagles, and the last nine miles of road are in **Chilkat Bald Eagle Preserve.** Where there are eagles, there is good fishing, and the river is great for rafting, too.

Tatshenshini-Alsek Wilderness

The west side of the Haines Highway, from the Yukon border to Customs, travels along the edge of Tatshenshini-Alsek Wilderness Provincial Park. This park, which is contiguous with Kluane and Wrangell-St. Elias parks, forms part of the largest protected wilderness area in the world.

The Tatshenshini-Alsek wilderness area was set aside in 1993, in response to a particularly stupid mining plan. The proposed mine would have dumped tailings and poisons into the Alsek, and threatened the entire area's wildlife. The mining company said that all the poisons would be contained behind an earthen dam and wouldn't have hurt anything. Yeah, right.

Summer snow is common along this stretch of highway.

There was a public outcry – part of the complication being that the mine was going to be in Canada, with most of the damage downstream in Alaska – and this beautiful park was the result. For once, the good guys won.

∎ Rafting

Because it is a wilderness area, no motorized vehicles are allowed. Experienced rafters who have been on the waiting list for several years and whose number has finally come up can shoot the Tatshenshini or the Alsek, both of which have Class III-IV whitewater and both of which are increasingly popular. But you'd better know what you're doing. The currents in the canyons are very tricky, and the water is cold enough to give you hypothermia in a matter of moments. If you're in a hurry, you can do the Alsek in five days, but it's kind of pointless. Better to take 10 and enjoy yourself. This is one of the best river trips in the world, a marvel of scenery.

Permits are required for most river trips on the Alsek or the Tatshenshini. Check at the Kluane Park headquarters, ☎ 867-634-2345. Only one launch a day is allowed on the upper Alsek, and half of those permits are reserved for commercial companies. If your trip is going to go all the way down to Glacier Bay, you'll need a permit from Glacier Bay National Park (☎ 907-697-3341) – and it'll cost you $25 just to get on the waiting list. Be prepared to wait a very long time.

If you've got to go this year, book with **Alaska Discovery**, 5449 Shaun Drive #4, Juneau, ☎ 907-780-6226 or 800-586-1911, www.akdiscovery. com. They have 10-day trips on the Tat, which includes Class III water through the Tatshenshini Gorge. It'll run you around $2,500. Twelve days on the Alsek – rougher, more remote than the Tat, water up to Class IV – runs about $2,750, including an airlift past the unrunnable Turnback Canyon. Good people, part of the larger Mountain Travel/Sobek family of adventure travel companies.

∎ Mountain Biking

Old mining roads in the park make for good mountain biking. Try the trailhead at **Parton River, Stanley Creek**, or about a mile and a half above the **Selat Viewpoint**, where you can ride on the original Haines road.

> **WARNING:** Remember, weather conditions change quickly in the park. Go prepared.

Haines

The town of Haines offers scenery and proximity to the best boonies in the state; Skagway gives you a different kind of scenery, and some of the more interesting history you'll find. The Haines Highway, though, connecting the town to points north, is, quite simply, the most beautiful road we've ever been on, anywhere in the world.

■ History

Haines was almost always a way to get somewhere else. The Chilkoot and Chilkat Indians lived in the Haines area, using it as a trading base. Its position on the coast gave them access to groups in the Interior, as well as to the riches of the coast and the islands. The modern Haines airport is on the site of the old village of Yendestakyeh. Other major Native settlements were along the Chilkat River (Klukwan survives today) and on Chilkoot Lake.

The Russians passed Haines by, and it wasn't until 1881 that Hall Young, a missionary who had first seen the region two years before when traveling with John Muir, established a mission in the area. Although the locals called the mission Dtehshah, or "end of the trail," the new settlers chose the name Haines, after Mrs. F.E. Haines. Although she was never actually in the city that bears her name, Mrs. Haines was an important fundraiser for the mission.

The mission settlement grew quickly. With the base population stable, canneries were built and, during the years of the gold rush, Haines was an alternative to the more popular (and crowded and lawless) Skagway. When the gold petered out, the military moved in. In 1902, construction began on Fort Seward. During World War II, the presence of the base and the large contingent of soldiers made Haines an important point on the planned supply route to the Aleutians and the Interior, in case of Japanese attack. The Haines Highway was built to connect the coast with the Alaska Highway and the Interior, to further ease transport of supplies.

Since the war, things have calmed down. The town survives on tourism, lumber, and fishing, and on its convenience as a middle point between other destinations. It thrives on its beautiful location. Haines is one of the most attractive towns in Alaska and also the fastest growing – *Outside* magazine named it as the place to live if you've just won the lottery and don't have to worry about making a living. The next few years will reveal how growth and beauty mix in this spectacular setting.

■ Basics

The **Alaska Marine Highway** (☎ 907-766-2111, 800-642-0066) stops at Haines almost daily in the summer, with direct runs to

Skagway and Juneau and connections to all points south. The route to and from Haines is simply lovely, as the ferry travels along the Lynn Canal, with great views of Davidson, Garrison, and Ferebee glaciers and the Eldred Rock Lighthouse, which looks like the prototype for all lighthouses. The fast ferry, the *Fairweather*, cuts the ride between Haines and Juneau in half. For more on the AMH, see the last chapter of the book, or pick up our other book, *Adventure Guide to the Inside Passage*.

Most cruise ships skip Haines and dock in Skagway; however, the towns are so close that a lot of the activities the ships book are actually in Haines.

The **Lynn Canal**, at 1,600 feet deep and more than 90 miles long, is the longest and deepest fjord in North America.

If you want to park or camp in Haines and still see Skagway without driving the long haul back (360 miles by road, 15 by water) or getting back on the AMH, **Chilkat Cruise's Water Taxi** offers an alternative to the ferry. The taxi makes two daily round-trips between the towns and takes no vehicles (except for bikes). A one-way trip takes about a half-hour, and in high summer, it's a good idea to make reservations in advance. Fare is $45 round-trip, $25 one-way. Call ☎ 907-766-2100 or 888-766-2103 for schedules and information. There are also trips to Juneau – it's only two hours, as opposed to 10 or so on the ferry. There's a $129 deal that takes you to Juneau, gives you a quick tour of town and a stop at the glacier, and gets you back in Haines (dinner on board the boat) before evening.

Of course, if you've got your own kayak, this is a great paddle.

The Haines Highway connects the town with the Interior of Alaska, British Columbia and the Yukon. The 150-mile road was built by the Army Corps of Engineers in 1943 shortly after the completion of the Alaska Highway. It passes through one of the prettiest concentrations of scenery in the state. It's a hard highway to drive, because you're gawking so much.

Skagway Air, ☎ 907-766-3233, **L.A.B. Flying Service**, ☎ 907-766-2222, and **Wings of Alaska**, ☎ 907-766-2030, all fly out of Haines to Southeast, and offer charter flights as well.

If you fly, boat, or bus to another city, you can still leave your vehicle in town and pick it up on the way back. **Bigfoot Auto**, ☎ 907-766-2458, and **J and D Rental**, ☎ 907-766-3398, offer vehicle storage.

Haines Shuttle & Taxi, ☎ 907-766-3138, runs tours of town. The 45-minute trip includes the harbor, Fort Seward, Dalton City, and a stop to see totem pole carvers.

The **Tourist Information Center** is at Second Ave. and Willard. It's open 8-7, Monday to Friday, 9-6 on weekends. ☎ 907-766-2234, www.haines.ak.us.

Internet at **Northern Lights Internet Lounge**, 715 Main St., ☎ 907-766-2337; or you can get on free at the library, at 3rd and Willard.

The zip code for Haines is 99827.

QUICK TOUR: Head out to the Chilkat River. Take a look at Fort William H. Seward.

DON'T MISS: Raft the Chilkat. Fly out to one of the tiny valleys behind town and be intimidated by the size of the state.

BEST FREE THING TO DO: In fall, Haines has the largest concentration of bald eagles in the world. If you're there too soon, the river the eagles like to hang out on will amaze you. It's the quick tour, it's the best thing to do: head out and get a look at the Chilkat.

■ Museums & Attractions

 Sheldon Museum & Cutural Center is a good first stopping point in town is this center, on Main Street near the boat harbor. The museum is open daily in the summer, but you need to check for opening times, which can be slightly irregular. The small but excellent museum shop has a good selection of Alaskana books. Haines was a center for the Tlingit Indians, and you can see their local history illustrated beautifully here. Don't miss the blankets on the second floor. Make sure to pick up any of the free historical sheets on topics that interest you. ☎ 907-766-2366. Admission is $3.

Right across the street from the Sheldon Museum is the **Hammer Museum**. Yep, really. Hammers. A couple of thousand of them. And the thing is, this is incredibly cool. It's hard to explain why – we have to admit upfront we have no real interest in hammers, but still managed to spend an utterly fascinating hour in the place. It's a labor of love, and maybe the only chance you'll ever get to see triple clawed hammers, sledge hammers, and Tlingit war hammers, all in the same room. Do this museum even if the mere thought of hammers makes you want to fall asleep. You won't regret it. This is a good thing in the world, a person doing something he loves – collecting hammers – and sharing it with all. 108 Main St., ☎ 907-766-2374. Admission is $3, and it's a bargain.

The American Bald Eagle Foundation and Natural History Museum, at 2nd Ave. and the Haines Highway, ☎ 907-766-3094, is a spot to take a look at our national bird in its environmental context – who lives around it, who it lives around. A good place to get an idea of what goes on in the Chilkat Valley. $3 admission.

The **Alaska Indian Arts Workshop**, ☎ 907-766-2160, by the totem village, is where you can see Native carvers and artists at work making totem poles, masks, and jewelry. It's open 9-5 weekdays. The workshop is housed in what used to be the hospital for the old **Fort William H. Seward**. The fort was built just after the turn of the century, after the Protestant mission deeded 100 acres of land to the government to establish a base. Fort

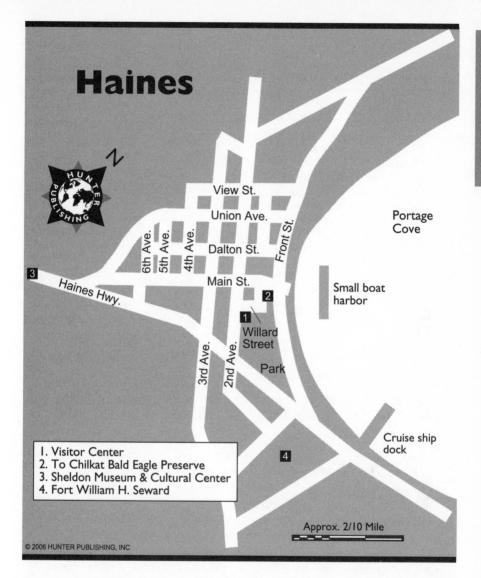

Haines

N

View St.

Union Ave.

Portage
Cove

Dalton St.

6th Ave.
5th Ave.
4th Ave.
Front St.

Main St.

Small boat
harbor

1

2

Haines Hwy.

3

Willard
Street

3rd Ave.
2nd Ave.

Park

Cruise ship
dock

1. Visitor Center
2. To Chilkat Bald Eagle Preserve
3. Sheldon Museum & Cultural Center
4. Fort William H. Seward

4

Approx. 2/10 Mile

© 2006 HUNTER PUBLISHING, INC

Seward was used as a training base in World Wars I & II. After World War
II, the fort was decommissioned, and it lay vacant until it was purchased
by five World War II veterans in 1947, and has since been declared a National Historic Landmark. Pick up a walking tour map of the fort at the visitors center and explore the parade grounds and other areas. Most of the
buildings have been taken over by private concerns and are now shops or
hotels. There are also quite a few private residences among the fort buildings. If in doubt, ask.

The highlight of Haines is the 48,000-acre **Chilkat Bald Eagle Preserve**,
which each winter hosts the largest gathering of bald eagles in the world.
The birds generally come here from November through February to feast
on the late chum salmon run. There can be almost 4,000 eagles along the

river at peak times. There are few sights as impressive as a bald eagle swooping down for a fish (it's also a lot of fun to watch them miss).

EAGLE ERROR

When eagles are hitting in the rivers after fish, an interesting fact of eagle biology can take over: They can't unlock their claws on the upswing. This means, if they're trying to gain altitude, whatever is in their claws is stuck there (there's some debate about this, but it's still widely accepted). If the bird has grabbed something too big and can't take off, it ends up doing a header into the water; from there it either has to swim to shore (they're very good swimmers, using their wings as you use your arms in the water) or sometimes they get dragged down and drown. No wonder Benjamin Franklin wanted to make the turkey the national symbol.

Take a good camera, fast film, and warm clothes on your eagle-watching expeditions; in winter months the sun is up only from about 10 am to 3 pm in December and January, and there's likely to be rain or snow. About 200 eagles live in the area year-round. Haines has started an annual **Bald Eagle Festival,** held in November, with educational talks, films, tours, Native dances, photography workshops, and more. ☎ 907-766-3094.

BALD EAGLE SPOTTING

There are a few rules to obey when you're looking for eagles.

First, remember the birds have better civil rights protections than you do. Hassling the birds can get you a $10,000 fine. When you're in the preserve, stay off the flats—that's where the birds are, so it's where you shouldn't be. The parks people want you between the river and the highway, which gives the birds a nice buffer zone. This does not mean stop your car on the roadway. There are turnouts. Use them, or keep your insurance company phone number handy. The best views are usually somewhere between miles 18 and 21 on the highway.

Alaska Nature Tours, ☎ 907-766-2876, has guided hikes along the Chilkat Valley for $50. **Keet Gooshi Tours,** ☎ 907-766-2168, does a tour of the eagle preserve, along with a visit to Klukwan, where you can see the totems and the fine screen. The 2½-hour trip runs $65.

Tsirku Canning Company has tours of a small-scale salmon canning operation. The good thing here is that the can-maker is still working – probably your only chance to ever see one of these, as most canneries order their cans from down south. The tours are only $10 and are held at 1 pm. It's well worth it to see what fueled the Alaska economy for so long. And, oh, yeah, you get a chance to buy fish at the end. They're at 5th and Main, ☎ 907-766-3474.

During the second week of August, Haines plays host to the **Southeast Alaska State Fair**, logging shows, games, rides, and contests. Once, years ago, it may have also hosted the world's only Frisbee pig. Book your hotel well in advance.

Nightlife in Haines is not as eventful as it was in the early gold rush days, but there are still a few things going on. At the **Chilkat Dancers Story-telling Theater**, see the **Chilkat Dancers**, who do a dance and storytelling show, featuring traditional masks and costumes. Okay, sometimes some of the dancers are white kids from the local high school. Still, it's all well meant, well done, and for $10, a nice way to spend some time. Shows are most weekdays; check at Tourist Info for the latest schedule.

▪ Out & About

There's enough stuff to do around Haines to keep you busy for months. The trick is narrowing down the list.

Portage Cove Adventure Center, ☎ 907-766-2100 or 888-766-2105, www.chilkatcruises.com, on the street at 142 Beach Road, is a booking service for a number of expeditions around town. One good package includes a round-trip to Skagway on the water taxi, with a ride on the White Pass & Yukon Route Railway for $125.

Right when we think we have the best job in the world, we meet somebody who, just maybe, has it even better. There's no reason at all why you would have heard of Steve Kroschel, but you know his work: this is the guy who trained the wolves for the incredible movie *Never Cry Wolf*. He's trained the animals – everything from ferrets on up – for a bunch of other movies, too, and if that weren't enough, he's also one of the premier avalanche photographers in the world.

Out on **Steve Krocschel's Wildlife Park**, a few miles outside of town, he has a minitheater, so you can see some of his work. Then there's the fun stuff: meeting the animals. Steve is, really, having a wonderful time. There are few things as enjoyable as watching somebody do what they were born to do, and hanging out while Steve plays with his animals is a wonderful experience. You meet the wolves, maybe feed a reindeer or two, and you might even get a chance to pet a baby porcupine. Along the way, you'll learn a lot about the animals that live in Alaska. It's a great way to spend a couple of hours. Admission is $20 for adults, $10 for 18 and under. Call ahead to see when tour times are. ☎ 907-767-5464.

Out near the ferry terminal is **Takshanuk Trail**, an ATV operation. For $75, nice lunch included, you get to drive an ATV up into the Southeast Alaska rainforest, getting a better look at it than most people have time for. At the top of the ATV trail is a lovely meadow, and the views stretch on forever. If you've never driven an ATV, no worries; these are pretty much fool proof. ☎ 907-209-9929, www.takshanuktrail.com.

Hiking

Haines has some pretty good hikes. There's the **Mt. Ripinsky Trail**, a five-mile hike up the mountain. From there you can walk along the ridge before heading back down. If you do the ridge walk, figure on overnight camping, or a really long day of hiking. The trailhead is off Young Rd. (keep left when the road forks). The first 1,600 feet are relatively easy, but it gets steeper at the end, peaking out at 3,650 feet, where you've got killer views of Haines, the Lynn Canal, and more snow-covered mountains than you can imagine. Obviously, with the elevation gain, this is not an easy hike, so go prepared, and figure it might be 10 hours round trip. There are other trails up the mountain at Piedad Road and Seven Mile, on the Haines Highway.

At **Seven Mile**, the trail leads up to the Seven-Mile Saddle, a 2,400-foot mountain pass, below the peak of Ripinsky. Go prepared for mud. This is not for beginners; figure five hours just to get to the saddle.

Mt. Riley is a little easier. Pick up the trail on Mud Bay Road, and hike just over two miles to the summit. Allow three hours or so, filled with good views of the river and the canal. There are alternate ways up the mountain via Lily Lake (2.8 miles each way). The trailhead is off the FAA Road behind Officer's Row in Ft. Seward. The trail is more gradual than the Mud Bay alternate, plus you get a lake along the way. Finally, you can get up from Portage Cove, a four-mile hike, one-way. There's only one steep section on this trail, which leads you to a muskeg meadow a few hundred yards below the summit.

Seduction Point is 6.8 miles to where the Chilkoot and Chilkat inlets meet. Allow 10 hours, but it's a fairly easy forest and beach walk, with are good views of Davidson Glacier, and a great chance to look at both inlets. The trailhead is at the Chilkat State Park Campground.

Kayaking

If you have your own canoe or kayak (or have rented one), head to the **Chilkat River**. It's a relatively sedate Class I, with excellent animal-watching; look especially for eagles, moose, and bears. The best place to put in is at Mile 19 on the Haines Highway, then you can paddle back to town.

Deishu Expeditions, ☎ 907-766-2427 or 800-552-9257, www.seakayaks.com, has a nice introductory paddle on a lake near town. They're also the people to call if you want to rent a kayak.

Biking

Sockeye Cycle, ☎ 907-766-2869, in Ft. Seward, rents bikes by the hour or day. They also have quite a variety of tours. Best of all, you can rent a bike here and take it over to Skagway, returning it to their office there, giving you a chance to peddle in both towns. It's only an extra $5 to load a bike onto one of the fast ferries.

If you have a car, you can get your bike up to the edges of the Tat-Alsek park, where there are a lot of old mining roads that make for good mountain biking. Try the trailhead at Parton River, Stanley Creek, or about a mile and a half above the Selat Viewpoint, where you can ride on the original Haines road.

> **WARNING:** Remember, weather conditions change quickly. Go prepared.

Flightseeing

For a look at an incredibly remote part of the world that's only a few minutes away from Haines, take the day tour with Glacier Valley Wilderness Adventures. You fly from Haines back to the **Tsirku Valley**, a landscape that looks like the glaciers pulled back only yesterday. It's about a half-hour flightseeing trip before you land at Nugget Creek Gold Mine, an operating mine until early last century. The most impressive thing is how obsessed the miners were about finding gold, digging 30 and 40 feet into hardscrabble hoping for a glimpse of color. There's still a lot of mining equipment around, and it gives you a good chance to see how gold mines worked.

After you've looked around, there's a quick airboat ride up the Tsirku River to **Deblondeau Glacier Cabin**, which sits at the foot of a glacier in a little spike of land surrounded by wilderness: look one way, it's Glacier Bay; look the other, it's part of the Kluane-Wrangell-St. Elias Wilderness Area. It's an astounding spot. You end up back at the mine for lunch and gold panning, and then get a flight back to town. It's quite a day, and the scenery is different than anything else you're going to see on your trip. Check rates and schedules at ☎ 907-767-5522, www.glaciervalleyadventures.com.

River Trips

All through the gold rush, the goal for the miners was to get up the **Chilkat River**. They were missing the point; it's a whole lot more fun to come down.

It's not a whitewater river; what you're in for is an incredibly beautiful float, with mountains ranging both sides of the wide flats, where there are almost always eagles, and where you also stand a really good chance of seeing moose, and maybe the occasional bear. There are few sights quite as beautiful as a mother moose and calf walking across the flats.

Chilkat Guides, ☎ 907-766-2491, www.raftalaska.com, takes you out to Klukwan, then brings you back to town in a raft, for $79. The trip takes about four hours. These people have been doing this excursion forever, and it's a great way to spend an afternoon. Highly recommended. They also do runs on even more remote rivers. If you don't have time for a full trip on the Tat or Alsek, and you're looking for something a little more remote than the Chilkat, check into trips on the Tsirku or the Kleheni.

Serious Adrenaline – the Mountains

If even the thought of rafting the Alsek is a little too tame for you, there's still plenty for you to do in Haines. Give **Alaska Mountain Guides** a call, ☎ 907-766-3366, www.alaskamountainguides.com. Start off with their two-day mountaineering course, where you'll take a ski plane somewhere north (depends on conditions) and then get to learn ice conditions, hiking, ropes – in short, everything you need to know at altitude. The two-day course is a good place to start, but if you're really serious, there are longer courses, up to a full three weeks, available. This will get you ready for one of their peak assaults – Denali, say, or Mt. Bona. They also lead international climbs—little jaunts in Greenland, Patagonia, or perhaps a run up Aconcagua, peaking out just below 23,000 feet.

This is also the place to come to learn ice climbing. Some of the best ice in the world is in their neighborhood, as is back-country glacier skiing. Play in the ice while we still have it.

This company offers some of the best ways to get where no one else is that you're going to find. Good people, good programs, good deals.

■ Shopping

 Since Haines doesn't get the number of tourists that Skagway does, downtown is more for locals than travelers. Still, there are a couple things worth checking into.

The Far North, on 2nd Ave. across from Visitor Info, has lovely ivorywork, walrus whiskers, and other items from Inuit lands. Everything here is Native made.

Buy some fish for the road ahead at either the **Tsirku Canning Company** (see above, for info on their tour) at 5th and Main, or at **Dejon Delights**, in Ft. Seward. Buy some wine to go with your fish at **Great Land Wines**, ☎ 907-766-2698. They're a ways out of town, but the liquor stores will have their local wines, made from, among other things, rhubarb, onion, "porcupine carrot gold," and a wide variety of berries.

Finally, just because you can, check out the **Lost Coast Surf Shop**. It's a block up from the fast ferry dock. Really. We're not making this up. It's really a surf shop.

■ Food

Some of the best places to eat in Haines are a way out of town. The **Thirty-Three Mile Roadhouse**, ☎ 907-767-5510, is out past the Chilkat Bald Eagle Preserve and Klukwan. Try it for hamburgers and the view. Dinners start at $14. For true gourmands, try **Weeping Trout's** Saturday night dinner. You get an astonishing meal at the resort, which is located on the edge of a lake well outside Haines (it takes two boat rides to get there). The basic price includes transport from the first boat landing; for a bit extra, you can get ride all the way from town. It's going to run you $100 for a couple. Go early and play a round of golf at the resort. A chance to do something really different.

The local choice in town is the **Bamboo Room**, open all day, right downtown. Burgers from $7, steak for around $20.

Fort Seward Lodge, ☎ 907-766-2009, makes a good night-out dinner. Steak and seafood from $10, and all-you-can-eat crab dinners for around $25.

The **Chilkat Restaurant and Bakery**, at 5th and Dalton, has the town's best baked goods. Also soups, sandwiches, and salads.

Mountain Market, at 3rd and the Haines Highway, is the town's health food store. They also have a nice deli inside, a perfect place to grab a picnic lunch.

Finally, **Howsers Supermarket**, on Main St., has a deli next to the groceries that offers sandwiches, chicken, and ribs, cheap.

■ Accommodations

In Haines, much of the lodging is located in or around Fort Seward, and thus many of the buildings are historic sites. Nothing is really cheap.

Try the picturesque **Hotel Halsingland** for historic accommodations; you may get a room with a claw-foot tub. $$$$. ☎ 907-766-2000 or 800-542-6363, www.hotelhalsingland.com.

HOTEL PRICING

Prices are in US dollars.

under $50 . . . . $
$50-$100 . . . . $$
$100-$150 . . . . . . $$$
above $150 . . . . . $$$$

Another lovely old house turned into a hotel is the **Fort Seward B&B**. On the National Register of Historic Places (it used to be the surgeon's living quarters), it's very small, so book early. You can get a double for under $$$. They'll pick you up at the airport or ferry terminal. ☎ 907-766-2856, 800-615-NORM, www.fortsewardbnb.com.

Fort Seward Condos offer one- and two-bedroom apartments complete with full kitchens year-round. There's a two-day minimum, with rooms in the low $$$s. ☎ 907-766-2708, www.fortsewardcondos.com.

Haines Highway

Chilkat Eagle B&B is in Ft. Seward in an old officer's house. Friendly, quiet, a nice spot to retreat. $$-$$$. ☎ 907-766-2891, 800-354-6006, www. eagle-bb.com.

Downtown there is slightly more generic lodging. Nicest is **Captain's Choice Motel**, ☎ 800-247-7153, in Alaska, 800-478-2345, outside 800-247-7153, www.capchoice.com, starting around $100 and heading up. A bit cheaper are the nearby, comfortable **Thunderbird**, ☎ 907-766-2131 or 800-327-2556, www.thunderbird-motel.com, and **Mountain View**, ☎ 907-766-2900, 800-478-2902, www.mtviewmotel.com, which has some rooms with kitchenettes.

A lovely option out of town is the **Weeping Trout Sports Resort**. It's about 90 minutes from town, on Chilkat Lake and you can get there only by boat. Packages, including boat use, start a bit upwards of $200 a day. It's rustic – there's no hot water in the very comfortable cabins – but how many other places have you been where you can play a round of golf and fish without going more than a hundred yards from where you slept? ☎ 907-766-2827, www.weepingtrout.com.

As in most towns in the North, B&Bs come and go. Some that have been around awhile and are around $75-100 include the **Summer Inn**, at 117 Second Ave., ☎ 907-766-2970, www.summerinnbnb.com, and **Sheltered Harbor**, at 57 Beach Rd., ☎ 907-766-2741.

Dalton Street Cottages are quite nice and close to downtown at 116 6th St., ☎ 907-66-3123. The cheapest places to stay in town are the pleasant **Bear Creek Cabins**, Box 1158. They offer cabins from around $50, as well as tent and dorm space. ☎ 907-766-2259, www.bearcreekcabinsalaska. com. They'll pick you up.

Camping

There are four lovely state park campgrounds in Haines: **Chilkat State Park**, seven miles south of town on Mud Bay Rd.; **Chilkoot Lake**, 10 miles north of town off Lutak Rd.; **Portage Cove** on Beach Road, just under a mile out of town; and **Mosquito Lake**, at Mile 27 on the Haines Highway. All of them have water and toilets along with good fishing. Sites cost $5 to $10 a night.

If you require hookups, there are several choices: **Haines Hitch-up RV Park**, at Main and Haines Highway, ☎ 907-766-2882, www.hitchuprv.com, is convenient, with nearly 100 spaces. **Port Chilkoot Camper Park** is at 2nd Ave. and Mud Bay Rd., ☎ 907-766-2000, www.hotelhalsingland.com. Farther from town, Mile 27 on the Haines Highway, is the **Swan's Rest RV Park**, ☎ 907-767-5662.

Chapter 9

Dawson City & the Dempster Highway to Inuvik

We admit right upfront that this chapter covers some of our favorite places in all the North. Plain and simple, high latitudes make us happy. From the kicky little town of Mayo, to the Mackenzie River port of Inuvik, this is the high north, and it is seriously cool. If you come up this way, the more time you spend, the more richly you'll be rewarded.

We covered the usual way to get from Whitehorse to Tok in the *Alaska Highway* chapter, but there is an alternative: north via the Klondike Loop. It takes you from Whitehorse to the Alaska-Canada border by way of Dawson City, where the road becomes the Top of the World Highway, which connects to the Taylor Highway, leading down to Tok. It sounds confusing, but it's really just one road with three names.

The Canadian side of this trip features excellent road and amazing views. The Alaska side on the Taylor has some of the worst "paved" road in the North, with stretches where you can only dream about going 30 mph. The Taylor Highway is actually a good road through the middle section. It's the beginning and the end that are so bad, especially approaching the border, where the road is paved with sharp shale rocks. Check all your tires, and don't forget the spare.

There's also an alternative to the alternative road: the Campbell Highway. It bypasses Whitehorse, taking you from Watson Lake to Carmacks, where you meet up with the Klondike Highway.

 HIGHWAY TIP: Before setting off on any of these roads, check with the Information Center in Watson Lake, Tok, or Whitehorse for current road conditions; it's not uncommon for the roads to be closed due to fire during the summer months or snow during the winter. They can also be closed due to severe washouts. You don't want to end up waiting for the bulldozers to finish their work.

Eastern Roads to Dawson City

■ The Campbell Highway

 If you decide to skip the stretch of the Alcan from Watson Lake to Whitehorse on your northbound trip, you can take the Campbell, which skirts the Liard River and the Campbell Range in the Pelly Mountains.

The road is named for Robert Campbell, a trapper/explorer who was in the employ of the Hudson's Bay Company. He's credited with discovering the Yukon River, and the Campbell Highway follows the fur trading route he laid out for moving around the southeast Yukon.

What you get for taking this road instead of the more traveled route is some great scenery – the Pelly River is beautiful – and the satisfaction of being on a road not many people bother with. If you're looking to avoid traffic, this is the way to go. There's not a whole lot on the road, though, so if you want towns for amusement, stick to the main southern route.

 HIGHWAY TIP: Most of the road is gravel. Remember that headlights are required at all times in the Yukon, and watch out for big trucks blasting down the road.

At Mile 36, you cross the **Frances River bridge**. The river was named after the wife of Sir George Simpson, the man who ran the HBC through its glory days. Simpson was bon in the Scottish Highlands around 1786. He was born out of wedlock, which was rather a major handicap in those days, but thanks to some family connections, he was able to get work at a sugar broker in London. This company, Graham and Simpson, merged with Wedderburn and Company, the president of whom was a bigwig at the HBC. In other words, it was pure luck that got Simpson his post, but he turned out to be brilliant at it. He came to North America in 1820, and immediately began exploring the territory he was in charge of – pretty much all of what's now Canada. For 40 years, Simpson made canoe trips into the wild, and he was a major source of support for arctic explorations, including both Franklin expeditions and a number of the Franklin rescue efforts, especially the Rae expeditions, which opened up more Canadian territory than any other journeys.

Although his wife Frances makes the history books as little more than a footnote (except, of course, to the descendants of her five children), the river named after her was a major part of the fur trade route the company used to open the western portion of the continent.

Camp at Mile 50.3, at **Simpson Lake**. You can fish the lake for trout, grayling, and pike.

There's another campground at Mile 110.5, **Frances Lake**. It's got 24 sites, and the fishing is about the same as at Simpson Lake. The campground was built around the **Frances Lake Historical Site**. In 1842, Robert Campbell established a trading post at the south end of the lake. It was the first fort built by the Hudson's Bay Company. The company didn't find this particular one to be very profitable, and they abandoned it in 1851.

At Mile 149 is the **Finlayson Lake Historical Site**. This lake sits by the continental divide. Waters drain southeast via the Wind River to the Mackenzie River, but rivers to the north drain into the Yukon system. The lake is about 10 miles long, and makes for a good day paddle.

Canol Road

The junction with the Canol Road, Yukon Highway #6, is at Mile 220. The road leads up to the border between the Yukon and the Northwest Territories. Six miles up the road is the town of **Ross River**, population 400, the site of an old trading post. The village is now mostly Kaskav Indians, part of the Ross River Indian Band. The town makes its money as a departure point for mineral exploration and hunting camps. There's a lot of mining in the area and good fishing and canoeing along the Ross River. In town you'll find gas and mechanical services, a general store, and a hotel.

The Canol Road was originally built during World War II. It was designed to bring oil from wells in the Northwest Territories burg of Norman Wells to Whitehorse. The project never was finished, and it was abandoned at the end of the war. Since that time, the entire road has been declared a National Historic Site. In local terminology, the road between Johnson's Crossing (near Teslin) and Ross River is the South Canol Road; everything else is the North Canol Road.

The road, just over 513 miles, is not very heavily traveled, and it's not recommended for RVs or trailers. It's steep in places and very slippery when wet; there are also still some one-lane bridges. If you're in a four-wheel drive or a good car, this is a great trip.

The junction of the Campbell and the Canol also gives you a chance to bail out if you don't want to stick on the Campbell to the Klondike. Instead, you can head south on the Canol and get back to the Alcan proper. If you decide to take the Canol all the way to the end, there's camping at Mile 47.9, near the headwaters of the Big Salmon River system. The drive from Ross River to the end of the road at Macmillan Pass should take about four hours. Once you're at the end, you have no option but to turn around and go back the way you came. Beyond this point the abandoned Northern Canol Road continues another 231 miles – it's a designated heritage trail.

■ The Campbell, continued

 Back on the Campbell, at Mile 233.7 is **Lapie Canyon Campground**. It's got 21 sites, and nice little walks around with overlooks of the Lapie River.

Faro

The town of Faro, on the banks of the Pelly River, is six miles off the Campbell, with the branch road at mile 257.5. It's a mining town, and Canada's largest open-pit zinc mine is nearby. As with most mining operations, there are boom and bust periods. Faro's in a boom right now, and the mine is one of the biggest producers of lead and zinc in the world. Despite the mining, there are lots of animals around, including Fanin stone sheep, a rare sub-species of Dall sheep. There's also a pretty good local population of moose and grizzlies.

In Faro – yes, the town was named after the card game – you can stop at the **Campbell Region Tourist Info Centre**, just across from the RV park, for the latest on fishing in the region or information on touring the mines. The **Faro Hotel** (☎ 403-994-2400) is open year-round, as is the **John Conelly RV Park** – only 10 sites, but not many RVs brave this road. You can also get gas and mechanical services in town.

Check out the **Blind Creek Sheep Viewing Sites**, a five-mile round-trip off Blind Creek Road. You can also paddle on the **Pelly River**; check in town for canoe rentals.

> **HIGHWAY TIP:** Back on the highway, from Faro to the junction with the Klondike, the road is hilly and narrow, with frequent sharp curves. Watch carefully for trucks heading to and from the mines.

You can camp at Mile 266, **Johnson Lake**; Mile 321, **Little Salmon Lake**; or Mile 342, **Frenchman Lake**.

The **Yukon River** comes into view at Mile 351, at **Eagle's Nest Bluff**. This bluff was an important marker for riverboats navigating on the river. You come off the Campbell just north of the town of Carmacks. From here it's 160 miles south to Whitehorse or 300 miles north to Dawson City.

■ The Klondike Highway

 There are two parts of the Klondike Highway – the southern part goes down to Skagway (see *Chapter 7*); the northern part, which concerns us here, is a smooth, paved road between Whitehorse and Dawson City. There are frequently some breaks in the pavement for construction, but they are short and smoothly graveled.

The Klondike Highway more or less follows the original route of the stampeders – while most of the miners went on the river, there was an overland alternative, and this was it, an old Native trading trail – going north along the Yukon River, past Lake Laberge, crossing and recrossing the Dawson Trail and the Yukon River. Fishing is great all along the route. For would-be gold-panners, most of the land is claimed, so it's not advisable to try your luck. There's hardly an inch of ground that hasn't been turned over a dozen times anyway.

Leaving Whitehorse, at Mile 925.4 on the Alaska Highway, take the junction to the Klondike Highway.

 HIGHWAY TIP: In the first stretch of the highway, as far as the junction with the Campbell Highway, watch out for the huge mining trucks.

Takini Hot Springs Road Cutoff is at Mile 123 (it's really a suburb of Whitehorse). The springs – which are nonsulphurous – were used by local Natives and greeted with great delight by highway construction crews. They're not nearly as nice as the springs at Liard, but if you need a soak, stop in. The springs, which are cooled from 118° down to 102° , are open from 8 am to 10 pm daily in the summer. There's camping on site.

At Mile 140.5 is **Lake Laberge Campground**, a Yukon government site up to the territory's usual high standards. The lake is probably the best-known piece of water in the North, outside of the Yukon River itself, thanks to Robert Service's poetry. It was on the banks of this lake, according to Service, that Sam McGee was cremated:

> *There are strange things done in the midnight sun*
> *By the men who moil for gold;*
> *The Arctic trails have their secret tales*
> *That would make your blood run cold;*
> *The Northern Lights have seen queer sights,*
> *But the queerest they sever did see*
> *Was that night on the marge of Lake Lebarge*
> *I cremated Sam McGee.*

You stand a better chance of getting through Ireland without hearing "Danny Boy" than you do making through a trip in the North without hearing "Sam McGee" a couple of times.

The campground is about two miles off the road; along the way, you'll pass **Mom's**, a great place to stop in for fresh-baked bread, pastries, and coffee, and **Kimberly's Place**, a convenience store. You can rent boats at Kimberly's and head out on the 40-mile-long lake. Lines in the water bring up pike, trout, and grayling, but be prepared for sudden storms.

At Mile 154 is the **Fox Lake Campground**. At Fox Lake, one Lt. Schwatka completed surveying the entire length of the Yukon River in

Dempster Highway

1883. There's a beach and a boat launch at the lake, and the campsites are gorgeous.

At Mile 185.5 is the **Whitehorse Trough Conglomerates**, a formation created by an underwater landslide and volcanic mud flows about 185 million years ago (in the early Jurassic period). This mess solidified into huge sheets; the formation stretches from Atlin to north of Carmacks. The conglomerates also form the rocks that make up the famous Five Finger Rapids on the Yukon.

Camp at Mile 191.8, and stop in at the **Montague Roadhouse,** at Mile 200.7, to see how people used to travel. The roadhouse, which dates to 1899, is what remains of a chain of roadhouses (placed about every 20 miles) on the road between Whitehorse and Dawson Creek. It makes for an interesting stop.

Carmacks

Carmacks is the only town of size along the Klondike Highway. It's located near the ancestral home of the Ts'awlnjik Dan First Nation people, and it's the approximate boundary between the North and South Tutchone First Nation peoples, whose settlements in the area date back more than 10,000 years. The modern town was named after George Carmacks, who opened a trading post here but failed to find gold in the early 1890s. He eventually moved to Fortymile, where he hit the big time as one of the discoverers of the granddaddy of them all, the Klondike strike.

Carmacks was a refueling point for riverboats headed north during the rush of '98. The town is still a supply center for surrounding mines.

The **Tourist Info Centre** (☎ 867-863-6271) has all the usual items, plus information on villages in the area, and the staff can point you to the best places to hunt for the local agates. They'll also help you book trips to the Five Fingers Rapids or along the Pelly River. There's a 1.2-mile wheelchair-accessible boardwalk that goes from the Info Centre along the Yukon River and leads to a nice little park.

The **Northern Tutchone Interpretive Center** offers a look at the traditional lives of the Natives, with indoor and outdoor interpretive displays. It's well worth stopping in, especially for – get this – the mammoth trap. Yep. They claim it's the only working mammoth trap in the world, but what it really seems to be is a bunch of very large rabbit snares set up in the trees. The idea was, the mammoth would get herded into the snares, caught in them, and then could be neatly dispatched.

This all makes a certain amount of sense. This area of the Yukon is part of what was a vast steppe, called Beringia, a warm spot in the middle of the last ice age, a place where mammoths and camels, horses and giant steppe bison, beavers the size of ottomans and sloths the size of Volkswagons, could go out and play. And if you read the literature, it's entirely possible that the extinction of mammoths – the last once disappeared less than

4,000 years ago, while the Egyptians were busy building pyramids – maybe the first ecological crime humans committed.

But that's not what the mammoth trap is about. According to the model of the trap in action, "The mammoths, as they were nearing extinction, became a threat to people.... The Northern Tuchtone devised this elaborate snare system to rid their land of this most feared predator. People dressed up in their best clothing in case they died in the fight with the mammoth."

And as the coup de grace, "The last mammoths were not eaten, since the Northern Tuchtone did not eat any animal that ate humans."

Yes, man-eating wooly mammoths. That creature of our ice age dreams, a cross between a puppy and an elephant. Mammoths had four teeth, shaped and sized much like bricks. Very fierce, very threatening. At least to grass and twigs.

Love it. Don't miss it.

You can stay at the **Carmacks Hotel** (☎ 867-863-5221), but you'd get better views at the **Tantalis Campground** on the Yukon, which has RV and tent sites.

At the north end of the bridge, stop in at the **Northern Tutchone Trading Post** for gas, food, Native crafts, fishing and hunting supplies.

You meet up with the Campbell Highway at Mile 223.5 (see above for details).

Stop at Mile 236.4 for the **Five Finger Rapids Recreation Site**. The rapids used to be about the biggest hazard on the Yukon for boat traffic, but in the early 1900s they got blasted with dynamite until they were about 20 feet wider, slowing the water down and making the trip considerably easier. You can take the partially staircased trail down to a viewing platform that gives great views of the river and the rapids. Check with operators in Carmacks for ways onto the water.

Camp at **Minto Resorts**, at Mile 267. Minto, at Mile 268, was another riverboat stopping point, situated at the junction of the Pelly and Yukon rivers. There's a campground here, too. Just 10 sites, but it's pretty and it's cheap. This is the turnoff for those with boats who want to see **Fort Selkirk**, about 25 miles upriver. The fort was established by the Hudson's Bay Company in 1848 and was destroyed by Chilkat Indians in 1852, who were somewhat perturbed at this new addition in their traditional summer home. There are quite a few buildings still standing, and if you've got a boat or want to book a boat, it makes for an interesting side-trip.

The town of **Pelly Crossing** is at Mile 288. Home of the Selkirk Indian Band (all sorts of ironies there that it's best not to go into), the town has the **Selkirk Heritage Center**, with a self-guided tour of displays of First Nation items. Camp outside of town at Ethel Lake. Tight for RVs, but great for tents.

Mile 333.9 is **Stewart Crossing**, the junction between the Klondike and the Silver Trail. The Silver Trail is about 70 miles long and leads up to the tiny mining towns of **Mayo, Elsa,** and **Keno** – a really cool side trip, if you have the time. Stewart Crossing was established as a trading post in 1886 by a trio of prospectors who decided it was easier to get rich by selling to prospectors than it was by being one. These guys, particularly Arthur Harper, were way ahead of the curve, prospecting the North before anyone else. They built a roadhouse and got rich on riverboat traffic. Jack London stayed here, his only Northern winter, on his way north to the goldfields. There's gas in town and an RV park.

If you've got a kayak or canoe, you can do a nice float trip down the **Selkirk River** to the Yukon and up to Dawson City. The rapids are behind you, and the trip takes an easy five days. You can also head up the Silver Trail to Mayo and start the trip there.

The Silver Trail

If you're in the mood for a side trip, the Silver Trail is a nice drive off the main route, and Keno, where it ends, is one of those really, really cool places in the world, although it can be a little hard to explain why. The town just has a vibe.

The trail traces its history to around 1901, when a party of Swedes who arrived too late to get in on the Klondike rush found gold on Duncan Creek. In the next two years, every inch of ground along Duncan, Minto, and Highet creeks was staked, and yet another rush was on. However, while they were looking for gold, quite a few miners had more luck with silver. On Galena Creek, the Silver King strike turned out over 2,500 tons of high-grade ore in just 10 years.

The problem was getting these riches south. Even by the mid-1920s, it cost roughly the same to get the ore from Keno to the Stewart River as it did to get the ore from the river to San Francisco. The government stepped in, and the Silver Trail road was built.

Mayo

The town of Mayo was the end of the 42-mile trip the ore had to take from Keno down to the river. Mayo thrived on this – it's always good to be a transportation hub. The village is now mostly home to the Na Cho Y'y'ak First Nation peoples. Stop in at the **Binet House Interpretive Center** (open 10 am to 6 pm in summer) for great geological displays and informative stuff on local flora and fauna.

Stay at the **Bedrock Motel** (☎ 867-996-2290), $$, or the **North Star Motel** (☎ 867-996-2231), which is a couple of bucks cheaper. You can camp just past town at Mile 35.8, **Five Mile Lake Campground**.

Mile 42.9 has the junction with the Duncan Creek/Minto Road. Duncan Creek Road follows the original Silver Trail to Keno. If you take this turnoff (head right) you can make a loop up to Keno and then back down the regular Silver Trail road. It's not recommended for larger vehicles or those towing.

Turn off at Mile 47.1 for the **Mount Haldane Trailhead**. The trail is about four miles long, with a 4,000 foot rise. It's ambitious. What's really hard to believe is that these switchbacks were cut by miners. Gold does weird things to people. Figure on the round-trip taking about six hours, although it always takes us longer because we love Keno.

The village of **Keno** and the end of the road are at Mile 70. In 1919, silver ore was found in the nearby Sheep Mountains. What was once a boom town is now a sleepy village of about 50. There's a hotel (☎ 867-995-2312), a very small but lovely campground, and a mining museum, open in summer from 10 to 6 daily.

One of the surprises of Keno is its good museum, which has lots of big equipment lying around outside (you wonder what kind of demented greed made people bring all this stuff in here). Inside are far-above-average exhibits about mining and daily life. This is one of our favorite museums in all the North – and we've been in every single one of them, from the US-BC border to Nome.

The main thing about Keno is its wonderful end of the road vibe. A surprising number of people find their way here, and we've never met anybody who went away disappointed. Okay, so there's not a lot to do. It's a great place to sit and relax, think about where you've been and where you're going next.

■ The Klondike, continued

 Buy your gas in Carmacks. The next chance is Dawson City, 112 miles away.

Moose Creek Lodge, Mile 349.2, has small and rustic cabins, and there are no private baths, but it's a clean and friendly place. We recommend it. Open May to September.

Camp at **Moose Creek** at Mile 349.5, a territorial campground with a couple of dozen RV sites and six tent-only sites, or the commercial **Spruce Grove RV Park** at Mile 364.2. No hookups, no power.

At Mile 409.2 is the **Tiina Trench overlook**; stop and see proof of the theory of plate tectonics. A plaque explains what you're looking at, but it boils down to this: you're looking at a fault line.

Mile 421.5 takes you to the junction of the Dempster Highway, which heads north to Inuvik. See the end of this chapter for more details.

Camp at Mile 433.8, the **Klondike River Campground.**

When you left Whitehorse, you might have noticed that the road was lined with tall trees; approaching Dawson City, the road is lined with tailings, the leftover rocks from mines. As you approach Dawson City, the landscape looks like nothing more than a bombed-out war zone. Literally, no stone has been left unturned here. It's as if the earth has been put through a giant blender. At Mile 439.4 you can stop and see tailings and the **Yukon Ditch**, part of a 70-mile pipe, ditch, and flume system used to bring water to the mines on Bonanza Creek.

At Mile 444.4 is what remains of **Guggieville** – not much more than a signpost now – once the largest gold mining operation in the Klondike, owned by (who else?) the Guggenheim family.

The Western Road to Dawson City

Although the western route to Dawson City involves two highways – the Taylor and the Top of the World – it's really one road that just changes its name at the border. The only difference between the chunks of road is that on the Alaska side, the road stinks. As soon as you're in Canada, however, you hit one of the nicest stretches of road in the North.

■ The Taylor Highway

While it's nothing compared to what it used to be when there were fields of sharp shale in the road, the Taylor Highway can still be hard road to drive. Although the section from the Alcan to Chicken has been paved – a vast improvement over the old days, when this road was big chunks of sharp shale – it's still not a road to hurry on, and it's best not to figure on hitting the right side of your speedometer very often. From Chicken to the Canadian border, things are not bad, but can be difficult, and in addition, there are many mountains to climb and sharp curves to round.

> **HIGHWAY TIP:** The Taylor has sections that require very careful driving. It's mostly hard-packed gravel, but it's prone to washouts and mud bogs. Don't let this scare you, though: we've driven the road in a tiny Hyundai.

It is quite scenic, though. Sweeping mountain vistas and long stretches of unspoiled county greet you whenever you raise your eyes. The roadside is lined with wildflowers: wild rose, Labrador tea, arnica, and lupine. All along the road are interesting mining sites; they are all, however, on private property, so you cannot explore them. Everywhere you look is a private gold claim, so don't go picking up rocks or panning in the streams.

The road took seven years to build, from 1946 to 1953. It was built to provide access to the **Fortymile district**. Fortymile was the richest gold mining district in all of the Yukon, with ore assaying at $20,000 a ton in 1881, long before the Klondike strike. The area was also a haven for trappers, some of whom ran trap lines more than a hundred miles long. By the time the road was built, miners had settled in to less feverish placer mining, and there are still tons of gold being pulled from the area.

Although the road has undergone massive improvements since we wrote the first edition of this book, it can still be rough, with frequent washouts, and days when it may be unpassable for passenger cars, RVs, or those hauling trailers. There are some serious grades on the road – it climbs to over 3,500 feet three times. Check in Tok or Dawson City for conditions before you start off. Really. We mean this.

The road starts at Tetlin Junction, just outside Tok. Miles are from the junction.

This was not the original route used by miners headed into Fortymile. At around Mile 9, the original trail headed up the Dennison Fork to Chicken. The route to the Canadian border took about 36 hours when it was a horse trail.

The weird bumps in the landscape around Mile 31 are pingos. These are formed when water gets between layers of permafrost and temporary frost; the ground is heaved up as high as 30 feet.

Mount Fairplay Summit, at Mile 33, is the first of the road's climbs. From the top you can see how the forests around all seem to be of different ages – this is a high-risk forest fire area, and some part of it burns almost every year. We've driven this road with trees all around us on fire.

Logging Cabin Creek, at Mile 43, is the southern boundary of the **Fortymile National Wild and Scenic River System**, which is composed of almost 400 miles of river. Know what you're doing before you head out. For the experienced paddler, this is a dream trip. If you've got your boat with you and somebody to pick you up, you can take the Fortymile and its connecting rivers all the way up to Eagle, although you will have to be prepared to portage over shallow stretches. Where the water runs deep, it can get to Class V.

 CUSTOMS CONTROL: Remember that if you're going to take the river into Canada you have to check in with Customs for both countries.

Popular points to put in for short trips are the West Fork Bridge (Mile 49; there's also a campground here) and the Mosquito Fork Bridge, Mile 59. The water is usually too shallow at both spots for much of a boat, but give them a look.

At Mile 66.6 you'll see a road leading to the west. This is a private road to Chicken. Just stay on the highway and you'll hit the town anyway.

This area was worked by the largest dredge used in the Fortymile district, and at its peak the dredge ran 24 hours a day for two weeks straight. A good run like this would bring in about $40,000 in gold. There are a lot of fossils in the tailing piles, brought up when the dredge went by.

> **WARNING:** You can check for mammoth bones, but try not to look as if you're searching for gold. Remember, practically every inch of ground you see is part of someone's gold claim, and they will not be happy if they find you messing around on it.

Chicken

The town of Chicken had about 175 people living in it at the turn of the century. Now there are perhaps 25 year-round residents. The town was supposed to be named Ptarmigan, because there were so many of the birds around. However, the story goes that nobody could spell Ptarmigan, so they settled on Chicken. Gold was first found here in 1896, and they're still out there looking for more. This town is the new Chicken – the old town site is about a mile north and not accessible.

 Ann Purdy's famous book, *Tisha*, is about her time as a teacher in Chicken.

Along the highway is a trading post/gas station. You can pick up a gold pan in the store and try your luck in the stream at the other side of the parking lot, where there's free RV parking.

In town, there's the café, a general store, and a gas station. Stop in at the **Chicken Creek Salmon Bake** if you're coming through at dinnertime. Overall, the town looks like a small trailer park set in a bomb crater.

Once you leave Chicken, you also leave the pavement. Conditions largely depend on when the graders last ran through.

At Mile 75.3 is the **South Fork Bridge**, where you can put your boat into the river. Thirteen miles downstream is the abandoned town of Franklin, site of the first gold strike in the area. Not much is left – nobody's lived there for 50 years – but there are still a few buildings that haven't entirely fallen over.

Camp at Mile 82, in the **Walker Fork Campground**. There's a short hiking trail to the top of the bluff.

Even though you have to keep away from mining claims, there is one place you can explore: 86 miles from the junction is the **Jack Wade Dredge** (Gold Dredge Number 1), which was abandoned in 1942. It's not the biggest dredge around – that honor belongs to Number 4, in Dawson City – but it's an interesting place to stop, rest your kidneys from the bumps in the road, and get a close-up look at how the miners used to eat up rivers whole. The dredge was one of the first bucket-line dredges used up here, and it stayed in service longer than any of the others. The rusting metal has turned a shade of gold, and it's almost impossible to take a bad picture of it. Stay back from it, though, as it is falling apart and very unsafe inside.

Wade Creek, where the dredge ended its days, is a prime example of how land was carved up by mining claims (usually 20 acres were given in a claim). In 1900, there were more than 200 claims along the banks of the creek.

Mile 96 is Jack Wade Junction. Head north to Eagle or east to the Canadian border and Dawson City.

Eagle

It's 64 miles from the junction to Eagle (area code 907). The road is gravel, narrow, steep, and winding, and you can't do much more than 30 mph.

The town of Eagle (population around 150) was originally a supply point for Yukon miners. It's only 10 miles from the Canadian border, so it was an important crossroads for miners who'd made the trip to the goldfields through US territory. At the height of the rush, there were more than 1,700 people in town. The local Athabascans had, of course, been using the area for hundreds of years. They had a huge camp about three miles east of where the town is now.

The first trading post was opened in 1874. The US Army arrived in 1889, and founded Ft. Egbert to enforce US law in the Interior. At this point Alaska had been part of the US for only a few years, and Washington still wasn't sure what to do with it. Most of the territory was ignored; it was only gold and the stampede that brought government forces to Alaska, and once they got here, they settled in to stay. A courthouse was built in 1900, and in 1901 Teddy Roosevelt made Eagle the first incorporated town in the Interior of Alaska.

Because of its location, they've been trying to figure out ways to link Eagle to the Gulf of Alaska for years. All the plans have died on the drawing board, and the only way in is the way you just came – through nasty roads.

COMPLETING THE NORTHWEST PASSAGE

An odd moment of history occurred in 1905, when Roald Amundsen, whose boat *Gjöa* was frozen in ice in the Beaufort Sea, wandered into town. Amundsen – who was later the first to reach the South Pole and, debatably, the North Pole – was the first man to finally put together the threads of the Northwest Passage and sail the whole thing, east to west. While other explorers – notably, the doomed Franklin expedition – tried to beat their way against the ice, Amundsen took his cue from Fritjof Nansen's spectacular drift toward the poles a few years earlier and decided to sit it out. He allowed the boat to get frozen into the pack ice, and let the current drift take him where he wanted to go. The trip took three years, but he and his small crew made it in good shape. He dog-sledded down to Eagle, crossing another 500 miles of unexplored territory and crossing over 9,000-foot mountains in the Brooks Range, where he was able to telegraph out news of his expedition. During the three years the crew spent in the ice, they took scientific measurements, chased polar bears, got really bored and (thanks to brilliant planning on Amundsen's part) they got fat like "prize pigs."

In his book, *The Arctic Grail*, Pierre Berton writes that Amundsen's expedition "in that same environment where others had suffered hardships and death [had] survived and thrived." It had taken over three hundred years to solve the riddle of the Northwest Passage, starting with Frobisher's first voyage in 1576. But in the end, the trick was to get a good boat and just sit tight.

Amundsen was the last excitement in town for a long time. The residents of Eagle settled back down to mining.

Today the town is very well preserved, and it's worth a side trip for the historically inclined in a good vehicle. Eagle actually has the largest museum system in the state. There are daily walking tours offered in the summer. Tours start at 9 am, and at $5 they are an excellent deal. Stop in at the **Eagle Historical Society and Museum**, in the old Courthouse (B St and 1st Ave.) for local goings on, great historical displays, and a good museum store. Check the bulletin board here for information on events at **Eagle Village**, a traditional fishing village for the Athabascans, who use fish wheels to farm the rivers. The locals don't discourage visitors, but they do discourage gawkers.

The **Yukon-Charley Rivers National Preserve Visitor Information Centre** is on the Yukon Riverbanks, off 1st Ave. If you're going to try a serious river trip, stop in here first. It's open 8 to 5 weekdays. The only other road access to the preserve is from Circle, Alaska.

Fort Egbert has been restored and renovated. There are historical photos on display and an old storage barn, more than a 150 feet long, filled with uniforms, weapons, tools, and everything a good army camp needs.

Stay at the **Falcon Inn** (☎ 907-547-2254), which offers river views and log cabins, $$, or the **Eagle Trading Company** (☎ 907-547-2220), a few bucks cheaper. You can also camp at Eagle Trading, at the BLM Campground, or on the far side of Ft. Egbert. Eat at Eagle Trading, with reasonable café food.

You can rent canoes at **Eagle Canoe Rentals** (☎ 907-547-2203), float and paddle to Circle, through the Yukon-Charley Rivers National Preserve, and leave the canoe there, for a small extra fee. Figure on the trip taking five days. It's about four days by boat to Dawson City, all upstream. Check your paddling muscles.

Eagle is the last chance on the road between Tok and Dawson City where you can get full mechanical services. Gas will be expensive enough to make you cry, though.

There is gas in Boundary, back on the Taylor, but no other services.

Boundary

The settlement of Boundary is 10 miles before you hit the Top of the World Highway. Buy gas here; it's your last chance if you're heading north, and while the price will strike you as ludicrous, it's still cheaper than it will be once you cross the Canadian border.

Once you leave Eagle and get back on the Taylor, you're almost to the Top of the World Highway. One of the shorter highways in Canada, it leads from the Alaska border to Dawson City. It may be short, but the views are astounding. The world drops away beneath you, and it's easy to see where the road got its name. It's a long, gradual climb to the border, with a lot of curves, as you leave the tree line well behind.

 CUSTOMS CONTROL: The US/Canada border is three miles east of Boundary. It's open from mid-May through mid-September, 9 to 9 (that's 8, Alaska time). It's a good idea to double-check the opening times in either Tok or Dawson City, because you cannot cross the border unless the post is open. Also keep in mind the one-hour time difference between Canada and Alaska.

The Customs post is only a mile shy of the highest part of the road, a stretch where the altitude is 4,515 feet, and it looks like the land to the side of the road is dropping all the way down. The views are stunning along here and, after the hard driving on the Taylor, this is a dream – or at least less of a nightmare. It's still slippery when wet, and there are quite a few steep grades and winding patches, but, especially if you hit it right after the graders have gone through, it's a lovely stretch of road all the way to the short, free ferry ride across the Yukon River to Dawson. The ferry is operated by the government, 24 hours a day, seven days a week, from mid-May through mid-October (except Wednesdays between 5 am and 7 am, when it's closed for servicing). The ferry can hold only 10 cars or four RVs at a time, so waits to cross the river can be long, particularly since commercial vehicles get priority.

With a couple of minutes of travel across the water, you reach Dawson City, a town built entirely from the echoes of one man standing in a river screaming *GOLD!*

Dawson City

Dawson City was once the focus of an entire continent's obsession. This is where the Klondike gold rush happened. Yeah, you hear it as the Alaska gold rush, but all the real action was in Canada. This is the place all

Dempster Highway

the hopefuls climbing the passes from Skagway or Haines, or taking ships in from Nome and traveling along the Yukon, were trying to reach. This is gold rush central.

■ History

Gold was discovered in the absolute middle of nowhere, on Bonanza Creek, August 17, 1896. When the yellow stuff was first found, there probably weren't more than 20 white people in a hundred-mile radius of the creek (the Han had been here forever, of course, but gold didn't excite them too much; more on them shortly). However, only two years later, in 1898, 27,000 people headed north along just one of the pathways to the goldfields. And each and every one of those people – as well as the thousands like them on the lesser-known routes north – were all hoping to strike it rich. The odds of hitting the powerball are better, though. Almost none of these would-be miners found a single flake of gold; actually, by the time most of the stampeders arrived in the Klondike, all the land had long been claimed. One estimate is that of the more than 100,000 people who tried to come north for the rush, fewer than 20 actually got rich.

But if you were making your money off something other than gold, you could do really, really well. During the first two years of the boom, lots that had originally sold for ten bucks an acre had jumped to as much as $40,000. So there was money to be made – just not by the miners. Southern cities, such as Seattle and Vancouver, were getting rich outfitting the miners, who were required by Canadian law to carry a year's supply of necessities with them. On July 17, 1897, *The Seattle Post-Intelligencer* printed a suggested provisions list, which included 100 to 200 pounds of bacon, 400 pounds of flour, 100 pounds of beans... the list goes on to include a "small assortment of medicines." (For one version of the full list, see page 12.)

AN ORIGINAL, STILL IN BUSINESS

Back in 1898, they didn't have Gore-Tex and ultra-light nylon fabrics. They had canvas, and just the tent for most of these guys weighed more than a modern camper's entire kit. But if you could forget the weight, the equipment was pure luxury, and properly taken care of, could last a lifetime.

There is, actually, a company still in business that started out making things for the miners. **The Filson Company** (☎ 866-860-8906, www.filson.com), headquartered in Seattle, not far from where the first ship loaded with Klondike gold docked in 1897; more than a century later, they're still making items out of the same tough materials that survived the Klondike. We are firm believers that when you buy any kind of tool – and clothes can be a tool – buy well, buy once. In a 1914 catalog, Filson summed it all up nicely: "The goods we quote must not be confounded with the cheap and vastly inferior grade with which the market is over-run. Such goods are not only useless for the purpose for which they are intended, but the person wearing them would be better off without them."

The first piece of Filson goods we bought were rain hats; over the years, we've put them through more abuse than can be imagined, and they're still comfortable and work beautifully. In a single year, Ed put his Filson briefcase through nearly 100,000 miles of travel, and it didn't even scuff. Serious rain gear, luggage... you can plan to hand down to your heirs.

No, we don't get any kind of kickback from this. We just love things that are well done, and we love the company's link to history. Do yourself a favor and check them out.

One way or another, these supplies had to be hauled to the Klondike. The most famous route was over the Chilkoot Pass, which required miners to trudge back and forth on steep grades in the dead of winter, carrying their ton of supplies on their backs over the mountains (figure fifty or sixty pounds per trip, then remember that famous photo of the miners headed up the steep slope in deep snow – and then think of making that climb forty or fifty times). Then, the stampeders would build a boat, heading out on Lake Bennett as soon as the ice broke. That didn't always work so well, since most of these guys had no idea at all how to build a boat. Known drownings, though, are fairly few.

There's no telling how many hopeful miners' hearts broke when they got to Dawson City, only to find they were too late.

Dawson City still thrives on mining; somehow, despite the valiant efforts of thousands of men over more than a hundred years, they didn't quite get all the gold. Modern techniques and sheer determination still manage to pull up enough nuggets to make mining operations profitable; those who don't mine make their living off the modern gold rush, the summer tourist season.

Today Dawson City is a funky town with a mood all its own. Even though the town's population is only around 2,000 people, it's very crowded in the summer. The campgrounds are full before noon, and there's a mad scramble for the last hotel rooms by 2pm. Plan ahead.

QUICK TOUR: You can easily walk around Dawson in an afternoon, from the river back to the Service Cabin and the museum. It's a town made for walking, since every corner is going to bring something new and interesting.

DON'T MISS: Play gold rush: hit one of the dredges, try some panning yourself.

BEST FREE THING TO DO: Dawson, flat out, is the best place in the Yukon to just sit and watch the river flow. This whole town has an end-of-the-world vibe that can't be beat. Watch the river, listen to what the Han called "the voices of the ancestors," and imagine yourself here in winter, digging down towards bedrock, hoping to strike the sheen of gold.

■ Things to Do

 There's quite a variety of sights in Dawson City – it's small, but it's not at all hard to find enough things to keep yourself busy for at least two or three days.

Best of all, the town is small enough that you can walk to almost all of attractions. Any walk around town will bring delightful discoveries of charming old houses and remnants of the boom days. It's especially good to head to the south side of town, where the vintage buildings look like they might fall before you get a chance to take a picture.

The **Visitor Reception Centre** is on Front Street, near the paddle wheeler. They show films here and are quite helpful pointing out the charms of the town. There's also a notebook with menus from most of the town's restaurants, so you can take a look before you head out for food. A second notebook details the hotels. Depending on the number of people around, the staff may help you locate a place to stay, but if it's high season, late in the afternoon, you might well end up thinking about how best to arrange the blankets on your car seat.

COMBO PASSES

The most important thing you can do at the Info Centre is buy tickets for the town's attractions. This can save you quite a few bucks. There are various combinations – for instance, a deal that gets you a steamwheeler tour, into the Han Centre, and a museum pass, for a good look at Dawson's history. Don't even bother with individual tickets at the attractions – most of which run in the $8-15 range. Come here first, and you'll see twice as much for half the price.

Right across the street is the information center for the **Dempster Highway**, the British Yukon Navigation Building. The Dempster is the northernmost public road in the Canada. It leads to Inuvik, in the Northwest Territories, and includes more than 200 miles of driving above the Arctic Circle. (Watch for Northwest Territories license plates on cars – the plate is shaped like a polar bear, and when Nunavut was split off from the NWT, one of the biggest issues was who got to keep the polar bear plates.) The road north is good, the scenery fantastic, the mosquitoes the largest in the world. (See the *Dempster* section, below, for more details.)

HIGHWAY TIP: It is imperative that you stop at the information center to get the latest updates on road conditions before you head out on the Dempster Highway.

Next door is the **Steamer *Keno***, a nicely restored old paddle-wheeler. The steamers were used to bring gold down to Whitehorse and supplies up to the miners; compare this ship with the S.S. *Klondike* in Whitehorse. The Keno was first launched in 1922, and was parked here in 1960. Tours of the ship give you an idea of what it took to keep the thing moving, and there are some nice displays, including some highly informative ones on the First Nations influence on paddle-wheeler culture. An awful lot of the guys who worked these things were Han.

To find out just who the Han were and what they were up to, head to the **Dänojà Zho Cultural Center,** at Front and York Streets, next door to the ship. This is a great spot, built by the local Han (just try and get your tongue around Tr'ondek Hwechi'in, what they call themselves, and you'll see why the trappers just called them Han) First Nation people. There are films, displays, and, of course, a crafts shop. A bit sparse in places, but one of the few chances you'll have to get a realistic idea of what life was like here for thousands of years. $5.

Dawson has a lot of historic buildings, many with interpretive signs and museum-quality displays in the windows. **Harrington's Store**, at 3rd and Princess, offers a photo exhibit of the early days of the town. At 3rd and King is the **1901 post office**, still operating, and the **Palace Grand Theatre**, which opened in 1899. The Palace has been restored and offers free guided tours from June to September 15. It's a beautiful old building, well worth stopping in to see. Nightly except Tuesdays, the **Gaslight Follies**, a gold rush-era variety show, plays at 8 pm. This is a Dawson staple.

Another must-see is **Diamond Tooth Gerties**, at 4th and Queen, where you can see a fun can-can show. Open from 7 pm to 2 am, it was Canada's first legal casino. It's also the northernmost casino in the world. There's a $5 admission charge, and you must be 19 to get in. The best show is watching people pour their money into machines the way miners once poured theirs into shovels and picks. On the good side, it's billed as a nonprofit gambling hall, and all proceeds go to community projects.

At Fifth and King is the **Firefighters' Museum**, which has exhibits of classic equipment.

Many of the other buildings downtown show historical photos and exhibits in their street-front windows. The Visitor Reception Centre does have walking tours of the town, but you'd probably be just as happy discovering stuff on your own.

The great bard of the North, **Robert Service**, spent some time in Dawson City. You can visit his restored house on 8th Ave. In the summer, there are readings of his poetry at 10 am and 3 pm – the afternoon show is better.

The restoration has been done well. Even if you don't like the poetry, it's worth stopping in to see a typical miner's cabin – although Service was never a miner. Admission is $6.

Nearby is the **Jack London Interpretive Center**, at 8th and Firth, open every day. It's is a replica of a cabin Jack London actually lived in, although nowhere near here. There are also daily talks about London's time in the Klondike at noon and 2:15. The museum is open 10 am-1 pm and 2-6 pm.

With both the Service cabin and the London cabin, check show times and current schedules at the Info Centre before you head out.

The **Dawson City Museum** is at Church and 5th; admission is $4 for adults. The museum has quite a nice display of gold rush items – far and away the best in the North – as well as a very comprehensive look at the geography and flora and fauna of the region. Dawson, during the last ice age, was pretty toasty warm, part of a transcontinental steppe now called Beringia. This is where the wooly mammoths and giant sloths played – check out the piece of wooly mammoth meat in the stairwell.

Outside, there are the remains of a failed dream: a train line that was to take ore out of the goldfields and down to the river. It failed because the owners of the claims didn't want to give up any of their land – the railroad right of way might have been just the spot where the gold was, after all. What remains are the engines and a couple of cars, brought north in a fit of optimism.

Guggieville is a huge RV park/tourist shop on Bonanza Creek Road, where it meets the Klondike Highway. Big parking lot, big gift shop, chance to pan for gold.

■ Out & About

There are two main attractions just outside of town. The largest gold dredge in North America, **Gold Dredge Number 4**, is 16 miles out Bonanza Creek Road. Built in 1912, it was in operation until 1959, and produced as much as 800 ounces of gold a day. Open daily in the summer. Admission is $5.

Eight miles south of Dawson City, on the Klondike Highway, is a **gold dredge support camp**. This huge, sprawling complex features a blacksmith's shop, a complete machine shop, and living quarters. Tours take about 45 minutes; admission is $3 for adults, $2 for children.

If you can't stand to have come all this way without panning for gold, there's free panning at Claim #6, a bit past gold dredge #4. You can rent a goldpan there, or bring one in from town. This is sponsored by the Klondike Visitor Association, and it's great PR for them.

There's a marker where George Carmack first hit the big time – $4 in a single pan of gold fired the hopes of millions – 10 miles southeast of town. Unless you're a hard-core historian, it's not really worth the trip, though.

Considerably farther out, you can tour either the **Goldbottom Mine**, about 30 kilometers south of town, where you can pan after the tour of the mine works, or the Brewery Creek Operations Mine, 43 miles from Dawson City, toward Whitehorse. The mine was reopened in November 1996, and makes for an interesting contrast to old techniques. In essence, tons of chemicals are poured on ore until the rock melts, leaving the gold behind. Fear over a similar operation in the Alsek region caused an uproar in both Alaska and Canada, and led to the formation of a new wilderness area. See the mine's office at 2nd and Queen in Dawson City to book a tour.

There are quite a few ways to get out into the bush for a look around. Ancient **Voices Wilderness Camp** combines a salmon bake/barbecue with a trip out to see First Nation dancing and culture. ☎ 867-993-5605.

Eagle Canoe Rentals (☎ 867-993-6823 in Dawson, ☎ 867-547-2203 in Eagle) rents canoes for trips on the Yukon. For a rental from Dawson to Eagle, which is a bit over 100 miles, and will take you three or four days, the charge is $110 for the canoe (big enough for two people and all the gear you'll need). Dawson to Circle, which is a 10-day trip, will run you $270 for the rental. You can drop off the canoe at an arranged spot when you get to your destination, but you're on your own for getting back to your put-in point.

■ Shopping

Dawson City first thrived as a spot to sell things to people passing through, and it serves the same purpose today.

Dawson Trading Post, 5th and Harker, has fishing gear, canoe rentals, and Army surplus supplies. For $5 you can pan for gold in the trough out front. If you need something to read for the night, buy books at **Maximillians Gold Rush Emporium**, on Front and Queen. Maximillians is also a general-purpose drugstore.

For groceries, hit the **Dawson City General Store**, right by Maximillians, across from the bandshell.

■ Food

Almost all the hotels have dining rooms, serving standard hotel fare. If that's not to your taste, the great concentration of restaurants is down on Front Street, or just off it near the corners.

Klondike Kate's Restaurant, next to the cabins, has a $5 breakfast special that might be the best deal in town. Good food and plenty of it. Lunches and dinners start at around $8.

River West, on Front St., is the place for health food. You can get out with your lunch running about $6, and it's a good change from all the greasy burgers you've probably been eating.

The Grubstake, on 2nd Ave., has pizza, subs, and a patio where you can eat your lunch and watch the town go on about its business. A good spot, under $10.

The Back Alley, on 2nd behind the Westminster, has good pizza and Greek specialties. You'll be quite nicely full for around $20.

The Jack London Grill, in the Downtown Hotel, is one of the tonier places to go. Open for all three meals, prices range from $10 to $27.

■ Accommodations

All the hotels are clustered in the downtown area. Don't forget to make your reservations early. It's jammed here.

HOTEL PRICING
Prices are in US dollars.
under $50 . . . . $
$50-$100 . . . . $$
$100-$150 . . . . . . $$$
above $150 . . . . . $$$$

Starting on the luxury end, there's the **Westmark Inn Dawson City** (☎ 867-993-5542 or 800-478-1111, www.westmarkhotels.com), with all the usual amenities and rooms, $$$. They've also got cabins.

The Downtown Hotel (☎ 867-993-5346, www.downtown.yk.net) is also quite luxurious. There's a dining room, lounge, Jacuzzi, and satellite TV. $$$.

Also in the same price range are the **El Dorado** (☎ 867-993-5451, www.eldoradohotel.ca), 3rd and Princess, and the **Midnight Sun Hotel** (☎ 867-993-5495), 3rd and Queen.

Klondike Kate's (☎ 867-993-6572, www.klondikekates.ca) has cabins of various sizes, $$$. Some of the rooms are huge, and they're all quite nice. Good attention to detail here, the little things that make a night's stay more comfortable. This is where we usually end up ourselves. Get as far away from the restaurant as you can, though, since on nice nights, the patio area can be really noisy. **The Bunkhouse** (☎ 867-993-5566) is simple, but affordable. Very clean and nice, and one of the few places that doesn't point and scream when you ask if they take pets. They're at Princess, near Front.

Camping

The **Yukon Government Campground** is just across the Yukon River from Dawson City – you have to take the ferry to get there. It's very nice, with 77 sites suitable for RVs and 20 tent-only sites. This one fills up very early.

The **Gold Rush Campground**, at 5th and York, is a large parking lot with 15 serviced sites, 25 partially serviced, and 50 unserviced. For RVs only, and only for people who don't mind being packed in like sardines. For an alternative, there's GuggieVille, two miles outside of town, which does have hookups. Phone for reservations: ☎ 867-993-5319, 866-860-6535.

The Dempster Highway

If you're looking to take a road no one else is on, look no further. The Dempster, the northernmost public road in Canada, leads from Dawson City to Inuvik, on the Mackenzie River not far from the Beaufort Sea.

The road is open year-round, except during spring ice breakup and the first stages of the winter freeze, but it's not really a road you want to be on in winter unless you've spent a lot of your life driving in extreme conditions. Even in mid-summer they may be waiting for snow passes to clear and for ice to break up on the Mackenzie so they can get the ferry across (at Mile 380, free).

The road, which was begun in 1959 and not finished for 20 years, is gravel with some clay areas, and in summer even RVs shouldn't have any trouble on it; a decent car should be able to maintain 60 mph without any real difficulty on a sunny day, although it's always a good idea to keep an eye on how much mud and dirt has covered your brake lights.

Not that anybody is likely to be behind you.

 HIGHWAY TIP: Before heading north, stop at the Northwest **Territories Information Centre** in Dawson City, next to the riverboat, for the latest information, or phone the **Arctic Hotline,** ☎ 800-661-0788. For general road and weather information, ☎ 800-661- 0752.

There are only three places to buy gas along the road: Eagle Plains, Ft. McPherson, and Inuvik. Prices aren't all that painful, but they are going to be higher than farther south. There are plenty of places to camp along the highway, but if you want a bed for the night, again, your options are Eagle Plains (a good halfway point), Ft. McPherson, and Inuvik itself.

As with traveling on other roads into the bush, you should plan to be self-sufficient during your trip. Carry spares, make sure your tires are in good shape, and figure your windshield stands a good chance of getting cracked by flying gravel. Also pack extra bug repellant. The farther north you go, the nastier they get.

THE LOST PATROL

The Dempster Highway was named for Corporal W. J. Dempster, a man who was in the Lost Patrol. This group of four Mounties headed out in 1910, leaving Ft. McPherson by dog sled, headed for Dawson City. They got caught in bad weather, their guide got lost, and they wandered over about 600 miles of the wrong trails, eating their dogs and boiling their bootlaces to try and stay alive. They finally decided to head back to the Fort. Their remains were later discovered about 40 miles away.

You get on the road by heading south out of Dawson City on the Klondike Highway. The junction is at Mile 301.5 on the Klondike. From here on out, all mile markers noted are the distance from this junction.

Right at the junction is the **Klondike River Lodge,** offering gas, food, lodging, and an RV park. It's your last chance to gas up for quite a ways, so make sure the tank's full. Just past the lodge there's a one-lane bridge over the Klondike.

From Mile 12 you should have good views of the Ogilvie Mountains to the west. The mountains were once heavily glaciated.

There's a highway maintenance camp at Mile 41. The staff will help you out in an emergency, but it will cost. Four miles farther down the road is the **Tombstone Campground**, with 31 sites. There's a nature walk that leads out of the campground. An Interpretive Center here is open from mid-June into early September, and its helpful staff is ready to answer almost any question you can come up with about the region. A shelf of reference books makes for nice browsing, and there are a wide variety of nature displays to help you figure out the things around you.

Hikers should head out the **Tombstone Mountain Trail** for the best views. The mountains here look like they were drawn by a little kid who just found a very sharp box of crayons; even if you don't want to take the entire highway, it's worth coming up this far just to see the mountains.

From Mile 52 to Mile 72, the road travels along the **Blackstone Uplands**. Lots of birds nest here, including Arctic terns, several different falcon species, and the usual loons, ducks, and pipers. If you're around Chapman Lake in mid-October, you should see the Porcupine caribou herd pass through on its migration route, and in the summer, keep an eye out for actual porcupines walking alongside the road; we've seen some the size of large dogs.

The area around Mile 100 includes the breeding grounds for some species of moth and butterfly found nowhere else in the world. It's amazing they can survive this far north; it's also refreshing to know that there's insect life out there not trying to drain your blood.

Engineer Creek Campground is at Mile 120.6. It offers 10 sites. Picnic tables and firewood are available. There's another highway maintenance camp at Mile 121 – again, don't stop here unless you absolutely have to.

The road moves along the Ogilve River, which is rushing toward the Beaufort Sea. At Mile 231 is the small town of **Eagle Plains**; it has one hotel (☎ 867-993-2453) – basic, but comfortable and friendly, $$, and offers gas as well as food.

Just past Eagle Plains, at Mile 234, is a picnic site with an info plaque on the "mad trapper of Rat River."

THE MAD TRAPPER

Albert Johnson, who was hanging out in Ft. McPherson and acting suspicious, was stopped by the Mounties one day in 1931. A few days later, a Mountie headed to Johnson's cabin with a search warrant – and no real idea what he was looking for. Johnson shot him. A posse quickly arrived, surrounding his cabin for three days. They used dynamite to blow off the roof, but Johnson somehow managed to chase them off. Yet another posse was sent out, this one bigger and better armed. By the time they got to Johnson's cabin, he was gone, and for the next month he eluded pursuit, staying out in the open of the Mackenzie River Valley during the dead of winter. He managed to cross the Richardson Mountains, but he was finally caught and shot to death on the Eagle River. To this day, no one is sure what all the fuss was about.

You cross the **Eagle River** at Mile 235, a good place to put in and float toward Alaska via the Porcupine and the Yukon.

THE FRANKLIN EXPEDITION

The Eagle is the main drainage for the Richardson Mountains, which were named after Sir John Richardson, the naturalist on the doomed Franklin Expedition searching for the Northwest Passage. Franklin went out with two ships and 134 men in 1845. He was never heard from again, and the search for his party – spearheaded by his indefatigable wife, Lady Jane Franklin – continued for 30 years. They never did find him, but they managed to map a lot of the Arctic coast in the process. It wasn't until well into this century that the full sad tale of the Franklin Expedition was known – after freezing up in the ice for a couple of years, the men who were left struck out across country. Being British and proper gentlemen, they were badly underdressed – wool ain't the thing to get you through an arctic winter; they were also very weak from eating provisions that had been stored in lead-lined cans. Top all that off with good doses of scurvy, and you know things were pretty bleak. About the last record we have of any of the men is the recollection of some Natives, who recounted to members of George Simpson's 1855 search party, which went overland along the Slave Lake watershed (partly hoping to refute rumors of cannibalism among Franklin party survivors, rumors which had surfaced the year before, after Dr. John Rae, one of the supermen of arctic exploration, reported finding bodies: "From the mutilated state of many of the bodies and the contents of the kettles [Franklin's crew had started across the arctic hardpack dragging tons of equipment on sledges], it is evident that our wretched Countrymen had been driven to the last dread alternative, as a means of sustaining life."

This didn't go down big in London. In fact, it pretty much ruined Rae, who would otherwise have a place alongside Peary and Amundsen in the annals of arctic exploration. Actually, if things were fair, he'd be number one on the hit parade, he covered so much ground.

However, because cannibalism simply wasn't possible among British gentlemen, Rae was destroyed for even suggesting such a thing, and officially, there was still no statement as to the fate of the party. Everyone knew they were dead, but no one wanted to admit it. And so Simpson's expedition went out. They found artifacts of the crew – monogrammed spoons, and such – but no people. Still, they spoke to Natives who claimed to have seen encampments of 10-12 whites, just beyond where Simpson's men turned back.

The rumors weren't enough; although Lady Franklin continued the search for the rest of her life, she died disappointed; although searchers had come within miles of where much of the crew died, and although there were food caches not far from where the final members of the crew starved, no one survived from the Franklin Expedition.

For a great account of this expedition, check out Pierre Berton's *The Arctic Grail.*

You are officially in the Arctic yourself at Mile 250, when the road crosses the Circle, latitude 66 degrees, 33 minutes. There's a big sign and a pullout (you can't miss it), and there are some lovely views, especially to the east. Take a walk on the tundra and check out some of the flowers and other plants. The great thing about tundra is the closer you look, the more appears.

Camp at **Rock River Campground**, Mile 277, if you can stand the bugs.

> **AUTHOR TIP:** *The Yukon-Northwest Territory border is at Mile 292 – don't forget to move your watch ahead an hour.*

Peel River Ferry is at Mile 334. The ferry is free and runs from 9 am to midnight, from mid-June to mid-October. From December to March, you can cross the river on ice. This is where the road closes during the season of ice breakup and ice formation.

At Mile 340 you'll find the **Nitainlii Campground**. There's an interpretive center here, staffed from June to September.

■ Fort McPherson

 The town of Ft. McPherson is at Mile 346. The First Nations name for the spot was *Tetlit Zheh*, meaning house above the river. It's the largest Gwichin (a tribe of the Dene) settlement in the Northwest Territories and home to the head office of the tribal council. The fort was named for Murdoch McPherson, an employee of the Hudson's Bay Company, which moved in and caused endless trouble, as trappers and First Nations people fought for a decade. Much of the town's economy is still a traditional subsistence economy, built on fishing and trapping.

Buy gas here, or stay at the **Tetlit Co-Op** (☎ 867-952-2417). The town also has a community center, with visitor information and crafts for sale; it's open in summer.

The other reason to stop in town is to check out **Fort McPherson Tent and Canvas Company**, ☎ 867-952-2179, which makes beautiful tents, bags, and other canvas items. They're not light, they're not cheap, but they'll last forever. We were 160 km/100 miles above the Arctic circle in a major storm in one of their larger tents – jammed in with a half dozen or so Gwich'in, having a bite or two of Arctic ground squirrel (tastes like dark meat turkey), and no matter how the wind blew, the tent held, and we were warm inside.

Cross the Mackenzie River at Mile 380 on the free ferry. It runs from 9 am to 1 am, the same season as the Peel River Ferry. Again, in winter, this is an ice crossing.

Tsiigehtchic, on the other side of the river, has gas and groceries. The town is another Gwich'in village, maintaining a largely subsistence economy. There is lodging at the **Sunshine Inn** (☎ 867-953-3904), and you can book boat tours at the **Red River Band Store**.

Camp at Mile 430 or Mile 457, or drive the last couple of miles to Inuvik.

Inuvik

A town of 3,000 or so, Inuvik is the largest city in Canada north of the Arctic Circle. It lies on the east channel of the Mackenzie River. If you came looking for a traditional First Nations village, though, you're in for more than a few surprises... Inuvik was largely built between 1955 and 1961, mostly with relocated people from the village of Aklavik. The majority of the population is either Inuit or Dene, and the town itself is perfectly modern, complete with enough traffic to make downtown parking difficult during the summer months.

Situated as it is in the Mackenzie River Delta, there's great birding here in summer, and a huge muskrat population. Hike down to the river, fly north to Banks Island, or do what most people do and simply hang out for a day or two before taking the long drive south.

■ Things to Do

 The **Visitor Information Centre** is on Mackenzie Road, across from the hospital. ☎ 867-777-8618, www.inuvikinfo.com. There's not much to do in Inuvik – getting here is largely the point. However, we always have a good time, just hanging out, walking the trails around the lake, checking out the igloo-shaped Our Lady of Victory Church, or watching the Mackenzie flow by – it's huge and braided here, and can be quite spectacular in late summer, very late at night, when the sun is finally starting to go down.

Let's face it: places at the end of the road have a vibe about them, and there simply aren't all that many spots more end of the road than this one. If you enjoy that particular vibe, you're going to have a good time.

If you get this far and wish you'd done more homework on the area, stop in at **Boreal Books** on Mackenzie Road. It has a great selection of stuff on the Arctic and the local people.

Inuvik is often the site of the **Arctic Northern Game**s (if they're not held in town, they're in one of the nearby villages), which are held in July and feature traditional Inuit and Dene games, dances, and crafts.

In mid-July, Inuvik hosts the **Great Northern Arts Festival**, which brings arctic artists from around the world together. Lots of speeches, dances, blanket tosses (sooner or later, you'll hear the ambulance on that one), and it's a great chance to see what kind of art the far north is producing now. Make lodging reservations in advance, as the town really fills for this. For more, ☎ 867-777-3536, or check out the website at www.gnaf.ca. We've been in town for this, and it's a really, really interesting time to make the run north.

■ Out & About

 There are a couple of operators who can take you out of Inuvik onto the Mackenzie. **Arctic Nature Tours** (☎ 867-777-3300) runs the river and into the Beaufort Sea. Rent canoes from **Western Arctic Adventures** (☎ 867-979-4542); they also run eco-tours. **Aklak Air** (☎ 867-777-3777) charters planes that can get you just about anywhere in the area. They also offer guided fishing trips with remote fly-ins.

■ Food

The hotels have dining rooms, or you can try **Café Gallery** and **Tamarack** Health Foods, both on Mackenzie Road.

■ Accommodations

There are quite a few places to stay in town. Expect to pay $100 to $125. **The Eskimo Inn** (☎ 867-777-2801), the **Finto Motor Inn** (☎ 867-777-2647), and the **Mackenzie Hotel** (☎ 867-777-2861) are the largest places. There are also some B&Bs – check at the Visitor Information Centre for current listings.

HOTEL PRICING

Prices are in US dollars.

under $50. . . . . $
$50-$100 . . . . $$
$100-$150 . . . . . . $$$
above $150. . . . . $$$$

Camp at the **Chuk Park Campground,** just before you hit town.

Once you're done in Inuvik, there's nothing to do but turn around and head back to Dawson City. Gas up before you leave, and check your spares.

Chapter 10

The Glenn Highway: Tok Cutoff to Anchorage

Alaska Route 1, the Glenn Highway, heads southwest out of Tok. The first part of the road, usually called the Tok Cutoff, takes you through willow and birch woods and excellent moose country before it begins skirting the edges of the Wrangell Mountains, offer-

ing stunning landscape views. The second part of the road, from Glennallen to Anchorage, takes you through deep, heavily forested canyons – more prime moose country – and past the Matanuska Glacier, one of the biggest in the state. The road is mostly in great shape, with only a few bumps and frost heaves.

If you couldn't find a place to stay in Tok, the **Eagle Trail State Recreation Site**, at Mile 109.5, has 40 campsites. From the campground you can take a one-mile hike along an old prospecting trail.

> **WILDLIFE WARNING:** There may be more moose on this stretch of road than anywhere else you go. Be especially careful along here – that goes double if you're traveling in something other than a car. We were on a motorcycle on this road when a moose decided we were a threat to her baby and charged us. Luckily, we had better acceleration than she did; otherwise she would have won the confrontation.

Mentasta Summit, 2,434 feet, is at Mile 80. There's a good chance of seeing Dall sheep on the hillsides.

Camp at Mile 64, at **Porcupine Creek**. It has beautiful sites, but you must obey all bear precautions.

The **Wrangell Mountains** soon come into view. There's a pullout at Mile 63 with an explanatory sign. The most conspicuous of the peaks are Mt. Drum (12,010 feet), Mt. Sanford (16,237 feet), and Mt. Wrangell (14,163 feet). On a clear day, the mountains fill the sky – but clear days are few and far between. Like all big mountain ranges, the Wrangells create their own weather patterns, which involve a lot of clouds and rain. In addition, Mt.

Wrangell is an active volcano, the largest in Alaska; a vent near its summit pours out steam on cold days.

Three miles past the viewpoint, at Mile 60, is the junction with the Nabesena Road, which leads 45 miles into **Wrangell-St. Elias National Park**, and back to the old mining town of **Nabesena** (no services). Open only in summer, it's mostly a good gravel road, although there are some unbridged stream crossings past Mile 29. The only reason for taking this road is to get a different access point into the park, but for the most part you're better off on the McCarthy Road. There's a ranger station at Slana, just down the Nabesena Road, which is open 8 am to 5pm daily in summer. They've got maps and books and can give you local trail conditions and bear sightings. Hikers might look into staying a night in Slana, where there is a reasonably cheap hotel and a lot of trails nearby. You can hike up to **Suslota Lake** or **Copper Lake**, with trailheads at Mile 11 and 12.4, respectively. At Mile 25 you pass the watershed divide between the Copper and Yukon rivers, and there are small campgrounds at miles 17.8, 21.8, 27. 8, and 35.3.

Back on the Glenn, you'll have good views of the Copper River and the Wrangell Mountains to the south – particularly Mt. Drum and Mt. Sanford – at Mile 39.

Mile 3 is the village of **Gakona**, a word that means "rabbit" in the local Athabascan dialect. Fish wheels are still in use here. The **Gakona Lodge and Trading Post** has been operating since 1901, and is worth a look. There's also an RV park in town with full hookups.

Mile 0 is the junction of the Tok Cutoff and the Richardson Highway. The roads travel together for 14 miles into the town of Glennallen. Although you've been on the Glenn all this time, the road is renumbered from here, now showing miles from Anchorage. So at Mile 189, you have the option of heading straight on the Richardson and going down to Valdez, or turning right – southwest – for Palmer and Anchorage. (For more on the road into Valdez and Prince William Sound, see *Chapter 11*.)

■ Glennallen

 The town of Glennallen was named after two early explorers in the Copper River Valley: Captain Edward Glenn and Lt. Henry Allen. Allen was a descendant of Reuben Sanford, for whom the highest peak in the Wrangells is named.

Stop in at the **Greater Copper Valley Visitors Center**, on the east side of the highway. It's open daily in summer, 8 am to 7 pm. Glennallen is the best place to buy gas and groceries if you're headed into the Wrangells. While everything is more expensive here than it was in Tok or will be in Anchorage, Glennallen is the only town of size in the area.

The **Caribou Café**, next to the hotel, has breakfast, burgers, and sandwiches for $5 to $12.

If you want to stay in town, the **Tolsona Wilderness Campground**, at Mile 173, has tent sites or hookups. The sites are nicely treed and by a creek. You can also camp at the **Dry Creek Campground**, at Mile 190, which has 58 sites and a healthy mosquito population.

There are also a couple of hotels in town: the **Caribou Hotel** (☎ 907-822-3302, 800-478-3302, www.caribouhotel.com), $$$.

There's a big **Fourth of July** bash here, and the area is a fisherman's paradise – about 40 lakes in the area are stocked with rainbow trout, grayling, lake trout, whitefish, burbot, and more. Get the flyer at the information center telling what's stocked where, pick a lake, and go to it.

If you want to go to McCarthy/Kennicott, there is a **shuttle service** from Glennallen, where they beat up their car instead of you yours. ☎ 907-822-5292.

Leaving Glennallen, if the weather is clear, check the rearview: you can get marvelous views of the massifs over in Wrangell/St. Elias.

Mile 160 is the junction with the Lake Louise Road, which leads 19 miles north off the Glennallen. There's **camping** 17 miles back on the road – lovely sites – and there are two lodges on the lake. At the **Point Lodge** (☎ 907-822-5566, www.thepointlodge.com), $$$; for a few bucks more, you get a room, bike, and canoe to use during your stay, plus dinner and breakfast. **Lake Louise Lodge** (☎ 907-822-3311 or 877-878-3311, www. lakelouiselodge.com) can rent you boats to get out on the lake, where the record catch for a lake trout is 41 pounds.

Mile 129 is the **Eureka Summit**, the highest point on the highway, at 3,322 feet. Descending, you move into moose country and the territory of the Nelchina herd of caribou. To the south you'll see the Chugach Mountains and the Nelchina Glacier, and to the northwest the Talkeetna Mountains. The summit ridge is also the dividing point of the Susitna, Matanuska, and Copper river systems.

The road gets worse from here to Palmer, with more frost heaves, and is winding and mostly shoulderless. It's also really, really pretty.

■ Matanuska Glacier

 The Matanuska Glacier comes into view at Mile 113. The Matanuska is but a finger – albeit a large one – of the **Chugach Icefields**, which cover 8,300 square miles, an area nearly the size of New Hampshire. There are several pullouts for viewing the glacier and the icefields, which disappear over the tops of the mountains, which include Mt. Marcus Baker (13,176 feet) and Mt. Witherspoon (12,012 feet). There's even a **campground** down near the glacier's path where you can enjoy the view all night long. Hike down close to the ice to see the deep shades of blue. Glacier ice is so thick that the other colors of the spectrum are absorbed by the ice, leaving only a dazzling blue. Matanuska is 27 miles long, and once reached all the way to Palmer. The terminus is four miles across at its widest point and averages two miles. When we wrote the first edition of this book, we wrote that "The glacier has pretty much sat here for the past 400 years, neither advancing nor retreating much." But now, more than a dozen years later, it looks like half the thing is gone.

Between Miles 112 and 108 is the range of a herd of mountain sheep. If the road isn't twisting too much, take a look up above you on the slopes.

The **Long Rifle Lodge**, ☎ 907-745-5151, www.longriflelodge.com, is at Mile 102.4. It offers food – great baked stuff – and lodging. The road down to the glacier is at Mile 102. Camp at Mile 101, **Matanuska Glacier State Recreation Site**. It offers a dozen sites, grand glacier views, and easy hiking trails.

On the road, you climb into the Talkeetna Mountains and then begin a long descent into the Ma-Su Valley and the town of Palmer.

Camp at Mile 85.5 or 83.2 – both campgrounds are on small lakes. More camping is available at **King Mountain**, at Mile 76. At Mile 61 you go through the town of Sutton, which was once a coal mining town, and by Mile 55, you're on the outskirts of Palmer, in rich farming land.

One of the best things to do in Alaska is at Mile 50.1, the **Palmer Musk Ox Farm** (☎ 907-745-4151, www.muskoxfarm.org). It's the only place in the world where musk oxen are raised domestically, and its foundation was in no small part responsible for the musk ox coming back from the verge of extinction.

The origin of this herd goes to Greenland; a bunch of musk oxen were taken from there to the Alaskan island of Nunivak, in the Bering Sea. In 1964, the Nunivak herd was fairly well established, so an expedition, sponsored by the University of Alaska and the Institute of Northern Agricultural Research, was sent out to round a few of the animals up. This was all under the charge of John Teal, whom Peter Matthiessen, in his book about the expedition, *Oomingmak*, calls "friend of the musk ox."

Capturing a musk ox is not an easy thing. Matthiessen writes that they first tried using an airplane to round the animals up, but that "Musk ox will not only stand and face a diving airplane, but the bull may actually leap upward like a giant goat, trying to gore it." Their final solution was to drive a few animals into the water – they can swim, but they don't really like to – and then lasso calves as they separated from their mothers. This actually depressed the entire expedition, as there were a couple of inadvertent drownings. "The cow's tongue was white with running and her chest heaved... The tired cow was mean as slag; she made several rushes, hooking and snorting. She would not be forced back toward the lagoon, despite hurled sods and stones and imprecations, but fixed angry red eyes at every man in turn. Once in a while, the head of the calf would poke out from behind her flank and stare at us, reproachful. The calf looked surprised, as if to say, 'Have you gone mad? What do you want with us?'"

There are accounts of musk oxen, which have very strong heads, butting vehicles and coming out the winner. Musk oxen do not attack unless attacked – hence their famous line formation – but when they do decide to charge, as John Teal summed it up best: "Once a musk ox decides to go for you... you've had it."

After a stop over for a few years in Fairbanks, the herd was eventually relocated to Palmer, where it formed the basis of those raised by the Oomingmak cooperative.

These musk ox are raised for their qiviut, the softest fabric imaginable. The wool is combed from the animal, in a process that takes from one to three hours, depending on the animal's mood. One combing gets about six pounds of qiviut, enough to keep the Native weavers of the co-op busy for some time. Unlike the musk ox farm in Fairbanks, where you see the animals from quite a distance, here they are only inches away. And despite their serious demeanor, you may get a chance to see them playing rugby or keep-away. Tours are $8.50 for adults; children under age six free. You can take a tour, then stay in the yard area as long as you want. Don't miss this look at the last vestige of the ice age. The farm is open 10 to 6 daily in the summer, with tours every 30 minutes.

SOFTER THAN SOFT

Clothing made from qiviut makes cashmere feel like steel wool. It's eight times warmer than sheep's wool, has a greater tensile strength, and is a startlingly beautiful shade of brown. Figure on about $200 for a basic scarf, a bit over $300 for one of the heavier duty ones. Worth every penny.

The Hatcher Pass Road is at Mile 49.5. Hatcher Pass includes **Independence Mine State Historical Park**, **Summit Lake Recreation Park**, and a fair chunk of **Little Susitna River**, where there's great kayaking. The area is laced with hiking and biking trails, and in winter it's a perfect place for cross-country skiing. Used more by locals than tourists – visitors are more likely to head farther south into the Chugach – it's a pretty spot if you're staying in the Palmer area.

To reach **Independence Mine**, take the road back 17.5 miles, then follow the mine road, which is another eight miles of gravel. The mine was run by the Alaska-Pacific Mining Company in the 1930s. Before it closed in 1955, more than 34,000 ounces of gold were taken out. It's $2 per vehicle to get into the site, another $3 per person if you want a guided tour. The road to the mine is open only in summer, 11 am to 7 pm.

Palmer

Palmer is only 40 miles northeast of Anchorage and, while it serves as a bedroom community for the big city, Palmer has a charm all its own. As a visit to the musk ox farm will show, Palmer is home to some of the more unusual ranches found anywhere.

■ History

Palmer is considered the center of the Matanuska and Susitna valleys (called the Mat-Su). The town was established as a depot for the Alaska Railroad; then FDR, as part of the New Deal, sent a bunch of farmers up from the Midwest. Once they got over the shock, the farmers discovered they could grow just about anything – and that it would grow very, very big – in the rich soil and long days of summer. Sixty-pound cabbages were common.

Still, before the crops came in, the first year was rough. The settlers lived in tents while they built their houses, and to celebrate getting through the rough times, they held a big festival, which, over the years, mutated into the Alaska State Fair.

■ Things to Do

If you drive out the Springs Road system, or the Farm and Bodenburg Loop Road, or Fishook Road, you can see some of the original buildings these settlers erected. There are more at the **Colony Village** (free admission) at the fairgrounds, open Monday through Saturday, 10 am to 4 pm. For a different kind of historical building, take a look at the Church of 1,000 Trees, at 707 S. Denali, which was built in 1937 by local parishioners. It's a masterpiece of local material building.

The **Palmer Visitors Center and Museum**, across the railroad tracks on South Valley Rd., is open 8 to 7 daily in the summer, 9 to 4 weekdays in the winter.

■ Out & About

In addition to the great Musk Ox Farm, a visit to Palmer offers a chance to see other unusual animals. The Bodenburg Loop Road features a **reindeer farm**. Open from June to September 1, 10 am to 6 pm, the reindeer farm is a family-run operation that lets you get close enough to pet and feed one of Santa's favorites. **Wolf Country USA**, on the Glenn Highway at Mile 52, breeds and sells hybrid wolf pups. Tours of the kennels are available. In the gift shop you'll find a one-of-a-kind item: yarn made from wolf hair.

If you're in Palmer just before Labor Day, go to the **Alaska State Fair**, which features over 500 events and 20,000 flowers. **Colony Day**, the third weekend in June, has events that memorialize the first settlers.

There are endless hiking trails around Palmer. The 1.5-mile **Matanuska-Susitna Community College Nature Trail** is an easy hike. For more of a challenge, try the series of trails in **Matanuska River Park**, .4 miles east of Gulkana St.. The **Lazy Mountain Trail**, with the trailhead off Huntley Road, is a two-mile climb with great views at the top. Figure on four hours for the round-trip, more if you want to stop and enjoy the subalpine tundra. The **Crevasse Moraine Trail System**, which you can get to from Mile 1.98 on the Palmer-Wasilla Highway, has 13 connecting loops, for a total of 6.7 miles. Any individual trail is short and easy, and all give a good look at glacial deposits, including eskers, kames, and a few kettles.

Leaving Palmer, you can either head south to Anchorage on the Old Glenn Highway (cutoff at Mile 42.1; the road rejoins the new highway at Mile 29.5), or keep heading south on the New Glenn Highway. The turnoff for the Palmer-Wasilla Highway, a 10-mile shortcut to Wasilla, is at Mile 41.8.

The junction with the Parks Highway is at Mile 35.3. Turn north for Fairbanks and Denali.

The exit to **Eklutna** is at Mile 26. Eklutna is an Athabascan settlement dating back to about 1650. In the 1830s, most of the villagers were converted by missionaries to the Russian Orthodox Church, and right off the road is the heavily photographed chapel. Thirty-minute tours are given from 8 am to 6 pm in summer. This is actually a very cool thing, very much worth the time. Not only do you see one of the oldest functioning religious sites in Alaska, you also get a look at the beautiful Athabascan spirit houses, which are sort of graves, sort of not graves, and are a fascinating look at how old traditions can blend with new ideas. Another attraction in town is the **traditional chief's house**, on the right side of Village Road.

In 1924, the **Eklutna Industrial school** was built in town, run by the BIA. It drew about 100 students, from all over the state. At the school, they were taught "industrial arts" – including ivory carving. School breaks were timed to coincide with fishing seasons.

Eklutna Village Historical Park is open 10 to 6 daily. The $6 admission gets you in to see the church, the spirit houses, and to hear how the Tanaina – a subtribe of the Athabascans – lived traditionally.

Taking Eklutna Road to the east will take you to the **Eklutna Lake Recreation Area**, in Chugach State Park. Eklutna is the largest lake in the park, and there are good mountain bike trails all around it.

At Mile 13.5 is the Eagle River Road exit, which offers access to the Chugiak and Eagle rivers. The **North Anchorage Visitors Center** and **Southcentral Alaska Museum of Natural History** are nearby – after you get off the highway, turn north. Admission to the museum is $3; it has good displays of wildlife, flora, fauna, and dinosaurs.

Glenn Highway

Chugach State Park

The real reason to get off the highway here is to take the Eagle River Road 13 miles out to the Chugach State Park and Eagle River Nature Center. It's open daily 10 am to 7 pm in summer and is the place to load up on hiking, biking, and boating information for the Chugach. There are interpretive displays and guided nature walks, as well as some self-guided hiking trails nearby. One of the best is the **Rodak Nature Trail**, a quick 15-minute walk that takes you past a salmon stream. For something a little longer, the **Albert Loop Trail** leaves from the center and takes you on a three-mile course along the Eagle River.

Also from the center, you can get on the trail of the Iditarod at the Crow Pass Trail. The **Iditarod Trail** starts in Seward and goes to Nome (the dogs run from outside Anchorage to Nome). Most of it is a winter-only trail, but the Crow Pass section (26 miles, with lots of easy places to break the hike into shorter bits), is quite hikeable and entirely authentic. Along the way, you'll see mining ruins, glacier views, and lots of wildlife. This is one of the better hikes around.

Chugach State Park is the natural playground for the entire Anchorage area – from here clear down to Girdwood. When Anchorageites want to get out and see what Alaska really looks like, this is where they come. There are countless hiking trails in the park (more listed in Chapter 15), enough lakes to ensure you can get one to yourself, lots of wildlife, and perfect places for a day's escape from town. Because you're on the outskirts of Anchorage, it also means that things can get pretty crowded during the weekends.

Fees for the park are fairly steep. It's $5 for day use, $10 to $15 for most of the camping sites, and (depending on where you are) there may well be a boat launch fee.

From the section of Chugach between Anchorage and Eklutna, some of the best hiking is on the **Eklutna Lakeside Trail**, a 12.7-mile one-way trek to Eklutna Glacier. You walk along the lakeside for seven miles, and most of the rest of the trail is on an abandoned roadbed. It's long, but easy, and offers a good chance to see mountain goats along the way. Branching off this trail is the **Bold Ridge Trail**, 3.5 miles one way, that takes you straight up to the ridgeline for lake views. The trailhead is off the Eklutna Lake Campground – take the Eklutna exit and head toward the mountains, following the signs. Camp at the lake. There's another trailhead here, the 3.2-mile **Twin Peaks Trail**, a steep scramble up above the tree line with great lake views from the top.

Off the Glenn Highway, Mile 21, there's the **Peters Creek Trail**, five miles long and open to bikes. There's another 11 miles of trail, unmarked and unmaintained, at the end of the bike road, which heads up to the tree line and the tundra.

Chapter 11

The Richardson Highway to Valdez

With Side Trips on the Denali & Edgerton Highways, & the McCarthy Road

From Delta Junction, you can keep on to Fairbanks – the actual end of the Richardson Highway – or head south to the beautiful coastal town of Valdez (for those heading west, if you're looking for a straighter shot to Valdez, head due south from Tok – don't bother to come this far).

Leaving Delta Junction on the Richardson, watch for bison, part of the herd that was transplanted here in 1928. Most of the scenery from here to the Tok Cutoff is low rolling hills, with views toward the big mountains – the Wrangells to the east, the Alaskas to the west. Once you get past the cutoff, the territory gets a little wilder.

The Donnelly Dome turnoff is at Mile 246 (see the Delta Junction section for hiking details). You'll see the pipeline at Mile 245, and you can camp at Mile 238: **Donnelly Creek** has 12 sites.

At Mile 185.5 is the junction with the Denali Highway. Before the George Parks Highway was put in, linking Fairbanks and Anchorage with Denali, this was the only way to get to the park.

The Denali Highway

In the old days, the George Parks Highway wasn't the way to get to Denali. The Richardson was the only north-south highway, and to reach the park, travelers took the Richardson to the Denali Highway. The road is now largely overlooked. If you want a very scenic side route not used by many people, this is a good choice.

The Denali Highway is open only in summer – snow closes the road from October to mid-May. The road is all gravel, except for paving on the first 20 miles to Paxson. There is a paving project in the works, but don't expect it to be finished any time soon.

Richardson Highway

HIGHWAY TIP: The road quality varies greatly, depending on how the weather has been – anything from somewhat rough with a few washboards to seriously potholed. If the weather's been dry, it's going to be dusty.

The road is mostly used by paddlers and hikers who want to get into the Delta River system, but if you're looking for a scenic drive with great chances to see animals, this is the place to come. There are important **archaeological sites** around Tangle Lakes, and the **Nelchina caribou herd** uses this area on their migration route. The herd numbers about 50,000 animals, and when they pass through in fall, with the tundra a hundred shades of red, gold, and orange, it's something to see. Along the road there are great glacial features, from kettle lakes to moraines. While fishing stinks in Denali, there are some non-glacial streams here that make angling for grayling and trout worth a try. In winter, when the road is closed, this is a paradise for cross-country skiers.

If you take the road, buy gas before you head out. There's nothing between Paxson and Cantwell – at Mile 210 on the George Parks Highway, near the Denali Park entrance – except scenery.

After you leave Paxson, from Mile 13.3, you should get good views of the Wrangell Mountains to the southeast. Mt. Sanford (16,237 feet) is the big one on the left. Mt. Wrangell itself (14,163 feet) is the one in the middle.

Tangle Lakes Archaeological District is at Mile 16. More than 500 sites have been found here, some of which show inhabitants using the area more than 10,000 years ago. You can look around, although you can't take your car off the roads and it is illegal to collect artifacts.

Camp at **Tangle Lakes Campground**, at Mile 21.5. The Tangle Lakes are a series of lakes connected by rivers into a long, narrow system leading mostly north and south. It's part of the **Delta National Wild and Scenic River,** and you can do a seriously nice float trip – you'll have a half-mile portage around a couple of waterfalls – from the campground. If you have more time, you can do a seven-day trip from here down to the take out at the **Sourdough Creek Campground** on the Richardson Highway (Mile 147). You'll hit some Class IV water, so be prepared. (See the Gulkana River section on the Richardson – right where we pick back up on that highway – for details.) There's a boat launch at Mile 21.7, where you can get started.

There are a couple of good hiking trails around the campground. Closest is the **Landmark Gap Trail**, which is actually two trails – one heading north, the other south. The south trailhead is at Mile 24.7. It takes you 11 miles down to Osar Lake, and it's not a good option if there has been a lot of rain. The north trail, with the trailhead at Mile 24.6, is only four miles up to Landmark Gap Lake. The trail can be mountain-biked, but there are some wet areas.

Just past Tangle Lakes, at Mile 22.4, is **The Gap**, a pass carved by glaciers and used by caribou on migration.

By Mile 36, you're in the foothills of the Alaska Range, at about 4,000 feet. Maclaren Summit is the second highest road summit in Alaska. From here you have great views of Mt. Hayes and the Maclaren Glacier.

If you didn't take the Landmark Gap South Trail to Osar Lake, there's another trail at Mile 37 that will get you there. It's an eight-mile hike along glacial eskers that you can do on bike or on foot. From the same spot is a quick hike to the Maclaren Summit. The climb isn't too steep, and you'll get great views, particularly of the Maclaren River.

The **Sevenmile Lake Trail**, a six-mile trail up to Sevenmile Lake, starts at Mile 40. The trail leads from the highway along a fairly flat landscape, turning in between 6,000-foot mountains about three-quarters of the way along. After the first mile and a half – a marshy area – you can bike it, but you will have to carry the bike for that first stretch.

There are pingos at Mile 40.8 – the one you see here is actually a partially collapsed pingo.

Your best views of **Maclaren Glacier** are at the viewpoint at Mile 42. You can mountain-bike south on Maclaren River Road. Head south for a great ride. It's 13 miles to the glacier, and you will have to ford the west fork of the Maclaren River.

The next few miles serve up a variety of natural features. **Crazy Notch**, at Mile 46, was cut through a glacial moraine by a stream. **Eskers**, at Mile 59, consist of a ridge of sand, silt, gravel, and rocks that were deposited by a stream flowing inside a glacier. The gunk was contained by the ice walls, and when the glacier melted away, these deposits were left behind.

You'll cross the Susitna River at Mile 79.5. The river is considered unrunnable from here because of Devil's Canyon, downstream.

You can camp at one of 18 sites by the **Brushkana River**, at Mile 104.

You cross the Nenana at Mile 116. The **Nenana River**, which you'll see a lot of if you head to Fairbanks, takes water from the Nenana Glacier. The Nenana meets up with the Tanana, which eventually flows into the Yukon. You can do the whole thing in a river kayak.

If the mountain – Denali – is out, you should be able to see it from Mile 130. 1, where there's a turnout for photographers.

The town of **Cantwell** is just three miles off the junction. It's an Alaska Railroad flag stop – stand by the tracks and you can wave the train down. If you're heading east, figure Cantwell as your last chance to buy gas before Paxson.

Richardson Highway

The Richardson Highway

At Mile 175 is **Paxson Lake Campground**. It's about 1.5 miles off the road, and has 50 sites. The campground is the main launch site for floating the **Gulkana River**, a National Wild River. It's about four days to the take-out at the Sourdough Creek Campground, Mile 147.5. Along the way there's a stretch of Class IV at Canyon Rapids, and about eight miles of Class II and III. You can portage around the worst of it. Bring your own firewood and camp only in established sites.

The Gulkana River Valley was inhabited by Ahtna Athabascans roughly 1,000 years ago. They hunted the huge caribou herds, splitting animals off from the herd, driving them to the lake, and then spearing them from boats.

At Mile 115 is the junction with the Glenn Highway, at the town of Glennallen (see the Glenn Highway section for details). The two highways run together until Mile 129, if you're headed north.

If you're headed south, from here to Valdez, the Richardson Highway drops down through the Chugach Mountains from Glennallen; this means long, steep descents and ascents, as well as a lot of twists and turns. It also means you're on one of the most beautiful roads in the entire North. Put some George Gershwin on the tapedeck, and get ready to be blown away.

The road is in excellent shape and is fairly heavily traveled, as it skirts the edges of Wrangell-Saint Elias National Park and Preserve. Fishing is excellent all along the road south, and there are many nice campgrounds.

At Mile 105.5 you come to the headquarters of **Wrangell-St. Elias National Park**. When combined with the abutting Glacier Bay, as well as **Kluane National Park** in Canada and a few more nature spot, this is the largest protected wilderness area in the world. It also forms part of a World Heritage Site, as designated by the UN, when combined with Kluane, Tatshenshini-Alsek, and Glacier Bay.

Nine of the 16 highest mountains in North America are in Wrangell-St. Elias, including Mt. Wrangell, a volcano that last erupted in 1900. You can still see it smoke from time to time. There's also Mt. St. Elias, which, at 18,000 feet, is the second highest mountain in the US. All told, there are four mountain ranges in the park: the Wrangells, the St. Elias, the Chugach, and the tail end of the Alaska Range, which is usually shown on maps as the Nutzotin and the Mentasta Mountains. This gives the park nine peaks over 14,000 feet, and 14 over 10,000. There are so many mountains in the park, and the park is so remote, that there are mountains bigger than anything you've got back home, but here they don't even have a name.

Also inside the park is the **Bagley Icefield**, the largest subpolar icefield on the continent; just one of its glaciers, the Malaspina, is bigger than the state of Rhode Island (yeah, once again, everything up here is bigger than

Rhode Island). So much soil has been deposited on parts of the icefield that there are actually forests growing on it.

No backcountry permits are needed to go into the park, but if you're heading into the wild, check in at the ranger station. (It's actually easier to get into the backcountry from Chitina or McCarthy, though; you're closer to the deep wild.)

You can camp anywhere in the park, as long as you can walk there or fly in, but be aware that there are a few inholds and some private property inside the park boundaries. Anywhere in the park – and this includes in McCarthy and Kennicott – be ready for bears. And if you're bushwalking, remember that the rivers are cold, nasty, and faster than you think. Having swum a few, we can tell you that losing your footing when crossing is something best avoided, so you'd better know what you're doing.

There are also nine public-use cabins inside the park. These are not yet hooked up to the statewide cabin reservation service; it's strictly a first-come, first-served basis. You can check at the ranger station to see if any are open, and then look at booking a charter flight in. The cabins are small – the biggest is only 20 x 24 feet – but probably you will never again have a chance to get this far into the wilderness. Bring your own bedding, fuel, and bear protection.

Park headquarters are open daily 8 to 6 in summer, weekdays 8 to 5 in winter. They've got some good video programs and some very useful maps. They've also got a nice map of state campgrounds, for only a quarter.

■ Copper Center

The town of Copper Center is just off the road at Mile 106. The road to the town loops around and puts you back on the Richardson at Mile 101. Copper Center is an historic town, dating back to 1898, once rich from the massive amounts of ore taken from the Wrangell Mountains. It was a stopping point for miners headed north from Valdez; they got here, the ones that survived the trip over the Valdez Glacier Trail, and pretty much collapsed from exhaustion.

Today, Copper Center is a sleepy little village of about 500 people that makes for an interesting side-trip. Stop in at the **Copper Center Lodge** (☎ 907-822-3245), $$, an original structure dating from the town's foundation. It used to be the Blix Roadhouse, the first roadhouse in the interior to have electricity and indoor plumbing. The restaurant inside serves excellent breakfasts – their sourdough starter is said to be over 100 years old – and don't miss taking a look at the one of a kind diamond willow staircase. Next door is the newly expanded **George I. Ashby Memorial Museum**. It has displays on the history of the area, with an emphasis on mining. You can also see what they claim is the record moose rack ever taken in Alaska – nearly six feet across.

Chapel on the Hill.

Heading back out, you pass the **Chapel on the Hill**, which dates from 1942. Admission is free. When the chapel was built, supplies were short and pews had to be made from packing crates. There's a worthwhile slide show inside that has a nice program on Copper River Basin history, and best of all, it's free.

Back on the Richardson, you hit the cutoff for the Edgerton at Mile 91. The actual junction with the Edgerton isn't until Mile 83 – this is a seven-mile shortcut over a gravel road.

At Mile 89 is a pullout with an interpretive display of the Wrangell Mountains – the peaks you see to the northeast. **Willow Lake**, at Mile 88, offers excellent views of the Wrangells – although from here, the highest, Mt. Wrangell, looks to be one of the lowest – and a viewpoint for the **Trans-Alaska Pipeline**, with an interpretive plaque. The pipeline goes in and out of view, all the way down to its terminus in Valdez; another pipeline viewpoint is at Mile 64.

The Edgerton Highway & McCarthy Road

Just past the first pipeline viewpoint is the turnoff for the Edgerton Highway. If you've got a sturdy vehicle, this trip can't be missed. The road goes straight into Wrangell-St. Elias Park, 33 miles to the town of **Chitina**. From there, you can go another 60 miles to McCarthy and the ruins of the **Kennecott Copper Mines**.

The road to Chitina is paved and smooth. The road from there to the Kennecott mines – the McCarthy road – is something of a nightmare. Every year we see people in low-slung cars stuck and not knowing what to do; every year, people try to take RVs down the road and discover that they have made a very big mistake. The park service says that "under normal summer conditions most two-wheel drive vehicles can make the trip." True – there are tour buses on the road now – but there is the question of how much you want to beat up your car. If you don't have a good car with decent clearance – and if it's been raining, four-wheel-drive – don't go past Chitina.

If you're driving in yourself, you can camp at **Liberty Falls**, at Mile 24. With only five sites, no hookups, no water, and lots of wind, it still beats the alternative campground in Chitina. If you camp anywhere near Chitina, keep in mind that the local peat is highly combustible – fires get out of hand easily here. It's also bear country, so obey all the usual precautions.

■ Chitina

Chitina (pronounced CHIT-na) was founded as a railroad town in 1910, to take ore from the Kennecott mines down to Cordova. Passengers could arrive in Cordova by ship, take the train to Chitina, and then go by sledge, sleigh, or cart to Fairbanks or other points north. The railroad is long gone (although a truly ambitious hiker can follow its old path down to the coast at Cordova; plan on at least two weeks, and go very well prepared, or tell people back home where to start looking for your body), but Chitina retains much of its old flavor. It's kind of a weatherworn town, with some nicely restored buildings. It's one of the few places where you'll see dip-netting, a now mostly illegal means of fishing for salmon: large nets on aluminum poles scoop the fish right out of the river. There are also some fish wheels working around town.

Eat at the Chitna Cafe, where you can get filled up for $5 to $10. There's a combination gas/grocery store in town; stock up on both here if you're heading out to McCarthy. If you've blown a tire, your last chance for repair is here.

After taking a look around town, stop at the **National Park Service cabin.** The cabin is located at the beginning of the McCarthy road, right past the pond with the old truck half sunk in it. (Yes, that is how directions are given around here.) The ranger station has slide shows, and you can ask about the road to McCarthy before you set out. The station is open daily in summer. There's a **campground** nearby, but it's prone to avalanches and buried campers, so we can't really recommend it.

The McCarthy road is about 60 miles of twisting, bumpy, unpaved track in miserable condition through spectacular scenery. At its end, you are rewarded with a look at McCarthy and a chance to wander the ruins of the Kennecott Mines. These were once the richest copper mines in the world, now abandoned and slowly rotting away as movements to have the site declared historic falter.

> **MINE HAZARDS:** Use great caution, and don't go into the area alone. The mines may be abandoned, but they are not entirely safe. Numerous hazards lurk.

Going out to Kennecott should take a full day. Two days are better if you really want to explore.

Richardson Highway

HIGHWAY TIP: Right from the beginning, the road to Mc-Carthy is bumpy, rough, and rocky. It's heavily wash-boarded, and there are deep holes ready to swallow your car, as well as huge rocks just waiting to rip out your oil pan. Don't take this road at more than 20 mph, and don't let your attention wander. The nearest oil pan for whatever car you're driving is a long way off. There are small pylons to mark particularly hazardous bumps along the way.

There's a private **campground** at Mile 11, and at Mile 17 is the **Kuskulana Bridge**, a single lane spanning 525 feet – about 385 feet of that over the river. Though everybody does it, this is not a good bridge to stop on. There's a gravel pullout on the far side. You can park there and walk back to take pictures of the river.

At Mile 28 is another one-lane bridge, this one over the Gilahina River. There's an old railroad trestle to the north, part of the long-abandoned Copper River Northwestern, which closed in the 1930s. Climb the hill on the east side of the river for the best views. Along the road, you'll hear people tell you to look out for railroad spikes – you will likely see some ties along the way – but the spikes have long been harvested and taken to the souvenir stores. There may be one or two still in the roadbed, but the odds of finding one are against you.

If the road is dry, you'll probably be choking on dust by now. If it's raining, you'll probably be wondering what the hell you're doing out here and looking desperately for a place to turn around.

At Mile 57.3 there's an overlook pullout with views of McCarthy and the Kennicott Glacier. The road ends at Mile 61, at the river; the town and the mines are on the other side. Park here – if you can't find one of the few free spots, you end up paying $5 to leave your car, $10 if you want to camp – and head across the footbridge, a bridge that has the locals seriously pissed off. They're mad that the Park Service has come in and interfered in their town. Before the bridge, you had to get across the river on a handtram, which worked fine for decades. You've probably already seen film of the handtram – it's a staple of any Alaska documentary. The problem with it (as far as tourists were concerned) was that it only took two people across at a time; some days, you'd be waiting upwards of an hour just to get across the river. From the town's point of view, of course, this helped prevent them from getting overrun.

Most people expect the government-contracted footbridge to go at the first decent flood on the river, anyway. But the loss of the handtram is a loss of part of the town's identity, and a true Alaskan classic.

McCarthy is in the middle of the Wrangell-St. Elias National Park, but it is private property. The tussles between inholders and government will probably never end.

Once you're across the river, you can head into town (about a mile) by taking the right fork, or to the mines (about 4.5 miles) by taking the left fork. There's a free shuttle to town; for $8, they'll take you to the mine. If you've got a bit of patience, you can also probably hitch, and if you've got a mountain bike, it's a great ride back.

■ McCarthy

 The town of McCarthy is a nice, self-contained place. Check out the **McCarthy-Kennecott Museum** in the old railroad depot for historical displays.

The Kennecott Mines got their start in 1900, when a couple of miners looking for gold found copper instead. In 1901, Stephen Birch was sent to the area to see how much copper was there, and what it would take to get it out. His report caught the eye of some rich bigwigs – the Guggenheim family and J. P. Morgan – and the Kennecott Copper Corporation was formed.

The first problem was that the rich guys didn't know how to spell. It's the Kennicott River and the Kennicott Glacier, both named after Robert Kennicott, an early explorer who'd traveled through here. But if you've got more money than anybody else, those around you are usually afraid to point out your errors. And so it's the *Kennecott* Mines on the *Kennicott* River.

After they decided it wasn't worth changing the letterhead (although today you'll see it spelled both ways by the less detail oriented) to be correct, the second problem they encountered was how to get the copper out. In the spring of 1908, construction began on the Copper River Northwestern Railway. The railway started in Cordova and stretched 196 miles to the mines here. Over the years, it hauled out more than $200 million in copper ore.

The company town of Kennicott (they were spelling it right again) sprang up, boasting a hospital, a grade school, a dentist's office, and even a dairy. Being a company town, it was subject to company rules – which were very strict and proper – so it lacked the usual boomtown amenities, like bars and a red-light district. And so the town of McCarthy sprang up, to fill the gap. At the peak of mine operations, more than 800 people lived in the two towns.

The mines closed in 1938. The railway, with nowhere to go, shut down at the same time. The railway line was donated to the federal government in 1941, in case the government wanted to build a road along the right of way. The government didn't, and the area ended up protected in the park; more recently, there has been considerable controversy over this right of way. Ex-governor Walter Hickel (a man who never met a patch of concrete he didn't like) decided that there should be a road through here, and damn the wilderness. Wally's road, of dubious legality, was started; but, before too much damage could be done, Hickel was voted out of office.

It's the classic battle in Alaska between pro- and anti-development forces. Hickel was classically pro, although he had served as Nixon's Secretary of the Interior in the early 1970s. When he became governor of Alaska in the '80s, he actually received fewer votes – it was a split ticket – than the initiative to legalize marijuana. There's a story that says a man who lived near the governor's mansion painted the front of his house with huge letters: "Pot got more votes than you, Wally." Hickel never stood a chance for a second term.

You can wander around the mine buildings yourself, or take one of the guided tours from town. **Wilderness Guides** (☎ 800-664-4537, www. kennicottguides.com) has a 90-minute tour for $12.50. There are also longer tours, lasting two to three hours, for $25. **St. Elias Alpine Guides** (☎ 907-554-4444, www.steliasguides.com) has a deal that's pretty much the same. There's a walking guide to the area available at the museum for a buck. If you're on your own, stay out of the buildings. Many of them are private property, and many more of them are condemned and unsafe.

Out & About

Since the town is so deep in Wrangell-St. Elias, it's a good jumping-off place for the backcountry. Wilderness Guides offers trips ranging from the quickie mentioned above to four-hour glacier hikes, to a three-day trip to the Stairway Icefall. They also feature some women-only programs, and they arrange fly-ins and drop-offs. They've been here forever and are a good choice. St. Elias Alpine Guides also has multi-day bush trips and trips on the river. Seven days on the Copper run about $2,500. Either one of these companies can get you anywhere you're likely to want to go in the parks. Both of these are good outfitters.

If you head out onto the waters by yourself, keep in mind that the rivers change rapidly here; rain a considerable distance away can affect where you are. Be prepared.

Wrangell Mountain Air (☎ 800-478-1160 or 554-4411) and **McCarthy Air** (☎ 907-554-4440) have flightseeing trips that will take you up for good looks at the glaciers, the mountains, the park, and the mines. Wrangell Mountain also does fly-in hiking trips, glacier trekking, and they can get you out on the rivers.

Food & Accommodations

Food choices are pretty limited, and your best bet, if for some reason a picnic isn't appealing, is probably the **Kennicott Glacier Lodge**. That's also the town's swank address, which doesn't necessarily mean you won't have to share a bathroom. (☎ 907-258-2350, 800-582-5128, www.kennicottlodge. com), $$$$. Other choices include the **McCarthy Lodge** (☎ 907-554-4402, www.mccarthylodge.com), and **Ma Johnson's Hotel**, run by the same people.

Camping in town is difficult; it's all private land. There is a small **National Park campground** back across the bridge and up the road a mile, or you'll see signs around town with people letting you pitch a tent on their land for $5 or $10.

> **AUTHOR NOTE:** *McCarthy/Kennecott has no garbage dump; whatever you take in, take out.*

As mentioned above, if you want to see McCarthy and the mines, but don't want to drive yourself, from Glennallen you can catch the McCarthy Day Shuttle. It's $109 if you do the round-trip in one day, an extra ten bucks if you come back a different day. Contact **Backcountry Connection** at ☎ 907-822-5292, www.alaska-backcountry-tours.com.

The road to McCarthy is one of the meanest in the state of Alaska. But it's well worth every bump to get out and see the mines.

The Richardson, continued

Back on the Richardson, you can camp at Mile 79, **Squirrel Creek**. At Mile 78.5 is the **Bernard Creek Trailhead**, a good 15-mile loop mountain-bike trail. It's mostly uphill, though.

The road climbs to **Thompson Pass** and the nearby Worthington Glacier (Mile 29), home to some of the worst weather in the state. The record snowfall for Thompson Pass is five feet two inches in 24 hours. Worthington Gla-

Coming out of Thompson Pass.

cier is a study in glacial blue on a sunny day; take some time off to peer into its crevasses and to listen to its slow melt. The glacier has three fingers leading off the main body of ice. Fifteen years ago, when we did the first edition of this book, you could drive right up to one of them. Now it's a fair hike up the hill and over a moraine. From the parking lot – where there's a small gift shop and some outhouses – you can hardly see the thing now. The glaciers are going fast, and it's difficult to describe how it feels to us, watching them get smaller year by year.

> **WARNING:** Worthington Glacier is still one of the most accessible glaciers you'll find, but don't be tempted by it – hiking on it is strongly discouraged. There are a lot of berry bushes around the glacier, but a few of them are poisonous. Know what they are before you pick.

From Thompson Pass, the road drops. It's almost as if the bottom falls out of the world as you descend 2,800 feet to sea level. You can camp at **Blueberry Lake** (Mile 24), or keep heading downhill until you enter Keystone Canyon, 16 miles from Valdez.

Keystone Canyon is one of the loveliest spots along the Southcentral coast. The canyon walls are mossy green, and there are lots of waterfalls; **Bridal Veil Falls** and **Horsetail Falls** are close enough to the road to mist your car as you drive by. The canyon was once fought over by nine different companies, each hoping to get a railway line through. This came to a head when someone was killed fighting over turf, culminating in a spectacular murder trial, a turn-of-the-century O.J. circus. All nine companies went bust, and the railway never did get through. Mile 3 (the mile markers are not entirely accurate, as they measure distance from the old city site) is the turnoff to the pipeline terminal and the Allison Point Fishery (see below for details).

Keystone Canyon was part of an alternate route from Valdez to the Klondike goldfields. In 1898, Captain William Ralph Abercrombie, hearing rumors of a possible way to bypass Canada on the way to the goldfields, came up to the Copper River area to look for a route. He spent a year mapping the territory, but by the time his maps were ready, the anxious prospectors had already passed him by, trying a route that involved climbing the Valdez Glacier, then dropping down the Klutina Glacier onto the Klutina Lake and River. This was tried by about 6,000 people. Only 300 of them survived. None of them made it to the goldfields.

The prospectors weren't exactly the brightest people on earth. Greed had brought them into a territory they knew nothing about, and as anyone who has walked in the Alaskan bush can tell you, it's not a forgiving territory. If you know what you're doing, it's the gentlest land in the world, full of things to eat; for the unfamiliar, it's a death trap. The prospectors showed up, treated the land like it was some cakewalk back east, and dropped like flies.

One of the biggest problems was snow blindness. When prospectors got up on the glaciers, reflected light burned their corneas. This is an astoundingly painful condition – blinking feels like someone raking nails across your eyes – and, of course, stumbling around blind on a glacier is not the best thing in the world to do. By the time Abercrombie showed up in Valdez in 1899, he found a huge graveyard and a lot of would-be prospectors talking about a "glacier demon" that prevented people from getting north. The 1939 Federal Writer's Project guide to Alaska sums this up as "Many had gone mad and talked of a 'glacier demon,' an unearthly being that threw men off the glacier." Abercrombie wrote, "Many of these people I had met and known the year before were so changed... that I do not think I recognized one of them. Some were more or less afflicted with scurvy, while not a few of them had frost-bitten hands, faces, and feet... the saliva and breath of those afflicted with scurvy gave forth a stench that was simply poisonous as well as sickening to a man in good health, and sure death to one in ill health." The few surviving miners were crammed into cabins the size of single-car garages, up to 20 men waiting for someone else's death to open up a little more space. Abercrombie fed everyone able to eat, shipped most of them back down to Seattle, and added a few of the healthier ones to his exploratory expedition. Nobody got to the goldfields this way.

The mile markers through the canyon are not entirely accurate – they are measured from the old site of Valdez, which was destroyed in the 1964 earthquake. Right after you run out of markers, you can take the turnoff for the **Valdez Glacier**, and the **campground** nearby, or just keep on going into town.

Valdez

Valdez, terminus of the Trans-Alaska Pipeline, is not the town it once was. The original site, like an old lurking ghost, is located three miles outside of what's now Valdez. In the old or new location, Valdez is in one of the most beautiful spots in Alaska.

Valdez has made world news twice. The first time was on Good Friday in 1964, when a great earthquake struck Alaska. The town was leveled by the quake and the resulting tidal wave. The old town site was deemed unrecoverable, so everyone packed up and moved down the coast.

The second time Valdez made headlines was 25 years after the first, when the tanker *Exxon Valdez* ran aground on Bligh Reef in Prince William Sound. (For the details of the spill and it's effects, see The Spill section, below.)

Oil never came near the beaches of Valdez; tides and wind pushed the huge oil slick south. What the spill meant for Valdez was boomtown status. While the world gasped in horror at pictures of oiled otters and birds, workers here made upward of $16 an hour for aiming hoses at beaches; boat captains got several thousand dollars a day for the use of their boats. There was not a hotel room to be found in town, and the Alaska Highway was jammed with travelers headed for Valdez. The population of Valdez rose from its usual 4,000 to more than 12,000 people (no more than half of which were news crews) hoping to strike it rich from the ecological disaster. Rumor has it that truckloads of kitty litter were being brought up by one entrepreneur, in the hopes it would soak up the oil.

But the spill and the earthquake were only two bad moments in an otherwise peaceful history.

■ History

Captain Cook sailed into Prince William Sound, mapping out the land in 1778. He named it Sandwich Sound, after his patron and the inventor of the hoagie, the Earl of Sandwich. By the time Cook got back to England, however, Sandwich had fallen out of favor (the earl, not the food), and the area name was changed to Prince William Sound.

The name of the town came from Don Salvador Fidalgo, one of the Spaniards trying to grab up land in Alaska before the British and Russians took all the good bits. Fidalgo was also responsible for Cordova's Spanish name.

The area was first settled in the winter of 1897-98, when prospectors came looking for a route into the goldfields through only US territory. Both the Chilkoot and the Chilkat Trails crossed Canadian territory, and the Mounties imposed heavy taxes and restrictions on miners. Several thousand would-be miners passed through the budding town of Valdez, some staying behind to sell to other would-be miners. But, of course, as mentioned above, nobody made it to the goldfields.

An 1898 government survey of the region, completed before the rush, showed a small village called "Valdes" at a time when what's now Anchorage didn't even merit a blip on the map. The surveyors reported that when they landed on April 7, snow was 6 feet deep and "the reindeer counted on for transportation had not been brought." They went on to say, "about a dozen white men have married into the native tribes and have become residents there, being engaged in trade or some other industry, such as blue fox raising." The official government description of Prince William Sound was quick and to the point: It had "the topography of a submerged coast."

The fortunes of the town rose and fell with mining and the railroads. Cordova was chosen as the railhead for the Kennecott mines, and Valdez languished, interrupted only by the earthquake. This was the situation until the late 1960s, when the town was chosen as the port for the Trans-Alaska Pipeline. (For details on the engineering marvel of the pipeline, see page 371.)

And, except for the year of the spill, Valdez has remained a quiet town of about 4,300 people making their living off oil, fish, or tourism. Despite its two moments of bad luck, Valdez is a nice little town – especially once you get away from the small downtown area. Most people stop by just long enough to see the pipeline and the Columbia Glacier, but Valdez is a good place to stay for rest and recuperation.

■ The Spill

 While it's not really fair to talk about the spill in the context of a chapter on Valdez, the fact is, this is where the ship went out, and this is where most of the action was in the weeks after the spill. While in today's Valdez you'll see no traces of the spill at all – in fact, oil never came anywhere near the town, as the reef and the wind kept it away – to understand what's going on in Coastal Alaska, why people are so angry about roads being built to reach the Sound, and how much fear there is over another spill, you need a little background on one of the greatest disasters in Alaskan history.

The Contingency Plan

On March 24, 1989, Alaska suffered its first big oil spill – the largest ever in United States history – when the *Exxon Valdez*, an oil tanker heading south after taking on a full load of crude, ran aground on Bligh Reef in Prince William Sound.

Although an extensive plan had been previously laid out as part of the Alaska pipeline system's emergency procedures in the Alaska Regional Contingency Plan, planning and reality separated drastically. The plan was prepared only for a tiny oil spill, one that could be contained by a couple of booms. The *Exxon Valdez* was putting thousands of gallons an hour into the waters of Prince William Sound.

One example of how the official plan was grossly inadequate for the size of the *Exxon Valdez* oil spill was demonstrated by Exxon's attempts to fly in chemical dispersant to treat the spill. The commissioner of Alaska's Department of Environmental Conservation, Dennis Kelso, estimated that the stockpiles called for in the contingency plan were only 9% of the chemical dispersant needed to treat a spill of this size on the day of spill. It was like throwing paper towels at the ship and hoping they'd soak up the mess.

And so, while the federal, state, and Exxon authorities fumbled over a workable plan of action and tried to assess blame – there was a lot of that going on – very little was done to actually contain the oil flow into the Sound during the three calm days after the spill. The days following were not so calm, and as the wind and the waves kicked up, the oil spread rapidly, heading south.

In the end, 11 million gallons of crude poured from a gash in the ship's side. Legal battles were more furious than the efforts to save the Sound's wildlife (Exxon lost an appeal in the summer of 2000, 11 years after the spill, to try and avoid paying reparations to fishermen). Was the captain drunk? Was he even awake when the ship struck the reef? Why were there no containment booms in place for more than 24 hours after the spill? Why was

Exxon being allowed to measure damaged coast in straight linear miles, instead of following the contours of the shoreline (which meant 10 times more coast was damaged than the news was reporting)?

Because of the failure to contain the oil immediately, more than 1,500 miles of coastline were affected by landed oil, which spread southwest from Prince William Sound into the Gulf of Alaska and along the Alaska Peninsula.

The Effects

The ecology of Prince William Sound was devastated. The spill, which happened at a critical time of year from a wildlife reproductive standpoint, immediately killed an estimated half-million marine birds, 4,000-5,000 sea otters, 600 bald eagles, 200-300 harbor seals, and an unknown number of other marine and land animals, including bear, deer, mink, river otters, whales, and orcas. While an extensive animal rescue program was funded by Exxon and got a lot of TV time, the number of animals helped was comparatively small. Only 1,589 sea birds and 344 sea otters were brought to treatment centers (about one-third of the otters died after release). Meanwhile, the beaches were littered with corpses. It wasn't just the animals in the water, the otters and the birds, that were affected, but the animals that fed on them, too. The entire food chain became slick and greasy.

For the towns near the spill – Valdez, Cordova, Kodiak, and quite a few native villages – fishing catches were dramatically down, and the fish caught were feared to be dangerous for consumption. How could they be edible when they'd been swimming in an oil can? Hatcheries were threatened by the advancing slick, and damage to them could have ruined the entire fishing industry.

Clean-up efforts were difficult at best and the results were often uncertain. Three days after the spill, the weather turned windy and stormy, whipping the oil into a hard-to-clean froth. Even in the best of circumstances, only a fraction of oil can ever be recovered in the event of a spill. Methods of recovering or treating spilt oil range from chemical aids such as dispersants or sinking agents, to mechanical helpers, such as skimmers, pumps, dredges, and containment booms. Some slicks may be burned, and oil is often washed from beaches using high-pressure hot water or by the use of chemical dispersants. Not much of this worked in Alaska.

A handout you can pick up in Valdez on the spill says that "The actual cleanup process was time consuming and ineffective in many ways. Workers would wipe down a beach, the tide would change, and oil-laden water would cover the rocks with a new coating of oil. Clean-up crews sprayed rock faces with steam hoses and manually wiped smaller rocks clean. By mid-summer new techniques and technologies were employed. Microorganisms that 'ate' crude oil were sprayed onto some of the beaches, and new materials were used in wiping operations."

A lot of money was thrown at the problem. The same handout says that "On average it cost Exxon $1,000 each day to support one worker on a beach cleanup crew." There were about 10,000 people out there cleaning at the height of the efforts, but, and forgive the pun, it was all just a drop in the bucket. A somewhat more objective source, the Oil Spill Recovery Institute, says that in the three years after the spill, cleanup cost more than $2 billion. However, "oil is still present.... A casual scan of the shoreline reveals little evidence of oil but weathered oil remains trapped beneath rocks and in the subsurface of the more heavily oiled beaches."

This is a way of saying nicely that they tried (although most will tell you they didn't try very hard), but in many ways failed to clean up after the spill.

The causes and results of the spill are still being debated. Meanwhile, there are still polluted beaches – turn over rocks on many small islands in Prince William Sound and you'll think you've struck oil. The only lesson learned may be that red tape conquers all. More than 15 years after the spill, there is no evidence that it can't easily happen again. Retrofitting oil tankers with double hulls would cost too much and raise oil prices more than people are willing to pay – although there's a law that says double hulled tankers must be in use in Prince William Sound by the year 2015, what are the odds it will really happen?

In September 1990, the *Exxon Valdez* – renamed the *Exxon Mediterranean* – was back at sea. And, about the same time, in an odd publicity coup, a division of Exxon bought Anchorage's major newspaper, squashing a fair amount of reporting on the downside of the spill.

The original court settlement for the spill required that Exxon pay out $900 million over a ten-year period; total fines and penalties came to around $6.5 billion (as of 1999, by the time the entire penalty was to have been paid, Exxon had actually only paid out about $1.5 billion of the total due). Almost half of this was to go to habitat protection. However, in August of 1993, a report was issued from the General Accounting Office, saying that nearly 15% of the money Exxon paid out for the clean-up has gone to reimburse government agencies and Exxon itself. That has meant, for Exxon, a tax rebate of over $40 million!

At almost the same time as the financial dealings were being disclosed, fishermen blocked the oil terminal for three days, protesting Exxon's failure to abide by the clean-up deal. Catches had declined steadily since 1990, and five years after the spill, in a meeting with Interior Secretary Bruce Babbitt, Valdez fishermen laid oil-covered rocks out on the conference table. Before the spill, to buy a salmon seine license for commercial fishing would have cost you about $300,000; now it's worth maybe a tenth of that. A lot of fishermen went bust. Exxon is still in business. In 1999, Captain Joseph Hazelwood, captain of the *Exxon Valdez* when it struck the rock, began serving his sentence for his part in the spill – one month a year for five years of community service, picking up trash in Anchorage.

Richardson Highway

The Long Term

Even now, more than 15 years after the spill, the effects are still being felt and are still debated hotly throughout Alaska. Chambers of Commerce and pro-development people try to paint a rosy picture, but those people making their living in the waters of the Sound present a different viewpoint. Fishing catches have been noticeably down, although there is some debate as to how much of this can be attributed to the spill, and how much is simply a matter of overfishing.

Bird populations have yet to recover. So many species were wiped out right before hatching that the young which did manage to hatch had no adult birds to teach them proper behavior. That practically wiped out the species in the region, creating an entire population of baby birds starving to death. The murre population is never expected to recover, nor is the short-tailed shearwater. It's estimated that 96% of these species in the Sound region were killed by the oil. The numbers are nearly as high for the fork-tailed stormy petrel and the tufted puffin. Overall, an estimated 64% of birds in the Kodiak region were killed by the spill. The total number of birds killed was more than 250,000.

A report compiled 10 years after the spill says that "Harlequin ducks, three species of cormorants, pigeon guillemots, killer whales from the AB pod (the largest family group of killer whales in PWS prior to 1989), and the common loon are among species listed as 'not recovering.'"

The same report notes that "The population of PWS pacific herring collapsed.... None of the seven seabird species injured by the spill has been declared recovered. Recreation, tourism, and subsistence activities also are still affected by the presence of residual oil on some beaches, or the reduced availability of fish/wildlife in parts of the spill region."

Overall, of the 28 main species listed as effected by the spill, only bald eagles and otters have recovered to their pre-spill populations.

Other areas of the ecosystem which were immediately affected by the spill still show long-term effects. At the most basic level on the food chain, zooplankton, the tiny animal food of the larger animals, are highly vulnerable to dispersed and dissolved oil. All the way up the food chain, animals have been affected in a variety of ways by the oil; many are mutated, while others ingested the oil and died. Larger animals eating those contaminated by the oil suffered poisoning or disruption of their thermal regulation.

In most intertidal zones, the oil has caused decline in the populations of plants and animals. Some oil is still visible pooled under mussel beds and beach sediments. Heavily oiled mussel beds are thought to have contributed to continuing reproductive problems of harlequin ducks, sea and river otters, and pink salmon ("higher than normal egg mortality for pink salmon in oiled streams continued through 1994").

Terrestrial mammals, such as river otters and brown and bears, and Sitka deer, which feed in the intertidal zone, have been observed with oil-patched coats, indicating that they have been exposed to the oil hydrocarbons. The short- or long-term effects of the spill on these animals are uncertain.

How Will The Spill Affect You?

Still, all is not doom and gloom. While the murre, marbled murrelett, harbor seal, sea otter, Pacific herring, and sockeye salmon in the Kenai and Akalura systems are showing no signs of post-spill recovery, sockeye at Red Lake are making a comeback, as are the bald eagle populations, black oystercatcher birds, mussels.

As a traveler in the Sound, you're not likely to see any outward effects of the spill at all. Obvious signs have been removed, and you'd have to walk fairly remote beaches to find blatant traces of the spill. That's not to say your trip won't be affected. Because of the spill, you're missing what Prince William Sound once was. It remains a startlingly beautiful place but, as you travel through it, picture how much better it used to be when there was abundant wildlife here.

Imagine what it was like when it was still pure.

Alternative Viewpoints

The Spill demonstrates two unfortunate features of human behavior. The first is that you can find someone willing to justify anything. The second is that when there are too many people justifying, too few functioning, the result can be disastrous.

For the other side of the picture, see the story in the June 29, 1997, *Anchorage Daily News*, which suggested that the breakdown of oil molecules into simpler carbon molecules and the fact that carbon is the basis of life on this planet has encouraged fish reproduction, and that dumping all that hydrocarbon into the ocean was "somewhat like fertilizing your yard."

Most biologists would agree the newspaper may be dumping fertilizer on the issue.

For the last word on the Spill, in August 1992, the U.S. Fish and Wildlife Service made the frozen carcasses of more than 35,000 birds and 900 otters, all killed by oil, available for "scientific" study. This made a Dave Barry column, bringing in requests from around the world, but in the end only about 3,000 bodies got dished out, mostly to scientists and museums. Fish and Fur officials acknowledged that, once thawed, the carcasses would pretty much be rotted beyond recognition. There was also the complication that, for some reason, the heads had been cut off all the otters.

Nobody claimed the frozen poodle that had found its way into the giveaway.

Richardson Highway

A Good Thing

There was one very good thing that came from the Spill. A man named Phillip McCrory saw news reports of oiled otters. He thought that if their fur was that absorbent, if it soaked up that much oil, maybe hair was a natural way of cleaning oil. McCrory, a hairdresser, gathered some hair from the floor of his shop, stuffed into an old pair of his wife's nylons, and behold, the stuff sucked oil right out of the water. Cleanup using McCrory's hair method costs about $2 per gallon of oil, compared to about $10/gallon with standard methods. McCrory sold the idea to NASA, and it could be the wave of the future.

▪ Basics

i If you're looking to get out of Valdez without getting back on the highway, the town is served by the Alaska Marine Highway almost daily, connecting the town to Cordova and Whittier. (To get around to Seward from Valdez, see the end of the *Valdez* section.) Valdez is also a stop on the once-monthly cross-sound trip, which means you can jump on a boat here and go to Juneau. Local number for the ferry is ☎ 907-835-4436.

The **Visitor Information Center** offers daily films about the pipeline and the great quake. Located on Fairbanks, off Hazlett, it's open 8 am to 8 pm in summer. ☎ 907-835-INFO, www.valdezalaska.org.

The zip code in Valdez is 99686.

> **QUICK TOUR:** Take a look at the pipeline as it heads into town. Then check out the mountain behind – the horizontal lines are the scoring of glacial action, as the ice moved back and forth on the mountainside.

> **DON'T MISS:** Kayak Prince William Sound and pretend you're an oil tanker. Head to the museum for the cool fire truck. Charter a chopper and scare yourself to death in the most extreme skiing in the world.

▪ Museums & Attractions

Start your visit at the **Valdez Museum**, at the corner of Tatitlek and Egan (☎ 907-835-2764), open daily. The museum houses an interesting collection of objects, including the first fire engine in Valdez, a 1907 Ahrens Steam Fire Engine. There's also a reconstruction of a miner's cabin, a bar, and the lens from a lighthouse dating to 1840. Just by the exit is a short history of the pipeline. Admission is $3, under 18 enter free.

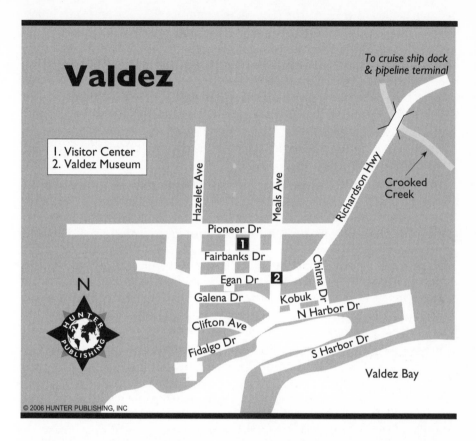

Valdez

To cruise ship dock
& pipeline terminal

1. Visitor Center
2. Valdez Museum

Hazelet Ave

Meals Ave

Richardson Hwy

Crooked
Creek

Pioneer Dr

1

Fairbanks Dr

Chitna Dr

Egan Dr **2**

Galena Dr

Kobuk

N Harbor Dr

N

Clifton Ave

Fidalgo Dr

S Harbor Dr

Valdez Bay

© 2006 HUNTER PUBLISHING, INC

The **Maxine and Jesse Whitney Eskimo Museum**, 300 Airport Rd. (at the airport), ☎ 907-834-1690, has nice displays of traditional Eskimo boats; also a good assortment of Native arts and rafts. The Whitneys traveled Alaska for 50 years, and they had both money and taste. The collection is open from 9 am to 8 pm, and there's a $4 admission charge.

The **old town site** of Valdez is beyond the Alyeska complex. There's not a whole lot to see out there, just fragments of a ghost town.

The Alyeska **pipeline terminal** is the largest economic force in Valdez – about 30% of the town works for the pipeline in some respect, and the pipeline remains one of the best examples of the balancing act that goes on continually in Alaska. People move here for the vast tracts of untouched wilderness, but they still have to make a living. And, despite the impassioned pleas cries of environmentalists, the US is not a country likely to give up driving.

It used to be that you could tour the terminal, and check out all the big machinery. That went out the window soon after 9/11. Check out the wording on a Senate bill, the Maritime Transportation Security Act of 2002 (S. 1214): "The intent of this legislation is to increase security at our nation's ports by providing the structure, coordination, and planning needed to pro-

Richardson Highway

tect ports nationwide. At the request of Senators Stevens and Dan Inouye (D-HI), the conference report includes language highlighting Alaska's and Hawaii's unique dependency on marine trade, stating that the states' economies and quality of life are directly tied to their ports. The report language further specifies that the Secretary of Transportation consider Alaska's and Hawaii's unique dependency in regard to federal waterfront security grants....

"Attention will be given to deterring and responding to such incidents, and an overall evaluation will be provided on the potential threat level of maritime terrorist attacks.

"This port security assessment is imperative for our State of Alaska, which has roughly one-half the coastline of the United States. Alaska's economy and quality of life are directly related to the functionality of its numerous ports. The majority of our Alaskan communities, including Juneau our State Capitol, are not on the road system and depend almost exclusively on marine trade for the delivery of basic goods. A terrorist attack at a port in Alaska, or anywhere on the West Coast, would cause significant interruptions in maritime service to our State, greatly affecting our way of life.

"In addition, there are several other ports in Alaska vital to Alaska and the rest of the nation. This is especially true of the port of Valdez, which is the southern terminus of the 800-mile-long trans-Alaska oil pipeline. Valdez is an important off-loading terminal for our nation's domestic energy supply. A terrorist incident here would impact U.S. oil production, and have a devastating affect on Alaska's fisheries. Dutch Harbor is consistently the top commercial fishing port in America, processing and shipping product to the rest of the world. Kodiak has the largest Coast Guard presence in the nation and the island of Kodiak has launch facilities that make it an important staging area for future military and NASA operations that are vital to our nation's national missile defense system."

So much for pipeline tours. And just pretend you don't notice the 800 miles or so of pipeline that crosses wilderness, and is absolutely, freely accessible to anybody with a car and some spare time.

The **Alyeska Terminal** does have a history prior. It was once the site of **Fort Liscum**, which operated from 1900 to 1923. The fort was established to provide security for gold miners and to see what could be done about punching a road into the Interior. At its peak, 172 men were stationed there.

Outside of Valdez, in Mineral Creek Canyon, is an interesting old **stamp mill**. The mill was used to crush ore; while the crushing was going on, water was mixed in and the mixture was placed on amalgamation plates, where the gold mixed with mercury. After the excess mercury was removed, the mixture was heated, melting and separating the purified gold and the mercury. An efficient method, if the mercury poisoning doesn't bother you. Mineral Creek is a great place for berry picking, and the scenery is lovely.

Theater

Yes, theater. Valdez hosts an astounding **theater festival**, in June. The quality of actors, directors, and producers who come here for the festival is simply astounding, so if you're looking for a chance to bump into Holly Hunter, this may be your best shot. Check with Visitor Info for dates and schedule, but plan early, because the already busy hotels get jammed for this.

■ Out & About

Hiking

There's a lot of good hiking in the Valdez area. The most popular trails are the Solomon Gulch and Goat trails. **Solomon Gulch Trail** is 1.3 miles toward Solomon Lake. The hike is not an easy one, but it offers panoramic views of the town. Pick it up off Dayville Road. Part of the trail goes by the pipeline. Figure about two hours for the hike, round-trip.

The **Shoup Bay Trail** is a more challenging 6.5-mile hike. Pick the trail up at the west end of Egan street. The first part of the hike is easy with boardwalks but once you head uphill, you'll know you're working. You do have to cross a couple of small streams on this trail, but at the end, you're up where gold miners once played.

Goat Trail begins in Keystone Canyon and follows the road that was once the only connection between Valdez and the Interior. The hike is about a five-mile round-trip, and after the first very steep incline, it levels out some and gets easier. An offshoot of the trail takes on a part of the original gold rush trail.

Somewhat easier are the **Mineral Creek Trail**, a bit under two miles, which picks up on the end of Mineral Creek Drive and follows the creek valley. The trail ends at the old stamp mill.

Dock Point Trail is quick – a half-hour or so – and easy. Start across from the boat launch ramp on Kobuk drive. You head right up the hill, and then drop into a lovely meadow. Take the boardwalks for views.

> **WARNING:** Any hikers on any trail should be very wary of bears. Valdez, with its salmon runs and berry bushes, is prime bear country.

Because the original mining trail north to the goldfields, to put it bluntly, sucked (see hike below), the military put in an alternate route. Head out the Richardson Highway Loop to mile 12.5. where you'll find the trailhead. Nice views of the canyon and the Low River; after a bit of hiking, you end up in Horsetail Falls Valley. It's a fairly easy hike, one of the prettier around. Figure two hours for the trip.

Richardson Highway

This hike actually links up with the 1899 **Trans-Alaska Military Trail** – as does the Goat Trail hike. One of the original builders of the trail wrote "The effort of climbing over, under, and through this brush on a side hill so steep as to scarcely afford a foothold; falling stumbling, grasping at devil clubs [a type of wild ginseng, which can cause rashes when touched]; bruised and beaten by the stout alder branches, and, at the same time, endeavoring to blaze out a line with a uniform grade or on a level is simply inconceivable to one who has not tried it." The trail is still undergoing restoration, but at least this bit of hiking gives you an idea of what it was like during the gold rush.

This hike will, eventually, link up with the **Eagle-Valdez Trail** – a trail from the coast to the goldfields, far inland. Until roads were built, this was one of the only ways into the Interior – and the only way that didn't involve entering Canada.

If you follow it (figure on a couple of weeks and some serious bushwhacking, plus some unpleasant walking along the side of the highways), you'll more or less follow the path of the Richardson and Glenn highways before heading across wild territory north of Tanacross (just west of Tok). Know what you're doing and go prepared – or be prepared to die. Rough maps are available in Valdez, but you'll need serious topo maps for this one.

 When you're in the Valdez Museum, pick up a copy of their brochure on Valdez trails – worth it for the "Hiker's Bible," which features wisdom such as: "Mosquito dope or spray will keep the demons of the air off thee."

Kayaking, Fishing, Rafting

While Columbia Glacier is Valdez's main attraction – more people come to see it than anything else – there is lots of other beautiful wild territory in the area. If you're good with a boat, you can run the rivers – the one-hour runs through Keystone Canyon or on the silty Love River are great – or kayak with the nice people at **Pangaea** (☎ 907-835-8442, 800-660-9635, www.alaskasummer.com). They lead short trips to Duck Flats for $55, slightly longer trips around Gold Creek, for $75, full days to the Shoup Glacier for $159, or Columbia Glacier for $199.

Anadyr Adventures, ☎ 800-TO-KAYAK, www.anadyradventures.com, has also been in Valdez for a long, long time. Quality programs, everything from short day paddles to multi-day trips.

Kayaking Valdez is not really kayaking Prince William Sound, unless you head out for several days. If you want to kayak the Sound, take a ferry from Valdez to Cordova, where things are less crowded and considerably more open (and where the Copper River Delta offers prime wildlife viewing, birding, and rafting in glacial waters), or go around to Whittier to put in – just be ready to get out of Whittier quick (see below).

Either company can arrange drop-offs, customize long trips, or lead you on multi-day paddles.

Charters

If you're interested in the Spill, get a custom charter and head out to the beaches to see what effects linger. Most charter captains in Valdez were part of the cleanup efforts so they know where to go (Exxon was paying $3,000 and up a day, post-Spill, for boat rental).

Easiest is to call the central charter booking outfit in town: **Fish Central**, ☎ 907-835-5090, 888-835-5002, www.fishcentral.net. Call a week or so before you get to town, tell them what you want – fishing, sightseeing, whatever – and let them worry about the details.

Skiing

In winter, Valdez hosts the world **Extreme Skiing Championships** in Thompson Pass. Downhillers zigzag and jump on slopes most folks wouldn't even think of attempting. Valdez and Cordova are bases for the nutcases who do "extreme" skiing – if you can't handle a 50-degree slope, don't even think about wasting the time of the helicopter operators who take the skiers out.

Ice Climbing

In February, the town hosts the **Ice Climbing Festival**. Valdez is justly famous as a Mecca for ice climbers, and the waterfalls in Keystone Canyon serve as great big frozen monkeybars. Check with the Visitor's Center for details, ☎ 907-835-4636, and dress warm.

Columbia Glacier

Most people go to Valdez for one reason: to see Columbia Glacier. Part of the same icefield that includes the Matanuska Glacier, Columbia is famous for its towering wall of ice, calving into the open ocean. The cheap way to see the glacier is to take the ferry to Whittier. The drawback of this way is that you don't get so close, so you'll need a good pair of binoculars. In fact, over the past few years, with the retreat, you're not likely to see much at all except for some bits of ice floating around the shore. If you really want to see the glacier, you're going to have to spend money, and there are quite a few tour companies and countless boats for charter. These allow you to get considerably closer to the glacier, and you may even glimpse seals basking on ice floes as the new icebergs plunge into the ocean around them. Expect to pay a bit over $100 per person for a trip to the glacier. Many people feel glutted on glaciers long before getting to Columbia, but the sight of a house-sized block of ice dropping into the ocean is unforgettable.

In addition to the charter operators listed above, all of whom can get you to the glacier, specialists include **Stan Stephens Cruises** (☎ 907-835-4731, 866-867-1297, www.stanstephenscruises.com), which runs nine-hour

Richardson Highway

tours of Columbia and Mears glaciers. They offer a six-hour trip that saves you a few bucks, but you'll see a lot more on the full version. They can also arrange longer packages that include a stay at the Growler Island Camp.

The **Glacier Wildlife Cruise/Lu-lu Bell** is a bit shorter – around five hours, but a lot of fun. Not so slick as the other operators, and church services are held on board on Sundays. ☎ 800-411-0090, www.lulubelletours. com. It's the choice of locals taking friends or relatives out.

■ Food

Overall, food prices in Valdez are high, but so is the quality. **Mike's Place** is the night out spot, with steaks, pasta, and seafood, from about $15. Almost next door is **Oscars on the Waterfront**, on Harbor Drive. Dinners from $10 and up. Oscars also has an all-you-can-eat barbecue for $15 – come early if you want to sit down and don't like waiting in line.

For faster seafood, try the **Alaska Halibut House** at the corner of Meals and Pioneer, where you can get fish and chips from $7. Get Chinese food at **Fu Kung**, on Meals Ave.: lunches from about $7.

If you're heading out hiking, kayaking, or camping you can get vacuum packed fish at **Peter Pan** – it's cheap and it's good. The perfect pick me up for a night around the campfire.

■ Accommodations

There are no bargains here. Valdez can fill up fast, and it costs. At the swank end of things is the **Totem Inn**, 144 E. Egan, ☎ 907-835-4443, 888-808-4431, www.toteminn.com, $$$-$$$$, with huge rooms, free DSL, and a few cottages. Other good choices include the **Keystone Hotel** (☎ 907-835-3851, 888-835-0665, www.keystonehotel.

HOTEL PRICING
Prices are in US dollars.
under $50 . . . . $
$50-$100 . . . . $$
$100-$150 . . . . . . $$$
above $150 . . . . . $$$$

com), 401 W. Egan, $$$. For chains, there's the **Best Western**, at 100 Fidalgo, ☎ 907-835-3434, 888-222-3440, www.valdezharborinn.com, and the **Aspen Hotel**, 100 Meals Ave., ☎ 907-835-4445, 800-478-4445, www.aspenhotelsak.com. Both are good choices, although not all that easy on the wallet.

If this is not your idea of a good time, try one of the many B&Bs, but you're still looking at $100 per night. These go in and out of business, as people with spare rooms open and close. You can check out the stacks of brochures in the Visitors Center.

Camping

A quick drive through downtown Valdez makes you think of the elephant graveyard: there are so many RVs parked, white butts facing the ocean, that you've got to think this is where they limp off to die. The RV parks in Valdez are very central, very crowded, and very ugly, with the usual charm you expect from a parking lot.

There are several campgrounds in Valdez. **Bear Paw Camper Park**, near the small boat harbor, has full hookups or dry camping. It's a good spot and, unlike most RV parks, they have a tent sanctuary a couple of blocks away – down by the ferry terminal at the end of Hazelet Avenue. Here you'll find 15 sites nestled among trees and berry bushes. Of course, there's still a huge line of RVs between you and the water, but at least the showers are hot and it's only a few minutes' walk from the center of town.

If that's full, try the **Eagle's Rest**, just off the Richardson Highway and Pioneer Drive – probably the best place for tents. Finally, there's the **Valdez Glacier Campground**, behind the airport. This is also a great spot if you're in a tent. There is unofficial camping along **Mineral Creek** or along the dirt road that leads up to the water tower. Just be inconspicuous, and don't start any fires.

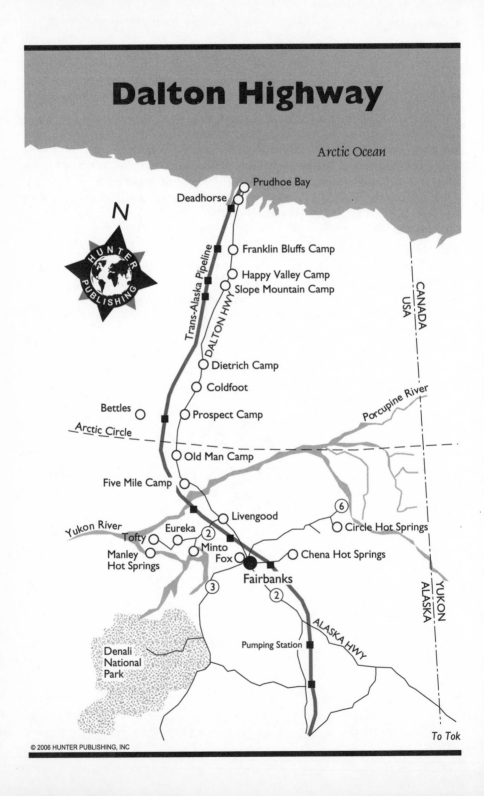

Chapter 12

North from Fairbanks
The Trans-Alaska Pipeline, The Dalton, Steese & Elliott Highways

O ne of the best things about Fairbanks is how easy it is to get out of it. If you're looking for places where wild Alaska hasn't given way to gravel-pit RV parks, simply get in the car and drive north.

The Pipeline

I f you head north out of Fairbanks, you're going to be following the path of the pipeline. In fact, if not for the pipeline, there probably wouldn't be much in the way of a road heading north.

The Trans-Alaska Pipeline stretches from Prudhoe Bay to Valdez, crossing 800 miles of tundra, mountains, permafrost, and caribou migration trails. The pipeline is an engineering marvel, completed in 1977 at a cost of about $8 billion, to take North Slope crude on a long journey south to the marine terminal at Valdez. Although much of the pipeline is buried, it does come above the ground near Valdez. At the northern end of the state, along the Dalton Highway, it is nearly always visible above ground because the permafrost prevented the pipe's burial. Oil in the pipeline is 145° Fahrenheit, which would turn the permafrost into a bog, bending and ruining the pipes.

In its above-ground sections, the pipeline is made up of sections of 48-inch diameter pipe, elevated on special supports, which carry heat up through the structure to finned radiators, above the level of the pipeline. The supports are located about every 60 feet, and the pipeline can move on the support, so it can react to earthquakes or expansion and contraction due to heat variations. The zigzag path the pipeline follows also helps it adjust to movement; at one point (on the Denali Fault), the pipeline's design allows up to 20 feet of horizontal and five feet of vertical movement. Every 800 to 1,000 feet, there is an "anchor" to help prevent uncontrolled movement.

Where the pipeline is buried, it lies at a depth of between eight and 35 feet, on an insulated bed, and is covered with gravel padding and soil fill. At three points along the pipeline it was necessary to bury the pipe under permafrost, to allow the highway and the caribou migration to cross. At these points, the buried pipe is refrigerated. Loops of pipe carrying chilled brine circulate around the oil-bearing pipe.

The pipeline itself is insulated with 3.75 inches of fiberglass throughout its length and is jacketed in galvanized steel.

Construction of the pipeline was preceded by five years of study on the fragile Arctic terrain and wildlife, the climate, and the impact of the pipeline. The entire route was surveyed by archaeologists. On November 16, 1973, construction began, and by August of 1975, 21,600 workers were on the project. The first oil was pumped on June 20, 1977; it was loaded in tankers headed south by August 1. About two million barrels of oil a day are now pumped through the pipeline. Despite all this technological marvel, and the fact that the pipeline has flowed smoothly for 20 years, there are subtle things to undermine your faith. A brochure passed out by Alyeska titled "What to do in case of a pipeline-related emergency" explains how to recognize a leak ("a pool of dark liquid") and offers useful tips if you do spot a leak ("Do not create sparks, light matches, start an engine, switch on a light, use a camera flash or a cellular telephone.") For more information on the pipeline, write to **Alyeska Pipeline Service Company**, Public Relations Department, 1835 South Bragaw St., Anchorage, AK 99512.

For more on what happens when it all goes terribly wrong, see Chapter 11, the section on Valdez.

The Dalton Highway

The Dalton Highway, leading north from Fairbanks to the Arctic Circle and up to Prudhoe Bay, is the subject of endless horror stories.

 HIGHWAY TIP: Most people will tell you there's no way to drive the Dalton without flattening at least one tire, or even two. The road is in terrible condition, it swallows cars whole; the truck drivers are crazed and dangerous, the tour bus drivers are even worse. No one gets out alive.

The stories, if taken with the appropriate grain of salt, are largely true. But it ain't that bad.

Formerly called the North Slope Haul Road, and still referred to as the Haul Road by most locals, the Dalton Highway was built between April 29, 1974, and September 29, 1974, to give access to the rich oilfields of the far North. Construction required moving more than 32 million cubic yards of gravel, three million man hours of construction time, and $125 million. The road runs parallel to the Trans-Alaska Pipeline, and it is the only road in the United States that crosses the Arctic Circle. It also crosses the Brooks Range and skirts the massive Gates of the Arctic National Park and Preserve (called "Alaska's ultimate wilderness" – a bit over 8 million protected acres, including the Noatak River, which the Park Service calls "one of North America's largest mountain-ringed river basins with an intact ecosystem," which just means it's still like it always was), the Yukon Flats National Wildlife Refuge, and the Arctic National Wildlife Refuge, which, despite the vote in late 2005 not to drill, remains threatened by politics and the deposits of oil that lay under its surface.

It's 511.9 miles from Fairbanks to the end of the Dalton Highway. For the first 20 years the road was there, you could drive only 290 miles of it – the rest was closed to the public. However, the road opened in 1994, and you can now drive all the way to Deadhorse.

But the question is, is it worth it? Probably not. It's one of those things that's fun to say you've done, but not really worth the effort of doing. If you're going up to spend time in the refuges and bush out around the road, it's a lot easier to fly in from Fairbanks. If you're driving simply because you have to go to the end of the road, take one of the tour buses and save your car and your nerves.

Even taking the road only as far as the Arctic Circle, 200 miles from Fairbanks (that's about where most people give up and decide to turn around), requires a bit of advance planning. It's not a trip to take lightly.

Yet despite all stories, the road really is in pretty good shape most of the year; it has to be, to support the number of trucks that travel to Prudhoe Bay carrying supplies. The road surfacing is hard-packed gravel treated with a special compound that is supposed to (but doesn't quite) keep dust down, and it will allow sustained highway speeds. This is the first danger. Large trucks move at faster than highway speeds. During dry spells, the dust and gravel fly so thick from the passing trucks that there is virtually no visibility; you just have to wait it out until you can see again, and hope there's nobody coming up behind you or stopped in front of you. If you haven't cracked your windshield yet, you probably will on this road. You might also note that the road is treated with calcium chloride to help control dust. The downside of this is that the chemical eats car paint. Plan on hitting the carwash as soon as you get back to Fairbanks.

HIGHWAY TIP: The road is also hard on tires, and there are few places to get repairs. Any mechanical breakdown on the Haul Road can be serious. Employees of Alyeska, the company in charge of the pipeline and the trucks, are not going to stop and help, nor are the people at the pipeline pump stations going to offer any help, not even in an emergency. Other traffic is sparse. Make sure your vehicle is in top shape before you set out. The official line from the pipeline people is this: "Travelers need to be informed and prepared for this remote road." Drive with your lights on at all times, and carry along basic survival gear: food, water, some blankets, spare parts, maybe some extra gas. Should you encounter problems, get your car completely off the road. Always keep the heavy truck traffic in mind, and watch for wildlife in the road, especially bears and caribou.

Services are few and far between. Only at **Yukon River** (140 miles from Fairbanks), **Coldfoot** (260 miles from Fairbanks), **Wiseman** (14 miles north of Coldfoot), and **Deadhorse** (another 225 miles north) are you likely to find help. Take cash along, because they will not always accept credit cards. Also remember that the farther north you go, the more expensive everything gets. Buy your gas and picnic supplies in Fairbanks.

If this has scared you off from trying the road yourself, we list some tour companies back in the Fairbanks section who will do the driving for you. One advantage of the organized tours is that almost all of them include getting all the way to the Arctic Ocean in the price. If you drive to Deadhorse yourself, you still end up having to get with a tour operator who is authorized to cross the oilfields – otherwise, your trip ends quite a ways from water, with nothing but a view of bored pipeline workers who are looking back at you.

MOSQUITO ALERT: *One final warning about the roads heading north. The bugs here make those in the rest of the state look like your best friends. Get out of the car anywhere and you will be swarmed to the point where you feel like one of those guys wearing a bee beard in the freak show. You cannot breathe without inhaling a bug. Remember that the biomass of the mosquitoes (not to mention the blackflies and other assorted nasties) is greater than that of the caribou up here. If you get out of your car without every inch of your skin covered with cloth and DEET, you will make the bugs very, very happy. After only a few minutes – when they're past your skin and starting to gnaw on your bones – and you'll wonder how this many bugs find enough to eat when you're not around. This is not the place to forget the DEET, particularly if you're planning to do some fishing.*

All along the highway in July and August you can try your luck for grayling, with the larger rivers having runs of pike, whitefish, and burbot.

■ Leaving Fairbanks

 It's a long drive from Fairbanks to the beginning of the Dalton Highway, and before you get to it, there are a couple of really nice options – west to Manley Hot Springs, or east to Circle.

Note: All distances are from Fairbanks.

Leave Fairbanks by taking the Steese Expressway toward the city of Fox. For the first 7.9 miles, the road is good and four-lane; the pipeline comes into view at Mile 7, and then is rarely out of sight again if you stick to the Dalton. Mile 8.4 offers a pipeline viewpoint, with informational signboards. The exit to see Gold Dredge Number 8 comes a mile later.

At Mile 11, the Steese Expressway becomes the Steese Highway.

The Steese Highway

The Steese, the first side-trip option as you head north, is 162 miles of road into the Alaskan bush. The first section – about 45 miles – is paved, the rest is packed gravel. The same cautions noted above apply here.

There are really only two towns along the Steese – Central and Circle – so come prepared.

The Steese Highway was completed in the late 1920s to provide an alternative to taking the Yukon River to Circle. Pretty much every inch of land you pass along the highway has been searched for gold a dozen times.

The first couple of attractions along the way – the gold dredge and the Howling Dog Saloon at Mile 11.5 – are detailed in the Fairbanks section. You're really still in what passes for suburbs at this point.

At Mile 28, turn right for a trip to the **Chatanika Lodge** (☎ 907-389-5760). This is a great hotel and restaurant – we mention it in the Fairbanks section as an excellent alternative to staying in town. It's loaded with character, at very reasonable prices – doubles start at just $50. Situated in what used to be a working gold camp, it's worth the trip out for a meal – they serve a great Sunday brunch – even if you aren't going to stay the night. Stroll the grounds and see what things were like during the height of a gold rush.

The settlement of **Welltown** (population four) is at Mile 36. There's a campground at Mile 39, the **Upper Chatanika River State Recreation Site**. The sites on the Chatanika River are a great alternative to staying in Fairbanks.

At Mile 42.5 is the trailhead for the **McKay Creek Trail**. This is a 17.5-mile hike with an elevation change of a bit over a thousand feet. Most of the climb comes right at the beginning, in the first five or so miles before you hit the ridge line. After you peak out, you drop down, cross a couple of creeks, including the Ophir and Beaver, and eventually end up at the

Cache Mountain Cabin, run by the Bureau of Land Management. Four can sleep comfortably in the cabin. Contact the BLM in Fairbanks (☎ 907-474-2350) for reservation information. You can book up to 30 days in advance.

Around Mile 57, you'll see a large pipe that was part of the **Davidson Ditch**, an 83-mile-long construction project originally made to bring water from the Chatanika to the goldfields to float the dredges. The Davidson Ditch included more than seven miles of pipe and, at the peak of operations, moved more than 50,000 gallons a minute. Also here is the turnoff for the Creek Road – it's rough, but seven or eight miles takes you back to **Nome Creek**, once a prime gold panning area and now a good place for a picnic.

This is in the middle of a caribou migration route. In season, there can be more than 50,000 caribou on the move through here.

There's another campground at Mile 60, the **Cripple Creek Campground**. It's got RV drive-in sites, an old trapper's cabin, and lovely views of the Chatanika River, and you're welcome to pan for gold in the river.

The river is close enough to the road for the next 30 miles or so that you can put your canoe or kayak in and have somebody meet you at a pre-arranged spot up north. It's an easy Class II, so it should be fine for the novice. In a dry summer, you may have to portage, so check with the BLM before striking out.

Birch Creek Canoe Trail starts at the launching point at Mile 94. Birch Creek is a designated wild river, with no development along it (except, of course, for the endless traces of mining). The river is a good intermediate trip, with mostly Class I and II water and a few Class III rapids. For a really nice trip, take a week or so and do the 126 miles down to the Birch Creek Bridge, coming out at Mile 142 on the Steese.

Mile 107 has a trailhead for the **Pinnell Mountain National Recreation Trail.** It's mostly popular for midsummer views. Around the solstice, you won't see the sun setting here, even though you're more than 50 miles south of the Arctic Circle. There are a couple of emergency shelters on the trail, but they're just wooden boxes that let you get out of the weather. Be self-sufficient when you hit the trail.

If you're packing a tent, consider the trail from Eagle Summit. This is a three-day hike through the White Mountains, with incredible views toward the north. You don't have to hike the whole thing to pop your tent for the night and enjoy being away from the road, but if you do want to do the whole thing, stop in at Public Lands in Fairbanks to get the latest scoop on conditions and to figure out the topo maps you'll need.

Eagle Summit, Mile 108, is the highest point on the road, at 3,624 feet.

■ Central

Central, the first of two settlements along the road, is 128 miles from Fairbanks. Central saw a gold rush as recently as 20 years ago. As gold rushes go, it was fairly small – a success story is of a miner who pulled $26,000 of gold in six years, or rather less than he would have made slinging hamburgers – but the promise of gold does strange things to people. If you're going to stay in Central, check out the **Central Motor Inn** (☎ 907-520-5228), $$; some tent sites outside. However, because of the influx of miners looking to work the short summer season, don't expect to find an empty room.

Remember this is a mining town and in no way genteel. There's a good **mining museum**; if it's open, it costs $1 to get in. It has great displays of mining stuff, dog sledding accoutrements (the Yukon Quest race route passes through here), and the first printing press hauled north of Juneau. Take a look at it and try to imagine setting type – little bits of lead – with your bare hands when the temperature is below freezing.

If you've already run out of the groceries that, with your great foresight, you stocked up on in Fairbanks, you can get more of the same stuff for only double the price or so at **Crab's Corner**'s, the store/café/laundromat in town.

Just past Central is the turnoff for **Circle Hot Springs**, about eight miles down a good paved road. You can camp at Mile 5.7, or stay in the lodge at the springs themselves, where there's also a restaurant. The lodge was built in the 1930s, and it still has a great frontier flavor to it – the building is on the National Register of Historic Places, and there are enough old mining artifacts around to allow the ambitious to start full mining works again.

The springs were discovered in the fall of 1897, when George Growe went chasing after a moose he'd wounded. The moose led Growe across a stream, which was odd, because the water wasn't frozen. The next spring, Growe went back. The story says he picked up some wild parsnip for lunch, but there's a problem with that, as the roots of wild parsnip are poisonous. It broke his health, and he remained a virtual invalid until he died.

The water from the hot springs comes out at 139° F; it's cooled to about 100°, and then drained into an Olympic-sized pool. You can stay in the water all day for only $8, and you don't have to be a resort guest to use the pool. However, the resort is a great place to spend a night or two. A room at the **Circle Hot Springs Resort** is pretty reasonable, $$$ for a double or a cabin, or stay in the dorm for about $20 (☎ 907-520-5113).

■ Circle

After a night soaking road stiffness from your bones, it's less than an hour to the end of the road at Circle.

North from Fairbanks

The first settlers came to Circle after gold was found in the area in 1893. It boomed for a few years and was billed as "the largest log cabin city in the world." Well, everybody needs some claim to fame.

Right on the banks of the Yukon River, Circle was just a couple of days' float downstream from what's now Dawson City – and what was then nothing but a bunch of trees until most of Circle's residents fled there as soon as they heard of the Klondike strike. Those who'd made it to the rush in Circle had quite an advantage over the masses who headed north out of Seattle in 1898.

There's not much in Circle. The main attraction is the **Yukon River** and access for the **Yukon-Charley Rivers National Preserve**. You can camp on the riverbanks, look at the devastation 100 years of mining have caused, sit back in a motel room at the **Yukon Trading Post** (☎ 907-773-1217, $$), or do what most people do: look around for a few minutes and then head back to the hot springs before you get back on the road north.

The Elliott Highway

If the Steese doesn't sound like your thing, stay left at the fork, on Alaska Route 2, which becomes the Elliott Highway, headed for Livengood and Manley Hot Springs. The road is rougher from this junction, with a narrow shoulder; watch for patching and frost heaves for as long as the road holds out.

You can catch the **Ski Loop Trail** at Mile 28. It's a quick five-mile hike with only a 460-foot elevation change. On a good day, you can see Denali from the trail.

Right past the trailhead, the pavement ends on the road. From here on out, it's just gravel, and big trucks churning up the gravel. The road narrows and is winding and hilly.

The land beside the road is heavily forested, mostly with spruce. Watch for permafrost areas, where the black spruce trees are shorter and may lean.

Camp at **Mosquito Creek Campground**, Mile 57 (they're not kidding with the name), or stay in the car and continue past **Livengood**, 78 miles from Fairbanks. There's a two-mile spur road to Livengood, where about all you'll see is a hundred people looking for gold. There are no services in town. The Elliott branches west (the Dalton heads north) at Mile 84.

Along the Elliott, there's a branch road to **Minto** at Mile 110. Minto is an Athabascan village of about 200 people situated on the banks of the Tanana River. There's an **arts and crafts center**, and you may be able to find a room for the night. The 1898 US survey of the region reported, "The Indians of the Tanana compare very favorably with the other Indians of the Interior. They are kindly, peaceful people, whose skill at certain crude handicrafts has long been known, and so far as our information goes they are trustworthy and reliable." This from white guys wearing wool in freezing winter rain.

■ Manley

 Back on the road to Manley, there's not a whole lot else except stunning views – the Alaska Range to the south, the Tanana River – until you get to **Manley Hot Springs**, 152 miles from Fairbanks.

Manley used to be a really popular day trip from Fairbanks, but when the lodge closed, it fell off dramatically. You can soak in the springs for a few bucks, but there's not much else out here, and overall, you're better off headed to Circle.

The Elliott Highway ends just past the hot springs. Drive out to the end for the best river views.

The Dalton Highway

The Narrow Road to the Deep North

If you avoid the temptation of hot springs to the east or west and instead follow the right fork of the highway at the junction just past Livengood, you will find yourself on the Dalton Highway. Cross your fingers and pack your good luck charm. This is the road to the end of the world.

Mile numbers are now given to match the mile markers on the Dalton Highway.

There's a small campground at **Hess Creek**, at Mile 23.8. Fish here for whitefish and grayling. The road crosses the **Yukon River** at the settlement of Yukon River at Mile 56. Gas and repairs are available here, but they're costly compared to Fairbanks.

There's a **BLM visitor center** here at the crossing, which is the best place to stop for current information on what the rest of the road is going to be like. Also some nice pipeline info.

If you've got your own canoe or kayak and are feeling brave, this is a good place put in to the river and fish for pike, burbot or, in season, king salmon. Check for current restrictions.

You can camp here, at the new spot four miles north, or stay in the lodge run by **Yukon Ventures Alaska** (☎ 907-655-9001) and look out your room window at the only bridge in Alaska that crosses the Yukon River.

A few miles farther down the road, at Mile 60.6, is an undeveloped **campsite**. There is an outhouse, and water from an artesian well is available.

The Ray River loops and swirls through numerous oxbows; watch for it at Mile 70.

Mile 74.8 brings a feature of the road known as the "roller coaster": a steep downhill, followed by a very steep uphill. Check your brakes before you try it.

As you head farther north, notice that the trees get smaller and smaller. Besides the ubiquitous black spruce, plants include resin and dwarf birch, alder, willow, and cottongrass.

There's a lovely viewpoint at Mile 90.2 of the tundra, the pipeline, and the road sweeping off into the horizon. From Mile 96, the road rises above the tree line for about five miles.

Finger Mountain, or Finger Rock, at Mile 97.5, is the most interesting of the tors – the large granite formations resulting from erosion. It points to the sky and is used by aviators as a landmark. If you get out to hike around the tors, try to stick to the paths. The tundra vegetation is extremely fragile.

This area is technically alpine tundra. The plants may be very small, but also very old, hanging on in the short growing season. Among the more common plants are dwarf birch, willow, blueberry, saxifrage, and lichens. There's a parking lot here where you can get safely off the road, an outhouse, and a quarter-mile of trail with wheelchair access and interpretive signs that explain the local flora and fauna. Tors are visible from the road for the next several miles.

The road crosses the **Kanuti River** at Mile 105.8. There's good fishing for grayling, burbot, and pike.

The **Arctic Circle** lies 200 miles from Fairbanks, at north latitude 66 degrees, 33 minutes. The Circle is defined as the line where the sun does not rise on the winter solstice (December 21) or set on the summer solstice (June 21). Once you've crossed this line, you have truly entered the land of the midnight sun. There's a pullout, a sign board (with a viewing deck so you can get a good look at this imaginary line), some bare bones campsites, a picnic table, and an amazing number of hungry mosquitoes and biting flies. Be sure to dose up on insect repellant before getting out of your vehicle.

This is where most people give up on the Dalton and head back south, figuring crossing the Circle is enough. But if you're stout of heart, there are delights awaiting you farther north.

The road penetrates the Arctic, remaining winding and narrow, with many hills. One such hill is **Gobbler's Knob**, Mile 132, which offers panoramic views from its 1,500-foot peak. On a clear day, you may see the Brooks Range on the northern horizon. To the northwest, nearer at hand, are the Endicott Mountains and the Koyukuk River system, which was first explored by Russian expeditions in 1842. The first US expeditions began in 1885, under the leadership of Lt. Henry Allen. To the east is **Pump Station Number 5** for the pipeline.

Mile 144.1 brings you to the **Jim River**, suitable for gentle canoe or kayak trips. If you've got somebody to pick you up, you can take an all-day float trip as far as Prospect Camp.

Chapman Lake is visible at Mile 160. You can see a trail used for dog sled racing, and the foothills of the Brooks Range. Other mountains visible include Twelvemile Mountain (3,190 feet) to the west, and Cathedral Mountain (3,000 feet) to the east.

■ Coldfoot

Access to Coldfoot is at Mile 175. Gas, food, and lodging are available; these are the last services on the road until Deadhorse, more than 200 miles away.

Coldfoot once prospered as a mining camp. The place was originally called Slate Creek, but stories say its name changed around 1900, when miners reached the town, headed north, but got cold feet and changed their minds. (Kind of like the Arctic Circle sign for drivers.) There's a visitors center in Coldfoot, open from June 1 through Labor Day. Check the **Slate Creek Inn** (☎ 907-678-5201) for a motel room or campsite.

This is your last chance to buy gas until Deadhorse – 239 miles north. Check all fluids here. You want to be fifty miles north and have to wait for a towtruck from Fairbanks?

To the west of the road is the **Gates of the Arctic National Park and Preserve**. No roads lead into the park, and there are no facilities. Do not venture into the park unless you are an experienced outdoorsman and you're packing everything you need. Plan on bears being everywhere, and remember that no water in the park is safe to drink – there aren't any people around, but there are a lot of animals who have multiple uses for the streams. Don't go in thinking you've got to get out on a specific day – particularly if you fly in to a drop-off point, expect the pilot to have weather delays for the trip back out. That also means you have to carry extra food. Gates of the Arctic covers roughly 8.4 million acres of land – like practically everything else in Alaska, that's bigger than Rhode Island. (What do people in Rhode Island do? Compare themselves to Luxembourg or San Marino?)

If you go in Gates of the Arctic without proper planning, there's plenty of space in which to get lost and die in a fairly unpleasant fashion – after you've rudely wasted a lot of taxpayer money on the search parties. If you go in knowing what you're doing, you'll enjoy the views in one of the last great wildernesses in the world, encompassing alpine lakes, glaciers, and long open fields of tundra.

This far north the tree line lies at only about 2,100 feet, so it takes almost no time at all to get above the trees and get views that go on forever. If you can fly in with a collapsible kayak or inflatable river raft, there's serious fun to be had on the John, the Noatak, Alatna, the Koyukuk, the Wild, and the Tinayguk rivers. Again, this is a serious wilderness area, for the experienced only. If you don't know what you're doing, there are easier and cheaper ways to die. If you do know what you're doing, we offer this: we spent a night on the Noatak with a musk ox above the camp, and a wolf howling nearby at regular hours. It doesn't get much better than that.

For more information, write: Superintendent, **Gates of the Arctic**, PO Box 74680, Fairbanks, AK 99707-4680. You can also get information on the park at the Public Lands Office in Anchorage or Fairbanks. Buy your topo maps in the cities.

Marion Creek, five miles past Coldfoot at Mile 180, has the only developed campground along the Dalton. You'll find water and picnic tables, but no RV dumping.

The road continues parallel to the pipeline and, through here, the **Middle Fork Koyukuk River**. Fish from Middle Fork Bridge Number 1, Mile 188.5, for Dolly Varden, grayling, and whitefish. There are very rough roads here leading to **Wiseman** and **Nolan**, active mining areas, with a year-round population of about 25. There's a small trading post and campground in Wiseman. Gold was discovered in the area in 1911, and they're still out there looking for more. Be sure to respect all structures as private property.

Around Mile 194, watch for views of the Wiehl and Sukakpak mountains to the north. Most anthropologists consider these as the boundary between the Athabascans to the south and the Eskimos to the north. To the Natives, of course, they were simply big mountains it wasn't worth the effort to cross. On either side, evidence of inhabitation goes back more than 10,000 years.

On the Sukakpak side, at around Mile 204, you'll find limestone formations that have been dated to about 375 million years ago. The odd bumps you see are created when water gets trapped under the soil surface between permafrost and a seasonal frost. The water freezes and the soil around heaves upward into a formation called a *polsas*.

It used to be you could get no farther than **Dietrich**, at Mile 209, without a permit. Those days are past, and there's really no reason to stop in Dietrich now. Just keep heading north.

Mile 237 is the **Chandalar Shelf**. If you follow the stream – a tributary of the North Fork Chandalar River – you'll see fossils (mostly brachiopods and horn coral) in the shale upstream. There are also herds of Dall sheep in the area.

Nine miles farther on, you hit the **Atigun Valley viewpoint**. This 4,739-foot pass marks the continental divide on the Dalton. Streams to the south flow to the Bering Sea, while streams to the north flow into the Arctic. Once you've crossed this point, there probably isn't another spot around that doesn't have a thick layer of permafrost beneath it.

Mile 286 has the Toolik Lake overlook. **Toolik Lake** is a glacial lake, pretty much held under a monopoly by the University of Alaska. Ostensibly they're studying global warming, but who knows what they're really doing. No camping is allowed in the area.

From here on to Deadhorse, there's not a lot except for tundra scenery, but you should keep your eyes open for musk ox. To the east are the Romanzof and the Phillip Smith mountains; to the northeast are the Shublick Mountains. To the west side of the road, most of the land is simply shelf and drainage; the largest river is the Colville.

You pass several pipeline stations and finally roll into Deadhorse at Mile 414. This is as far as you can drive. To get the last few miles, you're going to have to hook up with a tour operator who is allowed to cross the oilfields and take you to the Arctic Ocean. There's nothing to do in Deadhorse itself – it's just an oil rig support station and a security gate for the oilfields to the north.

You can stay and eat at the **Arctic Caribou Lodge** (☎ 907-659-2368, 877-659-2368) – they're actually authorized to take you to the ocean. The lodge is run by the local Native corporation, and you'll get a better deal here than working with one of the groups based in Fairbanks. Of course, by this point you've done the hardest part of the road yourself.

North Slope Oil Fields

If you book onto a bus that takes you from Deadhorse on to the ocean, you'll through the Prudhoe Bay oil fields. These are not the ones people are arguing about developing; these are here, and they'll stay here, for at least a few more years, until the wells run dry.

The North Slope actually includes 19 oil fields, not just one. Over those fields are scattered 3,900 separate oil wells, pumping out over a million barrels of oil a day, or enough oil to run the US for a little over an hour and a half.

Development of the North Slope was the biggest thing to happen to Alaska since the Russians stopped bopping fur-bearing animals on the head and shipping their skins off to China. When the pipeline was being built, the entire state felt like it was raining money. Now, when worldwide oil prices catch a cold, Alaska catches the flu.

Still, there's enough money coming off the slope to pay for Alaska's Permanent Fund, a stockpile of money that gets shelled out to residents in yearly chunks. Each year, everyone in the state gets a check for around a grand, thanks to you and your gas guzzling car that you drive around down south. Actually, when the fund was first set up, back in the early 80s, there were suggestions for more amusing ways of paying out the money, including dropping bags of silver dollars from airplanes flying over the bush. That way the people who worked the hardest to get it would get the biggest share of the change.

The North Slope oil is what keeps Alaska moving. No denying it. There's a reasonable safety record around the wells, and most environmentalists have given up fussing about little minor details like the waste pits that dot the landscape like periods dot this page. The battle now – and for the foreseeable future – is for ANWR, the Arctic National Wildlife Refuge.

■ Alaska National Wildlife Refuge

 One good reason to visit Deadhorse and the Slope is to see how your federal government is hoping to kill yet another wilderness area for the sake of short-term development. While the North Slope/Prudhoe Bay oilfields are huge – they've been pumping oil for the past 30 years – the disputed fields in the Alaska National Wildlife Refuge (ANWR) are really quite small. Some estimates say that they'd be dry in well under seven years if they were developed. It's roughly enough oil to run the US for six months. That's it.

Each year, pro-development forces descend upon Congress, begging them to start punching holes in the land. Every year, so far – but don't count on the holdouts lasting much longer – sanity has prevailed and ANWR has remained protected. But if you want to see it before they kill it (and the massive Porcupine caribou herd with it) – if you want to see the tundra while it is still pristine and unscarred by drilling rigs, jeep trails, gravel roads, and workmen looking desperately for entertainment – go now. ANWR is one of the most endangered areas in the state, perhaps surpassed only by Prince William Sound, which (thanks to the road to Whittier and its proximity to Alaska's population center) may already be doomed. ANWR's remoteness is keeping it safe for the moment, but don't expect that to last much longer.

ANWR covers most of the area east of the Dalton Highway, from the Chandalar River to the Beaufort Sea, stretching to the Canadian border. There are no roads in, but you can arrange to fly in from Fairbanks or Coldfoot. As with Gates of the Arctic, you have to know what you're doing to survive in ANWR. Being unprepared is a messy way to die.

There are great rivers moving through the park, including the Porcupine, the Ivishak, the Wind, and the Sheenjek. This is as far out as you can get and still be in the US.

The land has been home to various groups of Natives for thousands of years, and there are still a few villages inside the boundaries of the reserve. There are also countless archaeological sites, which should be left entirely alone.

ANWR is more wild than Gates of the Arctic, and less visited. Expect to see bears, wolves and, if you're really lucky, musk oxen, part of a herd reintroduced into the refuge in 1969. Just to see that is worth the trip. There are also about 140 species of bird that nest in the refuge, including six types of owl, six kinds of falcon, and eight species from the family Accipitridae, which includes harriers, hawks, and eagles.

Book a flight and buy your topo maps in the cities. You're on your own out here. That's a big part of the reason it's so incredibly beautiful.

There is no way to express the beauty of this landscape; it's difficult to imagine anyone wanting to damage it, but greed and stupidity do run rampant in the halls of government.

> **WEATHER ALERT:** Plan on weather days. Weather here changes fast and with very little warning. Try to stay dry – if you get wet, hypothermia can hit very, very quickly.

The ANWR Fight

ANWR covers 19.6 million acres. The idea, when it was set aside – at the same time as Ivvavik and Vuntut, in the Yukon, which are contiguous and under much better, more sane management – was that ANWR would be safe from development forever. That lasted almost 10 years. In 1980, Congress set aside eight million acres as wilderness; as for the rest, they more or less rolled their bellies up and invited oil companies to come scratch them.

ANWR is the last place in this entire country that has not been gutted by human development. When you travel through Alaska, you see wide swaths of territory that looks pristine to you, but the truth is, it's been mined, developed, folded, spindled, and mutilated for at least the past hundred years. ANWR is this nation's last hope for retaining a piece of the world in its natural state.

Okay, great, hard to argue with that, especially as it's stuck off way up in a corner of the country where nobody wants to go anyway, right?

But there's oil there. And no matter how we – and we include ourselves in this – complain, the truth is, we're not giving up our cars anytime soon, much less any of the billion items made of plastic that we use every day. And so this marvelous chunk of territory, home to musk oxen, grizzly bears, wolves, the Porcupine caribou herd, and more than 135 species of birds, is ultimately going to get sacrificed on the altar of the weekend trip to the mall.

Didn't you get the hint when George Bush named an oil company executive as his running mate? It's inevitable. The balance of power will sooner or later shift and the powers that be – the people we ostensibly trust to act in our interest – will open the reserve to drilling, chop out hundreds of acres of tundra for airfields and support crews, and there will be roads, slowly sinking into the permafrost. There will be new plans for pipelines and towns where a half gallon of milk costs $6.

To justify it, they'll tell you that we're decreasing dependence on OPEC (only four of the top 10 countries the US imports oil from are even in OPEC), and especially with terrorists and, well, the oil companies' money at stake, what do caribou matter (before the Iraq war, that country supplied about 8% of US oil imports).

And so what do we lose? Really?

Besides destroying miles and miles of habitat, species that have been running around the planet since time began, what we lose is something more philosophical. The US was built on the idea of wilderness, on the idea that there was room for everyone and everything. The country got the best and the brightest from around the world because it was so big, because the possibilities were endless.

Don't kid yourself that you're seeing this original ideal when you go to Yellowstone or Yosemite. Your lawn is less groomed than they are.

ANWR is the last chance the United States has to prove that people can be worthwhile, that they're not simply a destructive force.

As Gary Snyder wrote, "The world is watching: one cannot walk through a meadow or forest without a ripple of report spreading out from one's passage. The thrush darts back, the jay squalls, a beetle scuttles under the grasses, and the signal is passed along. Every creature knows when a hawk is cruising or a human strolling. The information passed through the system is intelligence."

We need the intelligence, we need the wild, a lot more than we need another week's supply of oil reserves.

Write to the president, write to Congress. Get ANWR set aside not as a refuge, but a monument – it's the difference of a word, and it's the difference between land that's open to people ruining your national heritage and keeping the world open for growth and thought.

Chapter 13

Denali Park & the George Parks Highway

The George Parks Highway, Alaska
Route 3, drops down from Fairbanks
to Anchorage, through the heart of
Alaska, touching the edge of Denali Park,
the most popular tourist attraction in the
state and home of North America's tallest
mountain, Denali (or, if you must, Mt.
McKinley).

The George Parks Highway to Denali

The George Parks Highway is one of the best roads in the state: smooth –
except for the inevitable frost heave from time to time – easy to drive,
with plenty of passing lanes on the hills (there are numerous hills heading
south from Fairbanks). The road winds and curves through a heavily forested area, roughly paralleling the tracks of the Alaska Railway.

> **WEATHER ALERT:** If you're driving this road in win-
> ter, check weather and road conditions before you start
> out – the highway gets some nasty storms.

■ Ester

The first point of interest is only seven miles south of Fairbanks:
the old gold rush mining town of Ester. Back in the gold rush days,
gold was discovered on Ester Creek, Cripple Creek, and Eva
Creek. Like developers flocking to pristine beach, the miners rushed in.
What's left today are the restored buildings of the **Ester Gold Camp**. Although it's now mostly run as a side trip for bus package tourists, it's still
kind of interesting. There's a good assortment of original buildings to ex-
plore, and a hotel, $$; also RV parking. The camp has a buffet dinner, and
show at the **Malamute Saloon**, daily at 9 pm. The show is a gold rush-era
variety show, complete with Robert Service poetry readings.

■ Nenana

 Fifty-three miles from Fairbanks is the small town of Nenana. The Athabascan name meant "a good place to carry between two rivers," and the name makes sense. Situated at the confluence of the Nenana and Tanana rivers, Nenana has been the place to switch rivers for thousands of years.

ICE CLASSIC

Nenana is also the site of one of the great annual events in Alaska. Every year thousands of people lay wagers on when the ice will break up on the Tanana River. A large tripod is set up in the river, and when the ice begins to move, signaling the end of the long winter, the tripod falls. Betting was first laid on the river here in 1917, when railroad workers were looking for something to kill their boredom. That year, the ice broke on April 30, at 11:30 am, and prize money that year was $800; in 1996, it was $300,000 – it got split among the 17 people who'd chosen the right moment. While the ice averages 42 inches thick at the beginning of April, it's eaten away by warming weather from above and the water flow from below. The ice usually goes some time between April 29 and May 12, between the hours of 9 am and 4 pm. Guessing the exact day and time is what wins you the pot. You can enter your guesses at the Nenana Visitors Center (at the highway near the bridge) or drop your tickets in any of the red Ice Classic cans around town. Tickets are $2 per guess, and are sold from February 1 through April 5.

Nenana is also famous as the spot where the golden spike was driven (by President Harding, in 1923; one of the theories about his death is that he caught cold while doing it, which was the last straw for his already exhausted system; however, the people of Talkeetna also claim their fame for killing off a president) to mark the completion of the Alaska Railroad. The depot is still standing – it was heavily restored in 1988 – one of only four original depot buildings left in the state. It houses the **Alaska Railroad Museum,** open 8 to 6 daily. A bit dark and dingy inside, but good fun for rail fans.

For engineering fans, Nenana has a 701-foot-long **single-span railroad bridge**, the only one of its kind in the world. It's still used.

Nenana is a nice spot to get out of the car and stretch your legs for a while. It's still a working town, sending tugs with supplies up the rivers. Quite a few buildings around town have made the National Historic Register, so taking a short walk can be very rewarding.

The town also has some good **shopping**. For railroad fans, try the gift shop inside the museum. If you saw an Alaska souvenir somewhere that you've regretted not buying for the past 500 miles, try the **Tripod**, right across from the Visitors Center. If it's got an Alaskan motif, they've got it.

Nenana Cultural Center, down by the river on Front Street at E, has some Native craftsmen at work, and a few things for sale. Makes for a nice walk.

Nearby, at Front and B, is **St. Mark's Mission Church**, a pretty little log cabin church with beautifully engraved pews and altar. It's frequently open, so check the door.

Your best bet for food is the **Tamarack Inn**, which serves dinner only – steak and seafood – at prices up to $40. If it's lunch you're after, try the **Depot Café**, which features sandwiches, huge cinnamon rolls, and home-made pies, with prices from $2 to $10. **Two Choice's Café**, on A St., has good standard dinner food.

Leaving Nenana

If you missed the Tripod in Nenana and are back on the road, try the **Tatlanika Trading Company**, Mile 82, for a wide selection of hand-made goods. With furs and a few displays of items from Alaska's past, it's worth a stop.

By Mile 248.8, the town of **Healy**, you're more or less on the outskirts of Denali. For the next 20 miles or so there are outfitters, hotels, shops, and suppliers geared entirely toward people heading into the park.

Just east of the highway, in Healy, you can see a 36-cubic-yard walking dragline, which was used to expose coal seams. The machine moved 24,000 cubic yards of earth every 24 hours.

Nenana River.

The **Mt. Healy Overlook Trail** is a reasonably easy five-mile round-trip that gives you views toward Denali without the crowds you'll encounter closer to the park. The trailhead is near the Denali Park Hotel.

Denali Park, George Parks Highway

The Denali Outskirts

The closer you get to the park entrance, the more places there are ready to cater to your whims. This area is one of the fastest growing in the state, because everybody knows all tourist roads lead to Denali. This is where the luxury hotels and restaurants are, as well as a variety of outfitters for helicopter flights and rafting adventures.

■ Getting Here

If you're not driving yourself, there is a useful shuttle service with Denali stops on its route between Anchorage and Fairbanks. Contact **Alaska Shuttle**, ☎ 888-600-6001, on the web at www.alaskashuttle.com. Round-trip fares are: Anchorage-Denali, $137; Fairbanks-Denali, $83.

Or, you can take the train. **The Alaska Railroad** has Denali stops on its Anchorage-Fairbanks run. You leave Anchorage at 8:15 am, and you're at the park by 3:45; if you're coming from Fairbanks, you still leave at 8:45, but you get here by noon. Anchorage to Denali is $129 in peak summer season; Fairbanks to Denali is $56. The railroad also has packages with overnight stays and transport. Call them at ☎ 800-544-0552, or in Anchorage at ☎ 907-265-2494, online at www.alaskarailroad.com. A really nice way to travel to the park.

■ Out & About

Strung out along the highway outside of Denali Park are companies ready to take you on expeditions into the park or along its edges. All the hotels book tours, but they have the usual hotel markups. If you don't see what you're looking for here, check the Talkeetna section, too: Talkeetna serves as the general base camp for Denali climbers, and there are a ton of operators there who are probably a few bucks cheaper than what you can find right outside the park.

Rafting on the Nenana

One of the main reasons to stop here is for a chance to raft the Nenana River (that's it right beside the road). Traditionally, the Nenana wasn't of much use; it's too wild and too cold. That makes it perfect for rafting. There are Class IV rapids minutes from the park entrance.

Know in advance: you will be cold on the river, and if the water's running high, there's always a chance you'll get bounced out of the boat and have to swim a bit. If you find yourself in the water, point your feet downstream and ride with the current as if you were sitting in a chair – make sure you can see your toes. If something is going to bash into a rock, better your feet than your head. You'll get a safety lecture before you're allowed on the boat, and don't worry, the guides have had plenty of practice pulling people out of the water.

Nenana Raft Adventures (☎ 800-789-RAFT, www.alaskaraft.com) has three-hour trips through Class III and IV whitewater that run $75. You have a choice of going in the float raft – the guide does all the work and you concentrate on hanging on – or the paddle raft, where you and your fellow passengers paddle and have nothing to hang on to. They've also got overnights.

Denali Raft Adventures (☎ 907-683-2234, www.denaliraft.com) has two-hour runs on the same stretch of river that start at $72, with full-day trips running $159. You'll find some good whitewater and some easy floating.

If you've got time, you're better off with longer trips on the Nenana; the short trips follow the course of the road, and all too often your view is of the white backs of RVs. Take-out is right where it starts to get really scenic. However, as far as the water itself goes, there's plenty of good stuff in the short trip. If you just want to see what whitewater rafting is all about, the short trips will more than satisfy your curiosity.

The best thing about being on the Nenana, even for the short trips, is that it's a great, cheap introduction to rafting. There aren't many other places around where you can be in this kind of water this close to a road. Think of it as a good sampler to see if you want to do one of the big trophy rivers in the state – the Stikine, say, or the Alsek.

■ Food

Almost all of the hotels have dining rooms, but if you're looking for something different than hotel fare, you'll find some nice places to eat around Denali. All of these places are right in the main drag, unless otherwise noted.

Lynx Creek Pizza is the place of choice for locals. It's open from 11 am to 11 pm. Prices for a large pizza start at $13. Right across the street is the **Denali Salmon Bake**, where dinner will run you $15. **The Denali Smoke Shack**, just north of the park entrance, has vegetarian fare, plus serious barbecue, with prices from $10.

The Black Bear Coffee Shop has good veggie wraps for $8.

Just south of the park is **The Perch**, a great choice for breakfast, lunch, or dinner. The bakery opens at 6 am, and they make great take-out sandwiches to help the bus ride to Wonder Lake seem a little shorter.

■ Accommodations

If you don't want to camp in the park, or if you can't get a space inside, you should be able to find something around the park entrance. Start your search early in the day. In summer the whole area is jammed. In the winter, it's completely shut down.

In Healy, the **Totem Inn** (☎ 907-683-2420, www.toteminn.com) is a nice choice on the lower end of the $$$$ scale.

Closer to the park, **Denali River Cabins** (☎ 907-683-2500 or 800-230-7275, www.denalirivercabins.com) offers luxury cabins, $$$, with hot tubs and saunas. This is a very relaxed – and relaxing – spot to stay.

Sourdough Cabins (☎ 907-683-2773), Mile 238.8, is about as close as you're going to get to the park entrance. This beautiful, laid-back place has cabins under $200. In the same price range, next door are the **Denali Crow's Nest Log Cabins** (☎ 907-683-2723, 888-917-8130, www.denalicrowsnest.com), with great views, a rooftop Jacuzzi, and secluded cabins. Highly recommended. Their Overlook Café has great burgers.

Staying in the $150-200 range, there's the **Denali North Star Inn** (☎ 907-684-1560, 800-684-1560), Mile 248, and the **Denali Bluffs Hotel** (☎ 800-488-7002, www.denalialaska.com), at Mile 238. Both are good choices.

A bit cheaper is the **Denali RV Park and Motel**, at Mile 245 (☎ 800-478-1501, www.denalirvpark.com). Low $$$$, which is quite a bargain for the area.

McKinley Creekside Cabins (☎ 907-683-2277, 888-5DENALI, www.mckinleycabins.com) and **Carlo Creek Lodge** (☎ 907-683-2576, www.carlocreek.com) are both at Mile 224, a bit away from the park, but you can get cabins here for low $$$$. The advantage is that you're away from the hustle bustle of the strip at the park entrance.

Camping

Obviously, the places of choice to camp are inside the park. But if you need a night outside first, there are some good choices.

The best of these is six miles south of the entrance, **Grizzly Bear** (☎ 907-683-2696, 866-583-2696, www.denaligrizzlybear.com), which has the nicest campsites, with some tent sites are right on the riverbanks. They've also got full hookups for RVs, and bunch of cabins with varying degrees of comfort, starting at $$ without running water, moving to nice luxury for $$$$. Call first.

The **Denali RV Park and Motel** has good RV sites; showers are available. They're at Mile 245 (☎ 800-478-1501, www.denalirvpark.com).

Denali Riverside RV Park is just what it sounds like: if you're rafting the Nenana, these are the RVs you see parked on the cliff above you. It's at Mile 240, dry or serviced sites. ☎ 888-778-7700, www.denaliriversiderv.com.

Denali National Park

Denali is, bar none, the most popular attraction in Alaska. The park draws more than a million visitors a year – and while Yellowstone may get that in a couple of busy weekends, remember that only 500,000 or so people live in the entire state of Alaska.

■ History

The park was the idea of Charles Sheldon, a naturalist who first traveled the area in 1906 with his guide, Harry Karstens. Karstens was the first man on the peak of Denali. Sheldon and Karstens cooked up the idea for the park during late nights at the campfire. Sheldon came back in 1907, trying to map out a natural set of boundaries for his dream and, in 1917, his dream came true when Mount McKinley National Park was established. Sheldon had pushed for the name Denali, the local name for the mountain, but he was overruled. It wasn't until 1980, when the park's boundaries were redrawn (at the park's formation, Denali itself was not entirely within the park borders) that the park changed its name. Officially, the state of Alaska has also changed the name of the mountain to Denali – it means "the great one" – but the change has yet to be accepted by the national board in charge of such things. That's okay. They're the only ones not calling the mountain Denali.

The park has been designated a biosphere reserve by UNESCO.

■ Geography

The centerpiece of the park is the **Alaska Range**. This chain of mountains divides south-central Alaska from the interior plateau. Pushed up by the Denali Fault, the chain stretches for 1,300 miles, arcing to the Aleutian Islands, where it meets up with the Aleutian Chain. There are active volcanoes in the chain, and earthquakes are fairly common.

The centerpiece of the Alaska Range is, of course, the mountain. The mountain – call it Denali or Mt. McKinley, around the park it's just "the mountain" – is the focus of the entire park, even though its looming presence is seen by perhaps only 25% of all travelers to the area.

The mountain creates its own weather patterns, and clearly the mountain likes cloudy and cold. Moist air coming in from the south side of the mountain can't get over the massif, so rain and snow fall more to the south – which means there are more glaciers on that side. Winter temperatures of below 100° F. are not uncommon on the mountain, and winds of 150 mph have been measured. Over half the mountain is permanently covered in snow.

The mountain is the highest point in North America and the tallest mountain in the world. Everest, of course, is higher, but it does not have nearly the vertical rise of Denali. From base to top, Denali is it in the way of big mountains, with a vertical rise of 18,000 feet. Many peaks in the Himalayas are considerably higher than Denali, but they start on the Tibetan Plateau, at 8,000 feet or so above sea level. Comparing Everest and Denali is like saying a short guy standing on a chair is taller than Wilt Chamberlin.

The mountain is double-peaked. The higher of the two peaks, the **South Summit**, is 20,320 feet; the **North Summit** is 19,470 feet, and it was the first to be climbed. On June 21, 1989, a team of researchers determined that the mountain is probably a little bit higher than originally thought, but the arguments continue. Geologists say the mountain is still rising from the upward push of the Denali Fault.

The mountain is climbed by herds of professional climbers every year, most of whom start off from Talkeetna, fly in to base camp, Kahiltna, and start their climb there. About a thousand climbers a year try the mountain. Recently there has been considerable controversy over unprepared teams on the mountain forcing rescue workers to risk their own lives to save a bunch of yahoos. Climbing teams from Korea, Japan, and Taiwan are particularly notorious for nose-diving off the mountain and needing rescue – there's a section of the mountain called the Orient Express, famous for being where these climbers falling off. One Taiwanese crew got stuck, necessitating one of the most dangerous rescues ever attempted by the local heroes, and showed up on Everest the next year, having learned nothing. It could be a prime example of Darwinian lack of fitness, but the fine rescue crews keep pulling unprepared asses out of the fire.

There's a new climbing center in Talkeetna where you must register for the climb (60-day advance notice is required) and pay your $150 fee. With the increasing popularity of guided climbs – $5,000-20,000 gets you a shot at the summit with a seasoned climber – more and more yahoos will be falling off the mountain.

 Read Jon Krakauer's book, *Into Thin Air*, to see how well guided climbs work in the Himalayas. Another book of his, *Eiger Dreams*, includes a great look at Denali climbing culture.

The **Talkeetna Museum** has a large-scale model of the Denali massif, with clippings and a history of summit accounts. See the *Talkeetna* section, below.

How to Climb the Mountain

Denali, as one of the seven summits – the highest mountains on each of the continents – is a very desirable peak to bag. In the year 2000, 1,209 people tried to make it up Denali. Surprisingly, 630 of them succeeded, peaking out.

Here's what they had to do.

Thanks to being in the middle of a national park, Denali is one of the most accessible serious mountains in the world. It's also one of the cheapest – whereas a permit for many peaks in the Himalayas can run upwards of $20,000, to apply to climb Denali costs you only $150. You can't even buy a decent ice axe for that.

Climbing season is short on the mountain. A few climbers trickle onto Denali in late April, but over 90% of them take it on in May and June. After that, the snowmelt is uncertain, and the chances of avalanche are too high; before that, you're too likely to freeze to death.

There are more than 30 lines that have been climbed on the mountain, and there are 11 well-established routes, such as the Czech Direct, the Cassian Ridge, the Messner Couloir. However, like the season, the route for most climbers is pretty much predetermined: almost everybody heads up the **West Buttress**. Of the 1,209 climbers the mountain saw in the year 2000, 1,047 of them took this route. It's the shortest, it's the most accessible, and it's the one with the best hope of someone bailing you out when you run into trouble.

No later than 60 days before your proposed climb, you must send an application to the ranger station in Talkeetna. The application asks how you're planning to get to the mountain, how many people you're climbing with, and who to call if you never come back. There's also a half-page given over to describing your previous climbs.

However, here we hit a problem. The mountain is in the middle of a park, with guaranteed access to all. You have to apply, but they can't turn you down. Your arthritic Aunt Gertrude who hasn't left the front porch in 20 years is eligible to climb the mountain, as long as she fills out the form and sends in her fees.

If you are grossly unqualified – if you haven't bagged your share of serious mountains in the past – the rangers will do everything they can to discourage you. There is a mandatory check-in at the ranger station, which comes with an orientation and briefing; it's the rangers' last chance to keep the unprepared off the mountain.

The official handout states that climbers "will be carrying heavy loads (often 60-90 lbs.)... at altitudes between 7,000 and 20,000 feet. Temperatures may range from 90° F. to -50F.... Conditions may vary from intense snow glare to severe snow storms with whiteout and winds in excess of 100 mph.. .. Expeditions usually last from two to five weeks. Prolonged confinement within cramped tents or snow caves due to bad weather often occurs."

Just as a quick comparison, Everest is a fairly warm mountain; in October, long after everybody has gone home for the year, temperatures below zero hit. For Denali, that's a nice summer day halfway up the mountain. The official handout says "It is not uncommon to find it -50° F at the 17,200 camp in early May."

If you're going to do it, allow 25 days for your climb. Day 4 is your first actual day heading up hill; over the next seven days, you climb to 13,500 feet (the camp there is prone to falling rock), climbing high, sleeping low. After a rest day, you go to 16,000 feet (camp hazards: "high winds and icy, steep terrain; contaminated snow; limited space"), rest a day (you'll need it), and then spend two more days going up the next thousand feet, where you can camp in an avalanche zone while you take a couple more rest days. Hope to hit the summit between 18-21 days after you reach the mountain, if the weather gods are with you. Then, of course, you have to get down. And, as *Rock and Ice* magazine points out, "The headwall below Denali Pass is frequently the site of accidents, as tired climbers slip while descending."

If it still sounds like fun, you get a flight up to the glacier from Talkeetna. The glacier serves as base camp for all those who want to run up the hill. It's at about 7,000 feet, and it's scattered with tents, equipment, and the leftovers of people who didn't bother to clean up after themselves. Proper disposal of human waste is one of the biggest problems on the mountain. New regulations require that every climber bring out a bag of trash, but it'll be a long, long time before the mountain is clean.

Once you're up there, you get to start thinking about acute mountain sickness (AMS) and high-altitude pulmonary edema (HAPES). Both of these are nature's way of telling you that you're not supposed to be that far above the ocean. AMS can hit you anywhere above 8,000 feet. We can tell you from experience that even a mild case of this is no fun. You get a headache, you get dizzy, you're too tired to bother leaning over when the nausea hits you and you have to vomit. Once you decrease in altitude some, you start feeling better.

HAPES is rather more serious. It tends to appear above 9,000 feet, most often after you've been working too hard climbing during the day. You get tired, you can't breathe, you start to cough. After a while, you start coughing up bloody froth and your lips and fingernails turn blue. None of these are good things. The only treatment is to get downhill, as fast as your buddies can drag you.

There are a couple of other hazards of high altitude, but before you worry too much about them on the mountain, you have other problems. First is getting across the glaciers and icefalls. There's a horrific story of a pair of climbers in the Himalayas. One fell into a glacial crevasse and stuck, head down. His friend tried for nearly two days to get him out – to no avail. For much of that time, the stuck man was conscious and knew exactly what was happening to him.

And of course, there's always a chance for an avalanche.

The men and women who rescue stuck climbers on Denali are among the bravest people in the world, flying into storms, taking helicopters past their design tolerances, lowering themselves onto slopes where no one has any business being. The average cost for a helicopter rescue runs at least $7,500, and can go a lot higher, depending on where the climbers are stuck and what's wrong with them. The tragedies of death on the mountain are compounded when, as happens from time to time, rescuers are killed while trying to save others.

Despite all this, people do make it up the mountain. If you're not feeling up to leading the expedition yourself, you can hire guides to take you up – but all they can do is organize, the strength and fortitude have to be yours. Give a call to **Alaska Denali Guiding** (☎ 907-733-2649), the **American Alpine Institute** (☎ 907-360-671-1505), or **National Outdoor Leadership School** (☎ 907-745-4047) to see what it's going to cost you. Plan at least a year ahead, start training – say, by strapping a 50-pound backpack on and running up the stairs of the nearest 60-story building for a few hours. In *Rock and Ice* magazine's special guide issue, in the winter of 2000, they lay out a six-month fitness program.

If you're satisfied with an armchair climb of the mountain, there are plenty of good books on it. Start with *High Alaska: A Historical Guide to Denali, Mt. Foraker, and Mount Hunter*, by Jonathan Waterman. He's also the author of *In the Shadow of Denali*. Terris Moore's *McKinley: The Pioneer Climbs* is a great look back at the early days of mountaineering, when they used tent poles instead of ice axes.

FIRST ASCENT

Although Harry Karstens is credited with the first ascent of the mountain, there was one who made the claim before him: **Dr. Frederick Cook**, who later became yet more famous for claiming to reach the North Pole before Peary. The Pole claim is still up for debate – Cook may have really done it (although probably not), and Peary's own claims would entail having Superman pulling the dog sleds to get in the mileage Peary said he made – but there is no doubt Cook was faking McKinley.

Cook claimed to reach the peak on September 16, 1906. On the 27th of the month, Cook sent out a telegram that said, "We have reached the summit of Mount McKinley by a new route from the North." His summit account was given at a speech to President Roosevelt and company: "The top of the continent, our North Pole had been reached. To an ice ax the flag was attached.... We had been eight days in ascending, but remained only 20 minutes."

Cook and his crew were people dramatically unprepared for the landscape. Robert M. Bryce's *Cook & Peary: The Polar Controversy, Resolved*, the definitive account of the two explorers' travels, says that Cook's supplies included "an ordinary horshair rope, the silk tent, pemmican and an alcohol stove, two thermometers, three aneroid barometers, a watch, a prismatic compass... a rubber floor cloth, tent pegs, aluminum kitchen gear and a pocketknife.... They each worse lightweight underwear and a flannel shirt with wool trousers and socks." In other words, these guys were hypothermia deaths waiting to happen, and it's just as well they didn't head up the mountain – if they had, they'd probably still be up there like that popsicle you always forget is in your freezer.

Cook's account of reaching the peak reads, "We stood up under a black sky so low that we felt as if we could nearly touch it. We had reached the top. What a task!... Then followed a long gaze over the cold wide world spread out at our feet.... Here, under our feet, was the top of the continent, the north pole of our ambitions, probably the coldest spot on earth, and we were the most miserable of men at a time when we should have been elated."

This is all well and good, but the photos Cook brought back, reputedly of the peak, were of a different peak, nowhere near Denali and only 8,000 feet high. Sadly for Cook, all this came out only when his claim to have reached the North Pole was contested.

Traveling in September, it's doubtful Cook even saw the peak he claimed to have climbed. The weather just wouldn't have been in his favor.

The sad thing is that the controversy over his Pole attempt and his faked McKinley climb obscure what he really did: he managed an astounding journey across unmapped parts of Alaska at a horrible time of year. He went places no one had ever been before. If the same trip were made now, it would have corporate sponsors and a National Geographic special.

Nobody doubts his trip; just his walk uphill.

Your best chance to see the mountain is in August, in the mornings. It's a rare afternoon that the peak does not cloud up. There's absolutely no way to predict visibility. Stand around the Visitors Center for a few minutes, and you'll hear 50 people ask the harried rangers if the mountain will be visible tomorrow. The invariable answer: Who knows? It's almost a miracle that, in 1794, George Vancouver spotted the peak from Cook Inlet, reporting "a stupendous snow mountain."

The mountain is far from being the park's only attraction. In fact, since it's invisible most of the time, it's hardly an attraction at all. If you can't see the mountain, focus on the things closer to you. There are more than 430 species of flowering plant in the park, plus countless varieties of mosses, lichen, and fungi on the vast tundra plains. There are glaciers in nearly every direction, including **Mudrow Glacier,** which has such thick deposits of organic material that it is hard to identify as a glacier. Kettle ponds and other erosion features left behind by retreating glaciers dot the landscape.

■ Flora & Fauna

And then there are the animals. Besides the 159 species of bird that have been spotted – from the trumpeter swan to the northern harrier to the ptarmigan to ravens and Arctic terns – officials estimate a park population of more than 3,000 caribou, 2,500 sheep, and 2,000 moose in the north part of the park alone. That's not to mention the red fox, lynx, marmots, and pika. There are also about 150 wolves (very rarely seen) and 200 grizzly bears.

The grizzly bears are not the giant Kodiak bears, but a small subspecies, the **Toklat grizzly**. Eating less protein then their fish-stuffed Kodiak relatives, the Toklats are closer to black bear size. This does not mean that they are any less dangerous. Bear-resistant food containers are built into every campground, and the park requires that anyone headed out into the backcountry must use portable containers.

The land these animals inhabit is wildly varied. The park covers six million acres, which makes it bigger than Massachusetts, so there's plenty of room for diversity.

A **taiga forest** fills the lowlands. Taiga, mostly lying in the river valleys, is made up of spruce, willow, birch, and aspen. The tree line is at about 2,700 feet in the park, which is where taiga gives way to tundra. **Tundra** is land carpeted with low-lying fungus and lichens, as well as some species of dwarf trees – dwarf willows can be an inch tall and a couple of hundred years old. In autumn, the tundra is ablaze in color – one park driver says it looks like "a big bowl of Captain Crunch cereal." Above the tundra is the land of permanent ice and snow, the caps of the Alaska Range.

■ Getting In

Denali is a limited-access park. Past a certain point, the only way you can get in is by the park bus or on foot. This has kept intrusion to a bare minimum, and has kept the park from becoming a huge parking lot like Yosemite or Yellowstone. When you come to the park and see how beautiful it is, remember that a large part of this is due to the limited access – it's the only thing saving Denali from being overrun.

■ Development

The fact that the park is nice and clean and pristine but still manages to draw a million visitors a year causes problems. Developers, those who are never happy unless they hear a bulldozer engine running, are more than anxious to turn the park into a big wilderness strip mall. Hiding behind terms like "improvement," they seek to gut Denali and ruin it for everybody except themselves and their accountants.

At the forefront of this movement are the people who have inholds inside the park. These inholds date back to before the park's formation, and their current owners have a point – restricted access to the park means restricted access to their land. However, to open their land the entire park would have to be opened. There is a certain concept of the serving the greater good, not being selfish.

The Park Service itself (which, along with the National Forest Service, is famed worldwide for selling trees below cost to foreign countries) is anxious to build in the park. Never mind that the vast majority of Alaska residents are against it. There are two development plans headed for implementation, and a third being studied. They boil down to an increase of development along the road, and opening up the southern area of the park, which has traditionally been left entirely alone. The Petersville Road would be widened and paved clear to the mountain, and the Tokositna River's pristine flow would be trashed by opening services along its banks.

If this isn't ugly enough, because Denali is a "preserve" and not a "refuge," wolf hunting and trapping are allowed here. The annual legal wolf kill in Alaska amounts to nearly a quarter of the state's wolf population. For centuries there was a pack that made its home near the park entrance; the last of these wolves was killed in 1995.

When you go into the park, look at the trees, the mountains, the huge open vistas of tundra. It is incredible, and it is very, very beautiful. Then picture it covered with fast food restaurants and convenience stores. That's where it's headed. If you want a beautiful world – what Gary Snyder called a place with "ripe blackberries to eat and a sunny spot under a pine tree to sit at" – write to your representatives in Congress and raise holy hell before the Philistines and the troglodytes have their way.

To show your support for the protection of the park and its wildlife, contact **Alaska Center for the Environment**, 519 West 8th Ave, Anchorage, ☎ 907-274-3621; or **Alaska Wildlife Alliance**, ☎ 907-277-0897.

■ Inside the Park

 It costs $10 to get into the park, which gives you seven-day access. There's a carload fare of $20, covering up to eight people. This fee applies to anyone who goes past the Savage River campsite – and that's a long time before things get really good, so pony up. These prices do not include camping or bus trips, except on the green buses.

All trips to Denali begin at the **Visitor's Center**, at Mile 1.6 on the Park Road. There's a secondary center, at Mile .5, for wilderness access. If you've been to Denali before, the Wilderness Center is the old VC.

Hit the VC for educational films are shown on bears and other subjects, the bookstore, and general park information on the park's many programs, which include daily sled dog demonstrations at 10, 2, and 4. There are also daily talks in the hotel auditorium at 1:30 and 8 pm, and most of the campgrounds have ranger talks at night. The Wilderness Center is where to go for reservations for campsites and bus tours (although you're a lot better off if you did that way in advance; see above), and where you can get bear-resistant food containers.

 Be sure to pick up a copy of the park's newspaper, the **Denali Alpenglow**.

Hiking

There are ranger-led hikes in the park. The most popular is probably the **Discovery Hike**, a moderate three- to four-hour trip in the backcountry. You need to make reservations one or two days in advance.

From the Eielson Visitors Center (closed until 2007, but you can't miss the building), there's a quick and easy **tundra walk** daily at 1:30. To appreciate tundra, you really need to see it up close.

If you want to hike on your own on an established trail, as opposed to setting out into the backcountry, there are a few choices right around the VC. The **Rock Creek Trail** is 2.3 miles one way – the trip out is mostly uphill – which gives good views of Rock Creek and Mt. Healy. It connects to the **Roadside Trail**, which takes you back to the VC on flat land. The **Mt. Healy Trail**, which starts from the Denali Park Hotel parking lot, is a five-mile round-trip with a 1,700-foot elevation change. It's hard work, but it's got great views out toward the Nenana and deeper into the park.

To go into the boonies, see the *Backcountry* section below.

■ Transportation

Buses

 Two kinds of buses run through the park. **Camper buses** are old school buses with the back seats taken out to make room for gear – tell the reservations people if you're packing a bike or inflatable boat. When you make your campsite reservation, you should also book a bus ride. Once you've got your bus ticket you can jump on any bus past Savage River. So if you're hiking around and looking for a ride, you can just flag a bus down. If they're full, they'll keep driving and you have to wait for the next one.

If you're not camping, you can still ride the camper bus, only now it's called a **shuttle bus**. It's $12.50 for rides as far as Mile 53, $31 for trips to the end of the road. Advance reservations are wise.

A special **natural history tour bus** runs daily in summer. It gives you about a three-hour trip through the park with a narrated tour, which is pretty nice. However, for your $35 you go only 17 miles out the road. If your kidneys can handle it, about the same price and 11 hours round-trip gets you on the regular shuttle bus to Wonder Lake, where the mountain looks like a wall.

> **AUTHOR TIP:** *When you load your gear on the camper bus, be aware that everybody else on the bus is going to throw their stuff on top of yours. Before you toss, make sure you've got everything you want with you: snacks, camera, binoculars, water.*

Shuttle buses start running at 6 am, and leave every half-hour. There are rest stops along the way, but even if you leave your camera in your backpack to get smashed, you should take along some water and a snack. Warm clothes to layer on as needed don't hurt, either.

The bus ride out is really the only way to see much of the park. While you see only what's right by the side of the road, it's still pretty impressive. The bus drivers are experienced at watching for animals, and they'll stop when something's spotted. Watch for caribou beyond the Savage River, Dall sheep in the hills above the Savage and Sanctuary rivers, and bears, particularly between Igloo Creek and the Eielson Visitors Center. Watch for moose in tundra ponds and wolves around the Teklanika – and consider yourself incredibly lucky if you actually see a wolf.

The **Eielson Visitors Center**, Mile 66, has great views of the mountain, if the mountain is out. There are also some interpretive displays and, if you're on the bus to Wonder Lake, a much-needed chance to stretch your legs and stop bouncing for a while.

Driving

Every year, the park holds a lottery to allow a total of 1,600 cars to drive the length of the park road. Drawings are in the fall, your name won't come up, and even if it does, the odds of you being there in mid-September are minimal.

You are allowed to drive, year-round, without a permit as far as the Savage River Campground. This is about 15 miles in, and you won't see much. To enjoy the park, you've got to get on the bus.

Mountain Biking

The road is open to mountain bikers. You have to stop in at the VC to get up on the rules and to pay the park admission fee. If you're in shape, this is the way to go. You can book a bus ride, peddle as far as you want, then load the bike into one of the shuttle buses. Bikes are not allowed on any trails or in the backcountry. You might want to ride with a bandanna across your nose and mouth to prevent yourself from choking on dust when a bus goes by.

■ Camping

Campgrounds

To repeat what we say at the beginning of this section, all campgrounds can be booked at the Wilderness Center, but the sad truth is you're not likely to be able to walk in and get the spot of your choice. Advance planning is necessary. Only Riley Creek, Teklanika, and Wonder Lake are wheelchair-accessible.

You can make reservations by calling ☎ 800-622-7275, from the third Monday in February through August 31. Lines are open from 7 am to 5 pm, Alaska time. You can also mail reservation requests to Denali Park Resorts, VTS, 241 West Ship Creek Ave., Anchorage, AK 99501. Mail reservations must be received no later than 30 days before the dates requested. You can also fax requests, from December 1 through August 31, to ☎ 907-264-4684. With your reservation request and payment for the campsite, they'll want the park admission fee; it also costs an extra $4 above the fees to make the reservations. Credit cards are accepted.

There are seven campgrounds in the park. Quiet hours are observed – no loud noises between 10 pm and 6 am – leave the boombox at home. No fires are allowed outside established grates. If you take a pet into the park, it has to be on a leash at all times. All of Denali is bear territory, so keep your camp clean, don't cook directly on the fire grates, use the bear-resistant containers, and don't leave food out. Most of the campgrounds offer programs on the park and its wildlife nightly at 8 pm during the peak season.

- **Riley Creek Campground** is right by the entrance to the park. It's the only campground open year-round, with 100 sites, flush toilets, water, a sewage dump, and pretty much no scenery at all. A night runs $12 per site.

- **Morino Backpacker Campground** is at Mile 1.9 on the park road. There is no vehicle access to the campground, and you don't have to reserve a site – just register when you get there. No open fires are allowed, so bring a cook stove. Sites are $9, with a maximum of two people per site allowed. Drinking water is available.

- **Savage River Campground**, Mile 13, has tent and RV sites. There's drinking water, and on a very clear day you may be able to see the mountain. Sites run $18 a night.

- **Sanctuary River**, Mile 23, is a tiny, tent-only campground, with seven sites. There's no drinking water here, and open fires are not allowed. Sites are $9 a night.

- **Teklanika River**, Mile 29, is as far as you are allowed to go in a private vehicle, and you only come this far if you've got reservations for the campground. Beyond here, the only transportation is by bus or foot. The campground has 53 sites, water, flush plumbing, and a minimum three-night stay for vehicles – this helps keep traffic on the road down. Sites are $16 a night.

■ **Igloo Creek**, Mile 34, is another tiny tent campground, much like Sanctuary River. No open fires. Sites are $9 a night.

■ The most popular campground for tenters is **Wonder Lake**, Mile 85, the end of the park road. Wonder Lake is only 25 miles from the base of Denali, and on a clear day it looks like the sky ends in a wall. There is no way to describe how big the mountain is from here. We've hiked the Himalayas, and they're tiny compared to this. The bus trip out to Wonder Lake takes six hours or so, and you get to take in all the scenery along the way – multiple bear stops are common. Wonder Lake fills up fast – if you want a spot here, plan well in advance. It's one of the most beautiful campsites in Alaska.

> **WILDLIFE WARNING:** At any park campground, there's a good chance of animals wandering through. Keep your cool and don't approach them. Absolutely do not offer up any food. The general guidelines from the park say to stay a quarter-mile away from grizzlies and at least 75 feet away from anything else. If you see a nest or a den of anything, head away from it. If you see a bear, don't run – food runs. Talk to it in a low voice and show it you're not interesting. If you see a moose, haul ass outta there – moose food doesn't run.

Backcountry

There's no reason to stick to the established campgrounds. If you want to head out into the wild, all you need is a backcountry permit, a bear-resistant food container, and some comfortable boots.

The permit is free and available at the Wilderness Center. There are no reservations – just come in the day before you want to head into the bush. The Wilderness Center will loan you the bear-resistant food container, or you can buy one at the VC bookstore. If you're only going out for a hike and don't plan to camp, you can skip the permit, but the food container is still a good idea.

Denali's backcountry is divided into 43 units, and backpacker access is limited – only 12 permits per day for each unit. There's a quick, useful, and mandatory survival course before they let you head out.

You may not be able to hike into the area you want to, simply because it's at capacity (a very low capacity, but the park is trying hard to keep these places beautiful). Other areas may be closed off because of animal activity – for instance, a wolf kill will shut down an area.

At the Wilderness Center, they have **Backcountry Description Guides**, or you can buy **The Backcountry Companion**, which details the areas. Read through these, and then pick two or three areas to try before you go talk to the rangers. Polychrome Pass is especially popular – it's about 2.5 hours from the VC, with great mountain views.

Get a topo map before you go. It's easy to get lost out there. If you can't read a topo map, stick to the road.

The best mountain views are in units 5 and 6.

After you've registered, book a trip on the camper bus and tell the driver where you're getting off.

In the backcountry, stick to leave-no-trace camping – pack it in, pack it out, don't alter sites, and try not to cut new trails. Stay out of muddy areas, stick to small groups, and remember that open fires are not allowed. You'll need to pack in a camp stove.

> **WEATHER ALERT:** The weather is unpredictable, so pack warm clothes. In July temperatures can range from near freezing to a fairly toasty 75. Summer in the park is also rainy season – about two inches of rain falls during each summer month.

If you're crossing a river, remember the river is stronger than you. Before you get into the water, check the current, check the depth, and figure out a way to retreat quickly. If you get dunked, get into dry clothes (if your pack didn't get dunked) as quickly as possible. Your boots are probably not anywhere near as waterproof as the salesman told you, so bring extra socks and a quick-dry pack towel. Remember that even fish don't really like Denali's rivers – they're too cold and filled with too much glacial silt.

Before heading out into the backcountry, reread the sections of this book on how to react around bears and what to do in case of hypothermia. Official statistics, though, say there have only been about 20 human-bear encounters in the park over the past 50 years.

If you're hiking, stay out of willow thickets. The official word may be to run from moose, but the truth is, they run faster, and if you scare a mother taking her baby for a nice browse in the willows, you're in serious trouble.

A final warning for all park visitors: Pack lots of mosquito repellant. Mosquitos are the only animals you can feed legally in the park, and your footstep on the path sounds like a dinner bell to them.

Denali Park, George Parks Highway

The George Parks Highway to the Glenn Highway Junction

The last bit of the George Parks Highway parallels the edge of the two Denali Parks (see below) to the town of Talkeetna, then moves through the Mat-Su Valley until it joins up with the Glenn Highway for the final miles into Anchorage.

After you get past the last of the places built up around the park entrance, you head into absolutely gorgeous scenery for 80 miles or so. You go by the town of **Cantwell** (about two miles off the Parks Highway) and the junction with the Denali Highway at Mile 210 (see the Denali Highway side-trip in Chapter 11). **Broad Pass** is at Mile 201 – this is the divide of the watersheds for streams flowing into Cook Inlet and those headed for the Yukon.

Between Miles 169 and 132, you're not traveling along the borders of Denali National Park, but Denali State Park. **Denali State Park**, which abuts the national park, is another 325,000 acres of park land, much less developed than the national park.

Camp at Mile 147, **Byers Lake**, one of the better state-run grounds, with 66 sites. If that's full, try Lower Troublesome Creek, at Mile 137.

On a clear day, watch for views of Denali at Mile 135. Even if the mountain is clouded in, you should get a nice view of the Alaska Range's glaciers, glinting in the light.

Mile 115 is the junction to the Petersburg Road, which leads back to the small town of **Trappers Creek**, a mining and homesteading area. The road is about 40 miles long, all gravel.

Another road spur at Mile 98.7 is the Talkeetna Junction. Head north 15 miles to the town of Talkeetna.

■ Talkeetna

Talkeetna is the base for nearly every climbing expedition heading into the Alaska Range. The town started as a supply center – located at the junction of the Talkeetna, Susitna, and Culitna rivers, it was a natural stopping point. It later became headquarters for the construction of the Alaska Railroad. Today the town is centered along Main Street. It's a rough-and-tumble kind of town, inhabited mostly by people who seem brusque until they get to know you. **The Fairview Inn** charges 25 cents for answering a question about the town. It's a place where climbers, bush pilots, and true individualists seem to hold court, and it's a really cool place to spend a day or two – probably the closest thing you'll find to the Alaska in *Northern Exposure* reruns. The town isn't much more than a roundabout and a few shops, but it's got a feel to it.

Things to Do

The **Visitor Center** is back out at the road junction, inside the gift shop. If you're in town, head to the **Talkeetna Historical Society Museum**, located in the old schoolhouse a street back from the main roundabout. The main reason to stop in is to see the display of mountain-climbing gear and photos, and to check out the model of the Denali massif. Shrines to Bradford Washburne and Ray Genet are mixed with clippings and histories of Denali climbers. There's also a restored trapper's cabin and the old railroad depot.

The **Mountaineering Ranger Station** (☎ 907-733-2231) is open full-time in the summer, offering information on climbing the Alaskas. They've got reference manuals, videos, and the like.

To see the price that some pay to climb, check out the old cemetery across from the airstrip – there's a monument that lists everyone who has died trying to climb Denali; a surprising number of the individual markers are in Japanese or Korean. It's a very moving place, a memorial for people who died doing something they dreamed about.

Out & About

The town thrives on its proximity to Denali, and Talkeetna has got more than its share of flight companies that can take you over to the mountain. **K2 Aviation** (☎ 907-733-2291, 800-764-2291, www.flyk2.com) is the biggest. They've got Denali flybys for $150, $215 with a glacier landing. The best deal is the McKinley Climber/Summit Tour, which swoops you up around the peak of the mountain, giving you views no one else offers. It's $240 for two hours.

Doug Geeting Aviation (☎ 800-770-2366, www.alaskaairtours.com) has the flyby and glacier landing that K2 does, plus a $290 trip that takes you on a two-hour trip around Denali, Foraker, and Hunter, with a glacier landing.

If the two big ones are booked up, don't despair. **Hudson Air Service** (☎ 800-478-2321, www.hudsonair.com) and **Talkeetna Air Taxi** (☎ 899-533-2219, www.talkeetnaair.com) have similar deals. All of these outfitters spend a lot of their time in summer flying climbers to base camp, and the pilots on all of these are among the best in the world – they have to be, because of the changing weather conditions the Alaska Range creates. Keeping that in mind, you also have to stay pretty flexible for your Denali flight; there are days when everything is socked in, days when the mountain simply won't appear. If you're planning out your itinerary, never think "we'll fly Denali on Tuesday..." Sometimes the mountain has other plans.

Talkeetna started off as a river town, and the river is still a big draw. To get in the water, try **Mahay's Riverboat Service** (☎ 800-736-2210, www.mahaysriverboat.com). Their two-hour trip runs $55, 3½ hours for $95.

Good program, with naturalists and gold panning. They also do longer trips, and guide fishing.

If you want your time on the river without the sound of an engine, you've got a couple more choices. TRG, **Talkeetna River Guides** (☎ 800-353-2677, www.talkeetnariverguides.com) has two- and four-hour trips on the Talkeetna River or the Chulitna. The short trip is $69 for adults, $49 kids under 12; the longer trip is $115/95.

If you've got a collapsible kayak or your own raft, **Doug Geeting Aviation** (☎ 800-770-2366, www.alaskaairtours.com) has a nice trip with a drop off up on the Talkeetna River. It's a three-day float back from where they drop you – about 60 miles – with a little bit of Class III along the way. Know what you're doing, practice all proper bear precautions in camp.

Food

All that running around is going to make you hungry. All the eateries pretty much face each other on the street, so it only takes a minute to walk from place to place and see which one smells best to you.

The Talkeetna Roadhouse has a great bakery, and filling breakfasts and lunches from $6. Right across the street, the **West Rib Pub and Grill** can serve you up a caribou or musk ox burger for $8. Right next to **The Fairview Inn**, there's a barbecue tent: $17 gets you steak, salmon, or halibut. For take away, the **McKinley Deli** has subs from $7.

Accommodations

The place of choice for ambience on overnight stays is **The Fairview Inn** (☎ 907-733-2423), a building that dates back to the 1920s. It's got only seven rooms, and it can get a bit noisy, because its bar – you should stop in at the bar for a drink to check out the atmosphere no matter what – is the center of the town's nightlife.

HOTEL PRICING
Prices are in US dollars.
under $50.........$
$50-$100 ....$$
$100-$150 ......$$$
above $150.....$$$$

President Harding drank here during his trip to Alaska – he died several days later, although there's no connection. Lots of climbing stuff gives the place quite a distinctive air.

All the other places to stay are still within easy walking distance of town. **Denali Anglers** has cabins right by the Susitna River, easy walking distance to downtown. $$$

The Latitude 62° Lodge/Motel has 12 rooms, nice spot. ☎ 907-733-2262, $$-$$$.

Talkeetna Cabins is new and shiny, with nice spots that include a full kitchen, $$$. ☎ 907-733-2227 or 888-9933, www.talkeetnacabins.org.

The **Talkeetna Alaskan Lodge** is largely given over to package tours, but try here if you can't get a room elsewhere. $$$$. ☎ 888-959-9590, www. talkeetnalodge.com.

Camping

There are two campgrounds in Talkeetna. If you're a screaming masochist and like crowds, mud, and the ambience of a trailer park after a hurricane, turn left at the downtown intersection and follow the road. You'll see a dozen or so crowded sites. The advantage to this place is that, years from now when you're trading suffering travel stories with friends, you may win on this one.

If that's not your idea of fun, you have a great option: turn left at the airport, right onto the first road (at the graveyard), and you'll come to **Talkeetna River Adventures' campground**. Sixty sites in the woods, or if you've got an RV you can park it looking right over the river. A really nice spot. It wouldn't hurt to phone for reservations, ☎ 907-733-2604, but odds are they'll have an empty spot or two.

If the town is full, there are campgrounds or RV parks about every 10 miles or so between here and Anchorage.

Try to time your visit to Talkeetna for the **Moose Dropping Festival**, the second Saturday in July, for music, food, and moose chip tosses.

Back on the George Parks, from here down to Anchorage is serious dog mushing territory. Most of the best mushers – the people running the Iditarod and the Yukon Quest – live around here. You'll see signs for kennel tours and mushing trips. There are also a few wolf farms along the way, where wolf hybrids are raised.

Camp at **Montana Creek Campground**, Mile 97, which has 89 sites. Or try the **Deception Creek Campground** at Mile 71 – follow the Hatcher Pass Road 1.5 miles off the highway. Seventeen sites.

■ Willow

 Back out on the main road, you hit the town of Willow, Mile 69, which was the site of one of the biggest uproars in state history. Alaska has long suffered from having the most inaccessible state capital in the country. Juneau is inconvenient and the weather stinks, which makes it hard to fly in and out. It's also a very long way from the state's population centers. Because of all this, in 1976 the state electorate voted to move the state capital to Willow. This was done after a long and very expensive search for the best site. The logical choice, Anchorage, was voted out because half the state hates Anchorage. The next logical choice, Fairbanks, was voted out because Anchorage hates Fairbanks. Willow was a compromise, and land prices there shot up immediately.

Promptly after the vote, the people of Alaska began to wonder about the wisdom of their decision. Sponges were passed out with the word Willow printed on them – implying that it was going to do nothing more than soak up money to move the state capital. The project stalled, and in 1982 all funding was withdrawn. Then nothing happened for a very long time. And it's still not happening. Those who bought land in anticipation of the capital boom are getting the last laugh as Willow is becoming a bedroom community for Anchorage – even though it's a bit of a haul, particularly in the winter dark – and prices are rising daily.

What you see from the highway, though, is a couple of stores and a lot of driveways disappearing into the trees – and every second or third driveway will have a parked clunker for sale.

 For a good look at the early days of the capital debate, try the middle section of John McPhee's *Coming into the Country*.

The area around Willow includes the **Nancy Lake State Recreation Area**, south of town. There are more than 100 lakes in the park, all with great fishing and boating. There's also an extensive canoe trail system on the **Little Susitna River**.

■ Wasilla & The Iditarod

 The town of Wasilla, only 42 miles from Anchorage, has also become an Anchorage suburb. The town is the second starting point for the Iditarod, the 1,049-mile dogsled race to Nome. After the official photo-op start in Anchorage, the dogs and mushers are transported here, where they start again.

The town was named after a Dena'ina Athabascan chief. It's fairly new, and was built not on gold but on the railroad.

Visitor Information is at the **Dorothy G. Page Museum**, just off the Parks Highway on Main Street. It's open 10 to 6 in summer; admission to the museum is $3. The museum boasts good mining displays. Out back is the town site museum, with seven restored buildings. There's a farmers' market held here every Wednesday in summer, from 4 to 7 pm.

The **Alaska Transportation Museum** is at Mile 147 on the Parks Highway. It features trucks, trains, tractors, and planes. Admission is $5; the museum is open daily in summer 9 to 6, and if you're into this kind of thing, it's one of the better transportation displays you'll come across.

Since Wasilla hosts the Iditarod's second start, it's no surprise that the official **Iditarod Headquarters** is here. Turn on Knik Road, past the railway station. Inside, you'll see historical displays, examples of musher's equipment, and films of the race through the years. Admission is free, but they get you on the great stuff in the gift shop.

IDITAROD

The Iditarod itself starts on the first Saturday in March. Mushers use teams of up to 20 dogs to cover the 1,049-mile course, which leads to the coast in Nome. The original Iditarod Trail (for hiking information, see the *Seward* section, page 452) was used as a supply route to get food to bush villages and mining camps.

The legend of the Iditarod goes back to 1925, when a diphtheria epidemic threatened Nome, and a group of mushers headed up the trail in the dead of winter to deliver serum.

The Iditarod has gotten a lot of bad press recently from animal activists. These people have probably never seen a sled dog up close. There are no Fifth Avenue poodles more pampered and cared for than a sled dog. Along the course of the race are checkpoints and veterinarians, and no musher rests before the dogs are taken care of. The dogs are fed a better diet than the vast majority of people in the world. Most of all, these dogs love to run. One sled dog demonstration will convince you of that. It usually takes two strong guys to hold the dogs back, they're so anxious to get moving. All you have to do is walk near them with a harness, and they're ready to go. It's what they live for, and it's what the dogs love to do.

Sled dogs can run 12 mph at temperatures of 30 below – the best running temperature is right around zero.

It takes more than 2,000 people to handle the Iditarod – from checkpoint volunteers to pilots who fly in supplies. All this so the mushers – an average of 57 a year – can take their dogs out for a nice run. There is no separate category for male and female mushers – the first person to ever win the Iditarod four times was a woman, Susan Butcher (she has been doing shorter races recently, to stay closer to home and her children, but she told us she doesn't even feel like she's warmed up in the first 500 miles). More recently, Martin Buser and Jeff King have dominated the race.

After more than 1,000 miles of running, the races can be remarkably close. The 1978 race was decided by less than a second, as Dick Mackey and Rick Swenson sprinted for the finish line. In the 1997 race, just over three hours separated the top two finishers: Martin Buser and his team finished in nine days, eight hours, 30 minutes, and 45 seconds. The top 20 finishers will all come in within a day or so of each other, and even the slowest sleds aren't much farther back from the leaders than 24 hours or so.

Nobody's getting rich from the Iditarod. Prize money is only $50,000 for the winner. A team of 20 dogs eats about $10,000 worth of dog food a year – on the trail, the dogs are eating 10,000 calories a day – and runs up another $5,000 in vet bills. Most mushers keep 100 dogs or so.

There's more Iditarod stuff at the official website, **www.Iditarod.com**, or at the **Knik Museum**, Mile 13.9 on Knik Road. The museum is in a restored building left from the glory days of the town of Knik, and it houses the **Mushers Hall of Fame**. Stop in noon to 6, Wednesday through Sunday; admission is $2.

Four-time Iditarod winner, Susan Butcher.

Wasilla is fast changing from a quiet burg to a bustling suburb. It's an hour's drive into Anchorage, but this is where people are living now, and it's okay, except in winter, when you'll pass a couple of cars that have gone off the road each day.

Wasilla is in the lush **Matanuska Valley**, which includes some of the richest farmland in the world. The Matanuska River cuts through the valley and empties out into the Knik Arm, one of the two pinchers of Cook Inlet that enclose the Anchorage metro area.

The Matanuska Valley was first inhabited by Tanaina Indians, who lived north of the Matanuska River and along the Chicaloon. The Tanaina traded with coastal Indians, running the rivers down to the Knik Arm for trading. At the turn of the century the area saw its first gold rush, with gold found in Hope, Willow, and along Hatcher Pass. Trader George Palmer opened a trading post in Eklutna, and then opened a second, farther north on the Matanuska, and finally a third in the town of Knik. The town is long gone, but it was a major supply hub, sending goods from Talkeetna clear over to the Copper River.

The railroad came in, opening in 1923, bypassing Knik and building the town of Wasilla. As part of the New Deal, FDR sent homesteaders into the Matanuska Valley – 203 farmers were sent to join the few who were already farming the region. The homesteaders landed in Palmer (see the *Glenn Highway* section), and the results are the vegetable stands you'll see alongside the road.

There's an interesting little side-light to all this. Most of the homesteaders had never before been out of their home states – primarily Minnesota, Wisconsin, and Michigan. When they got to Alaska, they got land – lots were drawn at random – but equipment for actually clearing the land and getting started on it was provided by the Federal Emergency Relief Administration; most of the newcomers ended up so far in debt to the feds that they never got out – some families owed upwards of $14,000, when a skilled carpenter in the valley netted eight bucks a day. Add in epidemics of scarlet fever, measles, and chickenpox in that first year, and most of the new settlers were interested in nothing but going home.

The ones that did stay worked their butts off. By the end of the first year, there were houses and barns up, and the fields were starting to produce, although there was still a critical shortage of material. There were paved streets and a newspaper in the valley, and it only took another two years to bring electricity and telephone lines.

Today, the valley continues to grow, mostly as a long chain of bedroom communities feeding Anchorage.

At Mile 41 there's a junction on the Parks Highway with the 10-mile-long Palmer-Wasilla Road. If you're heading to Palmer, bypassing Anchorage, this cuts a few miles off the trip.

Mile 35.5 has the University of Alaska's **Matanuska Research Farm**. Free tours take about an hour.

The **Mat-Su Visitors Center** (☎ 907-746-5000), at the junction of the Glenn and Parks highways, is open 8 to 6 daily in the summer. It's the central clearing house for the whole region, so if you're looking for a quiet B&B outside of Anchorage, check here for offerings.

Mile 35 is the junction of the Parks Highway and the Glenn Highway. For the last few miles between here and Anchorage, see *Chapter 10*, which covers the Glenn Highway.

Denali Park, George Parks Highway

Chapter 14

Anchorage

Home to nearly half the state's population and the de facto state capital – certainly the power center – Anchorage doesn't even appear on maps from the turn of the century. As recently as 50 years ago, it barely classified as a town. But that's judging it by modern standards.

■ History

The history of the Anchorage area goes back at least 6,000 years, when the area was inhabited by Athabascan Indians. The village of Eklutna, just north of the modern city, has a continuous history of over 1,000 years.

The Natives first came into contact with European explorers during the late 1700s, as the Russians exploited the incredibly rich fur market. The contact was beneficial to the Russians, but extremely detrimental to the Athabascans, who suffered from slavery, disease, and random violence as they watched their heritage wiped out, bit by bit.

But the Russians, despite their strong presence, weren't big explorers. They were more likely to find a rich spot and stay there until they'd burned it up, and they were no different here. Rather than going out and taking a look around, the Russians made the Natives come to them; they set up trading posts and didn't move very far afield.

It wasn't until 1778 that Cook Inlet was found, by Captain James Cook, who was searching for an entrance to the Northwest Passage. Cook Inlet was nothing more than a dead end, and Cook – who had wasted weeks late in the season heading up every little cove, entirely against the advice of his lieutenant, William Bligh (yes, the Bounty guy – see *Chapter 15*, page 432) went on to his death as part of an entrée in Hawaii without finding a northern sea route around the Americas. With Cook's detailed and beautiful maps showing no reason to go into Cook Inlet, very little happened in the area, except for trapping and trading, over the next 110 years.

Then, in 1888, gold was found near Girdwood, at Crow Creek, about 35 miles south of what would become Anchorage. This discovery was quickly followed by more finds in the Matanuska and Susitna Valleys. Although the city of Anchorage did not yet exist, its site had become a crossroads. US Geological Survey maps from 1898 label the spot as a "village," and then go into great detail on the goldfields nearby. When the surveyors got to Cook

Anchorage

Inlet, all they wanted to do was get out. "We arrived at Cook Inlet on the 26th of April – a rather unfortunate time, since it was too late for ice and snow traveling and too early for winter travel, the rivers being not yet broken; moreover, we were delayed several days by heavy gales."

The official history of the city began in July of 1914, when the US government decided to build a railroad from Seward to Fairbanks and chose the tiny settlement of Ship Creek as a mid-point base. Ship Creek consisted of a few ramshackle huts and transient miners, but with the news of the coming railway, more than 650 lots were offered up at the townsite auction. They weren't much of a bargain; once you had the lot, there were, of course, no services on it. Fresh water was five cents a bucket, and you had to take your garbage down to the water to be carried out by the tide. But where there's construction, there's money to be made. A report at the time said that "The process of moving has been progressing steadily for the past three weeks and all available teams and wagons have been busy in this exodus at the rate of two dollars an hour." Common laborers made 37½ cents a day for working on the townsite; skilled workers raked in 50 cents a day.

The official lots weren't the only place undergoing development; nearby was a second townsite for what were referred to as "bohunks" – mostly railway workers. According to the Seattle newspaper, "it is desirable to keep them in the country."

When the dust settled, Ship Creek had been transformed into Anchorage. The town incorporated in 1920.

The railroad was completed in 1923, when President Harding drove the golden spike at Nenana. By the 1930s, there were more than 2,000 people in town and the first road links had developed, including 50 miles of road leading to Palmer – which featured a 2,007-foot bridge over the Knick River – and a town loop road nearly 20 miles long. For the time, it was enough.

Over the next 20 years, Anchorage grew slowly on the railroad and on aviation business (today Lake Hood is the world's busiest seaplane base, with more than 800 takeoffs and landings on a summer day). A shot in the arm was given in 1935, when more than 200 families moved into the Matanuska Valley as homesteaders. Anchorage was the nearest point of resupply for the people who set off to farm the rich land of the valley to the north. By 1940, Anchorage had a population of 7,724. And then the boom began.

With the advent of WWII, Anchorage became a major base protecting the North Pacific and the Aleutians – the only US soil that saw land battles. Fort Richardson and Elmendorf Airfield were under construction by 1942, and people flocked to the beautiful city. By 1950, the population had increased by 600% over the previous 10 years.

The city never looked back, getting a major international airport in 1951, which was used as a refueling stop for planes traveling from Europe to Asia. Prosperity was the word, and it was remarkably smooth sailing until

Good Friday of 1964, when an earthquake estimated at 9.2 on the Richter Scale devastated south-central Alaska. Property damage was over $750 million, and 130 people lost their lives. The quake is still talked about today in reverential tones.

Luckily for Anchorage, it wasn't too long before oil money started flowing. The 1970s oil boom brought unprecedented prosperity to the town, and the flow of money hasn't stopped yet. Anchorage has built a beautiful performing arts center and a green belt of parks, and generally has gone all out to make the city a better place to live, largely funded from oil revenues.

■ The City Today

Situated at the base of the **Chugach Mountains**, the Anchorage municipal area is roughly the size of Delaware. More accessible, and with better weather than Fairbanks (average high temperature in July is 65; in January, 20), Anchorage's growth has been largely unchecked. Today, more than 270,000 people call it home, with quite a few more in the outlying regions – commuters drive in from as far as Willow. The Anchorage branch of the University of Alaska (the main university campus is in Fairbanks) has begun to outgrow its mother institution (which does nothing but fuel the fires of the Anchorage/Fairbanks rivalry). Anchorage is the base for most of the companies working in the oilfields of the North Slope. The state's economic and political power is centered here – despite the state capital actually being in Juneau – and no matter what those from other parts of Alaska say ("Anchorage is just 30 minutes from Alaska"), Anchorage is a large, wholly modern city with some of the best living in the state. Anchorage has its problems – traffic stinks just like it does in every major city, it's one of the few places in the state where people have to lock everything up, and there's even occasional smog. But if Anchorage is "30 minutes from Alaska," that also means that it's only 30 minutes to pretty much anywhere you'll want to be or anything you'll want to be doing.

■ Basics

One thing about Anchorage you should know going in, and before you start looking at this chapter: the fun outdoor stuff is outside of town. Look to *Chapter 15* for activities south of town, *Chapters 10* and *13* for fun stuff to the north. Anchorage is still a hub, a stopping place on the way elsewhere. It's just now – unlike when the miners came through – you can have a lot of fun while you're stopped.

The main **Anchorage Visitor Information Center** (☎ 907-274-3531, www.anchorage.net) is in a log cabin with a lovely sod roof, at the corner of 4th and F streets. Though the center is jammed in the summer, the staff still finds time to be amazingly helpful. You can pick up the usual variety of brochures, or check out the attractions on a giant TV. Don't miss a copy of the *Anchorage Visitor's Guide*, which includes walking and driving tours of Anchorage and detailed information on every other aspect of the city. The volunteer staff at the Visitor Center will take the time to help you with questions; they'll also help you make reservations at local B&Bs. Open June through August from 7:30 am to 7 pm, May and September from 8 am to 6 pm, and October through April from 9 am to 4 pm.

There are several smaller branches of the Visitors Center, including three at the airport: one's in the baggage area of the domestic terminal (C Concourse), ☎ 907-266-2437, and the other two are in the international terminal, one in the lobby area, ☎ 907-266-2657, the other in a secure area, ☎ 907-248-0162. Another center is at the **Valley River Center Mall**, in Eagle River, north of Anchorage. A **touch-tone visitor guide** (☎ 907-258-5858) has weather information, train, plane, and ferry schedules, and up-to-date tips on what's going on in town. It's worth picking up their brochure just for the sections on "bearanoia," which tells you exactly what not to do around bears. It includes this gem: "If you find a bear cub, grab it and rub its belly." On the serious side, the "moose courtesy" section has a good description of what you should do when you're facing a moose, with these two important reminders: "Moose kick with both front and rear legs, and a moose with its hackles raised is a thing to fear."

Other phone numbers to remember are ☎ 907-276-3200 for a daily recording detailing events and activities in the city, and ☎ 907-276-4118 for emergency assistance in more than 30 languages.

The **Alaska Public Lands Information Center** (☎ 907-271-2737), across from the Visitors Center on 4th and F streets, is worth a stop. It's got educational films, information on parks, some wildlife displays, and a small bookstore. The center is open daily 9 to 5 in summer. If you're going up to Denali from Anchorage, you can make reservations for Denali buses and campsites here, seven to 21 days in advance. ☎ 907-272-7275 or 800-622-7275 for reservations and park information for Denali.

You can get excellent topo maps for all regions of Alaska in the same building, in room G84. You can also pick up reservation forms for Forest Service cabins all over the state.

In the same building is the office for the **Alaska Marine Highway**, Alaska's coastal ferry system. For more information, check out *Chapter 16* of this book, or call ☎ 907-272-2737 or 800-642-0066. The office is open 9 am to 5:30 pm, from May 24 through September 1.

Anchorage has an excellent bus system. The **People Mover Transit Center** (☎ 907-343-6543) is at 6th and G streets. A buck seventy-five (exact change only on the bus) will get you just about anywhere in the city. You can also buy day passes, which are available at the center or most of the town's Holiday convenience stores. The bus service runs a short-hop free bus around the downtown area. Buses run about every 10 minutes on weekdays, and go from K Street, by the Captain Cook hotel, to Cordova

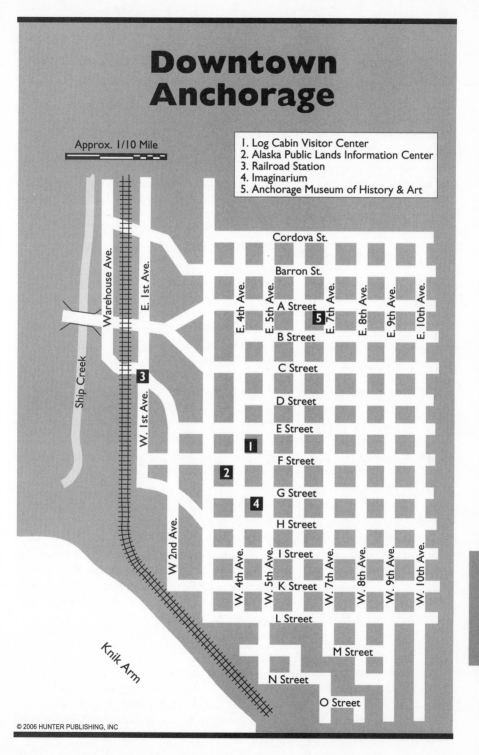

Downtown Anchorage

Approx. 1/10 Mile

1. Log Cabin Visitor Center
2. Alaska Public Lands Information Center
3. Railroad Station
4. Imaginarium
5. Anchorage Museum of History & Art

© 2006 HUNTER PUBLISHING, INC

Anchorage

Street, looping on 5th and 6th avenues. This is a great way to get around downtown.

Anchorage City Trolley Tours has an hour-long tour of the town, from Earthquake Park to Lake Hood and the Alaska Railway Depot. ☎ 907-276-5603. The big tour operators also have longer city tours – see the *Tours* section, below, for more details.

The Alaska Railroad Depot is at 411 W. 1st Ave. Rails run north to Fairbanks and south to Seward. The most popular trips are the ones to Denali, which run $129. Lots of good packages, with Denali stopovers. Don't even think about just taking the train straight to Fairbanks – you'll be glued to the window around Denali, cursing your choice. Runs down to Seward are $103 round-trip. Trains are good things. ☎ 800-321-6518, www.alaskarailroad.com.

■ Things to Do

 The **Anchorage Museum of History and Art** (☎ 907-343-4326), at 121 W. 7th Ave. (between A and C streets), is a must-stop. Downstairs is the permanent collection of art, including mostly what you'd expect in a city museum, plus some interesting historical etchings. Also downstairs is the temporary exhibit area, which is changed frequently. Between these two wings are a small café and one of the most impressive totem poles in the world – this one has, in fact, been taken on tour. But the real attractions for most visitors are upstairs. Here you'll see an entire history of the state – from Native dwellings to modern ships – as told through artifacts and interpretive exhibits. This is far and away the best collection of Native objects in the state, and it has to be seen to be believed. A self-guided tour is available with a prerecorded tape, and there are daily guided tours four times a day. Admission to the museum is $6.50 for adults, $6 for seniors; children under 18 are free. For $20.75, you can get a combo ticket that gets you into both the museum and the Native Heritage Center (see below). A very good deal if you want to hit both attractions. The museum is closed Mondays, but open from 9 to 6 daily from mid-May through mid-September, 10 to 6 on Tuesdays through Saturdays and 1 to 5 on Sundays the rest of the year. Check for the schedule of free films running in the summer. The museum also offers great classes. If your time in Anchorage is limited, spend it here. And it's only going to get better: the museum is in the middle of a massive expansion, which won't be done until 2009, to increase the art and history exhibits, and add an ice rink, as well as incorporate the Imaginarium into the mix.

Inside the museum building are two other attractions. The **Alaska Native Performance Series** is offered daily in the summer, usually with three 30-minute performances during the day. Different Native groups of singers and dancers perform here, so it's a good chance to see a small bit of a variety of Native cultures. Schedules and tickets are available at the museum.

Stuck off in a corner of the museum and open only from 10 am to noon, Tuesday through Friday, is the excellent **Museum Library and Archives**. This tiny room is stuffed to the rafters with information on every aspect of Alaska and its history, including an unmatched photo library with more than 150,000 historical photos. Admission is free; tell the ticket takers for the museum you are going to the library.

If all this museum-going has made you hungry, there's a small restaurant in the museum atrium.

One of Anchorage's most popular attractions is the **Alaska Native Heritage Center**. The center features films and speakers from Native groups around the state, plus there are craftsmen and women at work on the grounds (and, of course, the obligatory gift shop). But what sets the place apart is what's out back: grouped around a small pond is a collection of traditionally built Native houses, from different areas of the state. You can stop in and see how, say, someone in the Aleutians lived, as opposed to someone in Southeast. There are people there to help explain the culture, dances, and living style. The center also organizes special projects: for example, having someone from each group build one of their traditional boats, so that visitors can compare and contrast a qayak from an umiaq. Admission is rather steep – $20.75, but that's a combo ticket that also gets you into the Anchorage museum. Still, if you have limited time in the state and want to get an overview of what it was like before the Russians moved in and killed everything with fur, it's a good place to get a handle on things. The center is north of town: take the Glenn Highway to the Muldoon Road exit and turn west. From there, just follow the signs. It takes 10-15 minutes to drive in from the center of town. ☎ 907-330-8000 or 800-315-6608, www.alaskanative.net.

The Imaginarium (☎ 907-276-3179, www.imaginarium.org), at 725 W. 5th, is great for kids, with hands-on science exhibits, including stuff on Arctic ecology, the flora and fauna of Alaska, and rainforest and marine ecology and biology. Everything is explained in easy and interesting terms. Admission is $6 for adults, $5 for kids ages two to 12. It's open Monday through Saturday, 10 to 6, Sunday, noon to 5.

Nearby is the **Alaska Experience Theater**, at 705 W. 6th (☎ 907-276-3730). The center has a three-story high IMAX movie screen that folds around you 180 degrees as they show films of the state's scenery. Almost like being there, if you've had crappy weather and missed reality. They've also got an earthquake film/show where your seat and the ground beneath you shakes – remember the early '70s movie Earthquake with Sensurround? Like that, but updated. It's your best chance to find out what the big quake was like. Admission is $7 for the movie or $5 for the quake presentation; there's a combined ticket available for $10.

The **Alaska Heritage Library and Museum** is a huge private collection of Native art, shown in the lobby of the National Bank of Alaska building, on Northern Lights Blvd. and C St. Admission is free, and the collection can be viewed Monday through Friday noon to 5. The ivory carvings are amazing, and it's worth stopping in just to see the parka made of bird skins.

The pride of Anchorage is the **Loussac Public Library**, at 3600 Denali St. This impressive building cost the city $37 million, and it houses the largest collection of books on Alaska anywhere, with more than 15,000 titles, in addition to old documents, magazines, and maps.

The world's busiest float plane airport/harbor is at Lake Hood, and that's also where you'll find the **Alaska Aviation Heritage Museum** (☎ 907-248-5325), 4721 Aircraft Dr., which has been recently renovated, and features old photos, planes, and uniforms, with daily films as well. Stop in here to learn more about the Alaskan institution of the bush pilot, a brave and rare breed who flies anywhere, any time. There's a restoration center in the museum, a hangar with restored vintage aircraft and wrecks, and a good collection of artifacts from the battle for the Aleutians during WWII. The museum is open 9 to 6 daily; admission is $5 for adults, $3 for kids ages six to 12.

Also for aviation buffs, **Elmendorf Air Force Base** (☎ 907-552-5755) offers free tours. Elmendorf was established during WWII as the northernmost main defensive air base for the US and Canada. Call for reservations on the free weekly tour. There's also a huge, and free, wildlife museum on the base, open 10 to 2 weekdays, 1 to 5 weekends. If you prefer the army to the Air Force, **Fort Richardson** has self-guided tours of the base, including a rather smaller wildlife museum. ☎ 907-384-0431 for details.

The **Oscar Anderson House**, 420 M St., is said to have been the first wood-framed house in Alaska. Now it's a nice, small museum of Alaskana, a stop on most of the city tours. Admission is $3 for adults, $2 for seniors, $1 for kids. It's open 11 to 4, Tuesday through Saturday.

Moving farther afield, the **Alaska Botanical Garden** (☎ 907-770-3692), on Tudor Road near Baxter, is open 9 to 9 daily in summer. Its 110 acres include a demonstration garden, an herb garden, and a perennial garden. Admission is by donation, and there are frequent tours and special events.

The **Alaska Zoo** is at 4731 O'Malley, two miles east of the New Seward Highway. Open daily from 10 to 6, it's home to a good assortment of Alaskan animals (plus an elephant and a few tigers who no doubt spend most of their time wondering what's up with the weather) and nice grounds. It's not like seeing them in the wild, but if you've been unlucky with your animal-spotting, stop in. The zoo also often cares for orphaned moose and bear in the summer. Admission is $9 for adults, $5 for those 12 to 18, and $4 for children under 12.

Anchorage has a number of nice parks, good for picnics or just a day away from the bustle. The **Westchester Lagoon**, off Minnesota Blvd., is a waterfowl nesting area and a good place for lunch with the ducks – although, because of the delicate balance Anchorage maintains with its wildlife population, feeding them is a bad idea. There's a half-mile nature trail around the lake. **Resolution Park**, at the end of L St. and 3rd Ave., has a Captain Cook monument. In spring and fall, it's the place to go to watch beluga whales on their migratory route. **Earthquake Park**, near the airport on Northern Lights Blvd., is grossly overrated; there's a display board about the quake, a view of the city, and on a very clear day you might catch a glimpse of Denali. Much better is **Delany Park**, the "park strip" that once made up the firebreak for the original townsite and was later the town's first airstrip. The park stretches from A to P streets, between 9th and 10th avenues. In 1981, Pope John Paul II held mass here. Big renovations are ongoing, as the city puts in a rec center and more.

Downtown at 4th and E, next to the Anchorage CVB offices, you can hear open-air **concerts** twice a week in summer. Shows start at noon.

The **Campbell Creek Science Center** (☎ 907-267-1246), 6881 Abbott Loop Road, offers nighttime science programs in summer, from 7 to 9 pm. Programs change, but the offerings are excellent. Try to get in on the program about bugs, if you haven't had your fill of crawling and flying things already.

■ Out & About

Tour operators are listed below, in the *Tours* section. If you want to get out on your own, there are endless sporting and outdoor possibilities around Anchorage. Head up **Flattop Mountain** to watch the aurora borealis in winter; in summer, Flattop is a nice day hike. The peak sits at 3,550 feet, and from the top you get panoramic views of Cook Inlet, with some hope of seeing Denali on a clear day. The trailhead is off Upper Huffman Drive, in the Glen Alps Park. The hike takes one to two hours.

Alaska Backpackers Shuttle (☎ 907-344-8775) can arrange drop-offs and pickups in the bush for serious hikers.

Lakes around Anchorage are stocked with trout, grayling, char, and landlocked chinook salmon. Rules and regulations change regularly – particularly for ocean fishing anywhere near Cook Inlet – so before you drop a line, call the **Alaska Department of Fish and Game** (☎ 907-344-0541).

Most people head a bit farther out of town and go fishing or gold panning in **Chugach State Park**. This 495,000-acre park also has great hiking trails. Access is from Upper Huffman Rd., Upper O'Malley, and Rabbit Creek Rd. (see the *Eagle River* section, and the next chapter for details on activities in Chugach).

Easy walking and biking can be done on the **Tony Knowles Coastal Trail**, which follows the Knik Arm from downtown to Port Campbell. It's 11 miles long and crowded on weekends.

Anchorage

Because the city is built on water – sea, rivers, and lakes – it's a boater's paradise. **Goose Lake** is the place to go for swimmers (or ice skaters in the winter).

> **ALERT:** Do not even think about swimming in Cook Inlet. There are tidal rips and mud flats that make it a cold, very nasty place to die. Even wading in the shallows is not safe. Every year people drown when they get caught in the mud and can't get out before the tide comes in. This also means that Anchorage isn't the greatest place to drop your sea kayak in the water. While there are a lot of nearby lakes that make for nice paddling (Goose, Eklutna, Spenard, and Jewel are popular), if you want to get into the ocean, head south.

REI in Anchorage (☎ 907-272-4565) rents kayaks.

In winter, **cross-country skiing** is the sport of choice. There are over 120 miles of trails in Anchorage. Some of the best are in **Kincaid Park,** at the tip of the Turnagain Arm. For Alpine skiing, try **Alyeska**, with some of the meanest moguls in the world. It's about 40 miles south of town and has 60 runs. When the winter freeze hits, there's ice skating on Goose, Jewel, and Spenard lakes, and on Westchester Lagoon.

Any time you're outdoors, remember to watch for moose and bear; they are not afraid of the city. Anchorage is the only major city in the US where you might see wolves, grizzlies, beluga whales, and moose. Take care when driving, and never approach the wildlife. Watch for bald eagles in the Chugach Mountains or along Ship Creek (a good overlook on Whitney Road) during salmon spawning season. Dall sheep can be seen during the summer along (and sometimes on) the road to Portage, on the cliffs near Windy Point.

Rent bikes at **Downtown Bicycle Rental** (☎ 907-279-5293), 5th and C.

■ Seasonal Activities

Dog sled races are held at the Bicentennial Park in January, as the mushers gear up for the Iditarod.

Late February and early March brings the **Fur Rendezvous**, Anchorage's biggest annual event. For two weeks, the entire town goes crazy at the **Rondy Winter Carnival** with car races, theatricals, exhibits, balls, and fur auctions, as well as the World Championship Sled Dog Races. Or try snowshoe softball. You might just take a walk around and look at the snow sculptures. Expect a good time, but don't expect to be warm: Average temperature is 18° during the Rendezvous.

While furriers have been widely considered evil for the past decade or so, the simple truth is this: Without fur trapping, the United States would still be hugging the Eastern seaboard. It was trappers who opened up the West, and while there were problems – the Russians pretty much wiped out the sea otter population, which is only now at a reasonable level of recovery – carefully controlled trapping is still a major part of the Alaskan economy, particularly in northern villages. Trapping was the way Natives survived. The Rondy celebrates all that.

The greatest dog race of them all, the 1,049-mile **Iditarod**, starts in downtown Anchorage near the end of the Rondy (see the *Willow* and *Fairbanks* sections for more on dog sledding). Come up for the Rondy, stay a day or two extra to howl with the dogs.

April brings the end of winter and the **Alyeska Spring Carnival**, with the famous Slush Cup, and other events. In June, the **International Music Festival** is held. World-class musicians flock to Anchorage to participate. Finally, in late August, the **State Fair** is in nearby Palmer.

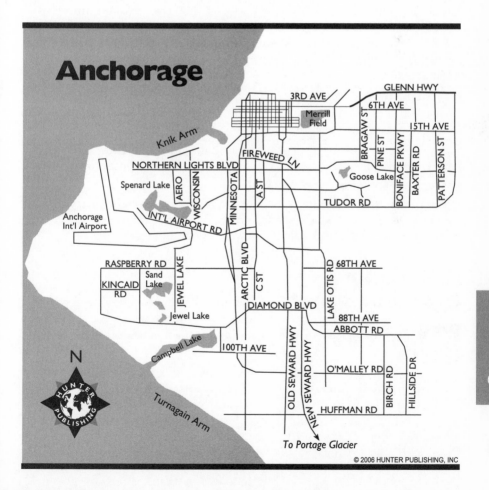

© 2006 HUNTER PUBLISHING, INC

■ Tours

Quite a few companies offer tours of Anchorage; these tours can be a good way to get your bearings and see what you want to come back to.

Gray Line (☎ 907-277-5581, 888-452-1737, www.graylinealaska.com), at 547 W. 4th, has a three-hour city tour, plus they offer trips to Portage Glacier, Columbia Glacier, and all around Alaska. Like Gray Line, **Princess Tours** (☎ 907-276-7711, 800-426-0500, www.princesslodges.com) will take you anywhere. These excursions are luxurious, and the city tours are a good value.

Flightseeing is available from **Sound Aviation** (☎ 907-229-7173), and **Aero Tech** (☎ 907-279-6558).

Nova has rafting tours on rivers near Anchorage. For $75, they'll take you to the Matanuska River, where you can paddle in front of a glacier; for $80, they'll put you in the whitewater lower on the river, onto Granite Creek. For serious excitement, try Six-Mile – where you can get into Class V water. $90. The company also has some nice hiking options, and pretty much everything can be done as day trips from Anchorage. ☎ 800-746-5753, www.alaskaone.com.

Most of the tour operators are trying to get you out of town, down to either Prince William Sound or Kenai Fjords. For details on these trips, see the *Whittier* and *Seward* sections, pages 438 and 445.

The same holds true for most other excursions you might think of: first, you have to get out of Anchorage, so you might as well drive closer to your destination and book with someone local.

If you're needing to get from Anchorage to somewhere else without your own transport, the **Alaska Shuttle** (☎ 888-600-6001) has service to Fairbanks, Dawson City, and Valdez, as well as points in-between.

■ Shopping

Whatever souvenir you've wanted, Anchorage is the place to buy it. The selection here is the widest and the prices the lowest. It's also the place to stock up on anything you might need for the rest of your journey.

The great bulk of the tourist shops are downtown, on **4th Street** around the Visitors Center. Just treat the whole area as one big gift shop; you can't walk more than 15 or 20 feet without hitting another treasure trove of t-shirts, packaged salmon and moose dropping earrings. Probably the best all-around shop for standard souvenir stuff is **Trapper Jack's Trading Post**, at 701 4th. It has great selection and the best prices.

It used to be you could come into Anchorage and buy serious Native art. That's a little more difficult now. One good option is to try the **Ship Creek**

Center, 4th Ave. and C St., where some really nice artisans ply their trade. The **Museum of History and Art** also has some good pieces, especially on ivory. Our stop of choice is the **Alaska Native Medical Center**, at Tudor Rd. and Bragaw. The gift shop is open 10-2 on weekdays, selling whatever pieces have been left there on consignment. This is the real deal: ivory carvings, scrimshaw, whalebone, and horn pieces that are impressive and very tasteful. Best of all, most of the money for the piece ends up back with the artist.

The arts of Alaska are as wide and varied as the state itself. The Native groups to the south – the Tlingit, Haida, and Tsimshians – produce highly geometric art that is nearly abstract. Usually done in blacks and reds, this is probably the most famous style of Alaskan art. Check for masks, paintings, and carved boxes. The Athabascans, from the Interior, make the best baskets and do the best beadwork. Beads are made from wood, seeds, quills, and shells, plus bone and other materials. When the Russians came, they brought glass beads for trade, which were quick to catch on. As for the Eskimo groups, the Inupiat, who live along the Bering Sea, produce some of the best ivory carving. The Yupik, from the southwest coast, also produce marvelous ivory items, plus beach-grass baskets. Out on the Alaskan Peninsula and in the Aleutians, the Aleuts make rye-grass baskets, once so highly prized they were used for currency. For more on local arts, see the *Introduction*.

There are some stores in the downtown area selling ivory and bone carvings. **Alaskan Ivory Exchange**, 700 W. 4th, ☎ 907-272-3662, has a good assortment of crafts, from the real to the tourist knock off. **Alaska Arts and Ivory** and **Alaskan Ivory Outlet** are in the 300 block of 5th street; they both have wide selections.

ARTWORK PURCHASES

Before you buy any artwork, make sure you know what you're getting. There are loopholes in the law that allow shops to sell junk made abroad without advertising it as such. Make sure the artist is Alaskan and the materials are Alaskan. On many items, there's a small sticker of a silver hand on the piece; this is a state program that authenticates the artwork. You'll almost never see this on soapstone; pretty much all of this soft green rock is now carved abroad. Before you buy, ask plenty of questions. If the store doesn't want to answer, go somewhere else. Finally, read the *Customs* section, page 83, for possible complications when you take your purchases home.

Anchorage

One of the best local craft shops is **Oomingmak**, at 604 H St. No, they don't have ivory or whalebone here, but it is the place to go for qiviut – the incredible wool from musk ox. Oomingmak is a Native, nonprofit co-op that provides employment to villagers. They also maintain the wonderful musk ox farm at Palmer. The musk oxen are combed and then the wool sent out to knitters around the state. Qiviut is not cheap – a scarf runs about $250 – but it's the softest, warmest fiber around; it makes cashmere feel like steel wool, and it's eight times warmer than sheep's wool. Check the website, www.qiviut.com. You're going to want some of this stuff.

For books, there's the great **Cook Inlet Book Company**, at 415 W. 5th (☎ 907-258-4544), which has the best selection of books on Alaska you'll ever find, plus a good magazine rack. For used and sale books, try **Title Wave**, 1360 Northern Lights Blvd., ☎ 907-278-9283, next to REI.

The **Myron Rosenberg Gallery**, 400 4th St., offers prints and posters by Alaska's master photographer. Rosenberg has shot some Alaskan classics; he's also made trips into China and Siberia. If you can't afford a print, there are many sizes of posters. Even the back of his business card has one of his photos.

If you're looking for something different, **Charlie's Alaska Trains**, 410 G St., has that certain item any train fan is going to want – an Alaska Railroad T-shirt or patch.

There are several malls in town; the best is the **Dimond Center**, at the corner of Dimond Blvd. and the Old Seward Highway. There's a bit of everything here, including theaters and an ice rink.

REI, 1200 Northern Lights Blvd., can fill all your camping needs. They've also got rental equipment at very reasonable prices – this is your chance to try a canoe or kayak on one of Anchorage's many lakes. There aren't cheaper outdoor prices in the state, so stock up here if you need to.

Alaska Mountaineering and Hiking, 2633 Spenard, is the place for ropes and crampons. For fishermen, the **Mountain View Sports Center**, 3838 Old Seward Highway, has the lure you need.

Anchorage is also a good place to get your film developed. The best place is **D & M Photo**, on the corner of Arctic and 36th. It's fast, friendly, and has prices you can afford for excellent quality photo processing.

Finally, you can buy Alaskan specialty food and get it shipped south or keep it for your nights in the bush at **10th and M Seafoods** (they'll also process and ship your catch). They've got two locations, at 1020 M. St (☎ 907-272-3477) and at 301 Muldoon Rd. (☎ 907-337-8831).

■ Food

 The specialty of the house in Anchorage is always seafood, and there's no shortage of places where you can get your fill of fresh catch. The best of them all is **Simon and Seaforts Saloon and Grill**, at 420 L St. Besides a wonderful array of seafood, try the steak or the Cajun cooking. Lunch is from $8 to $17, dinner is $25 to $30.

Tiny, expensive, and delicious is the **Marx Bros. Café** (☎ 907-278-2133), 627 W. 3rd Ave., with dinners from $18 to $30. Have your seafood with a waterfront view. Reservations are a must. Still in the expensive range is the **Crow's Nest** in the Hotel Captain Cook, at 5th and K. It's the place to be for Sunday brunch and affords a great view of the city. Another good brunch choice is the **Flying Machine** or **Fancy Moose** at the Millennium Alaska Hotel – where you don't get a view of the city, but you do get a great look at Lake Hood and Lake Spenard. It's at 4800 Spenard. Another place for view, high prices, and excellent food is the **Top of the World**, in the Hilton, at 3rd and E. It's got the state's biggest wine list, and a nice outdoor deck for warm evenings. The **Snow Goose Restaurant & Brewery**, 717 W. 3rd Avenue, also is a great place for sitting out on the deck and enjoying a microbrew.

If you're looking for something a little more accessible, there are a wide variety of steak and seafood houses in town. **Club Paris**, 417 W 5th Ave., serves lunch and dinner, with prices from $20 to $35. Their specialty is filet mignon. Or try **Corsair**, 944 West 5th Ave., for seafood. Prices start around $30.

The places listed above are all outstanding restaurants, but you can blow a bundle on them. While Anchorage eats tend toward the high range, there's no reason you can't have a nice dinner for under $20.

You can try an Alaska tradition at **Old Anchorage Salmon Bake**, 251 K St. They're open from late May to mid-September, and prices are moderate. If you're with someone who's determined to pass up the succulent salmon, they've also got steak and ribs. Or try **Phyllis's Café and Salmon Bake**, right downtown at 436 D St. The smell will draw you in as you're shopping.

Another place with true Alaska flavor is the **Sourdough Mining Co.**, on the corner of the Old Seward Highway and International Airport Rd. Furnished with antiques, the building is a replica of the old Independence Mine. The prices are fairly high, but the ribs are excellent. If you come here, be sure to walk across the street to see the chocolate waterfall at Alaska Wild Berry Products.

Another good spot in the same neighborhood – just around the corner, in fact – is the **Peanut Farm**, newly expanded and famous for hot wings, monster burgers and plenty of big screens for watching sports.

The **Kodiak Kafe**, 225 E. 5th Ave., is a good choice for breakfast or lunch. They serve great hamburgers from $6. **Sacks Café**, 625 W. 5th, is a popular downtown lunch spot with reasonable prices. Also downtown and crowded around peak lunch hours is the **Downtown Deli and Café**, at 525 W. 4th Ave. They serve sandwiches for around $7.

Gwennie's Old Alaska Restaurant is worth stopping in for a breakfast of sourdough pancakes and reindeer sausage. They're at 4333 Spenard, and you may be waiting a little while if you come at a peak hour – but it's worth it.

Right downtown, the **Snow City Café**, at 4th and L, doesn't look like much, but the crowd of locals hovering for tables should be your first tip that it's worth looking into. Try the omelettes for breakfast, or at lunch go for the huge sandwiches, a favorite of Anchorageites, and a couple can get out for under 20 bucks.

Anchorage has some good Chinese food. Try the **Golden Pond**, at 300 W. 36th Ave., or the **Peking Palace**, across from the Sears Mall, on Benson.

At 7305 on the Old Seward Highway is the **Mexico in Alaska Restaurant**, an Anchorage institution. Come in for the lunch buffet. For curry and nan, try the **Bombay House** in the Eagle River Shopping Center (☎ 907-696-6044). It's a bit of a drive, but if you're in the mood for tandoori, you don't have any other choice.

The Glacier Brewhouse, on 5th Ave. by the Imaginarium, is a microbrewery that also serves pizza, sandwiches, and pasta. You can get your fill for around $15.

One of the most popular spots for locals is **Moose's Tooth Pizza**, which also has a microbrewery, at 36th and the Seward Highway. Figure on $20 per person.

Finally, a little-known gem is the **Southside Bistro**, at Huffman and the Seward Highway. Lunch is around $15, dinner $20, and a lot of people think it's the best food in town.

In addition to these, you'll find all the familiar fast-food restaurants. If you've been having a junk food attack while camping in the bush, Anchorage is the place to get your fix, because they've got at least one of every burger, pizza, and chicken joint known to man.

■ Nightlife

 The Whale's Tail, in the Hotel Captain Cook at 5th and K, offers live entertainment, a bar, and a dinner menu. It gets crowded with package tourists out for a summer night. There's a younger crowd at the **F. St. Station**, at 325 F St. It's got a restaurant and bar in a very nice setting. **Chilkoot Charlie's**, 2435 Spenard, offers live music and serious rock and roll dancing on two separate dance floors. **Humpy's Great Alaskan Ale House**, 610 W. 6th Ave., has a microbrewery and live bands. It gets very, very crowded on weekends. **Rumrunner's**, at 5th and E, is also very popular for music and dancing.

Finally, **Mr. Whitekey's Fly By Night Club**, 3300 Spenard Rd., offers the "Whale Fat Follies," an Alaskan musical comedy. It's very popular, so call ahead (☎ 907-279-SPAM). There's a good restaurant – with a lot of Spam dishes – and a huge selection of imported beers.

■ Accommodations

There's a wide variety of places to stay in Anchorage, from four-star resorts to rundown shacks. There are, however, very few bargains. The important point for any of them is to make advance reservations; in summer, the town fills up fast.

The cheapest place to stay is the **Anchorage International Hostel** (☎ 907-276-3635, www.anchorageinternationalhostel.org), downtown at 700 H St. #2. It has dormitory-style accommodation for around $20, and some family rooms for $50 or so. The hostel has a kitchen, showers, laundromat, a four-night maximum stay, and an 11 pm curfew. The **Spenard Hostel** (☎ 907-248-5036, www.alaskahostel.org), 2845 W. 42nd Ave., is a good alternative. Convenient to the airport.

HOTEL PRICING
Prices are in US dollars.
under $50 . . . . $
$50-$100 . . . . $$
$100-$150 . . . . . . $$$
above $150 . . . . . $$$$

If these are both full up, try the **International Backpacker's Hostel**, 3601 Perkins Ave., ☎ 907-274-3870.

For hotels, consider $80 a screaming bargain, but figure on $100 and up for something that doesn't make you want to keep your shoes on as you walk the carpet. Prices quoted here are for the high season – rates drop dramatically outside the magic months of summer – and don't include Anchorage's hotel tax.

At the low end, **The Arctic Inn Motel,** 842 W. International Airport Road, ☎ 907-561-1328, has been around for a long time, $$$.

The Puffin Inn is a local favorite, at 4400 Spenard Road (☎ 907-243-4044 or 800-4PUFFIN, www.puffininn.net). $$$-$$$$.

The **Sourdough Visitors Lodge Motel** (☎ 907-279-4148, 800-777-3761, www.alaskasourdoughlodge.com), at 801 Erickson, has rooms with kitchens, $$$-$$$$. **Duke's 8th Avenue Hotel Suites** (☎ 907-274-6213 or 800-478-4837), 630 W. 8th Ave., also has suites with kitchens and is very convenient to downtown. $$$-$$$$. They allow pets "on approval," which is still better than most places on town.

The **Executive Suite Hotel** (☎ 907-243-6366 or 800-770-6366, www.executivesuitehotel.com), 4360 Spenard, has nice one-bedroom suites. $$$$. Another good spot in the mid-price category is the **Aspen Hotel**, 108 E. 8th Avenue, which has a good location and a nice indoor pool. Aspen pays a lot of attention to detail, which makes this a great place to stay. There also is a new **Aspen Extended Stay Suites**, near 36th & Seward Highway, with reasonable weekly rates. ☎ 866-GUEST4Um, www.aspenhotelsak.com.

Continuing to move up in price, **The Millennium Hotel Alaska** (☎ 907-243-2300 or 800-544-0988, www.millenniumhotels.com) is at 4800 Spenard Rd., on Lake Spenard. It has a dining room that serves excellent dinners and a health club. $$$$+. Right in the heart of downtown, at 5th Ave. and K St., is the **Hotel Captain Cook** (☎ 907-276-6000 or 800-843-1950, www.captaincook.com). It's got 600 rooms, but fills fast as it caters to tour groups. There are some good shops on the ground floor. Rates start upwards of two bills, and pass $1,500 for their best suite.

The usual hotel chains all have places in Anchorage. For the nicely upgraded and very convenient **Sheraton**, ☎ 800-325-3535; for **Super 8**, ☎ 800-800-8000; for **Days Inn**, ☎ 800-DAYS INN; for **Rodeway**, ☎ 800-228-2000. Pretty much any other chain you can think of – Marriott, Holiday Inn, Ramada – also have Anchorage properties.

There are also countless B&Bs in town. The easiest way to find one is to let the Visitors Center fill you in on who is currently open; the staff will also make reservations for you, or you can book a room online at www.anchorage.net. Prices start around $85, and you should call or hit the web at least a few days in advance.

A nice website, www.discoverourtown.com, also has a good listing of accommodations.

Camping

Your choices are pretty bleak if you've got a tent – your best bet is to head out of town. To the north, there are campsites near Eagle River, inside the Chugach Park; to the south, you shouldn't have to drive any farther than Bird Creek Portage to find somewhere.

> **WARNING:** In any tent site within easy reach of Anchorage, you need to be a little more security conscious than elsewhere in the state. There have been an increasing number of robberies – although still probably fewer than your neighborhood back home.

For RVs, there are quite a few choices in town. Still, just as with hotels, you'll be happier if you reserve early. **Ship Creek Landings** (☎ 907-277-0877, 888-778-7700, www.bestofalaskatravel.com), 150 N. Ingra St. and the **Anchorage RV Park** (☎ 907-338-PARK or 800-400-PARK, www.anchrvpark.com), 7300 Oilwell Rd. Both have sites with full hookups. Another place to try is the **Golden Nugget Camper Park**, 4100 Debarr Rd, ☎ 907-333-5311 or 800-449-2012.

Centennial Camper Park in Centennial Park, off Muldoon Rd. south of the Glenn Highway, is a scenic, convenient city-run spot with sites suitable for tents.

If all these are full, head north out of town on the Glenn Highway toward the **Chugach State Park**. The three campgrounds here have no hookups, but they do have outhouses and drinking water and are likely to have spaces when Anchorage itself is jammed. These are the best place to go if you have a tent.

Chapter 15

South of Anchorage

Portage Glacier to Homer

There's an entire peninsula south of Anchorage, much of it accessible by road. Figuring half of Alaska's population is in Anchorage, the Kenai Peninsula is where the biggest part of the state comes to play. Driving down the Kenai is an easy way to get into Prince William Sound, and if you're a fisherman, just keep driving until the road ends at the Homer Spit, and you'll find the best halibut waters in the state. The Kenai Peninsula combines the beautiful forests and mountains of Alaska's Interior with open expanses

of water and glaciers glinting on distant hillsides. If you've only seen the Interior of Alaska so far, you're in for a treat – this is a great chance to see the coast.

The Seward Highway

South to Portage

Although we describe this section of road from north to south, mile markers on the road show distance from south to north, beginning in Seward. The Seward Highway itself connects to the Sterling Highway, which can take you farther south to Kenai, Soldotna, and Homer.

 HIGHWAY TIP: Keep your headlights on at all times. The stretch from Anchorage to Girdwood has one of the highest accident rates in the state – it's full of people fleeing the city to remember why they live in Alaska – and everything you do to make yourself more visible helps keep you safe. Be especially careful watching for tourist cars stopped in the middle of the road while the driver gawks at whales or the herd of Dall's sheep you can often see from the road.

One of the most popular day trips from Anchorage is to follow the Seward Highway along the Turnagain Arm to Portage Glacier. The drive is really beautiful, with the Arm and its waters on one side, the mountains on the other as you drive along a narrow section of land that holds only the road and the railroad tracks. However, there is one drawback: No matter what the weather is in Anchorage, it's bound to be worse farther south. It tends to get better again the farther south you get, once you're out of the Cook Inlet influence, but there is nothing you can do except hope for the best. Pack a jacket if you're headed for Portage.

■ Turnagain Arm

Turnagain Arm is an extension of Cook Inlet. The story you'll here is that it got its name from Captain Cook, when he learned that he had yet to discover the Northwest Passage and he had to "turn again." That's more or less true, but there are some interesting sidelights to the story.

CAPTAIN COOK

By the time Cook got this far north, he was in a bad mood. A captain noted for keeping a ship with high morale, good health, and a happy crew had suddenly turned mean. Maybe he was just tired. Over the past decade he'd explored more of the world than anyone before him. He had sailed a huge ship through the Barrier Reef in Australia, a navigation hazard previously unknown to western sailors. He'd been around the world twice, and he had an astounding record of keeping his sailors alive – for example, on his first trip to New Zealand (he was the first to map it) not a single member of his crew came down with scurvy; a ship in the same seas at the same time had more than 60% of the crew out with the disease.But Cook also had teenage children he'd seen for perhaps six months of their lives. He was fifty years old, and we can guess all he wanted was to go home, not wander around looking for the Northwest Passage.

Cook had on his ship a man who was probably the second greatest captain of the age of sail, a man named William Bligh (yes, that one). All most people know of Bligh today is the movie Bligh – a nutcase who was rightly mutinied against. But even if that's all you know, consider this: the man was a good enough captain to keep his officers alive, in an overcrowded open boat, with very little food or water, while drifting in the open ocean for more than 2,000 miles. His account of the voyage of the *Bounty* is wonderfully written, far and away the most readable account of a sailing voyage.

Bligh, who had sailed with Cook for some time, looked at what we now call Cook Inlet and pronounced it a dead end. He had been one of the chief surveyors of the voyage, and he'd gotten a feel for the coastline.

Cook looked at the same waters and decided that they had to open up in just a few miles, that this was, had to be, the entrance to the Northwest Passage. He steered the *Resolution* up the inlet and found not a passage, but just another river. His diary for June 1, 1778, reflects his disappointment: "If the discovery of this River should prove of use, either to the present or future ages, the time spent in exploring it ought to be less regretted, but to us who had a much greater object in View it was an essential loss."

Cook sailed the coast for a few more weeks, and then headed south, away from the cold. On a beach in Hawaii, he was killed during a pointless altercation with some Hawaiians that got out of control. Maybe he was eaten, maybe not. Oddly enough, where that all happened was in a huge inlet that looks like the Hawaiian version of Cook Inlet, all steep mountains rising straight out of wild water.Bligh went on to greater fame.

For a good read, there are two essential books on Captain Cook: the first is the Penguin Classics edition of *The Journals of Captain Cook*. This is an inexpensive and accessible short version of the full journals, edited by J.C. Beaglehole (if you want to spend a grand or so, the full version was published by the Hakluyt Society a while back). Beaglehole also wrote the definitive biography of Cook, *The Life of Captain James Cook*, which you can pick up for twenty bucks or so in most Anchorage bookstores.

Turnagain Arm, besides being quite scenic, is home to some of the meanest tides in the world. The tidal fluctuation can be over 30 feet.

> **TIDAL ALERT:** At low tide, the entire Arm becomes an enormous mud flat, stretching for miles. It is extremely dangerous to venture out onto the mud flats; the mud grabs hold and does not let go until the water comes in. With a 30-foot tidal bore, by the time the water does return, it's too late. Several people drown here each year.

The second oddity is the phenomenon of the bore tide itself. The water comes surging into Cook Inlet, and then is funneled into the Turnagain and Knik arms. In the spring, the incoming tide may be a wall of water six feet high, moving at better than 10 knots. It can be quite a sight. Check the local tide tables for high tide, then head out to a viewpoint – from Beluga Point to Girdwood offers the best viewing – about two hours later.

■ Potter Marsh

Heading toward the Portage Glacier, the first point of interest is the Potter Marsh. This used to be named the Potter Point State Game Refuge; now it's the Anchorage Coastal Wildlife Refuge. It doesn't matter – everybody still calls it Potter Marsh. It's at Mile 117 on the Seward Highway, which puts it just barely outside Anchorage. It's also right beside the road. The 2,300-acre refuge is a great place to watch for duck, goose, swans, and moose. The refuge also includes nice habitat for the Arctic tern, a bird that winters in South America, then flies 11,000 miles or so to summer in Alaska. A boardwalk offers a good look into the marsh, and there are interpretive displays. When salmon are running, you can stand on the boardwalk over the streams and watch them right under your feet.

Potter Marsh gives you a good look at the main types of plant habitats in the state. It includes the coastal salt marshes (arrow arum grass, sedge, and silverweed); the sedge-bulrush marsh, which is permanently flooded and a favorite with ducks (northern pintail, northern shoveler, widgeon, canvasback) and the occasional mink; the shrub-bog, which is the transition between the wetlands and the drylands; and the deciduous area, pretty much what you've driven through to get this far.

Moose think the place is pretty cool, too.

Two miles farther on at Mile 115, you'll find the **Potter Section House**, which holds the **Chugach State Park Visitors Center** (☎ 907-345-5014); there's also a small railroad museum, with free admission, open Monday through Friday 8 to 4:30 year-round. Although the visitor's center for the park is here, it's really easier to get into the park from the Eagle River area (see that section of this book for more details).

> **WARNING:** Because you're so close to Anchorage here, be aware of crime at the trailheads. If you're parking your car and going off for a long hike, it is a temptation to thieves. Keep it as inconspicuous as you can, and hide the good stuff – inside the car is safer than in the trunk, as any yobo with a rock can pop a trunk in two seconds. This is one of the only areas in all of the North where crime can actually be a problem.

The Section House was originally the home of engineers working on the railroad. There's a hiking **trail** here that leads 3.3 miles to McHugh. The trail mostly parallels the road, and it's a good place to get out and walk along the Arm.

BELUGA POINT

The official whale-watching spot is Beluga Point, at Mile 110. There are interpretive signs and telescopes here. The whales chase salmon and smelt up the Arm, and the show can be pretty amazing. Beluga are small for whales – if you've gone through Southeast and seen humpbacks, beluga will look like big dolphins – but they are whales: toothed whales, to be precise. Over the past few years, Alaska's beluga population has dropped dramatically

– down 75% in some areas – but pods do still go by here. While working on the previous edition of this book, we sat and watched thirty or so go past the point; it took over an hour, and we could hear them honking, calling to each other across the water.

Mile 105 is the trailhead for the **Old Johnson Trail**. First used by area Natives, and then by trappers, miners, and missionaries, it offers a nice view of Turnagain Arm and another chance to see beluga whales. In season, check the bushes here for wild currants and blueberries.

Between Miles 107 and 110, watch for Dall sheep in the rocky areas on the north side of the road. They also come right down into the road, so drive carefully.

> **WILDLIFE WARNING:** There are many pullouts for sheep viewing. Don't stop in the middle of the road, and don't even think about trying to feed the sheep.

In mid-summer, there may be as many as 20 sheep down by the roadside; there's a total population of about 150 in the area. You may also see local rock climbers trying their luck and skill on the short cliffs by the roadside.

On weekends, this road can be packed – even pulling off at an overlook can make it difficult to get back on the highway.

This area is a good base for hikers heading into Chugach on the local trails, or you can camp at Mile 101.2 in **Bird Creek Recreation Area**. This has only 19 sites. Take the trailhead at the campground – the first five miles are open to bikes and ATVs – up to Bird Pass. The one-way distance is nine miles and, after you get off the bike path, it's a pretty steep trail. The **Indian Valley Trail** is just back up the road at Mile 102, and offers six miles of hard hiking up to mountain tundra. There's also a trailhead for the **Bird Ridge Trail** at Mile 100.5. The trail is one mile long and takes you above the tree line to the ridge. The trail is pretty steep, but it's the first trail in the Anchorage area to get completely free of snow in the spring.

■ Girdwood

The turnoff for Girdwood and **Alyeska Ski Resort** is at Mile 90. There's a convenience store and a small strip mall to mark the turnoff; just past the turnoff is a visitor center for the Chugach area.

Girdwood, two miles off the highway, was one of the original area gold mines, discovered in 1896. You can go to the old **Crow Creek Mine** from May to September and try your luck in the creek. There are also some great old buildings to explore. Admission, which includes panning, is $5 for adults, $4 for kids. It's a really nice place. ☎ 907-278-8060, www.akmining. com.

You can head out onto the rivers with **Class V Whitewater** (☎ 907-783-2004, www.alaskanrafting.com) in Girdwood. They've got simple floats on the Portage River for about $50, a fly-in trip on the Twentymile for around $225 – nice, because you're well away from the roads. Lots of other trips, serious hardcore whitewater.

Up Crow Creek Road is part of the early 1900s **Iditarod Trail**, which connected the Knik and Turnagain arms. There's a trailhead at Mile 7 that takes you 26 miles into the Chugach, with an elevation gain of 3,500 feet.

Another option is to head three miles down Alyeska Road, then turn left, heading toward the hotel. Just above the tram terminal is a trailhead for the **Upper Winner Creek Trail**, eight miles of fairly difficult hiking. Also nearby is the **Crow Pass Trail**, which picks up off Crow Creek Road, a mile back up the Alyeska Road. It's a 4-mile hike that's pretty difficult, but you pass the ruins of the Girdwood Mine, a waterfall, and top out at Raven Glacier. If you're equipped, the trail goes another 19 miles, ending up at the Eagle River Visitor Center.

Girdwood also houses the **Double Musky Inn** (☎ 907-783-2822), one of Alaska's best restaurants. Open Tuesday through Thursday, 4:30 to 10 pm, Friday through Sunday, 4 to 10. Try their Cajun seafood or one of the huge French pepper steaks. Dinner runs $15 to $20. The inn doesn't take reservations, but the food is worth the wait.

■ Alyeska

Alyeska Ski Resort, on Mt. Alyeska (3,939 feet), offers excellent skiing in the winter – a mogul-lover's dream – or berry picking in the summer. Watch for bears while berrying. At Alyeska, you can take the tram up the mountain, or, for only a few dollars more, you can do the **Glacier-Express tram/lunch combo**, so spend the extra couple bucks and linger. From the top of the mountain, you get sweeping views of the Turnagain Arm and seven glaciers. There's a short trail behind the sun deck for a different perspective. Rock climbing, golfing, hiking. You name it, it's right here. The resort is jammed in winter – the skiing here is famous worldwide – but in summer, you can get a deal at the **Westin Alyeska Prince Hotel**, $$$$. ☎ 907-754-1111 or 800-880-3880, www. alyeskaresort.com. There are a lot of more expensive places to stay in Anchorage, but none that can match the views here.

The **Twentymile River** turnout is at Mile 81. Fish here for hooligan, smelt, and pink, red, and silver salmon. The river is where local windsurfers come, and it can get pretty busy on a clear summer day.

Back in the good old days – say, before the summer of 2000 – if you wanted to get into Prince William Sound from here, you'd drive your car onto the Alaska Railroad at the depot at Mile 80.3. It'd take you on a short, surreal trip to Whittier, where you could jump a ferry to Valdez. Then somebody had the bright idea of building a road through (see *Whittier*, below). The train still comes through, but mostly the depot is a spot to stop and grab a few more brochures for local attractions.

■ Portage

At Mile 80.1 is the dead town of Portage. The townsite dropped 12 feet during the 1964 earthquake. For some reason, nobody wanted to live here after that.

At Mile 78.9 is the turnoff for **Portage Glacier**; it's five miles from the turnoff to the Visitors Center. Along the way, there are two lovely campgrounds (Williwaw, at Mile 4.1, is the nicer of the two), with no services, a total of 58 sites, nearly all with a glacial view. All of these sites are better for parking than trying to pitch a tent, but there are at least tiny spots of genuine grass near the fire rings.

There are many self-guided trails in the area, spectacular glacier views in nearly every direction, and excellent wildlife viewing. Watch for moose, beaver, bear, and eagles. Take a one-mile walk toward **Byron Glacier**, or try the **Moraine Trail** (at only a quarter-mile, barely enough to stretch your legs, but a great chance to see a moraine up close).

> **WEATHER ALERT:** For even the shortest stay in Portage, be sure to bring rain gear; the weather leans heavily toward nasty. Fifty-mile-an-hour winds aren't uncommon; wind here, in fact, has been known to lift box cars off the railway tracks.

The **Visitors Center** (open 9 to 6 daily in summer, 10 to 4 weekends only in winter; ☎ 907-783-2326) sits on the edge of **Portage Lake**, which was formed when the Portage Glacier began to retreat in 1914. While the face of the glacier is actually moving forward about 15 inches a day, it's melting backward a whole lot faster – official stats say that the glacier is advancing 500 feet a year, but melting about 520 feet per year. Fifteen years ago when we did the first edition of this book, you got a nice glacier view. Today, the glacier is not visible from the center, although icebergs sometimes still wash up right onto the building's foundations. Now that the glacier is out of the lake, its melt rate will probably slow down a fair amount.

> **HAZARD:** Do not walk on or near icebergs or lake ice. Ice is never as solid as it looks.

The Visitors Center is extremely busy; they run films, and there are good educational displays about glaciers. They keep a small chunk of fresh glacial ice so you can reach out and see what it's like (stand around for a few minutes and count how many people comment, "It's so cold," as if they were expecting glacial ice to be warm). A small notice board tells you when to expect the next bore tide. Park rangers offer iceworm safaris – proving that the iceworm is no myth, just hard to find and even harder to understand.

ICEWORMS

An iceworm is a tiny worm that lives in glacial ice, feeding off microscopic bits of algae. The worms are rarely more than an inch long, only one to two millimeters in diameter (about the size of a needle), and come out onto the glacial surface at night, burrowing down to escape the sun during the day. They are extremely delicate, temperature-wise, and can survive only in extreme cold.

Portage is also good for birders, just like the rest of the state. The Visitor Center has a nice handout that lists species you may see around the valley, including ospreys, harriers, and if you're really lucky, a northern shrike.

The Visitors Center itself is situated on a terminal moraine, dropped by the glacier in 1893. A moraine is a line of rocks pushed forward by a glacier's advance. When the glacier retreats, the rocks stay behind, showing the shape and place of the glacier's advance. The lake in front of the center was carved out by the glacier and is 800 feet deep in places.

Grayline (☎ 907-783-2983) offers tours of the glacial lake and a boat ride to the face of the Portage Glacier.

There are three other main glaciers in the Portage area, all readily visible: the Explorer Glacier and the Middle Glacier are both hanging glaciers, which means they're descending down the side of a mountain. There's a three-quarter-mile trail leading back to the Byron Glacier, which comes down a crevasse in the mountainside.

Whittier & Prince William Sound

Up until the summer of 2000, the only way into Whittier was by boat or train. If you look at the map, it's a long, long way around the Kenai Peninsula from Anchorage to Whittier – the nearest ice-free deepwater port – by sea; however, the peninsula is only a couple of miles wide at Portage, and so the train was a quick and easy, although somewhat surreal, trip. You loaded your car onto a flatbed, and off you went. When the trains weren't running, you couldn't get in or out of Whittier.

This system worked surprisingly well for a very long time. But then Wally Hickel became governor of Alaska. Being a man who never met a patch of concrete he didn't like, and frustrated by the opposition to his attempts to build an entirely illegal road to Cordova, he decided to build a road to Whittier.

Easy enough, right? The road is less than 10 miles long. There's one bridge. Should be the kind of thing a good road crew can do over a long weekend.

But it didn't work out that way. Surveyors came in, everybody chipped in with an idea, and only $90 million later (the original budget was $15 million, and in a sick piece of irony, the money was to come from the *Exxon Valdez* settlement), the road was finished.

Along the way, nobody seems to have noticed that a trolley car could have been run for a fraction of this cost. No, this is America, and dammit, we drive.

The main part of the expense was converting the railway tunnel to dual use. If cars were going to go through the tunnel, there had to be huge exhaust fans, to keep people from keeling over from carbon monoxide poisoning. There also had to be guards and information booths to keep people from driving through the tunnel when the train was coming. And then there were about $70 million of just-for-fun cost overruns.

So what did the town of Whittier get out of all this?

Well, they can now leave town more or less whenever they want to – or at least every hour, when the tunnel is open. If you've never lived on an island or in a remote community, you can't realize what a relief it is to know you can go somewhere.

Whittier is also now easily accessible for tourists who want to see Prince William Sound. These could be seen as good things.

But there is a large downside. Remember the line from Hunter S. Thompson's *Fear and Loathing in Las Vegas* where he says Vegas is what the whole free world would be like if the Nazis had won World War II? Whittier is what the whole world will be like when tourists take over once and for all. You've got a town of 300 people that's so crowded they had to put in parking meters. You've got traffic jams. You've got a cloud of pollution from bus exhaust. You've got crowds of people standing around wondering where the scenery is. You've got huge cruise ships, dwarfing the town, because Whittier is just a little bit closer to Anchorage than Seward, and so it's the new hot port for lines that offer Interior tours.

In 2000, already the sockeye fishery in the region was closed, and the arrival of more people is not going to decrease the stress on the fish. And now all the residents are trying desperately to be the first to think of new ways to fleece tourists. And those who can't fleece, resent.

Welcome to a little suburb of hell.

And that's a shame, because Whittier used to be a gorgeous town, and it's still the easiest way to get into Prince William Sound. It's the classic traveler's lament, best summed up by a couple of former British spies we met on a bus in Kathmandu: "Oh, you should have seen Albania before they ruined it." Oh, you should have seen Whittier before they ruined it.

■ The Tunnel

If you want in or out of Whittier, and you don't want to get on a boat, you have to go through the tunnel. It's almost worth it, just to see how desperately wrong planners can go if they really try.

The tunnel is now as much an Alaskan sight as a glacier, so live it up: if you don't have a car, hitchhike through – it's easy to get a ride, since everybody knows right where you're going.

Before you can go in the tunnel, you have to stop and get the tunnel brochure from the guardpost. This poor guy sits in a concrete bunker all day and watches cars line up.

There are lots of statistics about the tunnel. It's the longest highway tunnel in Alaska (technically, in North America, but it's hard to call this stretch of road a highway, and there are lots of longer tunnels on blue highways down south), and the first tunnel with computerized traffic control. It's built to work fine at temperatures of 40 below and with the wind blowing 150 mph.

The tunnel opens at specific times – about once an hour, each direction – so you'll likely end up sitting in line with other cars for a while.

Once you're inside the tunnel, the idea is to keep a steady speed, and keep your distance from the car in front of you. Headlights on at all times.

Inside, it's cold, it's wet, it's dank – hey, it's a tunnel – and keeping your car steady is not entirely easy, with the rough railroad bed, ties, and rails to contend with. Again, keep your distance from the car in front of you.

If you're claustrophobic, you will not enjoy this, but you're out faster than you think.

The tunnel was free for the first year. It's not anymore; it's a toll tunnel. They've got to pay for that $70 million in cost overruns somehow.

■ History

Whittier started off as part of a portage route for Chugach Indians who were traveling from Prince William Sound to fish in the Turnagain Arm. The city itself dates back to WWII, when it was an army camp, the primary debarkation point for the Alaska Command. The port is ice-free, and the armed forces made the most of it until 1960. Today about 300 people call Whittier home. Considerably more bears live in the area. In 1997, a black bear got into the grade school and wandered around for 45 minutes, before he curled up and went to sleep in the gym. During his ramble, he actually figured out how to open doors using the pushbars. Now that the RV crowd has taken over town, though, and a quiet backwater has turned into a boomtown, the bears are heading into the deeper woods.

■ Things to Do

Assuming you didn't take a look, gasp, and get back in line to drive through the tunnel, or immediately leap back onto the ferry, you'll quickly find that the best thing to do in town is leave – head into the mountains, or into Prince William Sound, but don't linger in town.

There's not a lot in the town. Whittier is dominated by the **Begich Towers**, part of a 1,000-room apartment complex, a leftover from military days, when it also housed a hospital, theater, pool, and virtually the town's entire population. Today it's got the post office and the library, and it's still got most of the town's people. It's kind of hard to look at the building now without shifting your gaze to the glacier on the mountain behind – it looks like the Blob coming down to eat the diner Steve McQueen is hiding in.

The town itself doesn't have a lot to offer. The **Visitors Center** is in an old railway car across from the small boat harbor. There's a historical museum in the first floor of the Begich Towers, open 1 to 5 Wednesday through Friday, which displays historical photos and some marine stuff.

■ Out & About

Hiking

The main reason to go to Whittier is to get out of Whittier. That's even more true now that the town itself has become unbearable. For hikers, there's the trail to **Portage Pass**. This is the old route used for thousands of years by Natives and for 100 years or so by hopeful miners. The trail took them from Prince William Sound to the Turnagain Arm. You can't take the whole route anymore – Portage Glacier has put itself in the way – but you can hike to the top of the pass in about an hour. You can camp at Divide Lake, or keep hiking along the side of the stream (the trail disappears and you're on your own) down to the glacier. Getting onto the glacier itself is a very bad idea, unless your idea of fun is falling into a crevasse and freezing to death while stuck head-first in a hole. The trailhead is at the foot of Maynard Mountain, about a mile behind Whittier Station. It's a great day trip.

Kayaking

Despite the hiking attractions, most people come to Whittier to get into the water. Whittier is heaven for kayakers – the only thing to watch out for are a couple of channels where you'll have to dodge cruise ships. The payoff is incredible scenery and endless wildlife, including otters, seals, Dall's porpoise, orca, and bald eagles.

Launch from the Whittier Small Boat Harbor. Check at the Harbor Office, where you can pick up tide tables, and pay your launch fee (this is the only town in Alaska that makes you pay to put in a kayak). It's worth stopping at the Harbor Office on the way back in, as well, not only to tell them you're back (because you told them where you were going when you left, didn't you?), but also to use the fire-hose-caliber hot shower they have. After a long paddle, it's the most fun you'll have for under $5.

An eight-mile paddle east through Passage Canal brings you to Decision Point (there's a nice camping spot near here, in Squirrel Cove, if you're putting in late in the day). From here, you can head north up toward Port Wells, or south into Blackstone Bay.

Most kayakers head to **Blackstone Bay**. It's about 10 miles east of Whittier and offers great views of tidewater glaciers in a relatively protected bay. Come bundled up, because the wind blows cold off the ice.

Port Wells leads north at the end of the Passage Canal to the biggest attractions around: the calving tidewater glaciers (the Coxe, Barry, and Cascade) of College (home to the Harvard and Yale glaciers) and Harriman Fjords. When a glacier calves, chunks of ice the size of houses can come off. It's not smart to get too close – kayaking in a 10-foot wave is never a good idea – but sitting back at a reasonable distance gives you a view of the ice crashing into the water and lets you hear the popping of the ice (it sounds like rifle shots) as it weakens in the warmer water. It's more than amazing, and the only drawback is the number of tour boats sharing the water with you.

Turn southwest at **Point Doran**, and Harriman Fjord continues another eight miles to the Surprise and Harriman glaciers. The several days of paddling it takes to see this area are definitely worth it. Dip your hand in the water and pick up a piece of glacial ice that could be 1,000 years old.

There are some cautions to remember if you're in the water here:

- Camp only above the high-water mark. Find where the color of the beach changes, and then move even further back.
- Bears are everywhere. Obey all proper bear precautions and stay out of the berry bushes.
- Wind comes off the glaciers, causing cold and choppy seas, which can make paddling difficult.
- Stay well back from a calving glacier – at least half a mile.
- Remember that cruise ships always have the right of way, because they're not paying a bit of attention to you.

If you're looking for kayak pickup or drop-off, try **Honey Charters** (☎ 907-472-2491, www.honeycharters.com). They've been working the area for a decade and can put you in at prime paddling spots. They also run day cruises that are a good value if you just want to sit back and enjoy the scenery.

You can rent kayaks from Honey Charters or **Alaska Sea Kayakers** (☎ 907-877-472-2534, www.alaskaseakayakers.com). Both also have guided kayaking tours. Standards are trips out to Shotgun Cove for a full-day paddle, or a half-day birding expedition. Day trips out to Blackstone Bay and back will run in the neighborhood of $300.

Cruises & Charters

As mentioned above, **Honey Charters** (☎ 907-472-2491) has good day trips into Prince William Sound from Whittier. Options include a three-hour cruise to Blackstone, four to six hours in the Barry Arm to watch glaciers calve, or an all-day whale-watching trip. The trips allow a maximum of six people, so you get a much better view of things than you would crammed onto a 70-foot ship with 100 other people. Honey Charters can also arrange fishing trips.

Major Marine Tours (☎ 800-764-7300, www.majormarine.com) has day trips into the Sound for $99. You'll get good glacier and mountain views, as you head down to Blackstone and Beloit Glaciers. **Phillips 26 Glacier Tour,** ☎ 907-276-8023, 800-544-0529, www.26glaciers.com, does 4½-hour trips into the Sound, taking in every bit of ice possible, for $129. These waters are so sheltered that Phillips has a "no seasickness" guarantee.

■ Food

Not a lot of options. For basic sandwiches and burgers, try **Café Orca Grill,** or **Frakie's Deli.** For a Whittier night out, there's **Swiftwater Seafoods**, which has a good selection of beer and wine, plus food that was swimming only a couple of hours ago.

To get your own food for a trip into the Sound, head to the **Harbor Store**, which has food and almost anything else you may need. If you've never seen a real general store, this is your chance.

■ Accommodations

The **Anchor Inn** (☎ 907-472-2394, www.whittierhotel.us), $$, has a loud bar and restaurant, so if you're looking for something a little more peaceful, try **June's Whittier B&B** (☎ 907-472-2396, 888-472-2396, www.breadnbuttercharters.com), $$. It's in the tower. They can also arrange local tours and charters. At the high end of things is the **Inn at Whittier** (☎ 907-472-7000, www.innatwhittier.com), new and shiny, and rooms with absolutely killer views. $$$$.

Camp behind **Begich Tower** in gravel for $7. There's a cooking shelter and the sites are okay, but you're better off taking your tent to **Salmon Run**, a free campground which is rather nicer, a mile east of town. This is an unofficial campground – the signs say no camping near the picnic area – but if you go back down to the gravel area past the picnic tables, it should be okay. Same with anywhere else outside of town – pitch your tent in the bush, and as long as you're not starting campfires, you'll be fine.

Farther Down the Kenai

If you've got time, it's well worth your while to keep heading south down the Kenai. The glaciers at Seward and the fish at Homer are waiting.

We pick up the Seward Highway again from Mile 79.9 – remember, distances are shown from Seward. All through this section of highway, the wildflowers in summer alone make it worth the trip out.

Mile 68.5 is the entrance to **Turnagain Pass Recreation Area**, a popular spot with cross-country skiers – you might find 12 feet of snow here in February. At Mile 63.7 is the **Johnson Pass Trailhead**, and you can camp at the **Granite Creek Campground**, Mile 63.

The junction of the Seward and Hope highways is at Mile 56.7. The Hope is a short road, only 17 miles, that takes you past the ghost town of Sunrise to the town of Hope. Site of another gold rush – one man pulled out 385 ounces in two months – the town was established in 1896. The road offers a good chance to see moose.

Fifteen miles up the road is the northern trailhead for **Resurrection Pass**. This is a 19-mile trail that's mostly fairly easy. In winter, it's a favorite cross-country skiing trail. The southern end of the trail comes out at mile 52 on the Sterling Highway.

The other reason to go to Hope is for whitewater – about the meanest in the state. **Class V Whitewater** (☎ 907-783-2004, wwwalaskanrafting.com) and **Nenana Raft Adventures** (☎ 907-683-RAFT, www.alaskaraft.com) offer trips on the Sixmile River, outside Hope. You can see part of the river from the main road – it's a tiny slot of water, boiling between big grey rocks. This is a trip only for those who have done whitewater before – no simple float, this trip is hard work. Nenana Raft Adventures wisely lists physical requirements for the Class V section: you should be able to swim 100 yards with a "strong, continuous stroke," and "run a mile without stopping." You'll be cold, wet (although Nenana puts you in dry suits), paddling frantically, and living with a good chance of having to swim a rapid or two when a wave kicks you out of the boat. There is a reason why rapids on the Class V section have names like "Suckhole" and "Jaws." The river drops more than 50 feet per mile – a huge descent – and flows between canyon walls that can rise more than 500 feet. For the serious whitewater junkie, this is pure heaven. Plan this one a bit in advance, and talk to the outfitter first.

Back on dry land, Mile 39.4 on the Seward has the trailhead for the **Devil's Pass Trail**. This is a 10-mile hike that links up with the Resurrection Pass Trail, taking you through the territory of the Resurrection gold rush. It's great for wildlife viewing.

The junction with the Sterling Highway is at Mile 37.4. Continue straight for the Seward, or turn right for the Sterling, which will take you to Soldotna and Homer.

The Seward heads almost due south at this point, dropping down past the **Trail River Campground**, Mile 24.2, with 64 sites right on the Kenai. It offers good fishing and berrying, and there are a number of trailheads around the campground. A bit further on is **Ptarmigan Creek campground**, set on the river, with an easy hike up to the lake. Nice spots, and you'll likely have the place to yourself.

You go through the tiny town of **Moose Pass** right before starting the final descent into Seward. There are a couple B&Bs in town, but it's mostly notable for how seriously they take their special speed limit zone. Slow down through here – there really are kids playing right by the road.

The turnoff for **Exit Glacier** is at Mile 3.7. The road is nine miles long; the first section is paved, but the final approach to the glacier can be a bit rough, with potholes and gravel. The ranger station is open from May to September, offering interpretive programs and hikes. This is the only part of the **Kenai Fjords National Park** that is accessible by car. (For more details, see below.)

Skip the turnoff for the moment, and you're in the town of Seward.

Seward

Located near the head of Resurrection Bay, Seward is one of the oldest communities in Southcentral Alaska.

■ History

The first community here was founded by Alexandar Baranov in 1781, when he came into the bay on Easter Sunday looking for shelter from a storm during his passage from Kodiak to Yakutat. Resurrection Bay came to serve the Russians as a shipbuilding port. The first ship launched here – the *Phoenix*, in 1793 – was probably the first European-built ship launched on the West Coast of North America.

The US history of the town begins in the 1890s, 20 years or so after the purchase of Alaska, when Captain Frank Lowell, along with his wife and children, settled in the area. They had the place pretty much to themselves until 1903, when the town of Seward proper was founded by John Ballaine, as an ice-free port terminus city for Alaska's then growing railway. Ballaine and his partners saw Seward as the future location of Alaska's major city, an easy route into the interior, and a perfect port, surrounded by stunning scenery. By 1904, the town's population was around 350.

The railroad was officially completed in 1923, when President Harding drove the golden spike. The railroad never turned out to be the cash cow Seward's founders had hoped for; except for a brief time during WWII, the railhead was largely neglected. In fact, the war sealed Seward's fate to remain a small town when the military developed the town of Whittier, much closer to Anchorage, as an alternate port. Seward was forgotten.

Historically, Seward also serves as a footnote to Alaska's most famous institution. The official story of the Iditarod dog sled race tells of mushers taking diphtheria vaccine to Nome; what's never mentioned is that the heroic mushers followed an existing trail, one that began in Seward. The trail was carved out by miners headed toward the **Iditarod Mining District**.

It was used until 1928, with as much as a ton and a half of gold being hauled out by teams of 46 dogs.

BALTO THE DIPHTHERIA DOG

As an interesting oddity, the last of the dogs that actually made that famous diphtheria serum run was named Balto; several dog foods were named after him. He spent many of his later years exhibited in a carnival, until a man from Cleveland purchased him for $2,000. Balto died in the Cleveland Zoo, then was stuffed, mounted, and displayed at the Cleveland Museum for years.

Seward made the news in 1926, when local resident Bernie Benson, just 14 years old, won a contest sponsored by Governor George Parks to design the state's (then territorial) flag. Bernie's design of Ursa Major on a field of blue is one of the most eloquent state flags in the US.

Seward was almost wiped out in the 1964 earthquake, which was centered just 95 miles from the town. Seward's shoreline dropped nearly six feet. Since that time, the town has moved along quietly, prospering as a terminus city, a vacation area for Anchorageites, and a fishing community. The current population of 2,700 gives the town a quiet, pleasant air, without the tourist wildness of Homer. It's one of those towns where you have a really, really good time just hanging out and watching the world go by. One of our favorites.

■ Basics

i Seward is the final stop for many cruises. From here, passengers take the train up to Denali, or to Anchorage, for the flight home. Cruise ships dock just north of the northern half of town, an easy walk to all attractions.

The **Alaska Railroad**, ☎ 907-224-2494 or 800-544-0552, www.alaska railroad.com, still stops in Seward. The line heads north to Anchorage, via Portage. The depot is at the small boat harbor. There is no passenger service between late September and mid-May; during the summer, departures are daily. Check with the Alaska Railroad for more details; there are some other nice package deals, like a train/cruise combo.

The town has two information centers: the larger is on the main road, which you'll see to the right as you drive into town (☎ 907-224-8051). There's also the Information Cache, at Third and Jefferson, at Mile 2 on the Seward Highway, inside an old Alaska Railroad car. In either you'll find the usual variety of helpful flyers. Both are open daily in summer.

If you're planning ahead for the off-season, write to the **Seward Chamber of Commerce**, Box 749, Seward, AK 99664. Be sure to get a copy of the town's walking tour – Seward is a place best explored on foot.

The town can easily be broken down into two pieces: there's the downtown area, where the Sealife Center is, and there's the harbor area, where most of the other attractions in town are.

The **Seward Trolley** – a little bus, actually – runs between downtown and the harbor. You can get a day pass for $3, but it's only a mile or so from the Sealife Center, at one end of town, to the harbor, at the other, and it's a nice walk. If you're going to park your car for the day, do it at the harbor side, in one of the big lots (don't forget to pay); it's a whole lot easier to park here than downtown.

On the harbor side, the **Chugach National Forest Service office** (☎ 907-224-3374) is at 4th and Jefferson. Stop in for current information on local hiking, fishing, and camping.

Headquarters for **Kenai Fjords** is at 1212 4th Ave. (☎ 907-224-3175, park infoline 224-2132), near the boat launch. Open daily mid-May through mid-September from 8 am to 7 pm, and Monday through Friday 8-5 in the winter, they offer slide shows that give you an idea of what the depths of the park are like. They've also got a small bookstore.

Seward's zip code is 99664.

> **QUICK TOUR:** If you've only got a couple hours, head out to **Exit Glacier.** Great scenery, one of the most accessible glaciers along the coast. Or do the **Sealife Center**.

> **DON'T MISS:** One way or another, you owe it to yourself to get to **Exit Glacier**. It's worth the trouble. If you've got the time and the money, a kayak trip around **Fox Island** will be a highlight of your whole trip.

> **BEST FREE THING TO DO:** Seward is a town made for walking. Head south, along **Resurrection Bay**. You'll pass the whole town, and then, on the dirt road, have the bay to yourself. If you're not in the mood for water, hike **Exit Glacier**, and see what global warming is doing to us all.

■ Things to Do

 Seward is rapidly adding to its list of visitor attractions. The challenge city boosters face, with Kenai Fjords so near, is getting people to look at the town instead of the scenery.

The **Seward Museum** (☎ 907-224-3902) is across the street from the Info Cache, on 3rd and Jefferson. Unusual for anything on the coast, there's a good Iditarod display here, plus a slide show of Seward's history and another of the Iditarod. There's also a good earthquake display and a collection of Native baskets. Don't miss the cow raincoats or the basket made out of porcupine quills. Open daily May 1 through September 1, 10 to 5; for off-season hours, phone before you go. Admission is three bucks.

Seward has also built a massive marine attraction, the **Alaska Sealife Center**, which is now the town's biggest draw. Funded in large part by a post-spill settlement from Exxon, the Alaska Sealife Center is right next to the Seward Marine Center. With the seven-acre site split roughly evenly between research and visitor facilities, the center has rookeries for otters, sea lions, and seals that have been rescued and deemed unfit to return to the wild, and they hope to draw in large colonies of sea birds.

Design for the center was intended to naturally recreate the world outside for the animals inside, including privacy areas where the animals can get away from people. There are also tanks where you can see salmon, a display where you can try to force feed a model otter (really), and a small petting tank.

The bigger areas include seals and sea lions – what's on view depends largely on what's been rescued recently, or what they haven't been able to rehabilitate. There's also a nice bird area, where you can see puffins swimming underwater – it's worth the price of admission just for this. The center also offers films and other programs.

All that said, visitor opinion on the center seems to be fairly divided. It's a research facility, but you aren't likely to see much research going on; and as far as the animal viewing goes, it's pretty sparse for your $15 ($12 for kids). We've talked to some people who found this the highlight of their trip; others have wandered through, looked at the bored seals swimming in loops, and wished they'd gone somewhere else. Our take on it is this: if you don't have a lot of time to go out on the water, and if you haven't seen what you wanted to in the way of animal life, give it a look. If you've been pretty lucky with your sightings, pass it by. The center is open daily in summer from 8 am to 8 pm. ☎ 800-224-2525, www.alaskasealife.org.

St. Peter's Episcopal Church, built in 1906, is one of the oldest churches on the Kenai Peninsula. Open by request (ask at the Visitors Center), the church is on the corner of 2nd and Adams.

If you're out to shop, walk along 3rd and 4th avenues for a nice assortment of galleries and gift shops. If you need charts for a trip out, head to **Northland Books and Charts**, at 234 4th Ave. You'll find all the hiking maps and navigational charts you need.

■ Out & About

 There's a lot going on around Seward. It's an ideal spot for kayakers. You can go from Resurrection Bay out to the glaciers, if you're experienced enough and have enough time.

If you want a guided trip, **Kayak Adventures Worldwide**, ☎ 907-225-3960, 800-288-3134, www.kayakak.com, offer a variety of programs suitable for all levels of experience, from one-day guided trips to multiday excursions. Full-day paddles run $120, half-day from $65. Lots of extended options, too.

Sunny Cove Kayaking has been working in Seward forever. Sunny Cove caters a little more to the cruise ship audience, but for the $250 neighborhood, what you get is a cruise into the fjords and then a paddle around glaciers. Both also run trips to Fox Island, for about $150, which offers great wildlife watching potential. ☎ 800-770-9119, www.sunnycove.com.

If you haven't kayaked anywhere else, this may be the perfect place for it. (See the Kenai Fjords section, below.)

Rent a bike from the **Seward Bike Shop** (☎ 907-224-2448) for around $40 a day for a mountain bike with suspension. Or if you want somebody else to provide the motor, **Bardy's Trail Rides** (☎ 907-224-7863, www.seward horses.com) has horseback trips down to the edge of Resurrection Bay.

If you're after furrier transport, **Ididaride Sled Dog Tours** (☎ 800-478-3139, www.ididaride.com) gives you a chance to play with the puppies and ride in a wheeled sled dog cart. $49 for adults, half that for kids. A good deal.

If you're after **wildlife viewing**, head into **Resurrection Bay**.

Six miles south of town is **Cains Head State Recreation Area**, an old WWII base, where there are still bunkers, a subterranean fort, and great beaches. You can't drive there; you've got to hike or boat in. Before the Alcan was built, Seward was the main transportation hub for the Alaska Command, and here's a bit of what was left behind.

Seward has one of the biggest **Fourth of July** bashes in the state, with games, parades, fireworks, and general madness. Plan ahead or you won't find a place to stay. In winter, there's cross-country skiing at the Snow River area – get to it via the Primrose Campground, at Mile 18 on the Seward Highway – or at Glacier Creek (see the *Exit Glacier* section, below). If you're in town in the winter, try the **Polar Bear Jump Off** in January. This is when insane people dress up in costumes, have a parade, and jump into the bay.

Exit Glacier

People come to Seward to see the glaciers in Kenai Fjords, but the glacier closest to Seward is the Exit Glacier, with a 150-foot-tall glacial face. You can drive to it from Seward by following Exit Glacier Road. The road is paved up to the Ranger Station at the foot of the glacier; if you continue north instead of turning off, you can reach several Forest Service cabins. This part of the road follows the river, and there are great views of the glacier up ahead, the silver water flowing from it.

The road past the Exit Glacier turnoff is dirt and can be hard on low-clearance vehicles. The glacial face is about half a mile from the parking lot.

You can hike all the way out to the main icefield from Exit Glacier, but allow yourself all day for the trip. It's only 3.5 miles out, but there's little maintenance on the path, so it's steep, rough, and often slippery. Much of the time the upper portion of the path is covered with snow.

If that's a bit much, there's an easy half-mile **Upper Loop Trail** that gives great views and takes you right up to the glacier's face. For the less ambitious hiker, the Ranger Station runs nature walks and hikes in and around the icefield. Check for current list of programs. (For more hikes, check the *Hiking* section, below.)

One of the most interesting things about Exit Glacier are the signs along the walkway: these show where the glacier was in the past. Like every other glacier in Alaska, Exit is on the way out. Thirty years or so ago, the glacier was where the parking lot is now; today, it's shrinking at a rate of about six inches a day.

Up at the top of the loop trail, you can get a good look at the glacial face, and by paying attention to the trail on the way in, you can see how glaciers impact the landscape. First, they obviously strip it all bare; then, over time, the forest returns. You can match up the date signs with the forest to see just how long it takes everything to return to full-growth.

Kenai Fjords

Kenai Fjords is the reason most people go to Seward. The park, which extends far enough south to abut Kachemak Bay State Park outside Homer, is most easily reached from Seward. All that separates town and park are a couple of 5,000-foot mountains.

Kenai Fjords are dominated by the **Harding Icefield**, one of the largest icefields in North America, from which 23 named glaciers flow. The icefield is approximately 35 by 20 miles; until the early 1900s, it was thought to be one huge ice system.

The Fjords themselves are an excellent place for **wildlife** watchers. More than 30 species of seabirds are seen in the area, including both tufted and horned puffins, and the waters are full of marine mammals.

If you don't want to take a kayak out (see above), there are plenty of people ready to take you out in ships.

Ship charters run out of Resurrection Bay, around Aialik Cape, and finally into the fjords themselves, usually for a stop at Holgate Glacier or, depending on the trip, Northwestern Glacier. In total, Aialik Bay has three glaciers flowing into it; McCarty Fjord has two, including the dramatic Dinglestatdt Glacier. McCarty Fjord also has a major seal pupping haul out.

On any trip, you're likely to see seals and sea lions, as well as more puffins than you thought possible – they're everywhere. On a good day, you might be lucky enough to see a whale or two, and maybe even a rhinoceros auklet.

There is a caveat to these trips: if you've come up through Southeast Alaska, or if you've been to Glacier Bay, this will probably seem a little bland to you. It's a nice introduction to Alaska's coast for people who've never traveled it before, but although it's pretty, there are better places around, so if they're on your itinerary, this might be a skip.

If you're going out, remember that the water can get rough out here; if you're prone to sea sickness, take pills before you get on the boat. Even on a calm, clear day, the sea can be pretty bumpy when they're taking you around to see the haul-outs. Also remember that, even on a bright, sunny day, it's cold on the water. Dress accordingly.

For your trip with the big outfitters, you'll get a spot on a large ship, narration from a naturalist, and lunch. All the full-day trips run the same range, around $125-150 for adults, half that for kids; most outfitters also offer shorter options, around $60, but you really don't get into the best scenery with this, and you're much better off taking the long trip.

To get into the fjords for a tour, try **Kenai Fjords Tours Inc.** (☎ 907-224-8068 or 800-478-8068, www.kenaifjords.com); it's a Native owned company.

Other good choices include **Major Marine Tours** (☎ 907-224-8030 or 800-764-7300, www.majormarine.com), and **Mariah Tours**, which has a 10-hour, 150-mile trip through the fjords. Other companies will pack you on huge ships with as many as 100 other people, but Mariah runs 43-foot boats with a maximum of 22 passengers. ☎ 800-478-8068.

All of these places have offices down by the harbor; stop by and talk to the staff, so you can pick one you like. It's not usually a problem getting a seat on one of the bigger ships.

There are dozens of charter operators running smaller boats with customizable itineraries. See the charter section, below.

To fly over the fjords, you can go with **Scenic Mountain Air** (☎ 907-288-3646), located in Moose Pass.

FOX ISLAND

One of the big sites in Kenai Fjords is Fox Island. There was a fox farm run here around the turn of the century, but the island's real claim to fame is that **Rockwell Kent** – perhaps the most famous illustrator of the early 20th century (his woodcuts for *Moby Dick* are amazing) – worked here. Kent had failed as an artist and was suffering from a crisis of confidence. He went to Alaska to get away from the pressures of down south, and he and his son were on the island for nearly a year, from the summer of 1918 to the spring of 1919. It would seem that their favorite activity while on the island was to sunbathe naked in snowdrifts and listen to the lady who ran the fox farm tell tales about her life – she was, from all accounts, quite a character.

Kent wrote of his time on the island that "So huge was the scale of all this that for some time we looked in vain for any habitation, at last incredulously seeing what we had taken to be boulders to assume the form of cabins."

That's how big it is up here.

If you're feeling in a Kent mood, **Kenai Fjords Wilderness Lodge** on Fox Island is a nice spot to get away. Overnight, with meals and transport runs $329/person, and there are extra deals with kayak trips and more. ☎ 800-4PUFFIN, www.kenaifjords. com. We don't suggest hanging out naked in snowdrifts, though.

Hiking

Just off the Exit Glacier Road, as you cross the bridge over the Resurrection River, is the **Resurrection River Trail**. This trail, which is 16 miles long, connects to the Russian Lakes Trail, which in turn connects to the Resurrection Pass Trail – about 70 miles of hiking in all. There's a cabin 6.5 miles in on the Resurrection River Trail.

Other good hiking includes **Devil's Pass**, which connects to the Resurrection Pass Trail. The trailhead is at Mile 39 on the Seward Highway. **Johnson Pass** is a 33-mile hike that starts and ends on the Seward Highway – at Miles 33 and 64, respectively. Along the way, it passes excellent fishing lakes, but watch for avalanches along the trail.

The **Carter Lake Trail**, Mile 32 on the Seward Highway, is only two miles long. It's steep in places, but takes you up to an alpine meadow.

WARNING: Everywhere around Seward is serious bear country. Act accordingly.

Charters

All around Seward you'll find outstanding fishing. The nine-day **Silver Salmon Derby**, held each year in August (book your hotel room well in advance), offers a $10,000 prize for the heaviest fish, but silver aren't the only game in town – head out for king, Dolly Varden, halibut, and more.

We're working on a mathematical formula that measures the relationship between the number of Subway shops in town and the quality of the fishing. Judging by this measure, the fishing in Seward is very good indeed.

There are dozens of charter operators working in town. You can get an idea of how their luck is running by going down to the docks around 5 pm, and seeing what the catch of the day has been.

Figure a day of salmon fishing is going to run you around $175; halibut will usually go about $25 more. Try to book at least a couple days in advance.

The **Charter Option** (☎ 907-224-2026, 800-224-2026, www.charteroption. com) runs more than 30 boats. Whatever you want, they've got the boat to handle it; they're also a good choice if you're looking for a sightseeing charter.

The Fish House (☎ 907-224-3674, 800-257-7760, www.thefishhouse.net) has full-day trips for salmon or halibut; they run almost as many boats as the Charter Option does, and they run a full-service tackle shop, across from the harbor.

■ Food

Seward has one absolutely killer restaurant, and then an assortment of dining attractions that are fairly run of the mill – except for the seafood, of course, which is wonderful almost everywhere. Most places serve entrées for $10 to $20.

For one of the best meals you'll have in Alaska, head to **Ray's Waterfront** (☎ 907-224-5606), 4th Ave. by the Coast Guard Station. They've been written up in all of the food magazines, and their cedar planked salmon is something you will not soon forget. Dinner from about $20, and worth every penny. Make reservations, or be prepared to wait a while.

The other choice for a night out is **Legends Restaurant & Pub**, 412 Washington St., ☎ 907-224-3161, with a mix of seafood, steak, Mexican, and American dishes. Great views from the dining room.

The **Harbor Dinner Club**, 220 5th Ave., is a good place for burgers and seafood. Figure on a complete dinner running about $20.

The **Resurrection Roadhouse** is a local favorite. It's .7 miles up the Exit Glacier road, and dinners of steak, seafood, or chicken start at $10.

Smoke'n' Alaska's Fish and Chips is down by the harbor. Fast, if you can get their attention, and cheap, with halibut and chips for under $10.

For breakfast, **Marina**, across from the boat harbor, is the place of choice. If you can't get in there, try the **Breeze Inn**, just a couple of doors down. Either place will fill you up for under $10.

If you want to eat healthy, check out **Le Barn Appetit** (☎ 907-224-8706), a health food store/bakery/B&B, at Mile 3.7 on the Seward Highway, the first right off Exit Glacier Road.

And for the classic Alaska dinner, **Exit Glacier Salmon Bake**, a quarter-mile up Exit Glacier Road, will do you up right. ☎ 907-224-2204.

■ Accommodations

The Van Gilder (☎ 907-224-3079 or 800-204-6835, www.vangilderhotel.com), 308 Adams (Box 2), is Seward's landmark hotel. Built in 1916, it's seen it all over the years, including a restoration. This is a registered National Historic Site, $$-$$$, depending on private or shared bath.

The **Best Western Hotel Seward** (☎ 907-224-2378 or 800-478-4050) is at 221 5th Ave. Doubles start at $$$ in the shoulder season and run to $$$$ in high.

The **Breeze Inn** (☎ 907-224-5237, 888-224-5237, www.breezeinn.com), by the small boat harbor, has nice doubles, $$$. **Murphy's Motel**, 911 4th Ave., is popular and pleasant, with doubles from $$.

The **Hotel Edgewater and Conference Center,** 202 Fifth Ave, ☎ 907-224-2700, 888-793-6800, www.hoteledgewater.com, has good ocean views, and complimentary continental breakfast. $$$.

HOTEL PRICING
Prices are in US dollars.
under $50. . . . . $
$50-$100 . . . . $$
$100-$150 . . . . . . $$$
above $150 . . . . . $$$$

Hotel Seward, 221 5th Ave, ☎ 907-224-2378, 800-478-4050; www.hotel sewardalaska.com, is downtown, and quite nice, with rooms that include VCRs. $$$.

Le Barn Appetit is a Seward landmark. They're on Old Exit Glacier Road – which is a sidestreet on the Exit Glacier Road – about 3.5 miles from town. They've got a room built around a tree ($$$), an efficiency apartment for the same price, or a three-room suite that can be rented whole for $$$$$, or in parts for less. But the real reason to stay is the food: gourmet, and healthy. There's also a small health food store here.

Take a look at the brochures in the Info Center, and you'll get the impression that half the town is running B&Bs. The percentage may actually be higher on that. Figure on around $100-150 for a double in a local B&B, and if the day is looking crowded, staff at the Info Center will help you find a place – vital during Salmon Derby days.

Camping

RV facilities are available at **Bear Creek** (☎ 907-224-5725), Mile 6.6 on the Seward Highway. **Kenai Fjords RV Park** (☎ 907-224-8779) also has full hookups, at Mile 1 on the Seward Highway.

Campgrounds spread out regularly along the **Seward Highway**. You'll find sites at Mile 17.4, Mile 23.2, and Mile 24.2.

There are also 12 tent-only campsites at **Exit Glacier**. There's potable water on site and a cooking shelter, but not much else except killer views. Come well prepared with lots of bug goop, because the flies are just nasty here. Sites are free, and they're all well hidden; check for a rock placed on top of the site number to show if somebody's already claimed the spot.

Closer to town, try the **Forest Acres Campground**, at Mile 2. Tents only.

Finally, there is the huge **Beachside Camping area**, across from Ballaine Blvd. – take a right from the ferry terminal and walk along the shoreline. You can't miss it, because there are hundreds of RVs parked here. It's managed by the Parks Department, and most of the spots have been graveled for RVs, but there are some grassy tent areas.

The Sterling Highway

By road, from Seward, you have to backtrack, to where the Seward Highway and the Sterling meet. Head back to Anchorage on the Seward, or take the Sterling for an easy drive through stunning scenery down to the town of Homer.

The attractions on the Sterling are not so much the small towns – Soldotna and Kenai – but the fact that, whatever your outdoor interests may be, this is the place you can come and play. All along the road you should watch for moose, Dall sheep, mountain goats, bears, and caribou. This is one of the richest fishing grounds in the world, and you have to be spectacularly unlucky not to catch your limit in the local lakes. And once you've fished the ocean around here, you'll think the lake catches were only good for bait. There's nothing quite like reeling in a 200-pound halibut.

It's only 57 miles from the highway junctions to Soldotna, but there's enough outdoor activity here to fill a book just on this area (and somebody did: try *55 Ways into the Wilderness in Southcentral Alaska*, by Helen Nienhueser and John Wolfe). We're not even going to try to be comprehensive. You'll like whatever you try. Miles listed show the distance from Homer.

This close to Anchorage, some of the sites can get full on weekends. Just move a little farther down the road and you should end up by yourself again.

Much of this stretch of road passes through **Kenai National Wildlife Refuge**. It was originally the Kenai National Moose Refuge, set aside by FDR in 1941 and expanded in 1980, both in area and in mission. The park, which covers roughly two million acres, has over 200 miles of hiking trails. If you don't hike them in summer, you can come back and ski them in winter. Some of the state's best berry bushes are in the park (watch for bears), and any spur road is likely to turn up some wildlife. Particularly good choices are the Skilak Lake Loop Road and the Swanson River Road.

We can only scratch the surface of what's available here. Figure out what you want to do – hike, fish, camp – then check in with the ranger station at Mile 121.5, just opposite the turnoff for the Skilak Lake Loop Road. They'll get you pointed in the right direction.

There are several lodges and campgrounds between the junction and Soldotna. Especially nice for campers are **Quartz Creek** (Mile 134.5, 31 sites on the lake); **Russian River** at Mile 127, two miles off the road (84 sites that get pretty crowded when the red salmon are running); **Hidden Lake**, 13 miles off the road at Mile 121.5 on the **Skilak Lake Loop** (a lovely campground with 44 sites); **Izaak Walton Campground**, at Mile 97.5, near the **Moose River Archaeological Site**, where you'll find evidence that Natives were hanging out here 2,000 years ago; and **Morgan's**

Landing, at Mile 95, five miles off the highway on Scout Lake Loop Road, which has good views of the Kenai River.

The small and town of **Cooper Landing**, Mile 131, stretches for several miles along the highway. You don't see much besides a couple of lodges and the giant Princess Hotel looming over the river on the opposite bank. The town is best known as a fishing hole and as the put-in place for raft trips down the Kenai River. The run through Kenai Canyon is about 14 miles, with the water ranging from Class I to Class III.

Alaska Wildland Adventures (☎ 907-595-1279 or 800-478-4100, www. alaskawildland.com) is based in Cooper Landing. They've got seven-hour raft trips on the Kenai for $110 – this is more of a float than whitewater – or a shorter trip for about $50. They've also got full-day fishing trips for $195 on the upper or lower Kenai. Head to the upper part of the river for sockeye and Dolly Varden; the lower portion is better in season for kings (May-July) and silver (August-September). If you want to stick around for a couple days they have a nice group of cabins right by the river. This company is one of the ones we recommend for taking you into the serious bush, as well, so they're good people to do business with.

Another good choice in Cooper's Landing is **Gwin's Lodge**, Mile 52, ☎ 907-595-1266, www.gwinslodge.com. Nice cabins, good restaurant, and they can book you any kind of outfitter trip you can imagine. Good place, been in business forever.

Alaska River Adventures (☎ 888-836-9027, www.alaskariver adventures.com) does trips on the Kenai for $169 for a full day. They specialize in fly fishing, so talk to them about throwing strings at water around here.

The town of **Sterling**, Mile 99, is in the middle of salmon country and is the place to bring your **canoe**. There are two great routes here; to get on them, take the Swanson River Road Turnoff at Mile 77 to Swan Lake Road. The **Swan Lake route** covers a total of 60 miles, connecting 30 lakes, with access to the Moose River. Put in at Canoe Lake (Mile 3.5 on Swan Lake Road) or the East Entrance to Portage Lake (Mile 9.5). There are no big portages to mess with, and the route takes about two days; add another day if you're going to continue on the Moose River.

The other great canoe route here is the **Swanson River route**, which is rather more strenuous – be prepared to portage. The put-in is at mile 12 on Swan Lake Road, and the route takes in 80 miles of water, including 40 lakes and 46 miles of the Swanson River. The hardest portage is about a mile and a half from Gene Lake to the Upper Swanson – you'll be climbing beaver dams and logjams. But once you're on the river, it's a beautiful float. Just make sure you've got good topo maps before you set out.

On either route, you have to check in at the log books that are set up by the put-ins. Group size is limited to 15 people, but who'd want a group that big to begin with? There are no designated campsites on either route, so try to find a place where others have already camped, to minimize your impact on the forest. Practice no-trace camping, and don't forget the bear precautions. Finally, remember that the weather can change fast, and you don't want to be stuck in the middle of a lake when a storm kicks up. Know what you're doing; these routes are in the middle of nowhere.

For fishermen, **Alaska Sunrise Fishing** (☎ 800-818-1250) and **Alaska Adventures** (☎ 800-262-9666) will take you out on the Kenai from around $125 a half-day, $195 for all day. Alaska Adventures also has guided canoe trips, canoe rental, and fly-in bear viewing at Katmai. To see the bears on a day trip starts at $295; this is a lot cheaper than operators in Homer offer. Still, for not much more, you could fly down to Wrangell or Juneau and spend a couple days at Anan or Pack Creek.

Alaska Mountain View Cabins (☎ 907-262-4287, 888-388-4827, www.alaskamountainview.com) has nice spots close to the river, if you want to stay around for a couple days. Or you can keep driving a couple more miles and hit the Soldotna/Kenai area.

Soldotna and Kenai are two separate towns – the road branches, with the southern fork taking you to Soldotna, the northern to Kenai – but they're really the same place for all intents and purposes.

For your purposes, if you're in a hurry, take the fork into Soldotna; it cuts a few miles off the trip down to Homer. But you didn't come up here to hurry, did you? So go into Kenai, spend a night out at Captain Cook State Park, and on the drive to Homer, you can cross the Kenai River delta, and stop and watch for birds. The Kenai fork has got the scenery.

■ Soldotna

Soldotna, at Mile 84, was first homesteaded by WWII vets just after the end of the war. They must have needed a little taste of paradise after what they'd been through. The town's commercial crossroads is at the junction of the highway and the Kenai spur road. While halibut fishermen keep driving south to Homer, salmon fishermen usually stop here. Besides the fishing, the town supports a large branch campus of the University of Alaska.

It's not a particularly scenic town; it's the kind of place that's great to live in, though, as is Kenai. Most visitors hurry through these twin towns, and so miss out on some fun stuff.

Attractions

Visitor Info is on the highway, just south of the Kenai River bridge. Open daily in summer 9 to 7; weekdays 9 to 5 in winter. ☎ 907-262-1337 or 907-262-9814.

The **Kenai National Wildlife Refuge Visitors Center** (☎ 907-262-7021) is off Ski Road (Mile 81.6). Open weekdays 8 am to 4:30 pm, weekends 10 to 6, they've got all the information you'll need to get you out boating, hiking, or camping. The center runs videos every hour, and there are some good dioramas. A nature trail leads from the center, and the Alaska Natural History Association keeps a small shop here.

The Soldotna Museum has a nice collection of early log cabins – including the very last of the Alaskan Territorial schools – and wildlife displays. It's on Centennial Park Road, just off the highway. Open Tuesday through Saturday 10 to 4, Sunday noon to 4. A good place to stop and see what homesteading was like.

Out & About

From here all the way down to Homer, there's great **razor clam digging**. Head out in the time window of an hour before to two hours after low tide (tide tables available in almost any store). There's a limit of 45 per day, and you need a fishing license to go clamming. To find them, watch for the dimple the clam makes in the sand when it buries itself; you can also watch for waterjets when it spits. Start digging next to the dimple, not on top of it – you don't want to smash the clam. Figure the thing is a foot to two feet under the sand, and dig the final few inches with your hands. Dig fast – you wouldn't believe how fast a clam can burrow.

But let's face it – if you're here or in Kenai and getting out of the car, you're doing it to **fish**.

A FISHERMAN'S TALE

The world record salmon was caught in the Kenai River, on May 17th, 1985: the fish weighed 97¼ pounds. The guy who hooked it, Les Anderson, got the fish in fairly quickly, but of course the net wasn't big enough, so they had to grab the fish and wrestle it to shore. Les and his fishing buddies, unusual for fishermen, weren't good at exaggerating – they thought they'd caught a big fish, but not that big – so they kept at it, working the river for another five hours. By the time they got around to having the thing weighed, it had probably lost at least two pounds. Les won $500 in the fishing derby, and now endures a lifetime of seeing publicity pictures of him with his fish (it's nearly as tall as he is).

You have three choices when you're going fishing. First, you can just find a good spot by the river and work it. Second, you can hire a guide to take you out. Or third, you can fly somewhere where there aren't a lot of other fishermen around.

For guides, try **Jughead Charters** (☎ 907-262-7433), **Bo's Fishing Guide Service** (☎ 907-262-5154 or 800-699-5154, www.boknowsfishing. com), or **Jeff King's Budget Charters** (☎ 907-262-4564 or 888-578-5333, www.jeffkingfishing.com).

Alaska Coastal Marine (☎ 907-262-4359, www.alaskacoastalmarine. com) does day and overnight fishing trips. They also work as hunting guides.

For more remote fishing spots, **Talon Air Service** (☎ 907-262-5452, talonair.com) has fly-ins that start around $200 per person. This does not include the guide – they just drop you off and pick you up at the end of the day. If you want a guide, add $50 to the per person price. Guided trips supply the gear; unguided, you bring your own. They can also arrange raft drop offs – remember, you can't fly a noncollapsible kayak on a plane. Good people, some really interesting package trips.

Food

Soldotna is home to every chain restaurant known to the human race. If that's not your style, try the **Hog Heaven Café**, right on the highway, for good omelets and breakfasts from $7. **Through the Seasons**, just past the road junction, has soups, breads, and great seafood, from about $20. The **Tide's Inn Supper Club**, across from the Kenai River Lodge, has steak and seafood dinners from $18 to $35.

There's a **farmer's market** on Saturdays in summer, so you can stock up for the night at the campsite.

Accommodations

If your tent has sprung a leak and you absolutely have to find indoor shelter, there is an assortment of generic hotels out along the main road where you can pretty much always find a room. If you're the plan ahead sort, give a call to **Kenai River Lodge** (☎ 907-262-4292, www.kenairiverlodge. com), $$$, or the **Soldotna Inn**, ☎ 907-262-9269, 866-262-9169, www. mykels.com, $$. There's also the **Riverside House** (☎ 907-262-0500 or 877-262-0500), $$, plus an RV park on the property.

HOTEL PRICING
Prices are in US dollars.
under $50.........$
$50-$100 ....$$
$100-$150 ......$$$
above $150.....$$$$

But if you have any choice at all, camp. The hotels are pricey and are set up to handle the summer influx of fishermen, which means people stomping up and down the hallway at 4 am.

For RVs, head to **Kasilof RV Park** (☎ 907-262-0418), a bit south of town. But see the Kenai section, below, for the Captain Cook option.

Campers should go to **Centennial Park Campground**, at the junction of the highway and Kalifornsky Beach Road, or **Swiftwater Park**, Mile 94.

> **AUTHOR TIP:** *For all accommodations in this area, plan early in June and July, when the fish run is at its peak. However, even while everything around town may be jammed, drive 20 miles in any direction, and you'll find places to stay.*

■ Kenai

 If you take the right fork at the Soldotna/Kenai junction, heading north, you end up in the town of Kenai, which is always a bit less crowded than Soldotna. It's also got better scenery. While it's the largest city on the peninsula (with a population around 6,700), it's a quiet getaway from the fishing furor that characterizes Soldotna and Homer.

The town used to be a Dena'ina village – when Captain Cook went by, looking for the ever-elusive Northwest Passage, he found a village called Shkit'uk; this translates to "Where we slide down," and who knows what that's all about.

In 1791, the area was taken over by the Russians, who were busy wiping out every fur seal they could find. The **Russian Lebedev Company** set up shop and proceeded to kill everything that moved, including many of the local Dena'ina. This led to a battle in 1797, in which more than 100 people were killed, and the Natives did succeed in more or less getting rid of the Russians; the Lebedev Company declared bankruptcy, and Alexandr Baranov, governor of the territory, looked around, saw there weren't enough fur-bearing animals left to bother with, and moved down to Sitka.

Gold was found in the 1850s, oil 100 years later. Today, the money comes from tourism and the gigantic fertilizer factory north of town.

Sights & Attractions

 Visitor Info is downtown in a complex with the cultural museum. You'll find good historical exhibits on the Russian history of the town. It's worth stopping in here; they have lots of brochures from places all around the peninsula, local art exhibits, and the museum is really a cut above average – and it's all free.

Leave the Info Center by driving away from the highway, and take the first right; you'll come to the **Holy Assumption of the Virgin Mary Russian Orthodox Church**, which was established in 1849. The building as it now stands was completed in 1895 – yes, it looks brand new and shiny, but it's real. The first missionaries were only about three years behind the first wave of fur traders. In 1845, Father Igumen Nikolai Militov came to Kenai from Sitka and established a permanent parish in the region. He did pretty well, converting about 1,500 Natives in the first ten years of his work.

If you haven't seen a Russian Orthodox Church anywhere else, stop in here – there aren't many in the interior; the best ones are in Kodiak and Dutch Harbor. When the church was built, it had river views; those have been given over to apartment complex views, but it's still a lovely spot. The church is open daily, but remember that it's a church – they still have services here Saturdays at 6 pm and Sundays at 10 am. Russian Orthodox services will seem familiar to Catholics or C of E members, but much of the iconography is quite different. An interesting fact about Russian-style icons is that real ones frequently have curtains that can be drawn – the icon is not simply a painting, it's a window on Heaven, and there are times when you don't want Heaven watching you. The other great thing about Russian Orthodox services is that you stand through the whole thing. As a priest once explained to us, "We don't believe religion is a spectator sport."

If the church is closed, you can phone ☎ 907-283-4122, or check at the Visitor Center to see when somebody will be around. Admission is free, but offer up a donation of a buck or two to help them keep the place in shape.

One of the best reasons to drive through Kenai, rather than Soldotna, is that it puts the **Kenai River Flats** on your path. Birders come here to add massively to their life list. If feathers don't interest you, there's a good chance of seeing beluga whales, although the population of them has recently suffered a dramatic decrease.

The Kenai River Flats have a boardwalk where you can get out and look at the marshy land the birds love so much. It's worth just stopping and hanging out for a while to see what shows up.

The delta area is part of the Kenai National Wildlife Refuge, which is a little unusual for wildlife refuges, in that it has towns in it. More common is to think of a remote place like ANWR as a proper refuge – but except from oil company greedheads, it's pretty safe, whereas the Kenai area sees 75% of the state's recreational fishing. The refuge here covers nearly two million acres, stretching from the tip of Turnagain arm down to where the refuge abuts the Kachemak Bay State Wilderness. Pretty much whenever you leave the road, you're in the refuge area, or nearby.

Food

Like Soldotna, there's at least one of every chain restaurant you've ever seen here. To avoid plastic food, eat at **Kitchen Express** – a coffee shop with good seafood from $5 to $15. Try the salmon scampi. **Paradisio's** has Italian, Greek, and Mexican food, from $6 to $20. **New Peking Chinese** has buffets that start at $8 for lunch, $11 for dinner. The **Old Town Village Restaurant** is between the Info Center and the church, set up in an old cannery building. Sandwiches from $9, seafood $15-20. **Burger-N-Brew**, by the Info Center, has dozens of different burgers, plus seafood and sandwiches. Prices start at $7.

Accommodations

The **B&B Assoc of Kenai** (☎ 866-436-2266, www.kenai peninsulabba.com) is your best call for choosing one of the countless B&Bs in the city.

There are a lot more hotels in Soldotna than in Kenai, but try the **Kenai Merit Inn** (☎ 907-227-6131, 800-227-6131), $$$.

As with Soldotna, if you can skip the hotel, you're better off heading to the campgrounds. RVs can stay at **Beluga Lookout RV Park** (☎ 907-283-

5999), **Kenai RV Park** (☎ 907-398-3382), or **Overland RV Park** (☎ 907-283-4512), all right near the visitor center.

However, if you have a tent, or if you're willing to skip the hookups, there's better stuff outside of town, in **Captain Cook State Recreation Area**, where there's Bishop Creek (15 sites), 15 miles north of town, and the Discovery Campground (53 sites), 29 miles north. Both are on bluffs overlooking the inlet.

■ Captain Cook State Recreation Area

Spread out along the shoreline north of Kenai is the Captain Cook State Recreation Area, a little-used treasure. The **Discovery Campground** has some of the prettiest sites in the state, and it's usually no more than half full.

To get into the park, just turn right onto North Kenai Road. You'll pass a huge, ugly factory, and then a bit farther on, you're in the park.

The park includes **Stormy Lake**, which has a boat launch at its north end and a boat-in only campsite at its narrowest point. There are cross-country skiing trails near **Bishop Creek Campground**, and the end of the **Swanson River Canoe Trail** is right by the Discovery Campground.

But the real reason to come out here is the views. On a clear day, you can see the mountains and volcanoes across a wide stretch of water. Pick a nice campsite, put your feet up, and relax. When it's time to stretch your legs, walk down on the beach. It's as good as it gets.

> **WARNING:** It is a very bad idea to go down in the mud beyond the rocky shoreline. Like in Turnagain Arm, the tides are very fast, the mud is very sticky, and people die every year.

■ The Highway to Homer

The Kalifornsky Beach Road reconnects Kenai to the Sterling Highway. Make sure to stop at **Clam Gulch**, at Mile 62. Get a license to dig for clams, go on a guided clam dig, or just stay at the **Clam Shell Lodge** and have a dinner that's the fruit of someone else's labor. If you've never gone clamming, it's a lot of fun. Clamming season lasts all summer. Other popular clamming sites are in Ninilchick, near **Deep Creek**, and at **Whiskey Gulch**.

Mile 44.5 is the turnoff for **Ninilchik**, half a mile off the highway. It's the oldest European settlement on the peninsula, settled by retired Russian sealers in the 1820s. The old village has some great cabins, with views of the volcanoes dominating the horizon: Mt. Redoubt (10,197 feet and still blowing regularly) and Mt. Ilianna (10,016 feet). There's a nice walking tour of the village, and a good **Russian Orthodox Church** that's still active. The church was originally built in 1901; services are at 10 am on the first and last Sundays of the month.

Stop at the **Village Cache** for nice Native and Russian art.

Camp at **Ninilchik View**, Mile 44.1, overlooking the ocean. (Of course, just about everything here overlooks the ocean.)

From Ninilchik, you keep heading south to **Anchor Point**, the westernmost city on the Kenai Peninsula – which means it's the westernmost point you can get to by road on the continent. The town got its name because somebody on Captain Cook's ship tied bad knots; the *Resolution* lost a large kedge anchor here when the tidal currents pulled it from the ship. There's not much in the town – a hotel, a liquor store, a couple small shops. **Halibut Campground**, part of the Anchor River State Rec Area, right outside of town, is the closest developed campground outside Homer – worth remembering if things are full down there.

The final miles into Homer offer some fine views of Cook Inlet and, as you round the point, the beautiful Kachemak Bay.

Homer

At the tip of the Kenai Peninsula, Homer bills itself as "the End of the Road." Stores sell a certificate of completion to people who have driven all the way out to the end of the spit, as far as you can go south of Anchorage by road. Popular radio figure Tom Bodett started here, broadcasting his NPR series, "The End of the Road." It's no wonder he's stayed even after hitting the big time. (Homer's other claim to fame, pop-singer Jewel, who grew up here, fled and now lives in Texas.) Homer is one of the great places in Alaska; it's got character to spare, and because almost all of the tourist activities are down on the Spit, the town itself stays safe, a charming little town that reveals its attractions only to the long-term visitor or resident.

■ History

Some of the finest fishing in Alaska is around Homer, and the Natives knew this for centuries before the RV crowd moved in. The Kenaitze Indians, an Athabascan group, had villages all along Kachemak Bay; their territory extended as far north as Cook Inlet.

Captain Cook claimed the Kenai Peninsula for England in 1778. Just seven years later, Grigor Shelikof sent an expedition to the Kenai Peninsula, and the Russian presence began. The first Russian settlement was at Alexandrovosk, or English Bay, south of present-day Seldovia. By 1787, the Russians had laid claim to the entire Cook Inlet area. To enforce their claims, they took hostages – mostly women and children – from the

Kenaitze to ensure the cooperation of the Native men when it came to hunting and gathering sea otter pelts.

This method of hunting was so successful for the Russians that, by 1800, the once huge sea otter population had been pushed to the brink of extinction. Unperturbed, the Russians packed up and moved to Sitka. The human population of the Kenai, estimated at about 3,000 in 1805, had dropped to 160 by 1880.

Homer got its start in the 1890s, when the English ran a coal mine at Bluff Point, just up the beach from the Spit. Although the mine closed in 1907, it was prosperous enough to inspire the building of a railroad from the mine to the dock at the Spit's end.

There was a brief heyday of gold mining in the Homer area, but what has kept the town going through booms and busts is the Spit, the tourists, and fishing. If you want to catch a 200-pound halibut, this is the place.

Today, about 4,000 people call Homer home. Most visitors never venture far from the Spit, but downtown Homer is not short on charms itself.

■ Basics

 There's a small **Tourist Information Center** annex on the Spit, about a mile from the ferry terminal. It may or may not be open, though. The main center is north of the Spit, on the ocean side, right at the crossroads as you're coming into town (next to the Ocean Shores motel), ☎ 907-235-5300.

Off-season, write to Homer Chamber of Commerce, PO Box 541, Homer, 99603. Homer is online at homeralaska.org.

Charter flight operators in Homer include **Emerald Air Service,** ☎ 907-235-6993, www.emeralairservice.com, **Bald Mountain Air,** ☎ 800-478-7969, www.baldmountainair.com, and **Kachemak Bay Flying Service**, ☎ 907-235-8924, www.alaskaseaplanes.com.

Homer is served by the Alaska Marine Highway's MV *Tustemena* several times a week, connecting the town to Kodiak, Seldovia, and Seward. ☎ 907-235-8449. The terminal is at the end of the Spit. Cruise ships don't come here.

📖 For more on the oceanic possibilities from Homer, see our other book, ***Adventure Guide to the Inside Passage***.

Jakolof Ferry Service runs back and forth to Halibut Point, on the edge of Kachemak Bay State Park. The ship leaves the harbor below the Salty Dawg three times a day; ☎ 907-235-2376 for departure times.

The zip code for Homer is 99603.

QUICK TOUR: Hit the **Spit.**

DON'T MISS: Get into **Kachemak Bay**: kayak, take a water taxi, something. It's some of the nicest scenery in Southcentral. Oh, yeah, the fishing's not bad, either. The **Pratt Museum** is one of the finest in the state. Well worth your time.

BEST FREE THING TO DO: Hang out at the **Fishing Hole**. Freak shows were a noble tradition in the circus world for years. Here's just a different kind of one, but the same idea.

■ Things to Do

Homer's tourist action is on **the Spit**, a 4.5-mile sandspit that projects into Kachemak Bay. The Spit is a glacial moraine – a deposit left behind by a retreating glacier – and, until the 1964 earthquake, was considerably larger. The quake put nearly half of it under water. An official guide to the city says that the Spit is "a source of artistic energy, a place to relax and get in touch with the rhythm of wind and water." Maybe. But you'd have to ignore the chaos to do any relaxing. And that's the fun of the Spit.

Come down at about 5 pm and watch the charter boats bring in the day's catch. This also gives you a chance to see the operators at work before you book. Or just hang out in front of the Salty Dawg and watch the people come and go. It's like a parade every day.

If you want to fish and don't mind basically fishing in a barrel, try the Spit "fishing hole." Salmon fry are released here in a dead-end inlet right off the Spit. When they're mature and suffering from the salmon instinct to return whence they came, the fish end up in this tiny pool – dazed, confused, and suffering from hormonal derangement while they look for freshwater to spawn in. There isn't any, but there are eagles waiting to pounce and "fishermen" snagging and casting for them. If dynamiting a stream is your idea of fun, this might be the place for you. On the other hand, to be fair, if you've got small kids, or for whatever reason can't get out on the boats, this is your chance to catch a big fish. It is wheelchair-accessible. Despite the side-show aspect, you'll still need a fishing license here, just like everywhere else you drop a line. There is a special deal where kids under 16 don't need the license. If you haven't brought gear, you can rent poles in the store next to the hole.

Walking along the beach at the Spit at low tide can be interesting, or you can stay up higher from the waterline on the paved trails that are popular with bikers and joggers. While you walk, watch for sea otters, which have made quite a comeback since the Russians left. There's also a wide variety of shore birds and a good bivalve community: butter clams and steamer clams on the east side of the Spit, razor clams on the inlet side and further up along most of Homer's beaches. Tide tables are available everywhere. Remember, clamming requires a fishing license, too.

One of the fun things about the Spit is that most places where you see brochures, there's also a bright orange flyer on what to do in case you're on the Spit when a tsunami hits. Homer, surrounded by volcanoes, is prime earthquake territory, and that means there is always a tiny chance of a big wave. If you see the water suddenly disappear and hear a siren blasting for several minutes, head for higher ground. No, this will not happen to you.

In town, the **Pratt Museum** is at 3779 Bartlett St., ☎ 907-235-8636, prattmuseum.org. The $6 admission gets you into one of the better museums in Alaska, featuring the usual historical displays, some excellent wildlife exhibits, and a selection of modern art. Their exhibit, "Darkened Waters," on the *Exxon Valdez* oil spill, won awards, spawned a traveling show, and made Exxon very unhappy. Lots of interactive displays. If you like museums, you're going to love this one; it's well worth the time.

The **Alaska Maritime National Wildlife Refuge** maintains a visitor's center at 451 Sterling Highway, next to the Ocean Shores motel. The AMNWR, which stretches from Forrester Island in Southeast to Attu Island in the Aleutians and north nearly to Barrow, totals more than 2,500 islands and three million acres of vital wildlife habitat. AMNWR claims that 80% of all seabirds in Alaska nest in the refuge. In addition to the visitors center in Homer, AMNWR also maintains an office in Adak, and puts naturalists onto the ferries to Seldovia, Kodiak, and Dutch Harbor.

At the center, there are films, a computer program that helps you identify birds, and a small bookstore. Guided bird walks are offered every Sunday and Wednesday from 1-2 pm, and there are sometimes beach walks, too. ☎ 907-235-6961.

Kachemak Heritage Land Trust offers a variety of summer programs, including nature walks, archaeological lectures, and more. Contact them at Box 2400, or ☎ 907-235-5263.

New to town is **Alaska's Island & Ocean Visitor Center**, 95 Sterling Highway, ☎ 907-235-6961, islandsandocean.org. The idea here is to give you a feeling for the ecology of Southcentral Alaska, through virtual exhibits, films, nature programs, talks, and more. It's worth the stop, and best of all, it's free.

In summer, **Pier One Theater** stages live weekend performances on the Spit. Past programs have ranged from performances by the Boston Pops Orchestra to productions of Woody Allen plays. Tom Bodett is a standard. Check the newspaper for current schedule, or ☎ 907-235-7333.

Homer's **Halibut Derby** runs May 1 through Labor Day. It's the state's biggest derby, with over $100,000 in prizes. There are prizes for the biggest fish (the 1994 winner was 346.7 pounds) and for specially tagged fish. Check with the Chamber of Commerce for more information, ☎ 907-235-7740.

May 10th through the 12th is the **Kachemak Bay Shorebird Festival**. More than 100,000 birds pass through the area in the first two weeks of

May. There's a birders' hotline for the latest sightings: ☎ 907-235-PEEP. The Tourist Info booth and the AMNWR office have a sheet with a checklist of local birds.

In August, there's the **Summer String Festival**, with a concert series and classes. Check with the **Kenai Peninsula Orchestra** (☎ 907-235-6318) for the year's programs.

Any time of year, take the drive out East End Road for great views of the bay and the rolling hills around Homer.

In winter, you'll find excellent cross-country skiing on **Baycrest-Diamond Ridge**, above town, on the **Homestead Trail**, and all around town. Get the free flyer on skiing from the Chamber of Commerce, or contact **Kachemak Nordic Ski Club** (☎ 907-235-6018).

OLD BELIEVERS

In Homer, you'll often see women in floor-length dresses and long head scarves. They come from the Russian villages south of Homer. The largest of the two villages, Nikolaevsk, is a town of "Old Believers," most of whom left Russia in the 1930s to escape persecution. (The schism between old and new believers dates back several hundred years, though; it was caused by a reformation in the rules of the Russian Orthodox Church. Old Believers didn't like the new rules. Today, there are about 1,000 Old Believers in Alaska.). The village of Nikolaevsk, founded in 1968, is a place where Russian is the de facto language and Russian culture thrives. The residents wear traditional Russian peasant garb and use old-fashioned tools. You can visit the village, but the residents do not seek or encourage tourists or attention. If you go, treat the people with respect.

■ Out & About

Booking Agencies

 Homer is activity central; sooner or later, everybody ends up here looking for stuff to do. Because of that demand, the town has three central booking agencies: one call to any of these can get you kayaks, fishing charters, bear watching trips, excursions over to Seldovia, and nights in one of the town's countless B&Bs. If you don't want to run around and track this stuff down yourself, let these people do it for you.

It's an especially good idea to let these people handle the details for you if you're coming into town on short notice in the high season. There are many days in summer when you have your choice of fishing boats to go out on, but there are also times when there's not a boat to be found for two or three days at a time. Calling one of these places early can save you a lot of frustration.

Central Charters (☎ 907-235-7847, 800-478-7847, www.centralcharter. com) is the town's original one-stop shop, with a huge office on the Spit.

Homer Alaska Referral & Booking Agency, ☎ 866-899-7156, www. homeralaskareferral.com, is another choice, or try **Tacklebuster**, ☎ 800-789-5155, www.tacklebuster.com.

We'd highly recommend letting one of these people get you a B&B if that's what you're going to want in town. Homer has more B&Bs per capita than any place in the North; let the booking agencies figure out which one is right for you.

Kayaking

Kachemak Bay is kayaking paradise, as long as you're careful to stay out of tidal rips. If you're going out on your own, check around before you pick a spot to paddle.

True North Kayak (☎ 907-235-0708, www.truenorthkayak.com) offers rentals and guided excursions around Homer. Their day trip takes you over for a paddle around Yukon Island, where there are plenty of otters to watch, for around $135. They also have overnight trips available, and best of all, unlike most guided paddles, you have a viable option of taking a single kayak out, rather than getting stuck in a double.

Seaside Adventures (☎ 907-235-6672, www.seasideadventure.com) has similar trips, as does St. **Augustine Charters**, ☎ 907-235-6126, www. homerkayaking.com. **Alaska Canoe and Kayak Base**, ☎ 907-235-2090, www.alaskapaddler.com, is another good option.

If you have your own boat, or are renting one for the day, there are several choices for drop-off. **Mako's Water Taxi**, ☎ 907-235-9055, www. makoswatertaxi.com, and **Jakolof Ferry Service**, ☎ 907-235-6384 – the town's original water taxi – run water taxis, rent kayaks, and can arrange for drop-offs and pickups. Another option is **Water Taxi Triton**, ☎ 907-235-7620, who are also good for hikers going to the Kachemak Bay trailheads. This is the only taxi service with dry landings.

Bear Watching

The growth industry in Homer the past couple years has been charter flights over to Katmai to see bears. Homer is the town closest to Katmai – sometimes referred to as the "land of 10,000 smokes," reflecting it's highly active volcanic past – and sometimes just called "the place you saw on TV where all the bears are." When you see the pictures of bears lined up at a waterfall, waiting for the salmon to jump, you're looking at Katmai.

There are tons of bears in Katmai, and they're fairly used to people, so they just go on about their business – trying to get fat before the weather turns – while you have plenty of chances to get pictures. These are some of the biggest brown (grizzly) bears in the world, and the chances of you not getting the best bear-watching you've ever imagined are remote. You will be amazed.

Now for the downside: a day trip out to watch the bears will run you in the neighborhood of $500. Yep, that's for the day trip. You fly from Homer to the park, and then hike in to a bear-watching spot. You'll want a good camera (don't even think about wasting your time with a little pocket camera), a better lens, and lots of film.

Bald Mountain Air Service (☎ 907-235-7969, www.baldmountainair. com), **Talon Air Service** (☎ 907-262-8899, www.talonair.com), and **Emerald Air Service** (☎ 907-235-6993, www.emeraldairservice.com) all offer similar trips over. Flying time is about 90 minutes each way.

Hallo Bay is an inholding in the Katmai Preserve, and it's worth checking out if you're looking for a more in-depth bear experience. They do day-trips, but what's really worthwhile is to stay in one of the cabins (big, comfortable tents, really) and hang out for a few days of serious bear-watching. We had a day out here with these people, watching two brown bear cubs playing on a log that was sticking out of the tideline like a diving board. It was one of the best days we've ever had in Alaska. ☎ 907-235-9461, www.hallobay. com. Day trips from Homer run $550 (don't waste your money on the shorter trip that's a hundred bucks cheaper); longer stays run $1,300 for two days/two nights.

If spending this kind of money on a day trip is a bit much for you, for around the same price you could fly or take the ferry down to Wrangell or Juneau, and then get a trip to Anan or Pack Creek, where the bear-viewing is equally amazing, plus you get to see another part of Alaska. If your time is short, though, these trips to Katmai are unforgettable.

TIMOTHY TREADWELL

Okay, back in the bear section of this book, we promised the Michio Hoshino story was going to be the only true bear attack tale we told. But we have to throw in one more, the saga of Timothy Treadwell, who was killed by a bear in Katmai in 2003.

Treadwell was an interesting guy. He'd spent numerous summers in Katmai, doing what he called "protecting" the bears; off-season, he wrote and lectured about bears, and no doubt brought the story of this beautiful chunk of the state to a lot of people who never would have heard about it otherwise. The guy did good conservation business in the off-season, make no mistake.

However, his summer activities were rather more controversial; many people thought he was doing good work, collecting good data; others thought he was bound to get chomped one day, because he was taking none of the standard precautions, and simply trusted his rapport with the bears to see him through.

It didn't work that way.

Bears, as anybody who has ever spent much time around them should know, have their own agenda, and it's not one we'll ever fully understand.

Power Trips

Finally in the tour department, there are some nice trips you can take around town. **Trails End Horse Adventures** (☎ 907-235-6393) has half-day rides for $65, full day for $110. For flightseeing, there's **Maritime Helicopters** (☎ 907-235-7771, www.maritimehelicopters.com) and **Kachemak Bay Flying Service** (☎ 907-235-8924, www.alaskaseaplanes.com), which flies a beautifully restored 1929 Travel Air 6000. Flying didn't always have the ambience of a fast food wrapper.

Hiking

The **Bishop Beach Hike** starts at Bishop Park. The full hike is 11 miles and passes a seal rookery and Diamond Creek. All along you'll have great views, but check a tide table before you set out. You can also pick this trail up at the Ocean Shores Motel – just head down the hill to the beach. It's not exactly a trail you're on here, just the beach, but it's a great walk, and as long as you're watching the water, you get great views and the place to yourself. Just be out of there when the tide is coming in. The British have a lovely term – embayed – that describes what happens when beach walkers get stuck by the tide. You could, maybe, climb the steep sand bluffs to get away from the incoming water, but you wouldn't really want to try.

The **Homestead Trail** is a bit over 6.6 miles, starting on Rodgers Loop Road. You climb through meadows and get great views of the bay. Walking the length of the Spit along the beach is also a great stroll – about five miles from the airport to the ferry terminal. You'll have the tideline to yourself.

Fishing

Okay, let's get to the reason why you came to Homer: serious fishing.

Homer is charter operator's paradise. An evening on the Spit will make you think more boats leave Homer than the rest of the state combined. And they're all here for good reason. If you're a serious fisherman, Homer is the place to find salmon, halibut up to 200 pounds and more, cod, and flounder.

If you're after the really big fish, you'll need an all-day charter. The biggest halibut are out around the point, in open water. It gets rough out there, so be prepared. If you're prone to seasickness, it will be a day in hell.

We suggest that you simply go to the oldest booking agency in town – **Central Charters** (☎ 907-235-7847 or 800-478-7847, www.centralcharter. com) and let them figure it out for you. They're linked with dozens of boats, and they're your best chance of getting exactly what you want. Take some time, talk to them, tell them what kind of fishing you're looking for, and let them match you up to the boat that will give you the best time.

Homer Alaska Referral & Booking Agency, ☎ 866-899-7156, www. homeralaskareferral.com, is another choice, or try **Tacklebuster,** ☎ 800-789-5155, www.tacklebuster.com.

Homer has so many independent charter operators that choosing one yourself can be a bewildering experience. Going down to the docks the night before you want to charter and talking to people coming in is one good way to pick a ship. The Homer Charter Association has certain standards that must be maintained, and membership is usually a sign of a good operation.

All the fishing charters are going to run about the same services. They'll provide you with the boat and fishing gear; you bring your own lunch. Beyond that, check what you're in for. Most operators will help you process your catch. If someone is drastically cheaper than everybody else, find out why. They may go to a different area, stay away from the deep water, or offer fewer services.

Most charter companies will clean your fish, but getting them back home is your problem. **Coal Point Seafood Company**, 4306 Homer Spit, ☎ 907-235-3877, can vacuum pack, freeze, and ship your fish.

A day's catch, Homer.

Kachemak Bay State Park

Homer's most famous attraction takes a little getting to. With over 350,000 acres, the park has a little something for everyone. It's located directly across Kachemak Bay from Homer and is accessible by boat. Many of the charter operators will offer drop-offs, or take the **Jakolof Ferry**, which runs back and forth to Halibut Point on the edge of the park. The boat leaves the harbor below the Salty Dawg three times a day; ☎ 907-235-2376 for departure times.

Kachemak Bay State Park varies between quite settled – Halibut Cove – and wild, with huge glaciers and strangely shaped rock cliff formations that are home to thousands of birds. Expect to see eagles, puffins, and more than 15,000 nesting seabirds on Gull Island.

The park has a variety of hiking trails. Trailheads are marked by large orange triangular signs at the water's edge. Some of the better ones are to

Grewingk Glacier, a 3.2-mile, flatland hike that takes you to the glacial outwash. You can get to the glacier itself, but it's difficult and dangerous. Another good hike is the **Lagoon Trail**, 5.5 miles from the Halibut Creek trailhead; it connects with the **China Poot Lake Trail**, 2.5 miles along three lakes below China Poot Peak. You can climb the peak itself from the lake – the two miles will take at least three hours, round-trip.

Fishing throughout the waters of the park is good. Salmon run in the rivers (some are also stocked behind Halibut Cove, but this is just a bigger version of the Spit's Fishing Hole), and in the deeper waters you'll find halibut, cod, flounder, and red snapper.

There's only one cabin in the park, and it's usually booked. **Campsites** are at the foot of the Grewingk Glacier Trail, the Lagoon Trail, and the China Poot Lake Trail. There's also a ranger station near the China Poot Lake Trail. There is no safe drinking water in the park; boil or treat before use.

> **TIDAL WARNING:** In the park, be aware that the tides in Kachemak Bay are tremendous. The vertical difference between high and low tide can be as much as 28 feet, with an average of 15 feet. Some of the passages get so narrow the tide flows in like a rapids, so take all proper boating precautions and stay off the mud flats. Don't kayak unescorted out here unless you really know what you're doing. And when you beach your boat, make sure you pull it up a lot farther than you think you need to.

■ Shopping

 Homer claims a number of **local artists**, and downtown you'll find galleries stuffed with their work. There are five galleries on Pioneer Ave. alone, and a couple more nearby. Exhibits change, and so do the tastes of the gallery owners.

Alaska Wild Berry Products (☎ 907-235-8858), 528 E. Pioneer, has all the standard tourist fare, plus candies and jams made from local berries. Shipping is available.

Inua and the **Roadhouse** – across from each other on the Spit – have good assortments of Native crafts.

■ Food

Homer has a great array of excellent, reasonably priced eateries for such a small town. The Spit is jammed with seafood places, offering cheap, very fresh fish. **Land's End**, at the very end of The Spit, has a good lunch special, starting at $6.

The **Cosmic Kitchen**, 510 E. Pioneer Ave, ☎ 907-235-6355, is the place in town for Mexican food. $8 for a steak chimichanga.

On the Spit is **Whales Cove Fish and Chips**, with a good, cheap lunch of halibut and fries for $8.

Café Cups (☎ 907-235-8330), 162 W. Pioneer, is the place for breakfast (they also serve lunch and dinner), with excellent coffees and teas and homestyle cooking from $8. They sport an art house decor, and their eggs Benedict will be a highlight of your trip.

The **Fresh Sourdough Express Bakery**, on Ocean Drive just off The Spit, serves great breakfasts with fresh-baked goodies, plus sandwiches for lunch. It's crowded and very popular – hard to find a place to park early in the morning. Lunch specials include spinach and cheese croissant turnovers and falafel burgers; for dinner, don't miss the lemon pepper crusted halibut. Lunch from $8, dinner from $15. They also have their own line of organic cocoa and coffee – buy a couple jars to take home.

Smoky Bay Co-op, on Pioneer, has vegetarian specialties and a health food store. Lunch runs around $7.

The **Homestead Restaurant**, 8.2 miles out East End Road, is the nice night out place. Prime rib, microbrews, and seafood that will make you start pricing property in Homer for your retirement. Make reservations. ☎ 907-235-8723.

The **Salty Dawg** was named one of the best bars in America by *Men's Journal* magazine. Yeah, maybe they were having a slow day in the editorial office, but the place does have atmosphere.

Finally, if you've got some spare cash and want a night out you won't soon forget, head to the **Saltry** in Halibut Cove (☎ 907-296-2223). You have to figure round-trip water-taxi fare into the price of the meal, but even with that, it's a deal. The place serves incredible seafood, caught fresh and prepared with an expert touch. With transportation, figure on at least $100 for a couple. This is a great place to eat.

If you're heading out to more remote areas, remember that Homer is the last town to shop in. Several **grocery stores** are convenient to downtown.

■ Accommodations

If you're determined to sleep in a hotel in Homer, call well ahead. In summer they are booked up. There are some good choices, though. The **Ocean Shores Motel** (☎ 907-235-7775, www.oceanshoresalaska.com) has a nice decor, water views from all rooms. $$$.

HOTEL PRICING
Prices are in US dollars.
under $50 . . . . $
$50-$100 . . . . $$
$100-$150 . . . . . . $$$
above $150 . . . . . $$$$

Land's End (☎ 907-235-2500, www.lands-end-resort.com) is at the end of the Spit. Doubles start at $$$ – if you want a water view, figure $$$$, but some of these rooms are really, really lovely.

The **Heritage Hotel** (☎ 907-235-7787, www.alaskaheritagehotel.com), 142 E. Pioneer, has doubles with a shared bath from $$, private from $$$. It's clean, but it can get noisy with the bar. It has a great log cabin decor, though.

The **Pioneer Inn** (☎ 907-235-5670, 800-782-9655), 244 Pioneer Ave., has pleasant rooms. Basic, but cheap. $$.

There's also a Best Western in town, the **Bidarka Inn**, ☎ 907-866-5000, www.bidarkainn.com. $$$, up to the usual good Best Western standards.

A quick look at the Visitor Center, and you'll think the entire economy of the town is supported by B&Bs. There are more of them here than you can even imagine. Talk to the **Homer B&B Association**, ☎ 800-473-3092, www.homerbedbreakfast.com, or **Homer's Finest**, ☎ 800-764-3211, www. homeraccommodations.com, or one of the other booking agencies, and let them do the work of finding one for you.

Camping

Camping on the **Spit** is bleak, windy, and barren, and you'll be surrounded by fishermen who haven't bathed in weeks. It's not as bad as it once was, though; since the cannery burned down, the number of permanent residents has decreased, and with them went much of the wildness. There are a couple private campgrounds on the Spit, and the one run by the city. You're right in the middle of the action.

Much nicer than anything on the Spit is the **city campground**, above the ball field off Bartlett and Fairview Ave. It has 33 nice sites, water, restrooms, lots of trees and privacy, and some good views of the bay.

Driftwood Inn & RV Park is right above the beach, so you get great views, and you're within walking distance of town. Full hookups are available. ☎ 907-235-8019, www.thedriftwoodinn.com.

Another choice is **Oceanview RV Park**, at mile 172 on the Sterling highway. Full hookups, nice views. ☎ 907-235-3951, www.oceanview-rv.com.

If all the camping is full, drive back up to **Anchor Point**, where there are several campgrounds.

Chapter 16

The Alaska Marine Highway

Wasn't it Oscar Wilde who said, "When choosing between two evils, I always choose the one I haven't tried before"? There are those of us who see the world as impossibly huge, too big for one lifetime, certainly too big to backtrack.

For these people, a one-way driving trip is enough; and for those folks, there is another way home, the Alaska Marine Highway, a journey like no other in the world.

Coastal Alaska's equivalent of a bus system, the Alaska Marine Highway runs to 34 ports, covering over 3,500 miles in two separate routes. The **Southeast Route** – what you hook up to from Skagway or Haines – is 1,600 miles long, the longest single ferry route in the world; the **Southwest Run**, which you can catch from Valdez and which connects Kodiak and Prince William Sound with the far-flung islands of the Aleutians, touches the most remote places you can get to in the US on public transportation.

There's even a once-monthly cross-Sound trip, which goes from Seward to Juneau, linking Southcentral and Southeast Alaska by passenger ship for the first time since World War II.

The statistics for the Marine Highway are staggering. The ferry system transports more than 400,000 passengers annually (most of them in the peak summer months) and more than 111,000 vehicles. The system directly employs almost 1,000 people and has an economic impact on Alaska's economy of more than $150 million.

Most AMH travelers find the main, Southeast section most useful. The Alaska Highway proper connects to the Southeast Alaska Marine Highway system in two places: at Haines, where a 152-mile road connects you to the Alaska Highway at Haines Junction, and at Skagway, where it's 99 miles to a point on the Alcan just south of Whitehorse. Haines is considerably more scenic, Skagway more historically interesting but sometimes overwhelming because of the numbers of people who visit the place.

From Canada, you can link up to either the Alaska Marine Highway or BC Ferries in Prince Rupert, which gives you a choice of heading north to Alaska, or south as far as Victoria, on Vancouver Island, where you can link up with yet more ferries to get you to Washington State.

■ Southeast Section

 The Southeast section of the Alaska Marine Highway travels through the **Inside Passage**, a region of lush rainforests, tiny inlets and bays, countless islands, and perfectly still and peaceful land between towns. This is the same view the cruise ship passengers get, but on the ferry, you get it more cheaply and with real Alaskans.

Taking the AMH is a vacation in itself, and a quick run down (roughly four days from Haines or Skagway to Bellingham) doesn't offer nearly the chance you'll want to explore the beautiful towns of Juneau (the state capital), Ketchikan, and Sitka, the old Russian capital of Alaska where the transfer to the US took place. (The first thing the US did after takeover? They built a ten-pin alley to keep the troops from mutiny. Alaska wasn't exactly a popular posting at the time.)

The scenery of Southeast Alaska can be compared to the fjords of Norway. The trees grow right up to the water's edge, and the forest is so thick it's nearly impenetrable. The light coming through a hundred shades of green is something you'll never forget.

There is abundant wildlife in Southeast. Bears and Sitka black-tailed deer are the most common of the big animals, but there are several varieties of birds, including the largest population of bald eagles in the world. The lucky traveler will also get glimpses of humpback whales, killer whales, seals, porpoises, and otters.

Life on board the ship is simple. This is not a cruise ship. There are no formal dinners, no theaters, casinos, or deck games. The entertainment is looking off to the sides, where land is almost never out of sight and the scenery is always beautiful.

> **WEATHER ALERT:** There is only one caveat to travel in Southeast: It rains here – a lot. Sitka averages 110 inches of rain a year; Ketchikan, 155. The standard weather joke in Southeast goes like this: "Summer was on Tuesday this year." So go prepared to get a little wet.

■ Southwest Section

 The Southwest Alaska Marine Highway connects to the road in Valdez, Whittier, Seward, and Homer. Starting in these towns you can go from Cordova to Kodiak, or, with proper planning, as far out as Dutch Harbor in the Aleutians. The scenery in the Southwest is remarkably different from Southeast, and the farther out you go, the more different it gets. Kodiak has enough shades of green to embarrass an Irishman; but if you go out toward the Aleutians, the mountains smoke and the rocks are bare except for sunning seals.

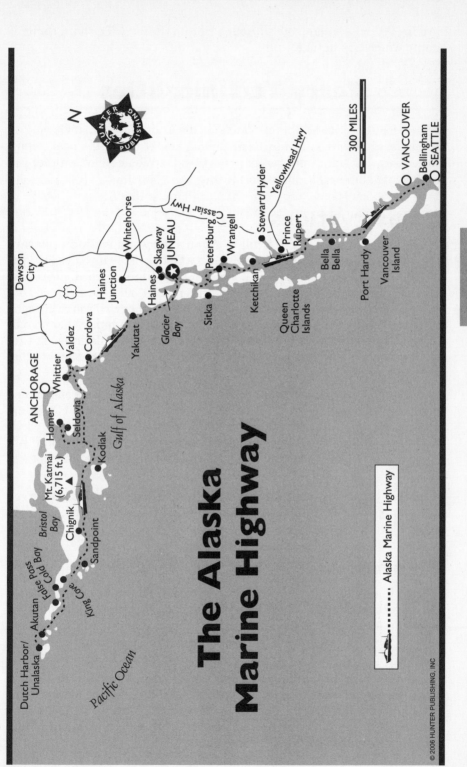

The AMH

The Alaska Marine Highway

Alaska Marine Highway

© 2006 HUNTER PUBLISHING, INC

No trip to Alaska is complete without a ride on the ferry. The hard choice is simply which trip to take.

Ferry Technicalities

First, for all would-be animal watchers, directions for animal viewing on the ferry are given in **nautical terms**: bow (front of the boat), stern (back), port (left side), and starboard (right side). Whales don't wait for you to translate ship-speak, so memorize these.

■ Reservations

 It is almost never difficult to get on a ferry as a **walk-on passenger**. If you're bringing a vehicle – which is likely if you've just gotten off the highway – or if you want a stateroom, you'll need to do some advance planning. Staterooms for the summer months can be sold out by January. Vehicle space is available a little later, although if you're bringing an RV or large truck, the sooner you plan, the better. In summer, there can be a two- to three-week wait for vehicle space on the more popular runs. In winter, however, the ferry is nearly empty. It's only from May to September that advance planning is essential.

Start planning by getting a **schedule**. ☎ 800-642-0066 to have one mailed to you, or log on at www.dot.state.ak.us/amhs/. In a slightly confusing, color-coded format, the schedule lists sailing times from each of the ports. Note that sailings from Bellingham leave only once or twice a week. If you have questions about the schedule, call and ask the reservations personnel.

The ferry system does maintain a standby list, with first-come, first-served hopes for specific dates. If your chosen sailing is full, you can ask to be put on the list.

■ Fares

Ferry costs vary with distance traveled. There are a couple of special price deals. Those 65 and older can ride for a 50% discount, on a space-available basis, on the *LeConte, Aurora*, and *Tustumena* ships. There are restrictions on this in the high season, and the rate applies only to your body. Cabins, vehicles, meals, and so on are all extra.

Passengers with disabilities can obtain a one-year, $25 pass that allows them space-available travel on the AMH. This deal is limited to those with 70% or more disability. The *Columbia, Malaspina, Matanuska, Taku*, and *Tustumena* have wheelchair access, and the AMH will try to make special arrangements. Call the office for more details.

Walk-on passengers can no longer book a through ticket, get off at stops en route for a day or two, and get back on any ship headed to the destination port. You'll need to book each stop for the ticket. However, to do this doesn't run more than $20 or so over the single-destination ticket with no stops.

Vehicle charges vary according to the size of the vehicle, and prices do not include the driver's transportation. There's also a fare category for kayaks, canoes, and bikes.

If you're driving a large RV, be aware that you will often have to back the vehicle down the ramp and into an assigned spot in a very tight location. Ferry personnel will help direct you, but you should get comfortable maneuvering your vehicle before leaving home.

If you're bringing a bike, motorcycle, kayak, or anything else that can roll, bring your own tie-downs. There are stanchions on the ferry floor. Car deck personnel will help you and, if they can find some, you might get some rope out of them, but it's better to come prepared.

■ Baggage Restrictions

You are permitted to carry as much baggage as you want in your car. Foot passengers are allowed only 100 pounds, although it's never checked. A baggage cart comes off the ship at each port in Southeast; load your stuff on that, and take it back once you've boarded. There are cheap storage lockers on all ships.

The ferry does not keep a refrigerator for your fish catch, nor does it allow explosives, flammable materials, or corrosives on board. You also must turn off your RV's propane tank before loading. Small gas containers are allowed, but they must be sealed and checked by ferry personnel before loading.

■ Pets

Pets are allowed on the ships, but they are limited to the car deck and they must be in a container. The ship does not make any facilities available for pets. You can go down to the car deck to tend to your animal only on car deck calls, which are limited to when the ship is in port and, on the longer runs, to three specific times per day. It's a cold, hard, lonely trip for an animal.

■ Check-In

Departure and check-in times are printed on the tickets. In larger ports, take the check-in times very seriously. If you're not in line, you can miss your spot. In some of the smaller ports, things are a lot more relaxed, but always check with the local terminal. In all but terminus ports, call the terminal an hour before check-in to see if the ship is running on time. The AMH does a remarkable job of sticking to the schedule, but delays do occur in the changeable weather of Alaska.

▪ Sleeping On Board

 Staterooms are booked for the entire run. The ships have two- and four-berth cabins (the *Aurora* and the *LeConte* do not have staterooms). Not all rooms have private bathrooms; rooms with full facilities are slightly more expensive, as are rooms with outside windows. Inside cabins should be avoided by the claustrophobic. They're comfortable, but dark and confining. It is occasionally possible to get a stateroom by going on the standby list. You generally stand a much better chance of getting a four-berth cabin on standby; if you choose to go standby for a two-berth cabin and don't get called, that's it. Check at the terminal, and again with the purser on board.

The *Kennicott*, the newest ship, and the one that makes the cross-Sound trip, has "roomettes" – basically two fold down platforms where you can pitch your sleeping bag. The roomettes are a good deal, though, as they're a lot cheaper than a regular room, and the ship is the absolute worst in the fleet for sleeping outside.

Because, on the other ships, if you don't want the trouble of a room, you can camp outside in the solarium or on the open area at the back end of the cabin deck on the *Columbia*. Tents are allowed (you have to get creative with ropes and duct tape), but only in these limited areas, and spaces fill up fast; every chair in the solarium will get occupied right away during high season. Still, when you're not surrounded by teenagers who just got off three months work at a cannery, sleeping outside is really nice. Just be sure to use the lockers for your baggage.

Those who don't want to sleep outside can sleep in the forward lounges and in the observation lounge. No baggage is allowed in the observation lounge, food and drink are not permitted in the forward lounge, and both places can get noisy. All these rules are widely ignored.

The advantage to the forward lounge and the observation lounge is that they are darkened at night, a blessing for those who find the white nights of summer a little much to take.

Technically, you cannot stake out a space by leaving your stuff in it. In practice, however, claims are usually respected.

▪ Food

Every ship has a dining area. Hours and services range from ship to ship. The dining area on the *Tusty* is open only three hours a day; the snack bar on the *Columbia* never closes in summer. There are also vending machines on the ships.

Snack bar and restaurant meals on the smaller ships are fairly limited, but are reasonably priced and quite good. At the other extreme of choice, the dining room of the *Columbia* will surprise you with its gourmet meals. Just-caught shrimp are picked up in port and cooked only an hour or two later. Non-seafood dishes are created with delicious sauces, and every attention is paid to detail to make the dining outstanding. In addition, you can't beat the view out the restaurant windows.

Bringing your own food is a good idea for some variety, but there is nowhere to cook on the ship and camp stoves are strictly forbidden. But there is always hot water available, which is good for instant oatmeal, soups, and teas.

A SHAMELESS PLUG

For full information on the Alaska Marine Highway and its stops, from Bellingham to Dutch Harbor, grab a copy of our *Adventure Guide to the Inside Passage and Coastal Alaska*, the only complete guide to the entire ferry system.

The AMH

Appendix

Recommended Reading

 One must-read book that jumps freely around the far North is Barry Lopez's **Arctic Dreams***, winner of the National Book Award. Although his concerns are largely farther north than the Alaska Highway, Lopez gives a masterful account of the relationship between the people, the animals, and the land of the Arctic. This is simply the best book on the North.*

 There has been a recent run of books on Alaska. Jon Krakauer's **Into the Wild** follows the misadventures of a young man who died in Denali Park. The book spent more than a year on the bestseller list.

For something a little less serious, the anthology, **The Last New Land: Stories from Alaska, Past and Present,** covers the history of people in the North. This is highly recommended.

Although a bit outdated, John McPhee's **Coming into the Country** offers a good look at life in some out-of-the-way places in Alaska. The middle section also gives a firsthand look at what's involved in moving a state capital.

Extreme Conditions, by John Strohmeyer, is the most complete look at Alaska's oil industry and the effects of the spill.

For those who like camping and hiking, **Soft Paths**, by Bruce Hampton and David Cole, offers advice on enjoying yourself and leaving minimum impact on the land.

If you're looking at the mountains, try **Alaska Ascents: World-Class Mountaineers Tell Their Stories**, by Bill Sherwonit.

Andrew Embick's **Fast and Cold** is a comprehensive guide to whitewater paddling in Alaska.

For those of a scientific mind, try **Roadside Geology of Alaska**, by Cathy Connor and Daniel O'Haire. They'll tell you anything you might want to know about the landforms around you. This is a great book to have on the front seat while you drive.

Pick up a copy of ***The Alaska Road Atlas***, which maps out every inch of the state.

 A must-have for the fisherman is Gunnar Pedersen's ***Highway Angler***, a how-to for all the lakes and rivers along the road.

One of the most popular birding books used by the U.S. Fish and Wildlife people is ***Seabirds: An Identification Guide***, by Peter Harrison.

Fishermen need a copy of ***Alaska Sport Fishing Guide***, by the Alaska Department of Fish and Game, and ***Fly Fishing Alaska***, by Anthony J. Route.

To get even farther out, state-wide, buy ***The Alaska Wilderness Milepost***, from Pacific Northwest books.

The first person to bring Alaska to the English reading public was John Muir. His ***Travels in Alaska*** shows a deep understanding and appreciation of the land. Muir would hit a village and immediately start looking for a trail into the mountains and icefields. (When you're reading it, don't worry – the dog Stikine comes out okay.)

Flat out, the best book about the gold rush is Pierre Berton's ***Klondike Fever***. Nothing else even comes close.

James Michener's ***Alaska*** was not well received within the state, but it will help pass the long nights. It can also be useful for leveling RVs when you can't find big rocks.

For the real history, there's a nice edition of the ***Journals of Captain Cook***, put out by Penguin books. If you're serious, though, about Cook, you'll have to go on-line to find a copy of the now out of print Hakluyt Society edition of Cook's journals – but it will run you at least a grand, and that's not including the map volume.

Not a single title, but an entire series for history buffs, ***Materials for the Study of Alaska History***, published by the Limestone Press, has wonderful Russian source material, beautifully translated. Some of the recommended titles include Two Voyages to Russian America, 1802-1807, by G.I. Davydov, and the two-volume Notes on Russian America, by K.T. Khlebnikov.

 Finally, there's ***Alaska Magazine***. It's slick, glossy, and full of useful advertisements.

BC has a great publishing industry all its own. There's no shortage of books on the province. Start by picking up a free copy of ***Read BC***, available at most Info Centres. This lists more than a hundred books on the province, broken down according to geographical region. It's a good place to start looking at what's available.

    Two books are absolute must-haves as you travel through BC: *The Beautiful British Columbia Travel Guide* covers almost every road in the province, with good maps, lots of interesting facts, and plenty of side trips. If you've used the *Milepost in Alaska*, it's like that, only without the endless ads.

    Cheryl Coull's *Traveller's Guide to Aboriginal BC* is a masterpiece of historic traveling. Over a 20-year period, she hung out with tribal elders, got their stories, their takes on the land around them. This is, flat out, one of the best guidebooks to Native culture and history ever written.

    George Bowering's *BC: A Swashbuckling History* is the perfect introduction to how BC became what it is. Bowering has a great grasp of the forces of history, and he makes it fun. You can read this book like a good novel, and only later will you discover just how much you've learned.

    Once you've got that nailed, pick up Rosemary Neering's *Traveller's Guide to Historic British Columbia,* another great one to have in the car with you.

    There's no way to travel around BC without wondering just what the HBC was thinking much of the time. Peter C. Newman's *Company of Adventurers* tries to answer that question. It's a little light on BC – the book is more interested in the HBC's early days in the East – but a must-read for understanding the second-oldest corporation in the world (behind the Zildjian Cymbal Co.).

    Robert Bringhurst won a ton of awards for his *A Story as Sharp as a Knife: The Classical Haida Mythtellers and Their World*. He deserved them all. It's a huge volume of Haida oral legend, beautifully translated and lovingly presented. You won't find a better book on the inner life of the coast First Nations groups anywhere. It's part of a series of three, so if you've got the time and the money, this is a must buy.

The Canadian Rockies Trail Guide, by Brian Patton and Bart Robinson, is what you need if you're going to spend a couple of weeks hiking in the parks – an area we simply can't give enough pages to in this book (although our *Adventure Guide to BC* is chock full of detail). There are other guides to the trails out there, but the Trail Guide is the one to own. Skimpy on the maps – you'll need topos, but then you'd need them no matter what – there are very detailed descriptions of the trails, and something in here for hikers of every level.

Index

Index

Index